WORLD WAR ONE CHANNEL WRECKS

VESSELS LOST IN THE ENGLISH CHANNEL 1914-1918

Neil Maw

UNDERWATER WORLD PUBLICATIONS

WORLD WAR ONE
CHANNEL WRECKS

A UB-class submarine. Together with the U- and UC-class submarines, they were the major cause of losses in the English Channel during World War One.

VESSELS LOST IN THE
ENGLISH CHANNEL
1914-1918

Book produced by DIVER Magazine

Edited by Kendall McDonald

Designed by George Lanham

WORLD WAR ONE CHANNEL WRECKS Internet site
http://www.divernet.com/channelwrecks

Published by Underwater World Publications Ltd
55, High Street, Teddington, Middlesex TW11 8HA.

© Underwater World Publications Ltd 1999

ISBN: 0 946020 29 9

Printed and bound by
Emirates Printing Press
P.O. Box 5106, Al Quoz, Dubai, UAE

CONTENTS

INTRODUCTION

THIS BOOK contains details of more than 750 ships sunk in the Channel between 1914 and 1918. The material comes mostly from the Admiralty's Weekly Reports from Coastal Stations, now in the care of the Public Record Office at Kew.

As you can imagine, covering the Channel in its entirety involved me in several years of work, particularly as I decided to include all ships sunk in the Channel during the period, regardless of their nationality or size. The biggest and the smallest are detailed here. The result covers every ship lost through enemy action in the four years of the war, and includes some vessels lost by collision as a result of war service.

Included too are details about the sinking of U-boats. Some of these reports, on which the maximum prize money of £1,000 was paid to the crews involved, together with medals and mentions in despatches, proved, after the war, to have been incorrect, with the submarines "definitely sunk" having returned safely to base. As there were at least three U-boats which have never been satisfactorily accounted for, I have graded some attacks as "probable" and others as "possible". The others are listed as confirmed kills.

If the number of ships sunk surprises you, then you should remember that the Channel was then, and is now, the busiest shipping lane in the world. The First World War, with its vast expenditure of men and munitions, particularly in the trenches in France, created a huge extra demand. Added to that, many raw materials had to be shipped to Britain to carry on the war effort. Coal, for example, was needed at home and abroad, and at later stages in the war there were special French Coal Trade convoys going back and forth across the Channel. It is therefore not surprising that a large proportion of the cargoes now lying on the Channel seabed are of North Country or Welsh coal.

Britain relied on shipping for much of its food, so it was common sense for the German navy to try and cut these lifelines. They had the weapons to do so – their Unterwasserbooten. These U-boats were built in three types. The U-class, which at first were small boats, but grew in size as the war progressed with both bow and stern torpedo tubes and a speed of 15 knots on the surface and capable of 80 miles at 5 knots submerged. Then there was the UB-class of boats. These attack submarines were slower at 13 knots and 4 knots underwater, but they carried more torpedoes and an 88mm deck gun. The UC-class were minelayers, capable of laying a field of 18 mines, but much slower at 7 knots on the surface and 4 knots submerged. These minelayers also carried torpedoes and a deck gun. All types had a range of thousands of miles from their bases.

Most of the submarines which appear on the following pages came from the Flanders Flotilla, based in Bruges after the Germans over-ran the Belgian ports such as Zeebrugge, which was connected to Bruges by canals.

At first, as you will see from the survivors' reports which are the basis of the material in this book, the German submarine commanders behaved impeccably towards the crews, though they were ruthless about sinking the ships they captured. Typical of this correct attitude are the last words of the German submarine commander who quite late in the war sank the *Norma* (see 9/22) to the crew in the boats: "Goodbye. I hope you will be safe". Earlier it was not unusual for the U-boat to tow the boats towards the shore or give them a course to steer.

However, due to the starvation conditions being endured by the German civilian population as a result of the British naval blockade of Germany, the Kaiser launched the "unrestricted" campaign on February 1, 1917. This said that all allied and neutral shipping was to be sunk on sight, without warning, in prohibited zones such as the English Channel, the western half of the North Sea, the western coasts of Scotland, Ireland, England and France, and extending 400 miles out into the Atlantic, and the Mediterranean.

The effect of the new U-boat offensive was disastrous for Britain. So much shipping was sunk that at one time there was only enough food in Britain to last three weeks. Germany's U-boats were winning the war.

Only the introduction of convoys, the entry of the United States into the war, the almost complete closing of the Straits of Dover to submarines with minefields, and the creation of the Northern Barrage of mines from the Orkneys to Norway, turned the tide.

The details in this book of each ship sunk and, in particular, the survivors' stories, give a fascinating insight into the ebb and flow of the U-boat war. Though there is a great similarity in many of the accounts, particularly the reports of the ships sunk by bombs planted by the U-boat crews, each adds a little bit more to the larger picture.

It is possible, for example, to note the growth of air power in the fight against the submarines by reports of crashes. Similarly, to sense the light-hearted way some of the young German U-boat commanders went to war. (The painting of the jaws and teeth of a shark on the bows of one boat [see 13/23], for example, must have been one of the earliest instances of modern war decoration – an art form which came to full flower with the aircraft decorations of World War Two.) The effect on the German submarine commanders of the Q-ships, pretending to be unarmed merchantman, but ready to drop the screens and blast the approaching submarine with their hidden guns, is clear in other survivors' reports, especially those of men held captive aboard the U-boats.

This vital material has been saved amid Admiralty records because every vessel kept a daily log and any occurrence worthy of note was submitted by the ship's captain to his area coastal station. These reports were collated and forwarded to the Admiralty as "Weekly Reports from Coastal Stations". Merchant ship sinkings and encounters with the enemy had to be given full treatment, and often area commanders were not satisfied with what they had been sent and asked for more details. This sometimes led to a Court of Enquiry. In the event of a Royal Navy ship being lost, a Court Martial usually followed, and the evidence was recorded in great detail.

As all this information arrived at the Admiralty, some of it could be removed from the original file and used to start a new one. For example, ships which were sunk by enemy submarines were filed separately from those sunk by mine or collision. However, the records were generally kept in area order and it would be quite unusual for papers concerning a vessel sunk in the Channel to be put in a file for one sunk in the North Sea.

This filing system, now collected together at the Public Record Office under the huge ADM 137 series, made my task slightly easier, though in one or two places there is an unaccountable shortage of information. Where I have added information from other and later sources, this has been made clear. The naval authorities who compiled the reports did not have the benefit of this hindsight and noted only what appeared correct to them at the time. This is particularly true when it comes to the position given for a sinking.

The fact that a complete list of crew members is not given does not mean that it is not in the records. It does mean that this book was becoming so weighty that the editor had to make cuts somewhere. Crew names of those involved in the action have been retained, as have the names of the gunners on the armed merchantmen where known. The reason for this is to help Britain's sport divers to identify "unknown" shipwrecks on the seabed. Gunners appointed to ships took their belongings and the tools of their trade aboard in wooden boxes, which often bore the owner's name and number on a brass plate. At least two ships have been identified in recent years by divers who have found the gunner's name on a little brass tag! Divers have also been responsible for identifying some ships which were sunk in darkness and whose loss and position were unknown to the authorities at the time. I have included some of these Channel casualties and made it clear where I got the information.

The coastal stations, whose weekly reports were consulted in the compilation of this book, include Falmouth, Penzance, Plymouth, Dartmouth, Portsmouth, Portland, Poole, Littlehampton, Newhaven and Dover.

NEIL MAW
1999

HOW TO USE
THIS BOOK

FOR THE purposes of this book, the boundaries of the Channel are defined by two imaginary lines: one in the west from Land's End (Latitude 50 03 00N; Longitude 05 40 00W), to the west of Ushant (Ile D'Ouessant, Lat 48 27 30N; Long 05 40 00W); one in the east from Dungeness (50 55 00N; 01 00 00E), to a point just south of Boulogne, (50 40 00N; 01 34 00E). Where a position has been given, no matter how vague, I have allocated a latitude and longitude to it. Within these boundaries, I have sub-divided the Channel into 14 convenient geographical areas, with a chapter devoted to each. Every vessel for which a position has been recorded has been given a number relating to the chapter in which it appears and (broadly speaking) its position in the 'chapter area', counting from west to east.

Vessels known to have been lost somewhere in the Channel, but for which no position has been recorded, are listed in an additional chapter, entitled "Unknown Wrecks", at the end of this book.

There is a companion Internet site which contains, where available, the lists of crew members for vessels mentioned in this book. See http://www.divernet.com/channelwrecks

CHAPTER AREAS

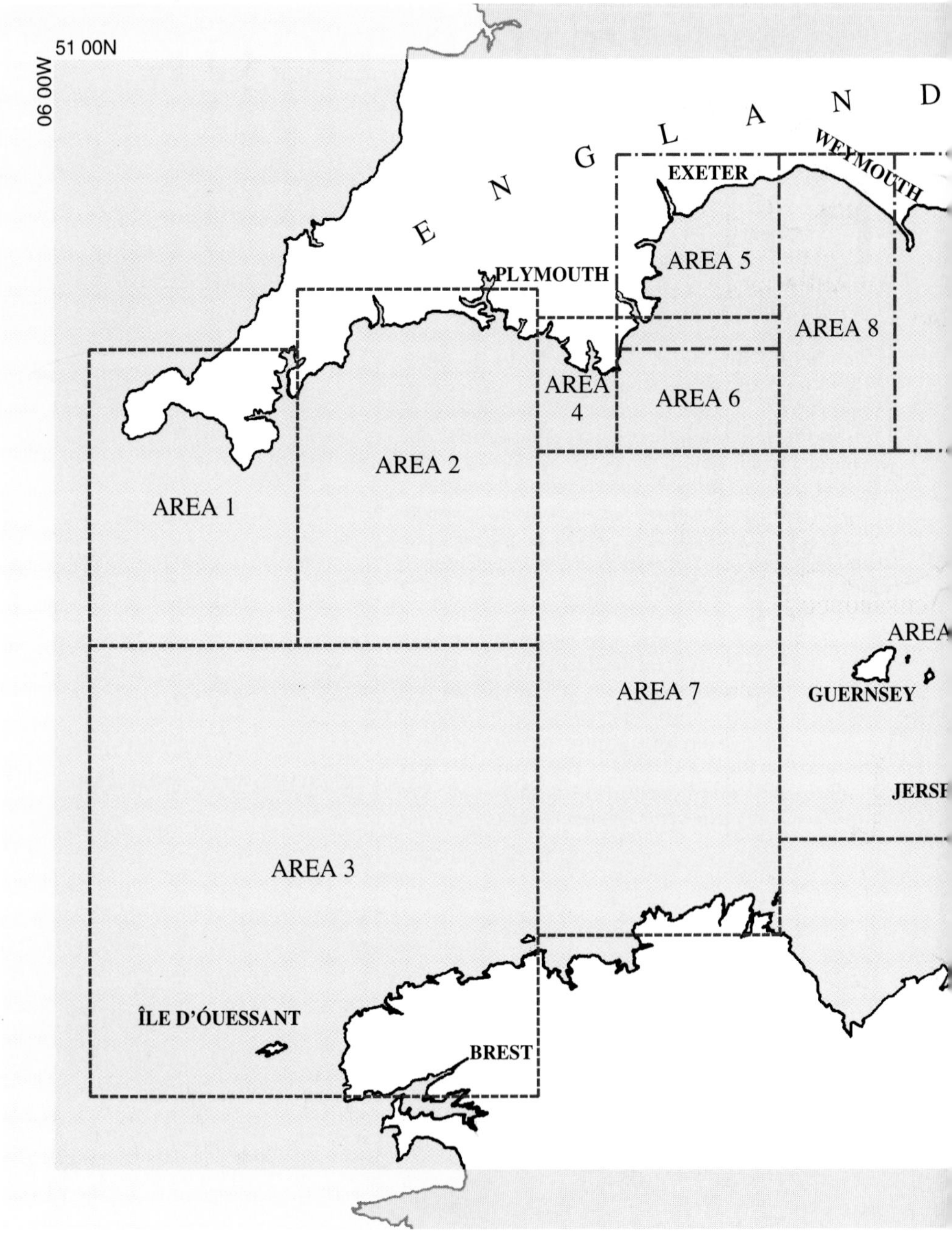

51 00N

06 00W

E N G L A N D

WEYMOUTH

EXETER

PLYMOUTH

AREA 5

AREA 8

AREA 4

AREA 6

AREA 2

AREA 1

AREA 7

AREA

GUERNSEY

JERSE

AREA 3

ÎLE D'ÓUESSANT

BREST

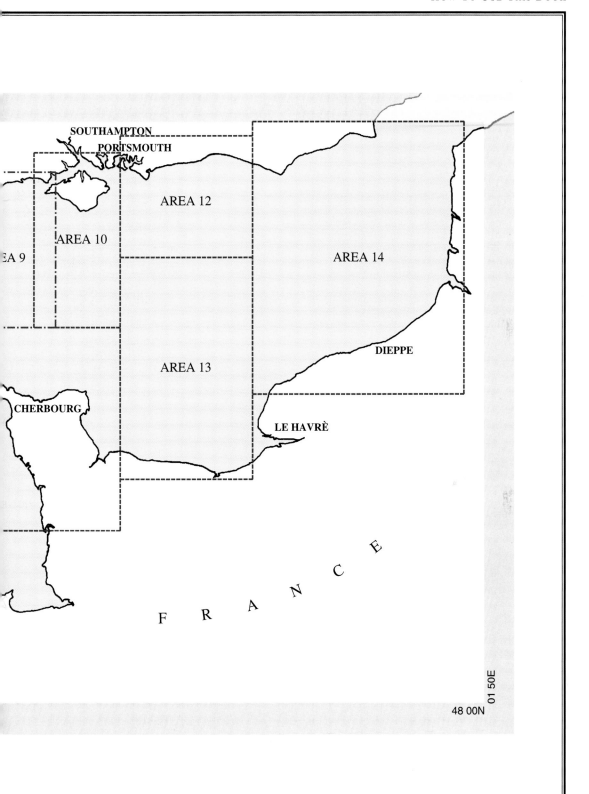

THE MILITARY REMAINS ACT

THE MILITARY REMAINS Act became law on September 8, 1986, and in the future may affect the wreck diver much more than it does at present. The main drive of the Act is to preserve the sanctity of "war graves", that is the wreckage of military ships and aircraft known to contain human remains of servicemen or women.

The wreckage of all military aircraft of any nation is automatically protected by the Act, but naval ships will have to be designated by the Secretary of State and will need a statutory instrument to do so. This means that ships to be named as "war graves" will have to be named and approved by Parliament in the same way that ships to be protected as historic wrecks need a statutory instrument passed through Parliament.

There seems no doubt that those who passed the Act had little idea of the number of ships which could fall under its terms, such as merchant ships with a naval gunner aboard – was he among the survivors? – and as a result no ships have yet been named under the Act. This does not mean that ships are not covered by the general thrust of the Act and divers should therefore treat all possible "war graves" with total respect.

However, once these ships have been named the diver commits an offence only if he or she tampers with, damages, moves, removes, or unearths remains or enters an enclosed interior space in the wreckage. Nothing in the Act prevents the wreck diver from visiting the site, examining the exterior or even settling on the wreckage. An offence is only committed if he or she disturbs remains or enters a proper compartment in the wreck. The punishment on conviction of an offence is a fine. This is, of course, a brief guide to the Act. Serious wreck divers should study the Act itself – your library or HM Stationery Office should be able to supply a copy.

THE MERCHANT SHIPPING ACTS

THE RECEIVER OF WRECK is responsible for the administration of the Merchant Shipping Acts 1894 and 1906 dealing with wreck and salvage. It is a legal requirement that all recovered wreck (flotsam, jetsam, derelict or lagan), whether recovered from within or outside UK territorial waters, is reported to the Receiver of Wreck.

Finders who conceal items are liable to prosecution, therefore any object – even if it appears to have little monetary value – should be declared as soon as possible. The Receiver of Wreck can then make a decision as to the future ownership of the property.

Wreck recovered from within UK territorial waters which remains unclaimed at the end of a one-year statutory period becomes the property of the Crown, and the Reciever of Wreck is required to dispose of it. This may be through sale of auction, although in many instances the finder will be allowed to keep unclaimed items of wreck in lieu of a salvage award. This, however, is at the discretion of the Receiver of Wreck and each case is judged on its merit.

For further information contact:

The Receiver of Wreck,
The Coastguard Agency,
Spring Place,
105 Commercial Road,
Southampton SO15 1EG.
Telephone: 01703 329474.
Fax: 01703 329477.

WORLD WAR ONE
CHANNEL WRECKS

◆

AREA ONE

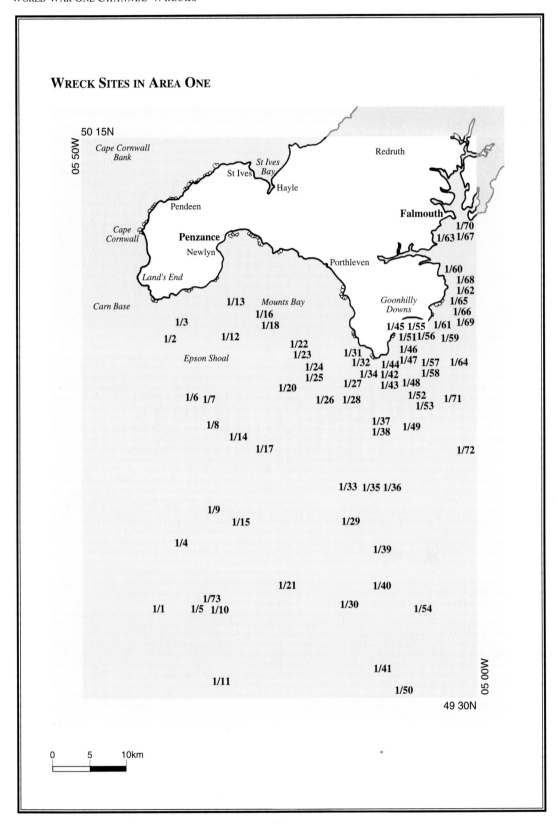

WRECK SITES IN AREA ONE

1/1: SIDMOUTH. *Country:* British.
Date sunk: 24/10/16. *Tons nett:* 2605. *Tons gross:* 4045. *Built:* 1903. *Type:* SS. *Rig:* schooner. *Owners:* Griffiths & Lewis, Cardiff. *Cargo:* Coal from Cardiff for Spezia. *Armed:* No. *Position:* 20 miles S by E of Wolf Rock (49 37 00N; 05 40 00W). *Master's name:* R. Hughes. *Crew:* 29. *Crew nationality:* 11 British, 18 others.

THE German submarine *UB-29* surfaced close to the *Sidmouth* and started to fire shells over her rigging. The message was clear enough to the master, stop or else. The master gathered his papers and put them in the bag he always kept ready, weighted with old shackles. He leaned over the opposite side to the submarine's approach and after dropping the bag in the sea, gave the order to stop engines.

The submarine came close, and the commander asked the master all the usual questions about his ship, where from, where bound etc. Having noted all the details he calmly told the master that he and his crew had better get away quickly as his ship was about to be sunk. The submarine moved menacingly around the *Sidmouth* to her port side.

Realising what was about to happen the master ordered his crew to take to the starboard lifeboat immediately. They got clear just in time before a torpedo slammed into the steamer amidships, blowing a huge hole in her.

From the boat the master and crew watched as their ship began to settle. However, they also spotted another ship in the distance which looked every bit like a British warship. It was in fact HMS *Cameleon* and she soon opened fire. One dropped close to the submarine which dived and got away.

1/2: GALLIER. *Country:* British.
Date sunk: 2/1/18. *Tons nett:* 2885. *Tons gross:* 4592. *Built:* 1914. *Type:* SS. *Rig:* schooner. *Owners:* Brys & Gylsen, 101 Leadenhall St, London. *Cargo:* In ballast from Havre to Barry Roads. *Armed:* 1 x 12pdr 12cwt gun, Mk 1, No 3608. Mount No 434. *Position:* 7½ miles ENE of Wolf Rock (49 59 30N; 05 38 00W). *Master's name:* Charles Albert Goodwin. *Crew:* 36. *Crew nationality:* 28 British, 2 American, 1 Italian, 2 Portuguese, 2 Belgians, 1 Russian. *Gunners:* J. Rowley, RMLI, No 13074 Portsmouth; Arthur Clover, RMLI, No 10682 Plymouth.

AFTER the first torpedo from *U-95* struck the *Gallier* under the saloon on the starboard side, Captain Goodwin immediately ordered the wireless operator to send the message, 'SOS ... ship torpedoed east-north-east of Wolf'.

It was 4.20am, the weather was particularly good for the time of year, a bright moonlit night with a moderate wind and sea. It was probably these conditions that helped the German U-boat commander to spot the *Gallier* as she was not showing any lights.

It was an excellent shot and the torpedo opened up a large hole in the steamer's number two hold. But for some reason the commander wasn't satisfied with the first hit and lined up ready to release another torpedo.

From his position on the bridge the master could see that his ship was settling rapidly and he calmly gave the order to the second mate to get the boats ready. He hurried to his room, gathered up his confidential papers and placed them in the weighted bag which was always ready for just such an occasion. As he joined the men assembled at the boats, he tossed the bag overboard, just as the second torpedo slammed into number one hold.

The crew left at speed as the steamer was now settling at an alarming rate, water pouring into the almost non-existent starboard side. They made it just in time, getting far enough away as the *Gallier* slipped below the surface and disappeared. In the bright moonlight the master looked around and saw a large submarine heading off to the south.

The radio message had not gone unheard. At 5.10am the trawler *Reeve* arrived on the scene and picked up all 36 of the crew, shaken but unhurt from their ordeal.

1/3: CLARA. *Country:* British.
Date sunk: 28/12/17. *Tons nett:* 1535. *Tons gross:* 2425. *Built:* By Richardson Duek & Co, Stockton in 1897. *Type:* SS. *Rig:* schooner. *Owners:* Burdick & Cook, London. *Cargo:* None. *Armed:* 1 x 13pdr gun. *Position:* 1½ miles SSW of Runnelstone (50 00 38N; 05 37 35W). *Master's name:* –. *Crew:* 24.

CLARA left Rouen on Christmas Day, 1917, bound for Barry Roads, to pick up a cargo of coal. She crossed the Channel and gradually made her way down the English side in the swept channel towards Land's End. At 10.30pm on December 28, her journey came to an abrupt halt when a torpedo slammed into her number four hold.

With his ship taking on water at an alarming rate and *UB-57*, the submarine responsible, only yards away, the master had no choice but to abandon ship. All the crew pulled clear and rowed towards the waiting submarine. The master was questioned by the German commander who wanted to know all his ship's details. Satisfied with the answers he received, the commander waved the master away and turned his attention to the sinking steamer. A few well placed shots with the deck gun finished her off and she sank at 11pm.

The crew rowed through the night towards the shore and were picked up around 10am by a patrol vessel which landed them at Penzance.

1/4: ZETA. *Country:* Dutch.
Date sunk: 22/1/17. *Tons nett:* –. *Tons gross:* 3053. *Built:* 1913. *Type:* SS. *Rig:* –. *Owners:* B. Fran Hengel. *Cargo:* –. *Armed:* No. *Position:* 22 miles

SW of Lizard (49 43 00N; 05 37 00W). *Master's name:* Jan Barf. *Crew:* 25. *Crew nationality:* All Dutch.

THE master of *Zeta* reported that the first he knew of his ship being in any trouble was at 11.15pm on January 22, 1917, when he heard a hissing noise on the port side of his ship. As he moved to have a look what was causing it a huge explosion occurred amidships about number two hold. He realised by then that his ship had been torpedoed.

Within five minutes *Zeta* was settling heavily in the water and the master ordered two boats to be lowered. All the crew with the exception of himself, the second engineer and the second mate left the ship but were instructed to stay close to her on the port side. Many blue rocket flares were let off and the ship's whistle was blown continuously in the hope of attracting attention. Just after midnight a searchlight suddenly lit up the starboard side of the steamer from something low in the water. The master said that because of the bright light he couldn't make out if it was a submarine or a patrol vessel. He shouted to his men in the boats on the port side to row around and see what it was but by the time they got there it had gone.

At 1am another vessel appeared close by but this time it was definite help in the shape of the steam trawler *Dynevor Castle*. Ropes were made fast to the sinking steamer and a tow was tried to the east with little success. In several hours they had only made about two miles due to the large amount of water inside her. At 8am the *Zeta* sank.

Dynevor Castle took all the crew on board and eventually landed them safely at Swansea.

1/5: DE VILLEBOIS-MAREUIL.
Country: French. *Date sunk:* 1/10/16. *Tons nett:* 30. *Tons gross:* 34. *Built:* Of wood. *Type:* FV. *Rig:* Smack. *Owners:* Madame Veuve le Moan of Douarnenez. *Cargo:* None. *Armed:* No. *Position:* 20 miles SSE of Wolf Rock (49 37 00N; 05 36 00W). *Master's name:* Bernard Surzur or Pierre Pevnes. *Crew:* 8. *Crew nationality:* All French.

WHY the *De Villebois-Mareuil* was returning home without any fish was not stated. In the late afternoon of October 1, 1916, a German submarine surfaced about 200yds astern of the little vessel. The first the crew knew of it was a loud bang as the enemy fired a blank shot. A voice came out of the conning tower but the master was unable to understand what was said. However, the man's arm signals explained everything, abandon ship at once or else!

As the crew pulled clear in their boat the submarine moved closer. Darkness was descending on the scene rapidly and the German commander appeared to be anxious to get on with the job in hand. Around 15 shells were fired from virtually point blank range into the wooden ship causing her to reel and lurch under each impact. The last the crew saw of her she was still afloat. The master reported that he saw the lights of another submarine close by but it took no part in the shelling.

For several hours the crew rowed towards the British coast and were eventually spotted by the schooner *Etoile Solaire* which picked them up at 1.30am the following morning, delivering them safely to Newport.

1/6: GARTHCLYDE. *Country:* British.
Date sunk: 15/10/17. *Tons nett:* 1319. *Tons gross:* 2124. *Built:* At Glasgow in 1917. *Type:* SS. *Rig:* schooner. *Owners:* William Garthwaite, 92/94 Gracechurch St, London. *Cargo:* 3000 tons coal for Bordeaux. *Armed:* 1 x 12pd 12cwt gun, No 4291 DAMS G. *Position:* 15 miles W by S of Lizard (49 54 00N; 05 35 00W). *Master's name:* John Stephen. *Crew:* 26. *Crew nationality:* All British. *Gunners:* Samuel Wilson, act LS RNVR, No TZ 5759; Sidney B.G. Fisk, AB RNVR, No LZ 5933.

GARTHCLYDE made Mounts Bay on October 14, 1917, in good time to join her convoy across the Channel. The next day 20 steamers escorted by four armed trawlers and five armed motor launches set off. The convoy was formed up in three columns abreast and *Garthclyde's* position was number four in the starboard column. She was 'dazzle painted'.

It was 6pm when a watchman on the bridge yelled to the master that he could see a torpedo heading straight for them on the starboard side. The master immediately ordered the helm to be thrown over hard to port but it was too late. The torpedo crashed into number three hold. The following explosion was so powerful that it completely ripped open the side of the ship. The steamer was in a hopeless situation, sinking rapidly, leaving the only option for the crew to get off quickly.

The lifeboat on the starboard side had been completely smashed by the explosion so all the men bundled into the port boat. The crew were clear in a trice which was just as well, the steamer sinking a few minutes later. One of the escorting trawlers was soon on the scene and picked up the crew. They were later transferred to another patrol vessel and taken to Penzance. The sinking was later claimed by *UC-79*.

1/7: POLYMNIA. *Country:* British.
Date sunk: 15/5/17. *Tons nett:* 1530. *Tons gross:* 2426. *Built:* 1903. *Type:* SS. *Rig:* schooner. *Owners:* Kaye Sons & Co Ltd, 118 Fenchurch St, London. *Cargo:* Iron ore and fruit, Huelva to Falmouth. *Armed:* 1 x 3pdr Vickers gun. *Position:* 15 miles W of the Lizard (49 54 00N; 05 34 00W). *Master's name:* A.H. Bonser. *Crew:* 27. *Crew nationality:* 25 British, 1 American, 1 Norwegian. *Gunners:* Grant; Lewis. *Casualties, drowned or killed by the explosion:* second mate; wireless operator; cook; donkeyman; Gunner Grant; 3 seamen.

IT was 6.30 in the morning when *Polymnia* was hit by a torpedo. It crashed into her starboard side just behind number three hold and the explosion blew in the engine room bulkhead completely. The water poured into the steamer and she started to settle immediately. Many of the crew managed to get themselves to the lifeboats but nine men were not so lucky and were either killed by the explosion or drowned when the ship sank so suddenly.

Although nobody had actually seen anything it was assumed that the ship had been attacked by an enemy submarine. It wasn't until *UC-75* surfaced alongside the first officer's lifeboat that it was certain. Fortunately for the survivors the weather was reasonable. The wind was light and the sea calm although there was some haze.

Both boats were making good progress towards the shore when at 9am they were given a helping hand by a passing Lowestoft drifter and taken into Falmouth.

1/8: LA ROCHE JACQUELIN.

Country: French. *Date sunk:* 14/11/16. *Tons nett:* 2199. *Tons gross:* 2400. *Built:* –. *Type:* SV. *Rig:* schooner. *Owners:* Buvean Freres et Baillerjean, France. *Cargo:* Maize. *Armed:* No. *Position:* 15 miles WSW of Lizard (49 52 00N; 05 34 00W). *Master's name:* Victor Rebillard. *Crew:* 22. *Crew nationality:* 21 French, 1 Dane.

A CALM day with light winds made sailing vessels such as the *La Roche Jacquelin* particularly vulnerable to attack from German submarines. This day was to prove no exception as about a mile off lay one such submarine, partially submerged, her commander observing the ship through the periscope.

On board the *Jacquelin* her officers were also looking through their binoculars trying to make out what the strange shape was in the water. It didn't take them long to work it out as the next moment the submarine was fully on the surface heading towards them with alarming speed.

It was pointless trying to get away from the menace as within a few minutes it was within hailing distance and a voice ordered the master to abandon his ship and go over immediately to the waiting submarine.

The master did as he was told and pulled alongside the enemy vessel. He noticed as he climbed aboard just what a scruffy bunch the submarine's crew were. They wore no real uniform just leather jackets and it looked like they hadn't had a wash or a shave for some time.

The Germans followed their usual pattern in such cases, a boarding party going over to plant bombs and to steal any food, instruments and valuable metals they could find. The master of the *Jacquelin* said that a German officer asked him in particular if they had any copper on board. The bombs did their job very effectively and within minutes the ship was sinking.

The crew in the boat made for the shore but were soon picked up by the Admiralty trawler *Kinaldie* which delivered them safely to Falmouth.

1/9: TYNE.

Country: British. *Date sunk:* 17/6/17. *Tons nett:* 1821. *Tons gross:* 2909. *Built:* 1900 *Type:* SS. *Rig:* schooner. *Owners:* Royal Mail Steam Packet Co, 18 Moorgate St, London. *Cargo:* Coal and benzol from Penarth to La Pallico. *Armed:* 1 x 12pdr gun. *Position:* 18 miles SW of Lizard (49 45 00N; 05 34 00W). *Master's name:* G.P. Matthews. *Crew:* 35. *Crew nationality:* 29 British, 2 Danes, 3 Americans, 1 Russian. *Gunners:* A. White; G. Balmer.

TYNE was part of a convoy heading from Mounts Bay to Brest. She was number three out of a total of nine steamers and was positioned behind the patrol ship No 2665 *Amroth Castle*. The weather wasn't particularly good with wind and rain.

Not a great deal was reported as to the circumstances of this sinking but that was probably because nobody really saw anything. All that can be said with any certainty is that at 10.30pm the steamer was hit by a torpedo, well below the waterline on the starboard quarter. She started to take in water quickly and the crew had to be sharp about getting off. But they all managed to get clear in time and 15 minutes later the *Tyne* sank.

All the crew were accounted for and uninjured when picked up by one of the patrol vessels. They remained on board for the rest of the journey to Brest.

The *UC-48* later claimed her as a 'kill'.

1/10: HENLEY.

Country: British. *Date sunk:* 10/4/18. *Tons nett:* 2111. *Tons gross:* 3249. *Built:* 1894. *Type:* SS. *Rig:* schooner. *Owners:* Watts, Watts & Co Ltd, Leadenhall St, London. *Cargo:* 4700 tons coal from Barry Roads to St Nazaire. *Armed:* 1 x 4.7in gun. *Position:* 24 miles SW by S of Lizard (49 37 00N; 05 33 00W). *Master's name:* Walter Rothwell. *Crew:* 39. *Crew nationality:* 28 British, 11 Others. *Gunners:* John McDonald, AB RNVR, No CZ152 Chatham; Richard Carty, AB RNR, No 2463 SD Devonport; James Edwardson, LS RNR, ONNK. *Casualties:* Evan Baker, third engineer; P. Murphy, sailor; Anton Baptista, fireman; Pedro Augustire, fireman; T. Bell, fireman; James Edwardson, gunner.

TWO other steamers were crossing the Channel under escort with *Henley* when she ran into trouble at 10.15pm on April 10, 1918. They were formed up three abreast with *Henley* on the port side, the Danish steamer *Hansen* about 400yds to starboard and the Greek steamer *Antonios* on the starboard wing. They were protected by three armed patrol vessels, one ahead and one on each side of the steamers. The weather was reasonable with light winds and a

The *Kalibia* – sank in just over a minute after being torpedoed by *UB-80*.

moderate sea, but the sky was heavily overcast creating a dark night.

The first anyone in the convoy knew of trouble was when a lookout on the escort trawler 3633 *George Burton*, which was positioned about 800yds on *Henley's* port side, reported that he had heard the hiss of a torpedo pass close by. A few seconds later a huge explosion boomed out from the *Henley*. The torpedo struck her on the port side at the break of the poop in number four hold. It opened up a massive hole in her, allowing water to rush in at an enormous rate.

She began to settle down rapidly and the master ordered *Henley* to be abandoned a few minutes later. Thirty-three men managed to get clear but six others were not so fortunate. The master stayed to the bitter end and was so devoted to getting his crew clear that he ended up having to jump into the sea as the steamer started her final plunge.

George Burton raced to the scene while another patrol trawler, *Amroth Castle* moved to the position where her commander judged the submarine to be and started depth charging. The crew in the boats were soon aboard the *George Burton* and the master was also fished out of the water rather cold and exhausted but otherwise unhurt. *UB-109* claimed to have sunk the *Henley*.

1/11: KALIBIA. *Country:* British. *Date sunk:* 30/11/17. *Tons nett:* 3149. *Tons gross:* 4930. *Built:* 1902. *Type:* SS. *Rig:* schooner. *Owners:* Clyde Shipping Co Ltd, 21 Carlton Place, Glasgow. *Cargo:* 6499 tons steel billets from

Norfolk, USA, to Bordeaux. *Armed:* Yes. *Position:* 29 miles SSW from Lizard (49 31 00N; 05 33 00W). *Master's name:* W.P. Bennett. *Crew:* 44. *Casualties:* 25.

THERE is literally only one form in the contemporary records dealing with the sinking of the *Kalibia* and the information on that form is very sparse. She was part of a convoy when she was struck by a torpedo from *UB-80*. The third officer is reported to have spotted the torpedo when it was just a few feet away from the vessel.

The resulting explosion was so severe and caused so much damage to the steamer that she sank in a little over a minute. It was 9.15pm, the weather was moderate but it was a dark cold night and anyone finding themselves in the water would not last long. Twenty-five members of the crew lost their lives in this sinking either by the explosion or drowning. However, 19 others were found by the escorting patrol trawler *Yokohama* and taken to Brest. The captain was among the survivors.

1/12: COMMANDANT BARATIER. *Country:* French. *Date sunk:* 19/2/18. *Tons nett:* 256. *Tons gross:* 324. *Built:* Of wood in 1900. *Type:* SV. *Rig:* Three masted barque. *Owners:* E. Louvet, St Malo, France. *Cargo:* 240 tons pit props from La Rochelle to Cardiff. *Armed:* No. *Position:* 8 miles S of Penzance (49 59 00N; 05 31 30W). *Master's name:* Francois Le Bourdais. *Crew:* 11. *Crew nationality:* All French.

WITH machine guns blazing at him, rifles cracking and bullets slapping through the sails of the *Commandant Baratier*, the master really had no other choice than to stop. The German submarine was only 400yds off, her commander displaying an unusually powerful show of strength against such a weak victim.

Once the barque had stopped sailing so did the firing. It was a bright moonlit night and the submarine was by this time plainly visible to the crew. Captain Le Bourdais watched as several men on top of the conning tower started to shout and make signals for him to abandon his ship and go alongside the submarine. The crew quickly obeyed and as the sea conditions were so calm it took them little time to reach the waiting enemy vessel. The master and mate were taken aboard the submarine to answer questions. Whilst this was going on several German sailors forced the crew of one boat to row them back to the *Commandant Baratier*.

After helping themselves to various provisions the German sailors planted two bombs on the barque, one in the hold and the other on the port side amidships. Happy with their work they were rowed back to the submarine where the master and the mate got back in the boat. Thirty minutes later the clear night was lit up by two explosions which tore the heart out of the barque and sent her plunging downwards.

Although the two boats from the *Commandant Baratier* were separated they both made it safely to the shore. The master and men in one boat rowed all the way to Penzance but the men in the other were given a helping hand by the drifter *Herty II* and landed at the same port.

1/13: HAAKON VII. *Country:* Norwegian. *Date sunk:* 7/9/17. *Tons nett:* 1379. *Tons gross:* 2180. *Built:* At Alblasserdam in 1907. *Type:* SS. *Rig:* schooner. *Owners:* Ivon & Christens, Oslo, Norway. *Cargo:* 3460 tons iron ore from Aznar Co, Bilbao to Cardiff. *Armed:* No. *Position:* 3 miles ESE of Land's End (50 02 00N; 05 31 00W). *Master's name:* Bjorn Gunderssen. *Crew:* 23. *Crew nationality:* 13 Norwegians, 1 Dane, 9 Swedes.

HAAKON VII sank so rapidly that the crew had no time to do anything except jump for their lives. One report stated that she sank in only 20 seconds after the torpedo struck.

It happened at 8.20am, the wind was light, the sea calm, ideal operating conditions for submarines. Nobody on the bridge saw anything. The torpedo slammed into the starboard side between holds three and four and opened up a hole that totally exposed her engine room to the sea. The effects were devastating and in an instant she slipped below the waves stern first. One donkeyman who was in the stokehold had no chance and was killed outright by the explosion.

The rest of the crew were left floundering in the water looking for pieces of wreckage to cling to. A minute or so later a lifeboat, a raft and then a dingy surfaced, having broken away from the steamer below. These were eagerly pounced on by the crew although two, the mess room boy and a seaman, couldn't hold on that long and drowned.

There were plenty of other vessels in the area and soon the survivors were picked up by a patrolling naval trawler and taken into Penzance.

1/14: FACTO. *Country:* Norwegian. *Date sunk:* 16/9/17. *Tons nett:* 1449. *Tons gross:* 2372. *Built:* At Sunderland in 1904. *Type:* SS. *Rig:* schooner. *Owners:* Stolt Nielsen, Haugesund, Norway. *Cargo:* 700 tons ballast bound for Cardiff. *Armed:* No. *Position:* 16 miles WSW of Lizard (49 51 00N; 05 31 00W). *Master's name:* Nicolai Abrahamsen. *Crew:* 23. *Crew nationality:* 12 Norwegians, 4 Swedes, 3 Danes, 2 Russians, 1 Dutch, 1 American.

ALTHOUGH the first officer was in charge of the watch on the bridge, the master was also there, doing some calculations and generally seeing to his paperwork. All was running smoothly, the ship was making nine knots, the lookouts were vigilant and ready for any eventuality. However, it was the master who first spotted the track of a torpedo about 500ft off, heading directly for the port side of his ship.

There was no time to do anything except to brace up for the impact which was violent, the torpedo smashing its way into the after hold. *Facto* started to settle by the stern within minutes. Twenty-one men managed to get clear in two boats, but two others, the second engineer and the carpenter, were missing, never to be seen again.

Facto was being watched by lookouts on a ship about six miles off, the American destroyer USS *Nicholson*. Her commander ordered his helmsman to make for the men in the boats and told his lookouts to keep a sharp watch for the submarine. The crew from the *Facto* were picked up but were not put ashore locally. They remained on board *Nicholson* until the next day when they were landed at Queenstown, Ireland.

1/15: GERMAN SUBMARINE (possible). *Country:* German. *Date believed sunk:* 2/12/16. *Tons nett:* –. *Tons gross:* –. *Built:* –. *Type:* –. *Armed:* Yes. *Position:* 17 miles SW of Lizard (49 44 00N; 05 30 00W).

A REPORT by Lieutenant M. Armstrong of HMS *Q9*, at St Mary's, Scilly Isles, on December 3, 1916. *Q9* sailed under the name of *Mary B. Mitchell*.

"Sir, I have the honour to submit my report on the engagement with an enemy submarine yesterday morning, December 2, at 10.25am.

"I observed the submarine two points on the starboard bow distant two miles. In the same direction there was a Brixham fishing boat and between the fishing vessel and ourselves there were four objects seen, the nearest of which was plainly distinguished as a submarine on the surface. The next two objects appeared to be boats and later turned out to be two boats with the crew of the Norwegian steamer *Skjoldulf*. The fourth object disappeared, being a second submarine. At 10.30am the remaining submarine opened fire at 1500yds coming towards us from the fore of our starboard beam, he had international 'A.B.' flying, so I ordered a panic party to clear away the boats and to launch them.

"After the submarine had fired three shots, the range having come down to 800yds I observed through the binoculars the man who was firing the gun suddenly clamped it in the fore and aft position and run towards the conning tower. The submarine then altered his course away from us so thinking they had observed something suspicious I opened fire with all guns, but unfortunately the lanyard on the 12-pounder carried away so I carried on with independent firing from six-pounders. Nine rounds were fired and two hits observed, the submarine going down.

"At 10.45am a periscope was sighted on the starboard quarter (the second submarine) and at 10.50am a torpedo was fired at us on the surface and by getting the helm hard a starboard quickly it just passed under our stern and missed the rudder. It is my opinion that the submarine observed an armed trawler bearing down which turned out to be the *Rosetta*. We cruised about in the vicinity for about two hours while the *Rosetta* picked up the crew and I afterwards had the Captain and mate aboard to interview them as they were quite close when I opened up."

A statement from the master of the Norwegian SS *Skjoldulf* said that his vessel had been sunk earlier several miles to the west. He said that the boats containing his crew were being towed by the submarine that had sunk his ship. Finding himself in the line of fire his crew rowed smartly to get clear and when he stopped to look at the scene again he noticed that part of the submarine's conning tower was missing.

The steamer's mate stated that it was the second shell from *Q9* that hit the conning tower as he saw the splinters flying from it in all directions. He thought that there was about six or seven men on deck, one man on the gun and the rest in the conning tower.

It was also stated by one of the crew on *Q9* that the fourth shot from the after six-pounder struck the submarine at the base of the conning tower making it list over to port heavily, righted again and sank vertically very quickly. As it sank a huge column of water was thrown up into the air from the side where she was hit.

The Admiralty agree after examining all the reports that the submarine was indeed sunk and they sanctioned the maximum payment of £1000 pounds to be paid to the crew of the *Q9*. Lieutenant Armstrong was awarded a DSO and others received the DSC and DSM. However, there is no German record of a submarine being lost on this date.

1/16: KILMAHO. *Country:* British.
Date sunk: 17/5/17. *Tons nett:* –. *Tons gross:* 2155. *Built:* 1898. *Type:* SS. *Rig:* –. *Owners:* J.Cory & Sons. *Cargo:* Railway material from Cardiff for Dunkirk. *Armed:* 1 x 12pdr 12cwt gun. *Position:* 10 miles WNW from Lizard (50 01 00N; 05 27 00W). *Master's name:* –. *Crew:* 22.

THE only person to survive the sinking of the *Kilmaho* was an Arab fireman who could give very little information.

He said that at around 11pm on May 16, 1917, he was awakened in his bunk by a loud explosion. The whole ship shook and he quickly rushed up on deck to see what was happening. As he made the deck he literally stepped into the water as the ship sank from beneath his feet. Amazingly, he managed to keep himself alive for six hours just floating in the cold water. He was picked up by a patrol vessel, feeling extremely cold but very much alive.

UB-20 later claimed to have sunk the *Kilmaho*.

1/17: CITY OF CORINTH. *Country:* British.
Date sunk: 21/5/17. *Tons nett:* 3773. *Tons gross:* 5870. *Built:* At Whiteinch in 1913. *Type:* SS. *Rig:* schooner. *Owners:* Ellerman Lines Ltd, Tower Buildings, Liverpool. *Cargo:* 8500 tons general, rice in bags and packages from Japan, Siam and Straits settlements to London. *Armed:* Yes. *Position:* 12 miles SW of Lizard (49 50 00N; 05 27 00W). *Master's name:* Charles Stuart Nelson. *Crew:* 68.

THE *City of Corinth* was to call at Falmouth to receive sailing instructions that would take her to London. Unfortunately she never made Falmouth, falling victim to *UB-31* lurking off the Cornish coast on Monday May 21, 1917.

It was 3.40 in the afternoon when the steamer was first attacked. She had been zig-zagging but the master felt that as he was in a dangerous rocky area he would stop. She was making just over 12 knots and lots of men were on watch.

The gunner on the gun platform aft had just been relieved by his mate when there was an enormous explosion on the port side. The steamer lurched violently and the master rushed about the ship trying to assess the extent of the damage. She had been hit in number six hold, a huge hole letting in water rapidly.

The master ordered the engines astern to take the way off her and had the order passed for all the Lascars and the Chinese crew to stand by the boats and to launch only when the steamer had come to a stop. All the crew got clear. Meanwhile the master and his officers put the engines ahead again to see if she could be beached. However, the engine room was soon deep in water, and the engines were shut down.

As the chief engineer joined his fellow officers on

deck the gunner, still standing by his gun gave a shout, "Torpedo." It was another streaking towards the steamer amidships. There was nothing that could be done to take evasive action but the gunner could see a foot or so of the submarine's periscope and in pure frustration opened fire on it. It was a plucky response considering that another loud explosion rocked the ship tearing open another hole in her side. It was time for the rest of the men to leave, the steamer heeling over rapidly. Four minutes later the *City of Corinth* had gone to the bottom.

All the men, apart from the odd cut and bruise, were uninjured and rowed towards the shore. However, with all the noise of the explosions it wasn't long before a patrol vessel had all the crew on board, landing them later at Falmouth.

1/18: VIGRID. *Country:* Norwegian. *Date sunk:* 31/12/17. *Tons nett:* 951. *Tons gross:* 2400. *Built:* 1914. *Type:* SS. *Rig:* schooner. *Owners:* Johan Vaage, Bergen, Norway. *Cargo:* 2102 tons coal from Barry to Rouen. *Armed:* No. *Position:* 8 miles ESE of Runnelstone Buoy (50 00 00N; 05 26 00W). *Master's name:* Frevold Anderson. *Crew:* 19. *Crew nationality:* 12 Norwegians, 6 Swedes, 1 Dane.

THE German submarine that sank the *Vigrid* with a torpedo could have hardly missed from a range of only 200yds. It was 1.30 in the morning and by the time the lookouts had spotted the menace in the darkness it was too late. The torpedo smashed into the steamer's port side, penetrating the boiler room and blowing almost the whole of the port side out. The explosion killed one engineer, two sailors and two firemen.

The steamer sank so fast that it was a marvellous feat of organisation to get the remaining 14 crew away in the only boat left intact on the starboard side. They did it with seconds to spare and managed to get far enough away to avoid being capsized by the suction as *Vigrid* plunged downwards.

A few minutes later the enemy submarine moved close to the boat and a voice asked for the details of the ship, name, where from, where bound, tonnage, and so on. The crew were spotted about two hours later by a lookout on the drifter *Hawthorne* which picked them up and landed them at Penzance.

1/19: NANNA. *Country:* Norwegian. *Date sunk:* 4/10/18. *Tons nett:* 699. *Tons gross:* 1125. *Built:* At Bergen in 1900. *Type:* SS. *Rig:* schooner. *Owners:* Albert Schjelderup, Bergen, Norway. *Cargo:* 1531 tons coal from Edgar Williams, Cardiff to St Malo. *Armed:* No. *Position:* 8 miles W by S of Lizard (49 56 00N; 05 24 00W). *Master's name:* John Halfdan Halvorsen. *Crew:* 15. *Crew nationality:* 7 Norwegians, 6 Swedes, 2 Danish.

NANNA was making her way around the Cornish coast in bad weather, heading up to Falmouth to join a convoy for France. The sea was rough which prevented the master from zig-zagging and he, along with the second mate, were on the bridge at 12.45 on the morning of October 4, 1918.

Nobody saw the submarine's periscope close by on the starboard side and nobody saw the white streak of the torpedo as it sped towards the ship. But everyone on board felt the impact as it smashed into the fore hold on the starboard side.

The master gave the order to abandon ship immediately. The *Nanna* sank in less than two minutes making it impossible for some of the men to gain the deck. The master managed to get away in the small boat with two sailors. He found two firemen still alive and soon had them aboard his little boat. At one stage he spotted a raft and another boat but when he reached them found they were empty.

The five men spent several hours being tossed around by the rough sea before help arrived in the shape of the French fishing vessel *Albert Robert*, which landed them later at Newlyn.

1/20: EROS. *Country:* Swedish. *Date sunk:* 20/3/18. *Tons nett:* 405. *Tons gross:* 762. *Built:* At Sunderland in 1905. *Type:* SS. *Rig:* schooner. *Owners:* Otto Hillerstrom, Helsingborg. *Cargo:* In ballast from L'Orient to Barry Roads. *Armed:* No. *Position:* 8 miles W of Lizard (49 55 00N; 05 24 00W). *Master's name:* Bernhard Nilsson. *Crew:* 14. *Crew nationality:* 6 Swedes, 2 Norwegians, 1 American, 1 Mexican, 1 Greek, 1 Spaniard, 1 Portuguese, 1 Chilian.

EROS was part of a north bound convoy consisting of 15 vessels. Her position was number five in the starboard column and she was in her correct position at 4.45am when she was picked out by a German submarine commander as the best target.

Just a few moments before the torpedo struck her, one of the lookouts had shouted to the second officer on the bridge that he could see a periscope. By the time the second officer had looked for himself it was too late, the torpedo smashed into the starboard side opening up a huge hole in the engine room.

The master appeared on deck instantly and after quickly surveying the ship decided that she wouldn't float for long. Three men were missing at the muster, two engineers and the cook. The master was told that they were down in the engine room and had either been killed by the explosion or had drowned as the engine room was by that time completely full of water.

It took only 10 minutes for the *Eros* to sink but the 11 surviving crew were well clear by that time. They didn't have long to wait as the patrol trawler *Sanson* was alongside their boat within five minutes, landing them later at Penzance.

1/21: GERMAN SUBMARINE (possible).
Country: German. *Date believed sunk:* 24/10/16.
Tons nett: –. *Tons gross:* –. *Built:* –. *Type:* –.
Armed: Yes. *Position:* 20 miles SSW of the Lizard
Light (49 39 00N; 05 24 00W). *Master's name:* –.

Q17 was commanded by Henry G.G. Westmore RNR,
and he later reported that at 6.20am he was on routine
patrol keeping an eye out for trouble in general, and,
in particular, enemy submarines. A watchman pointed
out a large tramp steamer off the starboard bow about
a mile off but of more interest a shape in the water
behind it. Temp. Lieutenant W.E. Sanders RNR,
quickly looked through his binoculars and confirmed
that it was indeed a submarine and immediately called
the crew to quarters, being very careful to keep all
apart from the designated deck hands to stay out of
sight.

Commander Westmore was called and he
immediately ordered his sailing ship to be close hauled
to the wind so as to get up as close as possible to the
enemy. At 6.45am the submarine's deck gun boomed
out as the Germans began their assault on the steamer,
Q17 remained silent but was getting closer by the
minute. Because the enemy was to windward it got
to the point where *Q17* had got as close as she
possibly could and at a range of about 1000yds the
order was given to down the screens and fire as the
guns came to bear.

The after starboard gun was the first to shoot but the
shell fell just short. This startled the German gunners
who immediately turned their deck gun towards the
approaching menace. *Q17's* forward gunners were
waiting to join the action but their screen jammed at
the vital moment. As the crew struggled to free the
screen the after gun let loose again, the shell finding
its mark, piercing the submarine's hull and exploding
inside. The German gunners loosed off one shot but it
whimpered harmlessly behind *Q17*. Having got the
range the rear gunners loosed off another shell with
equal effect piercing yet another large hole in the
submarine. Soon smoke and flames were pouring out
of the stricken enemy vessel and it sank with several
of her crew still on deck.

Commander Westmore would liked to have looked
for survivors but he couldn't. The position was
directly to windward and it would have taken too long
to get up to the site. However, more importantly,
another submarine had surfaced close to the tramp
steamer and had begun shelling it. The crew had
already abandoned their ship and were pulling clear in
the boats. At 4000yds it was a long shot as *Q17's* port
guns opened fire. None of the shells reached the
submarine but the gesture was enough to send it
scurrying off leaving the steamer crippled but still
afloat. The steamer turned out to be the Admiralty
Transport *Bagdale*.

The Admiralty were pleased with the actions of
Q17 and agreed that the submarine must have been
killed. They accordingly awarded the maximum £1000
prize money, to be divided among the crew as well

as decorating several men for their exceptional
performance during the action. Commander Westmore
was awarded a DSO.

German records do not show a submarine sunk on
this date.

1/22: TIRO. *Country:* Norwegian.
Date sunk: 29/12/17. *Tons nett:* 858. *Tons
gross:* 1442. *Built:* 1910. *Type:* SS. *Rig:* schooner.
Owners: Christensen & Paulsen, Sandefjord,
Norway. *Cargo:* 2800 tons coal from Barry to
Rouen. *Armed:* No. *Position:* 10 miles NW of
Lizard/Lizard bearing SE by E 7 miles
(49 58 12N; 05 23 00W). *Master's name:* Otto
Paust. *Crew:* 18. *Crew nationality:* 10 Norwegians,
2 Spaniards, 2 Swedes, 2 Russian/Finn women,
1 Dutch, 1 Eskimo.

TIRO was on charter to the Hudson Bay Company
when she was lost. The instructions contained in the
master's secret papers required him to pass close to the
west of Lundy and hug the coast south. He was to
pass inside of Longships, close around Land's End
and the Lizard to Falmouth. The master was carrying
out his instructions to the letter and was rounding the
inside of Mounts Bay when a torpedo struck the *Tiro*.

The wind was howling a full gale making the seas
extremely heavy. In fact, it was so bad that the master
wouldn't allow any lookouts up forward fearing for
their safety. But *Tiro* was still making a good eight
knots.

It was 5.30am when the torpedo struck her on the
port side at the after end of number two hold, striking
her with such force that a 30ft section was completely
blown out of her side. The explosion also killed the
chief engineer who was in the engine room at the
time. With such severe damage she started to go down
almost instantly, leaving little time for the crew to
get clear. However, four men did manage to get a
boat away and seven of the others climbed onto a
raft which floated free as the ship sank. Six others
though were not so lucky and drowned in the rough
waters.

Until that point nobody had seen or heard anything
of the submarine responsible. But as if out of nowhere
the U-boat appeared a few yards off the raft and
slowly cruised by. A man appeared at the top of the
conning tower and shouted down to the men, "What
nationality are you?"

The men on the raft were picked up at 9.30am by
the American warship *Houston* and taken to Penzance.
The four in the boat were picked up a passing steamer
and taken to Falmouth.

1/23: DEPENDENCE. *Country:* British.
Date sunk: 15/9/17. *Tons nett:* 99. *Tons gross:* 120.
Built: Of wood at Itchenor in 1874 . *Type:* SV. *Rig:*
schooner. *Owners:* J Marwood, 14 South Castle St,
Liverpool. *Cargo:* 180 tons flints from Hall & Son,

Fecamp to Liverpool. *Armed:* No. *Position:* 6 miles W of Lizard (49 57 30N; 05 22 00W). *Master's name:* William Jas Hooper. *Crew:* 5. *Crew nationality:* All British.

THE weather had been particularly bad for the *Dependence* as she made her way down the English Channel. At one stage it became so bad that she had to stop in St Austell Bay and stayed there for three days until the weather moderated. She weighed anchor at noon on September 14, 1917. A few hours later the wind began to blow strongly again and Captain Hooper decided he would make for Falmouth but the wind suddenly dropped.

With just basic steerage speed the *Dependence* headed on down the Channel past the Lizard. At 10.30am the next day the Master was below when he heard one of the watchmen shout, "Submarine" at the top of his voice. He scurried up on deck to find a German submarine about 100yds off. It quickly moved abreast of the schooner and opened fire with its deck gun. Although the shells were wide or high the master needed no more encouragement and ordered his men into the boat and rowed towards the waiting enemy.

Two men were ordered by the German commander to get aboard the submarine. The room was needed in the boat for several German sailors who demanded to be rowed back to the abandoned *Dependence*. The master was made to go back aboard and told to find soap, tea, and tinned meat. Whilst he was doing that, the Germans planted four bombs at various places around the ship. It was expertly done and as the crew delivered their unwelcome guests back on their submarine the bombs exploded, sending the schooner plunging down stern first. The crew rowed ashore without difficulty.

1/24: ATLANTIS. *Country:* Norwegian.
Date sunk: 3/10/18. *Tons nett:* 734. *Tons gross:* 1124. *Built:* 1906. *Type:* SS. *Rig:* schooner. *Owners:* C.H. Engelhart, Oslo, Norway. *Cargo:* 1450 tons coal from Barry Docks to Havre. *Armed:* No. *Position:* 6 miles W by S of Lizard (49 57 00N; 05 21 00W). *Master's name:* A. Stranger Thorsen. *Crew:* 18.

THERE are only basic details available on this sinking in the records, just enough to know what happened.

The weather was reasonable, the wind from the south-west, force 3-4, a heavy swell and a dark but clear night. It was one o'clock in the morning when *Atlantis* was spotted by a German submarine. One torpedo smashed into the port side of the steamer, exploding in the after part of number two hold and opened up a large hole.

She began to settle very rapidly indeed and it is amazing that 15 of the crew managed to get away in one boat in time. The steamer sank in under two minutes. Two men were not so lucky and were killed by the explosion.

1/25: THISBE. *Country:* French.
Date sunk: 6/9/17. *Tons nett:* 489. *Tons gross:* 1185. *Built:* At Sunderland in 1910. *Type:* SS. *Rig:* schooner. *Owners:* G. Lamy & Co, Caen, France. *Cargo:* 1374 tons coal, from The Main Colliery, Neath Abbey to Lamy & Co, Caen. *Armed:* 1 x 90mm gun. *Position:* 6 miles W by S of Lizard (49 56 00N; 05 21 00W). *Master's name:* Pierre Le Bitter. *Crew:* 21. *Crew nationality:* All French.

"IT is suggested this instance of what can be termed as foul murder might be published."

This was a comment in the Admiralty notes, caused by the graphic description given by survivors of the terrible death of the *Thisbe's* ship's boy.

The master and the mate were on the bridge at 12.15pm on September 6, 1917. Suddenly a shout went up from one of the lookouts followed almost instantly by a huge explosion. The lookout had seen the track of a torpedo when it was 10yds off the starboard side of the steamer, far too late to do anything about it. Both lifeboats on the starboard side were smashed to pieces but even worse was the state of the ship, filling rapidly and heeling over very steeply. Eight men managed to launch a boat on the port side and the rest just bundled over, or, as in the case of the master, were blown over by the explosion. The master landed in the water and although he was soon picked up by the boat, found that he had injured his back badly. In agony, the master looked back at his sinking steamer and was met with the awful sight of the boy's face at one of the portholes. The young lad stretched out his hand through the porthole as the ship heeled over more and more, his cries for help chilling the men in the boat. There was nothing anyone could do for him and in a few seconds more he was gone with the *Thisbe*. It was a double tragedy as the boy's father was the third engineer of the *Thisbe*. He was also lost with the ship, along with five other crew members, either drowned or killed by the explosion.

Six men in the water managed to clamber onto a raft that had floated free from the deck of the steamer.

Lieutenant Bartlett, commanding officer of the motor launch *334*, reported that he had observed a cloud of smoke rising high from the starboard side of the *Thisbe* and made to her assistance at full speed. Within two minutes the steamer had disappeared. He went in among the wreckage and picked up all the survivors. However, as he was doing so a lookout spotted the conning tower of a submarine about 500yds off to the south west. The gunners were immediately ordered to open fire on it but the submarine dived rapidly. After spending some time dropping depth charges, Lieutenant Bartlett went back to Penzance with the survivors of *Thisbe*.

1/26: BALLARAT. *Country:* British.
Date sunk: 25/4/17. *Tons nett:* 7055. *Tons gross:* 11120. *Built:* 1911. *Type:* SS. *Rig:* schooner. *Owners:* Peninsular & Oriental Steam Navigation

Co, London. *Cargo:* 9000 tons general.
Armed: Yes. *Position:* 6 miles SW of Lizard Light
(49 54 00N; 05 19 00W). *Master's name:*
G.W. Cockman. *Crew:* 150.

THE steamer *Ballarat* was a large ship and an
extremely tempting target for an enemy submarine
commander. She was also important because of her
human cargo of 1602 troops from Australia. With all
the escorts around her it would be hard to believe that
any enemy vessel would come within miles of the
convoy, but one did.

The *Ballarat* was zig-zagging about 23 miles to
the south-west of St Mary's, Scilly Isles, at about 10
knots. A lookout suddenly shouted that he could see
the wake of a torpedo heading for the ship but before
the officer on the bridge could react it was too late.
The torpedo slammed into the starboard side by
number five hatch. A huge explosion followed which
opened up a large hole in her side, smashed the rear
deck gun and starboard propeller.

As the water poured into her the master realised
that he had to stop the ship to try and slow down the
rate at which she was settling and hopefully get all
the troops and crew off safely. Destroyers and armed
trawlers descended on her from every direction. Whilst
some were busy taking off all the men from the
sinking steamer others were searching for the culprit
(*UB-32*) and trying to shield *Ballarat* from further
attack. Fortunately they were successful with the latter
and all the men were taken off without injury.

The master with six of his crew remained on board
to see what could be done for the ship. They were
joined by seven men from the naval vessel *Acasta*.
They found that the two after holds were completely
flooded and that water was up to the cylinders in the
engine room. Word had already gone out asking for
tugs to be sent to the scene but the reply was that it
would be some time before any were available.

At 6.30pm *Midge* got the *Ballarat* under tow and
slowly eased her towards the Cornish coast. They
were lucky through the night as the weather remained
calm allowing them to make some good headway but
the ship was badly crippled, taking on more and more
water as time went by. Eventually, as they approached
the Lizard the steamer was showing all the signs of
going down and the tow was dropped. At 4am she
rolled over and sank.

1/27: MABEL BAIRD. *Country:* British.
Date sunk: 22/12/17. *Tons nett:* 1568. *Tons
gross:* 2500. *Built:* 1901. *Type:* SS. *Rig:* schooner.
Owners: J.W. Baird, Montagu House, West
Hartlepool. *Cargo:* 3500 tons coal from Penarth to
Fecamp. *Armed:* 1 x 12pd 12cwt gun. Gun No 4082.
Mount No PI420. *Position:* 3½ miles SW from
Lizard Light (49 55 30N; 05 16 00W). *Master's
name:* John Rymer Parkinson. *Crew:* 27. *Crew
nationality:* 13 British, 6 Arabs, 7 Maltese,
1 Norwegian. *Gunners:* Matthew L Peeps, LS RFR,

No B4928 Devonport; Philip Callaghan, AB RNR,
No A6052 Devonport.

ALTHOUGH nobody actually saw the torpedo from
UB-57 strike *Mabel Baird*, the master was in no doubt
that it was a torpedo because he heard it. He claimed
that just before the explosion there was a loud hiss
and a thump on the steamer's starboard side. The
explosion that followed wrecked the engine room and
stokehold and killed five men – the chief engineer,
second engineer, a seaman and two stokers.

Mabel Baird was taking on water surprisingly
slowly considering the damage she had sustained. It
was 6.50am when she was hit and an hour later she
was still afloat, although the decks by then were just
about awash. The master ordered the boats to be
lowered and instructed his crew to stay about a
cable's length away and wait for help. There were
numerous other vessels around and it was only a
matter of time before help arrived. The trawler *James
Cumming* picked the men up and landed them later at
Penzance.

The Admiralty were not satisfied with some of the
answers the master gave to the interviewing officer
at Falmouth and wrote to his company at West
Hartlepool. They wanted to know why he was not ziz-
zagging, why he was so far from the land and why he
had dimmed stern and side lights burning. But there is
no record of a reply from the master and no mention of
any action taken by the Admiralty.

1/28: WESTWOOD. *Country:* British.
Date sunk: 3/10/18. *Tons nett:* 1070. *Tons
gross:* 1968. *Built:* 1907. *Type:* SS. *Rig:* schooner.
Owners: Furness, Whithy & Co, Collinwood St,
Newcastle. *Cargo:* 3000 tons coal from Barry to
France. *Armed:* 1 x 3in high angle gun. *Position:*
5 miles S of Lizard (49 54 00N; 05 16 00W).
Master's name: Robert Sebourne. *Crew:* 24. *Crew
nationality:* 16 British, 6 Arabs, 2 Japanese.

THE *UB-112*'s first torpedo to come streaking towards
the *Westwood* was spotted when it was only 50yds
off the starboard beam. It struck in number four hold
opening up a huge hole. It was 20 minutes past
midnight and the master was just altering course
which was why the second torpedo passed harmlessly
by the stern about 30ft off.

However, the one was enough and within a few
minutes the *Westwood* was well down in the water.
The order was given to take to the boats. One man,
an Arab fireman, M. Ali, fell overboard and had
disappeared by the time a boat could reach the spot.

With the wind blowing moderately from the west,
the sea was reasonably calm which helped the men
to get clear of the sinking steamer. Within 15 minutes
she had gone to the bottom, leaving the men to set
the sails as best they could to take them towards shore.
About three hours later a vessel in the distance altered
course towards them. It was the drifter *Primrose*.

Apart from loosing the man overboard the whole incident had not gone too badly for Captain Sebourne. Until he came to be interviewed by the senior naval officer at Penzance. When asked about his confidential papers, he said that they had been left in the wireless room which was not where they should have been. He also became very vague when asked about the pattern of zig-zagging he had been following. It all added up to negligence of sailing instructions. After learning that he had been in command of the *Westwood* for 21 days and before that four years in other steamers without incident, the master was given a warning by the Admiralty.

1/29: PRESIDENT. *Country:* British. *Date sunk:* 10/4/15. *Tons nett:* 257. *Tons gross:* 647. *Built:* At Troon in 1904. *Type:* SS. *Rig:* schooner. *Owners:* John Hay & Sons, 58 Renfield St, Glasgow. *Cargo:* 1715 tons coal tar pitch. *Armed:* No. *Position:* 14 miles S by W from Lizard (49 44 00N; 05 16 00W). *Master's name:* Neil Robertson. *Crew:* 10.

THE *President,* bound for St Malo, was making good time until a very unwelcome visitor appeared on the horizon. The master looked through his binoculars to confirm his suspicions. A German submarine was about five miles off heading towards another steamer that lay to the north. He shouted to the mate to get the boats swung out ready and to get as much speed from the engines as they would take. He hoped with a bit of luck he could be out of the area before the submarine had finished with the other steamer. He looked again through his binoculars and saw that the submarine had turned and was now heading directly towards him.

The engineers opened the engines up to the their maximum and the *President* was slicing through the water at over 10 knots. Unfortunately, it wasn't enough and the submarine soon caught up with her. A voice speaking through a trumpet ordered the captain to stop or face the consequences.

Two lifeboats were lowered and the crew pulled towards the submarine as instructed. Most of the men were ordered on board the submarine whilst three German sailors were rowed over to the steamer carrying a big bomb. The bomb was placed on the side of the ship and the fuse lit. Two minutes later it was all over for the *President* and she went to the bottom.

The crew rowed for some time but were eventually spotted by a fishing vessel at 6.15pm and taken to Brixham.

1/30: PELLEVIN. *Country:* French. *Date sunk:* 1/10/16. *Tons nett:* 31. *Tons gross:* –. *Built:* –. *Type:* SV. *Rig:* Smack. *Owners:* M. Larganet. *Cargo:* –. *Armed:* No. *Position:* 21 miles S by W of The Lizard (49 37 00N;

05 16 00W). *Master's name:* M Larganet. *Crew:* 6. *Crew nationality:* All French.

THERE is not at great deal of information on the sinking of the *Pellevin* apart from the fact that she shared the same fate as many other fishing vessels during the war.

The submarine had spotted her from several miles off and her commander soon made it very clear what his intentions were. Three shells were fired at the little fishing boat as the enemy drew nearer. They fell wide but were a warning to the master to stop. The master could do little else but to obey and ordered all the sails in.

The sequence of events although not recorded probably followed the norm with the Germans planting bombs aboard the *Pellevin.*

1/31: GJERTRUD. *Country:* Norwegian. *Date sunk:* 1/10/18. *Tons nett:* 299. *Tons gross:* 593. *Built:* At Newcastle in 1893. *Type:* SS. *Rig:* schooner. *Owners:* N. Mjelde, Haugesund, Norway. *Cargo:* 660 tons coal from Newport to St Malo. *Armed:* No. *Position:* 2 miles W of the Lizard (49 58 00N; 05 15 00W). *Master's name:* –. *Crew:* 14.

FROM a total number of 14 crew only three were to survive the sinking of the *Gjertrud* at 10.45 on the night of October 1, 1918. As the master and all the deck officers were among those who perished it was Seaman Johan Bohler, who gave the naval authorities details of her loss.

She was making her way up the Channel to Portland as per orders and hugging the coastline as near as safe navigation would permit. The chief officer was in charge of the watch on the bridge and Bohler himself was also on watch. Nothing was seen of either a submarine or a torpedo but the effect as it slammed into the starboard side of the *Gjertrud* was devastating. It hit her square on amidships blowing her completely in half and she sank in just 10 seconds. It was small wonder that so few people managed to get clear of her. Johan Bohler said that he just jumped into the water and by the time he surfaced, his ship had gone. After a few minutes he spotted the ship's raft floating nearby and swam to it. He was joined a little later by the steward and a fireman.

For three hours the men sat on the raft in the wind and cold wondering if they would ever see the comforts of home again. But then a sailing vessel passed close by them and they were able to catch the attention of a sharp-eared lookout. The ship was the British schooner *Cecilia* which landed them at Falmouth.

1/32: ASABA. *Country:* British. *Date sunk:* 6/12/17. *Tons nett:* 570. *Tons gross:* 972. *Built:* 1900. *Type:* SS. *Rig:* schooner. *Owners:* Africa SS Co, 23 Billiter St, London.

Cargo: 900 tons iron plates from Newport to Havre. *Armed:* 1 x 12pdr gun. *Position:* 2 miles WSW of Lizard (49 57 00N; 05 15 00W). *Master's name:* H. Pitt. *Crew:* 25. *Crew nationality:* 18 British, 7 Africans. *Gunners:* Jameson; Jobling.

ASABA was making six knots as she neared the Lizard about two miles off. It was 11am, the weather was fine with a moderate sea although there was a heavy swell from the south. The master and mate were on the bridge looking at the Lizard and generally making notes as to position and course for Falmouth. They too, were being observed, by two different people, one the lookout on the Lizard and the other the German commander of *UC-17*.

The torpedo hit the steamer on her starboard side directly in the engine room. Such was the force of the blast that it caused the *Asaba* to break in two giving little time for the crew to get clear before she went down. Some of those in the water were badly hurt, the master being one of them, and although he was pulled out of the water alive by the crew of the trawler *Croton*, he died a few minutes later.

The man who gave the information to the naval authorities at Falmouth was the second mate, Gwilym Davies. He had been lucky and survived with no major injuries. In all 16 men died in the incident.

The interviewing officer noted that he felt that the *Asaba* had been too far off the land in the conditions at the time. The lookout on the Lizard also said that she should have been hugging the land more closely.

1/33: LIBOURNE. *Country:* British. *Date sunk:* 29/9/18. *Tons nett:* 490. *Tons gross:* 1219. *Built:* At Glasgow in 1918 . *Type:* SS. *Rig:* schooner. *Owners:* James Moss & Co, Liverpool. *Cargo:* 1850 tons wines and spirits, and general from Bordeaux to Liverpool. *Armed:* 1 x 3in Howitzer. *Position:* 10 miles S by W of Lizard (49 47 00N; 05 15 00W). *Master's name:* John Richard Green. *Crew:* 30. *Crew nationality:* All British. *Gunners:* James Carson, AB RNVR, No CI2477 Chatham; Murdoch McDonald, AB RNR, No 7368A Chatham; Fred Davis, OS RNVR, No MZ1627 Devonport.

LIEUTENANT S. Keenan RNR, commander of the leading escort trawler *Thomas Dowding*, reported that at 4.45pm, whilst leading a north bound convoy from Brest, he heard a very loud explosion – the effects of which were felt on his ship from stem to stern. He looked around at the steamers in his charge and saw that the SS *Libourne* had been hit by a torpedo.

The weather wasn't good, the wind strong from the south-west and there were occasional banks of fog. It was while the convoy was emerging from one of these fog banks that *U-54* made her attack. The torpedo hit the *Libourne* on the port side between number one and two holds. The explosion almost severed the ship in two. However, even though

severely damaged, *Libourne* floated for 20 minutes giving the crew time to swing the boats out and get clear. Three boats were got away successfully but the small jolly boat ran into problems. Gunner Fred Davis, stated in his report that four men tried to lower the little boat but it capsized on reaching the water and three of the four men were lost. The rest of the crew searched for them without success.

Thomas Dowding was on the scene in a trice and after picking up *Libourne's* crew from the boats, got down to some serious depth charging. To the south, the French destroyer *Claymore*, and to the west, HMT 1204 *Ophir III*, were also depth charging, just in case they could strike it lucky.

Libourne sank by the head at about 5.15pm and after the patrol vessel commanders were satisfied that they had blanketed the area with depth charges, the convoy proceeded to Penzance. *U-54* escaped undamaged.

1/34: VAV. *Country:* Norwegian. *Date sunk:* 4/12/17. *Tons nett:* –. *Tons gross:* 1255. *Built:* –. *Type:* SS. *Rig:* –. *Owners:* Dampsk, Akties, Vestheim, Oslo. *Cargo:* Steel from Glasgow to Havre. *Armed:* No. *Position:* 2 miles SW of Lizard (49 56 30N; 05 14 30W). *Master's name:* –. *Crew:* 21. *Crew nationality:* 12 Norwegians, 5 Swedes, 1 Dane, 1 Spaniard, 2 Russian/Finns.

ONLY two young men of 18 and 19 lived to tell the tale of the sinking of the steamer *Vav*. Sverre Kristoffersen Freberg was an able seaman and told the naval authorities that he had been at the wheel from 4am to 5am. It was while he was on duty on the bridge that a large revolving light had been spotted on the British mainland. He didn't know at the time what it was but the interviewing officer concluded that it must have been the Lizard Light.

Freberg added that it had been a calm, moonlit night and the steamer was not showing any lights. After he had finished his stint at the wheel he went below for some coffee. He resumed his duties again at 6.30am which took him up on lookout to the crow's nest. Just as he arrived there he saw the white fizz of a torpedo. There was no time to warn anyone as a second later the torpedo slammed into the starboard side of the *Vav* just in front of the bridge. She sank almost instantly. Freberg reported that within a few seconds his position way up in the crow's nest was just a few feet from the water and he jumped clear.

The young seaman was dragged down with the suction of the ship but managed to fight free. When he surfaced he could see the ship's stern still showing above water. A loud explosion followed from deep within the ship, probably the boilers exploding as the water reached them and sent her plunging down, dragging young Freberg with it again. When he surfaced for the second time he swam around looking for anything to cling to and found an oar which gave him some buoyancy. He wondered if he was the only person to survive and was beginning to think he was when he found a firemen called Oskar Eriksen, cold and shaken but otherwise unhurt.

Both lads knew that a raft had been put on the deck of the *Vav* for emergencies such as this. It was deliberately left loose so that it would float free if the steamer sank. They had to find it if they were to have any chance of survival until help arrived. Their luck held out as they reached it a few minutes later and clambered aboard. They drifted slowly towards Black Head and were spotted at 8.30am by the patrol trawler *Fusilier* which took them in to Falmouth.

1/35: LORLE. *Country:* British.
Date sunk: 11/6/18. *Tons nett:* 1694. *Tons gross:* 2686. *Built:* 1896. *Type:* SS. *Rig:* schooner. *Owners:* Alexander Shipping Co Ltd, 4, St Mary's Axe, London. *Cargo:* 4050 tons iron ore from Bilbao to Heysham, Lancs. *Armed:* 1 x 12pdr gun. *Position:* 12 miles SSW of Lizard (49 47 00N; 05 14 00W). *Master's name:* James Gray. *Crew:* 27. *Crew nationality:* 25 British, 1 Greek, 1 Swede. *Gunners:* Giblin; Elvidge.

IT was just after midnight, June 11, 1918, when the *Lorle* was attacked by *UB-103*. The torpedo struck her in the stokehold, the explosion ripping her port side allowing tons of water to pour in. A minute later another series of explosions boomed out as the water reached her boilers. Her crew tried as best they could to get clear. The starboard lifeboat was swung out but the steamer sank in four minutes, throwing the crew into the water and turning the boat right over.

The chief officer, Martin Poulson, helped his badly injured colleague J. McDevitte, the second officer, towards the upturned lifeboat. Several men managed to cling to it in the cold, rough sea. About five minutes later a powerful light shone on them from the conning tower of the U-boat which had surfaced close by.

The mate reported later that just before daybreak he spotted a small, upturned dinghy close by with the master and some seamen clinging to it but they had disappeared at first light. It was then that the carpenter, K. Sjogren, began to lift the spirits of his fellow sufferers by suggesting that they right the boat and get a sail set. It wasn't an easy task and required a great deal of effort by the men, but they did it and, more to the point it kept them busy. It was relative luxury to be able to sit in the boat and the men soon had a sail rigged, and a course towards land. However, they were soon spotted by a lookout on a passing patrol trawler and taken to Brest.

Lieutenant J.R. Hodgson RNR, commander of HMT 2665, *Amroth Castle*, was the leading vessel of the southbound convoy in which the *Lorle* was lost. He reported on his return that Second Officer, J. McDevitte, had died of his injuries in hospital at Brest. This left only eight survivors of the sinking of the SS *Lorle*.

1/36: EVA. *Country:* Norwegian.
Date sunk: 31/12/16. *Tons nett:* –. *Tons gross:* 637. *Built:* –. *Type:* SS. *Rig:* –. *Owners:* T.C. Nordliu. *Cargo:* 1368 tons coal from Swansea to Rouen. *Armed:* No. *Position:* 10 miles S of Lizard (49 47 00N; 05 13 00W). *Master's name:* Toras Suendsboo. *Crew:* 14. *Crew nationality:* 10 Norwegians, 1 Greek, 1 Dutch, 2 Swedes.

THE submarine began to shell the *Eva* from about a mile off even though the weather was quite hazy. The international signal flags 'AB' were run up the small mast on the conning tower which meant 'Abandon Ship.' Certainly the master of the *Eva* knew what it meant and even if he didn't the shells whooshing over the rigging would have made it very clear.

The crew of the steamer abandoned the vessel as quickly as they could and rowed out to meet the approaching enemy vessel. The master was ordered to board the submarine by her commander, who demanded all the usual information: name, destination, cargo.

From a safe distance *Eva's* crew watched as their ship was pounded by the submarine's deck gun. The master said that when he last saw his ship she was still afloat but in a bad way. He added that she must have been on the verge of sinking when his view was lost in the poor visiblity. They rowed towards Falmouth and presumably made it safely to that port although it is not mentioned in the records.

1/37: POLJAMES. *Country:* British.
Date sunk: 2/10/18. *Tons nett:* 529. *Tons gross:* 856. *Built:* 46 years old. *Type:* SS. *Rig:* schooner. *Owners:* Managers: City of Cork Steam Packet Co, Cork. *Cargo:* 826 tons coal from Newport to St Malo. *Armed:* 1 x 90mm gun. *Position:* 6 miles S of Lizard (49 52 00N; 05 12 00W). *Master's name:* Francis Alexander MacMillan. *Crew:* 20. *Crew nationality:* 14 British, 4 Greek, 1 Russian, 1 Japanese. *Gunners:* J.H. Coe, RNVR; R. Norman, RNVR; C. Magne, RNVR.

THIS was one of the last British ships to be sunk in the Channel before the war ended.

Poljames met her sudden end at 1.30 in the morning of October 2, 1918. It was a dark night but clear with a fresh wind and moderate sea. A torpedo from *UB-112* struck her in the engine room on the starboard side opened up a large hole. She immediately took a list to port and began to settle down by the stern. Within a few minutes she had gone down completely taking 13 of her crew with her.

Seven men were later picked up by the passing Norwegian SS *Eikar*.

1/38: FRANCIS. *Country:* British.
Date sunk: 23/4/18. *Tons nett:* 45. *Tons gross:* 100. *Built:* –. *Type:* SV. *Rig:* Ketch. *Owners:* The

Marine Surveyor, Bride, Cardiff. *Cargo:* 70 tons coal. *Armed:* No. *Position:* 6 miles S of Lizard (49 51 30N; 05 12 00W). *Master's name:* Victor Belmont. *Crew:* 4. *Crew nationality:* 3 British, 1 Norwegian.

FRANCIS was dogged with problems from the very beginning when she tried to make her way from Swansea to Falmouth to catch the convoy for France. She encountered such powerful headwinds that she missed the convoy and had her sails blown to pieces. She tried over many days to get out of the weather and managed to lose an anchor. Eventually the tired crew got her around Land's End but were then battered by another gale that took away her sails yet again. Helplessly she was driven before the wind across the Channel, ending up a few miles from Guernsey, but then the wind shifted and proceeded to blow her back again, until she was off the Lizard. With such a run of bad luck it was probably no surprise to the crew when a German submarine surfaced near to them and opened fire with her deck gun.

The first shell crashed through the main tackle bringing down showers of rigging. The second smashed into her hull causing her to lurch violently and sent splinters of wood flying in all directions. By this time Captain Belmont had had enough and ordered his men to take to the boat and get away from his luckless ship. Even as they left, another shell slammed into the forward part of the *Francis* but luckily none of the debris harmed the crew. As they rowed away from their ship they watched as men from the submarine boarded her to plant bombs. The master said later that she went up in smoke and after a few more helping shots from the submarine's large deck gun she sank.

It would have been nice to have reported that the crew's ordeal was over at this point, but far from it. The four men drifted in their little boat for seven days before they were spotted by a lookout on the American ship *Medina*. But by then it was too late for two of them. The cook, Michael Hand, completely broke down under the strain and suffered severe mental problems before dying during the evening of April 27. The mate, Morgan Knocker, died from exposure the next morning. The master and the Norwegian seaman, Peter Johansen, were in a bad way when the *Medina's* men carried them aboard, but they lived to tell the tale.

1/39: LADY CORY WRIGHT. *Country:* British. *Date sunk:* 26/3/18. *Tons nett:* –. *Tons gross:* 2516. *Built:* 1906 . *Type:* SS. *Rig:* Collier. *Owners:* New Zealand government. *Cargo:* Munitions. Many tons of minesand depth charges. *Armed:* Yes. *Position:* 15 miles S of the Lizard (49 42 00N; 05 12 00W). *Master's name:* –. *Crew:* 40.

LADY CORY WRIGHT was another steamer requisitioned by the British goverment for use in the war effort. Her home port was in New Zealand but the records consulted do not specify exactly who her owners were. There is a letter addressed to the High Commissioner of New Zealand, Strand, London, from the Admiralty giving the bad news of her loss.

Lady Cory Wright had been earmarked to carry a vast consignment of munitions for the war effort and on February 18, 1918, she was moved into Millbay Docks. Here her holds were scrubbed completely clean to receive her lethal cargo. Her loading was carried out under the supervision of a Mr Petty in strict secrecy and only by men that had a high security rating. Thousands of mines, depth charges, detonators and other items of war, were carefully loaded.

At 8.15am on March 26, *Lady Cory Wright* left Plymouth accompanied by two escorts, HMT 3308 *Iceland*, commanded by Temporary Lieutenant Richard Brightman Young RNR, and HMT 2984 *Carency*, commanded by skipper John Edgar RNR. They headed out to the Eddystone and then altered course to west-south-west and began a zig-zag course down the Channel. They passed many patrol trawlers on the way which should have given the master of *Lady Cory Wright* even more confidence, but it was to prove no deterrent to the commander of *UC-17* waiting off the Lizard.

Skipper John Edgar reported that at 3.20 in the afternoon of the same day he heard a loud crack followed by a huge explosion. Looking to his port quarter to see if all was well with his charge *Lady Cory Wright*, he could see nothing but a huge cloud of black smoke rising some 800 feet into the air. John Edgar immediately altered course to get closer to the steamer but by the time the smoke had cleared there was nothing left of her. She had literally blown to pieces.

Drawn by the large cloud of smoke, airship *C9* arrived on the scene and from a height of 400 feet surveyed the area. The pilot couldn't belive his eyes as he saw a wide area of sea completely covered with floating mines from the holds of the *Lady Cory Wright*. He signalled to the *Iceland* and *Carency* below to be very careful.

By that time other patrol vessels that were in the area came speeding in on the scene. HMT *Kinaldie*, commanded by Lieut. J. Campbell, went right in among the dangerous wreckage to look for survivors. It was a brave gesture and one that paid off, for one survivor was found clinging to a mine! All the rest of the crew were dead.

The loss of the *Lady Cory Wright* was a blow to the war effort and a court of enquiry was held. The enquiry found that the explosion of the torpedo had set off either some mines or depth charges which had caused the ship to sink instantly. They were quite scathing, however, about the actions of the commanders of *Iceland* and *Carency*. It was said that Richard Brightman Young, commander of *Iceland*, appeared to have been entirely unnerved at the destruction of the *Lady Cory Wright* and his failure to launch a proper search and attack on the submarine, and his failure to search for survivors was strongly condemned. The same remarks applied to a minor degree to John Edgar of the *Carency* and both men were relieved of their commands and given shore duty.

1/40: QUO VADIS. *Country:* French.
Date sunk: 18/12/16. *Tons nett:* –. *Tons gross:* 110. *Built:* –. *Type:* SV. *Rig:* Schooner. *Owners:* J. Guegot, Papen Cia. *Cargo:* Coal. *Armed:* No. *Position:* 18 miles S of Lizard (49 39 00N; 05 12 00W). *Master's name:* J. Guegot. *Crew:* 6. *Crew nationality:* All French.

A MIRROR-CALM sea and no wind allowed an enemy submarine to surface right alongside the *Quo Vadis*. There was no need to fire shells as a warning or shout threats and abuse, the sailing vessel was going nowhere other than down.

Once on board the submarine, Captain Guegot was questioned by the commanding officer who asked for his papers. Whilst he was doing that several sailors were busy on the *Quo Vadis* looting whatever was not nailed down. They particularly wanted copper and went to great lengths to get it even unscrewing certain items from the bulkheads. Eventually they returned to the submarine laden with three full sacks of booty. Before leaving they left the finishing touches to their handy work in the form of several bombs, sinking the schooner instantly.

The crew were found and picked up by the British destroyer *Contest* and taken to Falmouth.

1/41: CHEVIOT RANGE. *Country:* British.
Date sunk: 21/2/18. *Tons nett:* –. *Tons gross:* 3691. *Built:* 1914. *Type:* SS. *Rig:* –. *Owners:* Furness Withy & Co. *Cargo:* General from Colombo to Manchester. *Armed:* No. *Position:* 25 miles S of Lizard (49 32 00N; 05 12 00W). *Master's name:* –. *Crew:* 36.

CHEVIOT RANGE stood little chance against the two submarines that attacked her at 0.45am on February 21, 1918. She wasn't armed and had no chance of out-running such fast opponents. The master ordered the wireless operator to send out an urgent SOS but his ship was a long way from shore and there were no patrol vessels around.

The master estimated that around 50 shells were fired at the *Cheviot Range* by the two submarines. Many of them hit the steamer, killing one man and injuring four others. Her hull was riddled with holes and she began to take on water at an alarming rate. Eventually, the master gave up and ordered his men into the boats. The master was still on board *Cheviot Range* when she sank.

The crew in the boats were in trouble also. One man fell over the side and was drowned and another died from exposure in the cold weather. Only nine men made it to shore, landing their boat at Bigbury, Devon. The men in the other boat were never seen again.

U-102 claimed this sinking.

1/42: GERMAN SUBMARINE U-93. *Country:* German. *Date sunk:* 7/1/18. *Tons nett:* 850. *Tons gross:* 1000. *Built:* 1917. *Type:* "Mittel-U". *Armed:* 16 torpedoes; 8.8cm deck gun. *Position:* 2 miles SSE of Lizard (49 56 00N; 05 11 00W). *Master's name:* Kapitan-Leutnant Hans Gerlach. *Crew:* 39.

U-93 was sunk in the early hours of January 7, 1918, by the SS *Braeneil* of Aberdeen, which was owned by J.&.P Hutchinson of Glasgow and had a gross tonnage of 424 tons. She was on her way from Swansea to Rouen, calling on the way at Falmouth for orders and was loaded with tin plate.

The master, Henry James Smith, said that he was on the bridge at the time with the helmsman when the ship was about two miles to the south-south-east of the Lizard making about nine knots. The weather was fine with light winds and the visibility was clear. At around 4.15am a lookout, Norman McLeod, shouted that he could see a submarine dead ahead. The master spotted it almost at the same time and said to helmsman, Thomas Richards of Swansea, "It's a German submarine." The submarine was showing it's port side to the steamer, heading north and the helsman altered his course a little as the master gave him permission to ram it.

"Yes it is," the helmsman replied with a grin. "I'm getting some of my own back." Thomas Richards had been shelled and sunk by German submarines twice during the war and relished the chance of getting even.

The *Braeneil's* bows smashed into the submarine just forward of the midship section. It was a tremendous impact. Fireman James Beattie, said in his statement that he was walking aft from the forecastle head when the impact happened and it was so violent that it knocked him completely off his feet. He got up and looked over the port side and could clearly see that the ship was right into a submarine. Bosun James Coutts, said he was nearly thrown out of his bunk at the time and rushed forward to see what was going on. He too looked over the port side and could see a conning tower and hull forward just awash.

The master ordered the engines to stop and then full astern to pull himself away from the grinding mass of metal. Whilst he was hoping he had done for the submarine, he was also hoping he hadn't done his ship too much damage. There was a strong smell of petrol and oil in the air and a few minutes later cries of help were heard in the distance in a foreign language. The master gave the order for the forward section of the ship to be checked for leaks, and the two gunners on *Braeneil*, Andrew Taylor and William Davies, stood by their gun just in case.

The reports from below were good and although the steamer had sustained considerable damage to her bows she remained water tight. The master said that he didn't go searching for survivors as he didn't feel particularly charitable towards the Germans, knowing of their treacherous character. Instead he continued to Falmouth and gave his report to the senior naval officer.

A search was made by several patrol vessels and an aircraft, and a considerable oil patch was seen to be growing at the position given by the master. The Admiralty were convinced of a successful submarine kill and awarded the full £1000 to the crew of the steamer. Captain Smith was awarded the DSC for his actions.

The Admiralty warned the *Braeneil's* owners to change her name immediately as the word would get back to Germany and revenge would be very sweet for German U-boat commanders.

1/43: BELLUCIA. *Country:* British.
Date sunk: 7/7/17. *Tons nett:* 2786. *Tons gross:* 4368. *Built:* 1909. *Type:* SS. *Rig:* schooner. *Owners:* Bell Bros & Co, 135 Buchanan St, Glasgow. *Cargo:* Wheat and flour from Montreal to London. *Armed:* 1 x 14pdr gun. *Position:* 2 miles SSE of Lizard (49 55 30N; 05 11 00W). *Master's name:* J. Kiddie. *Crew:* 40. *Crew nationality:* 32 British, 1 Russian, 1 Canadian, 3 Arabs, 3 West Indians. *Gunners:* Robert Smith, Pro LS RNVR, No 3589 Devonport; Patrick Lenehan, AB RNVR, No 3112 Devonport.

BELLUCIA was part of a convoy coming in from the Atlantic heading up the English Channel. The convoy came in as close as it dared to the Lizard Head and had just passed it when disaster struck the *Bellucia*. It was 3pm with the weather described as squally with a rough sea. One of the crew members stated later that he spotted the periscope of a submarine about 300yds off the port beam. However, before he could shout to anyone, the explosion occurred on the port side in the engine room. Four people were killed by the blast, the chief steward, third engineer and two firemen.

One of the escorts, HMS *Lyra*, was close to the *Bellucia* at the time. Her commander said that they were about one and a half miles east of Beast Point when a large explosion occurred on the steamer's port side. She began to sink almost immediately so he got in as close as possible to her and sent his whaler away to assist.

Two boats had managed to get clear but one had capsized and another was unusable, having been smashed by the torpedo's explosion. All the crew were picked up from the boats and the water and then a raft was dropped under the steamer's stern for those men still on board. They jumped and made the raft, ready to be picked up by the *Lyra's* boat.

The position given above is the one that is given by all the documents relating to the sinking. However,

one of the escorts stated that the *Bellucia* later grounded under the cliffs one mile north of Beast Point.

UB-31 later claimed to be the submarine concerned.

1/44: BORDER KNIGHT. *Country:* British.
Date sunk: 4/11/17. *Tons nett:* 2394. *Tons gross:* 3724. *Built:* 1899. *Type:* SS. *Rig:* schooner. *Owners:* Borderdale Ship Co Ltd, Princes Dock, Liverpool. *Cargo:* In ballast. *Armed:* 1 x 12pd 18cwt gun. *Position:* 1½ miles ESE of Lizard/2 miles off Black Head (49 57 00N; 05 10 00W). *Master's name:* A.B. Beedie. *Crew:* 38. *Gunners:* H. Christian, Act LS RNR, No 5790 A Portsmouth; J.G. Paines, AB RNVR, No WZ 3245; W.J. Atkinson, AB RFR, No 2403 Devonport.

THE investigating officer said that the master of *Border Knight* was to blame for losing his ship because he didn't carry out his sailing instructions correctly. The Admiralty took such a dim view of this that they summoned him to appear at the Admiralty offices to explain his actions further.

He said that from a position four miles south of the Eddystone he made a zig-zagging course for the Manacles Buoy. On sighting Black Head on his port bow he kept his ship's head more to the south so as to pass Black Head at a distance of two miles. At 10.40am Black Head bore north two miles so he steered west allowing for the tide which was running south, setting him off the land. He had been on this last heading for 20 minutes when a torpedo from *UC-17* slammed into the steamer's number four hold, opening up a huge hole.

The instructions given to the master didn't resemble anything like the actions he had taken. The Admiralty said that when closing the land at daylight the steamer should have been less than half way between Start Point and the Lizard and was not to pass any closer than two miles, not zig-zagging.

Even though the ship sank within five minutes, 37 of the crew managed to get clear in the boats before she went down. One man however, a Chinese cook called E. Joseph, stupidly ran back into the accommodation of the steamer to fetch clothes. When he returned the boats had left without him and he jumped over the side. The boats rowed towards him but by the time they arrived he had disappeared.

The Admiralty gave Captain Beedie a reprimand for not complying with his sailing instructions and a warning about his future conduct.

1/45: ARVOR. *Country:* French.
Date sunk: 17/3/18. *Tons nett:* 41. *Tons gross:* 52. *Built:* At Paimpol in 1896. *Type:* SV. *Rig:* Ketch. *Owners:* Le Gualet de Mezanbran & Kerviezic, St Brieux. *Cargo:* 85 tons coal from Swansea to St Brieux. *Armed:* No. *Position:* Half way between Lizard and Black Head, half mile from shore

(50 00 00N; 05 09 00W). *Master's name:* Albert Guilcher. *Crew:* 4.

THREE rifle shots were fired at the *Arvor* by the sailors on the conning tower of an approaching German submarine. They had the desired effect as the master of *Arvor* told his men to take to the boat and get clear.

There was little else they could do in the circumstances. The submarine was far too fast for them to try and outrun it and even then there was no wind to speak of. The crew watched the submarine go close around the *Arvor's* stern and then fire a single shell at virtually point blank range into her port side amidships.

The master said that he and his men rowed in the general direction of shore and eventually landed on the beach near Cadgwith. The last he saw of his vessel she was still afloat but when he looked a little later she had disappeared. As for the submarine, he saw that heading off in the direction of another sailing vessel, the *Anne Yvonne*.

1/46: ANNE YVONNE. *Country:* French.
Date sunk: 17/3/18. *Tons nett:* 76. *Tons Gross* 101.: *Built:* At Paimpol in 1901. *Type:* SV. *Rig:* schooner. *Owners:* Francois Jloux Gloux, Pleubian, France. *Cargo:* 148 tons coal from Emlyn Jones, Cardiff to Maupate, Paris. *Armed:* No. *Position:* 1½ miles E by S of Cadgwith, Cornwall (49 58 30N; 05 08 30W). *Master's name:* Francois Jloux Gloux. *Crew:* 5.

WHEN the German submarine commander spotted three French sailing vessels together, he couldn't resist sinking them even though they were quite close to the enemy shore.

The first the master of *Anne Yvonne* knew about any trouble was when three rifle shots drew his attention to the south. The submarine was having a go at *Arvor*, her crew having already abandoned her. The master watched as the submarine turned it's attention to *Anne Yvonne* and realised that he was helpless.

It was 6pm when the master ordered his men to take to the boat. It was easy going in the conditions with a light wind and virtually smooth sea. The submarine's gunner opened fire with the deck gun and several shells smashed into the *Anne Yvonne* but suddenly the firing stopped and the submarine dived rapidly. On looking around, the crew of the *Anne Yvonne* saw that a steamer had come into view and deduced that the German commander didn't like the look of her for some reason. Either that or he intended to sink her.

With the submarine out of the way the master decided to go back on board the *Anne Yvonne* to see if she could be saved. He found her, well down by the head, full of shell holes and splinters of wood scattered all around. He decided that it was pointless trying to save her and took to the boat again and began to head for the shore. It was just as well as the submarine appeared again and fired three more shots into the schooner sending her straight down.

The men from the *Anne Yvonne* eventually landed at Cadgwith.

1/47: ILSTON. *Country:* British.
Date sunk: 30/6/17. *Tons nett:* 1474. *Tons gross:* 2426. *Built:* 1915. *Type:* SS. *Rig:* schooner. *Owners:* Swansea Steamers Ltd, Swansea. *Cargo:* 800 tons railway material from France. *Armed:* 1 x 6pdr Hodgkiss. *Position:* 4 miles SE of Lizard (49 57 00N; 05 09 00W). *Master's name:* George John Jeffries. *Crew:* 28. *Crew nationality:* 19 British, 1 Portuguese, 1 Italian, 7 Arabs. *Gunners:* Michael Connor, Pro LS RNR, No A2548 Devonport; Duncan Ross, OS RN.

THE master was on the lower deck bridge just before the *Ilston* was hit. He reported later that he heard a loud hissing noise just seconds before a huge explosion occurred on the starboard side of the ship. Gunner Michael Connor, not only heard the torpedo but saw it as well and said that it slammed into number two hold on the starboard side, between the fore rigging and bridge.

It was immediately obvious that the *Ilston* was going to sink very rapidly as within a few seconds she was drastically down by the head and taking on a list to starboard. All the crew were ordered to make for the boats, but three couldn't respond, they had been killed by the explosion. The engineers had managed to shut the engines down but by the time the boats touched water there was still way on the ship. The starboard lifeboat got away with it but the port boat touched just as the steamer gave her final plunge and capsized.

Three men from the port boat were never seen again, but three others, the master and the two gunners swam around until they were picked up by the starboard boat. It had taken just over two minutes for the *Ilston* to sink from the time she had been hit.

As the crew in the starboard boat rowed around looking for more survivors they said that all that could be seen of the *Ilston* were the tops of her masts which helped them to stay in the area, but no further survivors were found. The men were eventually spotted by the patrol vessel *Betty* which took them to Falmouth.

1/48: GERMAN SUBMARINE UC-66. *Country:* German. *Date sunk:* 12/6/17. *Tons nett:* 427. *Tons gross:* 508. *Built:* 1916. *Type:* UC-class minelayer. *Armed:* 7 torpedoes, 1 x 8.78cm deck gun, 18 mines. *Position:* 2 miles SE of Lizard (49 56 00N; 05 09 00W). *Master's name:* Oberleutnant Herbert Pustkuchen. *Crew:* 26. *Crew nationality:* German.

IT was well known by the Navy that just to the east of the Lizard was a favourite spot where German submarine commanders liked to wait for victims. It was with this in mind that a flotilla of patrol ships with hydrophone listening equipment, were given instructions to search this area during their next patrol.

The trawler *Sea King* in company with *Sea Sweeper* was assigned to go into the area and drop a depth charge or two with the hope of stirring up any submarine that might be on the bottom there. The commander of *Sea King*, Lieutenant Godfrey Herbert, reported later that he dropped a 'D' type depth charge in the submarine resting ground. Just after it detonated he spotted the stanchion and jumper stay of a submarine about 400yds off his port bow. He immediately turned, along with *Sea Sweeper*, towards the enemy vessel with the intention of intercepting it with another charge. Both ships were so engrossed with their pursuit that they had a small collision but it was nothing serious and they managed to get depth charges down right on top of the submarine.

Reading the signal flags flying on both ships the rest of the flotilla also joined in the hunt, blanketing the area with depth charges so blocking off its escape. Lieutenant Herbert was convinced that his initial charge killed it, as six more explosions took place and a lot of oil had spread out over the surface of the water.

The signal was made for the flotilla to stop all engines as it was perfect weather for operating hydrophones. On *Sea King* was an expert in their use and after listening for some time he assured Lieutenant Herbert that there was no sound of a German submarine's engines in the area.

The Admiralty announced a little later that the attack on the submarine was successful and identified her as *UC-66*. Consequently the maximum award of £1000 was granted to be split up among the crews of *Sea King*, *Sea Sweeper*, commanded by Edgar W. Buchanan, *Nellie Dodds*, commanded by Sidney Court and *William H Hasties*, commanded by Charles Williams. Both Godfrey Herbert and Edgar Buchanan were recommended to be mentioned for their efforts.

1/49: PEARL. *Country:* British.

Date sunk: 30/9/16. *Tons nett:* 99. *Tons gross:* 143.
Built: Of wood at Malpas in 1875. *Type:* SV.
Rig: schooner. *Owners:* Thomas Waters, Carvonza Rd, Truro. *Cargo:* 210 tons coal from Carswood Coal Co, Wigan to Newham Coal Co, Truro.
Armed: No. *Position:* 6 miles SSE of Lizard (49 52 00N; 05 09 00W). *Master's name:* Pascoe Billing. *Crew:* 5. *Crew nationality:* 3 British, 2 Danes.

CAPTAIN Billing of the sailing vessel *Pearl* reckoned that the German U-boat commander was only about 28 years old. He seemed a pleasant enough fellow though, in spite of the fact that his men were at that very moment planting bombs aboard the *Pearl*. With the

standard questions out of the way the young commander broke into some small talk. "I shall be glad when the war is finished. How are your family. Do you have any children?" The master was quite taken aback and found himself responding to the man.

It was 11.34am, the weather was fine with a smooth sea. The submarine had crept up on the *Pearl* and began to fire shots at her as a signal to stop. The master felt he had no choice but to obey as the submarine was much faster and more manoeuvreable.

When the bombing party returned to the submarine the master was told he was free to go. As he waited for the Germans to climb out of his boat he saw that not only had they planted bombs but also plundered his ship as well. They carried coils of rope, charts, compasses and various provisions, making the master snap back into the reality of just what was going on. Just then a large swell caught the lifeboat as one of his crew, John Salmon, was getting aboard. The seaman fell between the boat and the submarine injuring his fingers and foot, but apart from severe bruising he was alright. The crew pulled clear of the attackers just as the bombs on board the *Pearl* exploded. Three had been hung over her sides, making big holes in her below the water line. Within three minutes she had gone.

The crew were picked up by the Danish schooner *Dragmer*.

1/50: CARMELA. *Country:* American.

Date sunk: 27/7/16. *Tons nett:* –. *Tons gross:* 1396.
Built: –. *Type:* SV. *Rig:* Barque with engine.
Owners: American Star Line, 25 Beaver, New York. *Cargo:* 1800 tons of foodstuff, oil and pig iron to Langstaff, Ehrenberg & Pollack of Havre.
Armed: No. *Position:* 28 miles S of The Lizard (49 30 00N; 05 09 00W). *Master's name:* John Alfred Johnson. *Crew:* 20. *Crew nationality:* 8 Americans, 5 Russian/Finns, 1 Russian, 1 Swede, 2 Norwegians, 2 Danes, 1 Spaniard.

ALTHOUGH the weather was fine and clear there was a strong westerly swell. *Carmela* was making good headway, her sails assisted by what was described as her auxilliary oil engine. At 6.30am her journey ended when a submarine appeared about 4000yds off and began a steady bombardment, firing about one shell a minute.

The master watched as the shells gradually got closer and closer. He realised he had no chance of out-running the submarine so ordered his crew into the boats. Very soon the submarine was alongside the *Carmela* and several German sailors went on board to plant bombs. It was over quickly, the American vessel blowing up and sinking immediately.

The crew headed in the general direction of the British coast and were spotted by the patrol boat *HMT BD68* at 10am and landed safely at Plymouth the same day.

1/51: BEATA. *Country:* French.
Date sunk: 17/3/18. *Tons nett:* 79. *Tons gross:* 103.
Built: At Paimpol in 1906. *Type:* SV. *Rig:* ketch.
Owners: M. Pitibon, Pleubian, France. *Cargo:* 157
tons coal from Norton, Swansea to N. Boulonga,
Paris. *Armed:* No. *Position:* Half way between
Lizard and Black Head, about 1 mile from shore
(49 59 30N; 05 08 30W). *Master's name:* Olivier
Libouban. *Crew:* 7.

THREE French sailing vessels left Swansea in
company on March 16, 1918, all loaded with coal
bound for Granville in France via Falmouth for
orders. Their crews didn't know it at the time but
they were all about to be sunk by the same German
submarine.

At a little after 6pm the next day, *Beata* was half
way between the Lizard and Black Head about a mile
from the coast. *Anne Yvonne* (see 1/46) was ahead
and *Arvor* (see 1/45) about half a mile off the port
quarter. Suddenly a conning tower was spotted by
one of the lookouts as it rose up close by the *Arvor*.
The master immediately shouted for the helmsman to
turn *Beata* towards the shore in the hope of finding
safety closer in.

Beata certainly had the better chance of getting
away as the submarine commander turned his attention
to the *Anne Yvonne* after he had sank the *Arvor*. But
half an hour later it was the *Beata's* turn. Her crew
were already in the boat being towed alongside her.
The master had been busy in his cabin destroying
confidential papers. When he saw the submarine
heading his way he jumped in the boat with his crew
and pulled clear.

As the submarine approached the *Beata* from the
stern, its gunner fired five shells into her but then
turned away rapidly to the south after a steamer that
had appeared a while earlier. The *Beata* was then still
afloat which tempted her crew to sneak back to her.
They rowed steadily in her direction hoping that she
wasn't too badly damaged, but at 7.15pm she rolled
over on her port side and disappeared.

However, her crew were spared the row into shore
by a passing motor boat which picked up their painter
and towed them into Cadgwith.

1/52: PROBA. *Country:* British.
Date sunk: 7/12/17. *Tons nett:* 88. *Tons gross:* 105.
Built: Of wood at Plymouth in 1891. *Type:* SV.
Rig: schooner. *Owners:* John L. Harris, Highfield,
Appledore, Devon. *Cargo:* 177 tons coal from
Swansea to Cherbourg. *Armed:* No. *Position:*
3 miles SE of Lizard (49 55 30N; 05 08 30W).
Master's name: William Thomas Braund. *Crew:* 4.
Crew nationality: All British.

PROBA was delayed by the master falling ill and they
put in to Appledore to allow him to recover. She
eventually sailed again on December 5, 1917, and
heading off to report in at Falmouth.

She passed the Lizard and the master headed north-
north-east. The weather was foggy with a heavy sea
and a strong swell from the south-west. At 4.40pm
the fog cleared a little, enough to allow a lookout to
spot a submarine to the south. It was headed straight
for them. Convinced that the only course of action
was to get away from his ship the master tore up his
confidential papers into tiny pieces, threw them over
the side, and ordered everyone into the boats.

The crew of the *Proba* were several hundred yards
away from their ship when the submarine came close
and threw them a line. The master made the rope fast
and they were towed back to the schooner. The
German commander needed provisions. Whilst his
men ransacked the schooner the master was
questioned by the German officer about his ship. As
he finished writing his notes the German added one
more question, "How is your country for food?"

The master thought about it for a second and
replied. "We have plenty sir, plenty."

The master jumped back aboard the small boat
which had returned from the *Proba*. Not only had the
Germans taken all the provisions they could find but
had planted several bombs. As they exploded, the
crew watched a huge hole appear in her starboard
side, sending her to the bottom instantly.

The men in the boat had to suffer a night at sea
and made the best of it by rowing to keep warm. The
next morning they were spotted by a lookout on the
French steamer *Renee Hyaffil* which landed them at
Penarth.

1/53: NOYA. *Country:* British.
Date sunk: 30/8/17. *Tons nett:* 2634. *Tons
gross:* 4282. *Built:* 1912. *Type:* SS. *Rig:* schooner.
Owners: English & American SS Co, Old Broad St,
London. *Cargo:* 615 tons crude oil, 6285 tons
barley. *Armed:* 1 x 12pdr Japanese gun. *Position:*
3 miles SE of Lizard (49 55 00N; 05 07 30W).
Master's name: Henry Philip Cove. *Crew:* 39. *Crew
nationality:* 34 British, 2 Spanish, 1 Russian, 2
Norwegian. *Gunners:* Reginald Sheppard, LS RNR,
No 1452X Ch; Joseph Denham, AB RNVR, No
4157BZ Ch.

THINGS hadn't gone well for the *Noya* since she left
Norfolk, Virginia, USA. She was part of a large
convoy crossing the Atlantic and had lost the convoy
in bad weather on August 27. The weather was so bad
that at one stage the master was forced to keep head to
the sea and just ride it out. When it moderated he
opened his secret sailing instructions to see what
options were open to him. At first he planned to pass
closely to the south of Wolf Rock, but then heard on
his wireless that an enemy submarine was known to be
active in that area.

Having spotted Bishop Rock Light near the Scillies
the master decided he would set a course to take him
directly towards the Lizard and then into Falmouth
for orders. In the early hours of August 30, *Noya*

approached the Lizard about seven miles to the south west. The master and second mate were on the bridge and both gunners were at their station aft keeping a sharp lookout for enemy submarines. They didn't see one, but the commander of U-62 saw them very clearly through his periscope and waited for the precise moment to release a torpedo.

It was a good shot and the torpedo smashed into the starboard side of the steamer, penetrating the engine room and bunkers, smashing the marconi house and lifeboat. The steamer went completely dark as all power failed, followed a few minutes later by the engines as the water crept up over the cylinders.

Although she was leaking badly, *Noya* suddenly showed signs that she had stabilised and the master waited and drifted with her for several hours. However, as she got closer to the Lizard she began to take a turn for the worse leaving the master no choice but to abandon her. The master complained later that when he looked back at his sinking ship from his lifeboat he could see her very clearly from over a mile off, made all the more easy by the bright light on the Lizard. He felt that this light had given the German commander an easy opportunity of sinking him.

Apart from one man who was killed by the explosion, the rest were unhurt and were later picked up by HMD *Concord*, which took them into Falmouth.

1/54: BORG. *Country:* British.
Date sunk: 10/6/18. *Tons nett:* 1308. *Tons gross:* 2111. *Built:* 1888. *Type:* SS. *Rig:* schooner. *Owners:* Cairns, Noble & Co, Tyne. *Cargo:* 2800 tons iron ore from Bilbao to Jarrow-on-Tyne. *Armed:* 1 x 18pdr gun. *Position:* 20 miles S by E of Lizard (49 37 00N; 05 07 00W). *Master's name:* Albert W. Parsons. *Crew:* 30.

THE north bound convoy left Brest on the morning of June 9, 1918, consisting of 10 steamers escorted by the trawlers, *Yokohama*, *Thomas Dowding*, *Cyrano*, *Isabella Fowlie* and the French destroyer *Fanion*. The weather was particularly bad with a strong northerly wind that whipped up a very rough sea. *Borg* was number seven in the convoy but in the bad weather convoy positions were difficult to maintain. By 10pm the following day the convoy was well scattered leaving many of the steamers unguarded and vulnerable to attack by German submarines.

The torpedo from *UB-103* hit *Borg* on the port side between number two hold and the stokehold. The explosion and damage that followed was very unusual in that it opened up a huge hole in her side that the hole was so positioned that it allowed her to fill with water almost instantly and she sank in an amazing 12 seconds. Sinking so quickly it is hardly surprising that so many of her crew perished, most of them would have been below decks at the time and would have had no chance of escape.

However, eight men were lucky. Five of the crew

and one passenger were picked out of the water by *Cyrano*. The chief engineer was found by *Fanion* and a gunner plucked to safety by *Isabella Fowlie*. As the master was among those missing, the duty of giving the information from which this report was taken, fell to John Rodsett, the Chief Officer.

1/55: CARMARTHEN. *Country:* British.
Date sunk: 26/7/17. *Tons nett:* 2690. *Tons gross:* 4262. *Built:* 1916. *Type:* SS. *Rig:* schooner. *Owners:* Jenkins Bros, Merchant Exchange, Cardiff. *Cargo:* In ballast from Genoa to Tees. *Armed:* 1 x 12pdr Japanese gun. *Position:* In Eagle Cove approx 1 mile W of Black Head (50 00 08N; 05 07 30W). *Master's name:* Griffith Roberts. *Crew:* 35. *Crew nationality:* 29 British, 2 Danes, 2 Swedes, 1 Norwegian, 1 Russian. *Gunners:* Walter Binstead, LS RNVR, No Z 305, Devonport; Edward O'Neill, LS RNR, No 8428A.

CAPTAIN Roberts said that he followed his instructions to the letter from the time of leaving Gibraltar on July 18, 1917. He hugged the coast as close as he could and was rounding the Lizard to make his way into Falmouth for further orders, when a violent explosion shook the ship. Captain Roberts ordered the engines to be slowed down whilst he investigated. He assumed that he had struck a mine. The engine room was taking in water fast, the deck plates being awash within a few minutes. All hands were ordered to assemble by their boats and stand by to abandon the vessel.

About four miles away, Commander J.A. Collett, of the patrol trawler *St Hubert* had heard the explosion and came alongside at 5.10pm. By this time the lifeboats had been launched and were clear of the steamer. All the crew were taken aboard the trawler and Commander Collett asked Captain Roberts for his confidential papers. Roberts had forgotten them. Collett then put it to Roberts that it looked as though the *Carmarthen* would float and they might just get a chance of beaching her if they got a move on.

Commander Collett sent out a radio message for assistance. Captain Roberts didn't think she would float long enough and from Collett's report it seems he was not over impressed with Roberts' negative attitude. Captain Roberts agreed to go back to his ship and have another look. He reported that the water was up to the boilers, which he felt would surely explode very soon. He rowed back to *St Hubert* and reiterated his point that she wouldn't float much longer.

Commander Collett was tiring, not only of the master's attitude but also of the *Carmarthen's* crew whom he had asked several times to help get the tow lines ready. Only two people volunteered. To get things moving he ordered three of his men, second hand C. Loft and deck hands A. Mitchell and W. Jackson, to get in the boat and get some cables attached to the steamer. By the time they got the cables sorted out, help arrived in the form of tugs and they commenced the tow. It was a good try and they made some headway, but at 8.05pm the *Carmarthen* grounded in 12 fathoms of water and became a total loss.

The Admiralty concluded that the *Carmarthen* had been torpedoed and not mined as the master had assumed. In fact *UC-50* claimed to have sunk her.

1/56: SKARAAS. *Country:* British. *Date sunk:* 23/5/18. *Tons nett:* 992. *Tons gross:* 1625. *Built:* 1882. *Type:* SS. *Rig:* schooner. *Owners:* Admiralty. Managed by English & Co, Middlesborough. *Cargo:* Admiralty cargo. *Armed:* 1 x 90mm gun. *Position:* 3/4 mile SW of Black Head (49 59 30N; 05 06 30W). *Master's name:* Robert Hilton Woodrow. *Crew:* 28.

THE steamer *Skaaras* sank so rapidly, in something less than 30 seconds, that the crew had no chance whatsoever of launching a boat. Consequently, 19 people died in this sinking. Even though the master survived there is surprisingly little information among the records. At the time she was hit, the chief officer was in charge on the bridge. The torpedo from *UB-31* struck the *Skaaras* at 6.45am on the port side in the engine room. Those that survived reported that the ship was completely enveloped in steam almost instantly and then they just found themselves in the water. Nine men were plucked out of the sea very soon after by a patrol vessel.

1/57: NYASSA. *Country:* British. *Date sunk:* 24/11/17. *Tons nett:* 1643. *Tons gross:* 2578. *Built:* 1897. *Type:* SS. *Rig:* schooner. *Owners:* Maclay & McIntyre, 21 Bothwell St, Glasgow. *Cargo:* 4000 tons coal. *Armed:* 1 x 12pd 12cwt gun. *Position:* 3 miles ESE of Lizard (49 57 30N; 05 06 30W). *Master's name:* David Macbeth. *Crew:* 26. *Crew nationality:* All British. *Gunners:* George Benjamin Savage, LS RNR, No 2093C; George Mackey, Seaman RNR, No 7771A.

SUCH was the power of the torpedo, fired from a bow tube by *UB-57*, which hit *Nyassa* on her port beam that the resulting explosion left the side of the ship in number three hold completely blown in. She took on water at an alarming rate, forcing the master to abandon the ship immediately.

It was 11am, the weather was rough and the sky overcast, making the whole episode even more gloomy than usual. In spite of the bad sea conditions, all 26 of the crew, after waiting for the ship to lose her eight knots of way, successfully got clear in the ship's boats before the steamer sank. They were later found by a naval drifter.

The contemporary notes on this sinking are very few but one written by the interviewing naval officer at Falmouth said that he felt that the master was not

hugging the land as near as safe navigation permitted. This referred to a paragraph included in most sailing instructions at the time.

1/58: ERATO. *Country:* British. *Date sunk:* 1/9/17. *Tons nett:* 1133. *Tons gross:* 2041. *Built:* 1911. *Type:* SS. *Rig:* schooner. *Owners:* Ellerman, Wilson Line, Hull. *Cargo:* In ballast from Dunkirk to Barry Roads. *Armed:* Yes. *Position:* 3-5 miles E of Lizard (49 57 00N; 05 06 00W). *Master's name:* C.A. Groves. *Crew:* 25.

AT the time, the Admiralty had great reservations as to whether the *Erato* had struck a mine or was torpedoed. Either way it made little difference to the crew of the steamer which ended up on the bottom within five minutes of the explosion.

The scant papers on the incident were placed among the 'Mined' files. (German records say that she sank after hitting one of the mines in a field laid by *UC-69*.)

The master's report stated the weather to be not very good, being overcast, the wind blowing from the west about force six and a rough sea. He said that an enormous explosion boomed out but does not say which part of his ship suffered the damage. He ordered his men to man the boats immediately, which they did, and all managed to get away just before she sank. They were later picked up by a drifter and taken ashore.

1/59: WAR TUNE. *Country:* British. *Date sunk:* 9/12/17. *Tons nett:* 1221. *Tons gross:* 2045. *Built:* 1917. *Type:* SS. *Rig:* schooner. *Owners:* Wm. France Fenwick & Co, 5 Fenchurch St, London. *Cargo:* 2660 tons coal from Barry. *Armed:* 1 x 12pd 12cwt gun. *Position:* 1½ miles SSE of Black Head (49 59 00N; 05 04 30W). *Master's name:* James Ernest Martin. *Crew:* 28. *Crew nationality:* 13 British, 8 Russians, 1 Spaniard, 6 Arabs. *Gunners:* Birch, acting bombadier RMA, No C7256; George Hamp, RMA, No P6632.

WHEN the shout went up, "Torpedo, starboard side," the master shouted to the helmsman to go hard to starboard immediately. He obeyed instantly and the ship began to respond, but not quite enough. The torpedo fired by *U-53* smashed into the starboard side in the after hold, opening up a huge hole.

It was one o'clock in the afternoon, the sea was rough and frequent squalls were coming through from time to time. However, the crew managed to get the boats away and would have got away with no casualties had it not been for an Arab fireman panicing and jumping out of the boat. A search was made for him but it was a hopeless task in the choppy sea.

It was a daring attack by the German U-boat, made even more so by the fact that *War Tune* had two patrol boats close by her at the time, one on either side. They came straight away to her assistance and one of them, *Forethought*, picked up the men.

The naval authorities said after the master had been interviewed, that he was not not 'hugging the coast as close as safe navigation permitted,'a somewhat ambiguous order included in sailing instructions at the time. The master answered that he felt he was as close as safe navigation permitted, something each master must decide for himself. They also questioned him as to why he was not zig-zagging but he answered that he was altering course at the time which rendered it impossible for him to do so.

A somewhat amusing note appeared in the documents concerning this sinking when it was noted that *War Tune* was not fitted with a crow's nest which was a great advantage point for a lookout, and, the note added, 'there is no reason why one should not be fitted.' Next to it in brackets one of their lordships had written, (There is now. The ship is sunk!)

1/60: VOLNAY. *Country:* British.
Date sunk: 14/12/17. *Tons nett:* 2928. *Tons gross:* 4610. *Built:* 1910. *Type:* SS. *Rig:* schooner. *Owners:* The Volnay SS Co Ltd, 8 Gordon St, Glasgow. *Cargo:* Admiralty munitions. *Armed:* Yes. *Position:* Half mile off Porthallow (50 04 15N; 05 04 02W). *Master's name:* Henry Plough. *Crew:* 41.

ON her way from Montreal to Plymouth the *Volnay* had in her holds a valuable military cargo of ammunition. It is also said that she carried luxury goods, although there is no detail in the naval records at the time to say just what those luxury goods were.

The master reported that at the time of the incident the night was dark with a moderate south-westerly wind and a fairly calm sea. It was about 45 minutes after midnight when the explosion occurred and it blew a large hole in number one hold. The master thought at first that he could probabaly limp into Falmouth but when he saw just how fast she was settling he decided to turn the *Volnay* towards the shore and try to beach her. It was a good try but she never made it, sinking in about 10 fathoms of water some half a mile from the shore. All the crew managed to get away in the ship's boats but the *Volnay* was completely submerged apart from her masts.

The *Volnay* struck a mine laid by *UC-64,* according to German records.

Being close to the shore and in fairly shallow water the *Volnay* is now a popular site for divers and much professional salvage work has been carried out. A lot of her cargo of 18pdr shells is strewn about the seabed and she is well broken up with her boilers exposed.

1/61: BAMSE. *Country:* British.
Date sunk: 2/10/18. *Tons nett:* 589. *Tons gross:* 1001. *Built:* 1881. *Type:* SS. *Rig:* schooner. *Owners:* Blow & Richards, Mount Stewart Square,

Cardiff. *Cargo:* 1225 tons patent fuel from Swansea to Dunkirk. *Armed:* 1 x 13pdr gun. *Position:* 1¹/₂ miles E by S of Black Head (50 00 00N; 05 04 00W). *Master's name:* William Ahern. *Crew:* 19. *Crew nationality:* 15 British, 2 Chileans, 1 American, 1 Russian. *Gunner:* W.H. Pullen, RNVR, No TZ10843.

IT was all over with very quickly for the *Bamse* at just after midnight on October 2. The weather was quite good with light winds and a slight sea. The master, chief officer and a seaman were on the bridge at the time she was attacked by *UB-112*, but none of them saw anything of the U-boat or the torpedo streaking towards them.

It smashed into her at the after end of number two hatch and must have opened up a huge hole, as she sank in just under one minute. The master said later that he stepped out of the bridge to see how badly his ship was damaged and found himself in the water with four of his crewmen. They clung to various bits of wreckage and just hoped that one of the sailing vessels they had passed earlier might spot them.

On board the French sailing vessel *Jean Bart* from Groix, the Master, Pierre Quere, was looking intently at an object that had been pointed out to him by his lookouts. It was indeed a German submarine and he shouted to his gunners to fire. It was about 400yds off, between *Jean Bart* and the land, and the first shot missed her but threw up a spout of water close by giving the gunner an indication of range. A second shell was about to follow when the submarine turned towards the shore and dived. Captain Quere cursed the submarine commander and turned in towards it. After a few minutes his lookouts reported that they could hear men shouting in the water ahead and a boat was sent out to check. It was five of the men from the *Bamse*, including the master. Three other men survived from the *Bamse* as a little later the British schooner *My Lady* came across them and took them into Falmouth.

1/62: LYDIE. *Country:* British.
Date sunk: 9/2/18. *Tons nett:* 1604. *Tons gross:* 2559. *Built:* 1900. *Type:* SS. *Rig:* schooner. *Owners:* Burdick & Cook, 34, St Mary's Axe, London. *Cargo:* 4000 tons coal. *Armed:* 1 x 12pdr 12cwt gun. *Position:* 1 mile E of Manacle Buoy (50 03 00N; 05 00 40W). *Master's name:* Henry Fellingham. *Crew:* 27. *Crew nationality:* 14 British, 1 Japanese, 1 Chinese, 3 Russians, 6 Arabs, 1 Dutch, 1 Greek. *Gunners:* H. Baillie, LS RNVR, No 1808C Po; Tuder Davies, AB RNVR, No 3740QZ Po.

AT 2.45pm the steamer *Lydie* was rounding the Manacle Buoy to start her approach to Falmouth Harbour. She was making eight knots and the master had just altered course from north-east to north-half-east when there was a huge explosion on her starboard side. A large hole was opened up, completely exposing the engine room to the sea. The torpedo from *U-53* killed the chief and third engineers.

The master could see that his ship was going down rapidly. He ordered his crew to the boats immediately, but that wasn't easy as the starboard lifeboat had been smashed to pieces by the explosion. However, five minutes later the port boat, in the charge of the mate, did get clear with 21 men, leaving the rest, including the master, to jump as the *Lydie* started to go down.

The mate quickly rowed around picking up the men who were in the water. A few minutes later the cause of all their problems showed itself in the form of a periscope a few hundred yards off. The German submarine commander, Oberleutnant Hans Rose, was admiring his handywork. Skipper W.J. Thompson of the armed drifter *Sunbeam II* had also seen what was going on and was soon bearing down at full speed. He had spotted the periscope and ordered his gunners to fire at will. But Rose spotted the *Sunbeam* a few minutes later and dived away.

Sunbeam II picked up the survivors from the *Lydie* and managed to draw several other patrol vessels into the hunt for the submarine.

1/63: N.G. PETERSEN. *Country:* Danish. *Date sunk:* 13/3/18. *Tons nett:* 803. *Tons gross:* 1282. *Built:* 1898. *Type:* SS. *Rig:* –. *Owners:* Charterers: Furness Whithy & Co. *Cargo:* 1900 tons iron ore. *Armed:* –. *Position:* 2 miles SW of St Anthony's Head (50 07 05N; 05 03 04W). *Master's name:* –.

N.G. PETERSEN sank as result of a wartime collision. Records of the incident are few.

The wreck today, in fairly shallow water in Falmouth Bay, is visited by many divers. It is well broken up and scattered over a wide area. Because of her position she was considered a navigational hazard and dealt with by explosives.

1/64: ALBION. *Country:* British. *Date sunk:* 30/9/15. *Tons nett:* 25. *Tons gross:* –. *Built:* At Galmpton in 1893. *Type:* SV. *Rig:* Cutter. *Owners:* James Summers, Berry Head Rd, Brixham. *Cargo:* Fish. *Armed:* No. *Position:* 6 miles E of Start Point (49 57 00N; 05 02 00W). *Master's name:* James Summers. *Crew:* 3.

NO one knows what happened to the fishing cutter *Albion* during the evening of September 30, 1915. She had been fishing with various other boats off Start Point.

Arthur John Phillips, skipper of the fishing vessel *Speranza*, also from Brixham, said that he saw the *Albion* on and off through most of the day. He was trawling in the same area as *Albion* and passed her at

various times. It was later on in the evening when he saw that the *Albion* had heaved to and was lying with her head to windward with her head sails lowered. He altered his course a little which would take *Speranza* close to *Albion* and shouted out, "What's the matter Jim?" Jim Summers replied that his trawl was foul of something but reckoned he would have it clear soon. *Speranza* kept on her course and put her trawl out again. At about 11pm Arthur Phillips said that he heard a loud explosion and he also felt the shockwaves of it on board his ship.

The crew of another vessel, the Belgian trawler *Hendrik* from the port of Nieuport, reported that they had seen a vessel blow up at about 11 the previous night. Her second hand, Louis Vijaene, said that he was on his way to Brixham and saw a large flash near to a small fishing cutter, this was followed by a large upheaval of water and a loud explosion. Fearing that he was entering a minefield he didn't stop but bore away and made his way to port.

Albion was never seen again and the authorities concluded that *Albion* must have netted a mine laid by an enemy submarine.

1/65: KROSFOND. *Country:* Norwegian. *Date sunk:* 22/11/17. *Tons nett:* 1075. *Tons gross:* 1737. *Built:* At Newcastle in 1904. *Type:* SS. *Rig:* schooner. *Owners:* Svithun Line, Stavanger, Norway. *Cargo:* 2100 tons coal from Newport for Rouen. *Armed:* No. *Position:* Half mile ESE of Manacle Buoy (50 02 30N; 05 01 45W). *Master's name:* Simon Bernhard Svendsen. *Crew:* 21. *Crew nationality:* 13 Norwegians, 1 Swede, 2 Danes, 2 Chilians, 1 Mexican, 1 Spaniard, 1 Portuguese.

IT was 9.20pm when Captain Svendsen of the Norwegian steamer *Krosfond* gave the order for all hands to take up their standby positions for entering port. It was standard procedure and nobody on board could have known that the ship was never going to make it into Falmouth. But worse still, 15 men were not going to make it at all

It was a fine, clear, moonlit night, with a beautiful smooth sea, ideal conditions for enemy submarines to operate in. The master of *Krosfond* had just given the order to the helmsman to change course when a torpedo hit the after part of number three hatch on the starboard side.

The steamer sank rapidly by the stern. The explosion had smashed the starboard boat to pieces. The port boat was lowered but not all the crew could get into it. The steamer sank whilst the boat was alongside and turned it over like a cork.

The master was dragged down by the ship but somehow managed to get free, surfacing to find only wreckage. In amongst it all was the ship's small boat, full of water but it gave the master enough support to get his breath back. Soon the second mate also made for the boat and together the two men emptied it and made their way around the wreckage looking for other survivors, but found none. However, five of the men from the upturned port lifeboat had found the ship's raft that had floated free of the deck when the *Krosfond* sank.

The second mate died from exposure at 3am the following morning. Later, while the master was being rescued by the passing steamer *Borgny,* the other five men were being picked up by a patrol boat.

1/66: SOMMEINA. *Country:* British.
Date sunk: 15/9/17. *Tons nett:* 2159. *Tons gross:* 3317. *Built:* 1899. *Type:* SS. *Rig:* schooner.
Owners: The Stella Shipping Co Ltd, 61, Bute St, Cardiff. *Cargo:* Admiralty cargo from North Shields for Leghorin. *Armed:* Yes. *Position:* Dodman Point bore NE, Pennare bore NW half N (50 02 45N; 05 01 30W). *Master's name:* A.J. Whyte. *Crew:* 31.

THIS ship struck a mine, or pulled a mine onto her, at 7.15am when her engines had been stopped to bring in her Otter Mine Defence gear. The area she was in had been swept that very morning and found to be clear of mines, though later *UC-69* was found to have laid mines close by.

After the explosion a fire broke out in the chart room, preventing the master from getting to his confidential papers. But it mattered little as the ship sank quickly, forcing the crew to take to the boats. They all got clear and were soon picked up by local patrol boats.

1/67: EPSILON. *Country:* Dutch.
Date sunk: 31/1/17. *Tons nett:* 2015. *Tons gross:* 3050. *Built:* At Rotterdam in 1913. *Type:* SS. *Rig:* schooner. *Owners:* Vrachtvaart Maatschappy Bothnia, Amsterdam. *Cargo:* 4760 tons maize in bulk and bags from Sandy & Co, Buenos Ayres to Dutch government. *Armed:* –. *Position:* 1 mile SSW of St Anthony's Lighthouse (50 07 37N; 05 01 24W). *Master's name:* Klaas Lieuwen.

IT was just pure bad luck that caused the loss of the *Epsilon.*

The master said that he left the anchorage in Falmouth at 2.20pm and his ship was under the command of the local pilot. The pilot took the *Epsilon* out towards the harbour entrance and left her when off Black Rock. The master ordered full steam on the engines and set her on a course of south by west. After only a few minutes there was a huge bang.

The explosion from the mine knocked holes in number one and two holds and the blast was so powerful that it blew the hatches completely off number one hold and part of number two. Water started to pour into the ship and the master immediately put the telegraph to stop, at the same time ordering the boats to be made ready.

As the crew scurried to their various boat stations

the master met the chief engineer who had just come from below. His report wasn't good, the water was already over the stokehold plates and rising rapidly. In just a few minutes more the forecastle head was underwater and Captain Lieuwen ordered the boats away.

It was a very smooth operation as all the boats were ready and the men just waiting for the word. They rowed off towards the shore but were soon met by the patrol vessel *Fezenta* which gave them a tow back into Falmouth Harbour.

The master said that although the *Epsilon* had sunk she was still quite visible in shallow water. Part of her poop was above and all of her masts. She must have presented quite a navigational hazard at the time, close to Falmouth Harbour entrance.

1/68: ERIC CALVERT. *Country:* British.
Date sunk: 22/4/18. *Tons nett:* 1173. *Tons gross:* 1862. *Built:* 1889. *Type:* SS. *Rig:* schooner. *Owners:* James Mitchell & Son, 39, Dock Street, Dundee. *Cargo:* 2400 tons coal from Penarth to Boulogne. *Armed:* 1 x 12pdr gun. *Position:* 2 miles SE from entrance to Falmouth Harbour (50 04 00N; 05 01 00W). *Master's name:* Peter Geekie Niven. *Crew:* 25. *Crew nationality:* 15 British, 1 Norwegian, 1 Swede, 1 Russian, 1 Dutch, 6 Arabs (Aden). *Gunners:* William Bird, seaman RNR, No 5915 A Chatham; John More, act LS RNR, No 6336 A Chatham.

IT was an excellent piece of timing on the part of Kapitan-Leutnant Hundius in *UB-103.* He had obviously been watching the *Eric Calvert* closely and knew that she would have to slow down soon. From the bridge of the steamer the master looked at the other vessel approaching the boom defences of Falmouth Harbour and realised that he would have to let her in first. He put the ship's telegraph to slow ahead and she gradually eased down to about four knots.

At 2am it was very calm with a bright moonlit sky, lovely conditions for entering harbour but also excellent conditions for enemy submarines to attack. With her speed much reduced *Eric Calvert* made an easy target and Hundius fired one shot from his bow tubes. It crashed into the steamer's starboard side just behind the engine room.

A huge explosion followed which just about tore the side of the ship out. Two men were killed by the blast. One was listed as an Arab fireman, but no name given, and the other, John Johnson, a cook, of Runwicks Boarding House, Bede Street, Tyne.

The steamer took on an alarming list to port and the master ordered the crew to the boats immediately. They made it by a whisker, managing to pull clear as she went down, just four minutes after being hit. They didn't have to wait long for help as the boom patrol boat was on the scene very quickly.

1/69: CAPE FINISTERRE. *Country:* British.
Date sunk: 2/11/17. *Tons nett:* 2803. *Tons
gross:* 4380. *Built:* In 1907. *Type:* SS. *Rig:*
schooner. *Owners:* Cape Finisterre SS Co, 124, St
Vincent St, Glasgow. *Cargo:* 5900 tons steel billets,
New York to Falmouth. *Armed:* 1 x 4.7in gun.
Position: 1 mile SSE of Manacle Buoy (50 01 40N;
05 01 10W). *Master's name:* James Lockhead.
Crew: 46. *Crew nationality:* 28 British, 1 Russian,
17 Chinese. *Gunners:* D. Morrison, LS RNR
Devonport; James Angus, AB RNVR, No 5205.

OWING to the huge loss of life in this sinking there is
little information as to what happened as *Cape
Finisterre* approached the entrance to Falmouth
Harbour. The master with all his officers, both deck
and engineer, were killed when the ship went down.
Out of 46 crew on board only six survived, the
wireless operator, a gunner, one seaman, one
apprentice and two Chinese hands.
The steamer was under escort from New York and
had just gone on to standby for entering port. It was
3.30pm and all the crew were at their stations when
suddenly a huge explosion occurred at the after part of
the ship. It was so violent that the ship sank in under
a minute.
The commanding officer of the escort vessel *Sea
King* said that he saw the explosion take a huge chunk
out of the steamer's stern and that she disappeared
almost instantly. He and another patrol vessel *Nellie
Dodds* headed at full speed to her assistance but when
they arrived found only six men alive.
UC-17 claimed to have fired the torpedo which
sank her.

1/70: HMT ST IVES. *Country:* British.
Date sunk: 21/12/16. *Tons nett:* –. *Tons gross:* 325.
Built: –. *Type:* Patrol trawler. *Rig:* –. *Owners:*
Admiralty (hired). *Cargo:* –. *Armed:* Yes.
Position: Half mile S by W of Black Rock
(50 08 00N; 05 01 00W). *Master's name:* Lieut
W.A. Carmichael, 346, The Boulevard, Hull.

A LETTER from the Commodore RNR, of HM naval
headquarters to the Admiralty, gave the news that
HM trawler 1192 *St Ives* was lost at 8.15am on
December 21, 1916, through striking a mine. He
enclosed the reports of two men, the commander of
HMT 1362 *Fezenta* who was with *St Ives* at the time
and a surviving officer of *St Ives*. The Commodore
added that he very much deplored the loss of
Lieutenant W.A. Carmichael, RNR, who was a very
zealous and efficient officer and had done most useful
and excellent work in the area.
St Ives went to sea at 7.45am the same morning to
commence mine sweeping operations outside
Falmouth Harbour. Richard Wright, a survivor, said
that they proceeded on a course south by west from
Black Rock about half a mile where they were about to
drop a buoy to commence a sweeping run.

Suddenly a huge explosion occurred under the
engine room aft. The majority of the crew who were at
the aft end of the vessel were killed by the explosion.
However, a few were still at breakfast in the forward
mess and were saved. The shout went up to take to
the boats but *St Ives* sank so rapidly that there was
no time to get any of the boats away.
Fezenta, commanded by W.G. Salsbury, got her
boats launched almost immediately and soon had the
surviving men aboard. Eleven men died.

1/71: ADAMS. *Country:* British.
Date sunk: 17/10/17. *Tons nett:* 1445. *Tons gross:*
2222. *Built:* At South Shields in 1887. *Type:* SS.
Rig: schooner. *Owners:* Brand/Adams SS Co Ltd,
Prudential Buildings, Newcastle. *Cargo:* 3100 tons
coal from H.A. Brightman & Co, Newcastle to St
Nazaire. *Armed:* Yes. *Position:* 6½ miles SE by E
from Lizard Light (49 54 30N; 05 03 00W).
Master's name: Alfred Barron. *Crew:* 25.

THERE was only one form made out and included in
the records of this sinking.
It was 5.45pm when *Adams* ran into trouble near
the Lizard. The weather was fine with a moderate
wind blowing and she was making a steady eight
knots. The master was on the bridge with the second
mate when without any warning a torpedo from *U-
62* struck on the port side in number one hold. The
steamer began to settle by the head almost instantly
and Captain Barron ordered the boats to be lowered
and for the crew to stand off but stay close to the ship.
A patrol trawler was soon on the scene and took
all the men on board. The *Adams* was still afloat two
hours later but at 8.25pm she started to settle again
and sank by the head. There were no losses or injuries
sustained by the crew who were landed later the same
day at Falmouth.

1/72: SABIA. *Country:* British.
Date sunk: 24/11/17. *Tons nett:* 1767. *Tons
gross:* 2807. *Built:* 1903. *Type:* SS. *Rig:* schooner.
Owners: Frumentum SS Co Ltd, 48, Moorgate St,
London. *Cargo:* 3600 tons iron and copper ore,
2800 tons bales of cork from Seville to Manchester.
Armed: 1 x 12pdr gun. *Position:* 10 miles SSE of
Lizard (49 50 30N; 05 01 00W). *Master's name:*
James H. McNeil. *Crew:* 28. *Crew nationality:*
24 British, 1 Dane, 2 American, 1 Dutch. *Gunners:*
Wm Evans, LS RNR, No 1773D; Cecil Alex Lifely,
OS, DJ 59187 Devonport.

LIEUTENANT T.H. Rothwell, RNR, commander of
HMT *Fusilier* reported that at 9am in a heavy sea
with a strong wind blowing, he was escorting the SS
Sabia when she was struck by a torpedo. It struck the
steamer amidships on the starboard side just before
the main mast. This was followed by a second torpedo
which also struck her on the starboard side. Lieutenant

Rothwell immediately went to her assistance but no sooner had he given the order to bear down on her than she sank, about two minutes after being hit.

Some of the surviving crew reported that the first torpedo had been spotted several hundred yards off but by the time the ship responded to the helm it was too late. There was no time to get the boats launched and those of the crew who were still alive found themselves floundering in the heavy seas.

Four naval patrol trawlers were soon on the scene and *Fusilier* managed to find 11 survivors. HMT *Fezenta* found three more as did HMT *Richard Roberts*. All of the 17 survivors were later taken to Falmouth.

U-96 was the U-boat involved.

1/73: CHATTAHOOCHEE. *Country:* American. *Date sunk:* 23/3/18. *Tons nett:* 6307. *Tons gross:* 8232. *Built:* 1911. *Type:* SS. *Rig:* schooner. *Owners:* USA Shipping Board. *Cargo:* 7300 tons cement, 120 motor lorries loaded with war supplies, 500 tons piping, 500 tons commissariat supplies, from London to St Nazaire. *Armed:* 1 x 12pdr 12cwt gun. Gun No C.4126, mounting pl/774. *Position:* 25 miles SW by S of the Lizard (49 38 00N; 05 35 00W). *Master's name:* Robert Carrol Law. *Crew:* 79. *Crew nationality:* 50 Americans, 6 British, 3 Greeks, 8 Spaniards, 7 Russians, 1 Dutch, 1 Swede, 1 Chilian, 1 Venezuelan, 1 Portuguese. *Gunners:* Hector McDonald, seaman RNR, No 4484B, Chatham; William Morris, AB RNVR, No MZ2072, Devonport.

IN view of the large size of the *Chattahoochee* and her valuable cargo, two additional trawlers were detailed to strengthen the escort. She assembled with the other steamers in Mounts Bay, Penzance, and waited for the order to sail in convoy for Brest. To shield her better from enemy attack, *Chattahoochee* was placed as the number two ship in the central column of the convoy.

The weather was fine and clear when the convoy set off. Until darkness fell, they were even escorted by an airship from Mullion station, as well as seaplanes from Newlyn. But after dark they were left to make their way across the mouth of the Channel. Escort trawler 1227, *Yokohama*, commanded by Alexander MacLean, RNR, was the lead vessel stationed ahead of the centre column.

From periscope depth a German submarine commander was studying his quarry. It must have seemed obvious to him that his target had to be the *Chattahoochee*. She was big and by the way some of the escorts kept close to her, full of valuable cargo. At 9.50pm, the U-boat fired two torpedoes. Both torpedoes slammed into the port side amidships of the big steamer.

On board *Chattahoochee*, the master on the bridge knew that a huge section of the port side had been blown out and the steamer was taking on a gradual list. Captain Law decided to abandon ship.

The escort commanders couldn't believe that a German submarine could have attacked such a well protected vessel. But they hurriedly closed the *Chattahoochie* and began to blanket the area with depth charges. HMT's 1863 *Sanson*, 3606 *Thomas Blackhorn*, 380 *Elk* and 472 *Ben Lawers*, completely circled the area with charge after charge.

The abandoned *Chattahoochie*, was still afloat nearly two hours later, but in a bad way. Her survival was no doubt aided by the calm weather conditions. Her master was discussing the situation with a patrol boat commander and planning to get back aboard her. The German commander had other ideas. He had kept out of the way after the first strike and watched the events from a safe distance. At 11.54 he released two more torpedoes, which both struck home on the starboard side of the *Chattahoochie*. The effect of these proved to much for the big steamer and she sank almost instantly.

There appears to be some confusion over the position of *Chattahoochie* when she sank. The Court of Enquiry records put her position as given above. Other sources put her position as, 41 miles NW by N of Ushant (49 05 00N; 05 35 00W), a difference of over 30 miles.

UB-55 claimed to be the submarine involved.

WORLD WAR ONE
CHANNEL WRECKS

◆

AREA TWO

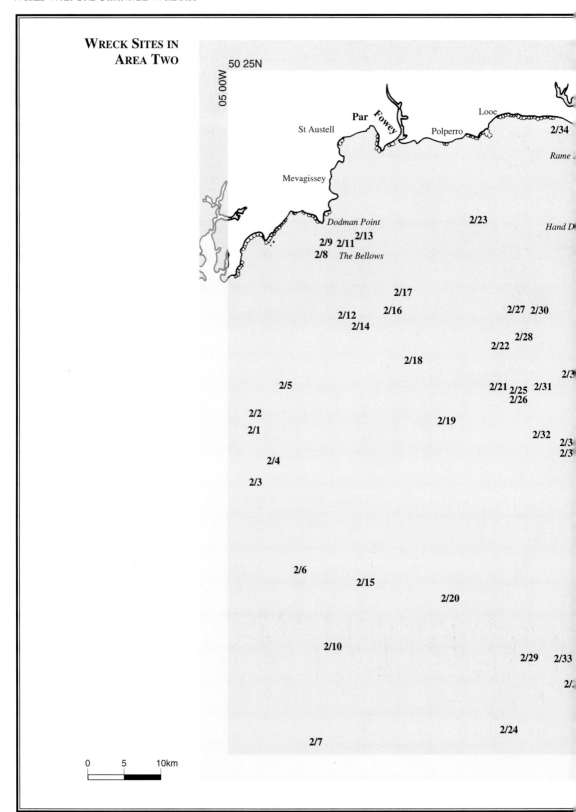

WRECK SITES IN AREA TWO

50 25N

05 00W

Par

Fowey

Looe

St Austell

Polperro

2/34

Rame

Mevagissey

Dodman Point

2/23

Hand D

2/9 2/11 2/13

2/8   *The Bellows*

2/17

2/12   2/16

2/27 2/30

2/14

2/28

2/22

2/18

2/5

2/21 2/25 2/31

2/26

2/2

2/1

2/19

2/32

2/3

2/3

2/4

2/3

2/6

2/15

2/20

2/10

2/29   2/33

2/.

2/24

2/7

0   5   10km

stoint

2/1: BRAMHAM. *Country:* British. *Date sunk:* 19/7/17. *Tons nett:* 1270. *Tons gross:* 1978. *Built:* 1891. *Type:* SS. *Rig:* schooner. *Owners:* J. Mitchell & Sons, Dundee. *Cargo:* Coal from Barry Docks to Rouen. *Armed:* Yes. *Position:* 10 miles E by S of Lizard (49 56 00N; 04 56 30W). *Master's name:* Jas Richardson. *Crew:* 24.

BRAMHAM was lost just after midnight. The master reported that the weather was fine but it was a very dark night. The ship was making her normal speed and all the usual lookouts were in position. A huge explosion boomed out from the fore part of the ship. The steamer started to settle slowly by the head.

None of the lookouts reported seeing anything suspicious, certainly no sign of a submarine, but then again it was a dark night. The authorities concluded that she must have struck a mine and this theory was strengthened by another steamer suffering the same fate in roughly the same position the following day.

The *Bramham* sank at around 1.40am and a muster of the crew revealed that one man was missing. Because of his position at the time of the explosion, being on the bows, it was assumed that he must have been blown overboard by the explosion. German sources say that she sank after striking a mine laid by *UC-47*.

2/2: BEATRICE. *Country:* British. *Date sunk:* 20/7/17. *Tons nett:* –. *Tons gross:* 712. *Built:* 1890. *Type:* SS. *Rig:* –. *Owners:* D.W. Cleeves & Co, Cardiff. *Cargo:* Coal from Penarth for Honfleur. *Armed:* 1 x 13pdr Japanese gun. *Position:* 10 miles E of Lizard (49 57 45N; 04 56 30W). *Master's name:* Thomas Lewis Nicholas. *Crew:* 17. *Crew nationality:* 11 British, 2 Russians, 3 Arabs, 1 Dane. *Gunners:* Scarborough, RNVR; Hillman.

THIS little known sinking happened at about 1.45am and at the time no one was certain whether by mine or torpedo. The fact that the *Bramham* had been sunk nearby on the day before made the Navy sure that they had both been mined. But the *Beatrice* was torpedoed by *UC-47*.

The explosion on the *Beatrice* was devastating, blowing a hole in her starboard side between the engine room and the stokehold. She sank so rapidly that 11 of her crew in their bunks stood no chance at all of getting clear and were lost. She went down in about one minute.

The survivors had to float about in the sea for two hours but were helped by lifebuoys which they grabbed just before entering the water. The Skelwith convoy came through the area later that morning and one of the steamers in the convoy, the Norwegian SS *Aslerund*, picked the men up and landed them at Falmouth.

2/3: MOUNTBY. *Country:* British.
Date sunk: 10/6/18. *Tons nett:* 2114. *Tons gross:*
3263. *Built:* 1898. *Type:* SS. *Rig:* schooner.
Owners: Sir A. Ropner & Co Ltd, West Hartlepool.
Cargo: 4500 tons admiralty stores from Swansea.
Armed: 1 x 12pd 18cwt gun. *Position:* 10 miles SE
of Black Head (49 52 00N; 04 56 00W). *Master's*
name: Arthur Earnest Bainbridge. *Crew:* 32.
Crew nationality: 16 British, 16 Spanish.
Gunners: David G. Robertson, LS RNR, No 632L
Chatham; Charles Tognola, AB RNR, No 6761A
Chatham; Alexander McJoor, AB RNR, No 2017C
Chatham.

A FULL gale was blowing from the north-west in the
early hours of June 10, 1918, and the sea state was
described as nasty. It was precisely 4.24am when she
was approximately four miles south-east of Black
Head, that a torpedo from *UC-49* smashed into the
port side of the *Mountby*, blowing open a large hole in
number two hold.

The master surveyed the damage and ordered his
crew to stand by the boats and wait for his instructions
There was no point in leaving the safety of the ship in
such bad weather unless absolutely necessary. She
was sinking and taking on a list to port but the master
decided to wait it out until help arrived.

About two miles to the north-west the watchmen
on the patrol trawler *Nellie Dodds* heard the explosion
and her commander, Lieutenant F. Padley, sped to
assist the *Mountby*. Once alongside he decided that
the steamer might well be saved if tugs could be got
out soon enough and he wirelessed accordingly. By
8am two tugs were at the scene, *Joseph Constantine*,
commanded by Lieutenant Frank H Taylor, RNR, and
Zaree, commanded by A.G. Downes.

By this time *Mountby's* fore deck was awash and
she had taken on a steep list to port, so the master
decided that it was time to get his crew clear.
Lieutenant Taylor asked for some volunteers to go
back to the ship and make fast the cables. Three men
stepped forward immediately, G. Moss, the second
mate; E. Grier, the bosun and C.A. Major, a steward.
They did the job well and soon had the tow ropes
fixed and the helm lashed ahead.

Both tugs took up the tow and started to make
headway towards Falmouth but it was very slow going
in the rough sea. Thirty minutes later *Mountby* gave a
large lurch which warned the tug skippers what was
about to happen and they cut the ropes a few seconds
before she went down.

All the crew were taken aboard the *Nellie Dodds*
and landed at Falmouth.

2/4: ULA. *Country:* Norwegian.
Date sunk: 9/1/18. *Tons nett:* 499. *Tons gross:* 839.
Built: 1899. *Type:* SS. *Rig:* schooner. *Owners:*
D. Tharldsen, Bergen, Norway. *Cargo:* In ballast
from Rouen to Barry. *Armed:* No. *Position:* 10
miles ESE from Lizard (49 54 00N; 04 54 00W).

Master's name: Eric Christensen. *Crew:* 14.
Crew nationality: 13 Norwegians, 1 Dane.

HAVING called in at St Helens Roads, Isle of Wight,
for sailing instructions the *Ula* continued on her
voyage down the Channel. The weather was clear,
but there was a strong wind which whipped up the
sea, making it quite choppy.

She was spotted by a German submarine
commander as she approached the Lizard. The
Admiralty said later that the steamer was much too
far out and the master should have had his ship much
closer to the land as per his instructions. He should
also have been zig-zagging, but he wasn't. At 10am
the torpedo slammed into number three hold and tore
open a huge hole in her side.

There was little time for the crew as the steamer
started to settle rapidly but all the boat practice paid
off as the 14 men scrambled into one lifeboat and
pulled clear. They were not on their own for long as
the patrol drifter *Forethought* was soon on the scene
and took them aboard.

2/5: VILLE DE THANN. *Country:* French.
Date sunk: 27/11/17. *Tons nett:* 888. *Tons gross:*
1416. *Built:* 1880. *Type:* SS. *Rig:* schooner. *Owners:*
Latham of Havre. *Cargo:* In ballast. *Armed:* 1 x
90mm gun. *Position:* 8 miles E of Black Head
(50 00 00N; 04 53 00W). *Master's name:* Fredrick
Perrault. *Crew:* 22. *Crew nationality:* All French.

WHEN foreign vessels sank close to British shores
during the war, the information concerning the
circumstances was often scant due to language
problems. The *Ville de Thann* was one such vessel
and apart from the bare essentials there is not much
written evidence about her loss.

There was an explosion at 8am – either of mine or
torpedo. The master was of the opinion that he had
struck a mine but the British naval authorities thought
that it was unlikely in view of the distance from land.
They thought the sinking was most probably caused
by a torpedo from an enemy submarine.

In spite of the ship eventually breaking in two, most
of the crew got away. However, two seamen and one
fireman were lost either by the explosion or drowning.

2/6: WILHELM. *Country:* British.
Date sunk: 7/6/17. *Tons nett:* 134. *Tons gross:* –.
Built: –. *Type:* SV. *Rig:* schooner. *Owners:*
Admiralty. Managers: Hannan Samuel & Co,
Fowey. *Cargo:* 260 tons coal from Glasgow to
Lannion. *Armed:* No. *Position:* 18 miles SE of
Lizard (49 45 00N; 04 51 00W). *Master's name:*
John Keeler. *Crew:* 5. *Crew nationality:* 2 British,
1 Russian, 1 Dane, 1 Norwegian.

At first there was a certain amount of confusion as to
whether the *Wilhelm* had been sunk or not. She was a

German prize and had been allocated the number of *CS 75* and put in the hands of managers Hannan Samuel & Co of Fowey. They kept the vessel busy on the coal run – which is what she was doing on the day she was lost.

It was 2pm according to the master when the first gunshot was heard. He looked around the horizon and spotted the shape off a German submarine heading directly towards his ship. After a short discussion with the crew, the master decided to abandon ship. However, in his hurry to get away the master forgot to destroy his secret sailing instructions.

Meanwhile the German gunners on the submarine had found the range of the *Wilhelm* and were scoring hits. Normally the submarine would have gone in for the kill but suddenly the patrol vessel *Badger* came into sight and made the enemy commander sheer off. *Badger* approached the crew in the boat and picked them up but nobody actually saw what happened to the *Wilhelm*. This is where the confusion arose but the last person to see her said that she was in a bad way and must have sunk very soon after the submarine left.

The Admiralty were not best pleased with the master for leaving his confidential papers on board and wrote to him demanding an explanation. He was very honest about the whole thing and said that during the rush to leave the ship with shells flying all around he just forgot about them. The Admiralty didn't appear to have taken it any further than giving him a warning.

2/7: MARJORIE. *Country:* British. *Date sunk:* 9/6/17. *Tons nett:* 60. *Tons gross:* 119. *Built:* Of wood at Milford Haven 1904. *Type:* MV. *Rig:* Motor ketch. *Owners:* W.A. Jenkins & Co, Baltic Buildings, Swansea. *Cargo:* In ballast from St Brieux to Swansea. *Armed:* No. *Position:* 30 miles SE by S from Lizard (49 31 00N; 04 49 00W). *Master's name:* Alfred Pooley. *Crew:* 4. *Crew nationality:* All British.

THE *Marjorie* was slightly unusual at the time in that she was a motor ketch, one of the early small traders to have motor and sail. She was obviously unusual to the Germans who captured her. Not only did they loot her of food, fixtures and fittings, but also tried to remove the engine to take with them as well. They were only thwarted in their attempt because they didn't have the right tools to do the job.

It was 2pm when the submarine first opened fire on the *Marjorie*. She was a long way off and the shells fell well short of their target. The crew of the *Marjorie* realised that against such a fast and powerful enemy they had virtually no chance of escape at all. The only sensible thing to do was to abandon ship before the German gunner came within range.

As the submarine drew alongside the crew in their boat the commander appeared and ordered the master and the cook to come on board. The two of them were

held whilst their boat was used by three German officers to plant bombs in the hold and grab whatever loot they fancied.

At 3pm the bombs exploded, blasting large holes in the keel of the ship. She slowly filled with water and within half an hour had gone down. The crew were left a long way from the shore and spent some 18 hours rowing and sailing towards the coast before being spotted by a patrol boat and taken into Falmouth.

2/8: BUTETOWN. *Country:* British. *Date sunk:* 29/1/18. *Tons nett:* 999. *Tons gross:* 1594. *Built:* 1891. *Type:* SS. *Rig:* As schooner. *Owners:* Harrison & Son, The Exchange, Cardiff. *Cargo:* 2392 tons coal from Glasgow to Portsmouth. *Armed:* 1 x 12pdr 12cwt gun. *Position:* 1½ miles S of Dodman Point (50 11 30N; 04 48 00W). *Master's name:* James Mitchell Anderson. *Crew:* 23. *Crew nationality:* 21 British, 2 Russian. *Gunners:* Murdo McDonald, LS RNR, No 4534B; James Southerland, AB RNR, No 9057A.

IN the files on this sinking is a letter to her master from the Director of Transport & Shipping, lightly chastising him as follows, 'In connection with the sinking of the steamer *Butetown* recently, I have to inform you that in accordance with paragraph 181 of war instructions for British merchant ships, you should not have been flying your colours and that the ziz-zagging should have been more irregular. Please pay particular attention to this point for the future.'

It happened at 10.35am on January 29, 1918. The weather was good, fine with a moderate sea although somewhat hazy in patches. The master was on the bridge at the time and said later that he saw nothing of the approaching torpedo (fired by *UB-40*) until it was too late. Several of his crew had seen it but could not warn the master fast enough for him to do anything about it. It struck the ship under the bridge on the port side and virtually blew the side out of her. The master ordered the ship to be abandoned immediately but at the muster it was discovered that two firemen were missing.

There was no time to search for the men as the ship was sinking rapidly. The rest managed to get clear just in time as the steamer sank, at the most 10 minutes from the time she had been struck. They rowed for the shore and managed to make it to Mevagissey.

2/9: CAROLUS. *Country:* Norwegian. *Date sunk:* 27/1/18. *Tons nett:* 643. *Tons gross:* 1041. *Built:* At Bergen in 1900. *Type:* SS. *Rig:* schooner. *Owners:* Jacob Lindvig, Oslo, Norway. *Cargo:* 1480 tons coal from Morgan Wakley & Co, Cardiff to Paris. *Armed:* No. *Position:* 2 miles S of Dodman Point (50 11 20N; 04 47 20W). *Master's* *name:* Alfred Toftenaes. *Crew:* 15. *Crew nationality:* 7 Norwegians, 2 Swedes, 1 Dane, 2 Dutch, 1 American, 1 Spanish, 1 Russian

IT was a dull, miserable day off the Cornish coast on January 27, 1918. The sky was overcast and a mist hung in the air with little wind to push it away. It was 3.45 in the afternoon and the *Carolus* was steadily making her way up the Channel past Dodman Point. The bridge watch was in the capable hands of the chief officer with one seaman at the wheel and another acting as lookout. The master wasn't far away, next door in the chart room plotting his course for the journey ahead. Suddenly the quiet scene was pierced by a shout from the lookout, "Torpedo off the starboard beam!"

The mate sprang into action and put the telegraph to stop, at the same time yelling to the helmsman to put the wheel over hard to starboard. It was a good try at avoiding the torpedo which zipped through the water at an alarming speed, but it wasn't good enough and it smashed into the starboard side of the steamer by the fore rigging. An enormous explosion followed and the *Carolus* slowly came to a halt. She started to settle and list to starboard.

Two boats were lowered successfully but somehow one of them took in water to the point where it became useless. Fortunately the boats were big and all the crew were able to get into one boat comfortably.

Within 10 minutes the *Carolus* had sunk by the head leaving the men to row for the shore. They eventually landed at Gorran Haven and walked to Mevagissey Coastguard Station.

2/10: YVONNE. *Country:* British. *Date sunk:* 6/9/16. *Tons nett:* 82. *Tons gross:* 152. *Built:* –. *Type:* SV. *Rig:* schooner. *Owners:* Yves Marie Barat. *Cargo:* –. *Armed:* No. *Position:* 25 miles SE of Lizard (49 39 00N; 04 47 00W). *Master's name:* Alain Marie Gelgon. *Crew:* 6.

THE German officer who stood on the side of the submarine shouted across to the crew of the *Yvonne* that they must abandon their ship as they were about to be sunk. He was very nice about it and told them they could take whatever they wanted with them. It was a calm day with light winds and there seemed to be an air of non urgency about it all.

The crew took their time and eventually pulled clear of the ship. The German officer shouted for them to come to him and ordered them aboard the submarine whilst a boarding party used their boat to plant bombs.

It was all over quite quickly. As the bombs exploded, the sailing vessel turned turtle almost immediately, but she didn't sink. It took a couple of well placed shells through her upturned hull before she went to the bottom.

2/11: ALMOND BRANCH. *Country:* British. *Date sunk:* 27/11/17. *Tons nett:* 2190. *Tons gross:* 3460. *Built:* Sunderland in 1896. *Type:* SS. *Rig:* schooner. *Owners:* F.M. Ritson, 30 West Sunnyside, Sunderland. *Cargo:* 1000 tons general, shipped by C. Howard & Sons from London to South America. *Armed:* 1 x 4in gun. *Position:* 2 miles SE of Dodman Point (50 11 30N; 04 46 00W). *Master's name:* George Donald, Waughton Cottage, Johnshaven, NB. *Crew:* 43. *Crew nationality:* 19 British, 21 Chinese, 1 Russian, 1 Dutch, 1 Swede. *Gunners:* George Townrow, L/Cpl, RM, No B1376 Ch; Frederick Fletcher, Pte, RM, No B1927 Ch.

THE shout went up from one of the lookouts at 8.05am, "Torpedo off the starboard beam!"

The master rushed to the starboard side of the bridge and saw the white wake of the torpedo streaking towards the ship. "Hard to port," he yelled to the helmsman who promptly obeyed the order. The ship's head started to come round but it was too slow and the torpedo slammed into the steamer's starboard side just behind the engine room in number four hold. The explosion that followed was enormous. The master looked aft to see number four hold's hatches blown completely off. Again he barked an order, "Engines full astern."

Knowing full well that it was most likely he would have to abandon his ship, the master wanted to get the way off her as soon as possible. Too many lives had been lost by trying to get boats lowered whilst the ship was moving. The engines responded well to the order and *Almond Branch* came to a steady halt. After a general look around his ship, Captain Donald knew that she was going down and gave the order, "All crew to boat stations and leave in an orderly manner."

In true tradition the master was last to leave. He stepped into the boat and gave the order to lower away. Three others had already got clear and were well away from danger. One man, Mr Drillot, an able seaman, had been reported missing and was presumed to have perished in the explosion. The master's boat was soon stopped by *UB-57*, responsible for the sinking. Oberleutnant Johann Lohs needed information for his log and asked the master all the usual questions, name, tonnage, where from, where bound, cargo etc. Captain Donald didn't feel much like giving the information but, looking down the barrel of a gun, decided it would be wise to co-operate.

At 8.50am the master watched as his ship gave a final lurch and sank. Three boats were picked up later by the SS *Halberdier* and the master's boat was given a tow by a local motor fishing vessel into Gorran Haven.

2/12: TREGENNA. *Country:* British. *Datesunk:* 26/12/17. *Tons nett:* 3705. *Tons gross:* 4380. *Built:* At South Shields in 1917. *Type:* SS. *Rig:* schooner. *Owners:* E. Hain & Son Ltd, St Ives,

Cornwall. *Cargo:* 6250 tons coal from Lambert Bros, London to Gibraltar. *Armed:* 1 x 4in gun, 2 x 7.5in Howitzers. *Position:* 12 miles E by S from Falmouth Gateway / 8 miles S of Dodman Point (50 05 30N; 04 44 30W). *Master's name:* Albert Benjamin Donald. *Crew:* 41. *Crew nationality:* 38 British, 1 Swede, 1 Italian, 1 Dutch. *Gunners:* A.H. Smith, LS RFR, No 188495 Chatham; Sam Ashton, LS RFR, No SS862 Devonport; George Temperton, OS RNVR, No TZ11037; F.J. Brasted, LS RNR, No 1890B Devonport; F.T. Barley, AB RNVR, No LZ4747.

LEAVING Falmouth in convoy, *Tregenna* was the sixth ship in single line ahead formation. They set off on an east by south direction from the gateway of the boom defence in Falmouth Bay to avoid a minefield to the south. After travelling 11 miles at six knots they altered course at 2.45pm to the south. Two minutes later it all started to happen.

The number five ship in the convoy SS *Benito*, was suddenly hit by a torpedo and the master of *Tregenna* looked through his binoculars to see what was going on. He saw more than he anticipated – the white wake of a torpedo speeding towards him, but it passed ahead of his ship. However, two minutes later another torpedo found its mark and smashed into *Tregenna's* port side in number two hold.

She heeled over and started to settle immediately and the master ordered the crew to the boats. Twelve minutes after being struck, *Tregenna* was on the bottom.

Help was at hand quickly from one of the escorting trawlers. The *Tregenna* was another victim of Oberleutnant Johann Lohs in *UB-57*.

2/13: EASTFIELD. *Country:* British.
Date sunk: 27/11/17. *Tons nett:* 1306. *Tons gross:* 2145. *Built:* 1901. *Type:* SS. *Rig:* schooner. *Owners:* The Field Line Ltd, Cardiff. *Cargo:* 3000 tons coal from Newport to Falmouth. *Armed:* 1 x 90mm gun. *Position:* 3$\frac{1}{2}$ miles ESE from Dodman Point (50 12 00N; 04 43 30W). *Master's name:* John Humphreys. *Crew:* 23. *Crew nationality:* 20 British, 1 Russian, 1 Portuguese, 1 Japanese. *Gunners:* Machasill; Macdonald.

THE torpedo that struck the *Eastfield* on her starboard side did enormous damage. It was described at the time as so violent that it completely blew the side out of her and smashed two of her three lifeboats to pieces. It also took the life of one man, a stoker, who was never seen again.

At the time the torpedo struck the steamer was making a steady eight knots. The master and the first mate were on the bridge but saw nothing of the submarine which once again was *UB-57*. However, they certainly saw the torpedo, but only when it was 200yds off.

Using just the one remaining good boat all the crew

got clear or had enough time to wait for the Mevagissey lifeboat to arrive. The lifeboat did pick up 22 men and landed them safely ashore.

There is a note in Naval Weekly Reports for the period that the patrol trawler *Vale of Fruin* picked up a boat off Eddystone marked *Eastfield* and some confusion ensued about the loss of the vessel.

2/14: BENITO. *Country:* British.
Date sunk: 26/12/17. *Tons nett:* 3021. *Tons gross:* 4712. *Built:* 1907. *Type:* SS. *Rig:* schooner. *Owners:* Elder Dempster & Co Ltd, Water St, Liverpool. *Cargo:* Coal and coke from Newcastle. *Armed:* Yes. *Position:* 12 miles ESE of Falmouth Gateway, 9 miles S by E of Dodman Point (50 05 00N; 04 43 30W). *Master's name:* A.W. Sulivan. *Crew:* 47.

IT would seem that the *Benito* was the first ship to be struck by a torpedo from *UB-57* after the convoy left Falmouth on December 26, 1917. She was number five in a single line ahead formation. The convoy steered east by south for 11 miles to take them clear of a minefield which lay to the south, before altering course to a more southerly direction. The torpedo struck *Benito* under her poop which smashed away her rudder and propeller, leaving her completely crippled.

Although she was crippled she was in no imminent danger of sinking and several patrol trawlers tried to get her in tow. It is at this stage that the information gets a little confused. The steamer behind her, *Tregenna*, was hit by a torpedo soon after and she consequently sank in 12 minutes. Apparently *Benito* was taken in tow for several hours but at just after midnight, whilst several patrol trawlers were still around her, she was torpedoed again by Oberleutnant Lohs and she sank soon after.

2/15: SPENNYMOOR. *Country:* British.
Date sunk: 28/5/15. *Tons nett:* 2544. *Tons gross:* 2733. *Built:* 1909. *Type:* SS. *Rig:* schooner. *Owners:* W. Ruciman, Newcastle. *Cargo:* General government cargo from Cardiff to St Sevan. *Armed:* No. *Position:* 50 miles SW by W of Start Point (49 44 00N; 04 43 00W). *Master's name:* –. *Crew:* 29.

SPENNYMOOR was under sealed admiralty orders heading for St Sevan. At 6.30am on the May 28, 1915, the shape of a submarine was seen by the watchmen on the bridge as it slowly rose out of the water about two miles off on the port bow. The master was sent for and immediately ordered the helmsman to turn away. As the steamer responded to the helm the sound of an enormous crash and splintering of wood was heard as a shell smashed into one of the skylights. The submarine commander meant business. A second shell went whimpering over the bridge but a third penetrated the engine room and the steamer slowly came to a halt. The master sent word to the engine room to ask what state it was in. Whilst waiting for a report he ordered all the firemen to go to the stokehold and ensure no fires broke out, but to his disgust they refused. As far as they were concerned the ship was done for and they all assembled by the boats.

The word from the engine room wasn't good. The shell had smashed a condenser rendering the engines useless. There was nothing for it but to comply with the signals flying from the approaching *U-41*, 'abandon ship.' The master reluctantly gave the order.

Two boats were lowered down into the choppy sea and the men began to pull clear of the steamer. The master's boat, however, got into trouble straight away and capsized. The mate, John Ohlsson, immediately went to help and pulled as many men as could be found to safety. For nearly an hour the men rowed around ignoring the submarine, hoping the German commander would show some mercy and wait until they had at least recovered all their shipmates. It was a slim hope as a torpedo smashed into the side of the *Spennymoor* and she sank within a few minutes.

Having given up hope of finding anyone else alive the saddened crew rowed towards the shore. Six men were missing – the master, bosun, a donkeyman, an apprentice and two firemen. At 11.45am the survivors were spotted by a lookout on the SS *Broadgreen* of Liverpool and taken into Falmouth.

Not unnaturally, their Lordships of the Admiralty took a very dim view of the firemen disobeying orders. The fact was highlighted within the records for this sinking but it is not recorded what action was taken.

2/16: PRUDENCE. *Country:* British.
Date sunk: 2/6/17. *Tons nett:* 24. *Tons gross:* 25.
Built: Of wood at Kingsbridge in 1907. *Type:* SV.
Rig: ketch. *Owners:* Alfred Lanfear (Snr), Park View, Galmpton, Brixham. *Cargo:* Fish. *Armed:*
No. *Position:* 15 miles WSW from Eddystone (50 06 00N; 04 39 00W). *Master's name:* Richard Brenchley. *Crew:* 3. *Crew nationality:* All British.

IT was a rainy, overcast and miserable day when the crew of *Prudence* started to trawl in the fishing grounds near the Eddystone. The ship was on the port tack and making good headway in the moderate breeze. The visibility wasn't particularly good but good enough for the master to stop what he was doing and concentrate on an object about two miles off on the port quarter. He wasn't sure but it looked to him every bit like a submarine, but was it friendly or hostile? A minute later his question was answered as a shell dropped close by, sending up a column of water.

The master shouted to the helmsman to turn away. The shells kept coming, each one getting closer and closer until the master decided that enough was

enough. The boat was got out and the crew left as fast as they could. Even though the German gunner had fired some 20 shells, many fell close, but not one hit the ship directly.

The submarine approached the crew in the boat but then veered away towards the *Prudence* as though the commander had just changed his mind about how he was going to sink her. From only a few hundred yards the German gunner let fly at the little sailing vessel, the first shot smashing off the bowsprit followed by two more which finished the job off and sent her to the bottom.

The enemy commander made no attempt to talk with the men of the *Prudence* which was unusual, but instead made off at speed to the east. The crew rowed towards the shore and kept a lookout for any passing traffic that might help them out. One such ship was the vessel *WE* of Ramsgate which picked up the men and dropped them off at Plymouth the next morning.

2/17: VICTORIA. *Country:* British.
Date sunk: 17/11/17. *Tons nett:* 573. *Tons gross:* 973. *Built:* At Bergen, Norway. *Type:* SS. *Rig:* schooner. *Owners:* The Shipping Control / Turnbull & Scott Co, London. *Cargo:* 1170 tons coal from Moxey, Savon, Cardiff for Dieppe. *Armed:* 1 x 13pdr gun. *Position:* 8 miles SE of Dodman Point (50 07 30N; 04 37 45W). *Master's name:* John William Hunter, 102 Clive Rd, Canton, Cardiff. *Crew:* 21. *Crew nationality:* All British. *Gunners:* Horice James Green Astill, AB RNVR, No BZ 5829 Ch; Isaac Henry Moore, AB RNVR, No BZ 3576 Ch.

THERE were no further instructions for the master of the *Victoria* when he arrived at Falmouth Roads at 7am on Saturday, November 17, 1917. He raised anchor and by 11am was heading off out to open sea again. He was zig-zagging his way in a north-easterly direction trying to hug the coast as best he could when he spotted a large sailing vessel that appeared to be under tow. He told the chief officer to stop the zig-zagging for a while and steady the course so as not to confuse the tugging vessel ahead. Seeing that all was well the master went off to the chartroom to sort out his courses.

To stop zig-zagging seemed to be the correct thing to do in the circumstances but it may have been that action which prompted the German submarine commander to strike sooner rather than later. At 1pm there was a deafening explosion on the port side of the ship and the *Victoria* started to settle down very quickly indeed.

The damage to the steamer was severe. Part of the bridge was blown to pieces, killing the mate, and the port lifeboat completely shattered. The master ordered the starboard boat to be lowered and the crew started to get into it. On looking around, the master shouted to the third engineer who was standing on the after part of the ship and ordered him to grab a lifebuoy. He looked again a moment later and the after part of the ship was underwater leaving no sign of the third engineer. The starboard boat was lowered but was soon in trouble when it touched the water, way on the ship causing it to break up. As men were floundering in the water and drifting astern of the steamer, some managed to get to the remains of the boat and shouted to others to do the same. Fortunately, they all managed to get to the boat and there were no more casualties. All this had happened in an amazingly short time as the steamer sank within three minutes of being hit by the torpedo.

Help came to the men fairly quickly when the SS *Trevisa* passed by and took them aboard. They were later transferred to a patrol trawler and the surviving 18 men taken into Falmouth. Most of them were cold and tired but otherwise in good order. The chief engineer was listed as injured.

A few days later the Admiralty wanted to know why the master was so far off the land and why he wasn't ziz-zagging. Captain Hunter had a very good reason why he wasn't ziz-zagging but made no comment as to why he was so far off the land. The Admiralty personally cautioned him and asked him to be more careful in future when carrying out route instructions.

2/18: FOYLEMORE. *Country:* British. *Date sunk:* 16/12/17. *Tons nett:* 2371. *Tons gross:* 3831. *Built:* In 1911. *Type:* SS. *Rig:* – . *Owners:* Johnson Line, Chartered by Furness Withy & Co. *Cargo:* Ballast from Calais to Manchester. *Armed:* 1 x 13 pdr gun. *Position:* 23 miles E by N of Lizard (50 02 00N; 04 36 30W). *Master's name:* Thomas J. Barkley RNR. *Crew:* 40.

THE weather was particularly bad at 5.20 on the morning of December 16, 1917. Heavy rain showers which at times turned into thick snow hammered the ship, as well as heavy seas. *Foylemore* was heading to Falmouth for instructions before carrying on with her journey north.

The first officer, Mr J. Dean, said that it was pitch black and the lookouts could see nothing. When the explosion occurred on the starboard side nobody knew if the ship had struck a mine or had been hit by a torpedo. The engine room bore the brunt of the explosion and the steamer began to settle by the stern. Fortunately for the crew she didn't settle fast which gave them time to gather up warm clothing and take to the boats. They got clear in about 15 minutes and the steamer sank soon after by the stern.

Eleven of the men including the master and the second mate were picked up by the American USS *Drayton* and 29 men in the mate's boat were picked up by another American ship USS *Benham*.

Even though the crew were unsure about what had caused the explosion the Admiralty were in no doubt that a German submarine was responsible. The Germans said it was *UB-55*.

2/19: ST ANDRE. *Country:* French. *Date sunk:* 19/12/17. *Tons nett:* 1337. *Tons gross:* 2456. *Built:* 1908. *Type:* SS. *Rig:* schooner. *Owners:* Societe Navale de L'ouest, Paris. *Cargo:* Approx 500 tons (3000) of empty casks from Rouen to Oran. *Armed:* 2 x 90mm cannons. *Position:* 17 miles SW by S of Eddystone (49 57 00N; 04 32 00W). *Master's name:* Jules Simon. *Crew:* 29.

IT was a very dark night when *St Andre* ran into trouble to the south-west of the Eddystone. The first officer was on the bridge at the time and reported later that conditions were terrible. The sea was rough and it was impossible to see anything at all.

The torpedo struck the steamer on the port side, amidships, and she immediately took on a list to starboard. Within a few minutes the engines ground to a halt as the water engulfed them and several smaller explosions boomed out. The master thought at the time that his ship was done for and ordered the crew to take to the boats. A fireman and a trimmer were killed by the explosion.

None of the crew saw what happened to their ship, all of them thinking that she must have sunk soon after they left. However, that wasn't the case. At 11am an airship from Mullion airship station circled over the *St Andre*, which was still afloat, although listing heavily on her starboard side. The pilot spotted a patrol trawler sweeping off to the east and signalled to her what he had found. The trawler was HMT 127 *Merisia* commanded by Lieutenant P.N. Taylor, DSC, RNR, who immediately made off to see what could be done for the stricken steamer. He arrived on the scene at 1.15pm and noted that there was no sign of the crew and that some of the lifeboats were missing. By this time the crew of the *St Andre* had already been picked up by the passing steamer *Borga*.

Lieutenant Taylor put men on board the *St Andre* with the idea of getting a tow line on her. But before they could get the lines attached the steamer gave another lurch before going to the bottom.

2/20: VEDA. *Country:* British. *Date sunk:* 2/1/18. *Tons nett:* 24. *Tons gross:* –. *Built:* Of wood at Rye in 1896. *Type:* SV. *Rig:* dandy. *Owners:* Cox & Davies, Canbrian Place, Swansea. *Cargo:* –. *Armed:* No. *Position:* 30 miles SSW from Eddystone (49 43 00N; 04 31 00W). *Master's name:* Walter Hewitt. *Crew:* 3.

IT was just as well the crew didn't know of the ordeal that lay ahead of them when they left Brixham for the fishing grounds on New Years Day, 1918. The weather was not particularly good, the wind quite strong with a choppy sea and, being January, it was cold.

Their troubles began at 7am the following morning. The second hand was in charge of the watch and the master was below having his breakfast when his peace

45

The White Star liner *Afric* – a victim of *UC-54* while en route from Liverpool to Australia via Plymouth.

was disturbed by the sound of gunfire. Hearing the distinct whistle of a shell pass close to the ship he immediately suspected an enemy submarine. Abandoning his breakfast he gathered up his secret papers and after tossing them into the galley fire went on deck to see what was happening. His suspicions were correct, a German submarine was very close and very threatening.

Captain Hewitt knew that it was pointless to resist such an assault and told his two men to grab some clothes and provisions and get in the boat quickly. No sooner had they pulled clear when the submarine moved in for the kill, the sixth shell sending the *Veda* down. The submarine commander made no attempt to talk to the crew. It seemed he had other things on his mind, such as sinking the other fishing vessels that were in the area.

All this would not have been so bad for the crew of the *Veda* had they made land or had been picked up fairly quickly. However, they drifted helplessly with the wind and tide for five days. It was January 7, when HMS *Cockatrice* found them about 30 miles to the south west of the Scilly Isles, cold, hungry and suffering from exposure.

2/21: AFRIC. *Country:* British. *Date sunk:* 12/2/17. *Tons nett: –. Tons gross:* 11,999. *Built: 1899. Type:* SS. *Rig:* liner. *Owners:* White Star Line / Oceanic Steam Navigation Co. *Cargo:* General, Liverpool via Plymouth to Australia. *Armed:* 1 x 6in gun. *Position:* 12m SSW

from Eddystone (50 00 15N; 04 25 30W). *Master's name: –. Crew:* 151, plus 2 passengers and 1 stowaway.

THE liner *Afric* had arrived about 3 miles ESE of Eddystone Light at 7pm on February 11, 1917. The master ordered the engines to slow ahead and he morsed for about an hour to attract attention. His ship was big and to get into Plymouth safely he needed a pilot. At 8.20pm he still had no reply and resigned himself to the fact that he was at sea for the night.

It was too dangerous to stay at slow ahead for long so he brought the engines up to full and headed off towards the Lizard. Most of the night was spent back and forth, Lizard to Eddystone. However, at 5.30am, her journey was to come to a very abrupt halt.

The chief officer was on the bridge. *Afric* was on a heading of east-north-east, making about 10 knots when he spotted the white streak of a torpedo, about 200 feet away, approaching at an angle of 45 degrees to the starboard bow. There was no time to do anything to avoid it. A huge explosion followed which knocked the generators out and plunged the ship into darkness.

The master immediately stuffed his confidential papers into the weighted bag and tossed it over the side. He looked around his ship to see what state she was in. She was listing over to starboard and a report from the engine room informed him that it was basically wrecked. Worse still, at least two engineers lay dead. He felt he had no choice but to abandon ship.

All the crew left *Afric* at 5.45am in eight boats and pulled away to a safe distance from the crippled steamer. At about 6am another explosion boomed out as another torpedo slammed into the port side of *Afric,* abreast of number one hold. At 6.20am the submarine surfaced and nosed her way in among the boats. An officer shouted down from the conning tower, demanding to speak to the master. On the side of the conning tower was painted *UC-54.*

The master had no choice but to obey the German commander and climbed onto the submarine. He was questioned for some time about the details of his ship. *Afric* was a good kill and the commander wanted plenty of details for his log.

By 7am the crew were rowing steadily towards Eddystone. They could hear the noise of shelling in the distance, the submarine's gunner pouring shell after shell into the *Afric.* One man counted 28 shots in total before she finally gave up and sank by the head at around 7.45am.

About an hour later a patrol boat arrived in the area to see what all the noise was about. It was too late to save the *Afric* but most of the men were picked up. However, one boat managed to get separated from the rest and at the time the report was written, it was still missing.

A Court of Enquiry was ordered to investigate the loss of the *Afric.* However, in spite of a frustrating search, the papers relating to it remain undiscovered. That it occurred cannot be denied as there is a reference to the Court of Enquiry finding that PNTO Liverpool was partly blamed for the route instructions issued to the master.

The master was apportioned some of the blame for cruising up and down at slow speed. Altogether five men died in the *Afric,* two engineers, two greasers and a cook.

2/22: WESTERN COAST. *Country:* British. *Date sunk:* 17/11/17. *Tons nett:* –. *Tons gross:* 1394. *Built:* 1916 at Dublin. *Type:* SS. *Rig:* schooner. *Owners:* Admiralty. *Cargo:* Ballast. Portsmouth to Barry for coal. *Armed:* –. *Position:* 10 miles WSW from Eddystone (50 03 00N; 04 25 00W). *Master's name:* –. *Crew:* 21.

THE only report of this sinking appears in Weekly Reports, which noted that the Naval Centre at Pembroke reported that *Western Coast* was sunk, believed mined. Four of the crew were picked up but 17 were missing. The captain was among the survivors. *UB-40* claimed to have sunk her.

2/23: K.L.M. *Country:* British. *Date sunk:* 21/2/17. *Tons nett:* 28. *Tons gross:* 40. *Built:* –. *Type:* FV. *Rig:* smack. *Owners:* W. Gearing, Plymouth. *Cargo:* –. *Armed:* No. *Position:* 8 miles NW of Eddystone (50 13 00N; 04 28 00W). *Master's name:* Edwin Alfred Crocker. *Crew:* 4. *Crew nationality:* All British.

ALTHOUGH the weather was moderate it was quite a hazy day out in the fishing grounds off Eddystone. Captain Crocker was just thinking about getting his trawl down around 8am, when, about a mile and a half off the port bow, a strange shape appeared. None of the men on *K.L.M.* could make it out at first, but after the first shell whistled over the rigging it soon became obvious just what it was. The gunner on the German submarine appeared to be deliberately firing high. The message was clear to the master, abandon ship or face the consequences.

He had no choice and a few minutes later the four men rowed away from *K.L.M.* The submarine crew did not waste time in planting bombs on the trawler, but just fired a few shells into her hull. It didn't take long and the *K.L.M.* went down at 8.30am.

The weather was reasonable and the crew rowed towards the shore. About an hour later they were spotted and picked up by the patrol boat *Young Roland* and landed at Plymouth.

2/24: IDUNA. *Country:* French. *Date sunk:* 26/10/16. *Tons nett:* 129. *Tons gross:* 165. *Built:* Paimpol in 1903. *Type:* SV. *Rig:* schooner. *Owners:* Deschornips, Rennes, France. *Cargo:* 227 tons coal shipped by Charles le Borgne of Llanelly to St Servan. *Armed:* No. *Position:* 50 miles SW by S of Start Point (49 32 00N; 04 24 00W). *Master's name:* Francois Cornillot. *Crew:* 7. *Crew nationality:* French.

IT was 9.15am when the submarine appeared about a mile off the *Iduna's* port side. The master watched as the menace got closer and closer. As the submarine got to within 30yds the master saw a man appear on the conning tower. He watched the man signal for him to stop.

Ten minutes later the crew of the *Iduna* were alongside the submarine in the ship's boat. Several of them were ordered aboard whilst three German sailors got in the boat, they were all clutching bombs in their hands.

It didn't take the sailors long to plant the bombs in the most damaging spots and at 10am the bombs exploded. *Iduna* resisted the explosions for some time, but sank some while later.

Unusually, the *Iduna's* crew were not put back in their boat and set adrift as was the normal practice, but instead were taken to a passing Norwegian steamer called the *Sorley.* Why the German commander should have wanted to pass up a steamer to add to his tonnage figures is unknown. However, the crew were landed safely ashore by the *Sorley* at 6pm the same day.

2/25: SATANITA. *Country:* British. *Date sunk:* 24/3/17. *Tons nett:* 30. *Tons gross:* –. *Built:* Of wood at Rye in 1900. *Type:* FV. *Rig:* ketch. *Owners:* William Gardener West,

68 Bellevue Rd, Ramsgate. *Cargo:* 15 cwt fresh fish. *Armed:* No. *Position:* 12 miles SSW of Eddystone (50 00 00N; 04 24 00W). *Master's name:* William Gardener West. *Crew:* 3.

THE skipper of the patrol vessel who spoke to the *Satanita's* master earlier that day was right, there certainly was a submarine in the area. The master had, in fact, just witnessed it sink the fishing smack *Alice*. However, he thought perhaps his luck was in as the submarine headed off in another direction. He could see that *Alice's* crew were heading towards him and a little later he took them on board.

It was the master of the *Alice* who spotted the submarine 45 minutes later. It was about three miles astern and gaining on them rapidly. A shot rang out – a signal to the *Satanita's* master to heave to. He had no choice, he was hardly moving as there was no wind to fill the sails. The German commander shouted for a boat to be brought to him. At this stage the *Alice's* crew also decided to leave as well, they had been through it before about an hour ago.

The bombs were quickly put into position by the German sailors who then disappeared down below. They were searching for something and eventually emerged with some butter and fat. The submarine's cook had obviously given them his shortages list. Minutes later the *Satanita* had gone.

The two crews kept in company with each other for some time but became separated at about midnight. At 7.30 the next morning the oiler *Osceola* spotted the crew of the *Satanita* and landed them at Milford Haven the next day.

2/26: ALICE. *Country:* British.
Date sunk: 24/3/17. *Tons nett:* –. *Tons gross:* 61.
Built: Of wood at Porthleven 1903. *Type:* FV.
Rig: ketch. *Owners:* Mrs Hannah Cook, Ship Inn, Carlton Rd, Pakefield. *Cargo:* Fresh fish.
Armed: No. *Position:* 12 miles SSW of Eddystone (50 00 00N; 04 24 00W). *Master's name:* William H. Aldred. *Crew:* 5.

THE crew of the *Alice* had been out in the fishing grounds for three days and had amassed quite a nice catch. They should have been heading for port by this time but there was no wind. About three miles to the south-east, an enemy submarine appeared and started attacking two other fishing boats.

It was inevitable that the submarine would notice the *Alice* and also another fishing smack in company with her, the Ramsgate trawler *Satanita*. Very soon it closed on her and the gunner fired two shots as a warning for the crew to get clear. They obeyed and rowed towards the beckoning German commander. He wanted the use of their boat and taking the master aboard as surety against any foolish ideas, two German sailors went over to the *Alice* and planted bombs on her.

She sank soon after the bombs exploded and the

crew were set adrift. They immediately headed off in the general direction of shore which also happened to be towards their companion the *Satanita*, while the submarine made off in another direction towards yet another victim. They made it to the *Satanita* and hoped the wind would pick up enough to allow them to get away but it wasn't to be. An hour later they had to go through the same procedure again as she too was sent to the bottom by the same submarine.

The two boats containing the crews rowed together for the shore. The *Alice's* crew were eventually picked up by the patrol boat *Buffalo* and the *Satanita's* crew by the oiler *Osceola*.

2/27: G.L.C.. *Country:* British. *Date sunk:* 12/5/17.
Tons nett: –. *Tons gross:* 24. *Built:* Of wood at Ramsgate in 1908. *Type:* FV. *Rig:* ketch. *Owners:* George G. Caseley, 10 Wilsons Rd, Ramsgate.
Cargo: ¼ ton fish. *Armed:* No.
Position: 6 miles SW of Eddystone (50 06 00N; 04 22 00W). *Master's name:* Alfred Ogben.
Crew: 3.

THE little fishing vessel *G.L.C.* was in the fishing grounds off Eddystone with her trawl out. A German submarine surfaced almost beside them.

The master was well enough acquainted with the methods the submarine commanders used and told his men to grab what they could of their belongings quickly and get in the boat. Once alongside the enemy vessel, the master was ordered aboard whilst two German sailors rowed over to the *G.L.C.* and hung a bomb on the side of her. Returning within 2 minutes the master was allowed back in the boat with his crew and after pushing them clear the submarine dived.

The master looked at his ship which was was only a 100yds away and asked the men if they fancied a go at getting back on board her to try and cut the bomb clear before it exploded. Naturally, most of the men thought he was completely mad as the bomb could go off at any time. They were just about to row back towards her when the submarine surfaced again; perhaps it wasn't a good idea after all. A minute later the bomb did explode and within three more minutes the *G.L.C.* rolled over and sank.

The crew were picked up and taken to Plymouth.

2/28: SNOWDROP. *Country:* British.
Date sunk: 20/2/18. *Tons nett:* 39. *Tons gross:* 47.
Built: Of wood at Brixham in 1897. *Type:* SV.
Rig: Ketch. *Owners:* William John Perring, 21, Anson Place, Plymouth. *Cargo:* Fish. *Armed:* No. *Position:* 8 miles SW of Eddystone (50 04 00N; 04 22 00W). *Master's name:* William John Perring. *Crew:* 4. *Crew nationality:* All British.

FISHING boats, during the 1914-18 war, had a particularly bad time of it because they were so vulnerable to attack from enemy submarines. What better way for the enemy to undermine British confidence than by sinking their fishing fleets.

The *Snowdrop* was another of those casualties. The submarine appeared about a mile off her starboard side. The first shell fired was close, landing only yards away from her starboard side. This was too close for the master who ordered his men into the small boat. It was a wise move as the next few shells found their mark and smashed large holes in the *Snowdrop's* side, sinking her almost immediately.

Leaving the four men to find their own way back to shore the submarine headed towards a fleet of fishing vessels which were hurriedly making for the safety of Plymouth. They would probably have all been sunk had it not been for the arrival of an armed yacht which forced the U-boat to dive.

2/29: MOUCHE. *Country:* French. *Date sunk:* 26/2/18. *Tons nett:* –. *Tons gross:* 61. *Built:* –. *Type:* SV. *Rig:* –. *Owners:* Societe des Carrieris de L'Ouest, Paris. *Cargo:* In ballast from Cherbourg to Swansea. *Armed:* No. *Position:* 38 miles SE by E of Lizard (49 38 00N; 04 21 00W). *Master's name:* Albert Blandin. *Crew:* 4.

IT was 8.40am when the submarine appeared on the surface about 3000yds off the port quarter of *Mouche*.

Two shells screamed across the open water between the two vessels, both slicing into the rigging and bringing down all manner of debris onto *Mouche's* deck. There was nothing the master could do apart from turn his ship enough to let the sails go as a signal that he was surrendering. Another shell passed close by and the master rightly interpreted this as a signal to abandon ship.

Before stepping into the boat with the rest of his crew, Captain Blandin threw the weighted bag containing his confidential sailing instructions into the sea. Once the boat had cleared the *Mouche* the submarine moved in closer for the kill, sinking her with a few more well placed shells in to her hull.

The men were a long way from land but rowed as best they could with the wind and sea. They were eventually spotted and picked up by the passing Grimsby trawler No 113, *Bromelia*, and landed at Plymouth the next day.

2/30: DIRIGO. *Country:* American. *Date sunk:* 31/5/17. *Tons nett:* –. *Tons gross:* 3005. *Built:* –. *Type:* SV. *Rig:* schooner. *Owners:* Axim Transport Co, chartered by Funch Edy & Co, New York, USA. *Cargo:* From New York to Havre. *Armed:* No. *Position:* 6 miles SW of Eddystone (50 06 00N; 04 21 00W). *Master's name:* S.A. Urquhart. *Crew:* 30. *Crew nationality:* 6 American, Danes, Russians, Norwegians and 1 Japanese.

FLYING the American flag was little protection against German submarines as the crew of *Dirigo*

were to find out. They left New York on May 4, 1917, for the last voyage that the big schooner would ever make. Crossing the Atlantic was easy enough, but the tricky English Channel was another matter. The weather was quite hazy, and the sea was choppy, making visibility poor at times. It certainly gave the submarine the edge when it surfaced about two miles from the *Dirigo* and began to fire shells at her.

Even from that distance the gunner was remarkably accurate and several shells hit the *Dirigo* square on. One passed through the rigging, bringing the topsail yard crashing to the deck. The master realised that he was in trouble and ordered his men to clear away the boat. Still the shells kept coming and it was amazing that nobody was injured, but as the boat was launched the first mate, John Ray, fell out. The crew desperately tried to reach him but by the time they got themselves organised he had disappeared.

While the commander questioned the master of *Dirigo* on board the submarine, the rest of the crew were made to row several German sailors back to the steamer. Once on board the German sailors quickly planted bombs at various places around the ship. Ten minutes later she blew up and sank.

The crew were picked up by the fishing smack *Faithful*, which took them into Plymouth later the same day.

2/31: HALFDAN. *Country:* Danish. *Date sunk:* 6/12/16. *Tons nett:* –. *Tons gross:* 1305. *Built:* –. *Type:* SS. *Rig:* schooner. *Owners:* L.H. Carl. *Cargo:* 1404 tons coke, Newcastle for Leghorn. *Armed:* No. *Position:* 11 miles S by W of Eddystone (50 00 00N; 04 20 00W). *Master's name:* O. Orpech. *Crew:* 19. *Crew nationality:* 14 Danish, 1 Russian/Finn, 1 Swede, 1 Spanish.

IT was 3.10pm when the master of the *Halfdan* saw a German submarine break the surface about 300yds off his starboard beam.

He watched as his worst fears were confirmed, the signal flags running up by the periscope read, 'A.B.' the international signal to 'abandon ship'. The crew left quickly in the two boats.

After the Germans had been on board the steamer and helped themselves to the chronometer and a bag of flour, a torpedo was fired at the *Halfdan* which hit her just behind the engine room. At 4pm she went down and the submarine started to tow the *Halfdan's* boats towards the shore in the general direction of Start Point. At 5.45pm they were slipped and left to row as best they could for the land. The master said that he spotted a number on the submarine's bow – *U5*.

2/32: PERSEVERENCE. *Country:* British. *Date sunk:* 4/10/17. *Tons nett:* 30. *Tons gross:* –. *Built:* Of wood at Galmpton in 1894. *Type:* FV. *Rig:* ketch. *Owners:* Charles Spratt, 44 Addington St, Ramsgate. *Cargo:* 4 cwt fresh fish. *Armed:* No.

Position: 15 miles S by W of Eddystone
(49 56 00N; 04 20 00W). *Master's name:* Robert
Crawford Miller. *Crew:* 3.

IT was a good day for fishing in the fishing grounds
around Eddystone. The *Perseverence* was close hauled
on the port tack with single reefed sails and her
trawling gear down. It was a blustery day with
periodic showers. The master was on deck when he
saw a submarine heading towards him. He kept his
glasses on it but then a sudden rain squall obscured it
from his view.

Five minutes later the squall had passed and the
visibility cleared. He didn't need the binoculars this
time, it was there again, still off the port beam about
half a mile. He warned his men of the danger and
told them to get the boat ready. A loud bang came
from the submarine and a shell screamed past the
ship, then another, again missing, but a lot closer. It
was enough for the master who gave the order to
abandon ship.

From a few hundred yards off the crew watched as
the German gunner began to pound the *Perseverence*,
one shot took away her mizzen mast completely.
About 10 shells later the master said that his ship was
very low in the water but after half an hour he lost
sight of her, presumably she sank.

The crew rowed for several hours, but for the first
hour the submarine seemed to follow them, the crew
catching glimpses of it from time to time. Perhaps
it's commander was hoping a ship would come to
their rescue, providing him with another victim to
add to his list for the day. Help did arrive – but
fortunately the submarine had gone. The Ramsgate
trawler *Star of Hope* spotted the men, delivering them
safely ashore at Plymouth at 3.30 the same afternoon.

2/33: ELIZA ANNE. *Country:* British.
Date sunk: 17/3/18. *Tons nett:* 31. *Tons gross:* 36.
Built: Newquay, Cardigan 1877. *Type:* SV.
Rig: ketch. *Owners:* David Davies, 21, Mount St,
Stuart Square, Cardiff. *Cargo:* In ballast.
Armed: No. *Position:* 40 miles SE of the Lizard
(49 38 00N; 04 18 00W). *Master's name:* Thomas
William Taylor. *Crew:* 3.

IT was just sheer bad luck that the *Eliza Anne* had to
drop out of the convoy whilst heading across the
Channel from France. the convoy was made up of 42
small sailing vessels, accompanied by four French
patrol boats. They were making good headway and
the *Eliza Anne* was keeping up very well, when
suddenly her main gaff snapped and the master had
to stop to make repairs.

By the time the repairs were finished the convoy
was out of sight. To make matters worse the master
spotted a submarine about two miles off the port
quarter. He had hoped he might be too small for
the submarine commander to worry about, but he
was wrong. It gradually came closer and moved

around to the little sailing ship's starboard quarter
and fired three shells, all of which missed, but only
just.

It was to close for comfort and the three men got
into the boat and rowed towards the submarine. Once
alongside they were questioned. They were then towed
in their boat back to the *Eliza Anne* and the Germans
stripped her of anything they fancied, finally leaving
her with a bomb in the main hatch. A few minutes
later the bomb exploded and she sank immediately.

After several hours of rowing the three men were
picked up by the patrol boat *Warbler* and landed at
Plymouth the same evening.

2/34: ROSEHILL. *Country:* British.
Date sunk: 23/9/17. *Tons nett:* 1685. *Tons
gross:* 2788. *Built:* 1911. *Type:* SS. *Rig:* schooner.
Owners: W.J. Tillett, Cardiff. *Cargo:* 3980 tons
coal, Cardiff for Devonport. *Armed:* 1 x 12pd 12cwt
Japanese gun. *Position:* 3 miles NW by W of Rame
Head (50 20 30N; 04 18 00W). *Master's name:*
Phillip Jones. *Crew:* 24. *Crew nationality:*
14 British, 3 Spaniards, 7 Somalis (Aden).
Gunners: J.W. Burton, acting bombadier, No 7207;
W.E. Parish, gunner, No 6816.

AT 6.05pm on September 23, 1917, the master was
in the chartroom sorting out positions and courses
when he heard a shout from the mate on the bridge,
"Torpedo coming!" By the time he got to the bridge the
mate had put the helm hard over, and to assist he rang
the engine room telegraph to full astern in a desperate
bid to swing the ship. *Rosehill* started to respond but
not fast enough. The master watched as the torpedo
sped closer, he got such a good look at it that he was
able to tell later that the nose of it was painted bright
red. It smashed into the side of the steamer just behind
the engine room in number three hold.

Rosehill sank 10ft down by the stern almost
immediately and the master at first thought that she
was going to sink quickly. He ordered the crew to
take to the boats but to stay close. An hour later she
appeared to be no worse and the master asked for
volunteers to go back with him to see if she could be
saved. To their credit all the crew volunteered and it
was left to Captain Jones to choose. It was the mate,
second mate, chief engineer, four seamen and two
fireman who accompanied their captain back on board
the *Rosehill*. They quickly examined the ship and
found that the engine room, after peak and propeller
tunnel were dry and that the bulkheads looked like
they would hold.

Two privately owned tugs arrived from Fowey,
Gallant and *Countess of Jersey,* and soon had a line
aboard the stricken steamer. At first the plan was to
take her to Fowey on account of her draught but it
proved a troublesome direction.

Torpedo boat number 104 found *Rosehill* eight
miles south of Fowey and asked for more assistance
from shore, this time by Admiralty tugs. Two arrived,

the *Woonda* and the *Atalanta,* who took over and shaped up a course for Plymouth.

At 1.50am, when in Whitsand Bay, the *Rosehill* started to show signs that she would founder and no sooner had everyone got clear of her than she broke in two and disappeared in 15 fathoms of water. Her position was fixed by the patrol vessels and marked with buoys.

There was a complaint by the Admiralty, over the use of privately owned tugs and the decision to tow the *Rosehill* at first to Fowey. They felt that had she been towed straight away to Plymouth she would probably have been saved.

UB-40 claimed to have sunk the *Rosehill.*

2/35: OCEANIAN. *Country:* French.
Date sunk: 24/9/16. *Tons nett:* 46. *Tons gross:* –.
Built: Of wood 1907. *Type:* SV. *Rig:* dandy.
Owners: Charles Boterf Mousters, Ile de Groix.
Cargo: 2 tons fresh fish. *Armed:* No. *Position:* 35 miles S of Eddystone (49 36 00N; 04 16 00W).
Master's name: H Boterf. *Crew:* 6. *Crew nationality:* All French.

IT wasn't certain that *UB-29* was resposible for sinking the *Oceanian* but it seems most likely. Members of the *Oceanian's* crew reported seeing the number 29 and later the Admiralty reported that the same submarine had sunk other vessels in the area.

It was a pleasant afternoon until 5.45pm when the U-boat numbered 29 surfaced about 500yds away and started to fire shells at the *Oceanian.* Several hit her rigging, sending down debris and spars onto the deck below. The master had already ordered the crew to take to the boat. The submarine came alongside and the master ordered to climb aboard.

Whilst he was answering questions, his crew were made to row two German officers back to the *Oceanian* to plant bombs. By the time the questioning had finished the Germans were back to watch the bombs go off. The wooden decks of the *Oceanian* opened up under the blasts and holes appeared in her sides. She lurched under each explosion and within a few minutes had gone to the bottom.

The crew rowed through the night and most of the next day, steadily making headway towards land. They were eventually spotted by the passing schooner *Jeanette* who later handed them over to the patrol trawler No 2958 *Resparko.* They remained on board her until September 26, when they were landed safely at Weymouth.

2/36: REINDEER. *Country:* British.
Date sunk: 24/3/17. *Tons nett:* 28. *Tons gross:* 39.
Built: Of wood at Galmpton in 1889. *Type:* FV.
Rig: ketch. *Owners:* Richard Brenchley, Ramsgate.
Cargo: 6cwt fresh fish. *Armed:* No. *Position:* 15 miles S of Eddystone (49 55 00N; 04 16 00W).
Master's name: –. *Crew:* 4.

THE *Reindeer* had her trawl out, heading north-west, very slowly with the tide. There was little wind and the sea was calm. However, the serenity of the scene was soon to be shattered – lurking close by was an enemy submarine. Slowly the submarine edged towards the little fishing vessel and rose so that her conning tower was just clear. A hatch opened and two sailors opened fire with small arms.

The master rushed to the side of his ship to see what was afoot. One of the German sailors shouted to him to abandon ship immediately or face the consequences. There was no alternative and the boat pulled clear a few minutes later.

Whilst the master was kept on board the submarine the crew rowed a German bombing party back to the *Reindeer.* A few minutes later the little ketch sank.

The crew were set adrift and told to find their own way back to the shore. They were picked up by HMS *Spitfire* and landed at Plymouth the next day.

2/37: ENIGMA. *Country:* British.
Date sunk: 24/3/17. *Tons nett:* –. *Tons gross:* 24.
Built: Of wood at Porthleven in 1898. *Type:* FV.
Rig: ketch. *Owners:* Henry Goodbourn, The Anchorage, Grove Rd, Ramsgate. *Cargo:* 1 ton fresh fish. *Armed:* No. *Position:* 14 miles S of Eddystone (49 55 30N; 04 16 00W). *Master's name:* Albert Bourner. *Crew:* 3.

THE submarine which had sunk the *Reindeer* a little earlier headed for the *Enigma.* There was nothing the master of the little smack could do. There was no wind. Wisely, he had a boat made ready and as the submarine approached, the crew pulled clear without being asked.

A German placed a bomb up in the bows and had a quick look around the ship. He emerged a few moments later from the hatch with a smile on his face, clutching a box of fresh fish; he and his fellow submariners would eat well that night.

The three fishermen watched from a distance as the bow of their ship was blown open and she plunged by the head to the seabed. HMS *Spitfire* passed by later with other crews who had suffered the same fate. She landed them at Plymouth at 11.30 the next morning.

2/38: RIO SOROCABA. *Country:* British.
Date sunk: 21/3/17. *Tons nett:* 2735. *Tons gross:* 4307. *Built:* Howdon-on-Tyne in 1907. *Type:* SS.
Rig: schooner. *Owners:* Peterson & Co Ltd, 6 Lloyds Ave, London. *Cargo:* 6400 tons sugar from Mauritius to Havre. *Armed:* No. *Position:* 10 miles S of Eddystone (50 01 00N; 04 16 00W).
Master's name: William James Jones. *Crew:* 35.

THE crew of the *Rio Sorocaba* had good weather for some time after leaving Port Louis in Mauritius on January 18, 1917. They called in at several other ports on the way – Durban, Cape Town, St Vincent –

eventually making their way up the English Channel on March 21. At 10am the steamer was midway between Lizard and the Start, making a good eight knots. The master was in charge on the bridge when a submarine surfaced just off the port beam about 300yds away.

Captain Jones immediately ordered the helmsman to turn away and as he did so he heard the first shell whistle over his ship. This was followed by several more. He looked behind to see how he was doing but, to his dismay, found that the submarine was closer than ever. After about the eighth shell the master ordered the engines to stop and blew his whistle three times as a signal to the German commander that he had surrendered.

Two boats were launched, the master had charge of one and the mate the other. A voice from the submarine was heard in clear English ordering the master to come alongside. As the master's boat rowed closer a line was thrown to them which the crew made fast to the bows. The submarine picked up speed and towed the men in the boat back to the *Rio Sorocaba,* where the enemy commander demanded that the master go back on board and collect all his papers. While he was doing this a boarding party not only planted bombs at various locations but also helped themselves to whatever they fancied.

The noise of the exploding bombs shattered the morning. The steamer listed first one way and then the other as water poured in through the gaping holes. A few minutes later it was all over for her and she sank. The crew in the master's boat eventually caught up with the mate's boat and they set off together towards the shore. A little later they were given a tow by the fishing vessel *Integrity* of Lowestoft.

2/39: AUGUSTE CONSEIL. *Country:* French. *Date sunk:* 12/3/15. *Tons nett:* –. *Tons gross:* 2952. *Built:* –. *Type:* SS. *Rig:* schooner. *Owners:* –. *Cargo:* 4200 tons coal Cardiff for Le Havre. *Armed:* No. *Position:* 6 miles S of Eddystone (50 04 30N; 04 15 00W). *Master's name:* Valentine Muller. *Crew:* 30.

THE circumstances of this sinking are a little strange as the master of the ship said that he saw his ship sink. However, the vessel *Rowan* passing later, found it abandoned but very much afloat.

The master of the *Auguste Conseil* said that he had loaded coal at Cardiff and was bound for Havre. He passed Longships and shaped a course to pass the Lizard by three miles, and from there head towards Cap la Hague. The weather was fair and he was making good progress. When the ship was about 22 miles south of Start Point he spotted a submarine in the distance which suddenly turned and headed towards the steamer. It didn't fire any shells but came very close alongside, a German flag flew from a short pole. It was a very clean submarine, freshly painted grey and had her number clearly displayed on the side

– *UB-29*. A voice shouted across, "You have 10 minutes to abandon your ship and get clear."

The crew left in two boats and rowed across to the submarine. One German officer and three sailors joined one of the boats and demanded to be rowed to the steamer, two of the sailors clutching bombs in their hands. One bomb was placed in the engine room and two in the stokehold. After helping themselves to various pieces of equipment they were rowed back to the submarine and waited for the explosions. The explosions failed to sink the steamer so the whole process was repeated with three more bombs. At this point the master reported in his deposition that his steamer broke in half and sank.

However, the commanding officer of HMS *Bittern* reported that he took the abandoned steamer *Auguste Conseil* in tow. He added that the steamer was in a bad way due to being bombed but he thought she might float long enough to be beached, but later she turned on her side near the Eddystone and sank stern first.

The *Auguste's* crew were towed in their boats behind the submarine for about six miles when the German commander stopped the Danish steamer *Excellence Pleske* and ordered her master to take the crew on board. At this stage of the war Danish vessels were considered neutral but that situation wasn't to last very long. As a parting shot to the French captain the German commander told him, "Please convey my compliments to Mr Churchill." The crew were eventually dropped off by the Danish vessel just outside Falmouth Harbour and left to row in.

2/40: EASTERN PRINCE. *Country:* British. *Date sunk:* 30/8/17. *Tons nett:* 1789. *Tons gross:* 2879. *Built:* At Sunderland in 1910. *Type:* SS. *Rig:* schooner. *Owners:* The Prince Line Ltd, Milburn House, Newcastle. *Cargo:* 4300 tons general from Philadelphia to Furness Withy & Co, London. *Armed:* 1 x 4.7in gun. *Position:* S 8 degrees E 23 miles from Eddystone/29 miles SW of Start Point (49 41 00N; 04 12 00W). *Master's name:* William Elias. *Crew:* 41, plus 5 passengers. *Passengers:* Commander Adair Hall RN, 4 Signal Ratings RN. *Casualties:* third officer and two signal RN ratings drowned. Fourth engineer, chief steward, mess room boy, two donkeymen, killed by explosion.

LEAVING Philadelphia on August 3, 1917, *Eastern Prince* called at Hampton Roads and joined a convoy to cross the Atlantic. All went well until 1.15pm on the 30th, when the second officer spotted a white streak heading straight towards him. He immediately shouted for the helm to be put hard to starboard but it was too late and the torpedo from *U-62* struck the ship on the starboard side just behind the engine room bulkhead. The explosion destroyed the engine room, brought down the main mast and killed several of the crew.

The boats were lowered towards the water but the master ordered that they were not to touch the water

Twenty-seven men lost their lives when HM destroyer *Foyle* struck a mine.

until the way was off the ship. Panic occurred in one boat as it was allowed to touch water too soon, and the men in it were immediately thrown out as it capsized. Three men were drowned as a result of this stupidity.

One of the escorting destroyers, *P16,* then came alongside and took off about 20 men that were still on board the sinking steamer. The master was the last to leave and did so only with about 30 seconds to spare before she sank. *P16* picked up the men in the boats and they were later taken to Plymouth.

2/41: CAMELLIA. *Country:* British.
Date sunk: 2/12/16. *Tons nett:* –. *Tons gross:* 46.
Built: 1879. *Type:* SV. *Rig:* ketch. *Owners:* J.T.
Walk, The Barbican, Plymouth. *Cargo:* Fish.
Armed: No. *Position:* Between Plymouth
Breakwater and Eddystone (50 15 00N;
04 12 00W). *Master's name:* Jaspar Lawrence.
Crew: 3.

IT is by no means certain what happened to the *Camellia,* but the circumstances and thin evidence all point to the probability that she either struck a mine or was unlucky enough to pull one up in her trawl.

She left Plymouth on the afternoon of December 1, 1916, and headed out to the fishing grounds. A cold wind was blowing from the east, the sky was overcast, but the sea was quite calm and certainly not rough enough to present any major problem to *Camellia.*

All that is known is that in the early hours of the next morning, around 2am, a loud explosion was heard from somewhere in the fishing grounds area. At daylight several bits of rigging and wreckage were found which were identified as belonging to *Camellia*. However, none of the crew were found.

2/42: HMS FOYLE. *Country:* British.
Date sunk: 15/3/17. *Tons nett:* –. *Tons gross:* 550.
Built: Launched 25/2/1903. *Type:* Destroyer.
Rig: –. *Owners:* Admiralty. *Cargo:* –. *Armed:* Yes,
1 x 12pdr, 5 x 6pdr, 2 torpedo tubes. *Position:*
2 miles SE of Rame Head (50 16 40N; 04 11
00W). *Master's name:* Lieut A.H.D. Young RNR.

THE incident of the sinking of HM destroyer *Foyle* was reported by her commander, Lieutenant A.H.D. Young, RNR, who said that his ship was patrolling the area off Devon known as the eastern area. In the early hours of the morning of March 15, 1917, when *Foyle* was just over three miles to the east of Eddystone Rocks, she struck a mine. The resulting explosion was enormous and not only ripped out the bottom of the ship on the port side but also destroyed some of the mess decks, killing 27 men in their bunks instantly and leaving two others critically injured.

Immediate checks were made around the ship to assess her situation and it was found that she was taking on water rapidly in two of her boiler rooms. Various watertight doors were closed and some of the bulkheads shored up to try and prevent them from collapsing. Three men were found to be trapped by twisted metal and a party led by the first officer went to their assistance. Two of the men were released successfully, although they were found to be badly injured. The third man however, couldn't be reached, although he was still alive.

A passing steamer was signalled and at about 8.30am the collier SS *John O'Scott* came alongside to help. All the injured men and most of the crew were transferred aboard the steamer which then took the *Foyle* in tow by the stern. By towing her stern first it was hoped that the twisted plates holding the trapped man might give enough to allow his release.

By this time HMS *Boyne* and *Bittern* were alongside and sent over men and tools to help get the man clear. They succeeded in getting him out but the man had to have his right leg amputated.

The towing hawser was transferred with the arrival of the tug *Illustrious* and she began to pull the *Foyle* towards Plymouth. Eventually, at 2.10pm she began to settle by the head and sank. Her commander gave the position as Rame Head bearing north 39 degrees west, the Breakwater Light bearing north 21 degrees east and Mewstone bearing north 75 degrees east.

2/43: AUSTRALBUSH. *Country:* British. *Date sunk:* 13/11/17. *Tons nett:* 2840. *Tons gross:* 4398. *Built:* At Glasgow in 1907. *Type:* SS. *Rig:* schooner. *Owners:* The Commonwealth Government Line of Steamers, London. *Cargo:* ballast, Le Harve for Barry. *Armed:* 1 x 6pdr Australian gun. *Position:* 7 miles NE of Eddystone LH / 8 miles NNW of Rame Hd (50 12 48N; 04 04 52W). *Master's name:* James Duncan, 168 Drakefell Rd, Brockley, London. *Crew:* 41. *Crew nationality:* 40 British, 1 Brazilian. *Gunners:* A.C. Ely, LS RAN, No ON 20; F. Riley, AB RAN, No ON 46. *Casualties:* W. Ogilvey, third engineer; F. Lewis, AB, both drowned.

AUSTRALBUSH was part of a convoy that left Le Havre on November 12, 1917, bound for Barry Roads. All went well until the next day when the ship lost the convoy off St Catherines Point and had to proceed on her own.

At 1.40pm the master went to the chartroom to check the next course change and left the second mate in charge of the bridge. The second mate sighted the white streak of a torpedo's wake only 200yds away. He had no time to manoeuvre and the torpedo hit the port side of the ship in number three hold. The force of the explosion not only ripped a hole in the port side but also penetrated right through to the starboard.

She began to sink rapidly by the stern. The master rushed onto the deck and ordered the boats to be lowered immediately. Whilst this was being done he headed back to the chartroom to fetch the ships's

papers, but owing to the bows being so high in the air he couldn't make it.

As the boats got clear of the ship the third engineer and one seaman held on to a lifeline that was hanging from the davits and an upward surge from the ship wrenched them clean out of the boat. It couldn't have been worse timing for at that moment the steamer sank. By the time a lifeboat was able to get back to the spot, both men had disappeared.

The Admiralty trawler *Vale of Fruin* was close by and its commander heard the explosion. In company with another patrol vessel, *Manx Hero*, the trawler sped to the scene and picked up the survivors and one body. They were eventually landed at Plymouth.

UC-31 claimed to have sunk this ship.

2/44: CLAVERLEY. *Country:* British. *Date sunk:* 20/8/17. *Tons nett:* 2441. *Tons gross:* 3829. *Built:* Sunderland in 1907. *Type:* SS. *Rig:* schooner. *Owners:* Sunderland SS Co Ltd, 38, Sandhill, Newcastle. *Cargo:* 5700 tons coal, from HA Brideman & Co, N.Shields to Cie L'Union des Gaz of Genoa, Italy. *Armed:* 1 x 4.7 inch gun. *Position:* 5 miles SE from Eddystone (50 06 30N; 04 04 10W). *Master's name:* Hugh Jones. *Crew:* 58. *Crew nationality:* 51 British (40 Lascars), 7 Portuguese. *Gunners:* Alexander Jack, Prov LS RNR No A5253; John Beer, AB RFR No 63296. *Casualties:* Three engineers, one apprentice and three lascars.

AT 2am on August 20, 1917, *Claverly* was steaming at her maximum speed of eight knots down the Channel. The night was clear and the wind a light south westerly. When off the Eddystone the mate took a four point bearing which gave him a position of four miles south-east of the Eddystone. On the bridge were the mate, accompanied by an apprentice, and the quartermaster.

The master had retired to his bunk earlier and left instructions to be woken when the ship was off the Eddystone. The mate had sent someone to do just that when the ship was shaken by a violent explosion which threw the master from his bunk.

On making the deck the master found the ship to be on her beam ends with a heavy list to port. The mate had already got the after starboard lifeboat away with some of the crew, so the master set about getting the forward starboard lifeboat ready. The rest of the crew assisted him, but had great difficulty in freeing the davits which had been twisted by the explosion. The first gunner had been sent to try to launch one of the port boats but returned to say that they were completely smashed. Finding the situation hopeless the master hailed the mate's boat to come closer and they all crammed carefully into it. It was just in time as the *Claverly* began to turn turtle. At that moment the second engineer appeared on deck with some of the lascars and the master shouted for them to jump clear, which they did.

At that moment two German submarines appeared close by and ordered the boat to stop, leaving the second engineer and the lascars floundering in the water. The smaller of the two submarines came alongside the boat and an officer asked for the master. The master misled the German and told him that he would be along in the next boat. The German then asked for details such as the name, cargo, destination and whether the *Claverly* was a "Clan boat or an Alfred Holt". Why he wanted the last information is unclear.

As the submarine pulled away the master noticed that another submarine had appeared making three in total around the victim. They stayed on the surface for 10 minutes and then dived. *UB-38* was later to claim to have fired the torpedo.

At 9.45am the steamer *Stream Fisher* came in sight and spotted the plight of the master and his crew. They went towards the *Claverly* which was still floating, but upside down, and found the second engineer and three lascars still alive.

Overhead, an airship had spotted the wreck of the *Claverly* and reported her position. Soon after HMT 125 *Agnes Wickfield* came on the scene and took all the surviving crew on board. Two engineers and seven lascars were taken to hospital.

The *Claverly* remained afloat and was judged to be a hazard to shipping. *Agnes Wickfield* fired eight shells into the hull and reported that the vessel sank in 36 fathoms of water.

2/45: LOCHWOOD. *Country:* British. *Date sunk:* 2/4/15. *Tons nett:* 1310. *Tons gross:* 2042. *Built:* Thornaby in 1900. *Type:* SS. *Rig:* schooner. *Owners:* The Constantine & Pickering SS Co, Middlesborough. *Cargo:* 3200 tons coal from Barry Docks to Rouen. *Armed:* No. *Position:* 25 miles SW from Start Point (49 52 00N; 04 02 00W). *Master's name:* Thomas Howard Scott, 10, Whitburn Terrace, Boldon, Newcastle. *Crew:* 21.

THE *Lochwood* was in the Admiralty employ and the master had been given sealed orders only to be opened at sea. He opened them when his ship was off Trevose Head and read that he was to proceed to Rouen. He set off around Land's End, hugged the coast up to the Lizard and was signalled from the station there at noon. The steady rain turned the visibility very murky and Captain Scott was glad to set a course east-south-east to take him away from the shore.

At 5pm the master was in his cabin getting ready to go to the mess for a meal when a steward brought a message from the mate saying that he had sighted a submarine. From the bridge the U-boat could be seen about a mile off. Orders were given to hoist the Norwegian flag and turn the ship keeping the submarine astern to present the least target possible.

The submarine commander, Oberleutnant Rudolf Schneider in *U-24*, obviously not fooled by the Norwegian flag, got into *Lochwood's* wake and rapidly caught up with her. At 5.45pm he released a torpedo which went zipping by the port side of the steamer. Ten minutes later he released another which sped harmlessly by the starboard side. Soon the submarine was broadside to the *Lochwood* and signalled her to stop. Weighing up the situation the master felt he had little choice, the submarine was much faster and more manoeuvreable. He stopped his ship and heard a voice from the enemy vessel telling him that he had ten minutes to clear the ship.

The port lifeboat was lowered with half the crew and they began to row away. As they did so the submarine released yet another torpedo which flashed straight past the boat and slammed into the port side of the *Lochwood*, just behind the engine room. An enormous explosion followed which hurled coal 150ft into the air and nearly swamped the port lifeboat in the process.

The master and the rest of the crew left in the starboard boat and after joining up with the port boat rowed towards a sailing trawler in the distance. She turned out to be the *Onward*. At 7.30pm *Onward* headed towards the shore and passed the swamped steamer just in time to see her disappear by the stern.

2/46: EAST POINT. *Country:* British. *Date sunk:* 9/3/17. *Tons nett:* 3305. *Tons gross:* 5234. *Built:* Sunderland in 1901. *Type:* SS. *Rig:* schooner. *Owners:* Furness Withy & Co, Billiter St, London. *Cargo:* 1350 tons general goods from London to Philadelphia. *Armed:* Yes. *Position:* 10 miles E of Eddystone Light House (50 11 00N; 04 01 00W). *Master's name:* Harold James Young. *Crew:* 42.

LIEUTENANT F.C. Baker, commanding officer of HMS *Tigress* was instructed to meet *East Point* and escort her out of the Channel into the Atlantic. He tried to contact her from 1pm onwards on the wireless but failed to get any response. At 5.20pm he spotted a steamer which turned out to be the *East Point*. When asked, the master said that the reason he didn't hear any wireless calls was because his wireless operator was totally incapable.

At the time the *East Point* was torpedoed the master was below having his tea, leaving the third mate on the bridge in charge of the watch. He said that he heard a loud bang and felt the ship shudder as though she had struck something. He immediately raced on deck to see what was going on and found that the hatch covers had been completely blown off number two and three holds and that the stokehold and engine room were filling rapidly. Within a few minutes the ship was heavily down by the head and the master decided to abandon ship.

Three boats were manned and lowered very rapidly. The master reported later that as he was getting into one of the boats he spotted the submarine about 100 feet off the port bow. It stayed in position for a while but disappeared as soon as one of the escorting drifters, 1899 *Expectant*, appeared on the scene. The commanding officer of *Expectant*, William Forder, reported that he searched around for the submarine but had to call the immediate search off because one of the *East Point's* boats was waterlogged and in danger of sinking.

The steamer sank approximately 15 minutes after being struck. All the crew survived and were soon picked up by several patrol vessels and landed later at Plymouth.

U-48 claimed the sinking.

2/47: ENERGY. *Country:* British. *Date sunk:* 21/2/17. *Tons nett:* 25. *Tons gross:* 38. *Built:* –. *Type:* FV. *Rig:* smack. *Owners:* Stephen Walter. *Cargo:* –. *Armed:* No. *Position:* Eddystone bearing NNW ¹/₂ N 10-12 miles (49 57 00N; 04 04 00W). *Master's name:* Stephen Walter. *Crew:* 4. *Crew nationality:* All British.

THE master of the *Energy* saw a German submarine start to attack another sailing vessel, the *Monarch*, and realised that, if he didn't run for it, he was going to be next.

Although all sail was put up it just wasn't enough and very soon the submarine moved towards the *Energy* firing several shells as she approached. The master could do nothing but stop.

Bombs were placed on board which, although they exploded with a loud noise, didn't sink the *Energy* and the Germans were forced to fire several shells to finish her off.

The crew were picked up four hours later by a patrol boat and taken into Plymouth.

WORLD WAR ONE
CHANNEL WRECKS

◆

AREA THREE

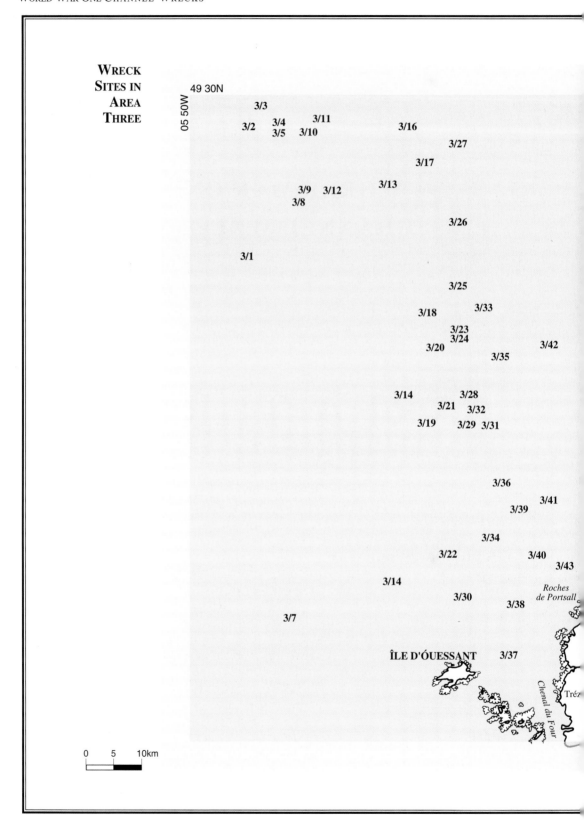

WRECK
SITES IN
AREA
THREE

49 30N
05 50W

3/3
3/2   3/4   3/11
       3/5   3/10   3/16
                                  3/27
                           3/17
        3/9   3/12   3/13
        3/8
                           3/26
3/1
                           3/25
                    3/18   3/33
                           3/23
                           3/24
                    3/20   3/42
                           3/35
        3/14   3/28
                3/21   3/32
        3/19   3/29 3/31

                           3/36
                           3/39 3/41
                           3/34
                    3/22   3/40
                           3/43
    3/14
        3/30   Roches
                           3/38   de Portsall
3/7

ÎLE D'ÓUESSANT   3/37

Chenal du Four   Tré

0   5   10km

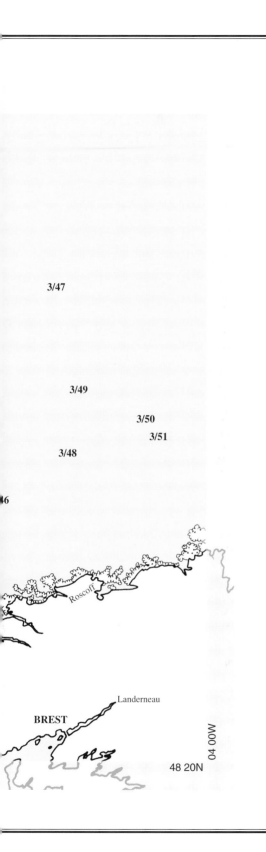

3/47

3/49

3/50

3/51

3/48

46

Roscoff

Landerneau

BREST

04 00W

48 20N

3/1: BEGONIA. *Country:* British.
Date sunk: 21/3/18. *Tons nett:* 1752. *Tons gross:* 2928. *Built:* 1918. *Type:* SS. *Rig:* schooner.
Owners: Stag Line Ltd, North Shields.
Cargo: Admiralty cargo from Tyne and Plymouth for Salonica. *Armed:* Yes. *Position:* 48 miles SSW of Lizard (49 13 00N; 05 40 00W). *Master's name:* C. Hunter. *Crew:* 38.

BEGONIA was in convoy and was hit by a torpedo from *UB-55* at 2.15am. The weather was listed as hazy with a light south-westerly wind and a heavy sea swell. She sank fairly quickly after the explosion but all the men managed to get clear in the ship's boats. Thirty of the crew were picked up by the French vessel *Vigilanti* and taken to Plymouth.

3/2: THEODOROS PANGALOS.
Country: Greek. *Date sunk:* 3/3/17. *Tons nett:* –.
Tons gross: 2838. *Built:* –. *Type:* SS. *Rig:* –.
Owners: Theodoros Pangalos. *Cargo:* Not stated, from Cardiff to Port Said. *Armed:* No. *Position:* 35 miles S of Land's End (49 27 00N; 05 40 00W).
Master's name: John Galakis. *Crew:* 22. *Crew nationality:* All Greek.

THE *Theodoros Pangalos* lies at the very western edge of the English Channel as defined by this book and virtually in the middle.
   The route instructions to the master ordered him to cross the mouth of the Channel by night but Captain Galakis had a problem. Having arrived off Land's End he calculated the distance ahead of him and realised that because of the slow speed of his ship he was never going to make the crossing in one go. Deciding that there was probably more danger on the French side he elected to leave the English side in daylight and make the French side by night. It was logical thinking in the circumstances but made no difference to the final outcome.
   The weather was not good, the wind was southerly force six, a dull overcast sky and a heavy sea. It was 11.40am when the master was informed by the officer of the watch that a submarine had been spotted about a mile off. As the master arrived on the bridge a shell came whistling over the ship. Captain Galakis ordered the helmsman to steer away from his assailant but the shells kept coming with more and more accuracy.
   Realising that he was in a hopeless position his immediate thought was for the welfare of his crew and he ordered them to get to their boat stations and stand by. He ran to his cabin, gathered his papers and stuffed them in a weighted bag. Making for the boats he tossed the bag over the side and jumped aboard with the rest of his crew.
   It was hard work in the boats, being tossed about by the rough sea. The crew watched as the submarine moved to within a cable of their abandoned steamer and fired a torpedo into her. A large explosion tore a

gaping hole in her port side, sending her to the bottom in a few minutes. The crew were later spotted by a keen-eyed lookout on the SS *Goshawk*, which picked them up.

3/3: IRMA. *Country:* French. *Date sunk:* 13/9/16. *Tons nett:* 462. *Tons gross:* 844. *Built:* 1911. *Type:* SS. *Rig:* schooner. *Owners:* Marcesche & Co, L'Orient. *Cargo:* 1050 tons coal from Newport to Montagne sur Garonne. *Armed:* No. *Position:* 28 miles S by E of Wolf Rock (49 29 00N; 05 39 00W). *Master's name:* Prosper Rio. *Crew:* 15. *Crew nationality:* All French.

THERE were two other steamers in the general area where the *Irma* was attacked. It was 7pm and the submarine made it very plain to the crew of the *Irma* that they must abandon their ship immediately. Shells were passing over her every 30 seconds, each one getting a little closer than the last.

The men pulled clear in their lifeboat and watched to see what would happen next. The submarine moved to within about 150yds and started to pound the ship with her deck gun. A Norwegian steamer about two miles behind had turned around and was now at full speed heading completely the other way. The same happened with the French ship SS *Molliere* about four miles ahead, she stopped on hearing the gunfire but when her master realised what was going on he headed off at full speed.

The *Irma* started to settle slowly, considering the amount of holes in her. At 7.30pm she filled and sank.

At midnight the patrol trawler No 955, *Star of Freedom*, spotted the crew and landed them at Penzance in the early hours of the following day.

3/4: AFRIQUE. *Country:* French. *Date sunk:* 25/9/16. *Tons nett:* 1120. *Tons gross:* 1730. *Built:* 1887. *Type:* SS. *Rig:* schooner. *Owners:* M. Hyaffil, 3 Rue Faitbout, Paris. *Cargo:* 1600 tons of pit props. *Armed:* No. *Position:* 38 miles S by E of Longships (49 27 00N; 05 35 00W). *Master's name:* Antoine Jacone. *Crew:* 26. *Crew nationality:* 23 French, 3 Spanish.

BY 10.30am a German submarine had fired several shells at the *Afrique*. None of them hit her but it served as a warning to the master that the submarine commander meant business. Captain Jacone had no choice but to abandon ship and, after ordering his crew to make the boat ready, went to his cabin to prepare himself. He grabbed his confidential papers and set fire to them in a metal container kept ready for just such an emergency. He then set about gathering up his personal items, money, sextant, coats, and dashed back on deck to join the others. He wasn't looking forward to taking to the boat, the wind was strong from the east, bitterly cold with a big swell running. Another shell whimpering overhead

reminded him he had no choice and he gave the order to get clear.

As they got further away from their steamer and closer to the submarine a voice in clear French ordered them to come alongside. The master was told to get aboard for questioning whilst his crew were made to ferry two German sailors back to the *Afrique* to plant bombs. It was soon done and they returned to the submarine 20 minutes later. The master was about to get back in the boat when he noticed that all the personal items he had left in the boat were gone. He turned to remonstrate with the commander but was just waved aside and told to leave.

A bitter Captain Jacone joined his men and rowed clear of the enemy vessel, out into the hostile weather and heavy seas. They rowed and sailed for most of the day and were beginning to resign themselves to a night adrift when the Lowestoft trawler *Splendour* picked them up at 5pm and landed them safely at Newlyn.

3/5: INKUM. *Country:* British. *Date sunk:* 4/6/15. *Tons nett:* 3074. *Tons gross:* 4747. *Built:* Limehouse in 1901. *Type:* SS. *Rig:* schooner. *Owners:* The Gulf Transport Co, Liverpool Ltd, 17 Water St, Liverpool. *Cargo:* 6000 tons general, shipped at New York and consigned to London. *Armed:* No. *Position:* 40 miles SW of Lizard (49 26 00N; 05 35 00W). *Master's name:* James Milligan. *Crew:* 41.

AT 4.35am on June 4, 1915, the *Inkum* was making a steady 11 knots. Weather conditions were particularly good – fine and clear with a long swell. The master had just left the bridge and handed over control to the chief officer. Almost as soon as the mate reached the front of the bridge he gasped as he spotted the white track of a torpedo heading directly for the ship on the port bow. He shouted to the helmsman to turn but it was far too late and the torpedo smashed into the side of the steamer under the bridge.

The master appeared again almost instantly and looked over the side of his ship. There was a huge hole in her and already she was beginning to settle down. He shouted to his crew to take to the boats, which was quickly done, and they pulled clear to see what would happen. Slowly the *Inkum* got lower in the water but then she appeared to stabilise. The master asked his officers for their views and between them they decided there might be a small chance of beaching her if they were left alone. On looking around there was nothing in sight so one boat started to row back towards the steamer. Just then the periscope of the submarine popped up in the water between the boat and the *Inkum* and a few minutes later a loud explosion occurred as another torpedo finished the job off.

At 6.05am the steamer sank, leaving the crew in their boats to row as best they could for the shore. They pulled for several hours but were eventually picked up by the Norwegian steamer *Wenale* which took them into Falmouth.

U-34 later claimed to have sunk her.

3/6: *(POSITION AMENDED)*

3/7: INDEPENDENT. *Country:* French. *Date sunk:* 15/1/17. *Tons nett:* –. *Tons gross:* 154. *Built:* –. *Type:* SV. *Rig:* Schooner. *Owners:* Edouard Levasseur, Fecamp. *Cargo:* –. *Armed:* No. *Position:* 18 miles WNW of Ushant (48 36 00N; 05 35 00W). *Master's name:* Julu Grieu. *Crew:* 6. *Crew nationality:* All French.

THE French schooner *Independent* stood no chance as the German submarine rapidly bore down on her. Although the enemy was flying a French ensign it hadn't fooled the master who indentified the "ship" almost at once as a U-boat.

A gun boomed out from the approaching enemy vessel, followed by a whimper as the shell passed over the schooner's rigging. The meaning was clear enough. The crew climbed into their boat and pulled clear.

As the submarine moved closer to the boat a man waved from the conning tower for them to come alongside. It was the usual tactic – three men were ordered to board the submarine while three German sailors took their place and were rowed back to the *Independent*. Several bombs were placed into position, fuses lit and left to do their destructive work. Within a few minutes the schooner had gone to the bottom.

However, instead of casting off the crew to fend for themselves, the German commander ordered them to be towed behind the submarine. In the distance the master had made out what he thought to be a Danish schooner. Whether the enemy commander intended to put them on board the Danish vessel or whether he intended to sink her as well, was not known. But either way it didn't matter, for on the horizon, close to the Danish ship was another vessel, a British patrol ship. The German commander obviously didn't fancy his chances with the armed patrol ship and quickly slipped the *Independent*'s boat. Within a few minutes the U-boat had submerged, leaving the men to be picked up by the patrol vessel TBD *69*.

3/8: TULLOCHMOOR. *Country:* British. *Date sunk:* 28/5/15. *Tons nett:* 2251. *Tons gross:* 3520. *Built:* Sunderland in 1899. *Type:* SS. *Rig:* schooner. *Owners:* Moor Line Ltd, Pilgrim St, Newcastle. *Cargo:* Ballast, Genoa for Tyne. *Armed:* No. *Position:* 52 miles N of Ushant (49 19 00N; 05 31 00W). *Master's name:* John Henry Koefod. *Crew:* 26.

THE crew of the *Tullochmoor* would probably have wished to stay in Genoa had they known what lay in store for them in the mouth of the English Channel. It was 7pm, the master was in the chart room, the second mate was on the bridge and an able seaman at the wheel. The steamer was making a steady nine knots on her way to the Tyne. The master had just finished laying in some course corrections on the chart when he heard a bang and dashed on deck. What greeted him was the sight of a column of water thrown up by a shell to the stern of his ship. A second bang followed, then a thud and a shuddering within the ship as a shell struck home somewhere along the port side.

As the third shell passed over the bridge the master ordered the engines to be stopped and told his crew to take to the boats. A large submarine was soon within a hundred yards of the steamer and sailors could be seen waving to the steamer's crew to get clear quickly. Once the *Tullochmoor*'s two boats were far enough away, the German gunner began to fire at the stationary ship. Soon her sides were riddled with holes, the master reckoned some 35 shells were fired at her. At 9pm the *Tullochmoor* could stand it no further and as her head dipped down she rose up from amidships, standing completely vertical before plunging downwards.

Immediately after she sank, the submarine, *U-41*, disappeared, her commander making no attempt to speak with the master or crew. They *Tullochmoor*'s crew rowed for the shore and later attracted the attention of the passing Spanish steamer *Olazarra* which dropped them at Barry Roads the next day.

3/9: HEATHDENE. *Country:* British. *Date sunk:* 7/9/16. *Tons nett:* 2277. *Tons gross:* 2541. *Built:* Sunderland in 1901. *Type:* SS. *Rig:* schooner. *Owners:* Dene SS Co Ltd, Guildhall Chambers, Newcastle. *Cargo:* 5600 tons iron ore from Mokta el Hadido, Benisaf, Algeria to South Shields. *Armed:* No. *Position:* 40 miles S by W of Lizard (49 20 00N; 05 30 00W). *Master's name:* John William Rigby. *Crew:* 28. *Crew nationality:* 22 British, 1 Russian, 2 Swedes, 2 Greek, 1 American.

THE master couldn't believe his bad luck when he saw the little speck on the horizon open fire on him. It looked a good four or five miles off but still the shells were landing fairly close to his ship.

It wasn't until the lifeboat pulled clear that the shelling stopped. At 2.30pm the submarine was only a few yards away from the boat. A man appeared at the top of the conning tower and climbed down to meet the men. The master was told to come aboard to be questioned about the *Heathdene*, her cargo, where from and to, her tonnage and all the relevant details the German commander needed for his log. Having finished he told the master to get back in the boat and pointed in the direction he wanted him to go, towards the French coast.

They crew never did see what happened to their ship but by the size of the explosion they heard sometime later it was pretty obvious that she had been sunk by bombs. They were found by the cruiser *Tamarisk* and landed at Falmouth the following morning.

UB-39 scored *Heathdene* as one of her kills.

3/10: COPSEWOOD. *Country:* British. *Date sunk:* 27/12/16. *Tons nett:* 352. *Tons gross:* 599. *Built:* Sunderland in 1908. *Type:* SS. *Rig:* schooner. *Owners:* The Meteor SS Co Ltd, Maritime Buildings, Middlesborough. *Cargo:* 668 tons pitwood from Bordeaux to Middlesbrough. *Armed:* No. *Position:* 34 miles SSW of Lizard (49 26 00N; 05 30 00W). *Master's name:* Albert Hawkins Perrin, 26, Kingsland Crescent, Barry. *Crew:* 14. *Crew nationality:* 9 British (including 1 stowaway), 3 Japanese, 1 Russian, 1 Swede.

IT was Christmas day when *Copsewood* left Pauilliac near Bordeaux to start her journey to Middlesbrough. It was uneventful until 7.45am, two days later, when the mate went to see the master to tell him the news that a lookout had just spotted a German submarine off the starboard beam. As he arrived on the bridge the first shell fired by the submarine went whistling past. The master immediately ordered the helmsman to bring the stern around to the enemy vessel and keep at full speed. Two more shells were fired with remarkable accuracy, making the master decide that he didn't have much chance of getting away.

Even after the ship had stopped and the crew were launching the lifeboats, the submarine's gunner continued his bombardment. One shell hit the starboard side in the fore part of the engine room, opening up a large hole as it crashed home. With all the noise the master suddenly spotted a new face appear on deck, that of a stowaway, who decided that now might be a good time to let someone know he was on board.

The two boats were rowed rapidly astern of the *Copsewood* to get out of the way of the shellfire. At least 12 or more were counted by the master, all hitting the ship. Eventually the submarine circled the vessel and fired a torpedo at her port side, causing a huge explosion, sending her to the bottom instantly.

The crew in the boats rowed through the night towards the Lizard and were picked up at daylight the next morning by a passing patrol vessel.

U-79 was the U-boat involved.

3/11: DUVA (renamed MADAME MIDAS). *Country:* British. *Date sunk:* 23/3/18. *Tons nett:* 715. *Tons gross:* 1203. *Built:* 1909. *Type:* SS. *Rig:* As schooner. *Owners:* T.G. Beatley & Son, 57/58, Leadenhall St, London. *Cargo:* 1800 tons coal from Cardiff to La Rochelle. *Armed:* 1 x 90mm gun. *Position:* 40 miles S of Penzance (49 27 00N; 05 28 00W). *Master's name:* John Nelson. *Crew:* 20. *Crew nationality:* 13 British, 2 Japanese,

2 Russians, 1 Italian, 2 Arabs. *Gunners:* William Pearce Collings, gunlayer, No B 2686; Henry B. Hatherley, second gunner, No C 2951.

TO make the Channel crossing, *Duva,* under her new name of *Madame Midas,* joined a convoy leaving Mounts Bay, Penzance.

At about half past midnight she ran into trouble when *UB-55,* lurking in the fog, fired a torpedo at her. It hit her on the port side in number three hold and blew a huge hole in her. The engine room was left completely exposed to the sea and several steam pipes had been shattered.

However, the engineers managed to stop the engines and the master sent up rockets. The steamer started to settle rapidly and took on a list to port then slowly rolled the other way to starboard – all signs that she was not going to stay afloat for long. The master wasted no time in ordering the boats away. By 1.15am all the crew had got clear of the stricken ship and just at that moment the dark shape of *UB-55* appeared out of the mist. Three shells were fired by the enemy's gunner into the hull and ten minutes later she rolled completely over and disappeared.

A voice from the conning tower demanded that the master come forward and climb on deck. Captain Nelson had little choice with about a dozen German sailors pointing rifles at him. The enemy commander wanted to know all the details of the ship he had just sank and once satisfied he waved the master away.

The boats were separated during the night but all made it to shore.

There is some confusion as to the position of the *Madame Midas/Duva* when she was hit. The position given in the general data is the one that was officially noted on the submarine attack form. However, Richard Headon, the Bosun, said that he had not long been off watch when the ship was struck and when he left the bridge the steamer's position was 49 20 00N; 05 15 00W.

The same German submarine commander sank three other vessels in the convoy. The Norwegian ship *Venborg,* the Spanish SS *Mar Baltico* and the American *Chattahoochee* were all also sunk by *UB-55,* commanded by Oberleutnant Otto Wenninger.

3/12: BASUTA. *Country:* British. *Date sunk:* 8/2/18. *Tons nett:* 1839. *Tons gross:* 2876. *Built:* 1897. *Type:* SS. *Rig:* schooner. *Owners:* The Italian Export Shipping Co Ltd, Cardiff. *Cargo:* 4200 tons coal from Newport to Blaye. *Armed:* 1 x 12pdr Japanese gun. *Position:* 47 miles S by W of Penzance/45 miles SSW from Lizard (49 20 00N; 05 27 00W). *Master's name:* John Luke Norwell. *Crew:* 31. *Crew nationality:* 28 British, 1 Norwegian, 1 Greek, 1 Italian. *Gunners:* William Armstrong Smith, Prov LS RNVR, No 6/217; Duncan McLean, AB RNR, No 2631B.

THERE is some confusion about where the *Basuta* sank and there are two references given. However, the latitude and longitude given is not accurate to either but rather a midway point between the two for expediency. A position was given in the records as 49 21 00N; 05 17 00W, but this was the position at which an escort trawler commander reported hearing an explosion.

Basuta was number four in a convoy of seven steamers bound to Brest, escorted by lead trawler 1277 *Yokohama*, HMT 1863 *Sanson* and HMT *Thomas Blackhorn*.

It was half an hour after midnight when the torpedo from *U-53* smashed into the port side of the steamer just under her bridge. The resulting explosion was so violent that it destroyed the port side of the bridge, killing one of the seaman on watch. The master immediately ordered the crew to assemble at their respective boat stations and to stand by for his instructions. Unfortunately, some of the crew started to panic and made a rush for the port boat. Finding that one of the falls had been damaged by the explosion they then made a rush to the starboard boat. By this time the steamer was settling down by the head and the master tried to calm the fears of the crew in the starboard boat by allowing them to lower away, but ordered them to stay close to the steamer.

Having examined the damage to his ship and finding that fire had also broken out, the master decided that he had no alternative but to abandon ship.

The rest of the crew set about sorting out the port lifeboat and once ready, the master and 18 men left *Basuta*. They stayed close to her for some time and at first light, around 5.30am, found that she was still afloat although well down by the head. The master could see no sign of the starboard boat but it was found some time later by HMTBD *Onslow* and the men in it taken to Plymouth. As for the master and his men, they were adrift in the wind and weather for 17 hours before they were finally rescued by HMS *Defender* and also landed at Plymouth.

3/13: AXPE MENDI. *Country:* Spanish. *Date sunk:* 7/6/18. *Tons nett:* –. *Tons gross:* 2873. *Built:* –. *Type:* SS. *Rig:* –. *Owners:* –. *Cargo:* Ballast, Middlesbrough for Bilbao. *Armed:* –. *Position:* 37 miles S by W of Lizard (49 21 00N; 05 17 00W). *Master's name:* –. *Crew:* 24.

THE only reference in the contemporary records to this sinking is on a convoy attack form which dealt only with facts that were relevant to convoy procedures. This provided very little information on the vessel itself but did explain to some degree what happened.

Axpe Mendi was part of a south bound French Coal Trade convoy and was the ninth vessel in position four, in the second column, line abreast. The weather was thick with hazy patches and the night was very dark. The convoy was protected by the escorting trawlers 3606 *Blackhorn*, 1863 *Sanson* and 3351 *Jane Ross*. The nearest trawler to *Axpe Mendi* at the time was *Sanson* and it was her commander who submitted the convoy attack form to his senior officer. He reported that at 3.40am on June 7, 1918, his watchmen reported hearing an explosion off the starboard beam and they immediately altered course to investigate. They approached the *Axpe Mendi* and could see that she had been badly holed by a torpedo and all her crew were in the process of taking to the boats. *Sanson* managed to rescue 22 men and the French trawler *Gaidon*, which arrived to assist, found one more man in a small, waterlogged skiff. Apparently one of the crew was missing, presumed killed by the explosion.

Gaidon stayed by the sinking steamer whilst *Sanson* continued with the convoy and the survivors to Brest. The *Axpe Mendi* didn't sink immediately but stayed afloat with her decks awash. To prevent her becoming a shipping hazard the *Gaidon's* gunners put a few shells into her hull to finish her off.

3/14: MARTIN. *Country:* British. *Date sunk:* 14/1/17. *Tons nett:* 1207. *Tons gross:* 1904. *Built:* 1897. *Type:* SS. *Rig:* schooner. *Owners:* Sir R. Ropner, West Hartlepool. *Cargo:* 1900 tons pit props from Bayonne to Barry Roads. *Armed:* No. *Position:* 8 miles N of Ushant (48 36 00N; 05 16 00W). *Master's name:* John White. *Crew:* 20. *Crew nationality:* 18 British, 2 Danes.

THE mate called to the master to see what he made of the mass of bubbles and white water on the port quarter. However, before the master could look, it became all too obvious that it was a submarine, and a big one at that. A seaman, Harry Thompson, said later that he had a good look at the submarine during the time it was close to the *Martin* and said he saw the number *U-14*.

The master looked through his binoculars and read the signal flags being run up the small pole behind the conning tower, 'AB', abandon your ship. He turned and looked astern to see another Danish steamer still heading up behind the *Martin* and hoped that if the German commander spotted it, maybe he would leave him alone. However, a warning shell was soon screaming over the masts. There was nothing for it but to shut the engines down and take to the boats, the master with nine men in one boat and the mate with the same in the other.

As the boats pulled clear the submarine manoeuvred into position and began to pound the *Martin* with shells. For 15 minutes the bombardment continued only breaking off once when the Danish steamer came within range and a couple of rounds fired at her. Eventually the *Martin* was so full of holes she settled low in the water and sank at 10am.

The chief officer later stated that his boat was picked up by a patrol vessel and taken to Brest but he didn't know what had happened to the master's boat as they had become separated. The master's boat had in fact been found by the Danish steamer *Aurora* and he and his men were perfectly safe.

3/15: PRESIDENT LEROY LALLIER.
Country: French. *Date sunk:* 9/4/18. *Tons nett:* 1320. *Tons gross:* 1800. *Built:* –. *Type:* SS. *Rig:* schooner. *Owners:* Compangnie du Vapeur du Norde, Dunkirk. *Cargo:* 400 tons pitwood from Brest to Mounts Bay. *Armed:* 2 x 90mm guns fore and aft. *Position:* 30 miles N by W of Ushant (48 58 00N; 05 13 00W). *Master's name:* Ollivier Lucien Gerou. *Crew:* 32. *Crew nationality:* All French

THE majority of the crew and the master perished when the *President Leroy Lallier* sank.

She was part of a convoy which left Brest on April 9, 1918. The weather wasn't good with a strong easterly wind, frequent rain squalls and a rough sea. The convoy consisiting of 11 steamers was formed up into two columns and the *President's* position was number four in the port column. The master was on the bridge at about 11pm the same evening when the ship was struck by a torpedo on the port side in the engine room. She took on water so fast that she sank within two minutes, leaving no time for the boats to be manned.

Nine men were picked out of the water by the escorting trawler 382 *Pintail* but, unfortunately, two of them, the chief engineer and the third officer, died before reaching Penzance.

3/16: ANNA MARIA. *Country:* French.
Date sunk: 2/2/17. *Tons nett:* 104. *Tons gross:* 140. *Built:* 1897. *Type:* SV. *Rig:* brigantine. *Owners:* J. Legasse, Bayonne, France. *Cargo:* 144 tons salt, 47 casks wine, 8 casks oil for St Servan, France. *Armed:* No. *Position:* 30 miles S of Lizard (49 27 00N; 05 13 00W). *Master's name:* M. Libreuse. *Crew:* 6. *Crew nationality:* All French.

HAVING been stopped once already that day by a German submarine it was something of a nuisance when the *Anna Maria* was set upon yet again by another. She had come all the way from Bonanza, Nicaragua, leaving there on January 19, 1917, travelled all those miles unhindered only to be molested twice in one day. During the first incident the German commander took one look at the state of her lifeboat and let the ship go unharmed. However, she was not so lucky the second time.

When about 30 miles south of the Lizard she was shelled by the second submarine, boarded and then sunk by bombs placed in the forward and after cabins. The crew took to the boat and were eventually picked up by the passing steam drifter *Adventure* when about 10 miles south of the Lizard and landed at Newlyn, having spent 12 hours adrift .

The master of the *Anna Maria* said that when he was on board the submarine he pointed out to the second officer the terrible condition of his boat, hoping to get away with it once more, but the officer was having none of it and said that was his fault for not looking after it. When asked the number of the submarine the officer told him that she was *U-39*.

3/17: EUGENIE. *Country:* French.
Date sunk: 16/11/16. *Tons nett:* 52. *Tons gross:* –. *Built:* –. *Type:* SV. *Rig:* –. *Owners:* –. *Cargo:* Coal from Cardiff. *Armed:* No. *Position:* 35 miles S of The Lizard (49 23 00N; 05 11 00W). *Master's name:* Pierre Lageat, Treburden, Cotes du Nord, France. *Crew:* 4.

ABOUT one mile off the *Eugenie's* port side was a strange looking sailing vessel heading directly towards it. The master looked at it through his binoculars and although it seemed like a small sailing boat he felt very uneasy about it. He kept his glasses fixed firmly on it when suddenly he realised precisely what it was, a submarine and German at that.

It wasn't long before the submarine was within hailing distance and the master went to the ship's rail to listen to what the man had to say from the conning tower. Because of the wind he couldn't make it all out but heard the words in English, " Quick captain, we have no time." Captain Lageat knew exactly what the German commander was talking about, abandon ship and be quick about it.

On boarding the submarine the master was met by several German sailors and the commander. As the commander beckoned him, the sailors jumped into the boat and ordered the crew to row them over to the *Eugenie*. The master glanced at what they were carrying, a bomb, a big one. As the master gave his ship's details to the submarine's commander the bomb was being fixed to the starboard side of his ship under the main mast rigging.

When the boat returned about 20 minutes later the master was put back in it with his crew and told to be on his way. As they watched from a distance the bomb exploded but it didn't seem to do the damage it was supposed to have done and *Eugenie* stayed firmly afloat. The Germans must have been watching as well for they soon edged closer and proceeded to fire about a dozen shells to finish the dying ship off.

The master had a compass with him and shaped up a course for the English coast. They did remarkably well and soon the Lizard was well in sight. When only about two miles off they were spotted by a keen pair of eyes on the Penzance steamer *Pivoc* which landed them later at Dartmouth.

3/18: ECHUNGA. *Country:* British.
Date sunk: 5/9/17. *Tons nett:* 3863. *Tons gross:* 6285. *Built:* 1910. *Type:* SS. *Rig:* schooner. *Owners:* The Adelaide SS co Ltd, Currie St,

Adelaide, Australia. *Cargo:* 7324 tons oil fuel. *Armed:* 1 x 4.7in gun. *Position:* 40 miles N of Ushant (49 07 00N; 05 10 00W). *Master's name:* John William Balchin. *Crew:* 44, including 1 naval signal rating. *Gunners:* H. Parkyn, Prov LS RNVR, No LZ2697; J. Thompson, AB RNVR, No TZ9736; P. Elliott AB RNVR, No BZ9328.

ECHUNGA was chartered by the Saxon Patroleum Company and was part of the *Roxburgh* convoy consisting of 21 ships in total. She was stationed about eight cables astern of HMS *Roxburgh*, and keeping a steady eight knots.

However, everything came to a sudden end for her when she was blasted by a torpedo that smashed into her starboard side, opening up a huge hole in number two hold and bursting the deck above it. It was all over within four minutes as she plunged to the sea bed. Thirty-five of her crew did manage to get clear in whatever boats were intact after the explosion. However, nine men were killed.

U-52 was the submarine involved.

3/19: POLVENA. *Country:* British.
Date sunk: 17/10/17. *Tons nett:* 2970. *Tons gross:* 4750. *Built:* 1904. *Type:* SS. *Rig:* schooner. *Owners:* The Admiralty. *Cargo:* 650 tons lead, 700 tons asbestos, 2000 tons ore, 800 tons maize, 2000 bales of skins, Durban for London. *Armed:* 1 x 12pd 12cwt gun. *Position:* 27 miles N of Ushant (48 55 00N; 05 10 00W). *Master's name:* Charles King. *Crew:* 84. *Gunners:* Duncan Downie, Pro LS RNVR, No CZ 7928; Alfred Dunbottin, OS RNVR, No MZ 2411.

THE Admiralty were extremely unhappy with the events that took place on board the *Polvena* after she was struck by a torpedo from an enemy submarine. They were so unhappy that they directed that an enquiry should be made into the conduct of the master and officers of the ship.

Polvena was part of a convoy crossing the Channel and was the leading ship of 'U' column. There were five columns abreast and the whole convoy was protected by three warships and 10 armed trawlers. The convoy in general was making a little under seven knots and most of the steamers were keeping good positions. It came as a great surprise to them all when a torpedo from *U-53* hit the *Polvena* on the port side between number three hatch and the stokehold, killing two firemen.

The water poured into the engine room and the steamer began to settle rapidly. Apparently panic broke out, particularly among the Lascar crew who made for the boats on the starboard side and filled them to over-capacity. The chief officer, Mr H.C. Skinns, said that he went to the starboard side and found the boat there overflowing with lascars. Without any orders from the master he enlisted the help of the radio operator and sent the boat away, even though

the engines were still running and way was still on the ship. Soon afterwards the engines stopped as the water in the engine room had put the fires out.

The second officer, Mr L. Joy, was on watch on the bridge at the time of the explosion and ran down aft to get his boat away successfully. The third officer did the same but his boat was so overcrowded with Lascars and firemen that one fell out on the way down and was drowned. The third officer himself had to jump overboard but was picked up by his boat fairly quickly, even though it was full of men and lay helpless alongside the steamer.

It was said by other officers such as chief engineer, G.R. Buchan, and second engineer, Mr Symington, that the master left the ship with the chief officer, carpenter, Marconi operator, the distressed British seaman and three Lascars in the small boat. Captain King had not only left several of his crew still on board the *Polvena*, but had also left secret books and sailing instructions on the chartroom table. He rowed his boat off towards the escort trawler *Sea Searcher* and was taken aboard her, unaware of the men left stranded on the sinking steamer. The commander of *Sea Searcher* pointed this out to him and ordered a boat away to rescue the men.

The other boats containing the Lascars and firemen were picked up by the patrol vessel *Conway Castle*. The third officer's boat, although in a bad way, was rescued in a near sinking condition.

The Admiralty concluded that the master had left his ship prematurely. The master said that he had been given orders by a patrol vessel to abandon the ship immediately but could not say which patrol vessel had given him the order. They said that he should have also gone to the assistance of the third officer's boat that lay helpless alongside the steamer, because had the steamer sank, it would almost certainly have sucked the boat down with it. They felt that his coolness had deserted him in an emergency and he had failed to keep proper control when it was needed. He was also severely reprimanded for not destroying his confidential papers at the first sign of trouble.

The documents relating to this incident do not say what punishment, or indeed if any, was given to the master. The whole episode, they felt, was most unsatisfactory and suggested that the truth of what happened on the *Polvena* that day was being covered up. The Shipping Intelligence Officer wrote at the end of his enquiry, "I may add that the evidence of the chief officer and the gunlayer was given in an extremely unsatisfactory manner, continual attempts being made to cloud the issue."

3/20: VICTORIA II. *Country:* Norwegian.
Date sunk: 6/7/17. *Tons nett:* –. *Tons gross:* 2798. *Built:* –. *Type:* SS. *Rig:* –. *Owners:* E.& N. Christian Evanson. *Cargo:* China clay, Fowey to New York. *Armed:* No. *Position:* 35 miles N of Ushant (49 04 00N; 05 08 00W). *Master's name:* H.B. Hansen. *Crew:* 24.

THE boat that Captain Hansen had been ordered to send over to the German submarine by her commander, returned to the *Victoria II* with far more than he bargained for. It contained not only his own crewmen but a German officer with four German seaman, clutching around 12 bombs between them. They informed the master that his boat was about to be sunk but first they were going to search the ship. The search, as it turned out, was nothing more than a plundering party as the Germans began to take everything of value they could lay their hands on. Nothing was sacred, they even robbed the master of his best set of clothes as well as his wallet, his cigars and the entire contents of his drinks cabinet. Happy with their haul, they planted the bombs at various places around the ship and made off in one of the ship's boats back to their submarine.

At 1.20pm the crew watched as the bombs started to explode sending bits of debris flying in all directions and opening up holes everywhere. It took five minutes for the steamer to sink.

The crew rowed off in two boats, the master in charge of one and the mate the other. The plan was to stay together, but during the night it became impossible and they lost sight of each other at around 10pm. The master's boat was spotted at 4.44am the next morning by a lookout on the USS *O'Brian*, which was on route to St Nazaire.

3/21: ARVOR. *Country:* French.
Date sunk: 21/7/18. *Tons nett:* –. *Tons gross:* 961. *Built:* –. *Type:* SS. *Rig:* –. *Owners:* –. *Cargo:* Coal, Cardiff for Lorient. *Armed:* –. *Position:* 30 miles N by W of Ushant (48 57 00N; 05 07 00W). *Master's name:* –.

OBTAINING information on this sinking is troublesome due to the fact that there is only a 'Convoy Attack' form available.

Arvor was part of a south bound convoy that left Mounts Bay on the morning of July 21, 1918. The escorting trawlers were HMT's 480 *Lark II*, 382 *Pintail* and 3633 *George Burton*. The French steamer was number one in the convoy and at the time she was sunk the convoy was reported to be in perfect formation. At 4.30pm an explosion blew out the side of *Arvor* although it is not stated what caused it. The master said later that he considered the explosion was internal as when he inspected the damage he found that the side and decking plates had been blown outwards. No reference was made as to what the authorities thought had caused it but it is more than likely that a torpedo penetrated the skin of the vessel before it's warhead exploded.

Arvor stayed afloat for 20 minutes, long enough for all the crew to take to the boats and get clear, where they were picked up by *Lark II*. Escort trawler *George Burton* moved to the area where her commander judged a submarine may have been and dropped a few depth charges. The convoy was soon

reformed and made Brest later that day without further incident.

3/22: BAGDALE. *Country:* British.
Date sunk: 1/5/17. *Tons nett:* 1934 *Tons gross:* 3045. *Built:* 1904. *Type:* SS. *Rig:* schooner. *Owners:* T. Smails, Whitby. *Cargo:* Coal, Clyde for Nantes. *Armed:* 1 x 12pdr gun. *Position:* 13 miles N of Creach Point, Ushant (48 41 00N; 05 07 00W). *Master's name:* Mennell. *Crew:* 27.

BAGDALE had come down from Glasgow on April 28, 1917, and joined up with the French Coal Trade convoy that left Mounts Bay on April 30.

The convoy made reasonable headway, around eight knots on average. The good weather helped progress considerably – light winds and a calm sea. However, the convoy was being watched.

At 7am a torpedo from *UC-66* hit *Bagdale* on the port quarter. Such was the power of the explosion that it snapped her back and she sank almost instantly. Only three crew members survived. The rest, including the master, went down with the ship.

By the time HMT 2665, *Amroth Castle*, got to the spot there were only pieces of debris and the three men in the water. One of the men was landed at Brest and the other two were taken back to Penzance. One of those two was the Chief Officer, David Williams. It was he who made a brief statement to the naval authorities. He had joined *Bagdale* just one week earlier.

3/23: ALLENDALE. *Country:* British.
Date sunk: 27/3/18. *Tons nett:* 1304. *Tons gross:* 2153. *Built:* At Sunderland in 1917. *Type:* SS. *Rig:* single masted. *Owners:* Furness Withy & Co Ltd, Billiter St, London. *Cargo:* 2900 tons coal from R.McKill Co, Ardrossan to Bordeaux. *Armed:* 1 x 4in gun. *Position:* 38 miles N of Ushant (49 05 00N; 05 05 00W). *Master's name:* George Thomas Presant. *Crew:* 33. *Crew nationality:* 27 British, 1 Norwegian, 1 Spaniard, 1 Swede, 3 Russians. *Gunners:* Joseph Garland, LS RFR, No 170392 Devonport; Thomas Milburn, AB RNVR, No TZ 6098 Chatham; John McConechy, AB RNVR, No Z 246 B Chatham.

ALLENDALE was the middle ship in a line of five merchant vessels under escort across the Channel. It was probably just pure bad luck that she was picked out by the commander of the waiting German submarine *U-101*. The master was on the bridge at the time with the second officer, Robert Rifferty Nugent. At 3.15am on March 27, 1918, a torpedo struck the steamer square on the port side amidships, tearing out a huge hole and blowing the hatch covers off.

The master gave the order to abandon ship but had his doubts about the state of the port lifeboat. He rushed off to have a quick look at it and promptly

A U-boat closes in to inspect the damage it has inflicted on a British steamer (vessel unknown).

fell down the bunker hatch injuring his wrist and breaking several ribs. He struggled to his feet and continued on to the port boat where he found that it had been completely smashed by the force of the explosion.

All the crew made for the starboard boat with the exception of a fireman, W. Rice of Glasgow. He was in the stokehold at the time and must have been killed by the explosion. The steamer started to take on a heavy list to port but by then the men had managed to get clear of her. At 3.40am, just 25 minutes after being hit, *Allendale* turned bottom up and floated for a minute or so before plunging downwards.

Lieutenant J. Pottinger, commander of the armed trawler *John Ebbs* immediately turned towards the stricken steamer. One of his men had spotted the periscope of the submarine responsible and he made straight towards it with the intention of ramming it. But the German commander dived his boat and got out of the area rapidly. All the crew of the *Allendale* were eventually landed at Falmouth.

3/24: PHILADELPHIAN. *Country:* British. *Date sunk:* 19/2/18. *Tons nett:* 3322. *Tons gross:* 5120. *Built:* Belfast in 1891. *Type:* SS. *Rig:* schooner. *Owners:* Frederick Leyland & Co Ltd, 27, James St, Liverpool. *Cargo:* 5000 tons general goods, 702 horses on deck from New York to London. *Armed:* 1 x 6in QF and 2 x 7.5in Howitzers. *Position:* 48 miles S of Lizard (49 05 00N; 05 05 00W). *Master's name:* William Ferrie Wood. *Crew:* 120. *Gunners:* Aaron Lumsden, Prov LS RFR, No 218195; Edward James Moore, Prov LS RFR, No 200003; Sidney Walter Land, seaman RNR, No 6792A; Arthur Davies, AB RNVR, No 9130BZ, drowned; Arthur Leslie Hill, ordinary seaman RNVR, drowned.

WHEN the master spotted the periscope of a submarine about 800yds off on the port beam he immediately shouted to the gunners to bring the port howitzer to the ready. The gunners eager for some action obeyed instantly and quickly sighted up the gun. The master watched as the periscope grew taller in the water and gave the order to the gunners to fire at will. As the first shell was fired by the gun another explosion came almost simultaneously from a torpedo already released by the commander of *U-82*.

It was 9.36am when the first of two torpedos slammed into the port side of the *Philadelphian* smashing a huge hole in number three hold. The force of the explosion threw up an enormous spout of water which crashed into the bridge with such force that it demolished the port side, smashed the wheel and telegraph, and knocked the master clean off his feet.

The volunteer gunner and quartermaster, Mr

Litchfield, who was at the wheel, calmly asked the master if he could be relieved to attend his post at the gun. A moment later another torpedo hit the steamer in number four hold with equal ferocity. Still the gunners carried on firing but had little more than the thin periscope to aim at.

The *Philadelphian* was sinking rapidly and the master ordered the crew to make for their boat stations and get clear. He watched as the men scrambled to the boats, the steamer's deck getting closer to the water by the second. He was thankful that the weather was quite good, fine with a moderate breeze, and also grateful that plenty of other ships were around. There were 10 steamers in the convoy altogether and these were escorted by five patrol vessels. He had already run up the distress flags and hoped that help was on the way. The horses were in the pens on deck and the horseman, Mr McGeehan, was trying his best to keep them calm.

Five minutes later the bulk of the crew were clear of the steamer in the lifeboats leaving only the gunners, the master and the chief cook on board. The master shouted to the gunners that it was time to go and ordered them over the side. Slowly the gunners left their post, and one, on reaching the water, got into difficulties straight away. His colleague Edward Moore, who was wearing a lifebelt instantly took it off and threw it to the man. Gunners Aaron Lumsden, and Edward Moore were at their gun to the last and only went over the side when the sea was washing around their ankles. Unfortunately, three of the gunners were killed including the volunteer, Mr Litchfield.

Last to walk down the starboard side of the listing *Philadelphian* were the master and the chief cook. They only had one lifebelt between them and sharing the support they swam clear as the steamer plunged to the bottom. One of the boats rowed quickly over to them and soon had them aboard.

It had taken seven minutes for the ship to sink from the time of being struck. All that remained was debris and horses, some already dead, some swimming for their lives. They stood no chance of survival, there was nowhere for them to go. Somewhere among the horses was the horseman, Mr McGeehan, who was never seen again. HMS *Lennox* was soon on the scene taking the men aboard. Four men were lost.

The Admiralty were very impressed with the way the master, his officers and crew had conducted themselves, and, in particular, the gunners. They were decorated for their actions that day and the master was given the DSC.

3/25: DIXIANA. *Country:* British.
Date sunk: 29/5/15. *Tons nett:* 2147. *Tons gross:* 3329. *Built:* At West Hartlepool in 1901. *Type:* SS. *Rig:* schooner. *Owners:* The Dixiana SS Co Ltd, West Hartlepool. *Cargo:* 2500 tons cotton, 2400 tons pig iron & general, shipped by Strachan SS Co, USA and consigned to Havre & Swansea. *Armed:*

No. *Position:* 40 miles N of Ushant (49 10 00N; 05 05 00W). *Master's name:* Alfred James Long. *Crew:* 27.

THE second mate was on the bridge of *Dixiana* with the master when they spotted a submarine. The master immediately ordered the helmsman to steer away and sent word to the engineers to give it all they could.

Dixiana responded well and raced away at nearly 10 knots but the submarine fired her deck gun and sent a shell screaming over the bridge of her quarry as a warning to stop.

Even while the crew were lowering themselves down into the boats the submarine continued to shell the steamer. The master was the last to leave and as he jumped into the starboard boat there was a huge explosion from the engine room. Several skylights were thrown into the air and one landed on the masters boat smashing the rudder. The two boats eventually pulled clear and stopped to watch as the bombardment continued followed by a well placed torpedo. At noon, *Dixiana* rolled over and sank.

The Germans in *U-41* made no attempt to speak with the master and turned their attention to another steamer that had appeared to the north-east. The master stated that he thought it was sunk but couldn't be certain. There is no record of another vessel being sunk on that day in that given position.

After rowing for about an hour the crew of the *Dixiana* were approached by a French steamer and offered a lift to Bordeaux which they declined, preferring instead to make for the British coast. It was 24 hours later that they were picked up by the Greek steamer *Zanos Sifnio*. They were landed at Barry Roads at 11am on May 31.

3/26: MAR BALTICO. *Country:* Spanish.
Date sunk: 23/3/18. *Tons nett:* –. *Tons gross:* 2023. *Built:* –. *Type:* SS. *Rig:* –. *Owners:* –. *Cargo:* Ballast, Port Talbot for Bilbao. *Armed:* –. *Position:* 48 miles N of Ushant (49 17 00N; 05 05 00W). *Master's name:* –.

MAR BALTICO shared the same fate as two other vessels in the convoy that left Mounts Bay at 6pm on March 23, 1918. Her position was number 10 in the starboard column.

She was hit with a torpedo at 5am fired by *UB-55* and sank soon after. One of the other vessels lost that night, the British SS *Duva (Madame Midas)*, is better described (see 3/11). However, the third, the Norwegian SS *Venborg*, is as short on detail as *Mar Baltico*.

3/27: WAR FIRTH. *Country:* British.
Date sunk: 4/9/18. *Tons nett:* 1860. *Tons gross:* 3112. *Built:* 1918. *Type:* SS. *Rig:* schooner. *Owners: Managers:* Joseph Chadwick & Sons, Liverpool. *Cargo:* 4700 tons iron ore from Bilbao

to Glasgow. *Armed:* 1 x 4in gun. *Position:* 33 miles S by E of Lizard (49 25 00N; 05 05 00W). *Master's name:* Percival John Greenhill. *Crew:* 39. *Crew nationality:* All British. *Casualties:* W. Turnball, third engineer; A. Adams, chief steward; C. Hanson, gunner, LS RNVR Portsmouth; J. Angus, carpenter; C. Davison, bosun; J. Carling, donkeyman; J. Laybourne, greaser. W. Fletcher (senior); H. Vile; W. Poole; J. Jones, firemen

THE weather was fine for the crossing of the convoy that left Brest on the morning of September 4, 1918. The visibility was generally good although there were slight hazy patches at times during the journey north. At 1.15pm the *War Firth* was singled out by the commander of *U-53* as the best target.

The torpedo was 150yds off the steamer when the watchman on the bridge shouted, but it was far too late to do anything about it and the torpedo slammed into her port side. Almost immediately the *War Firth* began to settle down. The master ordered her to be abandoned and one boat with 17 men got away successfully. However, as the ship sank, she dragged the remainder down with her.

The patrol trawler *Yokohama* was on the scene within minutes and first picked up the crew from the boat. The first, second and third officers, knowing that many of their colleagues including the master, were in trouble, urged the commander of *Yokohama* to make all haste to find them. Eleven men were picked up, but another eleven were still missing.

The survivors were taken to Penzance where the master made his statement to the naval examining officer. He couldn't sing the praises of his crew highly enough. He felt that their behaviour in such exceptional circumstances was exemplary. He recommended that his deck officers and the two surviving gunners be decorated for their services.

3/28: MERTON HALL. *Country:* British. *Date sunk:* 11/2/18. *Tons nett:* 2773. *Tons gross:* 4327. *Built:* 1899. *Type:* SS. *Rig:* schooner. *Owners:* Hall Line, Liverpool. *Cargo:* 7000 tons steel from New York to La Pallice. *Armed:* 1 x 12pdr gun. *Position:* 30 miles N by E of Ushant Light (48 58 00N; 05 04 00W). *Master's name:* A. Cameron. *Crew:* 69.

WHEN the *Merton Hall* was torpedoed at 6 oclock in the evening of February 11, 1918, by *U-53*, it resulted in an horrfic loss of life. Of the 69 men aboard her only 12 survived. Most of the crew were lascars and the only European to survive was Thomas Robert Carson, of 68 Hinoy Street, Limerick. He was the wireless operator and was called later by the naval authorities to be interviewed about the loss.

He said that he knew that a German submarine was responsible for the sinking as some of the lookouts had shouted that they could see the wake of the torpedo coming towards the steamer. It was a fine, clear night and the sea was quite smooth. In a matter of seconds it smashed into the port side of the ship. The effect was devastating, blowing a hole so big in the ship's side that she sank in less than 30 seconds.

Thomas Carson could remember little, other than being plucked from the water by the crew of a French destroyer. He said that the third mate was also picked up alive but died a little later from exposure.

3/29: BEGONA No 3. *Country:* Spanish. *Date sunk:* 23/5/17. *Tons nett:* 1718. *Tons gross:* 2862. *Built:* 1896. *Type:* SS. *Rig:* schooner. *Owners:* Sota & Agner, Bilbao. *Cargo:* Iron ore from Bilbao to Barrow-in-Furness. *Armed:* No. *Position:* 29 miles N from Ushant (48 55 00N; 05 04 00W). *Master's name:* Francisco Muntegue. *Crew:* 27. *Crew nationality:* All Spanish.

NOBODY on the *Begona No 3* really knew what happened on the night of May 23, 1917. Their ship was part of a convoy of some 10 or more steamers. Such was the organisation of that particular convoy that even the escorting patrol vessels were not aware of how many ships they had in their charge let alone the names of them. It was 10.40pm, the wind was strong from the south-south-west and the night was dark.

One of the escorting vessels was the armed trawler *Elk* commanded by J.A. Townend, who said that he felt the shock wave of the explosion in the distance. All he could do was to head off in the general direction of the explosion and see what he could find. After a while he heard voices trying to call above the noise of the wind and sea and he eventually found men clinging to pieces of wreckage strewn over a large area. He added that it was particularly difficult in the conditions to get the men aboard but after some time he managed to account for 13 crew of *Begona No 3*.

The Second Engineer, Manuel Pallister, was called on to make a statement to the authorities. He said that the ship suffered a violent explosion but he couldn't tell if it had been struck by a torpedo or had hit a mine. The steamer started to sink immediately and the next thing he knew he was in the water desperately trying to find something to hold on to. He was eventually picked up by HMT *Elk*.

Another seven men were picked up later by the steamer *Lady Madeline* which dropped them at Cardiff, leaving seven men unaccounted for, including the master and most of the officers.

3/30: CISSIE. *Country:* Norwegian. *Date sunk:* 16/6/17. *Tons nett:* 1943. *Tons gross:* 3030. *Built:* 1891. *Type:* SS. *Rig:* schooner. *Owners:* Torp et Winese, Bergen, Norway. *Cargo:* 4250 tons coal from South Shields to Blaye. *Armed:* No. *Position:* 7 miles N of Stiff Point, Ushant (48 36 00N; 05 04 00W). *Master's name:* Nikolai Stinessen. *Crew:* 25. *Crew nationality:* 22 Norwegians, 3 Russian/Finns.

IN a convoy, crossing the Channel for Brest, *Cissie* struck a mine.

The master reported that the weather was fine but occasionally foggy. The wind was light and the sea had a slight swell to it and at first it was assumed that she had been hit by a torpedo. However, if that were the case the track of it would have been easily visible. It was also nine oclock in the morning with plenty of daylight.

She started to take on water very rapidly and the crew were forced to abandon her. They all got safely away and were picked up by the patrol trawler number 472, *Ben Lawers*. The master of *Cissie* said that he didn't actually witness his ship sink as she disappeared from view into a fog patch, but the last time he saw her she was all but under.

3/31: VENBORG. *Country:* Norwegian. *Date sunk:* 23/3/18. *Tons nett:* –. *Tons gross:* 1065. *Built:* –. *Type:* SS. *Rig:* –. *Owners:* –. *Cargo:* –. *Armed:* –. *Position:* 28 miles N by E of Ushant (48 55 00N; 05 02 00W). *Master's name:* –.

A CONVOY left Mounts Bay at 6pm on March 23, 1918, to cross the Channel. Escorts vessels included were HMT 3351 *Jane Ross*, HMT 3564 *Samuel Dowden* and HMT 473 *Isabella Fowlie*.

It was to prove a disastrous crossing. Lurking in among the fog banks was the German submarine *UB-55*, her commander picked off the steamers at will. Three from the convoy disappeared including the *Venborg*, which was number seven in the port column. She was hit by a torpedo at 3am.

The other two vessels sunk were the British steamer *Duva* and the Spanish SS *Mar Baltico* (see 3/26).

3/32: BARGANY. *Country:* British. *Date sunk:* 24/12/16. *Tons nett:* 395. *Tons gross:* 872. *Built:* Greenock in 1911. *Type:* SS. *Rig:* schooner. *Owners:* The Bargany SS Co, 114, Bude St, Cardiff. *Cargo:* 1077 tons coal shipped by E. Marieschi & Co, Cardiff and consigned to same of Lorient. *Armed:* No. *Position:* 25 miles N by E of Ushant (48 57 00N; 05 02 00W). *Master's name:* Frank Bennett Hurrell. *Crew:* 15. *Crew nationality:* All British.

AT 3.50pm, when the light was fading fast the master saw a submarine off the port bow. The master made a run for it, but to his dismay the submarine gained on him with ease. One shell struck and shrapnel hit one of the crew.

With the order to abandon ship, the crew lowered the boats as best they could in the rough sea. The master remained at the helm on the bridge manoeuvering his ship to afford the boats protection from the weather while they launched. At 4.15pm the master joined the starboard boat with five other men and at last the submarine's gunner ceased firing.

After being questioned by the German commander of *UC-17*, the master was told to get his boats clear as they were going to sink the *Bargany*. The submarine moved off and took up a position close to the stern of the steamer to enable the gunner to fire several shells into her. The result was very effective and the steamer went down at the stern and sank.

The port lifeboat was in the command of the acting second mate, Edwin Lay, and he said in his statement that at dusk the two boats lost sight of each other. It was a rough night and the men rowed to keep their minds active and bodies warm. Help did arrive for the port lifeboat by way of the Norwegian steamer *Kingston* which picked up the nine men and landed them at Deal.

At daylight the master in his boat decided to shape a course for Ushant and was making reasonable progress when a passing ship spotted the men and took them to Cherbourg.

3/33: HURUNUI. *Country:* British. *Date sunk:* 18/5/18. *Tons nett:* 6824. *Tons gross:* 10644. *Built:* Glasgow in 1911. *Type:* SS. *Rig:* –. *Owners:* The New Zealand Shipping Co Ltd, London. *Cargo:* 8825 tons general from Wellington, New Zealand to London. *Armed:* Yes. *Position:* 40 miles N by E of Ushant (49 08 00N; 05 00 00W). *Master's name:* Thomas Shailer Weston. *Crew:* 91.

CONSIDERING the size of the *Hurunui* and the amount of cargo she was carrying it is quite amazing that only one solitary form exists in the records. It may well be that documents have been bundled in other files but at the time of writing the information remains very sparse.

The casualty occurred at 4.45am. The weather was good, described as fine and clear with light winds. She was struck by a torpedo on her starboard side in number three hold which tore open a huge hole. The master ordered an orderly abandoning in three of the boats. However, some of the crew panicked and jumped overboard. Most of them were picked up by the boats after launching but one, a trimmer called Smith, wasn't found.

It took two hours for the *Hurunui* to sink but sink she did leaving the men to row for the nearest shore. The boats were later spotted by a British destroyer which landed the crew at Plymouth around 10pm the same day.

U-94 claimed the sinking.

3/34: MONKSGARTH. *Country:* British. *Date sunk:* 19/8/17. *Tons nett:* 1052. *Tons gross:* 1928. *Built:* Glasgow 1907. *Type:* SS. *Rig:* schooner. *Owners:* R.& SH. Rea, 3, St Helens Place, London. *Cargo:* 2760 tons coal from Thomas, Cardiff to Midi Railway Co, Paris. *Armed:* 1 x 13pdr Vickers. *Position:* 17 miles NNE of of

Creach Point, Ushant (48 43 30N; 04 59 00W). *Master's name:* James Mitchell Anderson. *Crew:* 23. *Crew nationality:* 11 British, 8 Arabs, 2 Norwegians, 1 Swede, 1 Chilian. *Gunners Names:* A.J. Harry, No 2216; L. Garlthwaite, No 58300.

BY this stage of the war it was becoming increasingly necessary for steamers to cross the Channel in convoys. And even though the Channel convoys were heavily guarded by warships it still didn't stop the U-boat commanders from picking off the steamers. The *UC-48* for example, put an end to the *Monksgarth* at the western end of the Channel in the early hours of August 19, 1917.

The convoy was approaching Ushant with *Monksgarth* the second ship in the port column. It was 6.15am, the weather was good and the convoy was making a steady seven knots. Without any warning a torpedo slammed into the port side of the steamer below the fore part of the bridge. The explosion smashed the port lifeboat and the jolly boat to pieces, leaving only the starboard boat for the crew. The steamer took on water very rapidly and within five minutes was about ready to go down. There wasn't enough room for everyone in the starboard boat so the master and several others jumped as the ship sank.

It was fortunate that the weather was good and that the men in the water managed to swim to the starboard boat. Within minutes several patrol trawlers were in amongst the wreckage and took all the crew on board.

3/35: GLENCARRON. *Country:* British.
Date sunk: 19/2/18. *Tons nett:* 3232. *Tons gross:* 5117. *Built:* Irvine in 1917. *Type:* SS. *Rig:* schooner. *Owners:* Rio Cape Line Ltd, Milburn House, Newcastle. *Cargo:* 1700 tons powder, 1560 tons steel, 1200 tons flour, 2400 tons general from Philadelphia to London. *Armed:* 1 x 4.7in gun. *Position:* 35 miles N by E of Ushant (49 02 00N; 04 57 00W). *Master's name:* David Clunie Horne. *Crew:* 44. *Crew nationality:* 17 British, 2 Swedes, 2 Norwegians, 2 Finns, 1 Dutch, 1 Panamanian, 18 Chinese, 1 American. *Gunners:* James A. Budge, Prov LS RNR, No 7075A; Patrick Derrane, seaman RNR, No C2146.

GLENCARRON was part of a convoy of 10 steamers crossing the Atlantic accompanied by five escort boats. She was given the position of leading ship on the port column and throughout the journey the master and his officers kept station well. It was just bad luck on the master's part that he suddenly found himself three cables ahead of his station, when a course change at 10.30am combined with an opposite ziz-zag compelled him to slow his engines. At that moment *U-82* fired a torpedo at her.

It was a good shot. The torpedo slammed into the port side of the steamer , badly damaging one and two holds and the port side of the bridge. She began to settle by the head and the master concluded that his ship would not stay afloat for much longer. He was right – three minutes after the boats left her, *Glencarron* sank.

A few minutes later HMTBD *55* arrived and took the men aboard with no casualties.

3/36: SNYG. *Country:* Norwegian.
Date sunk: 26/2/18. *Tons nett:* –. *Tons gross:* 370. *Built:* –. *Type:* SS. *Rig:* –. *Owners:* –. *Cargo:* – Coal, Newport for Hennebont. *Armed:* No. *Position:* 20 miles NNE of Creach Point, Ushant (48 47 00N; 04 57 00W). *Master's name:* Johan Glenriksen. *Crew:* 12.

ALTHOUGH some records give her as mined, it is more likely that *Snyg* was yet another victim of a German torpedo. She was part of a convoy of 10 vessels from Penzance to Brest when she suffered a huge explosion. The master was asked later if he saw anything of a submarine but neither he nor any of the surviving crew members saw anything.

It happened at 4.45am when the weather conditions were bad with a strong westerly wind and a heavy sea. Even though several patrol vessels were quite close to the *Snyg*, the bad conditions prevented any of the lookouts from seeing or hearing the explosion. The first anyone knew of *Snyg's* fate occurred about 20 minutes later when HMT 3633 *George Burton* stumbled upon the survivors. Her commander, Lieutenant Culling, reported that at around 5am his lookouts spotted a dark object ahead and they closed to investigate. The object turned out to be a boat and a raft from the SS *Snyg* with eight men aboard including the master.

The men were picked up and later landed at Roscanvel, Brest. The master made a brief statement but it did not go into any further details apart from the fact that, sadly, four of his crew went down with the ship.

3/37: ADOLF ANDERSEN. *Country:* Danish.
Date sunk: 17/11/17. *Tons nett:* –. *Tons gross:* 981. *Built:* –. *Type:* SS. *Rig:* –. *Owners:* –. *Cargo:* 1160 tons coal, Newport for Nantes. *Armed:* –. *Position:* 5 miles E by N of Le Stiff, Ushant (48 30 00N; 04 56 00W). *Master's name:* –.

THE *Adolf Andersen* was torpedoed whilst in convoy and was reported by HMT 2665 *Amroth Castle*. The convoy was steaming at reduced power so as to enter the Channel at daybreak. All of the crew apart from one man who was lost, were picked up by the French trawler *Souffle* and landed at Brest.

Because the French were not as meticulous as the British in keeping records of these incidents there is virtually no information in the contemporary records for the period. A search of later documents however, might reveal more details.

3/38: SONNIE. *Country:* British.
Date sunk: 11/8/17. *Tons nett:* 1341. *Tons gross:* 2641. *Built:* Sunderland in 1917. *Type:* SS. *Rig:* schooner. *Owners:* Harris Bros & Co, Pembroke Buildings, Swansea. *Cargo:* 3465 tons iron ore from Bilbao to the Britton Ferry Steel Works, Port Talbot. *Armed:* 1 x 13pdr gun. *Position:* 8 miles NE of Le Stiff, Ushant (48 34 00N; 04 55 00W). *Master's name:* James Kinley. *Crew:* 25. *Crew nationality:* 24 British, 1 Norwegian.

THE sinking of the *Sonnie* was unusual only in that she sank in just over one minute from the time of the explosion taking place.

She was part of a convoy in two lines ahead. Her position was number two. Many of the surviving crew said that at around 9.35pm they felt a shock from the port quarter of the vessel and realised that she had been torpedoed or had struck a mine.

Amazingly, in the short time available two boats did manage to get away from the steamer but they were so close to her as she sank that they were capsized by the turmoil as she went down. It was probably at this moment that most of the missing men were killed. Eleven of the crew were lost, two engineers, two deck officers, three firemen, three seamen and a donkeyman.

The patrol escorts got in among the wreckage as best they could and picked up men, but it was particularly tricky in the large swell. The 14 survivors were landedl, five at Penzance and nine at Brest.

UC-77 was the submarine concerned.

3/39: JUTLAND. *Country:* British.
Date sunk: 19/11/17. *Tons nett:* 1829. *Tons gross:* 2824. *Built:* 1898. *Type:* SS. *Rig:* schooner. *Owners:* Anglo-Bretagne SS Co Ltd, 86, Merchants Exchange, Cardiff. *Cargo:* Iron ore from Bilbao to Brest. *Armed:* 1 x 12pdr gun. *Position:* 18 miles NE by N of Le Stiff, Ushant (48 46 00N; 04 55 00W). *Master's name:* Grees. *Crew:* 28.

THE commanding officer of the American patrol boat *Christobel* said that on the night that *Jutland* was lost his ship was part of the convoy and the flash of an explosion was plainly seen from his bridge. He immediately ordered his ship to turn to port to go to *Jutland's* assistance and put his crew to battle stations.

Suddenly a lookout shouted that he could see a dim light flashing and the ship was turned towards it. Wreckage started to appear, strewn over the choppy surface of the sea. Another shout came from a lookout who had spotted a hatch cover and clinging to the top of it was one of the *Jutland's* gunners, a man called Hopton Bishop. He was soon picked up and the search continued. The flashing light turned out to be a chemical light which was attached to a buoy and proved an invaluable aid to locating the spot. A few minutes later the wreck of the *Jutland's* radio house was seen floating and on it was another

man called Edwin Temburk, a Russian seaman.

These two men were the only people to survive from the torpedoed steamer. Edwin Temburk said later that at around 8pm he heard a dull explosion followed by a moaning sound as if the ship was breaking up. He ran on deck to see what was happening and saw that the stern of the ship was underwater, in another second he was underwater also, being dragged down by the sinking steamer. For what seemed like forever he remained underwater but suddenly he popped up to the surface and could see nothing but wreckage.

Gunner Bishop, said he was on watch at his gun when the torpedo struck and added that *Jutland* sank stern first almost immediately after. He was also dragged down by the suction of the ship sinking but eventually made the surface and found the hatch cover to climb on.

UC-79 was the submarine which sank her.

3/40: FARRALINE. *Country:* British.
Date sunk: 2/11/17. *Tons nett:* 765. *Tons gross:* 1225. *Built:* Leith in 1903. *Type:* SS. *Rig:* schooner. *Owners:* London & Edinburgh SS Co, 8/9, Commercial St, Leith. *Cargo:* 1200 tons pit props from Bordeaux to Cardiff. *Armed:* 1 x 13pdr Mk5 gun. No 1121. Mount No 404. *Position:* 14 miles N of Ushant (48 41 00N; 04 51 00W). *Master's name:* Thomas Parrott. *Crew:* 21. *Crew nationality:* 16 British, 5 Japanese. *Gunners:* Edward Fisher,L/Cpl. RMLI, No 12048 Chatham; Edward Stevens, L/Cpl. RMLI, No 17364.

FARRALINE was one of 19 ships in the convoy and her position was number 10 in the port column. It was 8.45pm when the shout went up from the bridge that the top of a submarine's conning tower had been sighted off the port side. The master rushed to pick up his binoculars and look for himself but he no sooner had them up to his eyes when the ship shuddered violently from a heavy explosion.

UC-69's torpedo had knocked a huge hole in the port side amidships of the *Farraline* blowing the engine room to pieces and killing one of the Japanese donkeymen who had been on duty at the time. She began to sink rapidly and the master wasted no time in ordering the boats away. The port lifeboat, in the words of the master had been, 'smashed to atoms', so the only boat left was the starboard. Captain Parrot watched from the bridge as the operation was swiftly carried out. However, seeing that his ship was about to make her final plunge, he ran to join the boat. He was just too late, by the time he had got half way the steamer sank from under his feet.

There were several others of the crew who had been caught out by the speed at which the ship sank, but along with the master they clung to various pieces of wreckage until their boat came and rescued them. A patrol vessel picked them all up and put them ashore at Penzance.

3/41: EASTLANDS. *Country:* British.
Date sunk: 25/1/18. *Tons nett:* –. *Tons gross:* 3113.
Built: –. *Type:* SS. *Rig:* –. *Owners:* C.F. Wilson, 61,
Church St, West Hartlepool. *Cargo:* 4300 tons
defence timber & sleepers from Bordeaux to
Dunkirk. *Armed:* 1 x 12pdr 12cwt gun. *Position:* 13
miles NW of Ile de Vierge (48 46 30N; 04 50 00W).
Master's name: David Lloyd. *Crew:* 28. *Crew
nationality:* 25 British, 2 Portuguese,
1 French/W.African. *Gunners:* Donald Bain,
No 2178A Portsmouth; John Burke, No 5045A
Portsmouth.

EASTLANDS was part of a convoy protected mainly
by French escort vessels when she ran into trouble.
At 7.45 on the evening of January 25, 1918, the
lookouts reported to the bridge that they could see a
submarine about 200yds off just showing her conning
tower. The gunners sprang into action immediately
and began to lob shells at the unwanted visitor but it
wasn't enough to deter the German commander,
Oberleutnant Wenninger of *UB-55*.

His first torpedo smashed into the port side of the
steamer opening up a large hole in number three hold.
This was followed quickly by another which hit a
little further astern on the same side. Still the gunners
kept up their fire but the blast from the second torpedo
lifted Gunner John Burke off his feet and threw him
over the side. He held on to the railings and by sheer
determination managed to get himself back on board.
Not content with saving himself he took up his
position at the gun again and managed to loose off
another seven rounds at the enemy.

The *Eastlands* was now in a bad way. Her port side
was completely smashed open, so much so that her
cargo was washing out and leaving a trail behind her.
The engine room was flooding rapidly and the
engineers decided that they could do no more,
expecting any moment another large explosion as the
water reached the boilers. At 8.15pm the master
decided he had no choice but to abandon his ship and
gave the order accordingly.

The crew were about to leave when the ship gave
a mighty lurch as if she was about to go down. Just at
that instant a fireman, a negro called C.W. Jackson,
appeared on deck in a very dazed condition. His crew
mates shouted to him to run to the boats quickly but
he seemed to ignore them all and wandered off again.
The master decided that it was crucial to get going if
the rest of his crew were to be saved and reluctantly
ordered the boats away.

As the boats got a hundred yards or so from the
steamer another torpedo was fired which hissed
straight under the chief mate's boat and slammed into
the steamer's side. All the men heard the explosion
but none could see the steamer clearly due to the
darkness.

Within a few minutes a French escort ship was
alongside the crew in the boats and they all boarded
her. The master asked the Captain if he would go back
to the *Eastlands*, if she was still afloat, to look for

the man that had to be left behind. But the Captain
had orders to stay with the convoy.

Both gunners received the highest praise by the
master of the *Eastlands* for their conduct. Their
Lordships of the Admiralty took note of their actions
and recommended that they both be mentioned in the
London Gazette and that gunner Bain be promoted to
the rank of Leading Seaman.

3/42: TREMEADOW. *Country:* British.
Date sunk: 19/1/17. *Tons nett:* –. *Tons gross:* 3653.
Built: South Shields in 1905. *Type:* SS. *Rig:*
schooner. *Owners:* The Hain SS Co, St Ives,
Cornwall. *Cargo:* Maize, Buenos Aires for Hull.
Armed: No. *Position:* 35 miles NNE of Ushant
(49 04 00N; 04 50 00W). *Master's name:* Arthur
Howell. *Crew:* 28. *Crew nationality:* 16 British,
9 Russian/Finns, 3 Sierra Leone.

AFTER calling in for orders at St Vincent on January
2, 1917, *Tremeadow* left two days later with
instructions to make for Hull. After two weeks she
arrived back in the Channel where she was to meet
her end. At 5pm on Friday January 19, the second
mate had the watch and saw a U-boat surface 50 yards
off the starboard bow.

Captain Howell acted immediately ordering the
helmsman hard to starboard and the second mate to
instruct the engineers below to give him all the speed
they had. The first shell loosed off from the deck gun
of *UC-21* passed right through the chartroom and
wheelhouse smashing the steering gear and injuring
the helmsman. The second shell missed.

Once the German commander realised that the
steamer was disabled and her crew were making
moves to abandon her he ordered his gunner to stop.
Two boats pulled away from the ship and fell astern.
He demanded that the master hand over his papers.
The master, obeying his instructions, had already
dropped his secret papers over the side in a weighted
bag and very conveniently had left the rest on the
steamer. The submarine left them, moved closer to
the stricken *Tremeadow* and began to pound her once
more with the deck gun. The master said that when
he last saw his ship she was still afloat but the onset of
darkness prevented him from witnessing her end.

The two boats tried as best they could to stay
together through the night but it was difficult. At 2am
they eventually lost contact with each other. At 9am
the master's boat containing 14 men was spotted by a
lookout on a British destroyer. They were picked up
and later landed at Plymouth. At the time the master
made his deposition to the authorities there was no
news of the mate's boat with the rest of the men, but
they were subsequently found.

3/43: PALACINE. *Country:* British.
Date sunk: 2/12/16. *Tons nett:* 2094. *Tons
gross:* 3286. *Built:* Dumbarton in 1904. *Type:* SS.

Rig: schooner. *Owners:* The Imperial Oil Co Ltd, Sarnia, Canada. *Cargo:* 4000 tons lubricating oil, from Standard Oil Co, New Jersey to Bedford Patroleum Co, Paris. *Armed:* No. *Position:* 18 miles ENE of Ushant (48 40 00N; 04 46 00W). *Master's name:* George Patterson. *Crew:* 32. *Crew nationality:* 5 British, 21 Malays, 2 Swedes, 1 Dutch, 1 Italian, 1 Dane, 1 Spaniard.

THE Atlantic crossing from New York was a fairly uneventful one for the *Palacine* – until 7am on Saturday December 2, 1916. The master was on the bridge when a shout from a keen eyed lookout reported a German submarine surfacing about a quarter of a mile off the starboard bow. Captain Patterson immediately stashed his secret sailing instructions into the weighted wallet always at hand and tossed it over the side.

As the master expected, shells soon started to whistle all around the steamer, some astern, some forward and then one directly over head. It was enough of a warning for the master to order the engines to be shut down and the boats to be manned.

First to leave was the mate's boat containing 15 men followed closely by the master's with the rest of the crew. Both boats gradually fell astern of the *Palacine* but the mate's was intercepted by the submarine and towed back to the steamer. The cook was ordered to board with several German officers who demanded that he show them where the food was kept. At the point of a revolver the cook had no choice but to obey. The submariners were obviously hungry as they loaded every scrap of food and anything they thought of value into the bridge boat before lowering it down to the water. They did however, to their credit, throw down a bundle of clothes to the crew in the boat below.

The enemy raiders then placed several bombs down the aft ventilators and beat a hasty retreat. The crew waited about 100yds off their ship. However, the submarine came alongside them and told them in no uncertain terms to go away.

Although the explosions were particularly violent the steamer refused to sink and the master stated later that the last he saw of his ship was around 10am and the submarine was still circling her. He thought however, that a torpedo was fired later and then she must have sunk instantly.

The crew all made the port of Weymouth after being picked up by a passing steamer, SS *Ortolan* of London.

3/44: NAGATA MARU. *Country:* Japanese. *Date sunk:* 30/11/16. *Tons nett:* 2156. *Tons gross:* 3512. *Built:* –. *Type:* SS. *Rig:* –. *Owners:* S. Nagata Allatini & Co, Saigon. *Cargo:* 4480 tons rice, Japan for Le Havre. *Armed:* No. *Position:* 23 miles N of Isle-Vierge (49 10 00N; 04 42 00W). *Master's name:* T. Yamamoto. *Crew:* 49. *Crew nationality:* All Japanese.

IT was a very confused and sad captain who wrote an account of the sinking of his ship for the authorities. Not only had he lost his ship but also six of his crew who died as a result of the incident.

He said that a submarine appeared very close to his ship and although it raised a signal flag, which he subsequently learned meant abandon ship immediately, he felt that the Germans gave him no time to do anything. Before he knew what was happening the submarine opened fire with her deck gun. The first two shots missed the ship but were very close, the third hit home, killing two men instantly and wounding eight more. The master ordered his crew to leave the steamer in the ship's three boats and tried to tend to the wounded men. Three were so badly injured that they died before they could be got into a boat.

The master rowed over to the submarine and was taken on board for questioning. After handing over his papers Captain Yamamoto asked the commander if he could return to his ship to recover the bodies of his dead crew. As the commander intended to send over a bombing party anyway to finish the ship off, he gave the master five minutes. He succeeded in finding three of his fallen men but could not find the other two. With his five minutes up the master was compelled to leave and watch as the bombs did their dirty work.

The master equipped with a pocket compass set a course for the French island of Vierge and they rowed and sailed for 10 miles in that direction. However, the Swedish steamer *Phyliss* picked them up and took them to Brest. The wounded were sent immediately to the Mariners Hospital where another of the men died of his injuries.

3/45: TORRIDAL. *Country:* Norwegian. *Date sunk:* 15/11/16. *Tons nett:* 367. *Tons gross:* 688. *Built:* –. *Type:* SS. *Rig:* –. *Owners:* Ingval Bjornebo of Christiansand. *Cargo:* 712 tons pig iron, 80 tons bunker coal, Middlesbrough for Hennebont. *Armed:* No. *Position:* 30 miles NE of Ushant Light (48 51 00N; 04 39 00W). *Master's name:* Abraham Abrahamsen. *Crew:* 14. *Crew nationality:* 11 Norwegians, 1 Dane, 1 Italian, 1 Swede.

BOUND for Hennebont in France the *Torridal* was making good progress until just after midnight on November 15, 1916. The wind was fresh with a heavy swell on the sea but the night was quite clear. Clear enough in fact for a watchman to make out the shape of a submarine's conning tower about two miles off on the port beam. The master was informed and at first he ordered that the ship be kept going as fast as possible – until a shell whistled over the ship's bow.

When the engines stopped a signal came from the submarine ordering the master to take his ship's papers over to the submarine. The first mate volunteered and with other crew members rowed over to the Germans. The commander studied the papers and without handing them back ordered some of his men to take the mate's boat over to the steamer.

They planted two bombs, one in number two hold and the other in the bunker. After helping themselves to various instruments the bombers informed the crew that they had five minutes to get clear. They then rowed back to the submarine, handing the boat back to the mate and his men.

Within a few minutes of the crew leaving *Torridal* the bombs exploded, and in just a few more minutes she had gone. The men set about rowing towards the nearest shore but were picked up by another Norwegian steamer *Theodor William*, who landed them at Brixham around 10.30 the same morning.

3/46: WESTLANDS. *Country:* British.
Date sunk: 23/11/17. *Tons nett:* 2001. *Tons gross:* 3112. *Built:* 1905. *Type:* SS. *Rig:* schooner. *Owners:* J.F. Wilson & Co, 61, Church St, West Hartlepool. *Cargo:* 4500 tons coal from Leith to Cherbourg. *Armed:* 1 x 12pd 12cwt Gun. *Position:* 10 miles N by W of Ile de Vierge Light House (48 48 00N; 04 37 30N). *Master's name:* Thomas Brown. *Crew:* 28. *Gunners:* Knott, No 215292; W. Corrin, No 1474D.

IT was said by the interviewing officer, with some justification, that the master of *Westlands* was a little hasty in leaving his ship after it had been torpedoed. After all, the steamer was armed with a rear deck gun and had two gunners aboard who were more than capable of firing it. It was felt by the authorities that an ideal opportunity had been missed to have opened fire on an enemy submarine which at one stage of the incident was only 200yds away from the steamer.

The torpedo fired by the German submarine *U-53* at 5am had struck the steamer between number one and two bulkheads but the damage was not very severe. Although she did begin to settle it didn't amount to much but the master ordered all hands to take to the boats and leave. They stayed close to the steamer to see what would happen to her and finding that she was holding up well, the master decided to go back on board and see if she could be saved after all.

Once back on board it became clear that she could probably limp into port somewhere or be beached but suddenly the enemy submarine appeared on the surface close by. Captain Brown immediately ordered the crew to take to the boats again perhaps forgetting that he had a large gun sitting aft doing nothing.

Once the crew were clear of *Westlands* the submarine moved in for the kill and pounded her with the deck gun. A few well placed shells just below the waterline was all it needed to complete the job, sending the steamer to the bottom at 7.35am.

3/47: ANNA. *Country:* Danish.
Date sunk: 13/5/17. *Tons nett:* –. *Tons gross:* 610. *Built:* –. *Type:* SV. *Rig:* barquentine. *Owners:* –.

Cargo: 663 tons logwood from Jamaica to Havre. *Armed:* No. *Position:* 53 miles SE of Lizard (49 12 00N; 04 26 00W). *Master's name:* Eric Christensen. *Crew:* 12. *Crew nationality:* 7 Danish, 2 Dutch, 2 Swedes, 1 Russian/Finn.

ANNA was basically a sitting duck as she almost drifted up the Channel making barely 3 knots in the very light wind. She was flying the Danish flag in the hope that it might afford her some immunity from attack, sometimes it worked but unfortunately for her, not this time. A German submarine suddenly appeared off her port quarter and caught her up with amazing speed. Several shells were sent whistling over her rigging and some crashed into her sides throwing up great splinters of wood. The master had no choice but to stop.

By the time the submarine was within hailing distance the crew had already rowed away from their ship in the lifeboat. A voice shouted across for them to approach the submarine and for the master to climb on board. Whilst the German commander questioned Captain Christensen about the details of his ship, three German sailors were being rowed over to the *Anna* by her crew to plant bombs. Several were hung on the outside of the ship and they rowed quickly back to the submarine. As the master rejoined his crew the bombs exploded and a few minutes later *Anna* was gone.

Her crew rowed for some time but were picked up by the trawler *Ocean* and taken to Spithead.

3/48: TAGUS. *Country:* British.
Date sunk: 6/9/16. *Tons nett:* 509. *Tons gross:* 937. *Built:* Dundee in 1898. *Type:* SS. *Rig:* schooner. *Owners:* Ellerman Lines Ltd, Water St, Liverpool. *Cargo:* 750 tons general from Oporto to London. *Armed:* No. *Position:* 40 miles ENE of Ushant (48 54 00N; 04 25 00W). *Master's name:* Thomas Quick Jarvis. *Crew:* 21. *Crew nationality:* 14 British, 5 Portuguese, 2 Russians, plus 2 passengers.

PASSING Ushant at a distance of four miles at 2.18am on September 6, 1916, the master ordered a course to be set to take the vessel towards the Casquets. She had been on that course for several hours when suddenly the sound of a shell made everyone look up. It whimpered overhead and splashed into the sea throwing up a spout of water. The master appeared on the bridge at once. Another shell whizzed by but nobody could make out where the firing came from. The answer lay towards the sun, where *UB-39* was hidden by the glare, about half a mile off on the starboard bow.

It was 8.20am and the master was faced with a big decision. Should he try and make a run for it and risk being shelled unmercifully or give up now to save any injuries? He chose the latter course and ordered the engines to be stopped. The submarine stopped shelling and waited as the boats were lowered. Half way through the operation two shells were fired high over the steamer to get them to hurry things along. A man on the submarine waved at the crew as they pulled clear, making it obvious that he wanted them to come to him. Both boats obeyed and drew alongside the enemy vessel.

One boat was emptied; the crew told to join their colleagues in the other boat. Five German sailors climbed in and rowed over to the *Tagus* to plant bombs. It didn't take them long to position them but they did spend some time looking for provisions. With the fuses lit they left her and made off back to their submarine.

The bombs had been placed expertly and at 9am they exploded. Two minutes later, *Tagus* was gone. The crew having got their second boat back were towed behind the submarine for some time. It wasn't until another steamer appeared on the horizon that they were slipped and left to their own devices. They were spotted later in the day by a lookout on the SS *Beira* which picked them up and handed them over to a patrol trawler. They were landed the next day at Dover.

3/49: EUMAEUS. *Country:* British.
Date sunk: 26/2/18. *Tons nett:* –. *Tons gross:* 6696. *Built:* 1913. *Type:* SS. *Rig:* Owners: A. Holt & Co. *Cargo:* 6000 tons general from Port Said to London. *Armed:* 1 x 4.7in quick fire gun. *Position:* 24 miles NNE from Ile de Vierge (49 01 30N; 04 22 00W). *Master's name:* –. *Crew:* 34.

EUMAEUS was in convoy when at 3am on February 26, 1918, she was struck by a torpedo from *U-55* on the port side in number five hold. She was a big ship and at first it was thought she would remain afloat. Most of the crew were transferred to one of the escort boats and she was taken in tow.

Just over three hours later, at 6.15am, *Eumaeus* displayed all the signs of sinking and the tow lines were cast off. The last of the crew were taken off and she sank moments later. All her company were safe and landed later at Falmouth.

3/50: BARBRO. *Country:* Norwegian.
Date sunk: 14/10/17. *Tons nett:* –. *Tons gross:* 2356. *Built:* –. *Type:* SS. *Rig:* –. *Owners:* –. *Cargo:* Coal, Tyne for Torre Annunziata. *Armed:* –. *Position:* 13 miles SE by E of Ile de Bâtz (48 57 00N; 04 10 00W). *Master's name:* –. *Crew:* –.

THE only reference to the sinking of the *Barbro* came from the Weekly Reports. The naval authorities at Brest reported that she had been torpedoed in the above position and that survivors had been landed. Nothing else is mentioned
Lloyd's gave her position as '13 miles NNW of the Ile de Bâtz.'

3/51: FREMONA. *Country:* British.
Date sunk: 31/7/17. *Tons nett:* 1926. *Tons gross:* 3027. *Built:* Dundee in 1887. *Type:* SS. *Rig:* schooner. *Owners:* Cairus Noble & Co, Arkenside House, Newcastle. *Cargo:* 3500 tons grain, flour & lumber, from Robert Reford & Co Ltd, Montreal to St Nazaire and Leith. *Armed:* 1 x 13pdr gun. *Position:* 12 miles NNW of Ile de Bas (48 56 00N; 04 08 00W). *Master's name:* Arthur William Melling. *Crew:* 42. *Gunners:* Charles Edward Hughes, L/Cpl. RMLI, No IR 85; A. Green, Pte. RFA, No 609 Chatham.

AFTER crossing the North Atlantic from Montreal, *Fremona* called into to St Nazaire to pick up the escort which would take her up the English Channel and from there further north to Leith in Scotland. She left with a convoy of seven ships protected by the French warship *Troublom*.

In the early hours of July 31, 1917, Gunner Charles Hughes, was on the gun platform aft accompanied by the first mate and two apprentices, John Mann and John Short. It was very dark and the shapes of the other ships could barely be seen. However, at one stage Gunner Hughes said that one of the convoy came very close to *Fremona* and had two bright lights showing. Apprentice John Short also saw it and thought that it was a Greek steamer but couldn't be sure. At 1.20am Gunner Hughes said he saw the wake of a torpedo streak towards the ship but it went wide and passed about 20yds in front. He watched carefully to see if he could spot any further torpedoes or better still the submarine itself but nothing appeared for some time. At 2.30am he spotted another torpedo which slammed into the port side of *Fremona* amidships. There was a huge explosion which penetrated right through to the engine room.

Within three minutes the *Fremona* had sank and 31 of the crew just managed to get into the starboard lifeboat, the port boat having been smashed to pieces by the force of the explosion. Eleven men were missing: the first, second and third mates, third engineer, apprentice, chief cook, third steward, two sailors and two firemen. The survivors were quickly picked up by their escort *Troublom*.

There was a lot of controversy afterwards regarding the vessel which was seen with two lights on. The Admiralty maintained that if the lights had not been showing it was very likely that the attack might not have occurred. There were still letters flying around in November 1917 about the incident but they never got to the bottom of it and the culprit wasn't found The torpedo, however, came from *UC-47*.

WORLD WAR ONE
CHANNEL WRECKS

—◆—

AREA FOUR

WRECK SITES IN AREA FOUR

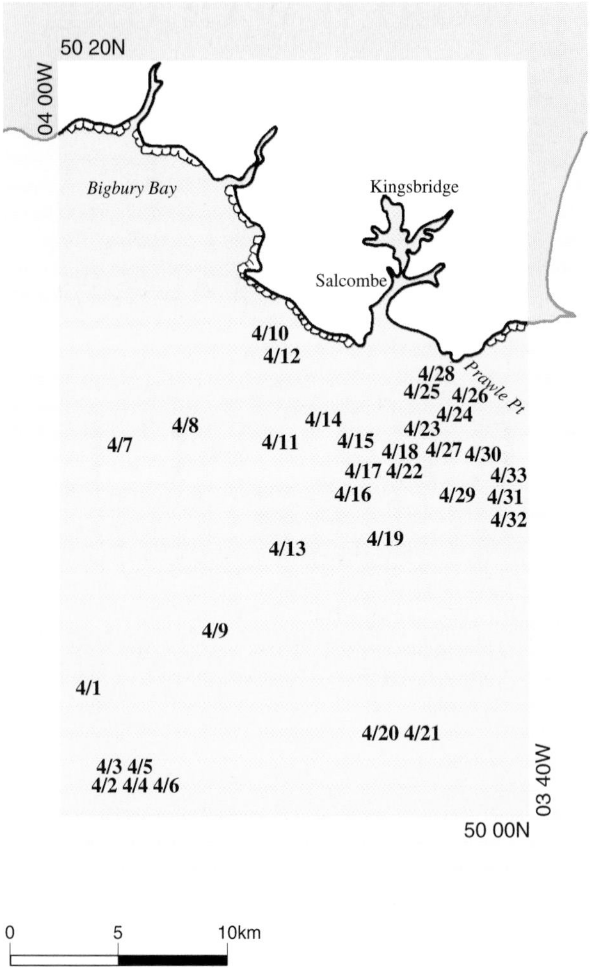

50 20N

04 00W

Bigbury Bay

Kingsbridge

Salcombe

Prawle Pt

4/10
4/12

4/28
4/25 4/26
4/24
4/8 4/14 4/23
4/7 4/11 4/15 4/18 4/27 4/30
4/17 4/22 4/33
4/16 4/29 4/31
4/32

4/13 4/19

4/9

4/1

03 40W

4/20 4/21

4/3 4/5
4/2 4/4 4/6

50 00N

0   5   10km

4/1: PURSUE. *Country:* British.
Date sunk: 28/4/17. *Tons nett:* 37. *Tons gross:* 50.
Built: Brixham in 1914. *Type:* FV. *Rig:* ketch.
Owners: Charles Scott, 12, Queens Rd, Brixham,
Devon. *Cargo:* None. *Armed:* No. *Position:* About
12 miles SW of Bolt Head *(50 03 00N;
03 59 00W)*. *Master's name:* Herman George
Gregory. *Crew:* 4.

PURSUE left Brixham on April 26, 1917, at 2.30pm
on the ebb tide and soon got into her usual area
south west of Bolt Head. The weather was fine and
clear with a light breeze blowing, perfect conditions
for trawling.

At 12.30pm on the 28th a submarine appeared
from nowhere. When it was about a mile off a shot
rang out and the boats jib disappeared in a mass of
splinters. The master ordered the fore sail to be
lowered and was no sooner done when another shell
struck the starboard bow just above the waterline.
The crew made for their boat. They shoved off and
drifted behind their ship only to have a third shell
fired directly at them which kicked up a spout of
water about 10yds off.

The submarine slowly came alongside the small
boat and ordered the crew to board. Four Germans
made three of the crew row them across to the
Pursue with three bombs. The bombs were placed
and the Germans went around the vessel helping
themselves to food and cooking utensils. Once back
on the submarine all eyes turned to the sailing vessel
which blew up within a few minutes and sank
immediately.

The submarine headed off to the east on the
surface and left the crew of the *Pursue* to row. They
were eventually picked up at 4.10pm by the patrol
vessel *Buffalo* and landed at Plymouth at 8pm. The
master was taken to Mount Wise to make his
deposition and it is interesting to note that he valued
his vessel at £1700.

4/2: MAYFLOWER. *Country:* British.
Date sunk: 24/3/17. *Tons nett:* 24. *Tons gross:* 38.
Built: Of wood at Lowestoft in 1898. *Type:* FV.
Rig: ketch. *Owners:* Lucy Ann Beck, Lowestoft.
Cargo: None. *Armed:* No. *Position:* 15 miles SE
of Eddystone (50 01 00N; 03 58 00W). *Master's
name:* Henry George Bydle. *Crew:* 3.

MAYFLOWER had been fishing for about six hours
and had her nets over the side. It was slow going as
she could only drift with the current, the wind
having died away to a flat calm. A submarine
surfaced just to the south-east and blew the fishing
vessel *H.C.G* to pieces. Mr Bydle ordered his men to
get their effects into the small boat and be ready to
abandon ship in a hurry.

As the submariners turned their attention to the
Mayflower the master gave the order and they pulled
away as fast as possible. However, the German

commander must have thought it was too fast and
a rifle shot zipped into the water close by them as a
signal to stop. They were in no position to argue
and made their way towards the enemy. The
Germans needed the use of their boat to plant bombs
on the ketch, which was soon done.

The submarine commander was in a hurry and
didn't even wait around to see the *Mayflower* sink.
Instead he sped across to another ketch, the *Qui
Vive*, and gave her the same treatment. *Mayflower's*
crew could only look on as first their ship sank and
then the *Qui Vive* joined it on the bottom.

The two crews joined forces and rowed for the
shore but it wasn't long before the special service
ship *Q12* picked them up and landed them safely at
Falmouth the next day.

4/3: QUI VIVE. *Country:* British.
Date sunk: 24/3/17. *Tons nett:* 22. *Tons gross:* –.
Built: Of wood at Brixham. *Type:* FV. *Rig:* Ketch.
Owners: –. *Cargo:* None. *Armed:* No. *Position:*
15 miles SE of Eddystone (50 01 20N;
03 58 00W). *Master's name:* T. Plumridge.
Crew: 4.

THE *Qui Vive* had drifted right into trouble as the
master first watched the *H.C.G* sink and then the
Mayflower. Captain Plumridge knew that shortly
his ship would become another entry in the
commander's logbook.

Then it was his turn and Captain Plumridge
ordered his men into the boat.

Within a few minutes it was all over and the men
rowed away to meet up with the crew of the
Mayflower.

4/4: H.C.G. *Country:* British.
Date sunk: 24/3/17. *Tons nett:* 24. *Tons gross:* 34.
Built: Of wood at Porthaven in 1907. *Type:* FV.
Rig: ketch. *Owners:* Henry Goodbourn, The
Anchorage, Grove Rd, Ramsgate. *Cargo:* one ton
of fresh fish. *Armed:* No. *Position:* 15 miles SE of
Eddystone (50 01 00N; 03 57 30W). *Master's
name:* George B. Evans, Ramsgate. *Crew:* 3.

LYING becalmed without a puff of wind was not
the ideal position to be in with an enemy submarine
lurking around. That was the unfortunate position
in which the master of *H.C.G* found himself. The
submarine surfaced about 300yds from the fishing
vessel and several sailors appeared from the conning
tower with rifles. They could have simply shot the
men on board the ketch but concentrated on giving
them a fright by sending bullets zipping through the
rigging or thudding into the hull. The master realised
that he didn't have a hope of getting away so
signalled to the submarine that he surrendered.

Obeying the German commander's instructions
the master and crew arrived alongside the

submarine. The master was ordered aboard whilst his crew were forced to row a bombing party back to their ship. As they arrived back at the submarine the bombs exploded sending *H.C.G* to the bottom.

The crew headed in the general direction of the shore. They rowed for four hours before being spotted by HMS *Q12* which took them on board and landed them at Falmouth the next day.

4/5: BOY WALTER. *Country:* British.
Date sunk: 24/3/17. *Tons nett:* –. *Tons gross:* 43. *Built:* Of wood at Yarmouth in 1909. *Type:* FV. *Rig:* ketch. *Owners:* Edward Beck, Whapload Rd, Lowestoft. *Cargo:* None. *Armed:* No. *Position:* 15 miles SE of Eddystone (50 01 20N; 03 57 35W). *Master's name:* James Henry Bryant. *Crew:* 5.

ALL Captain Bryant could do was look on as the enemy submarine casually worked it's way around the fishing fleet, sinking them one by one. He had every available sail up but there wasn't a breath of wind to fill them. Knowing it was only a matter of time before it was his turn he told his men to get their belongings together and put them in the boat ready to leave. It was a sensible move as sure enough the submarine's bows soon turned towards the *Boy Walter*.

There was no sense in risking being fired at so the master ordered his men to leave immediately and they rowed clear long before the submarine arrived. They were forced alongside and the master taken aboard whilst the boat was used to plant a bomb just below the ketch's waterline. It was well placed and she sank within seconds of the explosion.

The special service ship HMS *Q12* was of good service to the fishermen on this particular day. She already had several fishing crews on board who had suffered the same fate. *Boy Walter's* climbed aboard to join them and were landed at Falmouth the next day.

4/6: ENDEAVOUR. *Country:* British.
Date sunk: 24/3/17. *Tons nett:* 24. *Tons gross:* 35. *Built:* Of wood at Lowestoft in 1895. *Type:* FV. *Rig:* Ketch. *Owners:* B.F. Reynolds, 4 Herring Market, Lowestoft. *Cargo:* None. *Armed:* No. *Position:* 15 miles SE of Eddystone (50 01 00N; 03 57 00W). *Master's name:* Edward Reynolds. *Crew:* 4.

IT was Saturday afternoon and the master of *Endeavour* should have had half of his holds full of fish. It was doubly frustrating in that there was no wind which meant they were wallowing in the water. However, worse still, a German submarine had just sunk two of his colleagues a little to the south. He resigned himself to the fact that his ship was next. He planned to abandon the ship as soon as the submarine turned towards him.

It wasn't long before the German commander obliged and when about half a mile off, the crew of *Endeavour* pulled clear of their ship and rowed out to meet the approaching enemy. It was a carbon copy of the other attacks that day with German sailors being ordered to use the crew's boat to plant bombs aboard the fishermen. They returned to the submarine within a few minutes. In another few minutes the *Endeavour* had vanished leaving only a few pieces of wood on the surface to mark her grave.

Her crew should have at least been thankful that they had time to get their belongings together, usually these attacks left little time for such luxuries. However, it was not their day. When the patrol vessel found them about two hours later the boat had capsized throwing the master into the water together with all the crew's belongings. The master managed to cling to the boat and was hauled in but the rest of the gear joined their ship on the bottom.

4/7: STOCKFORCE. *Country:* British.
Date sunk: 30/7/18. *Tons nett:* –. *Tons gross:* 732. *Built:* –. *Type:* SS. *Rig:* Special service, Admiralty Q ship. *Owners:* –. *Cargo:* –. *Armed:* Yes. *Position:* 7 miles WSW of Bolt Head (50 10 00N; 03 57 30W). *Master's name:* Lieutenant Harold Auten. *Crew:* 44.

STOCKFORCE was a Q ship. To the eye she was just another merchant vessel, but in fact she was a well armed ship with guns hidden from view by special screens. She was also manned by naval personnel, well skilled in gunnery. Lieutenant Harold Auten, RNR, was the commanding officer and was first to give his report at the Court of Enquiry held at the Royal Navy Barracks, Devonport, on August 8, 1918.

The action started at 4.50pm on July 30, when the *Stockforce* was about 25 miles south-south-west of Start Point in position, 49 48 00N; 03 53 00W. Suddenly a torpedo was seen heading directly for the ship. The helm was immediately put over hard to port and the engines to full astern but it was too late. The torpedo crashed into the starboard side in number one hatch causing a tremendous explosion. Number one gun was put out of action and three men were injured, one of them trapped by the gun and unable to move. Huge showers of debris were sent flying, badly damaging the bridge and injuring four other men. A huge wall of water followed which battered the flaps screening number two gun but they held fast, which was to prove crucial later.

The bows of the *Stockforce* were in a terrible state but Lieutenant Auten ordered the abandon ship party away to keep up the ruse of being nothing more than a merchant ship. More than ever he wanted the enemy submarine to surface and come closer. The men obeyed instantly and went to their stations whilst the gunners kept their heads down ready for action. Reginald Starling, who was trapped under number one gun had to stay there.

As the abandon ship party pulled away from the stricken steamer the man in charge of the party, Lieutenant Louis Workman, although injured, signalled to his Captain that the submarine was ahead, on the surface about half a mile off. She remained still, no doubt many eyes peering through binoculars at the *Stockforce*, looking for anything suspicious. After 15 minutes she moved slowly towards the steamer, approaching her on the port side. Still the men on *Stockforce* remained hidden beside their guns.

Soon the U-boat was abeam of the port side, only 300yds off, directly in line with the two four inch guns hidden behind the screens. Captain Auten shouted the command and the screens fell away. The first shell passed just over the conning tower knocking off an aerial and periscope. The second was a direct hit in the centre of the conning tower, blowing part of it away and throwing a man high into the air. The next shot came from number two gun. This shell smashed into the submarine just below the remains of the conning tower, opening up a hole. Black smoke started to billow out of the submarine and her stern sank down raising her bow high into the air. She seemed in her death throws and presented an immobile target into which, Lieutenant Auten said, "We poured shell after shell until she sank stern first."

However, Lieutenant Auten still had the problem of saving the *Stockforce* which was listing heavily. He ordered full ahead on the engines and hoped he could make the nearest shore to beach her, but she sank at 9.15pm the same day. Two trawlers, *Lois* and *Kamu* had heard the gunfire and closed on the steamer just before she sank, and took off all the crew.

Many men from the *Stockforce* were decorated for their gallant efforts that day, and the highest award of all, the Victoria Cross, went to Lieutenant Harold Auten.

As well as the decorations the crew were awarded the maximum prize money of £1000 for sinking an enemy submarine. They were also granted 20 days leave each with the recommendation that on their return to duty they should be put together on a similar Q ship to continue their excellent work.

After all that, it is surprising to discover that *UB-98*, the submarine involved, managed to return to her base at Zeebrugge!

4/8: TASMANIA. *Country:* Italian.
Date sunk: 3/10/17. *Tons nett:* 2392. *Tons gross:* 3662. *Built:* 1900. *Type:* SS. *Rig:* schooner. *Owners:* Pittaluga of Genoa. *Cargo:* 5100 tons coal for Italian government. *Armed:* 1 x 76mm gun. *Position:* 8 miles W from Prawle Point (50 10 30N; 03 54 00W). *Master's name:* Emanuele Massone. *Crew:* 31.

Gunners: Salvermini Micile, Service No 89960; Alberto Castelleri, Service No 29340.

TASMANIA sailed from West Hartlepool and was bound for Ceivita Veccia. She had been given written orders from the Senior Naval Officer at Newcastle how to proceed down the west coast and was instructed to call in at Falmouth for further instructions.

The master complied with his instructions and was hugging the coast steering west by north making 8 knots when suddenly a lookout spotted the track of a torpedo very close to the ship. There was no time to take any evasive action. The torpedo tore into the ship on the port side by number two hold, completely destroying it along with the stokehold.

All the crew were safe apart from the master and chief engineer who were hurt when the lifeboat was thrown violently against the ship's side. They rowed for the shore but were eventually picked up by the SS *Lothbury*.

4/9: AIGLE. *Country:* French.
Date sunk: 26/4/17. *Tons nett:* –. *Tons gross:* 172. *Built:* –. *Type:* SV. *Rig:* ketch. *Owners:* Armatur Mossin en Gaz de Rennes. *Cargo:* 178 tons scrap steel, St. Malo for Briton Ferry. *Armed:* No. *Position:* 12 miles SW of Start Point (50 05 00N; 03 53 00W). *Master's name:* Francois Desbois. *Crew:* 9.

IT had been a pleasant trip across the Channel for the *Aigle* with the weather good, although the wind could have been a little stronger. At noon on Thursday April 26, 1917, the master confirmed through his binoculars that the point he could see ahead was indeed the Start as intended. Before putting his glasses down he turned them around the horizon out of sheer force of habit and was met with the alarming sight of an enemy submarine bearing down on him very rapidly.

A minute later the submarine opened fire. The first shot passed through the *Aigle's* rigging smashing up spars and sails in the process. It was a lucky shot for the next three shells all missed but they were close enough and the master ordered his crew to take to the two boats. Once close enough the German commander shouted for the master's boat to come alongside and he was taken on board for questioning. Whilst this was going on a bombing party borrowed his boat to plunder the *Aigle* of various bits and pieces such as, clocks, barometer, sextant, and as much food as they could carry. The bombs were set and they left very quickly. The fuses were short as the bombs exploded even before they arrived back at the submarine. Two minutes later, *Aigle* had gone.

The crew rowed towards the shore seeing the submarine several times on the way. At 6.30pm they saw it attack another vessel in the distance which turned out to be the fishing vessel *Boy Denis*. It shared the same fate as the *Aigle*. After seven hours of rowing they were picked up by the fishing smack *Gratitude* and taken to Brixham.

4/10: WREATHIER. *Country:* British. *Date sunk:* 3/12/17. *Tons nett:* 385. *Tons gross:* 852. *Built:* Stockton, Teeside in 1897. *Type:* SS. *Rig:* schooner. *Owners:* Allen Adams & Co Ltd, Southampton. *Cargo:* 886 tons coal from R.S. Dalgliesh, Newcastle to Jules Levee, Paris. *Armed:* 1 x 18pdr gun. *Position:* Prawle Point bearing E 3/4 mile/1 mile E from Bolt Head (50 13 00N; 03 51 00W). *Master's name:* Alfred Percey Read. *Crew:* 17. *Crew nationality:* 8 British, 1 Swede, 1 Russian, 7 Greeks. *Gunners:* Frank Smallshaw, Prov LS RNVR, ON No MZ 1536; Davey House, AB RNVR, ON No BZ 1509. *Casualties:* Robert George, chief engineer, (killed by explosion); Eli Walker, donkeyman, (killed by explosion); Davey House, gunner, (blown overboard, drowned).

THE loss of the *Wreathier* was noted in Admiralty records for the very bad behaviour of the crew.

After leaving Barry Dock she called into Falmouth for sailing instructions. On December 3, 1917, at 4.15pm she was struck by a torpedo on the starboard side in number three hold and began to sink rapidly. The master came on deck and his immediate thoughts were to try and beach his ship, but finding that the after deck was already underwater, decided that he had no choice but to abandon her. However, before he could give the order most of the foreign crew members had lowered the boats.

The master dashed back to the bridge and gave a succession of short blasts on the whistle to try and attract the attention of a patrol vessel about three miles away. He then telegraphed the engine room to cut the engines but got no reply, the crew by that time having deserted it.

The lowering of the boat on the port side was being supervised by the first mate and he joined the frightened crew as they pulled away from the ship. They started to make for the shore immediately but were eventually persuaded by the mate and a gunner to stop and look for others who might be in trouble.

The master joined the second mate at the starboard boat and tried to lower it. The ship was listing heavily. As the lifeboat touched the water, it was washed back towards the ship and cut in two by the davit pendant as the ship went down. Both men were sucked down by the ship but eventually surfaced and found a hatch cover to cling to. They were picked up by the other lifeboat. About 45 minutes later the patrol vessel *Mewslade* took them all aboard and landed them at Plymouth.

UB-35 was the submarine responsible.

4/11: LIVONIA. *Country:* British. *Date sunk:* 3/12/17. *Tons nett:* 1175. *Tons gross:* 1879. *Built:* Kiel in 1904. *Type:* SS. *Rig:* schooner. *Owners:* Managers: Lambert Bros Ltd, Cardiff & London. *Cargo:* 3000 tons iron ore, from Bilbao to Jarrow. *Armed:* 1 x 12pdr gun. *Position:* 15 miles E of Eddystone about 3 miles off the land (50 10 00N; 03 51 00W). *Master's name:* H.G. Orchard. *Crew:* 25. *Crew nationality:* 18 British, 1 Danish, 6 Arabs. *Gunners:* Sydney Benning; M. Wallie.

LIVONIA was formerly a Danish vessel. Out of 25 crew only two survived. The circumstances of the sinking were given to the authorities by those two survivors, Thomas Sinclair an AB, and John Henry Ryan, an ordinary seaman.

The ship left Falmouth and was going up Channel. Thomas Sinclair said that he was talking to the lookout on the forecastle head at 6.30pm when there was an enormous explosion on the port side. He said that the ship was broken in half and sank within 12 seconds. John Ryan gave a similar account and like Sinclair was lucky to be on deck, close to a lifebelt.

Both men found themselves in the water but in the darkness neither was aware of the other. They managed to find floating debris to cling to and Sinclair was picked up by the steamer *Northwick* and Ryan was found by a naval cruiser.

Shortly after the ship sank both men said that a submarine (*UB-35*) surfaced close by and then made off towards the east.

There is some discrepancy as to the position of this wreck. The official one is that she was sunk north-east of Start Point but that is the position given by *Northwick* when she picked up the survivor Sinclair. He had been in the water for eight hours so this position cannot be accurate. It is very probable that John Ryan's position is more accurate and is the one given. Another report states that she was sunk 15 miles east of Eddystone and a further report says she was more to the north-east of Start Point and this seems to be the more accurate.

4/12: MAINE. *Country:* British. *Date sunk:* 23/3/17. *Tons nett:* 2298. *Tons gross:* 3615. *Built:* At Glasgow in 1904. *Type:* SS. *Rig:* schooner. *Owners:* Atlantic Transport Co, 38, Leadenhall St, London. *Cargo:* 550 tons chalk & general, 50 tons cowhair/horsehair, fenugreek seeds, to Philadelphia. *Armed:* 1 x 4.7in gun. *Position:* About 1 mile from Bolt Head & Bolt Tail headlands (50 12 45N; 03 50 53W). *Master's name:* William Johnston. *Crew:* 43. *Crew nationality:* Mostly British but 1 Greek and some Russians & Norwegians. *Gunners:* Jno Ramsey; William Mackintosh.

THE weather was not particularly good as the *Maine*, formerly *Sierra Blanca*, slipped out of

London on March 21, 1917. It was raining and at times the rain turned to snow making visibility very poor indeed. The wind was strong and consequently the sea state rough. The master was on the bridge with the second mate and a helmsman, there was a lookout forward with a gunner at his station aft. The *Maine* was at full speed doing a steady nine knots and by 8am was about 13 miles south of Berry Head.

Looking through the periscope aboard the German submarine *UC-17,* Oberleutnant Ralph Wenninger watched the *Maine* carefully. At times she was in full view but occasionally she disappeared in a rain squall. The conditions were perfect for him to make his move and at 8.05am he released a torpedo with devastating effect.

On board the *Maine* there was a deafening explosion on the port side by number two hold and the hatches were blown open. Looking in the hold the crew could see it filling very rapidly with water. The master immediately sent an SOS on his radio and formed a plan in his mind there and then that he would attempt to beach his ship to the west of Start Point. The engines were kept at full ahead and the ship steered directly for the shore. At 8.45am the crew were forced to leave the stokehold and engine room due to the rising level of water and the engines gradually slowed down and finally stopped. *Maine* was in a bad way and at 9.30am Torpedo boat *99* came alongside her, followed by a British patrol boat. After assessing the situation both commanders decided they would try and tow her the rest of the way to the shore and promptly attached cables.

The two boats pulled her gradually towards Start Point but she was slowly getting lower in the water. At noon a tug arrived and took over the tow and began to make some good headway. By this time most of the crew had left the ship either in the port lifeboat or in the torpedo boat. The master, first mate, second mate, bosun and cook remained on board to assist with the towing lines as necessary. It was a good try but the situation grew more hopeless as the *Maine* settled down further by the minute. Soon, those that were left on board had to take to the gig and pull clear. They were picked up later by the yacht *Lorna* and stood by to watch their ship sink at 12.45pm.

Some time later there was a certain amount of controversy over the distance that the *Maine* had been from the shore. Subsequently, it was discovered that the master had been told to keep clear of a minefield. He was merely following orders.

Today the wreck of the *Maine* is owned by Torbay branch of the British Sub Aqua Club.

4/13: HAUGASTOL. *Country:* Norwegian.
Date sunk: 29/11/17. *Tons nett:* 1278. *Tons gross:* 2118. *Built:* 1896. *Type:* SS. *Rig:* –. *Owners:* Fearnley & Eger, Oslo. *Charterers:* Schneider & Co, Paris. *Cargo:* 2800 tons coal, Glasgow for Rouen. *Armed:* No. *Position:* Start Point bearing N by E ½ E 10-11 miles (50 07 00N; 03 50 00W). *Master's name:* Christofer Olsen. *Crew:* 20. *Crew nationality:* 15 Norwegian, 3 Danes, 2 Russian/Finns.

WHILST carrying out patrol duties off Start Point, Captain C.J. Locke, of the armed Trawler *Buffalo II*, heard a dull thud in the distance. He ordered his ship to approach some merchant ships ahead to see if one had been attacked but found all was well with them. One of the lookouts then shouted and said he could see a vessel in the distance taking on a strange shape. Through the binoculars the captain could see that it was a steamer with her stern high in the air. A moment later she was gone. At that moment a seaplane flew overhead and displayed the message, "ship sunk, follow me."

Haugastol had been attacked without any warning. The torpedo hit her on the port side between number one and two holds, sinking her eight minutes later.

Fortunately, there were no casualties and all the crew managed to get clear of the ship. The master reported that while they were in the boat the submarine headed for them in a menacing manner but quickly dived when the seaplane arrived.

Buffalo II picked up the crew and depth charged the area without result.

Another position for the wreck was given in Weekly Reports as 50 03 00N; 03 38 00W.

4/14: SKAALA. *Country:* Norwegian.
Date sunk: 26/12/17. *Tons nett:* –. *Tons gross:* 1129. *Built:* Bergen in 1906. *Type:* SS. *Rig:* schooner. *Owners:* Adolf H. Alvoosen, Bergen. Chartered by Hudson Bay Co. *Cargo:* 1515 tons coal briquettes from Port Talbot to Rouen. *Armed:* No. *Position:* 4 miles W of Prawle Point/1½ miles from land (50 10 54N; 03 49 06W). *Master's name:* Sven Tronstadt. *Crew:* 17. *Crew nationality:* 8 Norwegians, 1 Spaniard, 1 Chilean, 1 Cuban, 5 Swedes, 1 Dane.

AFTER calling in at Falmouth for orders *Skaala* left at 8am and continued on her journey up the Channel. The master's instructions were to hug the land as close as possible and this he was certainly doing when disaster struck. The weather was good, fine and clear, a light easterly breeze with a calm sea. She was about a mile and a half off the land making about 8 knots when at 2.45pm a huge explosion occurred on the starboard side. She had been struck by a torpedo from *UB-35* and so severe was the blast that the engine room immediately caught fire, killing the second engineer.

The master could see that his ship was sinking rapidly and ordered all the crew to make for the boats. However, a report came back to him that the starboard lifeboat had been smashed to pieces by the explosion leaving only the port boat serviceable. The master looked around for help, and saw another vessel about a mile ahead, a French steamer, but she forged away presumably avoiding trouble. All the men crammed into the port boat and pulled clear. Four minutes later the *Skaala* rolled over and sank.

Her crew didn't have to wait long for help. A destroyer turned up within 15 minutes to pick them up and search for the submarine responsible. The search proved fruitless and the men were landed later at Dartmouth.

4/15: NEWLYN. *Country:* British. *Date sunk:* 2/8/17. *Tons nett:* 2484. *Tons gross:* 4019. *Built:* 1913. *Type:* SS. *Rig:* schooner. *Owners:* Newcastle Steamship Co, Milburn House, Newcastle. *Cargo:* 6000 tons coal & coke. *Armed:* 1 x 12pdr 12cwt gun. *Position:* 2 miles S of Prawle Point (50 10 20N; 03 48 40W). *Master's name:* William Baker. *Crew:* 36. *Crew nationality:* 31 British, 1 Norwegian, 4 Swedish. *Gunners:* Thomas B. Quirk, Prov LS RNR No 5407; J.H. Day, AB RNVR No 1/321. *Casualties:* J.H. Day, second gunner; Mr Young, donkeyman; Mr Collins, fireman; Mr Brown, fireman.

THE SS *Newlyn* sailed from the port of South Shields on July 29, 1917, bound for Genoa, Italy. Just before her loss she was getting along nicely at nine knots. The master was on the bridge and he had four lookouts. The master didn't see it, but later it was learned that three of the crew caught a glimpse of a torpedo's wake very close to the ship. At 9.06am the torpedo, from *UB-31*, crashed into the stern of the ship causing a huge explosion which threw an enormous wave of water over the steamer. Such was the force of the explosion that part of the port lifeboat was hurled along the entire length of the deck. The second gunner, who was on watch, was assumed to have been blown overboard although nobody actually saw what happened to him. An indication of his fate was that a gold chain which he always wore around his neck, was discovered hanging over the stern.

The engine room was totally wrecked. The engines had been torn from their bed plates and the whole place was flooded. Two firemen and a donkeyman found themselves trapped by the rising water and their despairing faces could be seen under the deck grating. Two of them drowned. The third however, dived several times and eventually found a way out.

On deck, the crew ran to the starboard lifeboat and lowered it. By the time the master got there he found that the bosun had cut the boat's painter and was astern with only eight men in it. He cursed the bosun's stupidity and made for the jolly boat, managing to get it clear with 20 men. The rest of the crew took to the life rafts. The master thought he

was the last to leave but on looking back at his sinking ship he saw the gunlayer still on board. He shouted for him to jump which he did and the master picked him up. The boats were brought together and the men were distributed among them more evenly.

Soon, several patrol vessels arrived on the scene. Trawlers, *Lois*, *Agnes Wakefield*, *City of Carlisle*, *Max Pemberton* and also the Tug *Fortitude*, all started to search the area. The jolly boat under the command of the first mate was picked up by *Max Pemberton*. All the hands in the lifeboat were put aboard the *Lois*. The master called for volunteers to go back aboard but none were forth coming. He boarded the ship on his own by the stern and went forward where he joined a man named Green from the *Agnes Wakefield*. With Green's assistance a wire was got aboard from the *Lois* and they started to tow. However, *Lois* could not turn the ship and the wires snapped. The *Fortitude* came up and tried to pass a four inch wire hawser aboard but it was to big and awkward for two men to handle. The sea was by this time washing over the ship and the master decided that it was a hopeless situation. They left the ship just before it sank.

Mr Green was commended for his actions in assisting the master to try and save the ship. The Admiralty however, took a different view about the gunner, Leading Seaman Quirk. He had remained at his post until the ship had been abandoned and that was most praiseworthy, but they considered that he forfeited any merit he might have acquired in not volunteering to return to the vessel when called on by the master.

4/16: AMELIE. *Country:* Belgian. *Date sunk:* 13/11/17. *Tons Nett* 1135.: *Tons gross:* 1463. *Built:* Keil in 1883. *Type:* SS. *Rig:* –. *Owners:* Armement Adeppe, on government service. *Cargo:* In ballast, Harve for Cardiff. *Armed:* 1 x 15pdr gun aft & 1 x 37mm gun forward. *Position:* 7 miles SW of Start Point (50 08 45N; 03 47 45W). *Master's name:* Robert Diomede Godderis. *Crew:* 22. *Crew nationality:* 7 Belgian, 2 Argentine, 1 Japanese, 2 Dutch, 2 Danes, 1 Russian, 7 Spaniards. *Gunners:* Deridder; Anard De Brugne; C. Reve. *Casualties:* Deridder, gunner, Belgian; Wensel, second engineer, Dutch; Anderson, donkeyman, Dane; Ascenseo, cook, Spaniard; Poortinger, fireman, Dutch; Delgade, fireman, Spaniard.

WHEN Captain Godderis left Havre on November 12, 1917, the instructions he received from the French authorities were, according to the Admiralty, "rather lacking". They commented later that the instructions made no mention at all of the need for *Amelia* to zig-zag, and had she done so she might not have ended up on the seabed.

Bound for Cardiff, *Amelia* crossed the Channel in fine weather, the visibility was particularly good and the sea nice and smooth. These conditions alone should have made the master very aware of the danger of attack from German submarines.

The master reported that without any warning there was an enormous explosion caused by a torpedo hitting the ship amidships. The explosion was so violent that ship sank immediately leaving no time to even think about abandoning it. Sixteen of the crew found themselves floating in the water and managed to find bits of wreckage to cling to until picked up by a patrol vessel. Nobody had seen those that died and it was assumed they were below decks and unable to help themselves owing to the speed of the ship sinking.

4/17: NORTH SEA. *Country:* British. *Date sunk:* 31/10/17. *Tons nett:* 1089. *Tons gross:* 1711. *Built:* 1899. *Type:* SS. *Rig:* schooner. *Owners:* James Carnack & Co, Leith. *Cargo:* 2500 tons coal. *Armed:* 1 x 3in HA gun. *Position:* 3½ miles SSW of Bolt Head (50 09 00N; 03 47 00W). *Master's name:* George Donald Glennie. *Crew:* 25. *Crew nationality:* 21 British, 3 Swedes, 1 Russian/Finn. *Gunners:* William More, acting LS RNVR, No TZ 10166; William Haddick, AB RNVR, No TZ 10672; Patrick Shirley, AB RNVR, No CZ 8333. *Casualties:* C.B. Jorkstron, seaman, drowned.

THE master of the *Northsea* was obeying his instructions to the letter, making a zig-zag course and steering west half north. He had loaded at West Hartlepool and was en route to Pauillac, France.

At 12.30pm on October 31, 1917, his journey came to an abrupt end when a torpedo hit the port side of the ship. One of the gunners said that he had seen the wake of the torpedo before it had struck.

The ship began to list heavily almost immediately and the crew were ordered to take to the boats. As they pulled clear about five minutes later, the ship rolled over to port and sank. All the crew were saved with the exception of a Swedish seaman who had been ill for some days. He jumped overboard as the boats were being lowered and drowned before anyone could reach him.

Several miles away the patrol drifter *Vale Of Fruin* had been alerted to the plight of the *Northsea* by a passing Swedish steamer. She picked the crew up soon after and landed them at Millbay.

UB-65 was the submarine involved.

4/18: USKMOOR. *Country:* British. *Date sunk:* 5/3/18. *Tons nett:* 1977. *Tons gross:* 3189. *Built:* 1912. *Type:* SS. *Rig:* schooner. *Owners:* W. Runciman & Co, Newcastle. *Cargo:* Water ballast, Dunkirk for Barry. *Armed:* No. *Position:* 3 miles SW of Prawle Point (50 09 50N; 03 46 30W). *Master's name:* O.G. Owens. *Crew:* 32.

IN his brief report, Captain Owens, said that his ship was proceeding down the Channel heading for Barry Roads. At 6am on March 5, 1918, *Uskmoor* was struck by a torpedo on the starboard side just under the foremast. The ship took on water immediately and 10 minutes later she sank.

The crew managed to get clear in the boats and about two hours later they were picked up by HMS *Lysander* and taken to Dover.

UB-80 fired the torpedo.

4/19: NINA. *Country:* British. *Date sunk:* 2/8/17. *Tons nett:* –. *Tons gross:* 83. *Built:* –. *Type:* Hired Drifter. *Rig:* –. *Owners:* Admiralty. *Cargo:* –. *Armed:* Yes. *Position:* Prawle Point bearing NNE 5 miles (50 07 30N; 03 46 00W). *Master's name:* –. *Crew:* –.

SO far, the only information on this sinking comes from a snippet in Weekly Reports, which states: "at 10.30pm a G-type depth charge exploded on board the armed drifter 994, *Nina*, which vessel was employed on Hydrophone duty. As a result four deck hands were killed and six others injured. HMD *Morrison* took her in tow but soon after, fire broke out in the after part of the vessel. Following two further explosions she was cast adrift and sank at about 0.54am the next morning."

4/20: BOY DENIS. *Country:* British. *Date sunk:* 26/4/17. *Tons nett:* 41. *Tons gross:* 51. *Built:* Of wood at Brixham in 1907. *Type:* FV. *Rig:* Ketch. *Owners:* Emanuel Harris, Northview Rd, Brixham. *Cargo:* None. *Armed:* No. *Position:* 12 miles SSW of Start Point (50 02 00N; 03 46 00W). *Master's name:* Fred Rupert Tucker. *Crew:* 4.

THE fishing smack *Boy Denis* had been out in the fishing grounds for most of the day and had started to fill her hold with fresh fish. At 6.30pm she was on the port tack with her trawl out when a German submarine appeared out of nowhere and began to fire shells at her. Several whistled through the rigging. The crew took the hint and left their ship in the boat as quickly as they could.

The submarine was able to get alongside *Boy Denis* and a German crewman jumped aboard her. He was on her for several minutes no doubt helping himself to provisions. His leaving presents were two or three bombs which were effectively placed and sent the ship to the bottom instantly.

The crew by this time were well away and eventually met the fishing smack *Winnie* from Brixham which landed them later the same day.

4/21: FRISO. *Country:* Dutch. *Date sunk:* 16/5/17. *Tons nett:* 155. *Tons gross:* 171. *Built:* –. *Type:* SV. *Rig:* schooner.

Owners: –. *Cargo:* Pipe clay, Fowey for Amsterdam. *Armed:* –. *Position:* 12 miles SSW of Start (50 02 00N; 03 45 00W). *Master's name:* –.

THERE is just the briefest mention in Weekly Reports that this sinking happened, which notes: At 0800 *Frisco* from Rotterdam was sunk by a submarine. The crew were landed at Plymouth by a patrol vessel.

4/22: STANHOPE. *Country:* British.

Date sunk: 17/6/17. *Tons nett:* 1828. *Tons gross:* 2854. *Built:* Stockton in 1900. *Type:* SS. *Rig:* schooner. *Owners:* Letricheux & David, Swansea. *Cargo:* 4800 tons steel rails for the British Expeditionary Force, Dunkirk. *Armed:* 1 x Japanese 12pdr gun. *Position:* 6 miles SW of Start Point (50 09 00N; 03 45 00W). *Master's name:* Alfred James Harris. *Crew:* 26. *Crew nationality:* 18 British, 2 Russian, 2 Greeks, 1 Belgian, 1 Swede, 1 Cypriot, 1 Portuguese. *Casualties:* J.R. Richardson, first mate; Thomas Middleton, chief engineer; Arthur Morrell, second engineer; Jas Ashworth, third engineer; J. Trenchard, steward; Robert Petty, mess room steward, F. Morris, carpenter; E. Richardson, bosun; Alec Thompson, gunner, LS RNR; Jas Flynn, gunner, AB RNVR; Fred Ewes, Belgian, cook; G. Nelson, Russian, donkeyman; Mohamed Alee; F. Wetherell; R. Snowdon; G. Clark; R. Carter, seamen; X. Madri; Photo Chaniote; P. Anderson; Nicotan Johannes; Nick Souza; firemen.

THE last voyage of the *Stanhope* began from Barrow-in-Furness at 6.30 in the morning of June 14, 1917. She was headed for Dunkirk and her orders were to call into Falmouth for instructions. Having done that she left unescorted and followed the daylight route up Channel, close to the coast.

On Sunday 17th, she passed Plymouth at about three miles off. The master and the first mate were on the bridge with a helmsman at the wheel. A good lookout was being kept with one man on the forecastle head and another on the lower bridge. The ship's side lights were on but dimmed right down as there were a number of small sailing craft around. The engines were full ahead and she was making a steady eight and a half knots.

At 1am she was about midway between Start Point and Plymouth, some three miles off the land when it became hazy. The master decided to alter his course to bring his ship onto the night course and pass Start Point at about seven miles as per his instructions. At 1.40am the light on Start was seen on the port bow and the master went to the chart room to lay the bearing of the light onto his chart. As he put pencil to paper a terrific explosion occurred shaking the ship violently. Captain Harris immediately rushed to the bridge which was usually some thirty six feet above

the water level. Just as he made it he was instantly washed away as the ship sank from beneath his feet, just ten seconds after the explosion.

When he rose to the surface he called out to see if any of his crew had survived. Somebody replied and he swam around looking for something to cling to. He found one of the planks that he had stacked loose on the decks for just such an occasion. A few minutes later three of his crew joined him. These four men were the only survivors. They clung to their planks and the potato locker that had floated free and were eventually picked up by the patrol trawler *Earl Granard* which carried them to St Helens.

UB-31 was the submarine which sank her.

4/23: HMT NEWBRIDGE. *Country:* British.

Date sunk: 19/11/17. *Tons nett:* –. *Tons gross:* 228. *Built:* –. *Type:* Patrol Trawler. *Rig:* –. *Owners:* –. *Cargo:* –. *Armed:* Yes. *Position:* 2¹/₂ miles S of Prawle Point (50 10 00N; 03 45 00W). *Master's name:* –.

ONLY a brief mention exists on this incident, in Weekly Reports. It was noted that the patrol trawler 963 *Newbridge* was in collision with the SS *Macoris* and was taken in tow, but sank. A more thorough search of the records has failed to come up with any further information.

4/24: HAVBRIS. *Country:* Norwegian.

Date sunk: 5/7/17. *Tons nett:* –. *Tons gross:* 677. *Built:* –. *Type:* SS. *Rig:* –. *Owners:* Nils Nealde, chartered by Subbert Mottert, Paris. *Cargo:* 901 tons coal. *Armed:* No. *Position:* 5 miles SW of Start Point (50 10 00N; 03 44 30W). *Master's name:* Rasmus Wathne. *Crew:* 14. *Crew nationality:* 9 Norwegians, 4 Swedes, 1 Dutch.

BOUND for Honfleur, *Havbris* left Newport on July 3, 1917, called in at Cardiff and went from there to Falmouth. The master's route instructions were to keep close to the land during the day and seven miles off at night.

A good watch was being kept by the lookout on the bridge who had just noticed two drifters sweeping off the port bow. The ship was not zig-zagging as the master felt he was too close to the land. Maybe he should have been as suddenly a torpedo was spotted skimming along the water on the starboard quarter.

It was too late to do anything about it as it slammed into the starboard side, exploding with such violence that the stern of the ship was completely blown off.

The crew had just enough time to get clear before she sank. They were picked up at 11.55am by the patrol vessels *Young Henry* and *Leader* and landed safely at Plymouth.

4/25: RIVERSDALE. *Country:* British.
Date sunk: 18/12/17. *Tons nett:* 1785. *Tons gross:*
2805. *Built:* 1906. *Type:* SS. *Rig:* schooner.
Owners: R.E. Thompson, Maritime Buildings,
Sunderland. *Cargo:* 4000 tons coal for the Italian
State Railway. *Armed:* 1 x 12pdr 12cwt gun.
Position: 3/4 mile off Prawle Point (50 11 42N;
03 44 03W). *Master's name:* John Thorn Simpson.
Crew: 28. *Crew nationality:* 24 British, 1 French,
1 Swede, 1 Russian, 1 Dutch. *Gunners:* Corneleus
Simms, LS RNR, No ON 1319; Arthur Barber, OS
RNR, No ON A 6534 Chatham.

HAVING loaded her coal at Tyneside the *Riversdale*
sailed on December 12, 1917, bound for Savona,
Italy. Her journey was peaceful until she reached
Prawle Point.

One of the gunners, Corneleus Simms, thought
he spotted a periscope and promptly opened fire on
it with four shells. The periscope disappeared and
nothing more was seen of it. Shortly afterwards a
torpedo slammed into the port side of the steamer.
Number one hold took in water almost instantly.

Seeing that she was not filling too quickly the
master decided he would try and beach her. He
chose a small beach to the east of Gammon Head
called Elender Cove and made towards it at full
speed. After a few minutes he decided that she was
holding well and changed his plans to make for
Plymouth instead, turning her head to port. Almost
immediately the ship heeled over and started to fill
so it was back to the original plan to head for the
beach.

As she touched ground one of the stoves in the
forecastle must have been knocked over as flames
were soon leaping out of the portholes. To stop the
ship swinging broadside on to the beach anchors
were run out fore and aft but she wasn't holding.
Even when the Tug *Woonda* arrived and put a larger
cable on her, the force of the sea parted it and the
Riversdale swung onto the rocks.

She stayed in that position for several days whilst
salvage crews worked on her. Much of the coal was
thrown overboard and the holes in her hull plugged
where possible. Eventually she was refloated and
tugs started to tow her by the stern towards
Salcombe.The tow started at 6.15am on December
28, and all went well until she ran into a confused
swell and huge seas started to break over her. The
stricken steamer started to settle rapidly by the bows
and at 6.23am she gave a heave and went straight
down.

UB-31 was the submarine which torpedoed her.

4/26: LAERTES. *Country:* British. *Date sunk:*
1/8/17. *Tons nett:* –. *Tons gross:* 4541. *Built:*
1904. *Type:* SS. *Rig:* schooner. *Owners:* Ocean
Steamship Co, on government service. *Cargo:* In
ballast, Southampton to Montreal. *Armed:*
1 x 4.7in gun. *Position:* Prawle Point bearing NE

by N 1½ miles (50 10 45N; 03 43 30W).
Master's name: Fredrick Henry Towill. *Crew:* 55.
Crew nationality: 53 British, 2 Belgian. *Gunners:*
John Sheeham, RNR No C2183; Thomas Johnson,
RNR No A1322; Robert Watts, RNR No B1753.
Casualties: 14.

LEARTES received her sailing instructions as she
left Southampton on July 31, 1917. It was one of
the many lookouts who spotted a torpedo streaking
towards the ship. John Sheeham, a gunner, also saw
it and said it came in on the starboard side at right
angles to the ship. It struck the ship abreast of the
after hold and there followed a tremendous
explosion.

Within seconds the gun platform was awash
making it impossible to get forward and the after
well deck was completely below water. Two rafts
made of barrels and planks which had been stowed
on the after deck were soon afloat and various
members of the crew swam to them. One crew
member, Thomas Johnson, was knocked over by the
explosion and when he picked himself up found that
the port quarter boat was already afloat and
scrambled into it. But as the ship lurched over, the
boat was over turned. He surfaced a few moments
later and said that he saw another explosion on the
starboard side of the ship abreast of the engine room.
He was eventually helped into the upturned boat.

Another gunner, Robert Watts, was at the time
in his bunk and came rushing on deck. As he did so
the ship was in such an advanced state of sinking
that he had to jump straight into the water and swim
for a raft. He also says he saw a second explosion
and concluded that it was another torpedo. The first
torpedo demolished the stern, brought down the
main mast, flooded the engine room and blew the
hatches and derricks up. Only the fore part of the
ship remained above water. The second torpedo
from *UB-31* sank her completely.

The survivors were picked up by the drifter
Coulard Hill and eventually landed at Plymouth by
HMT *Bittern*.

4/27: GERMAN SUBMARINE (possible).
Country: German. *Date believed sunk:* 20/8/17.
Tons nett: –. *Tons gross:* –. *Built:* –. *Type:* –.
Armed: Yes. *Position:* 2½ miles S of Prawle Point
(50 09 30N; 03 43 30W). *Master's name:* –.

THIS "sinking" of an enemy submarine was reported
but not confirmed.

A submarine was seen to surface about 50yds on
the starboard bow of the patrol trawler *Lois*. *Lois*
immediately altered course with the intention of
ramming it. The U-boat dived. On reaching the
position a depth charge was thrown over and large
quantities of oil came to the surface. Another charge
was dropped and more oil came up. *Lois* then
dropped a sweep wire and cruised the area with a

single towed charge. The area was buoyed and watched.

The next day the position was swept again by trawlers *Lois* and *Warbler*. On four occasions the wires became fast in the same position as given. *Lois* dropped a depth charge with the intention of recovering some identifiable wreckage with no success.

No prize money was allocated.

4/28: BAYCHATTAN. *Country:* British. *Date sunk:* 11/10/17. *Tons nett:* 2417. *Tons gross:* 3758. *Built:* Glasgow in 1906. *Type:* SS. *Rig:* schooner. *Owners:* The Bay Steamship Co Ltd, 21, Old Broad St, London. *Cargo:* None. *Armed:* 1 x 13pdr quick fire Mk 5 gun. *Position:* ¹/₂ mile S of Prawle Point (50 11 30N; 03 43 10W). *Master's name:* Sydney Arthur Cornwell. *Crew:* 36. *Crew nationality:* 1 Norwegian, 1 Swede, 1 Portuguese, 1 American, 1 Russian, 31 British. *Gunners:* W.T. Richards, Prov LS RNR, No A3289; B.C. Holdsworth, Seaman RNVR, No B10064.

A NOTE in the documentation concerning the loss of this ship states that she was operating for the French government and she left Havre at 2pm on October 10, 1917. She crossed the Channel and then began to make her way down the coast towards Plymouth. Following her instructions she passed very close to Prawle Point and the master was on the bridge checking his ship's progress unaware that *UC-50* was lurking close by.

Suddenly the ship was rocked by a large explosion at her aft end. A torpedo had penetrated just behind number four hold and smashed the propeller shafts which instantly stopped the engines. Number four hold filled within three minutes and then started to spill into number three hold and the engine room, causing the vessel to settle rapidly by the stern. The master ordered the boats to be lowered and the crew to get clear but to stand by.

They watched from a safe distance as their ship sank lower and lower in the water. A patrol trawler arrived a little later and Captain Cornwell asked her commander if he would try and tow his stricken ship to shallow water. However, after assessing the damage to *Baychattan* the officer told the captain that any attempt at saving her would be pointless. He was proved correct as she sank very soon afterwards.

4/29: GERMAN SUBMARINE UC-51

Country: German *Date sunk:* 17/11/17. *Tons nett:* 420. *Tons gross:* 500. *Built:* Kiel in 1916. *Type:* UC-class minelayer. *Armed:* 7 torpedoes, 1 x 8.8cm deck-gun, 18 mines. *Position:* 4 miles S of Prawle Point (50 08 20N; 03 42 30W). *Master's name:* Oberleutnant Hans Galster. *Crew:* 26. *Crew nationality:* German.

AT 12.40pm on November 17, 1917, when trawler 951 *Lois* was 100yds east of the above position, a violent explosion occurred and a submarine was observed to be blown to the surface, turn over and sink. The explosion and sinking were so rapid that a full description of the submarine couldn't be obtained. *Lois* collected wreckage, consisting of several pieces of wood, one with a faint marking and one with pieces of human entrails on it, the top part of a sea boot marked with the name "Metzger". A chequered bed cover and a small piece of flannel shirting apparently of foreign make were also found in the oily water. At the time of the explosion a mine was observed to come to the surface a few yards from where the submarine sank, which trawler *Lois* exploded by gunfire.

On November 5 and 11, the Navy had laid 680 deep mines south of Start Point. At first it was thought that *UB-18* had been sunk, but Ewald Metzger was one of the crew of the mine-laying *UC-51*, and other checks confirmed that this was the minefield's victim. There were no survivors.

4/30: PERM. *Country:* Danish. *Date sunk:* 28/11/17. *Tons nett:* 675. *Tons gross:* 1112. *Built:* 1883. *Type:* SS. *Rig:* –. *Owners:* United Shipping Co, Copenhagen. *Cargo:* 642 tons coke, Cardiff to St. Malo. *Armed:* No. *Position:* 3 miles S of Prawle Point (50 09 30N; 03 41 00W). *Master's name:* Peter Clemment Henriksen. *Crew:* 20. *Crew nationality:* 11 Danes, 4 Norwegians, 3 Swedes, 2 Spanish.

ALTHOUGH the *Perm* was flying a Danish flag and had the marks of a neutral country along her sides, it made no difference to the commander of the German submarine that sank her.

She had left Falmouth earlier and was hugging the coast as instructed. She was making nine knots and had just altered course when a torpedo struck her in number four hold. The explosion was so violent that a big chunk of the after end of the ship was ripped off and the deckhouse was completely smashed.

The crew took to the boats and pulled clear as the ship sank leaving two men, the steward and the cabin boy, unaccounted for. The survivors were picked up by the patrol trawler *Darby* and taken to Dartmouth.

4/31: HAZELPARK. *Country:* British. *Date sunk:* 20/3/17. *Tons nett:* 1199. *Tons gross:* 1964. *Built:* At Grangemouth in 1916. *Type:* SS. *Rig:* schooner. *Owners:* J & J Denholm, The Sugar Exchange, Greenock. *Cargo:* 2900 tons coal from S. Shields to La Rochelle. *Armed:* Yes. *Position:* 5 miles S by W of Start Point (50 08 20N; 03 40 00W). *Master's name:* Malcolm Thomson. *Crew:* 24.

THERE was some confusion after the sinking of the *Hazelpark* about her position when she was struck by a torpedo from *UC-66*. The master gave his position as three and a half miles south by east of Start Point. But Lieutenant P. Nicholson RNR, commander of the patrol trawler *Maristo*, said that the position was very doubtful as several auxiliary patrol vessels were at that very spot waiting for a convoy at 9.45pm when the *Hazelpark* was sunk and that none of them saw anything of the sinking steamer. He argued that the position is much more likely to have been five miles south by west from the Start. It is his position that is recorded here.

Although it was a clear night when *Hazelpark* came to grief, the wind was strong and the sea somewhat choppy. The second mate was in charge of the bridge and the master had just stepped out of the chartroom when there was a huge explosion followed almost immediately by another. Both occurred on the port side, the second one blowing the hatch covers off and hurling coal many feet into the air. The steamer took on an immediate list to port and started to go down by the head.

The master ordered his crew clear. They did it but only just; the ship sank as the last boat pulled clear.

During the night the boats must have got separated as the master said later that he saw nothing of the submarine responsible, but the mate said that a submarine had approached his boat and a German officer had asked several questions about the *Hazelpark*. Both boats however were found by a patrol vessel around midnight and the crew landed at Devonport.

4/32: BOB. *Country:* Norwegian.
Date sunk: 29/11/17. *Tons nett:* 344. *Tons gross:* 678. *Built:* 1908. *Type:* SS. *Rig:* schooner. *Owners:* Fred Olsen & Co, Oslo. *Cargo:* 748 tons coal. *Armed:* No. *Position:* 8 miles SSE from Start Point/S 14 deg W 5 miles from Start (50 08 00N; 03 39 00W). *Master's name:* Carl August Fabricius. *Crew:* 14. *Crew nationality:* 8 Norwegians, 4 Swedes, 2 Spanish.

THE loss of the steamer *Bob* might well have been avoided. She was on her way to Rouen having left Falmouth the same day. At 10am a German submarine appeared on the surface about 1000yds off and started to shell her. The shots hit the ship every time and soon she was full of four inch holes.

The crew took to the boats and pulled clear but then the shelling suddenly stopped. The commander of the submarine, *UB-35,* had spotted a British destroyer and a patrol vessel approaching rapidly, and not wanting to tangle with them beat a hasty retreat. The crew of the *Bob* could have gone back to their ship as she was not at that stage showing any signs of sinking, but they continued to drift away until picked up by the patrol vessel *Lois*.

A little later it was discovered that in their haste to get away the crew had left behind the second engineer who was badly wounded and a female cook. *Lois* got alongside the steamer and with some difficulty got the injured man and the woman off, but the engineer died on the way to port.

Bob was still afloat and a wireless call was made for a tug. Volunteers had been sent to her from the destroyer and they managed to get some steam up in the engine room. Some progress was made but it was very slow indeed. However, when the tow was connected up things speeded up but so did the rate at which the ship took on water. Soon she had a list which got steadily worse and eventually *Bob* rolled over and sank.

As well as the dead engineer two others were lost, a steward who was killed by gunfire and a sailor who drowned.

The naval officers who were involved in the whole rescue were all of the opinion that had the crew of the *Bob* returned to their ship and worked on her quickly she could almost certainly have been saved. All the valves and cocks in the engine room were marked in Norwegian and it made life very difficult for the volunteer British crew.

4/33: GRELHAME. *Country:* British.
Date sunk: 30/8/17. *Tons nett:* 2363. *Tons gross:* 3740. *Built:* 1909. *Type:* SS. *Rig:* schooner. *Owners:* J.E. Gould & Co, Merthyr House, James St, Cardiff. *Cargo:* 6000 tons sugar. *Armed:* 1 x 4.7in gun. *Position:* 4 miles S of Start Point (50 09 00N; 03 39 00W). *Master's name:* Daniel J. Evans. *Crew:* 33. *Crew nationality:* 28 British, 4 Portuguese, 1 American. *Gunners:* W. Osment, PO, No 224268; J. Grimes, AB, RNR, No 4744; J. Sutherland, AB, RNR, No 7711.

GRELHAME was part of a convoy sailing up Channel on August 30, 1917. The naval vessel *P12* was in overall command of the convoy for the first half of the voyage and was then to be relieved by *P14*. Guarding the convoy were patrol boats *P29* and *P19*. *Grelhame* had originally sailed from Cuba and from there on to Norfolk, Virginia. Her orders were for Havre but to call in at Queenstown for instructions.

The story is taken from this point by the report of the commander of *P12*, H.E. Raymond who said that he was in command of the second division of the escort flotilla. At 3pm he was 27 miles southwest by south from Eddystone steering north, 87 degrees east at seven and a half knots. At 3.45pm he intercepted a radio message from *P13* who was in the area, reporting the sinking of the SS *Eastern Prince* about 12 miles ahead of him. He ordered an immediate alteration of course to steer north-north-east for Eddystone Light, zig-zagging at the fastest possible speed. When east of the Eddystone he turned the convoy to east-half-south to pass one mile from Prawle Point.

At 8.50pm, *Grelhame* was struck by a mine or torpedo. The convoy was steering a steady course although no order had been given to cease zig-zagging. The *Grelhame* was struck under the bridge on the port side and sank in four minutes. Captain Raymond immediately proceeded at full speed to pass under the stern of the *Grelhame* and tried to locate a possible submarine, at the same time ordering *P19* to stand by and pick up survivors. There was no sign of a submarine.

In Captain Raymond's opinion, as the *Grelhame* was the middle ship of three, she had probably been struck by a mine. He submitted that whereas, theoretically, convoying in line abreast order is the safer, in practice it is not adequate, mainly due to the inability of the merchant vessels to keep proper station. He advocated that in similar cases where there is an abundance of escorts, line ahead order would prove more satisfactory.

There was no loss of life from the sinking of the *Grelhame* but one man was reported missing. He was later found by the trawler *Zonia* and all were landed at Portsmouth.

In fact, *Grelhame* was torpedoed by *U-62*.

WORLD WAR ONE
CHANNEL WRECKS

◆

AREA FIVE

WRECK SITES IN AREA FIVE

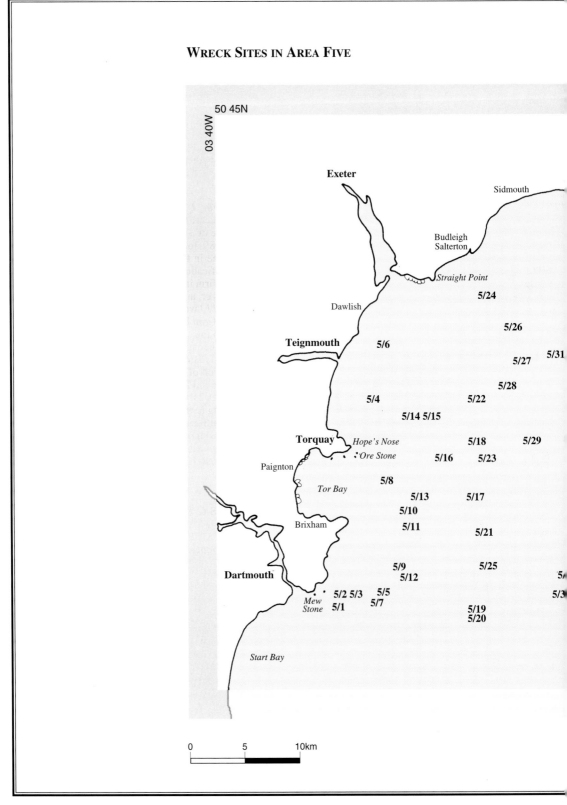

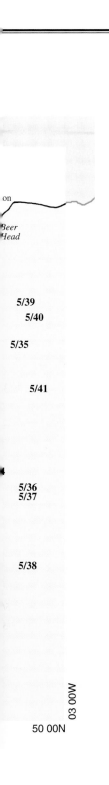

on

Beer
Head

5/39
5/40

5/35

5/41

5/36
5/37

5/38

03 00W

50 00N

5/1: GERMAN SUBMARINE UB-113

(probable). *Country:* German. *Date believed sunk:* 23/9/18. *Tons nett:* 510. *Tons gross:* 650. *Built:* 1918. *Type:* UB- class, Mark III. *Armed:* 10 torpedoes, 8.8cm deck-gun. *Position:* Off Dartmouth (50 19 57N; 03 29 54W). *Master's name:* Oberleutnant U. Pilzecker. *Crew:* 34. *Crew nationality:* German.

ALTHOUGH it is not certain that this is *UB-113*, the evidence would suggests that it is.

Her commander, Oberleutnant U. Pilzecker, sent a radio message to his home base on September 23 that he had just torpedoed the British steamer *Aldershot*. Nothing more was ever heard from him. On the same day a DH-6 seaplane reported dropping a 65 pound bomb on what he believed to be the periscope of a submarine in the same area.

In 1989 local divers found the remains of a submarine in this position and their description fits the specification of *UB-113*. More dives in the future may confirm it.

However, another source of information mentions that *UB-113* was captured and taken in tow and whilst en-route from Harwich to Falmouth the hawser broke. Owing to the sea conditions it proved difficult to get a line on her again so the hulk was ordered to be sunk. Apparently HMS *Kennet* did the sinking with gunfire.

A search of the log of HMS *Kennet* revealed the truth. She did indeed tow a submarine but on Sunday November 21, 1920. At 5.30pm her logs records that the towing hawser to the submarine broke when three miles south-east of Dodman Point Cornwall. She was considered a danger to navigation and consequently sunk by gunfire. The submarine in question however, was not *UB-113*, but *UB-118* which had surrendered to Britain at the end of the war.

5/2: ELSA. *Country:* Norwegian.

Date sunk: 24/1/18. *Tons nett:* 2304. *Tons gross:* 3581. *Built:* Newcastle in 1904. *Type:* SS. *Rig:* schooner. *Owners:* Norwegian African Australian Line, Oslo. *Cargo:* 2000 tons coal, 200 tons coke, 600 tons general. *Armed:* No. *Position:* Dartmouth Beacon bearing WNW 5 miles (50 20 00N; 03 29 30W). *Master's name:* Johannes Woxholt. *Crew:* 28. *Crew nationality:* 13 Norwegians, 3 Danes, 10 Swedes, 1 Dutch, 1 Portuguese, 1 Pilot.

ELSA had come a long way in the weeks before she was sunk. Her final journey began from Calcutta on August 28, 1917, and had taken her to Sierra Leone for an inspection. From there she joined a convoy at Dakar which escorted her to Falmouth. She left Falmouth on January 21, 1918, and was proceeding up the Channel when she received a message to proceed to Plymouth. The master promptly obeyed the instruction and remained there until the 24th. By then the master appears to have either ignored the authorities or became confused, as he seems to have left Plymouth without orders to do so.

Whatever the truth, the *Elsa* was torpedoed off Dartmouth by *UB-31*. She was struck on the starboard side about 35 feet aft of the engine room. Number five hold was completely destroyed and the hatch cover blown clean off. The steamer settled down by the stern immediately and the master ordered the crew away in the boats. She sank about 20 minutes later. All of the crew were picked up safely by two patrol launches and landed at Dartmouth.

The master had a keen eye for detail and made some extra notes on his position at the time of being torpedoed and wrote that the truncated pyramid on the hill on the east side of Dartmouth Harbour was bearing WNW five miles.

After this incident the Admiralty got quite irate about the fact that traffic had been suspended between Portland and Plymouth and said that the master of the *Elsa* should not have left Plymouth when he did.

5/3: HMT BENTON CASTLE. *Country:* British. *Date sunk:* 10/11/16. *Tons nett:* –. *Tons gross:* 283. *Built:* –.*Type:* Hired armed trawler. *Rig:* –. *Owners:* Admiralty. *Cargo:* –. *Armed:* Yes. *Position:* 4 miles S of Berry Head (50 20 00N; 03 28 30W). *Master's name:* –.

THE only useful document concerning this sinking is in the form of a letter written by the senior sweeper commander, Lieutenant Hamilton RN, commanding officer of HM trawler *Qumu*, who made his report of the incident the following day:

"I have the honour to report that in accordance with instructions I left Devonport at daylight on the 10th instant with minesweeping trawlers 128, 2972, 1972, 122, 760, 3281 for the purpose of sweeping a position where a floating mine had lately been reported by a steamer. On arriving at the position sweeps were being passed when three enemy mines were sighted. The mines were moored but were floating on the surface, it being nearly low water. They were sunk by rifle fire, there being too much sea to use guns, one mine detonating on reaching the bottom. As the conditions at the time were not favourable for sweeping with safety, it being low water and the weather misty at the time, I decided to wait for half flow before commencing operations.

"At 3.30pm the clearing of the channel was commenced by running a line on the leading marks on which line the mines had been laid. While towing on this line I regret to report that HMT *Benton Castle* struck a mine and was blown up. The attending trawlers took all steps to save life but only seven were saved, two of whom were dead and were brought in to Dartmouth. Medical assistance was obtained from the college with all speed and the remaining five were attended to by the surgeon. The mines were laid on a line with the leading marks of the harbour at a distance of two miles. The entrance has been swept

and no more mines have been found but another sweep will be required before declaring the port open.

"I wish to draw to your attention the conduct of skipper James William Smith and the ship's company of the HM trawler *Riskato* which was sweeping with *Benton Castle* when the latter was blown up. The seamanlike manner in which skipper Smith handled his vessel and the quickness of which the ship's company got out their boat to rescue survivors, was deserving of great credit and points to the fact that the discipline maintained on his vessel was good."

5/4: REAPER. *Country:* British. *Date sunk:* 21/2/18. *Tons nett:* –. *Tons gross:* 91. *Built:* –. *Type:* FV. *Rig:* Trawler. *Owners:* –. *Cargo:* –. *Armed:* –. *Position:* 2 miles NE from Teignmouth (50 30 30N; 03 27 00W). *Master's name:* –.

THE only information available on the sinking of the *Reaper* is that she struck a mine.

5/5: NERMA. *Country:* Danish. *Date sunk:* 20/8/17. *Tons nett:* 650. *Tons gross:* 689. *Built:* –. *Type:* SS. *Rig:* –. *Owners:* Marius Nielsien. *Charterers:* Souport Mattrart, Paris. *Cargo:* –. *Armed:* No. *Position:* 4 miles SSE from Berry Head (50 20 00N; 03 26 45W). *Master's name:* Soren Madsen. *Crew:* 14. *Crew nationality:* All Danish. *Casualties:* 2 deck officers, 2 engineers, 1 steward, 1 AB, 1 fireman

NERMA had her name in big letters painted along her sides to show that she was a Danish vessel. It was hoped that this might deter any attack from submarines but it was not to be. At noon when off Berry Head a torpedo crashed into her starboard side amidships, severely injuring the master and killing seven of the crew. The explosion was so severe that the ship sank almost immediately leaving no time for a boat to be launched. The survivors clung on to wreckage in the water.

The commanding officer of HMML 191 said that at 11.58am when on passage from Dartmouth to Torquay, he heard a heavy explosion and smoke rising on the skyline in a position about 3 miles to the south-south-east. He immediately made for the position and signalled ML214 to follow. In about two minutes the steamer disappeared and on reaching the spot the two patrol vessels found a mass of wreckage with survivors clinging to it. They both went in among the wreckage and picked up seven survivors.

5/6: GALICIA. *Country:* British. *Date sunk:* 12/5/17. *Tons nett:* 3778. *Tons gross:* 5922. *Built:* Newcastle in 1901. *Type:* SS. *Rig:*schooner. *Owners:* The Pacific Navigation Co, Liverpool. *Cargo:* Munitions and government

The *Galicia* – probably sailed into a German minefield off Teignmouth.

stores. *Armed:* 1 x 12pdr 12cwt gun. *Position:* 3 miles E of Teignmouth Pier (50 33 20N; 03 26 30W). Arthur William Pearce. *Master's name: Crew:* 53.

SAILING from London on May 11, 1917, *Galicia* made her way down the Channel heading for the warmer climate of Jamaica in the Caribbean. She arrived off Clerk Rock at Teignmouth at about 10am on the 12th May and was well on schedule. Fifteen minutes later a large explosion came from under the vessel below number one hold and she immediately started to sink by the head.

The master ordered the engines to be shut down and the crew to their boat stations whilst he assessed the situation. On a closer examination he could see all too clearly that his ship was sinking very rapidly and came to the conclusion that he was probably in the thick of a German minefield. He ordered the crew to take to the boats and get clear but to stay as close to the steamer as safety would allow. As the boats pulled clear another loud explosion occurred below number two and three holds and the bows of the ship immediately sank to the bottom. Within a few minutes the rest of the vessel followed.

The dazed crew couldn't believe the speed at which it all happened, but apart from a few receiving minor cuts and bruises they were all safe. The four boats headed for the shore but were soon taken in tow and landed at Teignmouth.

The records show that a salvage company called G. Shellabear & Son Ltd, Alton House, Mutley Plain, Plymouth, were awarded the contract to salvage

Galicia and they proceeded to remove what cargo they could. During their salvage they came across two packages of 12 and 14 pound shells. The gun had already been removed by navy divers. Then they discovered that there were row upon row of shells and through the Salvage Association the Admiralty were asked what they would like done with them. The Admiralty replied that if they could be removed they would pay eight shillings and five pence for each shell being half of the serviceable value. The rate of salvage agreed for the rest of the cargo was 20% of the value. The records however, do not state what the rest of the cargo was. However, subsequent letters show that the salvage contractors were unable to reach the bulk of the shells as they were stored away at the stem of the ship and could only be approached by the small side passages. It was therefore deemed uneconomical to recover them.

5/7: GERMAN SUBMARINE UC-49.
Country: German. *Date sunk:* 8/8/18. *Tons nett:* 420. *Tons gross:* 500. *Built:* 1916. *Type:* UC-class minelayer. *Armed:* 7 torpedoes, 8.8cm deck gun, 18 mines. *Position:* 4½ miles SSE of Berry Head (50 19 40N; 03 26 25W). *Master's name:* Oberleutnant H. Kukenthal. *Crew:* 26. *Crew nationality:* German.

A REPORT of this sinking was submitted by HMS *Onyx* at Torquay and says that the attack took place during the afternoon of August 8, 1918, approximately four miles east-south-east from the Mewstone, Devon.

In charge of the operations at sea was Lieutenant A.J. Baxter RNR, on board HMS *Opossum*, a torpedo boat-destroyer built in 1895.

At 12.10pm Dartmouth reported a steamer bearing south-east, five miles, stopped with steam escaping. *Opossum* and several motor launches closed to her assistance. They found that the SS *Portwood* had been torpedoed but was holding her own. A tug was sent for and the *Bramley Moore* and several motor launches got her safely into Dartmouth. With an enemy submarine on the loose three divisions of motor launches were ordered to take up a hydrophone watch on a line bearing north-west and south-east from Berry Head.

The whole operation was directed from *Opossum* and, she too, had her hydrophones out with an experienced man on listening watch. It was AB Sydney Herbert Iley, who reported that he could hear the motors of a submarine. Following his directions they tracked her for some time. Then the conning tower appeared above water. A lookout on ML *135* was the first to spot it and her gunners managed to fire two shells at it in 20 seconds before she dived. Both shells narrowly missing.

However, there were lots of patrol vessels around which immediately went into a well rehearsed routine and blanketed the area, or "browned" it (Navy slang), with depth charges. Soon a lot of oil came to the surface, but that was no real indication that the submarine had been hit. Many submarine commanders used to release oil when under attack to give the impression of being hit, then while the attackers concentrated on the oily area, the submarine could slip away.

But in this case there were other signs that the submarine had been hit. Huge volumes of air gouted to the surface bringing up small bits of wreckage. A light bulb was recovered bearing the mark "made in Vienna" and one vessel reported seeing a leather glove complete with it's owner's hand inside it!

The next day oil was still rising from the position and the yacht *Amy* made a thorough search of the area and managed to snag what was thought to be the submarine.

The £1000 prize money was shared among HMS *Opossum* and the motor launches No's 81, 85, 135, 191, 193, 195, 211, 281, 382, 385, 461, 467 and 490. Lieutenant Baxter of the *Opposum* was awarded the DSC and others were also decorated.

There were no survivors and the submarine was later confirmed as *UC-49*.

5/8: NORTHVILLE. *Country:* British. *Date sunk:* 17/2/18. *Tons nett:* 1552. *Tons gross:* 2472. *Built:* South Shields in 1897. *Type:* SS. *Rig:* schooner. *Owners:* Lowland SS Co, 3, Queen St, Newcastle. *Cargo:* 3400 tons steam coal, Newport to Dieppe. *Armed:* 1 x 12pdr 12cwt gun. *Position:* 3 miles NE of Berry Head (50 26 00N; 03 26 00W). *Master's name:* James Nicol Sim, 30, Cuba St, Sunderland. *Crew:* 26. *Crew nationality:* All British.

USING number four zig-zag pattern *Northville* headed up the Channel. At daylight on February 17, 1918, she passed Eddystone making eight knots. The weather was fine, the sea smooth and the visibility good.

When about three and a half miles south-east of Berry Head a lookout reported to the second mate that he could see a shiny object right ahead. The second mate lifted his binoculars and scanned the sea ahead but could see nothing. At the same moment the lookout added that it had disappeared and then a moment later reported that it had appeared again off the starboard bow. At first the lookout thought it was a motor launch but then recognised it as the conning tower of a submarine. Listening to the lookout's description the second mate immediately ordered the helmsman to bring the bows of the steamer to bear directly at the object. It was a wise move but alas made too late.

A few seconds later a torpedo hit the steamer on the starboard side aft. The hatch covers were blown off numbers three and four holds and the bulwarks completely smashed away. The master was soon on deck and after surveying the situation ordered the crew to muster at their respective lifeboats. He then asked the chief engineer if he would go down in the engine room and shut off the engines. He agreed without hesitation and wading through deep water he managed to shut everything down safely and got clear. This action later earned him a commendation.

The ship stopped, allowing the men to lower the boats safely and pull clear. A few moments later the *Northville* sank. In all only eight minutes had elapsed from the time of the explosion.

In the report that followed there was a certain amount of doubt cast on the second mate's actions by the naval authorities. They claimed that if he had indeed turned the *Northville's* bow directly at the submarine then the attack would have been thwarted.

The naval patrol vessels which later rendered assistance to the crew gave the position where the *Northville* sank as 50 25 00N; 03 23 00W.

The submarine involved was *UB-35*.

5/9: KENDAL CASTLE. *Country:* British. *Date sunk:* 15/9/18. *Tons nett:* 2438. *Tons gross:* 3885. *Built:* 1910. *Type:* SS. *Rig:* schooner. *Owners:* James Chambers & Co, King Street, Liverpool. *Cargo:* In ballast. *Armed:* Yes. *Position:* 4 miles SE of Berry Head (50 21 38N; 03 24 37W). *Master's name:* F.W. Hannah. *Crew:* 44.

THE *Kendal Castle* sailed from Havre on September 13, 1918, and crossed the Channel to Portland arriving there on the 15th. She left Portland the same day and headed down the Channel bound for Barry Roads.

At 2.05pm the vessel was about four miles off Berry Head. The second mate who was on the bridge suddenly spotted the track of a torpedo heading towards the port beam of the ship. He immediately ordered the helmsman to put the wheel hard to starboard but it was too late. The torpedo crashed into the side of the ship and blew out a huge hole.

The ship started to settle very rapidly and the crew rushed to the boats to try and get clear. They managed to lower two of them but had no time to unhook them from the falls before the steamer sank sending them all sprawling into the water.

Eighteen people perished either from the explosion or drowning: the master, first mate, second, third and fourth engineers, an apprentice, two gunners and ten Chinese crew. Twenty-six survivors were picked up by the patrol trawler *Tribune*, six Europeans and 20 Chinese, and were landed at Torquay.

Subsequent information has come to light to reveal that the submarine responsible for sinking the *Kendal Castle* was *UB-103*, commanded by Kapitanleutnant Paul Hundius, and he fired two torpedoes, both of which found their mark. It was the last kill for Hundius and *UB-103* as the next day he ran into the improved Dover Barrage and was blown to pieces.

5/10: SEVILLA. *Country:* Norwegian.
Date sunk: 25/4/18. *Tons nett:* 730. *Tons gross:* 1318. *Built:* Newcastle in 1913. *Type:* SS. *Rig:* schooner. *Owners:* Otto Thoresen, Oslo, Norway. *Cargo:* 1500 tons fruit, wine and general cargo, Valencia to Bergan. *Armed:* No. *Position:* 3 miles E by N of Berry Head (50 24 30N; 03 24 30W). *Master's name:* Anton Bang Neilsen. *Crew:* 22. *Crew nationality:* 20 Norwegians, 1 Swede, 1 Spaniard, 8 passengers.

Having arrived at Falmouth from Cadiz on April 25, 1918, *Sevilla* picked up her route instructions and continued up the Channel. She was flying the Norwegian flag and making 11 knots. Her route instructions required that she should make a zig-zag course but as it was very hazy and he could see some patrol trawlers ahead, the master decided it was unsafe to do so.

At 11.20am the steamer passed about one and a half miles off Berry Head and Captain Neilsen was about to alter course when a lookout shouted that he could see the track of a torpedo closing rapidly. There was no time to manoeuvre and the torpedo crashed into the side of the ship abreast of the boilers. A terrific explosion followed, the force of it killed one man in the engine room and injured two others.

The ship settled rapidly and the master gave the order to abandon ship. The last boat got clear in the nick of time as the steamer plunged to the bottom.

The patrol vessels *Lois* and *Iago* were swiftly on the scene and picked up the survivors, landing them at Torquay.

UB-80 was the submarine involved.

5/11: LEANORA. *Country:* British.
Date sunk: 21/2/18. *Tons nett:* 36. *Tons gross:* 37. *Built:* Of wood at Rye in 1897. *Type:* SV. *Rig:* ketch. *Owners:* Charles Richard Gander. *Cargo:* Fish. *Armed:* No. *Position:* 5 miles SE from Hopes Nose (50 23 30N; 03 24 30W). *Master's name:* Charles Richard Gander, Brixham. *Crew:* 4. *Crew nationality:* All British.

AS *Leanora* eased through the water with her trawl out the master was busy looking at an object about three miles out to the south-west. He looked more closely through the binoculars and saw that it was a small boat. Suspecting that it was a fellow fishing crew in trouble he immediately turned his ship towards it. Still looking around he then saw a fishing smack in the distance disappear, sink before his very eyes, revealing behind it an enemy submarine.

Realising that he now had to look after his own skin the master ordered the ship to bear away towards the land hoping that he could get close enough in time to put the German commander off the scent. It was a forlorn hope as several cracks were heard in the distance followed by the dull thuds as rifle bullets slapped into the sails. The small arms were soon replaced by the big stuff as a shell whimpered over the *Leanora's* bows, then another over her stern. The message was simple enough, 'Stop or else.'

The four men pulled clear of their ship as the submarine raced closer, rowing as fast as they could for fear of getting in the way of more shellfire. The German commander placed his vessel in a convenient position for his gunner who fired five more shells into the ketch, throwing up huge splinters of wood and opening great holes in her sides. Unable to withstand such an onslaught at close range the *Leanora* dropped like a stone.

The master decided to pull towards Exmouth, to go with the tide and wind, but was spotted by a lookout on the ship *Our Need* which carried them to shore.

5/12: BLEAMOOR. *Country:* British.
Date sunk: 27/11/17. *Tons nett:* 2400. *Tons gross:* 3755. *Built:* 1902. *Type:* SS. *Rig:* schooner. *Owners:* Bombay & Persia Steam Navigation Co, Bombay. *Cargo:* 5300 tons coal, Hull to Falmouth. *Armed:* 1 x 12pdr gun. *Position:* 4 miles SSE of Berry Head/4 miles SE ³/₄ S from Berry Head (50 21 00N; 03 24 00W). *Master's name:* Albert Blakey. *Crew:* 69. *Crew nationality:* 12 British plus 1 pilot, 57 Indians. *Gunners:* Peter Stickle, ON No 3988B; W. Astbury, ON No 1721 MZ Portsmouth.

BLEAMOOR left Hull on November 20, 1917, bound for Falmouth for orders. The very scant information available reports that at 12.30pm on the 27th she picked up a message on her radio that a steamer had been attacked off the Skerries Buoy and the master decided to play safe and head towards a patrol vessel for instructions.

As she altered course a torpedo hit the side of the ship in number one hold and she took in water rapidly. Within a few minutes she sank with the loss of eight men. The survivors were picked up by patrol boats and landed safely.

UB-80 was responsible for this sinking.

5/13: STRYN. *Country:* British.

Date sunk: 10/6/18. *Tons nett:* 1346. *Tons gross:* 2143. *Built:* 1901. *Type:* SS. *Rig:* schooner. *Owners:* Constantine & Duncan. *Cargo:* In ballast, Rouen to Barry Roads. *Armed:* 1 x 90mm gun. *Position:* 4-5 miles E from Berry Head/5-6 miles from shore (50 25 00N; 03 23 00W). *Master's name:* Magnus Johnston. *Crew:* 26. *Gunners:* F. Whiteley, LS RN No J52123; D. McCormack, RNR, No 1975A; D. Lang, AB RNR.

HAVING crossed the Channel from Rouen *Stryn* called into Portland and then continued her journey down towards Barry Roads. The weather was particularly nasty with a strong north-easterly wind and a rough sea. The steamer however, was making a steady seven and a half knots.

At 4.45am the good progress of the *Stryn* was violently halted as a torpedo slammed into her port side between the engine room and number four hold. Water poured into the engine room and on reaching one of the boilers, caused it to explode with such force that it killed five men.

The lifeboats were completely wrecked by the blast and the crew could only take to the rafts. The *Stryn* began to take on a steep list to port and the bows rose out of the water. The master ordered the gunner to fire a few shots to alert other ships of their plight. Gunner, Frank Whiteley ran to the gun and managed to fire off three rounds before he was forced to leave.

The *Stryn* sank in about 10 minutes, leaving the crew clinging to two rafts for 17 hours. Some of the men were swept off the rafts and the others hadn't enough strength to help them. The 18 survivors were later spotted by the escort trawlers *John Pascoe* and *Iceland*.

There was doubt cast by the naval authorities over the position given by the crew where the *Stryn* sank. If she had been in the position stated then she would have certainly been spotted by several minesweepers and three drifters which were working in that area at the time. The Navy concluded it was more likely that she was seven to nine miles south-east of Berry Head when she sank.

The submarine involved was *UB-80*.

5/14: PERONNE. *Country:* French.

Date sunk: 1/9/17. *Tons nett:* 3342. *Tons gross:* 3822. *Built:* 1882. *Type:* SS. *Rig:* schooner.

Owners: Compagnie Francaise Marine et Commerce, Paris. *Cargo:* Water ballast. *Armed:* 1 x French 90mm gun. Serial No 1. *Position:* 4 miles ENE of Hope's Nose (50 29 00N; 03 23 00W). *Master's name:* Emile Cazeils. *Crew:* 36. *Crew nationality:* 28 French, 8 Singelese. *Gunners:* Jessmeau, Moreneau, Chartis.

PERONNE'S last journey began at Havre on August 31, 1917, whilst bound for Barry Roads for orders. On making the UK coast the next morning, the weather worsened with a heavy sea and a strong wind from the south west.

When off Berry Head, the master was on the bridge when he spotted the white track of a torpedo speeding towards him. It was only about 150yds off and he had no time to take any evasive action. It struck the ship on the starboard quarter and blew a hole in her about 50ft long by 10ft deep. At the same time the master noticed a periscope close to his ship which circled around and then disappeared.

The *Peronne* was sinking rapidly. Suddenly there was an enormous groan and the after part of the ship fell away. The crew lowered two lifeboats and a raft and within five minutes were clear of the ship. Within another five minutes *Peronne* had sank.

Soon after, another steamer in the area, the SS *Landport* of Liverpool, picked the crew up and took them into Brixham.

The wreck of the *Peronne* was later declared a hazard to navigation with her mast showing 20ft above water.

Today the wreck is visited regularly by divers who report that the bows are reasonably intact but her stern is a mess. The 90mm gun fixed on her stern was laying on its side among twisted wreckage. On March 21, 1993, the gun was successfully salvaged by local divers and presented to the museum at Teignmouth.

UC-65 was the submarine which sank her.

5/15: BRETAGNE. *Country:* Norwegian.

Date sunk: 10/8/18. *Tons nett:* 860. *Tons gross:* 1382. *Built:* In Oslo in 1903. *Type:* SS. *Rig:* schooner. *Owners:* Fred Olsen Line. *Cargo:* 1888 tons coal, Barry to Rouen. *Armed:* 1 x 12pdr gun. *Position:* 7 miles NE of Berry Head (50 29 27N; 03 22 37W). *Master's name:* J.W. Johannesson.

THE sinking of the *Bretagne* was not directly as a result of enemy action and is not officially recorded as a war loss. But she was engaged in the Allies war effort.

She had loaded her cargo of coal at Barry Docks and was making her way up the Channel and eventually across to Rouen. A particularly thick fog had set in during the night and at dawn showed no sign of lifting. The master had doubled the lookouts and gingerly eased his ship along the coast.

Nobody on board saw or heard a thing but out of nowhere the French steamer *Renee Marthe* appeared and smashed into the starboard side of the *Bretagne*. As the French steamer eased away it was evident that she was badly damaged by the look of her crumpled bow. The *Bretagne* however was in a much worse state and took on water at an alarming rate. Her steering gear was smashed and she drifted helplessly, settling down by the stern.

Renee Martha made it safely to port under her own steam but *Bretagne* had to be taken in tow by the Drifters *Lerita* and *Expectant* and her crew, with the exception of the master and two men, were taken off. The three men tried in vain to free the crippled steamer's steering gear which was locked over to starboard and made towing virtually impossible. As the steamer settled down the master ordered his two men to give up and get clear. One did but the other decided he would fetch some personal possessions from his cabin. It was a fatal mistake for as he did so the *Bretagne* gave a lurch and sank, taking him with her.

The wreck today is owned by the Bristol Aerospace branch of the British Sub-Aqua Club. The position given is accurate and she has been positively identified by her bell.

5/16: IREX. *Country:* British.
Date sunk: 21/2/18. *Tons nett:* 16. *Tons gross:* 22. *Built:* Of wood at Brixham in 1887. *Type:* SV. *Rig:* Ketch. *Owners:* John Henry Skedgel. *Cargo:* Fish. *Armed:* No. *Position:* 5 miles E by S from Hopes Nose (50 27 00N; 03 21 00W). *Master's name:* John Henry Skedgel, Overgang, Brixham. *Crew:* 4. *Crew nationality:* All British.

TO say that *Irex* was a sitting duck was something of an understatement. Her trawl had snagged something large and refused to budge in spite of all the master's efforts. If he wanted to get his gear back in one piece the only option open to him was to wait until the tide turned. It was 3pm and the tide was due to turn within the hour. With a bit of time to spare the crew decided to go below, grab a bite to eat and a mug of tea and see what would happen when the tide shifted.

They never did get to clear the obstruction as no sooner had they gone below than rifle shots were heard. The master rushed up on deck. Looking to the south west he saw to his dismay a German submarine, about 500yds off, bearing down on him like an express train. He shouted to his men to get the boat out.

The German commander, Oberleutnant Gregor in *UB-33*, informed the master that he would require the use of his small boat for a while. Two German sailors ordered the crew to row them over to the *Irex* where they planted bombs on her forward keel. It was neatly done and the resulting explosion sent the fishing vessel quickly to the bottom.

As for her crew, they were left to row steadily to the shore but were saved going the whole distance by the passing ship *Florence*, which took them into Brixham.

5/17: GRELEEN. *Country:* British.
Date sunk: 22/9/17. *Tons nett:* –. *Tons gross:* 2286. *Built:* In 1894. *Type:* SS. *Rig:* schooner. *Owners:* J.C.Gould, Merthyr House, Cardiff. *Cargo:* Iron ore from Bilbao to Middlesborough. *Armed:* 1 x 12pdr gun. *Position:* 7 miles E by N from Berry Head (50 25 00N; 03 18 45W). *Master's name:* H. Clemants. *Crew:* 26. Plus one passenger

THE *Greleen*, previously known as *Ballater*, was not zig-zagging in the early hours of September 22, 1917. At 5.15am she was making a steady eight knots. The weather was fair although there was quite a strong swell from the west. Not zig-zagging may have been her undoing, as about half a mile off on her port beam was an enemy submarine (*UB-40*). By the time the watch keeper on the bridge spotted the periscope sticking up out of the water it was too late, the torpedo was already on its way. The helm was put hard to port in an attempt to swing the side of the ship out of the torpedo's path but she didn't respond quickly enough.

The explosion of the torpedo opened up such a large hole in her side that she sank almost immediately. Only eight people managed to get clear of the vessel before she went down, some jumped for their lives whilst others just found themselves in the water. However, others were not so lucky and the master, 17 crew and one passenger were killed.

Seven of the survivors managed to find an upturned boat and clung to it. The second mate said that at the time there were two steamers on his starboard side and on seeing the *Greleen* go down, they turned to the west and fled. To him it seemed a heartless thing to do, but their masters were only acting on Admiralty instructions, to get the hell out of it or join the victim on the bottom. For over four hours the men clung to the boat, cold and tired, but were eventually spotted by the Norwegian steamer *Bob*. She took them aboard and looked after them very well, landing them all at Torquay later in the day.

Having been alerted to the sinking of the *Greleen* several naval vessels were sent to investigate. HMS *Bittern* was soon in the area and located much of the wreckage from the sinking. Every piece they found was carefully checked for any form of life and this paid off when they found the chief engineer in a wrecked lifeboat, cold but very much alive.

The steamer's owners later wrote to the Admiralty saying that after talking to the survivors, they felt that the naval authorities could have acted much sooner and maybe have saved more lives. The Admiralty asked the Senior Naval Officer at Torquay for his views on the accusation. He said that he was informed by a passing Norwegian steamer that a vessel had been sunk. He immediately ordered several vessels to go to the area and they went as fast as they possibly could.

The Admiralty pointed out this fact to the owners and also added that the vessel was not zig-zagging when it should have been, but as the master was lost there was no point in taking the matter further.

5/18: LORD STEWART. *Country:* British. *Date sunk:* 16/9/18. *Tons nett:* 895. *Tons gross:* 1445. *Built:* Sunderland in 1905. *Type:* SS. *Rig:* schooner. *Owners:* David N. Grimes, Seaham Harbour. *Cargo:* In ballast, Cherbourg to Barry. *Armed:* 1 x 12pdr & 1 x Lewis guns. *Position:* Hopes Nose bearing E $^1/_2$ N $6^1/_2$ miles (50 28 00N; 03 18 35W). *Master's name:* James Edward Hardy. *Crew:* 21. *Crew nationality:* 19 British, 1 Swede, 1 Spaniard. *Gunners names:* H. Farquhar, No 7073A; H. Biles, No 1043WZ.

THE commanding officer of the third division naval patrol spotted the *Lord Stewart* heading down the Channel on a north easterly course. He ordered the other two patrol vessels to join him and escort the steamer as there were reports of submarine activity in the area. With three patrol vessels around the steamer she should have been safe, but she wasn't.

All went well until she reached the west end of Lyme Bay at 8.05pm on September 16, 1918, when a torpedo slammed into her port side forward, well below the waterline. The damage was severe and it was obvious she would sink quickly. The master ordered the crew to take to the boats and they all got clear with the exception of one man, a Spanish seaman, who was drowned.

As the steamer rolled over and sank four minutes later, Lieutenant Cassidy of *ML 135*, immediately made for the position where he judged the submarine to be and dropped four depth charges, but without result.

Meanwhile the crew were picked up by the other patrol vessels and later landed at Torquay.

The submarine involved was *UB-104,*

5/19: DAY SPRING. *Country:* British. *Date sunk:* 4/1/18. *Tons nett:* 35. *Tons gross:* 50. *Built:* Of wood at Brixham in 1903. *Type:* SV. *Rig:* ketch. *Owners:* John Kennar, Brixham. *Cargo:* –. *Armed:* No. *Position:* 8 miles SE from Berry Head (50 19 36N; 03 18 18W). *Master's name:* George Kennar. *Crew:* 4.

THE wind had dropped leaving the *Day Spring* with all sail up moving very slowly through the water. The trawl was at the ready in case the wind got fresher but in the event was never to be used again. The Second Hand, Harry Phillips, had heard something very much like gunfire and called the skipper. It was very poor visibility with patchy fog and nothing could be seen in the direction from which the noise was coming. Captain Kennar knew that something unpleasant was about to happen and dashed below to destroy his secret papers. He also gathered up some food, clothing and instruments and made his way back on deck.

His worst fears were confirmed when a German submarine appeared out of the fog about 50yds off. He shouted for his men to take to the boat which was

allowed to drift astern of their ship. The submarine made a pass around the men in the boat and pulled alongside *Day Spring*. A few minutes after they left, a loud explosion was heard. By this time they could not see the ship through the fog but had no doubts from the violence of the explosion that their ship had gone to the bottom.

In his deposition to the authorities, the master stated that as they rowed to windward they caught sight of the submarine on two occasions and both times they noticed that it was flashing morse signals from the conning tower. Whether this was some pre-arranged meeting signal with other submarines in the area was not known. The men in the boat were picked up by the *Rosebud,* a ship from their own port, which soon had them back home in Brixham.

5/20: GRATITUDE. *Country:* British. *Date sunk:* 4/1/18. *Tons nett:* 40. *Tons gross:* 49. *Built:* Of wood at Brixham in 1895. *Type:* SV. *Rig:* ketch. *Owners:* Albert Stokes Gempton, Bellevue Terrace, Ranscombe. *Cargo:* –. *Armed:* No. *Position:* 8 miles SE by E from Berry Head (50 19 36N; 03 18 18W). *Master's name:* Albert Stokes Gempton. *Crew:* 4.

WHEN the enemy submarine appeared so close to the *Gratitude*, there was little the master and crew could do about it. They were only making about two and a half knots at best so had no chance of escaping the fast and powerful vessel that stood only 400yds off the starboard beam. Four rifle shots cracked off across the gap between them, the bullets thudding through the sails above.

As the lifeboat left the *Gratitude* with all the crew on board the submarine drew up to meet them. The commander appeared at the side and asked the master a series of questions.

"Are you armed?"

"No," he replied.

"Are any of the fishing vessels in the fleet armed?"

"I don't know."

"Are there any armed cruisers in the vicinity?"

The master hesitated before replying,"It is too thick to see."

The commander strode off to talk to some of his officers. He was obviously worried about something. Maybe he suspected a trap with all the fishing vessels around, maybe one of them was a British Q ship, an armed vessel in disguise to lure hungry U-boats to their doom. The commander returned after 10 minutes and said to the master, "Go home in your rowing boat, I am going to sink your ship and as many others as I can."

The crew of the *Gratitude* rowed off to windward and watched as the submarine went alongside their ship. They saw the sails come down with the exception of the topsail. About 15 minutes later two explosions boomed out in the distance and *Gratitude's* topsail slowly sank down in the water before disappearing altogether.

There was nothing else for it but to row which the crew did with vigour to keep themselves warm. They spotted a fishing smack in the distance and decided to head for it. The *Boy Claud* of Lowestoft took them to Brixham.

5/21: HMD SILVERY HARVEST.
Country: British. *Date sunk:* 16/5/18. *Tons nett:* –.
Tons gross: 86. *Built:* –. *Type:* Patrol drifter. *Rig:* –.
Owners: Admiralty. *Cargo:* –. *Armed:* Yes.
Position: 7 miles E by N of Berry Head (50 23 00N; 03 18 00W). *Master's name:* –.

THERE is only the briefest of mentions in the records about the loss of the drifter *Silvery Harvest*. It notes that *Silvery Harvest* was one of three drifters acting as escorts for the returning Brixham fishing fleet. It was around 2am on May 16, 1918, and *Silvery Harvest* was showing no lights when she was rammed and sunk by the French SS *Picardie*.

5/22: GEFION. *Country:* British.
Date sunk: 25/10/17. *Tons nett:* 671. *Tons gross:* 1123. *Built:* Bergen, Norway in 1914.
Type: SS. *Rig:* schooner. *Owners:* Admiralty, managed by Mordey Jones & Co, Newport. *Cargo:* 1600 tons coal from The Federal Coal Co of Penarth to Honfleur, France. *Armed:* No. *Position:* 10 miles NE of Berry Head (50 30 00N; 03 18 00W).
Master's name: James E. Minto. *Crew:* 16. *Crew nationality:* 10 British, 2 Greeks, 1 Portuguese, 1 Dane, 1 Italian, 1 French.

IT was in awful weather that the *Gefion* came to grief off the Devon coast. The wind was strong with continual rain showers and squalls. She had called into Falmouth for instructions and was continuing her voyage up the coast making a steady 10 knots in spite of the rough sea.

The chief mate had the watch and was on the bridge keeping a sharp look out when he saw a torpedo approaching at an angle of 20 degrees to the beam on the port side. He immediately put the helm hard to port and the *Gefion's* head began to respond. However, it was just too late as the torpedo smashed into number two hold about eight feet below the water line, blowing a huge hole in her side.

The ship began to settle rapidly and the crew made for the starboard lifeboat as the port boat was smashed to pieces by the explosion. Nine of them managed to get away but the remainder just floated in the water as the ship sank from beneath them. Five men were found and picked up, but the master and a donkeyman were missing.

All the survivors were eventually picked up by the passing fishing smack *Rosebud* and landed safely at Brixham.

UB-40 was the submarine concerned.

5/23: GLOCLIFFE. *Country:* British.
Date sunk: 19/8/17. *Tons nett:* 1333. *Tons gross:* 2211. *Built:* 1915. *Type:* SS. *Rig:* schooner.
Owners: Humphries (Cardiff) Ltd. *Charterers:* Globe shipping Co. *Cargo:* 3300 tons coal. *Armed:* 1 x 12pdr 12cwt gun. *Position:* 9 miles WSW of Berry Head (50 27 00N; 03 17 00W). *Master's name:* R.T. Evans, 42, Victoria Park Rd West, Cardiff. *Crew:* 22. *Crew nationality:* 10 British, 1 Greek, 6 Arabs, 5 Russians. *Gunners:* E. Messenger, Chatham; J. Caddick.

GLOCLIFFE sailed from Cardiff on August 17, 1917, bound for Southampton. On reaching Falmouth the master adopted a zig-zag course up the Channel at nine knots. On passing Start Point the weather became thick with heavy showers and mist, and the master decided that it wasn't safe to continue zig-zagging. He also felt that he was too close to the land and altered the course away towards Beer Head.

Oberleutnant Howaldt in *UB-40* must have smiled as he watched yet another steamer target herself. The torpedo was released. The first anyone knew of it on the *Glocliffe* was when one of the crew spotted the wake about 150 feet away and screamed a warning to the bridge. The helm was put hard over but it was far too late and the torpedo struck the ship amidships on the starboard side in the stokehold killing two men. The rest of the crew got clear of their ship within a few minutes and only moments later at 5.25pm, the *Glocliffe* sank. They were later picked up by the armed trawler *Tribune* and landed at Torquay.

5/24: JOHN W. PEARN. *Country:* British.
Date sunk: 1/5/17. *Tons nett:* 68. *Tons gross:* 75.
Built: Of wood at Shoreham in 1874. *Type:* SV.
Rig: schooner. *Owners:* Kristian Andersen, Port Madoc, Carnarvon. *Cargo:* None. *Armed:* No.
Position: 40 miles SSE of Start Point (50 36 00N; 03 17 00W). *Master's name:* Kristian Andersen.
Crew: 3.

IT was a bright moonlit night on May 1, 1917, too bright in fact, allowing sailing vessels with all their canvas up to be spotted easily by marauding German submarines. Because of the conditions the master had extra lookouts posted and hoped he could spot trouble in advance. His hopes were in vain as, at 10pm, a shell came whistling towards the *Pearn* and threw up a spout of water about 50yds off the port side. Another shot followed which went equally as wide, before the master saw a big German submarine about half a mile off.

Having destroyed his confidential papers the master ordered his men to get the boat ready and leave as soon as the way was off the ship. Still the shells kept coming and some of them were getting perilously close. They were well clear when voices called from the submarine for them to head towards it. The commander wanted to know the name and details of the ship before he sank her. A few well placed bombs planted by three German sailors did the trick and at 10.30pm she sank almost as they exploded.

The crew of the *John W. Pearn* started to pull towards the British coast and the master fixed a course that he reckoned would get them somewhere handy to Plymouth. He stated that after the submarine left them it headed off towards two other vessels, one of which he thought was French and the other British. He saw flashes of gunfire in the dark and heard several loud explosions. He assumed that the two ships had probably shared the same fate as his own.

Pearn's men had to spend the night at sea, rowing to keep themselves warm. The next morning they were found by armed drifters and taken to Millbay.

5/25: ROTA. *Country:* British. *Date sunk:* 22/7/17. *Tons nett:* 1152. *Tons gross:* 2171. *Built:* Glasgow in 1915. *Type:* SS. *Rig:* schooner. *Owners:* Furness Withy & Co, Furness House, Billiter St, London. *Cargo:* 3700 tons iron ore. *Armed:* 1 x 15pdr gun. *Position:* 6 miles E from Berry Head (50 22 30N; 03 16 00W). *Master's name:* A.F. Thistlethwaite. *Crew:* 32. *Gunners:* R. Curtis, RN, Chatham; J.G. Ricketts, RN, No X1834 Chatham.

UPON leaving Benisaf, North Africa, on July 17, 1917, *Rota's* instructions were to proceed to Falmouth for orders and from there to Middlesbrough. She left Falmouth on the morning of July 22, and proceeded on her course steering north-east by north making about 10.5 knots. The first mate was on the bridge and the weather was clear with a light breeze. In his statement he said:

"When about six or seven miles east by south of Berry Head, I was on the bridge and suddenly saw the wake of a torpedo about 20yds off the starboard side. I immediately ordered the helm hard to port but before the ship could respond the torpedo struck us abreast of the engine room making a great breach in the starboard side. She immediately filled with water and sank in about two or three minutes. We had just time to get the port lifeboat over the side and 21 hands managed to get into it. When the ship had disappeared I rowed around and succeeded in picking up six men from the water. The remaining five, the master, two firemen, one donkeyman and the second steward all went down with the ship.

"I continued cruising round where the ship sank until 9pm when we were picked up by H.M. Motor Launch *214* which towed us into Torquay where I handed over the boat to the Lloyds agent."

UB-40- was the submarine which sank her.

5/26: COMMANDER. *Country:* British. *Date sunk:* 16/2/18. *Tons nett:* 47. *Tons gross:* 57. *Built:* Of wood at Brixham in 1899. *Type:* SV. *Rig:* ketch. *Owners:* Frederick Lang, Alexandra Rd,

Lowestoft. *Cargo:* Fish. *Armed:* No. *Position:* 8 miles SW from Beer Head (50 34 50N; 03 15 00W). *Master's name:* John Thomas Wilson. *Crew:* 4.

The *Commander* was doing well out in the fishing grounds of Lyme Bay. It was a nice day with the wind quite fresh, ideal for trawling. At half past twelve she was skipping along on the starboard tack heading east scooping up more fish when the first shell went across the *Commander's* bows with an ear piercing shriek. The master immediately ordered the helm to be set towards the land. He saw the submarine was about a mile off and bearing down on him rapidly. Ordering the trawl to be cut the master raced below and threw all his sailing instructions into the galley fire. Returning to the deck Captain Wilson saw that the enemy was getting nearer by the minute.

The second shell fell so close to the side of the ship that a large wave of water was sent washing over the *Commander's* deck. The third shell passed within inches of the mainmast and the master realised that if he didn't stop, someone on his ship was going to get hurt. He shouted for the ship to be brought to and the four men left the ketch as quickly as they could.

It wasn't long before the submarine was alongside the small boat and the crew were ordered to board whilst their boat was used by four German sailors. They proceeded to plunder the *Commander* of anything they could find of value before handing the small boat back to the four fishermen. As the men pulled clear they saw the bombs explode and their ship sink.

5/27: BOMA. *Country:* British. *Date sunk:* 11/6/18. *Tons nett:* 1720. *Tons gross:* 2694. *Built:* Barrow in 1889. *Type:* SS. *Rig:* schooner. *Owners:* British & African Steam Navigation Co, Liverpool. *Cargo:* 2000 tons general, hay & potatoes. *Armed:* 1 x 3in high angle gun. *Position:* 6 miles S of Sidmouth (50 32 10N; 03 14 10W) *Master's name:* Arthur Sutherland. *Crew:* 38. *Crew nationality:* All British. *Gunners:* N.J. Cummings, AB RFR, No Z0 9940 Po; C.A. Clayton, AB RNVR, No TZ 9799 Po; S. Miller, RNR, No A 7174 Po.

BOMA's journey originated in Belfast, destined for St Helens, Isle of Wight, calling at Falmouth. She left Falmouth at 12.30pm on June 11, 1918, and continued on her course up the Channel using the coastal route. The master should have been zig-zagging but the area was very busy with other traffic and he felt it unsafe to do so.

At 10 oclock the same evening she was off Sidmouth when a torpedo struck her on the starboard side causing a tremendous explosion. The steamer started to sink quickly and the master ordered abandon ship. In less than five minutes all the crew were in the boats and pulling clear of the ship. They got no further than 50yds yards before their ship sank.

At 1am the next morning both boats were found

by the Drifter *Veteran* and the crew were landed at Torquay.

UB-80 sank the *Boma*.

5/28: CITY OF SWANSEA. *Country:* British. *Date sunk:* 25/9/17. *Tons nett:* 809. *Tons gross:* 1375. *Built:* In 1882. *Type:* SS. *Rig:* schooner. *Owners:* Balgrave Murphy & Co, 17, Eden Quay, Dublin. *Cargo:* 1780 tons coal. *Armed:* 1 x 12pdr gun. *Position:* 15 miles ENE of Berry Head (50 31 00N; 03 15 50W). *Master's name:* Peter Furlong. *Crew:* 18. *Gunners:* Ernest Barry, RMAR No 1272; Walter Turvey, RMAR No 1331.

THE *City of Swansea* was requisitioned by the British government as a coal carrier and was engaged in such duties when she was lost.

She left Dunstan on the morning of September 21, 1917, and was bound for Bayonne. When she had reached a position about one mile off Portland Bill on the 25th she was hailed by a patrol boat which signalled that the commander wished to speak with the master. The master was instructed by the patrol vessel to go no closer to the land than five miles and a new course was set to comply with these instructions.

She continued on her way down Channel and was about 15 miles east-north-east of Berry Head when master saw a torpedo heading towards him and ordered the helm hard over. However, it was too late and it hit the port side in number four hatch about three feet below the waterline.

The crew had time to climb aboard the starboard lifeboat and get clear of the ship before she sank in 17 fathoms of water. They rowed and hoped that they would be found by a passing vessel but in the end had to row all the way to Budleigh Salterton.

The Admiralty were very curious afterwards as to why the ship was so far away from the coast. The master was very specific about the patrol vessel that instructed him to steer further out. The point does not seem to have been pursued.

UB-40 was the submarine concerned.

5/29: ADDAX. *Country:* British. *Date sunk:* 29/1/18. *Tons nett:* 31. *Tons gross:* 51. *Built:* Of wood at Brixham in 1910. *Type:* SV. *Rig:* ketch. *Owners:* Herbert Ford, Birmingham. *Cargo:* –. *Armed:* No. *Position:* 12 miles SE by E from Berry Head (50 28 00N; 03 13 00W). *Master's name:* Edward Henry Smith. *Crew:* 4.

CAPTAIN Edward Smith of the fishing vessel *Addax* had just spoken with the master of another fishing vessel, *Perseverance*, and had been warned that an enemy submarine was lurking somewhere in the area. He decided to keep a good lookout whilst hauling in the trawl and head back to port as soon as possible.

But at 2pm he spotted the submarine heading towards the group of fishing vessels. It was moving very fast, far to fast to outrun and all the master could

do was watch as the enemy commander decided which of the sitting ducks he would shoot first. The *Perseverance* was the closest and she was sunk by a well placed shell. The German commander then turned his attention to the *Addax*, opening fire on her from 350yds. The first shell was enough for Captain Smith who had already ordered his crew to stand by their small boat. As they pulled clear another shell cut the mainmast sending it crashing over the side in a tangled mess.

Seeing that the *Addax* was well crippled the submarine commander turned his attention to another sailing vessel close by, the *Ibex*. After despatching her he moved onto another the *General Leman*. Satisfied that no more vessels were within easy reach the enemy commander ran his submarine alongside the drifting *Addax* and put men aboard her, presumably to plunder what food they needed. Captain Smith said that he gradually lost sight of his ship due to the fading light but he was certain she was later sunk by bombs.

Addax's crew were given a tow into Brixham by the passing ship *Peace & Glory*.

5/30: PRECEDENT. *Country:* British. *Date sunk:* 11/4/17. *Tons nett:* 36. *Tons gross:* 48. *Built:* Of wood at Brixham in 1912. *Type:* FV. *Rig:* ketch. *Owners:* Charles Stanley Howe, 36, Station Hill, Brixham. *Cargo:* None. *Armed:* No. *Position:* 12 miles ESE from Berry Head (50 20 00N; 03 11 00W). *Master's name:* Charles Stanley Howe. *Crew:* 4.

CAPTAIN Howe stated that on April 11, 1917, around 11am, he was in the fishing grounds between Portland and Start Point with his trawl out and his ship under reefed sails. The first he knew of trouble was when a shell came whistling over his rigging, fired by a German submarine that had appeared about a quarter of a mile off. Within minutes the submarine was only 200yds off and her commander ordered the master to abandon his ship and row towards him.

He had little choice with the submarine's deck gun trained on him so ordered his men to comply. Whilst he was being questioned by the German commander his lifeboat and crew were used to ferry a bombing party back to the *Precedent*. This was nothing unusual but it was different in that the German sailors allowed the men to gather up their personal belongings before planting the bombs and leaving again.

After the bombs exploded the submarine cast the crew adrift and made off in the direction of another fishing boat, the *Collie* of Brixham, but, strangely, did not attack her.

5/31: URSA. *Country:* Swedish. *Date sunk:* 17/9/18. *Tons nett:* 789. *Tons gross:* 1740. *Built:* Grangemouth in 1902. *Type:* SS. *Rig:* schooner. *Owners:* Bernhard Inglesson,

Helsingborg, Sweden. *Cargo:* 2432 tons coal from Harrison Sons, Cardiff, to French goverment, Rouen. *Armed:* No. *Position:* 8 miles SSW from Beer Head (50 33 30N; 03 10 48W). *Master's name:* Robert Helge Andersson. *Crew:* 19. *Crew nationality:* All Swedish.

THERE was an agreement on board the *Ursa* between all the officers that if the vessel was hit by a mine or torpedo, the engines would be shut down immediately without any signal from the bridge. A simple enough arrangement but when the time came, totally ignored.

The *Ursa* had loaded her coal at Cardiff and was making her way up to Portland before crossing the Channel to Rouen. At 5.15am on September 17, 1918, the master was in the chartroom and the second mate was on watch on the bridge. Without any warning the ship was suddenly struck by a torpedo and a huge explosion boomed out from number one hold. Within a few minutes the steamer was down by the head.

Had the agreement about shutting down the engines been observed then the boats could have been launched easily. However, as a result of the engines running, one of them was tipped over on touching the water and three men were thrown out. Fortunately for them they were soon picked up. The *Ursa* sank about 10 minutes after being hit and as the crew watched her slip beneath the waves the German submarine responsible appeared alongside the lifeboats. The commander of the submarine ordered one of the steamer's officers to board. The second mate volunteered and was asked the usual questions about the details of his ship.

Once the second mate had returned, the crew rowed the two boats towards the shore and reached Beer at 8.30am.

5/32: GENERAL LEMAN. *Country:* British. *Date sunk:* 29/1/18. *Tons nett:* 44. *Tons gross:* 56. *Built:* Of wood at Brixham 1914. *Type:* SV. *Rig:* ketch. *Owners:* Thomas G. Bishop, Goodwick, Pembroke. *Cargo:* –. *Armed:* No. *Position:* 14 miles SE by E from Berry Head (50 21 00N; 03 10 00W). *Master's name:* Frank James Sanders. *Crew:* 4.

THE submarine commander who attacked the fishing fleet off Brixham on January 29, 1918, found it a simple operation.

General Leman was on the port tack heading eastward when the master noticed that *Perseverance* half a mile to the south had a flag hoisted which read, 'Enemy submarine close by.' Captain Sanders immediately shouted to his crew to trim the sails and make for the shore.

It was slow going but the master hoped he had acted quickly enough. To his dismay, he saw the submarine about four miles off to the east bearing down on the nearest fishing vessel to it, the *Ibex. General Leman* was still some 14 miles from Berry Head. The submarine caught up with them, firing two shells as she approached. Captain Sanders had no choice but to abandon his ship to the submarine's gunner. A few more shots were pumped into *General Leman*, to cripple her then the enemy moved on to the *Perseverance* and the *Addax* close by. With both those vessels out of the way the U-boat came back to the *General Leman* to finish her off. Her crew watched from a distance as their ship was sunk.

It was 6.20pm before any help arrived. The commander of the patrol vessel *Rinaldo II* had heard all the gunfire and came out to investigate. He was too late, but picked up the crews of the *General Leman*, *Ibex* and *Perseverance*, landing them later at Brixham.

5/33: W.H. DWYER. *Country:* British. *Date sunk:* 26/8/17. *Tons nett:* 1141. *Tons gross:* 1780. *Built:* Sunderland in 1913. *Type:* SS. *Rig:* schooner. *Owners:* Forwarders Ltd. *Charterers:* Solvey & Co. Paris. *Cargo:* In ballast, Rouen to Newport. *Armed:* 1 x 3pdr Vickers gun. *Position:* 13 miles E by N of Hope's Nose (50 31 00N; 03 09 00W). *Master's name:* Edward Stuart Whitton. *Crew:* 22. *Crew nationality:* 19 British, (inc 1 woman) 1 Russian, 1 Swede, 1 Norwegian.

W.H. DWYER crossed the Channel in a convoy on August 22, 1917, and after receiving her instructions off St Catherines, proceeded down the coast. The weather was particularly bad and getting worse so the master decided to return to St Helens and wait for it to moderate.

She eventually left St Helens on August 25, and continued her journey westward. All went well until 4.50am the following morning. The master was in the chart room when, according to his later report, an enormous explosion shook the ship. He immediately went on deck and discovered a huge hole in the port side between number one and two holds and that she was sinking by the head rapidly. He summoned all hands on deck and ordered the boats to be lowered. They all managed to get clear just before the *W.H. Dwyer* sank.

The master could only guess at the time that he had probably been hit by a torpedo. It was later confirmed by a lookout on the forecastle head who said that he saw the track of a torpedo a few seconds before it hit the ship.

The crew rowed towards the land and were eventually picked up by the French steamer *Aline Montreauil* who dropped them at St Helens.

The wreck of this ship was dived by some Teignmouth divers in 1985 and they report that it is in generally good condition. It lies in deep water and had probably not been dived since it sank. Proof that the wreck is *W.H. Dwyer* is backed up by the fact that the ship's bronze bell with her name engraved on it was recovered by one of the divers.

The submarine concerned was *UB-38*.

5/34: CURLEW. *Country:* British.
Date sunk: 22/3/17. *Tons nett:* 40. *Tons gross:* 51.
Built: Of wood at Brixham in 1904. *Type:* FV.
Rig ketch.: *Owners:* Joseph Whisher, 30, Hamilton
Terrace, Milford Haven. *Cargo:* None. *Armed:* No.
Position: 14 miles S of Beer Head (50 27 00N;
03 06 00W). *Master's name:* William John Shears.
Crew: 4.

IT was a hazy but breezy day with a choppy sea as
Curlew trailed her trawl nets in the fishing grounds
between Portland Bill and Berry Head. She was
headed in a north-westerly direction under reefed sails
when someone on board shouted that he could see a
periscope off the starboard bow. The master rushed
forward to have a look and sure enough there was a
periscope. It was moving quite quickly and getting
closer. The master shouted to his men to get a boat
ready. A few minutes later a German submarine rose
to the surface and four men came out of the conning
tower armed with rifles. Soon holes appeared here
and there and small thuds could be heard down one
side of the *Curlew* as the bullets slammed home. The
shooting stopped when the master waved to signal
that he understood what they meant and was going to
leave. A voice from the submarine ordered him to
send a boat.

When the German sailor arrived on board the master
had just finished burning his papers. It was obvious
what the sailor intended to do with the bomb tucked
under his arm. The master asked him if he could take
his clock and compass and some food to put in the
boat to which the German nodded. After grabbing a
ball of twine, a strange thing to steal, the German
sailor escorted the master back to the submarine. The
Curlew sank almost instantly as the bomb exploded.

The crew rowed towards the shore for some time
but were found the same afternoon by a patrol ship.

5/35: GALLIA. *Country:* Italian.
Date sunk: 24/10/17. *Tons nett:* 1733. *Tons
gross:* 2727. *Built:* In 1887. *Type:* SS. *Rig:* –.
Owners: Cerrano Giovanni, Genoa, Italy. *Cargo:*
3029 tons coal from the Tyne to Savona. *Armed:*
1 x 76mm gun. *Position:* 6 miles S of Beer Head/24
miles W by N of Portland Bill (50 34 15N;
03 04 54W). *Master's name:* Stefano Baracchini.
Crew: 26. *Casualties:* S. Lauzetta, fireman.

THIS ship was formerly the British *Olive Branch* of
Sunderland.

Having loaded her cargo of coal at Tyne Dock she
set off on her homeward passage at 8am on October
19, 1917. By Wednesday the 24th the weather had
deteriorated and the wind was very strong from the
south. Either a torpedo or a mine caused a large
explosion occurred on the port side which penetrated
the engine room.

What happened next is very confused and
presumably it was difficult due to language problems

for the interviewing officer to get to the bottom of it.
The Trinity House Pilot, Mr G.R. Green, stated that
the ship was abandoned amidst considerable
confusion. The majority left in a large lifeboat
leaving the master, pilot, officers and a few men to
get away in the gig. The lifeboat made sail and
headed towards an auxiliary patrol vessel which they
spotted off Lyme Regis. Patrol vessel *Wyndham*
picked up the large boat and towed the gig into
Weymouth about 9pm.

Mr Green also added that he was told by one of the
crew that the ship was hit with two torpedoes and that
the *Gallia* had opened fire with her gun. However,
he didn't consider this information to be reliable as
the man was wounded and far from well.

Lloyds records give the ship as "torpedoed".

5/36: PROVIDENT. *Country:* British.
Date sunk: 28/11/16. *Tons nett:* 38. *Tons gross:* 50.
Built: Galmpton in 1910. *Type:* FV. *Rig:* ketch.
Owners: William Pillar, Berry Head, Devon.
Cargo: None. *Armed:* No. *Position:* Portland Bill
Bearing E by N 24 miles (50 27 00N; 03 04 00W).
Master's name: William Pillar. *Crew:* 4.

THE crew of *Provident* were about to begin trawling
when, at 1.30pm, a German submarine appeared close
by. Her commander warned the crew to get clear as
their vessel was about to be shelled.

Having little choice in the matter the crew pulled
clear. The submarine moved closer to the abandoned
ship and fired several shells into her. Although she
was badly holed she refused to sink and remained
afloat. An officer from the submarine called to her
crew in their boat nearby to come to him and he along
with two sailors used the boat to plant bombs on the
ketch.

A few minutes later the bombs exploded, her deck
heaved up into the air and *Provident* disappeared..
The submarine made off towards a new victim, the
Amphitrite.

5/37: AMPHITRITE. *Country:* British.
Date sunk: 28/11/16. *Tons nett:* 44. *Tons gross:* –.
Built: Brixham in 1904. *Type:* FV. *Rig:* ketch.
Owners: Samuel F. Dugdall, King St, Brixham,
Devon. *Cargo:* Fish. *Armed:* No. *Position:* 24 miles
W by S from Portland Bill (50 27 00N; 03 04 00W).
Master's name: William George Norris. *Crew:* 4.

HAVING watched their companion the *Provident*
blown out of the water, the crew of the *Amphitrite*
gazed in horror as the submarine raced towards them.
They hoisted all the sails they could and tried to run
for it but it was hopeless.

Suddenly a shell whistled close by her rigging, as a
signal to stop. As the ketch came to a halt the
submarine was close enough to signal them to
abandon their ship and get clear.

This time the submarine's gunners made a cleaner job of it and, unlike the attack on the *Provident*, sank the *Amphitrite* with a few well placed shots.

The crew rowed away and eventually caught up with the men from the *Provident* and together they made for the shore. They were spotted later by the patrol vessel 391 *Lord Stanhope* and taken to Weymouth.

5/38: AVANCE. *Country:* British.
Date sunk: 21/3/17. *Tons nett:* 45. *Tons gross:* 64.
Built: Of wood at Porthleven in 1911. *Type:* FV.
Rig: ketch. *Owners:* Peter Hancock, Millford, Carnarvon. *Cargo:* 1½ tons fish. *Armed:* No.
Position: 25 miles WSW of Portland Bill (50 23 00N; 03 04 00W). *Master's name:* John Thomas Wilson. *Crew:* 4. *Crew nationality:* All British.

IT took most of the day sailing from Brixham on March 19, 1917, for *Avance* to reach the fishing area between Portland Bill and Start Point. She put her trawl down the same evening and began filling up her holds with fish. She was doing well until two days later at 8.30am on the 21st. The master was on deck when he noticed a strange vessel about three miles to the south. He picked up his binoculars and tried to make out what it was. He could see that it was generally heading towards him but then it veered off and started to circle keeping about two miles off. Gradually it got closer and when about a mile off the master could see that it was an enemy submarine.

Almost at the same moment a puff of smoke blew to one side of it in the wind, followed by a frightening scream as a shell passed over the rigging. The master shouted to his men to get into the boat. Before joining them he grabbed his confidential papers and tossed them into the galley stove.

The crew pulled clear leaving their little ship to the mercy of the German gunner who continued to pound her. The master said it was the ninth shot that finished the *Avance* and she sank stern first. The submarine commander made no attempt to talk to the crew but made off immediately. They rowed for 12 hours towards the coast and were eventually spotted by a patrol ship which landed them at Weymouth the next day.

5/39: GERMAN SUBMARINE (possible).
Country: German. *Date believed sunk:* 8/6/18.
Tons nett: –. *Tons gross:* –. *Built:* –. *Type:* –.
Armed: Yes. *Position:* 4 miles S of Beer Head (50 37 00N; 03 03 45W). *Master's name:* –.

INFORMATION on this incident was given by a pilot, Lieutenant H.R. Hutt, who claimed to have spotted and bombed an enemy submarine from his small patrol airship. His letter to the Admiralty dated the same day gives the following information:

"I ascended in *SSZ 49* at 10.45 today for patrol. At 13.35 in the position given I observed patches of water discoloured by sand and a small surface swirl. At 14.00 I decided that this was not due to natural causes and at 14.05 I dropped a 112 pound bomb from 100 feet high, 100 feet ahead of the swirls. About two minutes later I observed a thin streak of air bubbles which increased and five minutes later distinct traces of oil."

Having got the attention of two patrol vessels, he then proceeded to direct them to the position and they threw depth charges over the side. Lots more bubbles and oil rose to the surface and the pilot was of the opinion that a submarine was sunk.

The Admiralty don't agree and make the observation at the time that a submarine was still working in Lyme Bay and therefore he couldn't possibly have sunk it. However, there were very often more than one enemy submarine prowling the Channel which makes their conclusion possibly a little suspect, although there is no sinking at that date in German records.

5/40: ROSEBUD. *Country:* British.
Date sunk: 21/2/18. *Tons nett:* 44. *Tons gross:* 51.
Built: Of wood at Brixham in 1896. *Type:* SV. *Rig:* ketch. *Owners:* Thomas Henry Lane, Bolton St, Brixham. *Cargo:* Fish. *Armed:* No. *Position:* 5 miles SSE from Beer Head (50 36 00N; 03 03 00W). *Master's name:* Gordon Sparks Cumming. *Crew:* 4. *Crew nationality:* All British.

AS daylight arrived on the morning of February 21, 1918, the master of *Rosebud* had a good look around for British patrol vessels. He was a little worried that he couldn't see one anywhere and decided to shape a course to take the boat nearer to land. There had been too many scares about enemy submarines of late and he didn't fancy coming across one himself.

The first the master knew of any trouble was when rifle shots were heard very close off the lee quarter. A submarine had surfaced about 100yds off and several German sailors were on deck taking pot shots at the *Rosebud's* rigging. There was nothing the master could do but to order his men to leave their ship and get clear.

The German commander waved his arm, motioning the men to row the boat towards him. With several rifles pointing in their direction the four men had little choice. The boat was needed by the Germans as they wanted to visit the *Rosebud*, first to plant bombs on her, and second to help themselves to whatever food and goodies they fancied. It was soon done and 10 minutes later the bombs exploded sending the *Rosebud* straight down.

The four men were then allowed to go, leaving the submarine heading off towards another fishing vessel, the *Idalia*. The crew from *Rosebud* rowed towards Beer Head and were later picked up by the armed trawler *Lerita* which dropped them off at Torquay.

5/41: SPARKLING FOAM. *Country:* British.
Date sunk: 15/3/18. *Tons nett:* 175. *Tons gross:*
199. *Built:* Of wood at Sandwich in 1868. *Type:*
SV. *Rig:* barquentine. *Owners:* The Anglo French
Co, Paris. *Cargo:* 120 tons sand ballast from Caen
to Swansea. *Armed:* No. *Position:* 9 miles S by E
from Beer Head (50 32 00N; 03 02 00W).
Master's name: William Isaacs. *Crew:* 6. *Crew
nationality:* 3 British, 2 Swedish, 1 Dane.

ALTHOUGH she sailed with a convoy which included
several other sailing vessels the master somehow
managed to lose sight of them at dusk. He realised
that all alone he was completely vulnerable to attack
from enemy submarines and immediately altered
course to take him to the nearest part of the British
coast. With all sail up and the wind blowing a strong
breeze the *Sparkling Foam* slipped along at nearly
six knots.

It was 1.15pm when a submarine appeared about
three miles off to the south. The first shell threw up a
spout of water just short of the *Sparkling Foam*.

Having dumped his confidential sailing instructions
in the weighted bag overboard, the master joined his
crew in the boat and pulled clear. Several shells had
already struck home but none caused enough damage
to sink her. As the submarine slowed alongside the
crew in the boat a German officer ordered the master
and three men to come aboard. They did as they were
told and whilst the master was being questioned the
two men left in the boat were forced at gunpoint to
row a German boarding party over to the *Sparkling
Foam*. After helping themselves to all sorts of items
they planted several bombs near her keel and made
off back to the submarine. It was all over a few
minutes later as the bombs sent her to the bottom.

The German commander ordered the crew away in
their boat. They rowed for some time towards shore
but were soon safely aboard the trawler *Warbler* which
took them to Brixham.

Another victim of a WWI German submarine sinks in the Channel. Note the survivors in a lifeboat.

WORLD WAR ONE
CHANNEL WRECKS

◆

AREA SIX

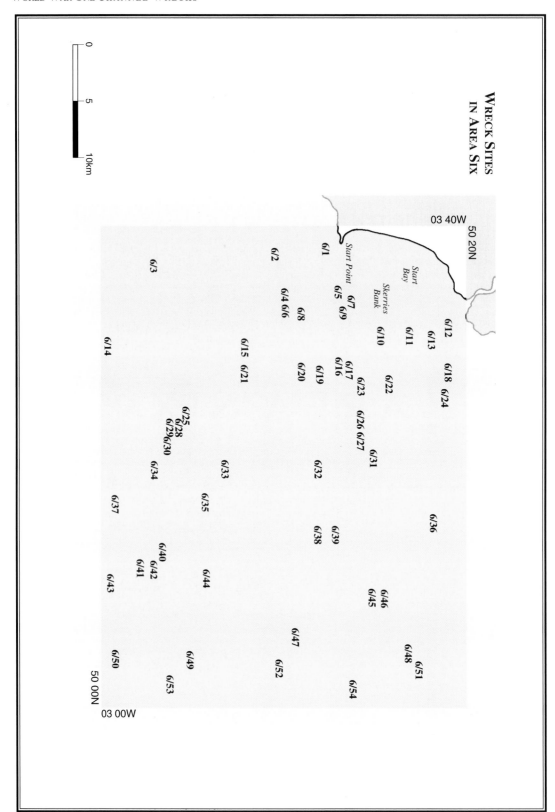

WRECK SITES
IN AREA SIX

03 40W
50 20N

0
5
10km

Start Point
Start
Bay
Skerries
Bank

6/1
6/2
6/3
6/5 6/9
6/7
6/4 6/6
6/8
6/10
6/11
6/12
6/13
6/14
6/15 6/21
6/16
6/17
6/19
6/20
6/18 6/24
6/22
6/23
6/26 6/27
6/31
6/25 6/28
6/29 6/30
6/32
6/33
6/34
6/35
6/36
6/37
6/38
6/39
6/40
6/41 6/42
6/43
6/44
6/45
6/46
6/47
6/48 6/51
6/49
6/50
6/52
6/53
6/54

50 00N
03 00W

6/1: NEWHOLM. *Country:* British.
Date sunk: 8/9/17. *Tons nett:* 2194. *Tons gross:* 3399. *Built:* Wallsend in 1899. *Type:* SS.
Rig: schooner. *Owners:* Newcastle SS Co, Milburn House, Newcastle. *Cargo:* Iron ore from Bilbao to Middlesbrough. *Armed:* 1 X 4.7in gun.
Position: 1 mile SSW from Start Point/2 miles E of Prawle Point (50 12 32N; 03 38 24W).
Master's name: Magnus Smith. *Crew:* 29. *Crew nationality:* 26 British, 1 Russian, 1 Dane, 1 Swede.
Gunners: P. McKeown, RNR; Frank Lee, RNVR; T. Martin, RNVR.

CAPTAIN Magnus Smith of *Newholm* said that he received his route instructions at Brest but the trouble was they were written in French and he didn't understand a word of them. However, in the circumstances, it would have made little difference to the fate of *Newholm* if he had.

The weather was fine and clear and the sea calm. It was 11am when the mine made contact with *Newholm's* hull. The huge explosion and blast ripped open number one and two holds putting the steamer down by the head almost instantly. The master was unsure if he had been struck by a torpedo or had hit a mine, but it mattered little at that moment, for *Newholm* was sinking very rapidly indeed. She went down so fast that none of the crew had time to get to the boats. Some jumped overboard as she slipped from beneath them, some didn't know how they got in the water. However, 20 of the crew went down with her.

Nine men, including Captain Smith, managed to cling to the wreckage that was left strewn over the area and hoped that help would arrive soon. It arrived very quickly in the form of two local crab boats. Mr W.J. Stone of Frogmore was in one and Miss Ella Trout from Hallsands was in the other with her cousin William Trout and a 10 year old lad. Both boats sailed in among the wreckage and hauled the exhausted men to safety. They passed them over to the patrol trawler 598 *Direct Me*.

Their Lordships at the Admiralty were very grateful for the help given by the two crab boats and they sent a letter to the owner of the boats, Mr Spencer Fox of The Gables, Salcombe, along with £3 for Mr Stone and £1 for young Ella Trout, as a token of their appreciation.

The mine was part of a field laid by *UC-31*.

6/2: AGNETE. *Country:* British.
Date sunk: 24/4/18. *Tons nett:* 705. *Tons gross:* 1500. *Built:* Kiel in 1893. *Type:* SS. *Rig:* –.
Owners: R.S. Dalgliesh, Watergate Buildings, Newcastle. *Cargo:* 1500 tons coal from Powell Duffryn Newport to same at Rouen. *Armed:* 1 x 13pdr gun. *Position:* 4 miles SSW of Start Point (50 09 42N; 03 38 00W). *Master's name:* Charles Henry Hudson. *Crew:* 20. *Crew nationality:* 10 British, 5 Greeks, 2 Russians, 1 Dutch.

THE master having perished in this sinking together with 11 of his crew, it fell to the first mate, Sidney Hawkes, to be interviewed by the naval authorities.

He said that he took charge of the bridge from the second mate at 8pm on April 24, 1918, and they were steering a zig-zag course as instructed. At 10.25pm the master, who had been on the bridge, went to the lower bridge. At the same time the first mate noticed a suspicious object on the starboard bow about half a mile away. He promptly ordered the helm to be put hard to starboard and physically jumped down to the lower bridge to assist the helmsman as the ship did not have steam steering gear. As soon as he touched the wheel he found himself hurled onto number two hatch by a terrific explosion and seconds later he was floating in the water.

The sinking had taken about a minute and the mate, still dazed, looked around to find something to cling to. Fortunately, there had been a raft left untied on number two hatch and he climbed onto it along with two other men. A few yards away he could see an upturned boat with a few men on it and also the waterlogged jolly boat with one man, George Palmer, the cook, clinging to that. The survivors eventually got together and bailed out the jolly boat and rowed around looking for others. Satisfied that there were no other survivors they rowed for the shore and landed at Lannacombe near Start Point.

6/3: EAGLE. *Country:* British. *Date sunk:* 4/12/17.
Tons nett: 73. *Tons gross:* 181. *Built:* Greenock in 1902. *Type:* SS. *Rig:* schooner. *Owners:* J.G. Piprell, St Peters Port, Guernsey. *Cargo:* Water ballast. *Armed:* No. *Position:* Start Point bearing N 10 miles (50 03 00N; 03 37 00W). *Master's name:* Edward Henry Playle. *Crew:* 9. *Crew nationality:* 8 British, 1 French.

THE master could hear the sound of gunfire and looked around for the source of it. It was 12.20am and dark. Suddenly a shell fell close to the *Eagle*. The master realised that whoever it was could see him and was now getting the range. More shots found their mark, slamming into the hull of the steamer.

The master ordered the engines to be stopped and instructed the crew to stand by the boats. As he did so the cause of his problems appeared out of the darkness just off the port bow. It was a submarine heading swiftly towards him and still firing.

The boats were lowered and the crew pulled clear of the ship. A shout came from the submarine *UB-35* in clear English which ordered the boat to go towards it. Two Germans then used the boat to plant two bombs on board the *Eagle*. Four British prisoners from the fishing vessel *Rion*, who had been on the submarine for three days, were brought up from below and ordered to get into the lifeboat.

Ten minutes later the *Eagle* exploded and sank stern first. The crew continued to row towards the Start and were found by a naval patrol vessel at 7.30 am.

6/4: PLUTON. *Country:* Norwegian.
Date sunk: 9/9/17. *Tons nett:* 858. *Tons gross:*
1449. *Built:* 1889. *Type:* SS. *Rig:* –. *Owners:*
Hennewig Torbjorsen, Oslo. *Charterers:* Hudson
Bay Co. *Cargo:* 1960 tons patent fuel, Port Talbot
for Rouen. *Armed:* No. *Position:* 5 miles SE of Start
Point (50 10 30N; 03 34 00W). *Master's name:*
Jacob Andersen. *Crew:* 20. *Crew nationality:*
1 American, 1 Russian, 1 Dutch, 4 Spaniards,
13 Norwegian.

THE first mate was on the bridge of the *Pluton* as she
made her way up Channel. The weather was fine and
fresh and the ship was making a steady eight knots.
The Norwegian flag was flying in the hope that any
hostile craft might be lenient and allow her to pass
but that was most unlikely in the light of the many
Norwegian casualties.

The mate, Christian Eek, was an observant man
and he spotted the submarine which had just appeared
on the surface close by. Suddenly the wake of a
torpedo was seen skimming across the surface and
the mate ordered the helmsman to bring the ship hard
to starboard. The torpedo was too fast and it struck
amidships with a dull thud. Nothing followed; it had
failed to explode. Counting his blessings, the mate
turned away from the submarine and rang the engine
room telegraph for more speed, hoping that they could
outrun the submarine. It was a good try but the
submarine was too fast and very soon another torpedo
slammed into the side of the *Pluton*. This time it
exploded and the ship started to settle rapidly.

The crew scrambled into the lifeboats and on to
raft as quick as they could and managed to get clear of
the ship in the nick of time. It was very dark and the
boat rowed towards the shore and made Dartmouth
by 2am the following morning. The raft with the
master and the nine other crew members were later
found by a patrol vessel and brought in safely

6/5: COLORADO. *Country:* British.
Date sunk: 20/10/17. *Tons nett:* 5349. *Tons gross:*
7164. *Built:* Glasgow in 1914. *Type:* SS. *Rig:*
schooner. *Owners:* Ellerman Wilson, Hull. *Cargo:*
8000 tons coal and coke, from Stephenson & Co,
Hull, to Parker & Co, Alexandria. *Armed:* 1 x 4in
gun. *Position:* 3 miles E by N of Start Point
(50 13 30N; 03 34 00W). *Master's name:* Tom
Collins. *Crew:* 45. *Crew nationality:* 38 British,
2 Swedes, 1 Dane, 1 Russian, 1 Greek, 2 others.
Gunners: A.E. Gardiner, RNVR No 5360;
R.G. Baringer, RNVR No BZ 3827.

ATTACHED to the records of this loss is a letter from
the master to the Marine Superintendent of Ellerman
Wilson Line and it sets out the circumstances as
follows:

"I regret to report the loss of the *Colorado* under the
following circumstances. We left Hull at 7am on
October 17, 1917, bound for Alexandria, Egypt, under

orders to proceed to Southampton for instructions. At
Southend I received orders to join the convoy at
Falmouth and proceeded in carrying out my admiralty
instructions to hug the land closely en route. At
9.10am on the 20th we passed the Skerries Buoy close
on the starboard hand and at 9.30am, when rounding
Start Point at a distance of 1.5 miles, a violent
explosion occurred on the port side abreast of the
engine room. This was followed a few seconds after
by another explosion further aft.

"As the ship began to rapidly settle down I ordered
the gun to be fired as our wireless and whistle were
both put out of action. All hands were ordered to stand
by the boats and it was found that the chief and fourth
engineers, a donkeyman and three firemen were
missing. I proceeded to the engine room, which by
this time was full of water, and found Mr Whiteley,
the Chief Officer, throwing a rope to the chief
engineer who was dangerously wounded and expired
a few minutes after being hauled up to the deck. Two
firemen were struggling in the water in the engine
room and both were rescued by the chief officer at
great personal risk.

"Finding there was no hope of saving the ship I
destroyed all my confidential papers and ordered the
crew into the boats. I just managed to get clear myself
when the *Colorado* turned on her port side and sank,
11 minutes after the first explosion.

"After being in the boats a short period the armed
trawler *Grackle* took us on board and landed us at
Dartmouth. I deeply regret that the fourth engineer, a
donkeyman and one fireman must have been killed
by the explosions.

"The behaviour of the crew was very good but I
must again point out the gallant conduct of Mr
Whiteley, who in a calm collected manner was of the
greatest assistance to me under the most trying
conditions and without his help both firemen in the
engine room would have drowned."

A note at the bottom of this letter read: "Mr
Whiteley to be awarded the silver medal for gallantry
for saving life at sea."

The patrol trawler *Casoria* was also on the scene
and had got there as the vessel sank. Her commander
calculated the position of the wreck and noted the
following sextant angles: Start Light House 103 deg,
Dartmouth Beacon 21 deg. Berry Head and Start Light
House bearing S 80 deg. W. Skerries Buoy N 56 deg
W. Dartmouth beacon N 4 deg E. Found no bottom
at 25 fathoms then being about three hours of ebb.
The above fix is about half a cable to the east of where
the ship sank.

It is interesting to note that there are numerous
cases in Weekly Reports, of patrol vessels depth
charging the wreck of the *Colorado* believing it to be
an enemy submarine.

The submarine involved was *UB-31*.

6/6: WARSAW. *Country:* British.
Date sunk: 20/12/17. *Tons nett:* 344. *Tons gross:*

608. *Built:* Greenock in 1864. *Type:* SS. *Rig:* schooner. *Owners:* James Currie & Sons, 16, Bernard St, Leith. *Cargo:* In ballast. *Armed:* 1 x 12pdr 12cwt gun. *Position:* 4 miles SE by E from Start Point (50 10 55N; 03 33 50W). *Master's name:* John Valentine. *Crew:* 20. *Crew nationality:* 14 British, 6 Japanese. *Gunners:* James Johnson, Workington; Mr Strickland, Newfoundland.

ONLY three people survived the sinking of this vessel, the first officer and two seamen. The cold water was the main cause of most of the deaths and the Chief Officer, George William Gunn, was at one stage rendered unconscious by the soaking. He said that they left St Malo on December 13, 1917, and were bound for Liverpool. They called in at Brixham for bunkers and left there just after midnight on the 20th.

George Gunn was in his bunk at the time *Warsaw* was attacked and was awakened by a loud explosion. He rushed on deck to discover that the vessel had been struck by a torpedo and was settling rapidly. Still in a state of undress he went quickly back to his cabin to grab his trousers and coat. Arriving back on deck he found that the crew were in both boats and had started to lower themselves down. At that precise moment the ship sank and both boats were swamped.

The chief officer found himself in the water and was dragged down by the steamer sinking. He eventually got free, surfaced and swam around until he found an upturned boat. A little later he was joined by four other men but two of them died from exposure. He recalled that they saw a submarine on the surface nearby which came close to them at one point but then disappeared. He remembered nothing else until he found himself on the warship *Roebuck* in Dartmouth Harbour.

The submarine seen by Gunn was *UB-31*, which claimed responsibility for the sinking.

6/7: WAIKAWA. *Country:* British.

Date sunk: 19/10/17. *Tons nett:* –. *Tons gross:* 5642. *Built:* 1907. *Type:* SS. *Rig:* –. *Owners:* Union SS Co New Zealand, Fenchurch St, London. *Cargo:* In ballast from Rouen to Barry Roads. *Armed:* 1 x 4in gun. *Position:* 4 miles ENE of Start Point/2 miles off Skerries Buoy (50 14 00N; 03 33 00W). *Master's name:* Henry Charles Hammond. *Crew:* 51. *Crew nationality:* 50 British, 1 Russian. *Gunners:* John King, Port Melbourne, Australia, No 617 RANR; Ellis John Hole, Bridgewater, UK, No BZ1755 RNVR.

AT the time of her loss the master was carrying out his instructions, and was zig-zagging. The ship was struck by a torpedo in the after hold below the waterline and she sank very rapidly. However, all the crew managed to get into the boats and get clear and were picked up half an hour later by the patrol trawler *Cassoria*.

The commanding officer of *Cassoria* stated that once he had all the crew safely on board he buoyed the position of the wreck and noted that it lay in 33 fathoms of water and had 18 fathoms clear over the top of her.

UB-31 was the submarine involved.

6/8: GRO. *Country:* Norwegian.

Date sunk: 22/8/17. *Tons nett:* –. *Tons gross:* 2667. *Built:* –. *Type:* SS. *Rig:* –. *Owners:* Biorn Biornstad & Co. *Charterers:* Snyder & Co, Paris. *Cargo:* 8100 tons coal, Clyde to Rouen. *Armed:* No. *Position:* $4^1/_2$ miles SE by E of Start Point (50 11 00N; 03 33 00W). *Master's name:* Niels Sorensen. *Crew:* 24. *Crew nationality:* 16 Norwegian, 3 Swedes, 3 Russian/Finns, 1 Spaniard.

ON the night of the *Gro's* loss the weather was cloudy and dark, and the sea had a slight swell. The ship was showing stern lights but dimmed right down and she was heading north-east by north at nine knots. There is little information recorded from the crew members about what happened. At 4am the third engineer saw the track of a torpedo very close to the ship. It smashed into the port side amidships, smashing the bunker and number three hold, and flooding the engine room.

The crew took to the starboard lifeboat and got clear of the vessel which, although in a bad way, was still afloat. They were picked up at 4.45am by a patrol vessel, transferred to another and later landed at Plymouth.

The commander of the patrol trawler *Lois* reported that he received a signal that there was a vessel in distress off Start Point and made all speed to her assistance. On arrival he found HMTBD 99 was towing the *Gro* and HMT *Derby* was cruising around to warn off any further submarine attack. At 6.30am HMT *Stanley Weyman* arrived on the scene to assist. *Lois* connected up on the *Gro's* bow whilst *Stanley Weyman* and *Derby* took up on the aft end. They had difficulty controlling the ship as there was nobody on board the steamer to help. Eventually the course was set for Dartmouth and some headway was made but she eventually sank.

UB-47 was the submarine involved

6/9: MEDINA. *Country:* British.

Date sunk: 28/4/17. *Tons nett:* 6700. *Tons gross:* 12350. *Built:* Greenock in 1911. *Type:* SS. *Rig:* schooner. *Owners:* The Peninsular & Oriental Steam Navigation Co, London. *Cargo:* 3100 tons of general. *Armed:* 1 x 4.7in quick fire. *Position:* 3 miles ENE from Start Point/8 miles SSW from Dartmouth (50 13 30N; 03 32 30W). *Master's name:* Henry Sandys Bradshaw. *Crew:* 358, plus 52 passengers and pilot.

MEDINA'S voyage began in Australia when she left Sydney on March 3, 1917. She called in at many Australian ports on her way stopping at Colombo,

The SS *Medina* was torpedoed by *UB-31* while returning from Australia in 1917. She was believed to be carrying a cargo of valuable antiques.

Bombay, Aden, Suez Canal, Malta, Marseilles, Gibraltar and finally Plymouth. Her cargo was listed as general but it was believed that she also carried a very valuable collection of antiques.

Having discharged her passengers at Plymouth she put to sea again and headed up the Channel for London. It was Saturday April 28, the weather fine with light winds and a smooth sea. At 6.05pm, unknown to those on board the *Medina*, she had been spotted by the German submarine *UB-31*. The liner was an enormous vessel and in the calm conditions must have presented an easy target for the German commander, Oberleutnant Bieber. One torpedo slammed into the side of the big liner, penetrating the after part of the engine room, killing five firemen and the fourth engineer.

Medina began to settle rapidly and the master ordered all the crew into the boats and to get clear. By 6.50pm she was completely abandoned and at 7.28 she sank in the position noted above. Another position given at the time was four miles SSE of Skerry Buoy.

Help was soon at hand and numerous boats came to the survivors' assistance.

In recent years the wreck of the *Medina* has been the subject of newspaper headlines. It seems that part of her cargo included Indian artifacts collected by Lord Carmichael of Skirling during his six years as Govenor of Madras. A firm of divers carried out salvage work on the wreck and at one point claimed that they had recovered the general's Masonic chain worth £500,000. Unless it was made from solid gold this is probably a little exaggerated! The value of antiques finally recovered proved to be disappointing.

6/10: FARN. *Country:* British. *Date sunk:* 19/11/17. *Tons nett:* 2735. *Tons gross:* 4393. *Built:* 1910. *Type:* SS. *Rig:* schooner. *Owners:* Farrar Groves & Co Ltd, 147, Leadenhall St, London. *Cargo:* 4500 tons general, London to Salonica, Greece. *Armed:* 1 x 4.7in Japanese gun. *Position:* 5 miles SSE of Dartmouth (50 15 30N; 03 31 00W). *Master's name:* A.B. Allen. *Crew:* 34. *Crew nationality:* 28 British, 4 Russian, 1 Dane, 1 Norwegian. *Gunners:* John Collie Campbell, Portsmouth RFR, No 14626 B1274; Charles Edward Tombs, Portsmouth RFR, No 13670 B1118.

THE steamer *Farn* was on her way to Salonica and was to call at Falmouth for orders. She was heading down the Channel steering a south westerly course and making just over eight knots. The weather was cloudy but the sea smooth.

The master and the mate were on the bridge and reported that they both saw the track of a torpedo when it was about 75yds off the starboard side. The helm was thrown over to starboard but it was too late and the torpedo hit the after quarter. The explosion ripped open number four hold and blew the propeller completely off.

She started to settle quickly and the order was give to abandon ship. The crew got away and half an hour later *Farn* sank. The men in the boats were later picked up by a patrol drifter and landed at Dartmouth. There were no casualties although one man in the engine room was scalded by escaping steam and slightly injured by shrapnel.

UB-31 was the submarine involved.

6/11: ALICE MARIE. *Country:* British.
Date sunk: 19/12/17. *Tons nett:* 1217. *Tons
gross:* 2210. *Built:* Sunderland in 1915. *Type:* SS.
Rig: schooner. *Owners:* The Rutland SS Co,
Newcastle. *Cargo:* 2950 tons coal from Pelton
Collieries, Newcastle to Rochefort for Union
Caziere of Paris. *Armed:* 1 x 12pdr 12cwt gun.
Position: 6 miles ENE from Start Point (50 17 00N;
03 31 00W). *Master's name:* Henry Ellison
Cousins. *Crew:* 26.

AT 11.55pm on the night of December 19, 1917, *Alice
Marie* was making her way down the Channel. She
should have been zig-zagging but couldn't because of
the large number of fishing vessels around. She should
not have been showing lights but had to for the same
reason. The wind was light and the sea smooth.

She must have presented an easy target for *UB-31*
which was lurking nearby. A few moments later a
torpedo was zipping towards the steamer. It smashed
into her starboard side and ripped a huge hole in her,
right through to the engine room.

It took eight minutes for the ship to sink which
gave ample time for the crew to get clear. The
submarine approached them and demanded to speak to
the master. The defiant crew told Oberleutnant Bieber
that they couldn't answer his questions as the master
and the mate were dead. Apart from obtaining the
ship's name and destination, the German commander
left them none the wiser.

The master and mate were in fact perfectly well as
were all the crew and they rowed towards the coast
reaching Dartmouth at 5am the following morning.

6/12: RION. *Country:* British. *Date sunk:* 1/12/17.
Tons nett: 39. *Tons gross:* 49. *Built:* Brixham in
1905. *Type:* FV. *Rig:* ketch. *Owners:* Mrs Annie
Rennels, Brixham, Devon. *Cargo:* In ballast.
Armed: No. *Position:* 8 miles N by E of Start Point
(50 19 00N; 03 31 00W). *Master's name:* William
Brinham. *Crew:* 4. *Crew nationality:* All British.

ALTHOUGH the loss of the little fishing vessel *Rion*
is small fry compared to the sinkings of the big
steamers, her story is quite an unusual one.

She made her way out to the fishing grounds. At
9.30am on December 1, 1917, the master spotted a
German submarine on his port side about a quarter
of a mile off. A few moments later the submarine
began to fire at the *Rion*.

The master ordered the crew to abandon ship and
get clear. The submarine turned towards the crew's
boat and shouted for them to come alongside which
they did. The German commander then spoke to the
master of the *Rion* in good English, "Why did you
not leave your ship before I fired?"

Before the master could answer a German sailor
appeared and jumped in with the crew with the
intention of planting a bomb to finish their ship off. At
that same moment the sea swell caused the submarine

to crash into the lifeboat and damaged it quite
severely. Seeing that the boat was filling with water
rapidly, the German jumped back on board the
submarine. The Commander looked down at the crew
in their water-logged boat and with a sigh said, "What
am I going to do with you?"

The master replied, "You'd better land me under
the Start."

The Commander shrugged, "Come aboard and get
below."

A few minutes later the *Rion* was sunk by a few
more shells from the submarine's deck gun.

The *Rion's* crew, consisting of three men and one
boy, were kept on board *UB-35*, commanded by
Oberleutnant Stöter, for three days. During that time
they were well treated and talked quite freely with
their German hosts. They reported in their interview
later that the submarine's crew consisted of 23 men.
The cook of the *Rion* helped the German cook on
several occasions and they ate with the submarine's
crew in their quarters. During one meal the German
second officer approached the prisoners and said,
"You can have some brown bread and coffee but you
cannot have any white bread as you are used to ashore
because we don't have any. But when you see us again
you cannot call us 'Bloody Germans'!"

The *Rion's* men witnessed the sinking of three
British steamers and noted that just after a torpedo
had been launched several of the crew would run
forward to compensate for the weight loss. The three
vessels that were sunk were the SS *Wreathier*, SS
Livonia and SS *Eagle*. The *Eagle* was sunk by bombs.
They also fired a torpedo at the steamer *El Uraguayo*
but it missed.

The SS *Eagle* was a small steamer and the
commander of the submarine must have seen her as an
ideal opportunity to get rid of his guests. Instead of
torpedoing her he shelled the crew into abandoning
it and called them over to him. The four crew
members of the *Rion* were then put in their boats and
ordered away.

It was a great adventure for the crew and one they
must have talked about for many years afterwards.
However, another report subsequent to the sinking,
did not show the master of *Rion* in a good light.

Because the authorities wanted to know all the
details of the crew's stay on the submarine,
Commander A.S. Keyes, was sent to interview the
men of the *Rion*. He made a report to the Commander-
in-Chief on December 5, 1917.

Commander Keyes interviewed the four men at
Dartmouth. His report of his encounter with Captain
Brinham was quite scathing: 'the skipper was drunk
when he came ashore from *Opossum* and was still
under the influence when I saw him. He continually
contradicted himself and was a very unreliable witness,
and seemed an untrustworthy person generally, and I
am of the opinion that he was deliberately lying. I took
no written statement from him, as it was evidently
worth nothing. The second hand and the boy cook
however seemed to have their wits about them.'

6/13: GREATHAM. *Country:* British.
Date sunk: 22/1/18. *Tons nett:* 1501. *Tons gross:* 2338. *Built:* 1890. *Type:* SS. *Rig:* schooner. *Owners:* Coombes Marshall & Co, Albert Rd, Middlesbrough. *Cargo:* Coal, Grimsby for Blaye, near Bordeaux. *Armed:* 1 x 12pdr gun. *Position:* 3 miles SE of Dartmouth (50 18 15N; 03 30 20W). *Master's name:* Robert Harrison. *Crew:* 26. *Crew nationality:* 17 British, 2 Russians, 7 Arabs (British subjects). *Gunners:* W. Harris, L/Cpl. RMLI, No 10592 Plymouth; H. Pointer, Pte. RMLI, No 10553 Portsmouth.

THERE is not a great deal of information on the circumstances but seven people died during the sinking. The explosion, which was presumed to have been caused by a torpedo, caused extensive damage to the after part of number two hold. The master reported that as the ship started to list heavily he ordered the crew to take to the boats. He saw the ship sink about 35 minutes later.

Six people were found to be missing: the chief officer, bosun, cook, Marconi operator, a sailor and a fireman. The master stated that he saw the cook, bosun and Marconi operator in the water but saw nothing of the other three. One man, an Arab, died in the lifeboat.

Greatham left Grimsby on January 16, 1918, destined for Blaye, and was, in fact, torpedoed by *UB-31,* which fired two torpedoes at the convoy in which the ship was travelling.

6/14: ETHEL. *Country:* British.
Date sunk: 22/1/17. *Tons nett:* 23. *Tons gross:* –. *Built:* Of wood at Galmpton in 1895. *Type:* SV. *Rig:* ketch. *Owners:* Walter Edward Fairbrass, 15, La Belle Square, Ramsgate. *Cargo:* Fish. *Armed:* No. *Position:* 30 miles SSE from Start Point (50 00 00N; 03 30 00W). *Master's name:* Walter Edward Fairbrass. *Crew:* 3.

IT should have been just another day's fishing for the three crew of the ketch *Ethel,* but it turned out to be one of the most frightening days of their life.

Having left Brixham at midday on January 18, 1917, they made for the fishing grounds and soon shot the trawl. It was a fine clear day with the light wind filling *Ethel's* sails and she made good way on the starboard tack. But suddenly, at around 3pm, an enemy submarine surfaced close by and fired a shell which passed just ahead of *Ethel.* The master told his two companions to make the boat ready. Two more shells followed which screamed over the rigging but the message was plain enough, abandon ship or else.

The three men reluctantly rowed over to the waiting submarine where the master was ordered to climb aboard. His place was taken by a German officer who demanded that the two men row him back to the *Ethel.* He promptly helped himself to whatever documents he could find and hurried back to his ship which had been circling impatiently. Once back aboard, a German gunner opened up and sent four shells crashing into the *Ethel's* wooden hull. She filled rapidly and sank.

For nearly two hours the crew were towed in their little boat behind the submarine. It wouldn't have been so bad had the submarine been heading towards shore but she was heading south further out to sea. Eventually the boat's painter was slipped and the men set about rowing themselves home. It was 6.30 the next morning before they were spotted by a friendly vessel, a Dutch schooner called *Ootsmudsum.* She later transferred them to a patrol vessel which took them home to Brixham.

6/15: LOFOTEN. *Country:* British.
Date sunk: 3/2/18. *Tons nett:* 552. *Tons gross:* 942. *Built:* Bergen, Norway in 1914. *Type:* SS. *Rig:* schooner. *Owners:* Cunard SS Co, Cunard Buildings, Liverpool. *Cargo:* 900 tons general from T.L.C. Duff & Co, George Square, Glasgow, to Havre. *Armed:* 1 x 12pdr HS. *Position:* Start Point bore NW by N 7 miles (50 08 00N; 03 30 00W). *Master's name:* Laurence Leask. *Crew:* 21. *Crew nationality:* 20 British, 1 Norwegian. *Gunners:* Coles, gunlayer, RNVR; Fred Pearson, gunner.

LOFOTEN collected her sailing instructions from Falmouth on February 3, 1918, and sailed out again within 10 minutes. She headed up Channel and at 11.30 the same evening was off Start Point when a torpedo struck her on the port side. The explosion was so big that the ship sank almost immediately. Some of the crew managed to make it to the boats but the steamer sank before they could be lowered.

Many of the men were dragged down by the suction of the ship and were never seen again but four were lucky, the Master, Second Mate, a fireman and a seaman were thrown clear. A few moments later one of the boats that had been dragged down appeared upside down on the surface and the four managed to cling to it.

The master reported that shortly after this a German submarine came close and threw a light on them. They called to it and shouted that they needed help but the submarine just turned away and left them. They drifted for nine hours and all four got colder by the minute. At one stage a vessel passed close by in the dark and they shouted to attract attention. She was a salvage ship and the crew had actually heard their cries of help and turned about to search but couldn't pinpoint where the cries were coming from. They noted the position of 50 18 00N; 03 19 30W and headed off towards port for help. Eventually they came across the patrol trawler *John Anderson* and gave her commander, Richard Cowling, the position.

The crew of the *John Anderson* soon found the freezing men and landed them at Dartmouth. The other 17 were not found.

UB-59 was the U-boat involved.

6/16: TORBAY LASS. *Country:* British.
Date sunk: 8/6/17. *Tons nett:* 38. *Tons gross:* –.
Built: Galmpton in 1907. *Type:* FV. *Rig:* ketch.
Owners: George Eveleigh, 3, Prospect Rd,
Brixham, Devon. *Cargo:* 3½ cwt fish. *Armed:*
No. *Position:* 5 miles E of Start Point (50 13 00N;
03 29 00W). *Master's name:* George Eveleigh.
Crew: 4.

THE crew of *Torbay Lass* had been fishing off Start
for several days and had made a reasonable catch. On
Friday June 8, 1917, she was lying becalmed but with
all sails set ready to catch the first breath of wind.
She was lopping around in the swell and the weather
had made the visibility hazy. The master reported that
he couldn't see the land but could hear the horn from
the Start Lighthouse. At 5.45pm he heard gunfire and
in the hazy distance he could see a submarine
attacking another fishing vessel. As he strained his
eyes to make it out a shot whimpered across the stern
of *Torbay Lass*. The master immediately lashed the
tiller hard to port and put the vessel before the swell
with her stern towards the submarine. He then
hurriedly burnt his notices to fishermen, gathered up
his other ship's papers and got into the lifeboat with
the crew.

They remained beside the *Torbay Lass* until the
submarine had got to within 50yds and a rifle shot
rang out. Understanding its meaning, the master and
crew pulled away from their ship. They all watched as
two German officers rowed past them in a boat
belonging to the other vessel they had just sunk called
Onward. Their mission was the usual one of planting
bombs which was soon done and the *Torbay Lass*
blew up and sank.

About 45 minutes later the crew were picked up
by the *Prevalent* which also had survivors of other
attack victims on board and all were taken to Brixham.

6/17: EVELINE. *Country:* British.
Date sunk: 20/12/17. *Tons nett:* 1660. *Tons gross:*
2605. *Built:* 1897. *Type:* SS. *Rig:* schooner.
Owners: Pyman Bell & Co, Newcastle. *Cargo:*
4070 tons coal and 8 tons general. *Armed:* 1 x 18pdr
gun. *Position:* 9½ miles SSW of Berry Head
(50 14 33N; 03 28 12W). *Master's name:* Benjamin
Burgess. *Crew:* 28. *Crew nationality:* 5 Arabs,
1 Russian, 1 Greek, 1 Dane, 2 Norwegians,
18 British. *Gunners:* Arthur Jones, LS RNR,
No 1392C Devonport; John Henry Whalley, AB
RNVR, No MZ 1563 Devonport.

EVELINE'S last journey began when she left Barry
Docks on December 15, 1917, and made for Falmouth.
She left Falmouth on the 19th, bound for Rouen.

At the time of her loss she was heading NE ¾ E
and was complying with her instructions to take a
zig-zag course. Just a little before 4am on December
20, a steamer was spotted ahead of the *Eveline* by a
lookout who confirmed that it was heading virtually

straight towards them. The order was given to turn
on the navigation lights until the danger had passed. It
was a bad mistake and at 4am she was struck by a
torpedo on the starboard side amidships in the after
part of the engine room.

She quickly settled in the water but still remained
afloat for about half an hour. The crew took to the
lifeboats and remained alongside the steamer until
she sank. They made for the shore but were picked
up soon after by the Drifter *Phingask*.

The submarine concerned was *UB-31*.

6/18: HMT PICTON CASTLE. *Country:* British.
Date sunk: 19/2/17. *Tons nett:* –. *Tons gross:* 245.
Built: –. *Type:* hired trawler. *Rig:* –. *Owners:*
Admiralty. *Cargo:* –. *Armed:* Yes. *Position:* 2½
miles ESE of Mewstone (50 19 00N; 03 28 00W).
Master's name: –.

THE commander of HMT 125 *Agnes Wickfield*, was
Lieutenant E. Davis RNR. He was in company with
the *Picton Castle*, or rather he should have been had it
not been for the terrible weather. He said in his later
report that the two vessels left Plymouth at 4.20am
on February 19, 1917. Their orders were to proceed to
Torbay and Dartmouth to carry out sweeping
operations. As the weather was extremely foggy they
anchored up in Plymouth Sound for a while to see if it
would clear. It did but only for a while as no sooner
had they put to sea than it closed in again even thicker.

The commanders of each vessel had been wise
enough to arrange a rendezvous point and it was also
agreed that *Picton Castle* would sound her whistle
regularly so that *Agnes Wickfield* could work out
roughly where she was. They took soundings regularly
as they rounded Start Point and altered course to bear
up to Berry Head. It was sometime soon after this that
Lieutenant Davis said he lost the sound of *Picton
Castle's* whistle.

When he judged he was about right for the
rendezvous point Lieutenant Davis waited for *Picton
Castle* but she didn't arrive. Even when the fog cleared
a bit there was still no sign of her. Lieutenant Davis
tried to call her on his wireless but the contraption
wasn't working properly. He thought it best to head in
to Dartmouth and speak to the Senior Naval Officer
who also tried to raise *Picton Castle* by wireless.

Nothing was heard of *Picton Castle* until 6.45pm
the same day when a patrol vessel picked up two of
her crew floating in the water off Dartmouth. They
were taken to the Cottage Hospital at Dartmouth and
later interviewed by a naval officer.

Reginald John Pearse from Newquay was a deck
hand but acting as a gunner on *Picton Castle*. He said
he was standing aft and judged that his ship was about
three miles off the land. He assumed that his
commander planned to go into Dartmouth to look for
Agnes Wickfield as she had just turned in that
direction. However, a few moments later there was
"a hell of a bang" and the ship sank rapidly. The other

survivor was Andrew Craig from Belfast who said much the same thing and reckoned that the ship had struck a mine amidships. Both men added that there were several other crew members in the water but they must have been overcome by the extreme cold.

The Admiralty list this one as "mined'.

6/19: CARIAD. *Country:* British.
Date sunk: 8/6/17. *Tons nett:* 38. *Tons gross:* 49.
Built: Brixham in 1904. *Type:* FV. *Rig:* ketch.
Owners: Samuel Partridge, Berry Head Rd, Brixham. *Cargo:* None. *Armed:* No. *Position:* Downend Point bore NNW 9 miles/6 miles E by S of Start Point (50 12 30N; 03 28 00W).
Master's name: Samuel Partridge. *Crew:* 4.

CARIAD lay becalmed in thick fog on the evening of June 8, 1917. Her fore sail was stowed and the helm hard to starboard waiting for the weather to clear. She was not alone as several Brixham fishing smacks could just be seen by the crew, out towards the east. Whilst looking at the other smacks, one of the crew suddenly spotted the conning tower of a submarine about half a mile off and alerted the master. The foresail was hoisted rapidly and the vessel turned towards the shore but with precious little wind it was hopeless.

A shot rang out and a shell kicked up the sea to the side of them. This was followed by two more which both missed but were too close for comfort. The *Cariad* was stopped and the lifeboat got ready. By this time the submarine was within hailing distance and a voice shouted across for the crew to leave their ship and approach the submarine. Once alongside, the *Cariad's* men were ordered to board the submarine while a German sailor used their boat to plant bombs in the fishing vessel's hold. No sooner had their boat returned to the submarine than the bombs exploded and the *Cariad* sank within a few minutes.

The crew were cast adrift in their boat and within 15 minutes a fast patrol vessel *TBD 24* came hurrying in from the east followed closely by another. On passing the *Cariad's* boat the commanding officer shouted, "Where's the submarine?" To which the master replied, "Close under your port bow."

Both boats disappeared into the fog and shortly after, the crew of the *Cariad* were picked up by a patrol trawler and later transferred to the smack *Prevalent* and taken to Brixham.

6/20: ST GEORGE. *Country:* French.
Date sunk: 21/5/15. *Tons nett:* –. *Tons gross:* 44.
Built: Of wood in 1884. *Type:* SV/SS. *Rig:* ketch with steam engine. *Owners:*-. *Cargo:* 16 tons fresh fish. *Armed:* No. *Position:* Dartmouth Castle bore NNW 10 miles (50 11 00N; 03 28 00W).*Master's name:* Jean Baptiste. *Crew:* 14.

ST GEORGE had just finished fishing in the Channel and was hauling in her nets for the last time before heading to Le Havre with her catch. It had been a good trip and the holds were full with 16 tons of fresh fish.

The master was watching the hauling operations from the starboard bow and two of his crew were standing beside him. Suddenly there was an enormous explosion and the ship was blown onto her port side, virtually tearing her in half.

Recovering himself from the deck the master shouted for his crew to get clear. No sooner had he said it the ship sank and he found himself in the water. On looking around he discovered that not only had his ship gone but there was no sign of any of his crew. He grabbed at a piece of wreckage that was nearby and scanned the horizon. There were several other vessels in sight and one in particular had seen his plight.

It was the Brixham fishing vessel *Sunstar* and her master later said that Dartmouth Castle was bearing north-north-west about 10 miles and he could see the *St George* about one and a half miles nearer the land. Suddenly he heard a strange hissing noise pass under the keel of his ship and he realised that it was a torpedo. He looked towards the French ship just in time to see the mid section surge into the air as the explosion occurred. He immediately went to her assistance and by the time he arrived on the scene only bits of wreckage remained. He searched around and found the master but no other survivors.

The master was later taken into Brixham by the *Sunstar* and landed safely at 9pm the same evening.

Meanwhile the armed trawler 1212 *Lord Salisbury* had been ordered to investigate the explosion and made a search of the area. He subsequently picked up the *St George's* lifeboat but no other survivors.

6/21: VERONICA. *Country:* British.
Date sunk: 11/11/16. *Tons nett:* 27. *Tons gross:* –.
Built: Of wood, 1907. *Type:* FV. *Rig:* Ketch.
Owners: Walter Painter, Padstow. *Cargo:* 16 tons fish. *Armed:* No. *Position:* 9 miles SE of Start Point (50 08 00N; 03 28 00W). *Master's name:* James Strong. *Crew:* 3. *Crew nationality:* All British.

WITH his vessel trawling under all plain sail on November 11, 1916, the master spotted an enemy submarine about a mile off on the starboard beam. No sooner had he spotted it than a shot rang out and a shell sliced into the water very close to the *Veronica*. The master ordered the top and fore sails to be lowered and after another shell came perilously close, rowed across to the submarine with his papers.

The German commander sent some of his men over to *Veronica* to plant bombs and after the deed was done they kept the three men on board the submarine for several days.

The master reported later that after they had been sent below in the submarine the Germans had come across a British patrol vessel in the fog and the submarine had to dive very rapidly. The water wasn't very deep and the submarine settled onto a large rock which made it roll over at an angle of forty five degrees and crash to the sea bed. They managed to right her and cruised underwater for quite some time.

The next day they came across a French schooner which they sank and later that day had a go at a steamer. However, as they got closer to the steamer it started to return fire and the German officers got into a panic and dived. The following day they sank another French vessel, this time a three masted schooner and the three crew men from this ship were also taken on board the submarine. Eventually, they attacked another sailing vessel which had a boat on board big enough to take them all and the Germans set them free. During the whole time the master said he and his men were treated very well and some of the Germans even gave them tobacco when they left.

6/22: GARM. *Country:* Norwegian.
Date sunk: 25/8/17. *Tons nett:* 309. *Tons gross:* 725. *Built:* Rotterdam in 1916. *Type:* SS. *Rig:* schooner. *Owners:* Alexander Prebensen of Rasar, Norway. *Cargo:* 880 tons coal from Bowater & Co, Liverpool to Eug Huret, Rouen as broker. *Armed:* No. *Position:* 8 miles ENE from Start Point (50 16 00N; 03 27 30W). *Master's name:* Einar Svendsen. *Crew:* 14.

GARM made her way down the west coast and came up the Channel to Falmouth. She received her route instructions and left shortly after. She hugged Start Point at a distance of one mile and altered course to east-north-east at 4.50pm making about eight knots. At 6.30pm a large explosion boomed out from her midship section which wrecked the bridge and chartroom, and blew the main mast over the side. Coal from the holds was also thrown up through the deck and sprayed all over the ship.

The crew only had one lifeboat on the port side as the starboard boat had been lost in a gale earlier. The boat was lowered with eleven men in it. One man panicked and jumped overboard while another two refused to get into the boat. As the boat touched the water it was immediately over turned because of the ship having way on her and all the men were thrown into the sea. Suddenly the ship was hit in her forward section by another torpedo and she sank immediately. The two men who had refused to leave found themselves in the water clinging to the upturned boat with the others.

The commander of HMT *Buffalo*, Captain S.J. Locke RNR, reported that he was in company with *Casoria* and said that they saw a steamer going east about two miles on their port beam, when suddenly there was a big explosion and the ship began to list heavily to port. They took up action stations and immediately closed on her as she continued to settle by the head. Suddenly the vessel took a final plunge forward and sank. They picked up all but one man who was missing when the lifeboat turned over. All 13

survivors were landed at Brixham at 7.30pm on the same day.

Several positions were given for the sinking of this vessel: Eight miles ENE from Start Point/Start Point bearing W by S seven miles/Berry Head bearing N by E seven miles.

UC-65 was the submarine which sank her.

6/23: BRUNHILDA. *Country:* British.
Date sunk: 11/7/17. *Tons nett:* 1467. *Tons gross:* 2296. *Built:* West Hartlepool in 1901. *Type:* SS. *Rig:* schooner. *Owners:* Arthur Capel & Co, Newcastle. *Charterers:* Herskind & Co. *Cargo:* 3400 tons aluminium earth (bauxite) and esparto grass. *Armed:* 1 x 12pdr 12cwt gun. *Position:* 7 miles E by S of Start Point (50 14 00N; 03 27 00W). *Master's name:* Richard Stonehouse. *Crew:* 23. *Crew nationality:* 14 British, 8 Russians, 1 Norwegian. *Gunners:* W.S. Daymond, acting L/Cpl. RMLI Plymouth, No 4763; F.W. Mosley, RMLI Plymouth, No 6464.

BRUNHILDA'S cargo was listed to be shipped from St Raphael and Bona and consigned to various people in Sunderland and Newcastle. It was from St Raphael her homeward journey began on June 1, 1917. She called in at Bona on the 4th to complete her cargo and left on the 9th. She called in at Gibraltar for sailing instructions on her way back to the UK and was ordered to proceed to Falmouth.

On arrival at Falmouth the *Brunhilda* got off to a poor start by striking the boom defences. The master must have been quite unpopular with the authorities as considerable damage was done to the defences but very little to his ship. The master pleaded that he had no knowledge of the boom and was not warned about it at Gibraltar. She left Falmouth to continue up the Channel to Newcastle. Her bad luck was to continue, for, as she zig-zagged her way past Start Point, a lurking German submarine fired a torpedo at her.

It was 1.50am and the first mate was on the bridge. The master had just gone below, when the torpedo slammed into the starboard side of the ship in number two hold. She began to settle immediately and the forward deck was awash in about one minute. However, the rate slowed considerably once the water reached the esparto grass in the holds. The master, in considerable pain after badly damaging his hand in the blast, ordered the ship to be abandoned which was quickly done with two lifeboats. They pulled clear and watched a U-boat, *UB-31*, appear about two miles off but it beat a hasty retreat as the British patrol boat *Lerita* came in sight. The *Brunhilda* sank about 20 minutes later by the head. The crew were picked up by *Lerita* and landed at Plymouth at 7.30am.

6/24: ALDERSHOT. *Country:* British.
Date sunk: 23/9/18. *Tons nett:* 1354. *Tons gross:* 2177. *Built:* Stockton in 1899. *Type:* SS. *Rig:*

schooner. *Owners:* Aldershot SS Co, 136, Fenchurch St, London. *Cargo:* 2830 tons coal, 2 boilers, for French government, Clyde to Nantes. *Armed:* 1 x 12pd 12cwt gun. *Position:* 10 miles NE by E of Start Point (50 19 00N; 03 26 00W). *Master's name:* Henry Hunter. *Crew:* 27. *Crew nationality:* 21 British, 2 Dutch, 4 Russians. *Gunners:* Thomas Rowland, LS RNVR, No TZ 5445; Ernest Warren, AB RNVR, No BZ 5270.

THE route instructions that the master of the *Aldershot* received at Falmouth were to zig-zag from Falmouth to Start Point, pass not less than two miles off the Mewstone and not less than five miles off Hopes Nose. A straight course was then to be steered on account of the numerous wrecks dangerous to shipping.

Aldershot was heading for St Nazaire and Nantes and was making a steady seven knots. Her journey came to a sudden halt at 5.45pm off Dartmouth when she was hit by a torpedo on her starboard side amidships. The engines were stopped immediately and the men in the engine room and stokehold had to flee the rapidly rising water. Two lifeboats were successfully launched and all the crew except one got clear. Gunner Thomas Rowland was missing. The mess room steward said that he was alongside him at the time of the explosion and a wall of water washed him overboard.

Soon the area was swarming with patrol vessels and several of them started depth charging suspicious movements in the water in the hope of crippling the marauding submarine. At one stage a DH-6 seaplane number 06667 from Prawle joined in the bombing, the pilot having seen the fate of the *Aldershot*. He flew around for a while and spotted what he believed to be a periscope moving through the water leaving a slight wash. He made a pass and dropped a 65 pound bomb on it but no wreckage was seen.

The *Aldershot* sank about 10 minutes after being hit. The crew were picked up by the patrol vessels ML *490* and *461* and landed at Dartmouth.

By recent research in German records, it has been discovered that the submarine responsible for sinking the *Aldershot* was probably *UB-113*, commanded by Oberleutnant U. Pilzecker. This sinking was the last kill that Pilzecker reported by radio and he was never heard from again. In 1989 divers found a submarine only three miles from the position of the *Aldershot* and this is most likely to be the remains of *UB-113*. Perhaps the bomb from the DH-6 seaplane did the trick.

6/25: HILDEGARD. *Country:* American. *Date sunk:* 10/7/17. *Tons nett:* –. *Tons gross:* 622. *Built:* –. *Type:* SV. *Rig:* barquentine. *Owners:* Hildegard Shipping Co, New Orleans. *Cargo:* 250 tons stone. *Armed:* No. *Position:* Start Point bearing N by W about 12 miles (50 05 00N; 03 25 00W). *Master's name:* Ben Thomas Bragg. *Crew:* 10.

Crew nationality: All American. 3 white, 7 coloured.

LEAVING Havre on July 7, 1917, *Hildegard's* orders were to cross the Channel from Cherbourg to Start Point, from there out into the Atlantic and on to St Thomas in the West Indies. Or, if the wind favoured, to follow the French coast to Brest. The wind obviously didn't favour as she was 12 miles off Start Point when she was captured by a German submarine.

W.H. Swann RNVR, commander of the armed trawler 1988 *Recono* takes up the story as he saw it:

"I have the honour to report that at 0800 today while in company with trawler 961 *Lois*, an enemy submarine was sighted attacking the USA Barquentine *Hildegard* 12 miles off Start Point. We were about four miles off Start and the commander of *Lois* gave orders for both vessels to proceed towards the barquentine, when at a distance of about five miles from her it could be seen that the enemy submarine was attacking her by gunfire. The submarine then manoeuvred around the barque and we opened fire at a range of 3500yds, but the shots falling short the range was altered to 5000yds and then 5500, but the shots still fell short. 17 rounds were fired from *Recono* without success and the submarine submerged. Both trawlers put out towed charges and searched the vicinity without result. The *Hildegard* was seen to sink and I took the crew on board and proceeded to Plymouth."

Lieutenant A.A. Crowther RNR, commander of HMT 961 *Lois*, said much the same in his report but added that *Recono* opened fire without receiving orders, the first shot passing close over his own ship. Apparently a rating on board *Recono* mistook an order and, no doubt, was severely reprimanded.

The master of the *Hildegard* was later questioned by the British naval authorities and said that he was becalmed at the time the submarine appeared, and could do nothing to prevent bombs being placed aboard his ship. He said that whilst the German crew were using his boat to plant the bombs the German commander questioned him about conditions in France. Did they have plenty to eat? He replied yes. Were there any shortages? He replied no. The German then told the master that the war would soon be over as they were going to sink every ship they saw.

6/26: ONWARD. *Country:* British. *Date sunk:* 8/6/17. *Tons nett:* 39. *Tons gross:* 50. *Built:* Galmpton in 1907. *Type:* FV. *Rig:* ketch. *Owners:* Edward Davis, 8, Trafalgar Terrace, Brixham. *Cargo:* None. *Armed:* No. *Position:* 9 miles E by S of Start Point (50 14 30N; 03 24 30W). *Master's name:* Edward Davis. *Crew:* 4.

LYING becalmed in the fishing grounds off Start Point the crew of the *Onward* waited for the wind to pick up. Another fishing vessel the *Oceans Pride* was nearby and within hailing distance. The mate suddenly heard a shot boom out and looked towards the other ship just in time to see a hole appear in her mainsail. Another shot was heard which this time was aimed at them. The master ordered the crew into the lifeboat and pulled clear but the Germans continued firing and shouted at them to stop.

They were ordered alongside the submarine and told to board whilst their boat was used to take German officers equipped with bombs around the three fishing vessels. Each boat in turn was paid a visit and all three, including the *Onward*, sank almost immediately.

The crew were picked up along with the other crews by the patrol boat *Prevalent* and taken to Brixham.

6/27: LA BLANCA. *Country:* British. *Date sunk:* 23/11/17. *Tons nett:* 5549. *Tons gross:* 7478. *Built:* Sunderland in 1905. *Type:* SS. *Rig:* schooner. *Owners:* British & Argentine Steam Navigation Co, London. *Cargo:* 3985 tons beef and 400 tons general from Argentine and Brazil to Havre. *Armed:* 1 x 4.7in gun. *Position:* 10 miles SSE of Berry Head/Berry Head bearing N 22 deg W 10 miles (50 14 30N; 03 24 00W). *Master's name:* Robert Alfred Smiles. *Crew:* 70. *Crew nationality:* 38 British, 8 Greeks, 2 Swedes, 2 Norwegians, 1 Manillan, 2 Dutch, 2 American, 2 Roumanians, 5 Spanish, 1 Chilean, 4 Russians, 3 Egyptians. *Gunners:* John William Talbot, LS RFR Chatham, No 173982; Henry P. Leddra, AB RNR Devonport, No A2220.

THERE was so much controversy over the sinking of *La Blanca*, that a Court of Enquiry was called by the Admiralty. This was held at the Royal Naval Barracks, Dartmouth, on Tuesday December 11, 1917.

Returning from South America with her holds full *La Blanca* called into Plymouth for orders and to pick up armed escorts to accompany her up the Channel. Two armed trawlers were made available, HMT 686 *Rinaldo II*, commanded by Temporary Commander William Main RNR, and HMT 707 *Zonia*, commanded by Temporary Commander Charles Llewellyn Kingdon, RNR.

Before leaving Plymouth, Captain Smiles asked both trawler commanders if they would be able to keep station with him as his ship was fast. They replied that they could make eight knots and there shouldn't be a problem. But there was. It became evident almost immediately every hour the master of *La Blanca* would have to slow down and allow the two escorts to get back on station, one off the port bow and the other to starboard. Captain Smiles wrote in his report to the naval control office at Dartmouth that the escort commander on his port bow seemed quite indifferent to station keeping and at times he couldn't tell if he was with him or not.

At the end of a long ziz-zag, around 11.30pm, and a subsequent alteration of course to allow the escorts to get on station *La Blanca* was attacked. The master said he only saw the torpedo when it was right under his bridge leaving him no time to take evasive action. It struck the steamer on the port side in number three hold blowing a large hole in her side and causing her to take on an immediate list to port. The explosion also brought down the mast and with it the crow's nest with a lookout inside it who went over the side.

Captain Smiles immediately ordered his officers to the boats to ensure that everyone was assembled and ready to go as soon as possible. This was quickly done but another life was lost when the chief steward slipped and disappeared overboard. All the boats got clear and one was ordered to stay close to the steamer. The master and officers on the bridge discussed the idea of getting *La Blanca* in tow and beaching her. But just then the man in the boat alongside shouted that she was settling more quickly which made up the master's mind for him. They all left and pulled clear, but after a few yards the master felt certain he heard a voice shouting from the steamer. He quickly put the others aboard the nearby *Zonia* and headed back.

Close alongside the sinking steamer he shouted to see if anyone would reply but heard nothing except a loud hiss as another torpedo sped past him and buried itself in the port bow of *La Blanca*. He was lucky, being just far enough away to escape the blast.

With this *La Blanca* gave up, rolled completely over and sank with her belly uppermost. Sixteen of her crew were landed at Plymouth by *Zonia* and 51 were landed at Dartmouth by *Rinaldo II*. This left one person unaccounted for, possibly bringing the total lost to three, though the official loss figure remained at two.

The findings of the Court of Enquiry blamed the escort commanders. The master of *La Blanca* should also have been hugging the coast and not taken a straight line from Start to Portland. The master said he was ordered to by a signal from *Rinaldo II*. The signalman on *Rinaldo II*, Hugh Keatings RNR, said that he had merely asked *La Blanca* if that is what she intended to do. Whatever the truth, the responsibility lay with the escort boats, particularly William Main of *Rinaldo II*, being the senior of the two. He was reprimanded for not organising routes and signals with *La Blanca* before leaving Plymouth, not keeping correct station, for showing lights and for not zig-zagging. He was relieved of his command and sent ashore to be put under the command of a commissioned officer.

Charles Kingdon was also censured for bad station keeping and showing lights but no other punishment was noted.

The position given is the one believed to be the most accurate. One of the escorts put their position as Start Point bearing WNW 16 miles with Berry Head bearing NNW 15 miles. However, a document in the Court of Enquiry papers gives a position of 50 11 30N; 03 13 00W.

U-96 was the submarine involved.

6/28: BEECHTREE. *Country:* British. *Date sunk:* 10/2/17. *Tons nett:* 778. *Tons gross:* 1277. *Built:* Antwerp in 1912. *Type:* SS. *Rig:* schooner. *Owners:* The Tree Steamship Co Ltd, Cymric Buildings, Cardiff. *Cargo:* 1776 tons coal from Coward & Son, Swansea to A. Lemone of Rouen, France. *Armed:* No. *Position:* 11 miles SE of Start Point (50 08 30N; 03 23 30W). *Master's name:* Daniel Wright Fowle. *Crew:* 15. *Crew nationality:* 6 British, 5 Greeks, 2 Russians, 2 Spaniards.

BEECHTREE commenced her final voyage from Swansea, leaving there at 7am on February 7, 1917. The weather was hazy with a light breeze. All was set for a fair crossing to France on the 10th and at 3.50am she was at full power making six knots, steering a course east allowing a quarter point for wind and sea.

Henry Burton, the first officer, was on the bridge. The next instant the calm was shattered by an explosion on the starboard side of the ship. The master immediately made his way to the bridge to find that *Beechtree* was badly damaged abreast of the foremast and was sinking by the head. Surveying the damage he could see that the hatch covers had been blown right off, the deck was torn up and large quantities of coal had been blown all over the ship.

He ordered all hands to the boats and they were all clear of the ship within three minutes. The *Beechtree* sank two minutes later with the last man to get clear being the master, who only quit her when the water was up to the lower bridge.

As they pulled away from the sinking ship the crew spotted a submarine on the surface near the second mate's boat which stayed a few moments before submerging. Meanwhile, they spotted a steamer and started to pull towards it in the hope of being rescued quickly. The steamer appeared to be about one and a half miles to the south and they rowed hard in the hope of converging with her but suddenly, another large explosion boomed out and the steamer sank.

The crew were found at 5am and were picked up by HMT *St Cuthbert* which landed them safely at Brixham at 10am on the same day.

The submarine involved was *UC-21*.

6/29: ELIZABETH. *Country:* British. *Date sunk:* 8/9/17. *Tons nett:* 48. *Tons gross:* 70. *Built:* 1859. *Type:* SV. *Rig:* ketch. *Owners:* E. Lloyd, Shipbroker, 118, Dock St, Newport. *Cargo:* 95 tons coal from Newport to Cherbourg. *Armed:* No. *Position:* 18 miles SSE of Dartmouth (50 04 00N; 03 23 00W). *Master's name:* John Morris Williams, 14, Victoria Place, Exmouth. *Crew:* 3.

AT 7pm on September 8, 1917, the master was at the wheel when he saw an object on the starboard bow about five miles off which he thought was a patrol vessel. The sea was quite choppy and it was difficult to make it out, but he thought there was something peculiar about it. He called the mate to take the wheel and called the boy up to have a look. The lad had been torpedoed twice before and so the master reckoned he should be able to recognise a submarine when he saw one. The boy looked through the binoculars and confirmed that it was indeed a submarine.

The master ordered the boat to be got ready. About 12 minutes later the submarine was about one point off the beam about four miles away and fired two shots at the *Elizabeth* in quick succession. The first shot missed but the second took the ships rudder away and made a mess of the stern.

The master ordered his crew to abandon ship and they pulled clear. The submarine didn't fire any more shots but came alongside the boat and ordered the master to board. He was questioned as to the details of his ship and informed that she would be sunk.

The *Elizabeth* still had some sail up and was moving quite fast as the submarine chased after it. The German crew, using the crew's lifeboat, tried to board her once but couldn't row fast enough. The submarine then towed the boat with the master and two German sailors in it ahead of the ketch and they eventually managed to get aboard. On boarding, the master was held at gunpoint and told to fetch the ship's flag. The ship was by this time nearly full of water and close to sinking. Whilst he fetched the flag the other German took whatever he fancied and then attached a bomb to the starboard mizzen rigging. They then left the ship quickly and rowed back towards the submarine. Just as the Germans climbed back on board the bomb exploded and the *Elizabeth* sank almost immediately.

The rest of the crew were ordered back in the boat with the master. Having been bashed around by the submarine whilst being towed, the boat was now very leaky. The master appealed to the German commander to tow them nearer to land but he refused and waved them aside.

They set a small sail and pulled for the land as best they could while all the time having to bale. An hour or so later the Norwegian steamer *Rodney* picked them up.

6/30: VISBORG. *Country:* Norwegian. *Date sunk:* 27/11/16. *Tons nett:* 762. *Tons gross:* 1300. *Built:* 1886. *Type:* SS. *Rig:* schooner. *Owners:* Brummnas & Torgersen, Haugesund, Norway. *Cargo:* 1760 tons coal from Barry Roads to Cherbourg. *Armed:* No. *Position:* 14 miles SE from Start Point (50 04 00N; 03 22 00W). *Master's name:* Ole Sorace. *Crew:* 17. *Crew nationality:* 4 Greeks, 2 Americans, 1 Swede, 10 Norwegians.

CAPTAIN Sorace gave a new heading to the helmsman, east half east, which would put the ship on a direct course for Cherbourg. He felt the vessel settle down to it's new track. Five minutes later he heard a bang and a shell threw up a spout of water several hundred yards off on the starboard side. Through his binoculars he could see the conning tower of a submarine about four miles off. Suddenly there was another bang on the port side. There was another U-boat much closer.

The master ordered the engines to reduced power and waited to see what would happen. He expected the nearest submarine on the port side to issue some instruction but the message came some time later from the other as it hoisted the signal FH, "Bring your boat."

The master had already thrown his confidential sailing instructions over the side in a weighted bag. He had with him though his ship's manifest and general papers belonging to the company. The commander of the submarine kept the papers and ordered one of his men to go back with the master to the *Visborg* and plant bombs. It was done very quickly and two boats left the steamer, the rest of the crew following after the master. As the German bomber climbed back aboard the submarine his bombs exploded sending the *Visborg* straight to the seabed. The commander appeared and pointed to a steamer in the distance and said, "There is a Belgian relief ship, we are not going to sink her, go on board."

The two boats rowed off towards the steamer which was the Belgian relief Ship *Queenstad* which picked the men up. They were later transferred to the patrol vessel *Monarch* which landed them at Weymouth.

The submarine was *UB-19*, commanded by Oberleutnant Erich Noodt.

6/31: IDALIA. *Country:* British.
Date sunk: 21/2/18. *Tons nett:* 23. *Tons gross:* 32.
Built: Of wood at Galmpton in 1896. *Type:* SV.
Rig: ketch. *Owners:* Alfred Henry Lanfear,
Paignton, Devon. *Cargo:* Fish. *Armed:* No.
Position: 10 miles SE by S from Berry head
(50 15 00N; 03 21 00W). *Master's name:* Samuel
Down. *Crew:* 3. *Crew nationality:* All British.

SKIPPER Samuel Down of the *Idalia* could see a fishing smack in the distance and wondered what the indistinct object was alongside it. His course took him towards it and every now and then he took glances to see if it was any clearer. He would have been wise to have studied it more closely beforehand as suddenly the smack, *Rosebud*, sank leaving the object clearly outlined as a German submarine.

Captain Down immediately shouted to his crew to bear *Idalia* away and make a run for the shore. *Idalia's* speed was no match for the submarine which caught up with her in no time at all. A few rifle shots cracking into her sails was enough to make her crew realise that there was no escape.

After the three men rowed clear in the small boat the German commander signalled them to come alongside. The crew were held aboard the submarine while the enemy used their boat to plunder and plant bombs. They helped themselves to clothing, oilskins,

boots, food and then left a bomb under the keel. Ten minutes later *Idalia's* men were back in the small boat, just in time to witness the explosion and watch their ship plummet to the seabed.

As the men rowed towards the shore the submarine made off to the east-south-east after yet another helpless fishing smack, *Leanora*. After rowing for about an hour *Idalia's* men were spotted by an armed drifter and taken into Torquay.

6/32: OCEANS PRIDE. *Country:* British.
Date sunk: 8/6/17. *Tons nett:* 50. *Tons gross:* –.
Built: Of wood at Brixham in 1901. *Type:* FV.
Rig: ketch. *Owners:* Edward Rowse Crocker,
13, Trafalgar Terrace, Brixham. *Cargo:* None.
Armed: No. *Position:* 7 miles SE of Berry Head
(50 12 00N; 03 20 00W). *Master's name:* Edward
Crocker. *Crew:* 4.

AT 6pm on the June 8, 1917, the fishing vessel *Oceans Pride* wallowed in the swell and waited for the wind to pick up. Unfortunately the crew had just spotted a submarine surfacing about a mile to the southward. A shell whistled overhead followed by two more which both missed their target. The submarine then dived and surfaced again on the other side of *Oceans Pride*. It opened fire again and this time with more accuracy as a shell carried away the beak halyards, damaging the mainsail and mizzen.

The master ordered the boat to be launched and the crew pulled clear. As they did so the Germans fired four or five shots at the small boat but aiming wide as a signal for them to stop. On looking around the crew could see that they were not alone in their plight. Two other fishing vessels the *Onward* and the *Torbay Lass* had also been threatened and their crews had taken to their boats too. The German commander ordered the crew of *Onward's* boat to get aboard the submarine and their boat was used to tow a bombing party around all three fishing vessels. One by one they exploded and sank.

The crew of the *Oceans Pride* were picked up later with other survivors by the patrol boat *Prevalent* and taken to Brixham.

6/33: OCEAN SWELL. *Country:* British.
Date sunk: 5/7/17. *Tons nett:* 163. *Tons gross:* 194.
Built: Of wood at Fowey in 1875. *Type:* SV.
Rig: barque. *Owners:* Edward Stephens, Fowey.
Cargo: 1200 bundles (34 tons) iron cask hoops,
from Pessie, Granville to ECC, St Austell.
Armed: No. *Position:* 15 miles SE from Start Point
(50 07 00N; 03 20 00W). *Master's name:* Charles
Henry Deacon. *Crew:* 6.

THE master of the *Ocean Swell* had made repeated requests to the French naval authorities for an escort to take him across the Channel. He was told that he would get one if he waited. He waited several days and was eventually informed that there wouldn't be an escort available for some time. The master then decided he would go ahead and reverse the route given to him on his outward bound journey from Fowey.

He timed his departure from Granville to try and sail across the Channel during the night and arrive close to the coast at daylight. All went according to plan until dawn when the wind fell, leaving *Ocean Swell* wallowing. At 9.30am the master had put her on the starboard tack and had all sail set trying to catch every breath of wind, when suddenly a shot rang out. This was followed by two more which sent up spouts of water very close to the barque. The master realised that he was under attack by a submarine which was approaching very rapidly.

As the master and crew pulled clear in their boat the submarine poured over thirty shots into the *Ocean Swell* and she sank by the bows very quickly.

The submarine then came alongside the crew's boat. A German officer ordered them to put their hands on their heads and had them covered by rifles whilst the commanding officer demanded to know the particulars of the ship. He then asked for the boat's compass which he kept and sent them on their way. They were eventually picked up at 6pm that evening and taken to Plymouth.

6/34: CONSOLATION. *Country:* British. *Date sunk:* 9/9/16. *Tons nett:* –. *Tons gross:* 47. *Built:* Of wood at Oulton Broad 1900. *Type:* SV. *Rig:* ketch. *Owners:* Albert E. Dexter, 23, Trawl Market, Lowestoft. *Cargo:* None. *Armed:* No. *Position:* 15 miles SE of Start Point (50 03 00N; 03 20 00W). *Master's name:* Edward Reynolds. *Crew:* 5.

ON the morning of September 9, 1916, the crew of the *Consolation* were busy repairing their trawl. So busy were they that the German submarine approaching them went unnoticed until a shell came whimpering over the masts. This was followed rapidly by two more which passed over the bows.

The five men quickly manned their small boat and pulled clear. The submarine closed on the *Consolation* firing shell after shell as it approached. The little sailing ship lurched violently under each impact but eventually could take no more and slowly slipped below the waves.

The submarine dived immediately, because a British destroyer appeared on the horizon. *Consolation's* crew made off towards the fishing vessel *Admiral Jellicoe* of Lowestoft and were whisked on board at top speed. Her master had seen what was going on and had his trawl already in. As soon as the men were aboard, the *Jellicoe* made off to Brixham.

6/35: PREMIER II. *Country:* British. *Date sunk:* 27/11/17. *Tons nett:* 23. *Tons gross:* 48. *Built:* Of wood at Brixham in 1904. *Type:* SV.

Rig: ketch. *Owners:* William Sanders, King St, Brixham. *Cargo:* 1 ton fresh fish. *Armed:* Yes. *Position:* 16 miles SE of Start Point (50 06 00N; 03 17 00W). *Master's name:* Fred Dyer, 93, Mount Pleasant, Brixham. *Crew:* 4. *Crew nationality:* All British.

PREMIER II was listed as an admiralty drifter, presumably part time as on the day she was lost she had been fishing. The weather was quite clear but a moderate gale was blowing and a strong westerly swell made conditions particularly rough. All the crew were on deck and the ship was on the port tack heading in a northerly direction. Nobody spotted the German submarine surface about 1000yds to the west until she fired the first shell. It crashed into the *Premier's* rigging bringing down the head sails and an assortment of blocks.

The master looked at the menace getting closer and wished he had a gun that would be of use against such a large submarine. She looked very big. He judged about 300ft feet long, painted grey, and he couldn't be sure but he thought he could see the remains of the letters *UC-1* below the fresh paint. Several more shells came whistling towards the *Premier*, most of them missed but two hit the hull square on, throwing up huge splinters of wood. The master told his men that it was time to leave and they rowed clear in the ship's boat.

It was a very nasty sea and it was all the men could do to keep themselves running with it. The submarine got closer and closer to the *Premier*, shelling her all the while until she sank. If the weather had been better the commander would probably have sunk her with bombs instead.

The *Premier's* crew made the best of it as they were swept up the Channel into the night. They rigged up a sea anchor to slow their rate of drift down and all took it in turns to row to keep themselves warm. At 5.30 the next morning help arrived when the transport SS *Lorburn* plucked them to safety. On board they were treated to some warm dry clothes and hot food before being landed at Sandown Bay later the same day.

UC-1 was sunk on July 19, 1917, so was not the submarine involved.

6/36: ORYX. *Country:* British. *Date sunk:* 21/2/18. *Tons nett:* 37. *Tons gross:* 49. *Built:* Of wood at Brixham in 1912. *Type:* SV. *Rig:* ketch. *Owners:* John William Upham, Brixham, Devon. *Cargo:* Fish. *Armed:* No. *Position:* 11 miles SE by E from Berry Head (50 18 00N; 03 16 00W). *Master's name:* Harry Williams. *Crew:* 4. *Crew nationality:* All British.

BY the time the German submarine commander got around to sinking the *Oryx* he seemed to be in something of a hurry. He had been busy that day and had already sunk several other fishing vessels in the vicinity. Maybe it was the appearance about six miles off, of a large convoy that was making him jumpy.

However, it made no difference to the fate of the *Oryx*. She was about two miles away from the submarine, her trawl out presenting her port side nicely to the German gunner.

At 2.15pm the first shell passed clear over the rigging, an intentional shot meant to inform the master to abandon his ship or face the consequences. There was no contest, such a small sailing vessel couldn't possibly have any answer to such a powerful vessel other than to give in. Her foresail was lowered and the four men on the *Oryx* rowed away in the small boat.

From about half a mile distance the German gunner opened up in earnest, the first shell striking *Oryx* low down on the port bow. The next smashed away the jib and the following two smashed more holes in the port side. It was more than enough to send her to the bottom about four minutes later.

The four men in the boat rigged up a sail out of an old rug and headed for Lyme Regis. At 4pm they were spotted by the patrol vessel *Rinaldo II* which dropped them later the same day at Brixham.

6/37: FAVOURITE. *Country:* British.
Date sunk: 9/9/16. *Tons nett:* –. *Tons gross:* 38.
Built: Of wood at Brixham 1905. *Type:* SV.
Rig: ketch. *Owners:* Stephen Richardson, Bond St, Brixham. *Cargo:* –. *Armed:* No. *Position:* 19 miles SE of Start Point (50 01 00N; 03 16 00W). *Master's name:* Edward Goldfinch. *Crew:* 4.

The crew of the *Favourite* had just hauled in the trawl and were jibbed over on the starboard tack under all sail heading towards Berry Head. The master saw a submarine about half a mile off which seemed to be chasing another fishing vessel which the master knew to be the *Paragon*.

The master shouted for the helmsman to bring the ship up a point and hoped he could get clear but suddenly a shell whistled close by. The submarine commander had turned his attention to the *Favourite* and the next shell smashed into the starboard side throwing up splinters and planks. Yet another shell followed which carried away the jib and the master realised that his ship was doomed.

He ordered all hands into the boat and pulled clear in the nick of time as several more shells made direct hits with devastating effect. Shortly afterwards, *Favourite* sank.

The submarine paid no attention to the men in the boat and sped off in pursuit of other fishing vessels in the distance. The *Favourite's* crew rowed towards a ship in the distance which turned out to be the *Boys Friend* of Lowestoft, which picked them up and took them to Brixham later that day.

6/38: IBEX. *Country:* British. *Date sunk:* 29/1/18.
Tons nett: 42. *Tons gross:* 50. *Built:* Of wood at Brixham in 1896. *Type:* SV. *Rig:* ketch. *Owners:* Andrew Upham, Brixham. *Cargo:* –. *Armed:* No.
Position: 16 miles SE of Berry Head (50 12 00N; 03 13 00W). *Master's name:* William John Shears. *Crew:* 4.

THE master of the *Ibex* lifted up his binoculars and looked at the *Perseverance* lying about a quarter of a mile off to the east. She was flying signal flags up her mast which read, 'Enemy submarine close by.' The trawl was out and Captain Shears told his crew of the impending danger. He urged them to get the trawl in quickly. It was a slow process, too slow as at 1.30pm the submarine appeared to the east, bearing down rapidly on the helpless fishermen.

From 100yds the submarine fired one shell which threw up a huge spout of water alongside the *Ibex*. The message to the master was clear, leave your ship now. The four men wasted no time in launching their small boat and no sooner were they clear than the submarine fired two more shots into the hull of the *Ibex*. She lurched under each impact, splinters flying high into the air, then she settled down as the water poured into her and she disappeared.

The submarine moved on to attack the rest of the fishing fleet, each vessel receiving similar treatment. The crew of the *Ibex* rowed towards other small boats from the *Perseverance* and *General Leman*. All of them were picked up at around 6.30pm by the patrol trawler *Rinaldo II* which ferried them into Brixham.

6/39: REINDEER. *Country:* British.
Date sunk: 12/3/17. *Tons nett:* 42. *Tons gross:* 52.
Built: Of wood at Brixham in 1914. *Type:* FV.
Rig: Ketch. *Owners:* Samuel S. Drew, New Road, Brixham. *Cargo:* Fish. *Armed:* No. *Position:* 15 miles SE of Berry Head (50 13 00N; 03 13 00W). *Master's name:* Edgar Thomas. *Crew:* 4.

THE *Reindeer* was under all plain sail in the area known as the fishing grounds between Berry Head and Portland Bill, when a submarine was seen. She didn't seem to be making for the *Reindeer* but was heading in the opposite direction at about 8 knots.

The master wasn't taking any chances and ordered his other three crewmen to make a boat ready. He looked at the submarine again and wondered if she was British. Slowly the submarine turned and started to head towards him. As she approached the first shell was fired. It missed but it was enough for the master to decide to take to the boat and pull clear. By the third shot the German gunner had the range and the main mast came crashing down. This was followed by many more shells, most of them throwing up huge splinters of wood and causing the ship to lurch under the impact.

The *Reindeer's* crew were by this time a safe distance away and watched as their ship took the pounding. Suddenly the submarine stopped firing and turned away. About a mile off a steamer had appeared and a sharp eyed German had spotted it. The submarine turned towards the steamer as the gunner loosed off a few shells at it which all fell short. The *Reindeer* was left still afloat but in a bad way.

The crew of the fishing boat rowed away as fast as they could and watched from a distance as their boat disappeared leaving the submarine to chase after the steamer. Later that day they were picked up by the trawler *Picotee* and were landed at Brixham at 2pm on the 13th.

6/40: SEA LARK. *Country:* British.
Date sunk: 28/11/16. *Tons nett:* 42. *Tons gross:* –.
Built: Brixham in 1900. *Type:* FV. *Rig:* ketch.
Owners: Robert Jackman Snr, Berry Head Rd, Brixham. *Cargo: Armed:* No. *Position:* 24 miles SE by S of Berry Head (50 03 00N; 03 12 00W).
Master's name: Wilfred Blackmore. *Crew:* 4.

THE master of the *Sea Lark* became extremely suspicious when he spotted another fishing vessel about a mile to leeward. He knew the vessel well, it was *Diligence*, and he knew that something was wrong as she was hauling down her mainsail. The only thing he could suspect was that a submarine was at work and he immediately told his men to cut the trawl and make a run for it. He was well aware of the method the Germans employed when dealing with small fishing vessels. They simply went round to each one in turn and sank them at leisure.

However, in spite of the master's shrewdness he was not quick enough as in the next instant a shell came whistling over the *Sea Lark's* sails; it was the signal to 'stop, or else.' The submarine was closing rapidly and the master ordered the crew to take to the boat. No sooner were they clear than the submarine opened fire, this time at close range and a few minutes later *Sea Lark* was sent to the bottom.

The crew rowed in a northerly direction for six hours and were eventually picked up by the vessel *Rosebud* and later landed safely at Brixham.

6/41: CATENA. *Country:* British.
Date sunk: 28/11/16. *Tons nett:* 36. *Tons gross:* –.
Built: Brixham in 1910. *Type:* FV. *Rig:* ketch.
Owners: Samuel Thomas Evans Locke, Mount Pleasant, Brixham. *Cargo:* –. *Armed:* No. *Position:* 25 miles SE by S of Berry Head (50 02 00N; 03 11 00W). *Master's name:* Charles Henry Locke. *Crew:* 4.

THE master of the *Catena* knew something was wrong as lots of the fishing vessels around him in the distance were behaving very strangely. Sails were going up and down, some were changing tacks very violently and others were disappearing. He didn't like the look or the feel of it one bit so he ordered the trawl cables to be cut and set the helm for shore.

She sailed on for some while and the crew hoped they had got away with it. However, a shell soon came

whistling past the foremast, and very close at that. The master ordered the sails down then destroyed his confidential papers. After gathering up some of his personal instruments he joined his men in the boat.

Three minutes later after a pounding from the submarine's gun the *Catena* had gone. After rowing for about an hour the crew were spotted by the vessel *Ethel Lilian* and taken into Brixham later that day.

6/42: ACORN. *Country:* British.
Date sunk: 26/9/17. *Tons nett:* 97. *Tons gross:* –.
Built: Aberystwith in 1864. *Type:* SV. *Rig:* schooner. *Owners:* E. Maynard, Overton, Plymouth. *Cargo:* Shingle ballast. *Armed:* No. *Position:* 20 miles SE by E of Start Point (50 03 00N; 03 11 00W). *Master's name:* George Gush.
Crew: 5. *Crew nationality:* All British.

LEAVING Granville on September 24, 1917, *Acorn* was heading down the English Channel on the afternoon of the 26th under full sail. A strong breeze was blowing with a heavy swell. The master was on watch and on looking to the west he noticed what he thought to be a steamer heading towards him. He kept his eye on it for some time and gradually the "steamer" turned into a submarine.

The submarine opened fire. The master ordered his crew to take to the lifeboat and abandon ship. As the crew pulled away on the opposite side to the submarine's approach they heard a crack as the flying jib was smashed away and sent crashing down. They got further and further away and still the submarine continued to pound the wooden ship. Soon the *Acorn* was lost to view by a rainstorm and when it cleared she had vanished.

The crew headed north towards the land and were picked up by the Brixham Trawler *Silver Lining* the same evening and landed at Brixham.

6/43: EINAR JARL. *Country:* Norwegian.
Date sunk: 12/3/17. *Tons nett:* 1112. *Tons gross:* 1849. *Built:* –. *Type:* SS. *Rig:* –. *Owners:* Norden Jeltske SS Co, chartered to a London firm. *Cargo:* In ballast. *Armed:* No. *Position:* 10 miles ESE from Start Point (50 0 700N; 03 10 00W). *Master's name:* Alex Fredricksen. *Crew:* 20. *Crew nationality:* All Norwegian.

EINAR Jarl sailed out of London on March 10, 1917 bound for Fowey and from there she was to proceed to Philadelphia, USA. On the 12th she was still heading down Channel when at about 12.30pm a shell cracked close by his ship. The master stopped the steamer's engines and ordered all the hands on deck. At that precise moment another shell came whistling in and hit the ship.

It was foggy and the master couldn't make out the submarine. A few seconds later another shell slammed into the coal bunker and exploded. Meanwhile, the first mate was now on deck mustering the hands assigned to the port lifeboat. The master had gone down below to snatch his papers from the saloon but as he arrived there a shell exploded nearby and knocked all the lights out. He immediately made for the deck again and as he arrived he was welcomed by a bullet in his right shoulder. Staggering and bleeding badly, the master managed to make his way to the boat on the starboard side. The shells were still coming and one smashed into the ship just as the master arrived, wounding two men severely.

Both boats eventually managed to get clear of the ship. The master's boat had taken quite a battering and the mate saw that his captain was in a bad way. The boat was swamped and full of bullet holes. He got alongside and transferred the captain and the two wounded men to his own boat and replaced them with fit men.

It was at this stage that the cause of all their problems appeared in the form of a German submarine about four ship's lengths away. It made no attempt to communicate with them but closed on the *Einar Jarl* and put a boarding party on her. About half an hour later they left and the ship sank soon after. The crew were rescued by the trawler *Chanticleer*.

6/44: MOTANO. *Country:* American. *Date sunk:* 31/7/17. *Tons nett:* 1742. *Tons gross:* –. *Built:* –. *Type:* SS. *Rig:* oil tanker. *Owners:* Standard Oil Co, New York. *Cargo:* 3581 tons fuel oil. *Armed:* 2 x 3in 50 cal guns. *Position:* 20 miles S 70 E of Start Point/16 miles 72 deg E from Start (50 06 00N; 03 10 00W). *Master's name:* L.S. Stratton. *Crew:* 46.

THE information on this loss is taken mainly from reports of patrol boat commanders.

The *Motano* had crossed the Atlantic from New York and was under escort to Portsmouth. HMS *B13* was one of the escorts and reports that at 7.35pm on July 31, 1917, the convoy was zig-zagging up the Channel making 15 knots. The weather was threatening to become misty and the convoy joined in single line ahead formation. There was one patrol boat at the head of the column and one on each beam.

At 8.15pm there was a heavy explosion from the *Motano* and her stern sank at once. The commander of *B13* ordered *P59* to pick up the crew immediately as the *Motana* could not lower any boats. *P59* says that she appeared to have been hit by a torpedo in the port quarter well under the waterline.

Twenty-four people were lost including eight US Navy ratings. The 22 survivors were taken off by *P59* and eventually landed at Portsmouth. Seventeen were merchant seaman and five US navy ratings.

Motano was a very deep draughted ship and lay upright but touching the seabed in 34 fathoms of water. She was completely submerged with the exception of the forecastle which stood up about 40ft above the surface. William Colegrave, commanding

officer of the naval vessel *Woonda* was sent to examine the situation and decide what to do with her. He found that the vessel was quite stationary and the sea and tide breaking against her with considerable force. He concluded she was beyond salvage.

The wreck posed a serious navigational hazard so he went back to Torquay to report and was ordered to sink her completely.

Once back at the scene he placed two charges made up of 16¼lb of gun cotton each and placed one under the port and starboard bilges as far down as he could get them. The charges were fired simultaneously with good effect. The mast was blown out of the wreck which fell over the port side and slowly she heeled to port, rolled over and sank. The *Woonda* made several passes over the wreck and declared her safe with not less than 15 fathoms clearance.

6/45: VARUNA. *Country:* British. *Date sunk:* 4/1/18. *Tons nett:* 40. *Tons gross:* 52. *Built:* Of wood at Galmpton in 1906. *Type:* SV. *Rig:* ketch. *Owners:* John Brusey, Brixham. *Cargo:* –. *Armed:* No. *Position:* 15 miles SE by E from Berry Head (50 15 38N; 03 09 00W). *Master's name:* John Brusey. *Crew:* 4.

THE submarine broke the surface about 250yds off. The third hand, Arthur Solomon, spotted her first and shouted for the skipper to come on deck quickly. Looking around they could all see a fleet of armed patrol ships about two and a half miles to the south. Four rifle shots were heard followed by four shells, all of which missed. It was a strange thing for the German commander to do considering the British patrol vessels were so close. The gunfire undoubtedly drew the patrol's attention. One of the patrol vessels opened fire but her shells fell well short.

By this time *Varuna's* crew had taken to their small boat and were clear, leaving the submarine to nudge the sailing vessel's starboard quarter forcing it over onto the port tack. Two Germans quickly boarded her and planted bombs, obviously with short fuses as a few moments after they left, the bombs exploded sending the *Varuna* to the bottom.

The last the crew saw of the action was the submarine heading off on the surface to the north with several of the patrol vessel's in hot pursuit. One of the patrol ships *Gene Stuart* stopped and picked the crew up who were landed safely the next morning at Brixham.

6/46: SJAELLAND. *Country:* British. *Date sunk:* 25/5/17. *Tons nett:* 878. *Tons gross:* 1750. *Built:* Kiel in 1872. *Type:* SS. *Rig:* schooner. *Owners:* R.S. Dalgleish SS Co, Watergate Buildings, Newcastle. *Cargo:* In ballast. *Armed:* No. *Position:* 18 miles E by N of Start Point (50 16 00N; 03 09 00W). *Master's name:* A. Macphee. *Crew:* 18.

SJAELLAND was formerly a Danish vessel and retained her Danish name when transferred to British ownership.

She left Havre Roads on May 24, 1917, at 1pm on high water and was bound for Barry Docks, Cardiff. On Friday May 25, at 6.40am, she was steering a course west by south and making a steady nine knots. About one mile off on her port beam a submarine had just surfaced and her crew were now pouring out of the hatch, making ready the deck gun. Within a few minutes they opened fire on the steamer and the first shot crashed into her port lifeboat reducing it to matchwood.

The master, who was on the bridge, put the helm over to bring the ship in line with the submarine and then stopped the engines. He ordered all hands on deck and was watching the men scurrying to their boat stations whilst at the same time keeping an eye on the fast approaching enemy. Another shot and the master was killed as a shell crashed into the bridge. The second mate also fell victim to the same shell and was seriously injured. Another shell followed, smashing the davits of the starboard lifeboat causing it to drop into the water and float away. The first mate seeing this leapt into the sea and swam to the boat and managed to row it back to the ship. The mate's gallant efforts gave the crew a means of escape and they pulled clear. The *Sjaelland* was by then full of holes and sinking rapidly, her decks completely awash.

The submarine finished off the *Sjaelland* with a well-placed torpedo and she sank at 7.20am. Having questioned the crew in the boat, the submarine commander hurried east in pursuit of another steamer. She was the *New Pioneer* and she had seen what was going on and made off as fast as she could. She was lucky and made it to safety.

Meanwhile, the crew of the *Sjaelland* had spotted another steamer, the *Seaforth* of Bristol, which picked them up and landed them at Torquay.

The submarine concerned was *UC-66*.

6/47: HMS FORMIDABLE. *Country:*
British. *Date sunk:* 1/1/15. *Tons nett:* –. *Tons gross:* 15000. *Built:* 1898. *Type:* Battleship. *Rig:* Twin-funnelled. *Owners:* Admiralty. *Cargo:* –. *Armed:* 4 x 12in guns, 12 x 6in guns, 18 x 12pdr. *Position:* 20 miles E of Start Point (50 11 00N; 03 06 00W). *Master's name:* Arthur N. Loxley. *Crew:* 780. *Crew nationality:* British.

THE sinking of HMS *Formidable* was a terrible loss during the early stages of the war. It brought home to the British Navy just what an effective weapon of war a submarine was. Over 500 men lost their lives during the early hours of New Year's Day, 1915. More might have survived had it not been for the bitterly cold weather.

The Fifth Battle Squadron under the command of Vice-Admiral Sir Lewis Bayly, had been ordered by the Admiralty to proceed to the English Channel for exercises and firing practice. During the last day of 1914, the squadron manoeuvred in Lyme Bay all day. However, rather than go in to Portland Harbour, Vice-Admiral Bayly decided to keep the squadron at sea.

The squadron consisted of *Lord Nelson*, the Vice-Admiral's flagship, *Agamemnon*, *Queen*, *Implacable*, *Prince of Wales*, *Venerable*, *London* and *Formidable*, with attached light cruisers *Topaze* and *Diamond*. They were about 20 miles east of Start Point, heading west at a steady 10 knots, in line ahead formation with *Formidable* to the rear. The attached light cruisers were one mile astern of the squadron.

The weather had not been too bad through the evening. It was cloudy but the visibility had been reasonable, up to two miles at times. However, in the early hours of New Year's Day, it started to worsen. The cloud thickened and the wind got stronger and stronger.

What nobody among the squadron knew was that they were being watched, and had been all day. From periscope depth Kapitanleutnant Rudolph Schneider in *U-24* studied the fleet. He fixed on *Formidable*, and decided to attack her.

At 2.20am the torpedo from *U-24* smashed into the starboard side of *Formidable* under A1 casemate, abreast of the forward funnel. Her steam pipes were ruptured instantly by the blast which put out her dynamos and plunged her into darkness.

Captain W.J. Law, commanding officer of *Topaze*, was alerted by the leading signalman of the watch. There was something wrong on board *Formidable*. He had heard a gun fire but couldn't get any response from her and she appeared to be listing to starboard. Captain Law immediately ordered his crew to general quarters and put his engines up to full speed. As *Topaze* circled *Formidable*, Captain Law could see the problem, a large hole in her starboard side and deduced it was the work of an enemy submarine.

Already boats were being swung out from the stricken battleship. Captain Loxley knew that his ship was badly wounded. He also knew that the submarine was most likely very close by and another torpedo was almost inevitable. One officer, Lieutenant Simonds, went to work the instant Captain Loxley gave the order to abandon. The Vice-Admiral noted later that he did a splendid job in hoisting out the boats in such dark conditions. It was those conditions that were to cause such problems, as the weather grew worse, the wind increasing to force eight or nine.

A barge managed to get clear of *Formidable* and was spotted by the lookouts on *Topaze*. Captain Law was about to try and pick them up when he got a message from Loxley on *Formidable*. There was a brightly lit steamer close by which could give valuable assistance. His orders were to intercept the steamer and ask the master to stand by to help. *Topaze* first swooped on the barge and picked up 43 men, then headed off towards the steamer. When close enough, Captain Law sent several signals to the steamer's master, urging him to follow. A signal eventually

The 15,000-ton battleship HMS *Formidable* – sunk by a torpedo fired from *U-24*.

came back from the steamer, "I will follow." *Topaze* turned away and headed back to the *Formidable*. She was made easier to spot by the numerous rockets and red flares being sent off from her. However, on looking back to the steamer, Captain Law was angry and dismayed to see that it had gone, full speed the other way. He put in his report that the master could have had no doubt that a ship was in trouble but just ran away

Back on board *Formidable*, the captain's worst fears had been realised. Another torpedo smashed into the port side, levelling up the ship but leaving her sinking rapidly by the head. By the time *Topaze* got back to her, her bows was virtually under. Captain Law brought *Topaze* as close as he dared to *Formidable* and watched the figure of Captain Loxley approach the rail and shout, "There is a submarine on my port quarter. You can't do any good here, you had better clear out or you will be hit." It was an order, he had to obey. He could also see the submarine and his thoughts were to attack it immediately, but as *Diamond* was close by, surrounded by men in the water, it would have been madness to try.

Around 3.30am the weather became even worse, with howling winds and a very dark sky. The men left on *Formidable* had to get a move on as their ship was about to go down. Some of them wore only the clothes they were sleeping in when they plunged into the cold water.

At 4.39am *Formidable* lurched downwards, bows first listing heavily to starboard. *Formidable's* stern was vertical and remained so, with both screws out of the water for four or five minutes, her bows resting on the bottom.

By this time many men, including Captain Loxley, were dead. Others adrift in boats were struggling for life in the mountainous seas and bitter winds.

The Admiralty were shocked by the loss of the *Formidable* and the loss of 547 men. Heads had to roll and their Lordships chose Vice-Admiral Bayly to provide the neck. They wrote to him accusing him of neglect and carelessness. They pointed out that the Channel was infested with submarines, that he prolonged his stay in those waters, and that he was going too slowly, with the result that a battleship and 547 men were lost. The final paragraph of the letter reads, "These facts as presented seem to their Lordships to affect your position most seriously, but, before taking a final decision they are willing to receive any statement you may desire to make in explanation of your action in this deplorable event."

It seems to have been very unfair. To say that the English Channel was infested with submarines at that early stage of the war, was quite an exaggeration. Defending himself in a return letter, Sir Lewis Bayly said that he had received no intelligence whatsoever of even one submarine, let alone an infestation of them. He also pointed out that he was in the English Channel because their Lordships had ordered him there. However, as Vice-Admiral, the buck stopped with him and he was later relieved of his command at sea and given a shore posting. His career though, was far from over and he went on to play an important part in naval tactics throughout the remainder of the war.

6/48: WESTERGATE. *Country:* British. *Date sunk:* 21/4/18. *Tons nett:* 1109. *Tons gross:* 1742. *Built:* 1881. *Type:* SS. *Rig:* –. *Owners:* Franco British Shipping Co. *Cargo:* 1800 tons coke and coal. *Armed:* 1 x 4.7in gun. *Position:* 17 miles ESE of Berry Head (50 17 00N; 03 05 00W). *Master's name:* T. Collier. *Crew:* 29. *Crew nationality:* 25 British, 4 others. *Gunners:* R.C. Kettle, AB RNVR; J. Farmery, AB RNVR; H. Pears; J. McLeod.

THERE were only five survivors from the sinking of this vessel and the information is taken from interviews with those people. None of the ship's officers survived and the position of the vessel when attacked is unclear.

The interviewing officer commented that the general opinion of the five men was that the *Westergate* had been steering a direct course between Portland Bill and Start Point and that she had not been zig-zagging.

Harold Pears, a gunner, stated that he was just coming on deck to relieve the gun watch when he heard an explosion. Gunner Farmery, already at the gun, informed him that he saw the track of the torpedo and that it struck forward on the port side. The ship was sinking extremely rapidly and by this time they were joined by the third gunner. They all ran to the lifeboats but as soon as they got there they were washed apart and into the water. Pears surfaced to find an upturned boat close by with three men on it and he joined them.

James Purcell, the senior wireless operator, stated that he was off watch when the explosion occurred and made his way to the radio room but the radio was dead. He then tried to find the master but couldn't and feeling the vessel sinking he grabbed his lifebelt and made for the port lifeboat. As the boat was being lowered the ship sank and the lifeboat was capsized. Eventually he managed to reach the upturned boat and stayed on it until rescued.

Gunner John Mcleod was on lookout duty on the forecastle head at 4.15am when the explosion occurred. He immediately made his way to the port lifeboat and noted that the well deck was already knee deep in water. He remembered the master shouting down to the men not to lower the lifeboat below the rail until the way was off the ship. As the boat touched water the ship rolled over to starboard and sank by the head sucking the boat down with it. A few moments later he and the boat surfaced and he managed to scramble on top of it.

Fireman James Collins said that as the ship sank he heard a tremendous bang from within the ship as the boilers exploded.

The five survivors were found by the patrol boat HMS *Morning Star* in position 50 25 30N; 02 58 00W, and taken to Plymouth.

UB-80 was the submarine involved.

6/49: BEHREND. *Country:* British. *Date sunk:* 30/11/16. *Tons nett:* 111. *Tons gross:* 143. *Built:* 1906. *Type:* SV. *Rig:* schooner. *Owners:* J. Livingstone, Grangemouth. *Cargo:* Guano. *Armed:* No. *Position:* 35 miles SW from Portland Bill (50 05 00N; 03 04 00W). *Master's name:* John Holt. *Crew:* 6. *Crew nationality:* 3 British, 2 Norwegian, 1 Dutch.

BEHREND was on voyage from London to Brest and met her end at 8.30 in the morning of November 30, 1916. A submarine surfaced alongside her and ordered the master to produce his ships papers. Looking down the end of the submarine's deck gun the master felt he had no choice and complied. The Germans boarded the sailing ship and after helping themselves to whatever they fancied, planted bombs at various positions around the schooner.

As the submarine backed off a little the crew of the *Behrend* pulled clear in the boat and stopped to watch as their ship lurched under the explosions that followed. The starboard side of her was blown completely out and she turned over and slowly sank.

The crew rowed for some time and were eventually picked up by the vessel *Vanatis* and landed at Weymouth.

6/50: VULCAN. *Country:* British. *Date sunk:* 28/11/16. *Tons nett:* 27. *Tons gross:* –. *Built:* Rye in 1897. *Type:* FV. *Rig:* ketch. *Owners:* William Robert Caseley, Ramsgate. *Cargo:* –. *Armed:* No. *Position:* 28 miles SE by S of Berry Head (50 01 00N; 03 04 00W). *Master's name:* Alfred Hodges. *Crew:* 3.

VULCAN was going about her normal routine in the fishing grounds between Start Point and Portland Bill. The master noticed that the wind was getting lighter by the minute and by 10.40am the ship was completely becalmed. With nothing to do but wait, the master had a look around the horizon with his binoculars and was not happy to see a submarine about one and a half miles off and headed towards him.

The U-boat came alongside the little ketch and four German sailors jumped aboard, clutching several bombs which were placed at various points around the *Vulcan*. As the bombers left they told the three crew men that they had five minutes to get clear.

The bombs did the work very effectively and the master and his two men watched as *Vulcan* heaved under the pressure and sank. They rowed in a northerly direction for about four hours and were eventually picked up by the Brixham smack *Seabelle* and landed later that day.

6/51: ROTORUA. *Country:* British.
Date sunk: 22/3/17. *Tons nett:* 7100. *Tons gross:*
11140. *Built:* Dumbarton in 1910. *Type:* SS.
Rig: –.
Owners: New Zealand Shipping Co Ltd.
Cargo: 5600 tons general NZ produce shipped by
various to British government. *Armed:* Yes.
Position: 24 miles E of the Start (50 17 30N;
03 03 15W). *Master's name:* Isaac Ashton Sutcliffe.
Crew: 148, plus 238 passengers.

IT was a long voyage from Wellington, New Zealand
to London. It had taken seven weeks from the time
of sailing on February 1, 1917, to arrive at Plymouth
where all the passengers and mail were landed at 6pm
on March 21.

The next day the master got together with the
Plymouth Pilot, Mr Bussey, and discussed the route he
should take up the Channel to London. The Pilot
pointed out to the master all the dangers spots on the
chart and also remarked that he should have had
written instructions of how to navigate the Channel
and, in particular, which headlands he should hug to
cut down the risk of submarine attack. At noon the
Rotorua began her passage up the Channel.

At 5.45pm she was speeding along at 13 knots. She
should have been five miles off the coast but was in
fact 28 miles off! It was a mistake and the ship was
soon spotted by the German submarine *UC-17*,
commanded by Kapitanleutnant Ralph Wenninger. A
ship the size of the *Rotorua* presented an easy target
for such an experienced submariner and a few
moments later a torpedo slammed into the starboard
side of the steamer just behind the engine room.

The master was below at the time and immediately
rushed on deck. He soon grasped what had happened
and ordered the whistle to be blown to summon all
hands to their boat stations. The first and third officers
were on the bridge and had seen nothing of the
approaching torpedo or the submarine which had fired
it. The master ordered the engines to be stopped and
an SOS to be sent out by wireless. He then threw his
ship's papers over the side in a weighted bag.

The ship was settling down fast by the stern and
as soon as she came to a standstill the boats were
lowered with all the crew. At this point, one man, Mr
Williams, the steward, was thrown out of the boat as
it touched the water and despite desperate attempts
to save him, he drowned. About 35 minutes later the
Rotorua sank.

At 6.45pm the British patrol boats *Sea Monarch*
and No 609 *Douraco* came to their assistance and
they were all landed at Weymouth at around midnight.

There was some flak flying after this incident and
the Admiralty were not impressed with the master's
actions. They also didn't believe that he had no proper
sailing instructions. However, there were no details
of any disciplinary action taken against him.

6/52: PERSEVERANCE. *Country:* British.
Date sunk: 29/1/18. *Tons nett:* 35. *Tons gross:* 51.

Built: Of wood at Brixham in 1906. *Type:* SV. *Rig:*
ketch. *Owners:* Herbert Ford & J.H. Ford,
Birmingham. *Cargo: –. Armed:* No. *Position:*
22 miles SE of Berry Head (50 10 00N;
03 03 00W). *Master's name:* Richard Foale.
Crew: 4.

THE German U-boat commander had spotted the fleet
of fishing boats busily trawling in the fishing grounds
off Berry Head and had decided that he would sink
the lot if he could. He surfaced alongside the port
quarter of the *Perseverance* and one of his men fired
a few rifle shots into her sails.

The master of *Perseverance* understood only to well
what the submarine commander was up to and ordered
his men into the small boat and to pull away. They
rowed towards the submarine but as they approached,
she submerged. A puzzled Captain Foale stood up and
looked around. To the south was a large convoy of
steamers and more to the point several patrol ships.
The German commander had obviously seen them and
wasn't taking any chances of being spotted.

Thinking it was their lucky day the crew rowed
briskly back to the *Perseverance*. They had left the
trawl out and hurriedly heaved it back in. Still there
was no sign of the enemy as they put up all sail and
left the area as quickly as possible, running a flag up
the mast to indicate to others that an enemy vessel
was in the vicinity.

At 2pm, the convoy long since passed, the
submarine appeared again among the fishing fleet.
Several of the vessels were fired on as a warning to
their crews to get clear. One shell screamed over the
rigging of *Perseverance* and the master realised that
his luck had run out. He ordered his men once more to
abandon ship which was quickly done. It was just as
well, as the next shell hit *Perseverance* full on,
sending her to the bottom instantly.

The German commander gradually worked his way
around the fishing fleet sinking most of them before a
patrol trawler arrived on the scene. *Rinaldo II* picked
up the crew of *Perseverance* along with the crews of
Ibex and *General Leman* and landed them at Brixham.

6/53: PITHO. *Country:* British.
Date sunk: 28/12/16. *Tons nett:* 128. *Tons gross:*
237. *Built:* Of wood at Swansea in 1868. *Type:* SV.
Rig: 3 masted schooner. *Owners:* K. Peterson,
The Docks, Gloucester. *Cargo:* 237 tons coal,
shipped by J. Mules, Cardiff and consigned to
Cherbourg. *Armed:* No. *Position:* 30 miles SE
from Start Point (50 04 00N; 03 02 00W).
Master's name: George Amy. *Crew:* 5.

THE submarine that surfaced close to the *Pitho* must
have been economising on shells for it fired two blank
shots at them. However, it was enough for the master
to take notice and stop his ship. The German
commander shouted to the crew to take to the boat
and bring the ships papers to him for examination.

They did as they were told.

While the crew were kept on board the submarine, several sailors rowed over to the *Pitho* and planted bombs. After helping themselves to various instruments and provisions they rowed back. A few minutes later the *Pitho* disappeared.

The crew were cast adrift and left to fend for themselves. Fortunately for them the weather was reasonable and luckier still, the Dutch steamer *Djember* came by and picked them up.

6/54: CHORLEY. *Country:* British.
Date sunk: 22/3/17. *Tons nett:* 2468. *Tons gross:* 3828. *Built:* Sunderland in 1901. *Type:* SS.
Rig: schooner. *Owners:* Brys & Gylser Ltd, 101, Leadenhall St, London. *Cargo:* 6525 tons munitions from Transatlantique, France.
Armed: Yes. *Position:* 23 miles E by S from the Start (50 14 00N; 03 02 00W). *Master's name:* Andrew Henry. 447, Fishponds Rd, Bristol. *Crew:* 27. *Crew nationality:* 3 Americans, 4 Russians, 2 Norwegians, 1 Swede, 1 Greek, 16 British.

HAVING received his sailing instructions from the British Consulate at Norfolk, Virginia, USA, Captain Henry sailed on March 3, 1917, and headed across the Atlantic to Havre. He passed Longships in the early hours of March 22nd and the Lizard at 8am the same day. At 5pm he passed Start Point and then set a new course to bring the ship close to Portland Bill. Once past Portland the master intended to cross the Channel under the cover of darkness with no lights as per his instructions.

At 7.45pm he was below leaving the second mate in charge of the bridge. Without any warning the night was shattered by a tremendous explosion as a torpedo smashed into the starboard side of the ship underneath the forecastle. The master rushed on deck and to his dismay found that his ship was sinking rapidly.

He ordered the engines to be put full astern and all the crew with the exception of a skeleton crew of engineers to get into the boats. At 7.55pm the engines were shut off and the rest of the crew ordered to make for the boats and get clear of the ship. As they pulled away the ship's bows were already awash.

Within minutes the patrol boat *Resparkoe* was among them and shone a searchlight at the *Chorley*. She was in a sad state with her bows under water and her stern high in the air. A few moments later she slipped below the surface. All the crew were safe and eventually landed at Weymouth.

From a patrol boat log dated May 29, 1917: the skipper was sweeping an area 1$^3/_4$ miles radius around a particular position. He came across an obstruction which moved when towed and noticed that his wire was marked by iron and he pulled up a section of iron mast. The exact position noted is 50 14 00N; 03 06 20W. This might be the wreck of the SS *Chorley*.

UC-48 was the submarine involved.

WORLD WAR ONE
CHANNEL WRECKS

◆

AREA SEVEN

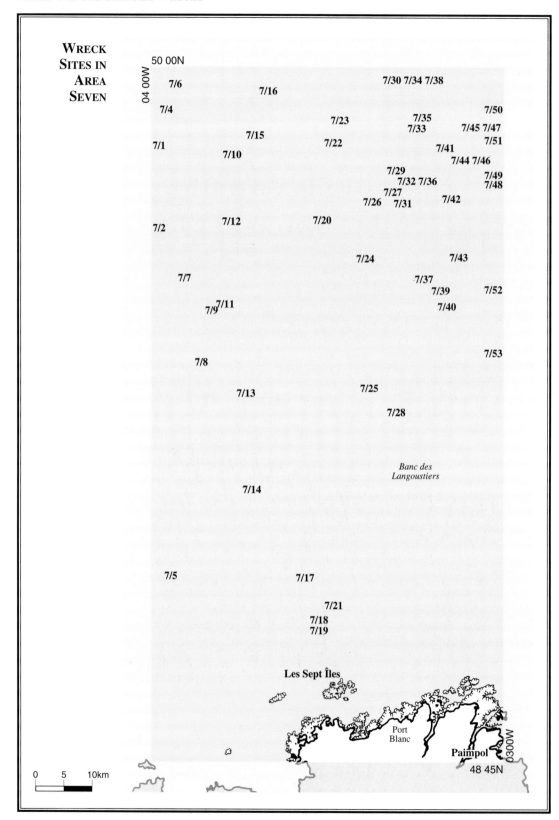

**WRECK
SITES IN
AREA
SEVEN**

50 00N

04 00W

7/6

7/16

7/4

7/23

7/30 7/34 7/38

7/50

7/35
7/33

7/45 7/47

7/15

7/22

7/51

7/1

7/41

7/10

7/44 7/46

7/29

7/49
7/48

7/32 7/36

7/27

7/26 7/31

7/42

7/2

7/12

7/20

7/24

7/43

7/7

7/37
7/39

7/52

7/9 7/11

7/40

7/53

7/8

7/13

7/25

7/28

*Banc des
Langoustiers*

7/14

7/5

7/17

7/21
7/18
7/19

Les Sept Îles

Port
Blanc

Paimpol

03 00W

48 45N

0   5   10km

7/1: EMILIE GALLIENNE. *Country:* French.
Date sunk: 13/8/17. *Tons nett:* 1944. *Tons gross:* –.
Built: –. *Type:* SV. *Rig:* barque. *Owners:* Societe
des Voiliers Francais, Paris. *Cargo:* 2550 tons
nitrate of soda from Taltal, Chile to Havre.
Armed: No. *Position:* 25 miles SSW of Start Point
(49 52 00N; 04 00 00W). *Master's name:* Jules
Frostam. *Crew:* 19. *Crew nationality:* 16 French,
2 Russians, 1 British.

AT 4000 yards the gunner on the German submarine
was doing a remarkable job of shelling the *Emilie
Gallienne*. Some of the shells were wide but others
were knocking off bits of rigging quite effectively. It
certainly made the master of the *Emilie* very worried
as he watched the submarine getting closer by the
minute and the shells becoming more accurate.

There was nothing else for it but to abandon the
ship. The crew pulled clear and rowed out in two boats
to meet the approaching submarine. The master was
ordered on board for questioning whilst his lifeboat
and crew were used to row a party of German sailors
back to the *Emilie*. Bombs were planted at various
points in her.

The master was allowed to rejoin his men and on
stepping into his boat the bombs on board *Emilie*
exploded. Huge lumps of deck and rigging were tossed
high in the air by the explosions and holes appeared in
her. She lurched over to port, raised her stern high
and sank like a stone.

Both boats pulled for the shore. At first they stayed
together but as the day went on they somehow
managed to lose each other. The mate and 10 men
were picked up at 4.30pm on the same day by the
patrol trawler 808 *Casorio*. Her commander, on being
told of the master's boat, started a search for him but
called it off when he learned that he and six hands
had been picked up at 2.30pm by HMS *Spitfire* and
landed at Plymouth.

It is mentioned in the documents about this vessel
that one man was drowned but there is no detail of
how it happened.

7/2: MIZPAH. *Country:* British.
Date sunk: 3/12/16. *Tons nett:* 51. *Tons gross:* 90.
Built: Of wood at Gorey, Channel Isles. *Type:* SV.
Rig: ketch. *Owners:* J.C. Renouf, 26, The Pier,
Jersey. *Cargo:* In ballast, St Malo for Charlestown,
Cornwall. *Armed:* No. *Position:* 30 miles SSE of
Eddystone Light (49 43 00N; 04 00 00W). *Master's
name:* Charles George King. *Crew:* 4.

AT 10am the wind was light and the ketch was
making around three knots. A large submarine
surfaced about 150yds off her port quarter and at first
had a French flag flying from her small mast. A shot
boomed out across the water and almost
simultaneously the French ensign was replaced with a
German flag.

The shell that whistled over the rigging was a

warning for the master to stop. He obeyed straight
away and along with his three crew, left the *Mizpah* in
the small boat. A man on the submarine beckoned the
master over. Using the *Mizpah's* boat and her crew
to row them, several German sailors boarded the
ketch. After helping themselves to food and anything
else that caught their eye they planted two bombs in
the hold. These exploded at 10.45am sinking the
Mizpah almost immediately.

It was over 24 hours later that help came to the
crew when they were spotted by a lookout on board
the Danish steamer *Laura* and landed at Ramsgate.

When the master made his deposition he added at
the end of his narrative that one of his men had spotted
the number *UB-37* in small letters on a part of the
submarine.

7/3: *(POSITION AMENDED)*

7/4: MONARCH. *Country:* British.
Date sunk: 21/2/17. *Tons nett:* 35. *Tons gross:* 45.
Built: –. *Type:* FV. *Rig:* smack. *Owners:* E.
Hellings, Milford Haven. *Cargo:* –. *Armed:* No.
Position: 14 miles SE of Eddystone (49 56 00N;
03 59 00W). *Master's name:* W. Brinham. *Crew:* 4.
Crew nationality: All British.

THE fishing vessel *Monarch* had just started fishing
and had her trawl out heading north-east by north.
The weather was quite good, perhaps a little hazy,
with a light wind blowing from the north-west.

At 7.30am the peace of the morning was shattered
when a German submarine appeared about 400yds
off her port beam.

Three shells were fired. Captain Brinham had little
choice but to abandon ship. The four men rowed clear
and made for the submarine.

The German commander adopted the usual tactic
of dealing with small sailing vessels. By using
Monarch's lifeboat bombs were hung over the port
side amidships. They did the trick, sending her to the
bottom at around 7.45am.

The crew were picked up by a patrol boat and
landed at Plymouth. The submarine set off after
another fishing vessel a few miles off. The *Energy*
was the next one to go down.

7/5: JOACHIM BRINCH LUND.
Country: Norwegian. *Date sunk:* 16/11/16. *Tons
nett:* 1063. *Tons gross:* 2500. *Built:* –. *Type:* SS.
Rig: –. *Owners:* Messrs T. Lund & Co, Bergen.
Cargo: Iron ore. *Armed:* No. *Position:* 60 miles NE
of Ushant (49 06 00N; 03 57 00W). *Master's
name:* T. Sjursen. *Crew:* 13. *Crew nationality:*
12 Norwegians, 1 Russian/Finn.

IT was left to the Chief Officer, Mr O. Nilssen, to
make the deposition to the British naval authorities

after the *Joachim Brinch Lund* was sunk. At the time, the lifeboat with the master and part of the crew were still missing and there is no mention of their fate.

The mate said that at the time they were attacked the vessel was making eight knots. The wind was strong, the sea quite rough and the visibility not particularly good. The first they knew of trouble was when a German submarine appeared about two miles off and began firing shells at the steamer. Although they missed, one or two were frighteningly close so the master ordered the ship to be stopped. The German commander ordered the men to abandon their ship and go across to the submarine which they did.

After using their boat to plant bombs on the *Lund* they were cast adrift. The mate was in charge of one boat and the master a second. They tried to keep together as best they could but the rough sea soon parted them. The mate was lucky as the passing steamer *Pluton* spotted their plight and came to the rescue.

7/6: HOLLY BRANCH. *Country:* British. *Date sunk:* 1/1/17. *Tons nett:* 2216. *Tons gross:* 3568. *Built:* In 1911. *Type:* SS. *Rig:* schooner. *Owners:* Nautilus SS Co Ltd, 30, West Sunniside, Sunderland. *Cargo:* 4479 tons oats in bags, La Plata for Le Havre. *Armed:* No. *Position:* 14 miles NE by N from Isle de Batz (48 59 00N; 03 56 00W). *Master's name:* John Henry Bell. *Crew:* 45. *Crew nationality:* 21 British, 1 Russian, 1 Dutch, 1 American, 21 Chinese.

ANOTHER well executed attack by a German submarine on a merchant vessel sank the *Holly Branch*. By the time the master knew of the submarine's presence it was just half a mile away and fired a well aimed shell that struck the ship square on. The master realising the hopeless position he was in ordered his crew to take to the boats. Even though it must been obvious to the Germans that the engines had been stopped and boats were being launched, they continued to fire regardless. Many of the shells struck the steamer but by some good fortune nobody was injured. The master stated that as he left the ship there were fires in several places.

Once the boats were clear the shelling stopped and the submarine approached the crew. One of the boats was ordered alongside and several of the men taken aboard while German sailors replaced them. They in turn ordered the remaining crew to row them over to the *Holly Branch* where, after helping themselves to various stores and provisions, they planted several bombs. At 1pm the bombs sent the steamer to the bottom.

U-41 was the U-boat involved.

7/7: ETHIOPE. *Country:* British. *Date sunk:* 28/5/15. *Tons nett:* 2474. *Tons gross:* 3794. *Built:* Hartlepool in 1906. *Type:* SS.

Rig: schooner. *Owners:* Elder Line, Colonial House, 20, Water St, Liverpool. *Cargo:* 5000 tons general goods in packages and bulk from Hull and London, to Canaries and Africa. *Armed:* No. *Position:* 40 miles SW of Start Point (49 38 00N; 03 55 00W). *Master's name:* James P. McDonald. *Crew:* 32.

IT was 8.50am when the master left the bridge of *Ethiope* to get some breakfast leaving the second mate in charge. No sooner had the master gone than a lookout signalled to the bridge that he had spotted something. The officer picked up his binoculars and focused on the object but couldn't make it out clearly. He sent word to the master who returned in moments. He too, gazed at it. There was no mistake, it was an enemy submarine. Captain McDonald shouted to the helmsman, "Hard to port."

Looking again through his binoculars the master saw that the submarine was gaining on him very rapidly and it was also flying the loathed signal, 'Abandon your ship.' There was a puff of smoke from her bows and a shell went screaming overhead. The helmsman looked at the master, "Hold your course," snapped Captain McDonald. A second shell streaked between the funnel and the bridge followed by another that threw up a spout of water very close to the stern. The master knew he was in a hopeless position and put the telegraph to stop at the same time ordering the second mate to spread the word to abandon ship.

Two boats pulled away from the steamer a few minutes later. The submarine commander allowed them to get clear and then moved in for the kill. One torpedo was enough to open up a huge hole in the *Ethiope's* side and three minutes later she had gone.

The two boats became separated. The master's boat was picked up by the SS *Saxonian* of London at 3pm but the other boat led by the chief officer was lost. It was later discovered that he and the crew with him were picked up by another passing steamer.

U-41 was the U-boat involved.

7/8: LA NEGRA. *Country:* British. *Date sunk:* 3/9/17. *Tons nett:* 4949. *Tons gross:* 8312. *Built:* Hebburn in 1913. *Type:* SS. *Rig:* schooner. *Owners* British & Argentine Steam Navigation Co, London.: *Cargo:* 3857 tons frozen meat from Buenos Aires and La Plata to the Admiralty. *Armed:* 1 x 6in gun with B3 mounting. *Position:* 39 miles S by W of Start Point (49 29 00N; 03 52 00W). *Master's name:* William Foot Dickers. *Crew:* 96. *Crew nationality:* 91 British, 2 Americans, 1 Belgian, 1 Norwegian, 1 Dutch. *Gunners:* James Jardine, RFR No 3931B; Michael Mccormick, seaman RNR No 2908A; Magnus T. Sinclair, seaman RNR No 1441L. *Casualties:* R. Wing, J. Doyle, J. Roach, stokers; W. Hunter, fourth engineer.

After surviving the first torpedo attack, the *La Negra* was seriously damaged in the second and sank in 40 fathoms while under tow.

LA NEGRA left Montevideo on August 3, 1917, and was to make for Spithead for orders. She joined a convoy at Sierra Leone and left with it on August 22nd.

As they approached the UK coast the weather stayed fine with light winds and a smooth sea. She was zig-zagging along with the rest of the convoy and the first mate was on the bridge with two lookouts and a helmsman. Suddenly the mate screamed out for the helm to be put hard to starboard. He had spotted the wake of a torpedo about 100yds off the ship's port side. With the engines at full speed the ship responded quickly, nearly clearing the torpedo. However, it slammed into the aft end blowing away the port propeller and rudder.

An immediate check was made to ascertain the damage and it was found that she was not holed. The propeller shaft tunnel was dry and only a small amount of water present in the aft peak. *La Negra* limped on her way whilst the escorting destroyers raced back and forth trying to track down the offending submarine.

After such a close escape *La Negra* deserved to make it but the U-boat commander obviously decided that she was just to big to leave alone. At 2.30pm another torpedo was spotted heading towards the ship. It was a long way off and the ship had only had one propeller and rudder and her steering was perilously slow. The torpedo slammed into the starboard side and into the boiler room. The resulting explosion killed four of the crew.

La Negra listed heavily to starboard and then righted herself but started to settle down. As the main deck was just about awash the crew left the ship and pulled clear. However, she seemed to hold her own for a while and the master and some of the crew returned to destroy confidential papers. At 6.30pm two torpedo boats arrived along with a tug. *La Negra* wasn't getting any lower in the water so it was decided to try and save her.

Progress was very slow as the steamer was an enormous dead weight in the water. As she was pulled so the worse she got and at 2.30am the next day she sank in 40 fathoms of water.

The position given by a naval patrol ship differs slightly from that given in the information above: 49 25 00N; 3 58 00W.

UC-50 sank her.

7/9: TORRIDGE. *Country:* British. *Date sunk:* 6/9/16. *Tons nett:* 4574. *Tons gross:* 5036. *Built:* 1912. *Type:* SS. *Rig:* schooner. *Owners:* The Tatem Steam Navigation Co, Cardiff. *Cargo:* In ballast, Genoa to Tyne. *Armed:* No. *Position:* 40 miles S by W of Start Point (49 34 00N; 03 49 00W). *Master's name:* George P. Sherbon. *Crew:* 33. *Crew nationality:* 20 British, 4 Norwegians, 2 Danes, 4 Greeks, 2 Russians, 1 Roumanian.

THE Mate, Osborne Richard Thomas, was in charge on the bridge as the *Torridge* made her way up the Channel at about eight knots. The master was below, when, in the early hours of the September 6, 1916, a German submarine appeared on the surface about 200yds off the port beam. The mate shouted for the master immediately; he was there in seconds.

He ordered the helm to be turned and signalled the engine room to put on every bit of steam they could muster. The Admiralty advice was to head directly at any submarine forcing it to dive or be rammed. All very well in theory but at sea with a four inch deck gun blazing away at you … This master was going to try and escape.

The shells came thick and fast and the master realised that he had little chance of out-running such a fast submarine. Captain Sherbon reluctantly ordered the engines to be stopped and looked towards the submarine to see what would happen. He didn't have to wait long as a minute later signal flags fluttered from the submarine's small mast, 'Abandon ship immediately.'

The crew left in two boats and pulled clear. The submarine went close to the *Torridge* and after passing under her quarter, two German sailors climbed aboard. They lowered the port jolly boat and returned in it to the submarine to pick up some bombs.

At 6.20am the enemy sailors left having planted four bombs at various positions around the ship. Ten minutes later they all exploded. She didn't sink straight away and had to be helped on her way by the submarine's deck gun, going down by the stern at 9.30am.

The crew had to row for most of the day until the Norwegian steamer *Astra* picked them up, landing them later at Cherbourg.

UB-29 was the submarine involved.

7/10: HENRY R. JAMES. *Country:* British.
Date sunk: 16/7/17. *Tons nett:* 1974. *Tons gross:* 3149. *Built:* 1909. *Type:* SS. *Rig:* schooner. *Owners:* Henry R. James SS Co Ltd, 8, Queen Square, Bristol. *Cargo:* 5300 tons iron ore from Bilbao to Middlesbrough. *Armed:* 1 x 12pdr gun. *Position:* 10 miles E by N from Ile de Batz (48 50 00N; 03 47 00W). *Master's name:* Francis Willey Stinchcombe Mogg. *Crew:* 28. *Crew nationality:* All British.

OUT of a total of 28 crew members aboard the *Henry R. James* only four men were to survive. The main reason for this large loss of life was due to the extraordinary speed at which she sank.

A Court of Enquiry was held later at the office of HM Consul General, Le Havre, and this was forwarded to the Admiralty. Three of the four survivors – Charles Tippetts Tucker, the Chief Officer; Morgan Henry Jones, the Second Officer; and Robert Quick, a seaman –told the court their stories. The Master, Francis Mogg was not well enough to attend and was still under medical care at Paimpol.

The *Henry R. James* left Brest in convoy, hugged the coast and continued close inshore as she passed along the French side of the Channel. Robert Quick was on lookout forward in the early hours of July 16, 1917. A huge explosion occurred on the starboard side of the steamer abreast of the main rigging. About ten seconds later another explosion boomed out, this time on the port side abreast of number three hatch. The blasts blew down the mainmast, rendering the wireless aerials useless.

The master immediately shouted to get everyone up from below. Robert Quick called the men in the fireman's forcastle and then ran back amidships and was amazed to see that the after deck was already awash. Seeing the master and the second mate in the jolly boat he ran to join them just as the ship plunged downwards. The jolly boat managed to stay afloat but was swamped as it touched the sea throwing Robert Quick clean out of it. He swam around for a while but soon spotted the chartroom of the steamer which was still above water. He clambered onto it and was later joined by a fireman called M.W. Jones who had a serious head injury and died a few hours later.

The first mate had managed to get away in the ship's scow along with the Chief Engineer, T. Robinson. Robert Quick said that at daylight he spotted the chief mate's boat about a mile away floating at the mercy of wind and tide, swamped with water. At 9am the cold proved to much for the chief engineer and he died.

The master and second mate's boat remained afloat even though waterlogged and remained in the vicinity of Triagoz Light House all day. They were eventually spotted by a French patrol boat and picked up as were Robert Quick and Chief Officer Tucker.

The Court of Enquiry and the Admiralty reached the conclusion that the *Henry R. James* had ran into an enemy minefield. However, *UC-48* claimed to have torpedoed her.

7/11: GEORGE M. EMBIRICOS.
Country: Greek. *Date sunk:* 22/10/16. *Tons nett:* –. *Tons gross:* 3636. *Built:* –. *Type:* SS *Rig:* –. *Owners:* –. *Cargo:* 5720 tons maize from Buenos Aries via St Vincent to Brixham. *Armed:* No. *Position:* 40 miles SSE of Eddystone (49 35 00N; 03 47 00W). *Master's name:* John Paleocrossas. *Crew:* 29. *Crew nationality:* All Greek.

THE wind was very strong from the south west and had been for most of the day. The *George M. Embiricos* was nearly at the end of her long journey from South America. Her final destination was Rotterdam where her valuable cargo of maize was to be handed over to the commission for relief in Belgium. She was to call at Brixham where she would have been painted with special lettering to show she was a relief ship. Before that could happen, and exactly at 4.30pm on October 2, 1916, she was caught by a U-boat

The first the master and crew knew of it came when two shells screamed past the rigging. Just two minutes later the shape of a submarine appeared through the dimness of the day. A voice boomed out through a megaphone ordering the master to take his papers for inspection. The master did as he was told and with a party of men rowed through the heavy sea in one of the ship's boats. Having examined the documents the commander coldly informed the master that his steamer was to be sunk and gave him 10 minutes to return to his ship, gather his crew and get clear. Captain Paleocrossas pleaded that his ship was a relief vessel and as such this should give him immunity from attack, his papers proved this beyond doubt. However, the German merely repeated his 10-minute warning.

The crew got clear just as the submarine manoeuvred into position and fired a torpedo into the starboard side amidships of the *Embiricos*.

By 5pm the steamer had gone to the bottom leaving the two boats to row as best they could for the shore. They stayed together as best they could but as darkness fell became separated. Fortunately for the master's boat the trawler *Penear* was in the area and a sharp eared member of her crew heard faint cries. The Skipper, Ralph Stamp of Bay View Road, Brixham, stated in a letter to the Admiralty that after hearing the faint cries he hauled to and listened in order to get a bearing on the direction. He subsequently found the 17 men, cold and tired and landed them safely at Brixham.

The mate's boat was not so lucky, they were found much later in a terrible state, the boat having been overturned in the rough seas. Five of the 12 were washed away, their bodies found days later around the shore. However, the survivors were picked up suffering from severe hypothermia.

There was much diplomatic activity over the loss of this ship and letters were directed via the American Embassy to Germany. The reply from Berlin stated that the steamer's papers showed that the vessel was not acting according to the rules of war, and was not showing the distinctive markings of a relief ship.

7/12: RAKIURA. *Country:* Norwegian.
Date sunk: 8/12/16 *Tons nett:* –. *Tons gross:* 3569.
Built: –. *Type:* SS. *Rig:* –. *Owners:* –. *Cargo:* Coal, Shields to Oran. *Armed:* –. *Position:* 45-50 miles WNW of Guernsey (49 44 00N; 03 46 00W).
Master's name: Grimstead.

THERE is only the briefest mention of this sinking in Naval Weekly Reports which stated that "*Rabiaura*" was sunk by an enemy submarine at 5pm on December 8, 1916. The captain and crew were landed safely at Guernsey. The captain stated that he picked up two men belonging to another Norwegian steamer sunk at 5.30pm the same day at approximately the same position. However, no mention is made of the name of this ship, though she may be the 433-ton *Saga*, in ballast from St Malo for Swansea.

Another report gives the correct name – Rakiura – and adds that the captain, Grimstead, and 15 crew landed safely at Guernsey. They reported being sunk by bombs from a U-boat at 4.15pm, on December 8. A boat with the rest of the crew was last seen being towed by the submarine.

7/13: SECUNDO. *Country:* Norwegian.
Date sunk: 20/10/16. *Tons nett:* 1214. *Tons gross:* 1512. *Rig:* –. *Owners:* Haaland of Haugesund, Norway. *Cargo:* Iron ore. *Armed:* No. *Position:* 40 miles W of Hanois Light, Guernsey (49 26 00N; 03 43 00W). *Master's name:* Havert Wallesverd. *Crew:* 18. *Crew nationality:* 6 Norwegians, 7 Spaniards, 4 Swedes, 1 Russian.

THE *Secundo* was bound from Santander to Caen.

The signal that flew from the German submarine's mast read: "Abandon your ship immediately".

This was instantly followed up by a few shells over the top of the steamer. The master complied, taking to the boats with his men and pulled clear.

The submarine closed on the boats and questioned the master about his ship's papers and destination. Whilst this was going on several German sailors borrowed one of the boats to carry bombs over to the steamer. They were placed in the holds and the engine room. They exploded and the *Secundo* sank at 4.30pm.

The crew were eventually picked up by a British warship and landed at Cherbourg.

7/14: TOFTWOOD. *Country:* British.
Date sunk: 13/11/17. *Tons nett:* 1961. *Tons gross:* 3082. *Built:* 1906. *Type:* SS. *Rig:* schooner. *Owners:* Constantine Pickering, Maritime Buildings, Middlesbrough. *Cargo:* 5000 tons of copper, steel, motor cars, ammunition, provisions and oil. *Armed:* No. *Position:* 23 miles NNW of September Isles (49 15 00N; 03 43 00W). *Master's name:* Frederick Milsom Jones. *Crew:* 25. *Crew nationality:* 13 British, 1 Dutch, 3 Norwegian/ Danes, 1 Montenegrin, 5 Chileans, 1 Japanese, 1 French.

WITH her cargo loaded by the French Translantique Steamship Company, *Toftwood* left New York on her journey to France. The master's sailing instructions required him to sail as close as possible to Ushant and then make his way to Havre. On reaching Ushant he should have been met a French patrol boat but it wasn't there so he pressed on.

Soon afterwards a shell whistled close by the ship. A German submarine was about 300yds off on the starboard side. Signal flags flying from her small mast ordered him to abandon ship. To back up the demand another shell cracked over *Toftwood's* mainmast.

The master put the ship's telegraph to stop. The

submarine drew closer and a voice shouted out to the master that he and his crew had five minutes to get clear. Two boats were launched and all the men managed to get away.

The submarine then moved in for the kill and fired several shells at the steamer. However, none of them appeared to have any effect on the vessel. The commander must have lost patience as a few minutes later a torpedo sent the *Toftwood* to the bottom.

The Germans made no attempt to talk to the men in the boats who were left to row for the shore as best they could. It was a long haul and took them over 19 hours but they eventually arrived at Trebeurden, France, at midday on January 14.

UC-18 was the submarine which sank her.

7/15: ABEJA. *Country:* British.
Date sunk: 9/3/17. *Tons nett:* 149. *Tons gross:* 174.
Built: Littlehampton in 1880. *Type:* SV. *Rig:* schooner. *Owners:* W.C. Phillips, Polkeyth, St Austell. *Cargo:* In ballast from Granville to Fowey. *Armed:* No. *Position:* 20 miles SSW from Start Point (49 53 00N; 03 42 00W). *Master's name:* Henry Cohring. *Crew:* 5.

THE weather, although pleasant didn't help matters when it came to keeping out of the way of enemy submarines. There was only a light breeze with a gentle swell and *Abeja* was finding it difficult to make any headway at all. It made the ship a sitting duck for the German submarine that broke the surface about one mile off on her port side.

The first shell came whimpering over the rigging. The next shot left them in no doubt as to the enemy commander's intentions as it smashed away the fore mast, leaving the ship completely helpless. The crew left her in a great hurry, so much so that the master didn't destroy his confidential sailing instructions. It was mentioned in the report afterwards that the master said he left them in a locked drawer in his cabin and added that the Germans never boarded the ship anyway. If they had done, Captain Cohring could have been in trouble with the Admiralty.

It took five shells and 15 minutes in all to sink the *Abeja*, the submarine heading off immediately after, leaving the crew to make their way towards the shore. They were saved the effort of rowing the whole distance by a patrol vessel which landed them later at Plymouth.

7/16: BELLE ILE. *Country:* Norwegian.
Date sunk: 27/11/16. *Tons nett:* 1128. *Tons gross:* 1883. *Built:* 1908. *Type:* SS. *Rig:* schooner. *Owners:* Fernley & Eger, Christiania, Norway. *Cargo:* 2960 tons iron ore from Bilbao to Middlesbrough. *Armed:* No. *Position:* 15 miles S of Start Point (49 58 00N; 03 38 00W). *Master's name:* H.V. Gallocksen. *Crew:* 21. *Crew nationality:* 15 Norwegians, 2 Danes, 4 Swedish.

THE vessel about one mile off the port side of the *Belle Ile* looked like a small fishing boat. It was flying a red ensign which meant she was a merchant ship and the master of the *Belle Ile* thought no more about it, leaving his steamer to push on at full speed. It wasn't until a shell went whistling over his ship followed by two more in rapid succession that the master looked through his binoculars more closely. He was startled at just how rapidly the vessel had gained on him and even more startled when he realised that the innocent little merchant vessel was in fact a German submarine.

As the last shell fell into the sea throwing up a spout of water, the master of *Belle Ile* gave the order for the ship to be stopped. He watched as the signal flags were run up the submarine's small mast, "Send off boats to me." He did as he was told and made his way over to the waiting submarine. The German commander asked the master for his ship's papers but the master replied that as he was carrying only iron ore he thought it wouldn't be necessary to bring them with him. It was a nice try but the German wasn't falling for it, telling the master that he had five minutes to go back to his ship, gather up his crew and his papers and get clear.

The *Belle Ile* was cleared in the five minutes allotted and the master duly delivered the papers to the submarine at about 1.30pm.

After examining the papers the commander moved his vessel closer to the *Belle Ile* on her starboard side and fired a torpedo from virtually point blank range. It smashed into her and blew open a huge hole in her side causing her to sink almost immediately head first.

The men in the boats were left to fend for themselves. However, two British patrol vessels were in the area and found them a few hours later, landing them in the early hours of the next morning at Weymouth.

7/17: THEODOR. *Country:* British.
Date sunk: 5/9/17. *Tons nett:* 196. *Tons gross:* 230. *Built:* Hammelwarden in 1909. *Type:* SV. *Rig:* schooner. *Owners:* Admiralty. *Cargo:* 100 tons sand ballast from St Malo to Fowey. *Armed:* No. *Position:* 13 miles N by W from September Isles, France (49 06 00N; 03 33 00W). *Master's name:* William Frederick Cort. *Crew:* 7.

THE first shot from the German submarine's deck gun was a very good one. From about half a mile the gunner managed to place the shell straight into her head gear bringing down all sorts of tackle and rigging onto the deck below. The master realised that he had better get himself and his men out of it.

The men got into the boat and pulled clear. The sea was fairly calm although there was a long swell. It was one of those typical autumn days in the Channel with the sky overcast and continual drizzle. It was 6.15pm and the light was beginning to dwindle; not the ideal time to be abandoning ship.

The enemy submarine arrived alongside the *Theodor* having fired about 30 shells in her general direction. Some had missed her but quite a few had found their mark. The commander shouted to the men in the boat to come close and demanded that the master hand over his papers. Captain Cort handed over his Certificate of Registry but said he had nothing else, that all his papers were in St Malo where he had delivered his cargo. He was telling the truth so had no need to worry.

A German officer motioned to two sailors and they used the *Theodor's* boat to go over to her. Once on board they plundered everything they could find of value, clocks, barometer, telescope, food, clothing, throwing it all in the boat before planting several bombs.

The bombs exploded about five minutes later making the sailing ship lurch under each impact. The bombs were well positioned and within another five minutes she had gone to the bottom.

The crew rowed as best they could for the shore through the night. The weather was kind to them and the sea remained fairly calm. They made a landing the next morning at about 9 oclock at the little French port of Lezardrieux.

7/18: EMMA. *Country:* British.
Date sunk: 5/9/17. *Tons nett:* 67. *Tons gross:* 73. *Built:* 1865. *Type:* SV. *Rig:* ketch. *Owners:* Felix Sildey, Epney, Stonehouse, Gloucester. *Cargo:* 25 tons ballast from St Malo to Fowey. *Armed:* No. *Position:* 8 miles N by W of September Isles, France (49 01 00N; 03 32 15W). *Master's name:* Joseph Thomas Warren. *Crew:* 4.

IT seemed inevitable to the master that his ship was about to be sunk. He had already seen the *Florence Muspratt* sunk by a German submarine and it was now shelling his other companion the *Francis* nearby. Two shots were fired and then the German gunner swung around and let two off at the *Emma*, a clear signal that the they meant business and that their ship should be abandoned immediately.

The four men left their ship and rowed clear. The men from the *Francis* had done the same and headed out towards the waiting enemy vessel together. A man on the conning tower had made it clear by waving his arms that he wanted both boats to come alongside. A German officer spoke to them and told the men to get into the *Francis's* boat which they did pretty quickly after looking down the barrel of a revolver. Their boat was then used by several German sailors to row to both ships, first the *Francis* and then the *Emma*, planting bombs. It was soon done and the Germans left with armfuls of stolen equipment and provisions.

From a safe distance the two crews watched as each of their ships heaved under the explosions and were gone a few minutes later. The men were later picked up by a French patrol boat which already had on board

two other crews who suffered the same fate a little earlier. All of them were taken to the French port of Lezardrieux the next day and landed safely.

7/19: FRANCIS. *Country:* British.
Date sunk: 5/9/17. *Tons nett:* 72. *Tons gross:* 89. *Built:* Falmouth in 1889. *Type:* SV. *Rig:* ketch. *Owners:* William Hutchings, Middle St, Padstow, Cornwall. *Cargo:* Ballast from St Malo to Fowey. *Armed:* No. *Position:* 8 miles N by W of the September Isles, France (49 01 00N; 03 32 00W). *Master's name:* John Hellyar. *Crew:* 4.

THE crew on board *Francis* looked on in dismay as the German submarine attacked and sank their companion *Florence Muspratt*. The submarine was about two miles off on the port side of the *Francis* and worse still it was heading directly for her.

When it got within a quarter of a mile it fired two shells at her which missed but only just. The German gunner then swung his gun around and fired at another sailing vessel close by, the *Emma*. It was a message to both boats: "abandon your ships immediately".

Both crews did just that and pulled clear as all the men watched the approaching submarine. It drew in between them and ordered them both to come close. A German officer appeared and in good English told the men from the *Emma* to join the men from the *Francis*, leaving a boat free for several German sailors to use. They rowed to each ship and planted bombs, after having a good look around them and stealing whatever they fancied.

The two crews rowed away from the area as fast as they could, stopping only to watch the bombs explode and to make sure that their ships were really gone. Eventually they were picked up by a French patrol boat which already had on board the crews from two other victims of the same fleet. All of them were landed the next day at the French port of Lezardrieux.

7/20: HEINRICH. *Country:* British.
Date sunk: 30/11/16 *Tons nett:* –. *Tons gross:* 98. *Built:* –. *Type:* SV. *Rig:* –. *Owners:* Charles Livingstone & Sons. *Cargo:* –. *Armed:* No. *Position:* 30 miles S by E from Start Point (49 44 00N; 03 31 00W). *Master's name:* –.

THE submarine that sank the *Heinrich* used a cunning tactic and approached the vessel disguised as a fishing boat. It had sails up and even had smoke coming out from behind the sails as if to show the galley fire was burning. As soon as it got close the sails came down and a shell was sent whistling through the rigging.

The Germans stopped the ship and demanded to know her details. Once satisfied, the German commander gave the crew a few minutes to get clear before *Heinrich* was pounded with the submarine's deck gun. Her port side was completely shot to pieces and she finally gave in and sank.

The crew in the boat rowed all the through the night and although they saw many ships none spotted them. They eventually made a landfall and came ashore close to Start Point later the next day.

7/21: FLORENCE MUSPRATT. *Country:* British. *Date sunk:* 5/9/17. *Tons nett:* 79. *Tons gross:* 104. *Built:* Burton Stather in 1872. *Type:* SV. *Rig:* schooner. *Owners:* Harry Manley, Porlock Weir, Somerset. *Cargo:* Ballast from St Malo to Newport. *Armed:* No. *Position:* 10 miles N of September Isles, France (49 03 00N; 03 30 00W). *Master's name:* John Wilkinson Redd. *Crew:* 4.

FLORENCE MUSPRATT was in company with four other sailing vessels making their way to Perros to join a convoy that would take them across the Channel. The weather was miserable, overcast with continual drizzle, but the sea was virtually calm.

The master reported that he heard gunfire a little earlier from the direction of one of his companion ships but couldn't see anything due to the haze. About half an hour later he heard gunfire again but this time a shell went screaming over his ship's rigging. This was followed by several more, many of which struck the *Florence* inflicting a deal of damage. He decided that he and his men should abandon ship. The mate agreed and ran to the cabin to collect some of his personal effects. As he entered, a shell smashed directly into the cabin killing him outright.

The other three men got into the boat and pulled astern. The U-boat was about a mile off, heading directly for them. As it drew closer a man appeared at the top of the conning tower and waved the men towards him. Once alongside, the master was questioned about his ship. The German then pointed in the direction the men should row to meet up with the men from the *Theodor*, the previous victim. As they left the area the master said that the submarine went closer to the *Florence* and sank her with more shells.

The three men didn't catch up with the crew of the *Theodor* until much later, and after they had been picked up by a French patrol boat. She had already found the *Theodor* crew along with the crews from two other sailing vessels, *Francis* and the *Emma*. They were eventually landed at the French port of Lezardrieux about noon the following day.

7/22: AIRSHIP C8. *Country:* British. *Date sunk:* 9/6/16. *Tons nett:* –. *Tons gross:* –. *Built:* 1916. *Type:* Coastal class, non-rigid. *Rig:* Blimp. *Owners:* Admiralty. *Cargo:* –. *Armed:* 2 Lewis machine guns, 448lb of bombs. *Position:* 22 miles SSE of Start Point (49 52 00N; 03 30 00W). *Master's name:* Lt Dickinson. *Crew:* 4.

EXTRACT from a letter from the Commander-in-Chief Devonport:

"At 10.50am on June 9, 1916, a report was received from Prawle Point signal station that at 10.30am airship *C8* was bearing south-east 10 miles in difficulties, apparently breaking in the centre and nearly down in the water. Prawle Point was immediately ordered to signal to any patrol vessels in sight to proceed to the assistance of *C8* and the destroyers *Boyne*, *Sunfish* and *Roebuck* of the local defence flotilla, were sent out to render assistance. Prawle Point signal station reported that at 10.40am *C8* was on the water bearing south by west 10 miles. HM ships *Larne* and *Nemesis*, who were on escort duty, received the signal from Prawle Point and proceeded to the spot. *Larne* arrived about 11.45am and took the airship in tow, the position then being 24 miles south of Start Point. At 4.50pm only a small portion of the envelope was remaining above the water and was deflating rapidly. At 5.35pm *Larne* reported that it was now impossible to save the remains and I ordered her to sink the airship. At 7.16pm the airship was blown up and sank.

"I regret to report that of the crew of one officer and three men, only one man was saved. His name is Andrew Douglas Wilkins, a W/T operator RNAS. The names of those missing are given as Lieutenant Dickinson, commander; Chief Petty Officer Eames, coxswain; Chief Petty Officer Palmer, engineer. A thorough search was carried out but no traces could be found of the remainder of the crew."

7/23: DORADO. *Country:* British. *Date sunk:* 9/9/16. *Tons nett:* 24. *Tons gross:* 36. *Built:* Porthleven in 1904. *Type:* SV. *Rig:* dandy. *Owners:* Charles Carter, 22, Harder St, Ramsgate. *Cargo:* Fish. *Armed:* No. *Position:* 20 miles SSE of Start Point (49 55 00N; 03 29 00W). *Master's name:* Charles Carter. *Crew:* 3.

The crew of the *Dorado* were busy fishing between Berry Head and Start Point. The catch was particularly good and at 6.30am they were hauling in another net full. Suddenly there was a bang and a shell landed close by, throwing up a spout of water. A German submarine was about two miles off and heading menacingly towards the little fishing vessel.

Dorado's crew lowered the fore sail and waited as the submarine drew alongside. The German commander ordered the crew to lower their boat between the two vessels and a man jumped down into it and attached a bomb to the trawling gear. The crew were informed very politely that they had two minutes to get clear which they did rather rapidly. The bomb exploded and the *Dorado* sank instantly.

The men drifted and rowed until about 9pm the same day when they were picked up by the transport *Imperial* and landed at Newport.

7/24: LE LAMENTIN. *Country:* French. *Date sunk:* 26/2/17. *Tons nett:* –. *Tons gross:* 716. *Built:* –. *Type:* –. *Rig:*–. *Owners:* –. *Cargo:*

Dyewood from Haiti to Havre. *Armed:* No.
Position: 30 miles WSW of Guernsey (49 40 00N;
03 25 00W). *Master's name:* Le Floch. *Crew:* 14.
Crew nationality: 13 French, 1 Haitian.

LE LAMENTIN was making her way up the Channel
to Havre when she was captured by a large German
submarine at around 3pm on February 26, 1917. Three
bombs were placed on board her and after the
Germans had plundered everything of use or value
they left her to blow up.

The crew were given a minute to get clear and they
were eventually picked up and taken to Guernsey.

7/25: LIZZIE ELLEN. *Country:* British.
Date sunk: 28/6/17. *Tons nett:* 85. *Tons gross:* 185.
Built: Cardigan in 1874. *Type:* SV. *Rig:* schooner.
Owners: Rhys H. Evans, 36, Mount Stuart Square,
Cardiff. *Cargo:* 170 tons scrap iron from Jersey to
Newport. *Armed:* No. *Position:* 30 miles NW of
Roche Douvres Light (49 26 00N; 03 24 00W).
Master's name: James Kerr. *Crew:* 4.

ALL sails were set and *Lizzie Ellen* was skipping
along nicely at four knots. The master was on deck
when a shell threw up a waterspout close by. Another
shell landed even closer and he stopped the ship. He
saw that he was being attacked by a German
submarine.

The master was ordered aboard the submarine while
his crew were made to row two German sailors back to
the *Lizzie Ellen*. Not content with planting bombs
they stole everything they could lay their hands on,
even the ship's wheel!

At 4pm the bombs exploded and the schooner sank
almost immediately. The next day HMS *Viola* picked
the crew up and landed them safely at Plymouth.

7/26: SIR JOSEPH. *Country:* British.
Date sunk: 16/3/17. *Tons nett:* 64. *Tons gross:* 84.
Built: Plymouth in 1879. *Type:* SV. *Rig:* ketch.
Owners: I.O. Nash, Plymouth. *Cargo:* 25 tons
ballast. *Armed:* No. *Position:* 30 miles SSE of Start
Point (49 46 00N; 03 22 00W). *Master's name:*
Anthony Bootyman. *Crew:* 4.

SIR JOSEPH left France for Plymouth on March 10,
1917, and made several stops on the way down the
coast. She was half way across the Channel at 7.45pm
on March 16 when a submarine had appeared from
nowhere and had fired a shell at them. Soon she was
only about 200yds off with her gun trained on the *Sir
Joseph*.

A voice boomed out across the water between them
ordering the master to bring a boat and his papers.
He had no choice but to obey and rowed across with
one of his men. Whilst he was talking to the German
commander two German sailors used his boat to row
back to the sailing vessel and planted two bombs, one

in the cabin and the other in the forecastle. The boat
having returned with the rest of his crew, the master
got in and was told to leave.

Within a few minutes the crew were completely
alone, their ship had blown up and the submarine had
dived. The master decided that from the last position
fix they would do best by rowing for the British coast,
and they reached Dartmouth the next day.

7/27: GLYNN. *Country:* British.
Date sunk: 5/9/17. *Tons nett:* 58. *Tons gross:* –.
Built: Wexford. *Type:* SV. *Rig:* schooner.
Owners: John Griffiths, 114, Bute Road, Cardiff,
Glamorgan. *Cargo:* 110 tons iron ore from Galibot
& Cie of Granville to Swansea. *Armed:* No.
Position: NW 32 miles from Hanios Light,
Guernsey (49 47 00N; 03 19 00W). *Master's
name:* Thomas Lesley. *Crew:* 4.

ON crossing the Channel from Granville the *Glynn*
made slow progress in the light south easterly wind
when she came under shellfire. A shell crashed into
the starboard side. That was enough for the crew who
climbed into the boat and rowed away. The submarine
continued firing.

The master said in his statement that even when he
was several miles away he could see his ship being
attacked, but then the submarine moved away from
it and chased after another schooner a few miles off.
He heard gunfire again and shortly after that the other
schooner disappeared. This turned out to be the
Industry. The master was starting to think about
returning to his ship when the submarine appeared
alongside again and finished her off.

The crew rowed through the night and most of the
next day and eventually arrived off Dartmouth where
they were given a tow by the patrol vessel *Morrison*
into Dartmouth Harbour.

7/28: TREVARRACK. *Country:* British.
Date sunk: 16/11/16. *Tons nett:* 2678. *Tons gross:*
4200. *Built:* South Shields in 1914. *Type:* SS. *Rig:*
schooner. *Owners:* The Hain Steamship Co Ltd,
St Ives, Cornwall. *Cargo:* 7290 tons maize from
Sanday & Co, Buenos Aires to Hull. *Armed:* No.
Position: 25 miles W of Guernsey (49 24 00N;
03 18 00W). *Master's name:* Nicholas John
Woolcock. *Crew:* 32.

THE last voyage of the *Trevarrack* began when she
left Buenos Aires on October 9, 1916, with orders to
proceed to Tenerife for further instructions. There
she was given instructions to proceed to Hull.

The ship followed the usual coastal route up the
French coast, changing her course at Ushant to set
her up the Channel. The mate, Charles E. Cleaves,
was in charge of the watch at 8.30am when he spotted
the conning tower of a submarine off the port beam.
He watched it for a few moments and then heard a

distant bang and the hiss of a shell as it passed overhead. The master, who had also heard the shell, rushed to the bridge and ordered the engine room to give him all they had in the hope they might lose their attacker. It was a brave attempt but luck was not with them as about half a mile away another, smaller, submarine appeared and sent another shell whistling close overhead. The master looked at the larger of the two submarines and could see it was flying a signal ordering him to bring his papers. As one last act of defiance he chose to ignore it and steamed on regardless. The submarine hoisted another signal, "Abandon your ship."

Watching the submarines closing on him rapidly the master realised he had no chance of escape and reluctantly ordered his men to muster at the lifeboats. As the crew rowed away the submarines began to pound her with their deck guns. Within half an hour the *Trevarrack* was sunk.

The crew continued to row away from the scene and were later spotted by the Brixham trawler *Peto*, taken on board and landed safely the same evening.

Only one U-boat claimed to have sunk *Trevarrack* and that was *UC-18*.

7/29: CONCORD. *Country:* British.
Date sunk: 30/11/16. *Tons nett:* –. *Tons gross:* 42. *Built:* Galmpton in 1898. *Type:* FV. *Rig:* ketch. *Owners:* John H. Skedgel, Bay View, Brixham. *Cargo:* Fish. *Armed:* No. *Position:* 28 miles SE by S of Start Point (49 49 00N; 03 18 00W). *Master's name:* William John Shears. *Crew:* 4.

ON November 30 there was no wind, but one of the crew of *Concord* shouted to the master that he could see what appeared to be the lugsail of a small boat heading towards them. The vessel was making extraordinary speed considering there was no wind. The master trained his binoculars on the vessel and suddenly a shell whimpered overhead. He looked again just in time to see the sail rise high enough in the water to expose the vessel as the conning tower of an enemy submarine.

There was nothing the master could do as the grey submarine moved closer towards him. He watched as the dummy sail was taken down and replaced with signal flags. "Come to me", he read.

On board the submarine the master was questioned about his ship. Although he knew it was hopeless, Captain Shears asked the German commander if he would spare his harmless little ketch. The determined German waved him aside telling him to get back into his boat, collect his crew and get clear. Two German sailors accompanied him carrying two bombs which they placed in the cabin and the hold. After helping themselves to ropes and chisels they ordered *Concord's* crew into the boat and demanded to be rowed back to their submarine which had dived several minutes earlier. The German commander obviously felt vulnerable on the surface in such a calm

sea and was watching the proceedings through his periscope. As the lifeboat drew nearer, the submarine surfaced. Having got rid of their unwelcome passengers *Concord's* crew watched as two explosions sank their ship.

For over four hours the men rowed in the direction of shore and were eventually spotted by the Norwegian steamer *Miralda I*. They were put ashore at Barry Docks the next day.

7/30: GERMAN SUBMARINE (possible).
Country: German. *Date believed sunk:* 10/7/17. *Tons nett:* –. *Tons gross:* –. *Built:* –. *Type:* UC-class. *Owners:* German navy. *Armed:* Yes. *Position:* 45 miles SW of Portland Bill (49 59 00N; 03 17 00W). *Master's name:* –. *Crew:* –. *Crew nationality:* German.

THE special service vessel HMS *Glen* was no stranger to submarine hunting. In fact she was disguised for that very purpose being made to look like an ordinary merchant ship. Her commander, Sub Lieutenant Keith Morris, had been first lieutenant in the same vessel two months earlier when she sank *UB-39* south of the Needles.

It was 2.30pm on July 10, 1917, when *Glen* was on a routine patrol carrying out her job of trying to tempt enemy submarines to attack her. Suddenly a lookout shouted that he thought he could see a submarine about 3000yds off on the port beam. The commander looked through his binoculars to see for himself, it was a submarine all right, a UC-class but no number was visible. He ordered his UC-crew to action stations and waited for the enemy commander to make the first move. It wasn't long in coming as a shell threw up a spout of water about 50yds off. Sub Lieutenant Morris looked again, she was still coming and hopefully had fallen for the ruse. At 1000yds men could be seen on the conning tower with rifles popping of shots in uneven bursts. *Glen* slowed down as if to stop but then speeded up again. Once more rifle shots popped off to reiterate the point that *Glen* should stop. The plan was working well and to complete the deception the 'abandon ship' party was ordered to leave the *Glen* whilst all other crew stayed out of sight.

The submarine commander was wary, lowering his vessel in the water until only the periscope was visible but he kept coming. It passed about 10yds around the stern of the *Glen* and stopped alongside her, gradually rising until her conning tower and half her side was clear of the water. A German officer appeared at the top of the conning tower and shouted at the abandon ship party who were some 100yds off but then he seemed startled and disappeared down the hatch rapidly. *Glen's* commander reacted quickly and ordered his gunners to open fire. The 12 pounder was directly on the submarine and fired off five shots in rapid succession, one missed but the other four hit home opening up big holes in the submarine's sides.

144

The three pounder couldn't bear directly but managed to get off three shots which hit her stern.

The submarine rolled in the swell gradually sinking but suddenly she rolled over violently to starboard and sank horizontally. White vapour, oil and air bubbles gushed to the surface in huge amounts turning the water in a mass of froth. *Glen* stayed over the area watching and listening on the hydrophones for some time. Oil and air continued to rise in large amounts but there was no sound of life.

The Admiralty accepted the fact that HMS *Glen* had sunk a submarine and awarded her crew the maximum £1000 prize money. Several of her crew also received medals for their exceptional efforts during the action. Her commander, Sub-Lt Keith Morris was awarded a bar to his DSC.

However, there is no German record of a submarine being lost on this date, and no identification number was given by the Admiralty.

7/31: GAUNTLET. *Country:* British.
Date sunk: 18/6/17. *Tons nett:* 52. *Tons gross:* 58. *Built:* 1875. *Type:* SV. *Rig:* ketch. *Owners:* J.E. Benoal, Knockhampton Villas, Jersey. *Cargo:* 30 tons ballast from St Malo to Par, Cornwall. *Armed:* No. *Position:* 30 miles NW of Hanois, Guernsey (49 45 00N; 03 17 00W). *Master's name:* Thomas Chevalier. *Crew:* 4.

THE master of *Gauntlet* couldn't work out where the shells were coming from. Two had screamed over the rigging about 30 seconds apart and a third took away part of his ship's fore mast. He decided that whatever it was, it was time to go, and told his crew to get in the boat and pull clear. As they left, the master saw a German submarine, a big one, about a mile off heading towards him very quickly.

Soon the submarine was alongside the crew in the boat and a rope was thrown to them. They tied it off and sat still as the submarine towed them back towards the *Gauntlet*. As they neared her a German officer pointed at one of the men, the Mate called Laurens, ordering him to board the submarine. He did as he was told and his seat in the boat was taken by a German sailor armed with several bombs. As the bomber went about his duty, planting the bombs and stealing items such as food, clocks, the barometer and flags, the submarine commander set about questioning the mate.

"When does the potato season start in Jersey? I don't want any lies now, I want the truth."

The mate replied, " In about a month."

"Are there many vessels left there now?"

"No, this is the only one."

The commander continued to ask questions about the quality of the harvest expected, obviously planning to ensure that he and his colleagues in the undersea world would disrupt the trade when the time came.

The *Gauntlet* sank within a few minutes of the bombs exploding and the mate was put back with his crew. They rowed for some time and eventually landed at Hanois, Guernsey, at two o'clock the following afternoon.

7/32: SEEKER. *Country:* British.
Date sunk: 3/12/16. *Tons nett:* 58. *Tons gross:* 74. *Built:* 1879. *Type:* SV. *Rig:* schooner. *Owners:* W.G. Waters, Wigmore, Chatham. *Cargo:* Sand ballast. *Armed:* No. *Position:* 30 miles NW of Hanois, Guernsey (49 48 00N; 03 16 00W). *Master's name:* Thomas Jas King. *Crew:* 5.

THE master of *Seeker* could see the strange object that had been pointed out to him, about half a mile off on the port bow but he couldn't make out what it was. He could see the sail quite clearly but there was something very peculiar about the vessel which made him feel very uneasy. His anxiety was fully justified as a few minutes later the sail disappeared to reveal the conning tower of an enemy submarine.

There was nothing Captain King could do, so he watched and waited to see what would happen. As the submarine drew closer he could see one of her officers waving as if to beckon him to approach. Realising it was the end of his ship he ordered the crew to take to the lifeboat and rowed towards the waiting enemy.

The message from the German commander was blunt, "Get clear, I am going to sink your ship," and pointed in the direction of Guernsey. *Seeker's* crew watched as the submarine manoeuvred close alongside their ship, sailors leaping aboard her to plant several bombs. A few minutes later it was all over for *Seeker* as she blew to pieces and sank. The crew reached Guernsey the next day.

7/33: UNION. *Country:* Norwegian.
Date sunk: 28/12/16. *Tons nett:* –. *Tons gross:* 511. *Built:* –. *Type:* SV. *Rig:* barque. *Owners:* J.B. Linaae, Sandefjord, Norway. *Cargo:* Logwood, Haiti for Le Havre. *Armed:* No. *Position:* 24 miles SE of Start Point (49 54 00N; 03 16 00W). *Master's name:* Frederick Eriksen. *Crew:* 11. *Crew nationality:* 5 Norwegians, 3 Russian/Finns, 1 Danish, 2 Swedes.

A WELL placed shell from the U-boat threw up a spout of water ahead of the ship.

The master of *Union* had no choice but to stop. He read the signal flags that had been run up the conning tower mast, grabbed his papers and went across to talk his assailants.

Captain Eriksen was obviously a man who could think clearly when the going got tough. He talked to the first officer of the submarine in a very light hearted manner even suggesting that it would be a shame to sink such a fine ship in the middle of the English Channel. The German seemed to agreed with him until the commander stepped in and said: "Your ship will be sunk, now."

Within a few minutes German sailors were clambering over the *Union* and planted three bombs, forward, middle and aft. They had obviously been at sea a long time as Captain Eriksen reported that they looked hungry, thin and very dirty. They made for the galley and proceeded to plunder whatever food they could find. They even tried to take the ship's chronometer but the master grabbed it and wouldn't allow them near it. Luckily the Germans didn't press the point and left.

A few minutes later the crew watched from their lifeboat as the bombs on board *Union* exploded. It made a mess of her but she didn't sink immediately. Twenty minutes later a piece of the stern was still showing. The crew rowed towards the shore and were spotted by the armed trawler *Sea Monarch* from Portland. They were landed at Torquay at 7am the next morning.

7/34: MURIEL FRANKLIN. *Country:* British. *Date sunk:* 9/9/16. *Tons nett:* –. *Tons gross:* 29. *Built:* Galmpton in 1916. *Type:* SV. *Rig:* ketch. *Owners:* A.C. Neby, Billingsgate. *Cargo:* Fish. *Armed:* No. *Position:* 20 miles SE of Start Point (49 59 00N; 03 16 00W). *Master's name:* George Sparrow. *Crew:* 4.

AT 9.30 in the morning of September 9, 1916, the master of *Muriel Franklin* was enjoying his breakfast. The weather was fine and all seemed set for a good day's fishing. His breakfast was ruined when the mate shouted down that he had just spotted a German submarine off the port quarter.

Captain Sparrow rushed up on deck. Estimating that the submarine was about two miles off he ordered the trawl nets to be got in quickly but it was a painfully slow process so he ordered them to be cut away instead.

On looking again the master could see that the submarine was attacking two other fishing vessels and thought that if he was lucky he could make a run for it. He ordered full sail to be put up and came about on the port tack. He watched both vessels in the distance gradually disappear from view, but his worse fears were confirmed when several shells came whistling in his direction. He ignored them to start with but as the shells and the submarine got closer, realised that to run was futile.

He ordered the ship to be stopped and told everyone to get in the lifeboat and pull clear. From a few hundred yards off, the crew watched as the submarine came alongside the *Muriel Franklin* and pumped about eight shells into her until she sank.

The Germans made no attempt to talk to the crew but just moved on to the next fishing vessel to dish out the same treatment. When the British destroyer *Manly* appeared, the U-boat made off and dived. The *Manly* searched for her and was joined later by the warship *Hornet* without success. The crew of the *Muriel Franklin* were landed at Weymouth.

7/35: COMTESSE DE FLANDRE.
Country: Belgian. *Date sunk:* 25/10/16. *Tons nett:* 1136. *Tons gross:* 1817. *Built:* 1906. *Type:* SS. *Rig:* schooner. *Owners:* Belgian Ocean Line, Antwerp. *Managers:* L. Drow & Co. *Cargo:* In ballast, Calais for Barry. *Armed:* No. *Position:* 35 miles WNW of Casketts (49 55 00N; 03 15 00W). *Master's name:* Charles Schmidt. *Crew:* 24. *Crew nationality:* 14 Belgians, 3 Danes, 3 Dutch, 1 Swede, 1 Russian, 1 British, 1 Chilian.

CAPTAIN Schmidt was below in his cabin when the first shot rang out. Another explosion boomed in the distance and another shell whistled close by.

The master knew that the submarine was ordering him to stop and felt he had no choice but to do just that. As the enemy drew closer an officer on the submarine waved his hand, beckoning the crew to leave their ship and get clear. They left in three boats but once clear the men in the small gig transferred leaving the master and 10 men in one and the mate with 12 in the other. The submarine began to pound the *Comtesse* on her starboard side and after about 20 shots she rolled over and sank.

The master stated later that the Germans made no attempt to talk to him or his crew and they were ignored from the moment they left their ship. The two boats tried to stay together but were eventually separated. The master and his men were picked up by the patrol boat *Sea Monarch* and the mate's boat picked up by another vessel and landed at Guernsey.

7/36: ALCYONE. *Country:* British.
Date sunk: 1/8/17. *Tons nett:* 69. *Tons gross:* 149. *Built:* 1893. *Type:* SV/MV. *Rig:* schooner. *Owners:* The Italian Export Shipping Co, Baltic House, Cardiff. *Cargo:* 200 tons coal from Cardiff to St Brieux. *Armed:* No. *Position:* 45 miles NNW of Roche Douvres (49 48 00N; 03 14 00W). *Master's name:* Matthew Craven. *Crew:* 6.

THE *Alcyone* was a little unusual for her time in that she was classed as a motor schooner having an auxiliary engine as a back up. She left Falmouth on August 1, 1917, and fell in with a convoy of steamers. She stayed with them until off the Eddystone at noon when she bore away for the French coast.

At about 4.30pm the master heard what he thought was gunfire and went on deck to investigate further. As he made the deck he heard another report followed by the whistling of a shell as it landed in the water close by. Several more followed one of which hit the fore part of the ship smashing away the head gear. He spotted the submarine, just off the fore quarter about a mile away. Another shell came screaming overhead and went clean through the fore sail causing it to flap wildly in the wind.

The master told his men to take to the boat. Even as they rowed clear the submarine kept up her bombardment, hitting the vessel with more and more shells. One shell took the mainmast clean out of the schooner throwing rigging and debris in all directions. Eventually she took on a list to starboard and at about 4.30pm slipped below the waves.

The German commander turned his attention to the boat and ordered the master to come on board the submarine at once. He gave the commander his ship's details but denied having any confidential sailing instructions on him at all, having destroyed them just before he abandoned ship. He was allowed to go and join his crew in the boat. They rowed for many hours and eventually landed on the group of rocks called the Roches Douvres where they stayed with the lighthouse keeper. He managed to get them a lift to the French port of Lezardrieux the next day.

7/37: KATE & ANNIE. *Country:* British. *Date sunk:* 19/6/17. *Tons nett:* 79. *Tons gross:* 96. *Built:* Bridgewater in 1894. *Type:* SV. *Rig:* ketch. *Owners:* Thomas Stamp, Ebney, Stonehouse, Gloucester. *Cargo:* 153 tons coal from D. Mules & Son, Cardiff to St Malo. *Armed:* No. *Position:* 25 miles NW by W of Hanois Light (49 38 00N; 03 14 00W). *Master's name:* Thomas Stamp. *Crew:* 4.

THE information on this sinking is taken mainly from a report sent to the Admiralty by the State Police at Guernsey where the survivors landed.

The master said that at 9.30am he was called by the mate to have a look at a strange craft he had spotted about four miles off on the starboard quarter. The master looked through the binoculars and recognised it immediately as an enemy submarine. The helm was altered a little to try and take the ship away from her but it was useless against such a fast and manoeuverable vessel. As she got closer the submarine's gunner opened up sending several shells over, around and through the ketch's rigging.

The master realised that he stood no chance of getting away and ordered his men to get clear as quickly as possible. An officer from the submarine waved to the crew beckoning them to come towards him. Once alongside they were all ordered out of the boat and to stand on the submarine and wait while several German sailors used the boat to visit the ketch. They took their time, filling boxes with food, taking clocks and barometers down, then leaving their calling cards of two bombs. One was placed in the forecastle and the other in the galley.

By the time the German commander had finished questioning the master the bombing party were back with their booty. All eyes turned to the ketch and one officer produced a camera to record the event. A few minutes later the bombs exploded and the *Kate & Annie* went down by the head.

As the crew clambered back into their now vacant boat the commander had his binoculars up studying another sailing vessel about four miles to the south east. She turned out to be the brigantine *Mary Ann*.

The crew rowed for several hours and eventually landed at Rocquaine Bay, Guernsey.

7/38: TOM ROPER. *Country:* British. *Date sunk:* 21/10/17. *Tons nett:* 92. *Tons gross:* 120. *Built:* Barrow in 1857. *Type:* SV. *Rig:* schooner. *Owners:* Harris & Sharp, 67, Hope St, Glasgow. *Cargo:* 60 tons ballast from Guernsey to Cardiff. *Armed:* No. *Position:* 22 miles SE of Start Point (49 59 00N; 03 13 00W). *Master's name:* Robert Fels. *Crew:* 6. *Crew nationality:* 3 British, 1 French, 1 American, 1 Venezuelan.

AT 4.15pm someone shouted to the master that he could see a strange sail off the starboard bow. The master looked through his binoculars, it was strange indeed, looking a bit like a sailing vessel, but there was something odd about it. At 4.30pm a bang was heard from the vessel's direction and a few seconds later a shell screamed over the rigging. The master looked again, it was an enemy submarine.

The order was given to reduce sail a little and get the boat ready. While that was being done the master tore his confidential papers into tiny pieces and threw them up to the wind, scattering the fragments over the waves. They pulled clear just in time as a shell took away the mainmast, followed rapidly by others which ripped through the rigging, splintering pieces of timber to matchwood.

As the submarine got closer to the men in the boat a German officer appeared and beckoned them to come towards him. Once alongside they were told to board and held at gunpoint whilst several German sailors rowed over to the *Tom Roper*, which was still afloat but in a bad way. The German officer asked the master if he had any lard, tallow or soap on board, to which the master confirmed he had. The boarding party soon found what they wanted and placed three bombs on her before leaving. With the bombing party back at the submarine the crew were told they could leave. It was quite dark by this time and great care was necessary in getting into the boat. One lad, a young Frenchman called Jean Brevost, lost his footing and fell into the sea. The others desperately looked for him but he just didn't come to the surface.

At 7pm three explosions were heard from the *Tom Roper* and she could be seen burning in the distance. Half an hour later the master said he could still see her but she seemed very low in the water and disappeared soon after. The five men rigged a sail and were soon blown up the Channel all through the night and most of the next day. They were fearful at one stage of having to spend a second night at sea but help came when drifter B71 *The Boys* found them, putting them ashore safely at Weymouth.

7/39: MARY ANN. *Country:* British. *Date sunk:* 19/6/17. *Tons nett:* 138. *Tons gross:* 163. *Built:* Kingston Moray in 1879. *Type:* SV.

Rig: brigantine. *Owners:* William A Jenkins & Co, Baltic Buildings, Swansea. *Cargo:* 180 tons pitwood from Nivel, St Brieux to Mr Morgan of Cadogan. *Armed:* No. *Position:* 21 miles NW by W of Hanois Light, Guernsey (49 37 00N; 03 11 00W). *Master's name:* William Henry Brokenshire. *Crew:* 5.

HAVING just sunk the ketch *Kate & Annie* the German commander set his sights on the brig that lay to the south east. It was the *Mary Ann*. After the second shell landed right under his stern, the master decided to abandon his ship.

It was 11am before the submarine got alongside the crew's boat, a German sailor throwing them a line as they closed. The same routine was employed as with their previous victim, and the crew were towed back to their ship. Sailors were then put aboard. The master said he was amazed at what they took – bits of brass fittings, nails, even two old brushes. However, they must have run out of bombs as instead of blowing her up they set fire to her.

The crew were told to go and rowed away. The *Mary Ann* was still afloat but burning fiercely. The submarine commander must have felt he needed to help things along as several shells were fired into her hull. However, in spite of it all she still didn't sink. The last the master saw of her he thought it was only her cargo of wood keeping her afloat.

The crew landed at Rocquaine Bay, Guernsey the next day.

7/40: YRSA. *Country:* Danish.
Date sunk: 3/12/16. *Tons nett:* –. *Tons gross:* 844. *Built:* –. *Type:* SV. *Rig:* –. *Owners:* –. *Cargo:* 1200 tons of lead and fruit, Garrucha to London. *Armed:* –. *Position:* 30 miles WNW of Guernsey (49 35 00N; 03 10 00W). *Master's name:* –. *Crew:* 16.

There is very little available on this sinking apart from two brief snippets. One in Naval Weekly Reports notes that the *Yrsa* was sunk by bombs at 8am on December 3, 1916. The master and 15 of the crew were landed at Guernsey.

Another report says that the captain and 15 men of the Danish steamer *Yrsa* bound to London with fruit and lead arrived in Guernsey in two boats. The captain stated that the steamer was sunk by bombs about 30 miles west-north-west of Guernsey at 8am on December 3, 1916. The submarine sank three sailing ships close by. The captain of *Yrsa* said he had been stopped previous to this on December 2, off Ushant, but the submarine fled on the arrival of a French patrol boat.

7/41: GERMAN SUBMARINE U-85. *Country:* German. *Date sunk:* 12/3/17. *Tons nett:* 808. *Tons gross:* 946. *Built:* Kiel in 1916. *Type:* Mittel-U.

Owners: German navy. *Armed:* 10 torpedoes, 10.5cm deck gun. *Position:* 28 miles SE of Start Point (49 52 00N; 03 10 00W). *Master's name:* Kapitanleutnant W. Petz. *Crew:* 39. *Crew nationality:* German.

Q19, a special service ship, looked every bit like a merchant steamer called *Privet*. But behind screens were guns manned by well trained naval gunners. In March she left Land's End and headed for the Channel Isles. At 2.50pm on March 12, 1917, the white wake of a torpedo was seen streaking towards the ship but in the last few yards it appeared to dive and passed safely under the boat. The crew were immediately ordered to quarters and a close watch kept in the direction of the torpedo's wake. Nothing was seen for another 15 minutes until a submarine slowly rose to the surface about 2000yds off.

The submarine commander must have been taken in by the *Q19's* disguise and opened fire on her. The first few shells missed but one caught *Q19* in her aft section. Lieutenant Commander Matheson was keen to keep up the sham and ordered abandon ship parties to leave *Q19* and pull away. With a bit of luck he hoped the German commander would come closer, allowing him to blow it out of the water. However, things didn't go exactly to plan as one of the submarine's shells burst very close to an abandon ship boat and caused several casualties. The lieutenant commander couldn't afford to wait any longer and ordered his gunners to open fire. They shot well and several shells made direct hits on the submarine causing great chunks of metal to be hurled into the air.

The submarine's stern sank very low in the water and her bows reared up. Vapour and smoke was seen by several of the men on *Q19*, pouring out of the holes in her sides as the U-boat slowly slipped below the surface.

The Admiralty awarded the maximum £1000 prize money. Several of the men were decorated for their actions. Lieutenant Commander Charles G. Matheson was awarded the DSO.

The submarine sunk was *U-85*, commanded by Kapitanleutnant W. Petz. There were no survivors.

7/42: BOSTONIAN. *Country:* British.
Date sunk: 10/10/17. *Tons nett:* 3668. *Tons gross:* 5736. *Built:* 1896. *Type:* SS. *Rig:* schooner. *Owners:* Fredrick Leyland & Co, 27, James St, Liverpool. *Cargo:* 7200 tons general from Crew Levick & Co, Philadelphia, USA, to Admiralty, London. *Armed:* Yes. *Position:* 25 miles SE of Start Point (49 46 00N; 03 09 00W). *Master's name:* W.F. Wood. *Crew:* 109.

THE *Bostonian* was on Admiralty service and in some of the records is referred to as HMS *Bostonian*, possibly due to the fact that she was the command ship in a convoy. She was a large steamer carrying a cargo of general stores which included grain, lubricating oil and munitions. She carried so much cargo that the lubricating oil had to be stacked in casks on her upper deck in rows, two deep. She left Philadelphia on September 20, 1917, carrying the convoy commander, Admiral Nelson Isard, who was on the bridge at the time of her loss, together with the master.

On that particular day the weather was overcast with a cold northerly wind and the *Bostonian* was making a good 12 knots. Nobody on board saw any sign of *U-53*,. which had just released a torpedo which smashed into the starboard side of the ship causing a huge explosion. Apart from a large hole appearing in her side the main steam pipe was ruptured sending clouds of boiling steam in every direction. The engineers managed to shut down the engines and were beginning to bring some semblance of order to the situation when a second torpedo struck, on the starboard side again, but behind the engine room. She began to settle down.

The crew had to abandon her very rapidly indeed, taking several boats and pulling clear. Everyone got away with the exception of four men who had been killed by the first torpedo strike. Help was on hand immediately from the destroyer *Cockatrice* which picked the survivors up and took them safely to port.

The convoy continued on up the Channel and just after midday the following day the tanker *Mira* struck a mine and sank off Beachy Head.

7/43: DANSBORG. *Country:* Danish.
Date sunk: 22/12/16. *Tons nett:* –. *Tons gross:* 2242. *Built:* –. *Type:* SS. *Rig:* –. *Owners:* C.K. Hansen, Copenhagen. *Cargo:* 3046 tons coal, Sunderland for Lisbon. *Armed:* No. *Position:* 40 miles SE by S of Start Point (49 40 00N; 03 08 00W). *Master's name:* L.K. Nielson. *Crew:* 22. *Crew nationality:* 16 Danish, 2 Spaniards, 2 Norwegians, 2 Swedes.

WITH a large Danish flag flying and her name in huge letters spelt on her sides, *Dansborg* headed out across the Channel for Ushant. Danish vessels were theoretically safe from attack by German submarines but in practice they were rarely spared.

The first shell was fired from several thousand yards and fell well short. Captain Nielson steadied his binoculars on the submarine and read the signal: "Stop. Bring your papers to me."

The *Dansborg* stopped. When the submarine came close enough he rowed across in the gig. As he boarded, several sailors dressed in oil skins stood around, some armed with revolvers, some with rifles, while another two had the deck gun trained on the steamer. Captain Nielson spoke to the commander in German and was told that his ship would be sunk. He protested but it had little effect for as they spoke a boarding party were on their way in his own gig laden with bombs. Three was enough to do the trick, all

hung on the rails on the outside of the ship, one port, two starboard.

The crew were told by the bombing party that they had eight minutes to get clear. Within five two boats were alongside the submarine. Exchanging the German bombing party for their master the two boats were tied off astern to the submarine and taken in tow. As they headed away the crew watched as the bombs exploded and their ship slowly disappeared.

For about five miles the two boats were bashed and battered as they were pulled along but then a sailor appeared and hurriedly cast them adrift. To the south east another steamer appeared, also Danish, the *Hroptatyr*. She was to be next.

The two boats from *Dansborg* were later found by the British patrol ship *Q13* which took them aboard and landed them safely.

7/44: C.E.C.G. *Country:* British.
Date sunk: 18/5/17. *Tons nett:* –. *Tons gross:* 47. *Built:* Jersey in 1869. *Type:* SV. *Rig:* ketch. *Owners:* J.C. Renouf & Sons, St Helier, Jersey. *Cargo:* In ballast from Jersey to Par, Cornwall. *Armed:* No. *Position:* 30 miles SSE of Start Point (49 50 00N; 03 08 00W). *Master's name:* Thomas King. *Crew:* 4.

IT was a miserable day with thick mist and continual drizzle, typical English Channel weather. The *C.E.C.G.* was making slow progress. At about 2.30pm a dull thud was heard in the distance followed by the whistle of a shell as it passed over the rigging. Another shot followed, which smashed into the jib knocking it completely off. As the third shell shrieked through the rigging one of the crew at last spotted the culprit, a German submarine coming straight at them from the east.

As the submarine drew closer the shelling stopped. All the crew were ordered onto the submarine's deck whilst several sailors used their boat to row over to the ketch to plant bombs on her. The German commander then decided that he was too high in the water and told the captured crew to climb onto the conning tower. They did as they were told and slowly the submarine sank down until only a few feet of it was showing above water allowing waves to break over it occasionally, soaking the men in the process.

Once the bombing party returned the submarine rose up to greet them and the crew were allowed back into their boat. Several German officers appeared at the top of the conning tower with cameras and took pictures as the bombs exploded.

The crew rowed the whole distance to Dartmouth reaching there at 7am on May 19.

7/45: COCK O' THE WALK. *Country:* British.
Date sunk: 21/10/16. *Tons nett:* 89. *Tons gross:* 180. *Built:* Millwall in 1876. *Type:* SV.

Rig: ketch. *Owners:* Fred Frend, 50, Harbour St, Whistable, Kent. *Cargo:* None. *Armed:* No. *Position:* 30 miles NW by N of Hanois, Guernsey (49 54 00N; 03 06 00W). *Master's name:* Fred Frend. *Crew:* 4.

THE *Cock o'the Walk* left Granville at 1pm on October 20, 1916, bound for Fowey, Cornwall. At 6am she was on a north-north-west course making good speed when the master heard two shots in rapid succession. Looking around he an enemy submarine about one and a half miles off. He immediately had the square sail lowered and put the ship over on the starboard tack in an attempt to get more speed. The submarine fired again and a shell screamed overhead taking the mizzen mast away with it.

The master realised that there was no way he could escape and ordered the ship to be hove to. The submarine drew alongside and after questioning the master as to his nationality, cargo and destination, the German commander warned the crew to get clear quickly as he was going to sink the ship by gunfire.

The crew watched from a distance as the submarine's deck gun did its deadly work. A few minutes later the *Cock o' the Walk* had gone.

The crew eventually landed at Fowey during the evening of the same day.

7/46: ENDYMION. *Country:* British.
Date sunk: 31/3/17. *Tons nett:* –. *Tons gross:* 67. *Built:* 1881. *Type:* SV. *Rig:* ketch. *Owners:* Charles H. Truscott, 2, Kingston Row, Charleston. *Cargo:* None. *Armed:* No. *Position:* 32 miles SE of Start Point (49 50 00N; 03 04 00W). *Master's name:* Alphonse Hurley. *Crew:* 4.

LITTLE is known about the fate of the *Endymion* as all four of the crew were lost. The master of the sailing vessel *Primrose* which was sunk on the same day reported speaking with her a little earlier. He also reported that after his ship was sunk he and his crew pulled to the north in their lifeboat and did spot a sailing vessel some distance off. However, before they could make her out the same submarine that sank the *Primrose* suddenly appeared and sank her as well.

The submarine's commander was particularly aggressive in the way he sank the *Primrose*, so if it was the *Endymion*, it would explain why there were no survivors.

7/47: DAPHNE. *Country:* Norwegian.
Date sunk: 11/11/16. *Tons nett:* 849. *Tons gross:* 1388. *Built:* –. *Type:* SS. *Rig:* –. *Owners:* Jacob Rabe. *Cargo:* 1993 tons coal. *Armed:* No. *Position:* 30 miles S by E of Start Point (49 54 00N; 03 03 00W). *Master's name:* Soren Sorensen. *Crew:* 18.

DAPHNE commenced her final voyage from Newport on November 9, 1916, and was headed for Rouen. The trip went well with no problems until, without any warning, shells started to rain down just ahead of the steamer.

The master stopped his ship and waited for the submarine to get closer and as it did so another shell exploded only a few yards from the side of the ship. Taking this as a signal to present his papers the master had a boat lowered and rowed across to the submarine. After the papers had been examined the German commander sent several sailors over to the steamer to plant bombs and the crew were told they had ten minutes to get clear.

Two lifeboats were lowered, one under the command of the master and the other by the mate. They pulled clear and in just under ten minutes the bombs exploded sending *Daphne* to the bottom.

7/48: PRIMROSE. *Country:* British.
Date sunk: 31/3/17. *Tons nett:* 95. *Tons gross:* 113. *Built:* Southampton in 1886. *Type:* SV. *Rig:* schooner. *Owners:* Edward Stephens, Fowey, Cornwall. *Cargo:* None. *Armed:* No. *Position:* 35 miles SE of Start Point (49 48 00N; 03 01 00W). *Master's name:* Alexander Doherty Steele. *Crew:* 4.

THE weather was not particularly good as *Primrose* made her way out across the Channel from Granville in France. The wind was quite strong with some very heavy gusts. Suddenly there was a flash in the near-darkness just off the port bow. A spout of water was thrown up by a shell about 20yds off. By this time the master had spotted a conning tower of a submarine and shouted for the boat to be got ready.

One of the hands, William Jackson, jumped onto the hatch coamings to release the falls of the lifeboat. At that instant the submarine's gun fired again. This time the shell made a direct hit on the hatch, blowing William Jackson to pieces. The three remaining men eventually cleared the lifeboat, but the submarine kept firing. As they pulled clear the submarine pressed closer, firing more and more shells until the *Primrose* settled down and sank.

The three men tried to row to the north towards the British coast but the weather got worse all the time. A ray of hope arrived when they spotted a sailing vessel in the distance but their delight was crushed when the same submarine appeared and sank her too! The wind increased to near gale force from the north-west and the boat was being tossed about like a cork. There was nothing the master could do but to put out a sea anchor and let the wind take them. He estimated that they would probably make the Channel Islands. He proved to be right and they landed at Alderney at 8.30pm the next day.

7/49: LADY OF THE LAKE. *Country:* British.
Date sunk: 28/11/16. *Tons nett:* –. *Tons gross:* 78.

Built: Bosham in 1876. *Type:* SV. *Rig:* ketch.
Owners: William Quance, Appledore, Devon.
Cargo: 150 tons coal shipped by Ocean Colliery
Co. *Armed:* No. *Position:* 35 miles SE of Start Point
(49 49 00N; 03 01 00W). *Master's name:* John
Nicholls Day. *Crew:* 3.

IT had been a troublesome journey from the very
beginning for the *Lady Of The Lake*. She left Cardiff
on November 16, 1916, and was forced into St Ives
through weather. She was unable to leave there until
the 22nd but was forced to seek shelter yet again at
Plymouth until the 27th. At last she headed out across
the Channel for her destination at Alderney.

At about 9.30am on November 28, she was half
way across when a sea-plane flying a French flag
landed beside her and the pilot warned the master that
a German submarine was only about one mile away
from him. Grateful for the information the master
pressed on and hoped he could keep up enough speed
under full sail to outrun the problem. However, a short
time later a shell whistled over the vessel's rigging.

The master immediately went below and burnt his
confidential papers and told his two crew men to get
the boat ready. Within a few minutes the submarine
was virtually on top of them and a German officer
stood on the decking waving for the three men to get
clear of their ship. No sooner were they a few yards
away than the submarine's gunners opened up – four
shells were sufficient to send the *Lady Of The Lake* to
the bottom.

The crew rowed for about an hour when they spotted
a lifeboat not far from them. They pulled towards it
and found that it contained fellow sufferers from the
vessel *Clematis* of Ramsgate which had been sunk by
the same submarine. The *Clematis's* boat being the
larger of the two the crew from the *Lady Of The Lake*
joined forces with them and rowed towards the shore.
They were eventually found by the trawler *Pencare*
and landed at Brixham the same evening.

7/50: MINIOTA. *Country:* British.
Date sunk: 31/8/17. *Tons nett:* –. *Tons gross:* 6422.
Built: 1914. *Type:* SS. *Rig:* –. *Owners:* Canadian
Pacific Ocean Services Ltd, London. *Cargo:*
Munitions, Montreal to Portland. *Armed:* 1 x 4in
gun. *Position:* 30 miles SE by E of Start Point
(49 56 00N; 03 00 00W). *Master's name:*
W. Haines. *Crew:* 54. *Crew nationality:* All British.
Gunners: James Gibson, Pte. Portsmouth, No RFR
600; Frederick Jourdan, Pte. Portsmouth, No RFR
8911; John Eustace, Pte. Chatham, No RFR 888;
Harry B. Evans, signalman, Chatham, RNVR.

THE convoy was formed in five columns and the
Miniota was the last ship on the inshore column. She
was making eight knots. The torpedo hit the *Miniota*
in the exact centre of the engine room cavity, 15 feet
below the waterline. It made an enormous hole and
the sudden inrush of water caused the boilers to

explode which brought the engines to an abrupt stop.

The master abandoned ship immediately and placed
his wounded men on the destroyer *Latin*. Two of his
men, one engineer and a fireman, were killed.

The steamer didn't sink immediately and various
attempts were made to take her in tow. The second
mate and some of the deck hands volunteered to return
to the ship and help with the salvage. The Admiralty
trawlers *Miura* and *Jeannie Stewart* were first to
attempt a tow but the lines parted. They tried a larger
five inch wire hawser but there were not enough men
on the *Miniota* to handle it and they lost the end. They
tried again with sweep wires and managed to tow all
night until the *Miura* received orders from *St Cuthbert*
to cast off the tow ahead and take up astern to assist
with the steering. *St Cuthbert* then took up the forward
tow. Good progress was made for an hour but
suddenly the stricken steamer began to list to
starboard, steadily settling down in the water.

The weather was getting worse with a strong wind
and a high sea and the whole salvage operation was
getting more dangerous by the minute. The crew on
the *Miniota* decided they had pushed their luck far
enough and got off. Shortly after, at 12.25pm on the
September 1, she sank by the head.

U-19 was the submarine involved.

7/51: MINNIE COLES. *Country:* British.
Date sunk: 19/11/17. *Tons nett:* –. *Tons gross:* 119.
Built: –. *Type:* SV. *Rig:* –. *Owners:* J.D. Bevan.
Cargo: 195 tons pitch. *Armed:* No. *Position:* 30
miles NW by N from Hanois, Guernsey (49 53 00N;
03 00 00W). *Master's name:* –. *Crew:* 4.

IT would seem that the crew of the German submarine
who sank *Minnie Coles* were rather hungry. When
they fired shots at her at 3pm on November 19, 1917,
the shots were just blanks. However, they had the
desired effect and the master of *Minnie Coles* stopped
his ship and waited to see what would happen.

The Germans boarded her straight away and they
knew what they wanted, food and lots of it. The
master commented later that the men were very
pleasant. The German commander explained that he
was sorry to have to sink the sailing vessel but that
was war. He also added that he and his men were very
short of food.

The master of *Minnie Coles* and his three crew left
in the small boat. After the Germans had gathered up
all the food, bombs were left which sent *Minnie Coles*
to the bottom at 4pm.

The four men in the boat rowed towards the shore
but were spotted by a patrolling French torpedo boat
and landed at Cherbourg.

7/52: HROPTATYR. *Country:* Danish.
Date sunk: 22/12/16. *Tons nett:* –. *Tons gross:*
1300. *Built:* –. *Type:* SS. *Rig:* –. *Owners:* Holm &
Vonsild, Copenhagen. *Cargo:* –. *Armed:* No.

Position: 16 miles NW by W of Hanois, Guernsey (49 37 00N; 03 00 00W). *Master's name:* Hinningsen. *Crew:* 17. *Crew nationality:* 16 Danish, 1 Swede.

"DANISH crew experience German savagery." That was the title of an article printed in the Danish, *Politiken* newspaper on December 31, 1916. It read:

"The survivors of the crew of the Danish steamer *Hrpotatyr* which was torpedoed on December 22nd off Ushant have arrived in Copenhagen. They give harrowing details of their experiences.

"A heavy sea was running when at about two oclock in the afternoon the *U-18* stopped the *Hroptatyr* and ordered the crew to leave the ship. The boats were lowered with the greatest difficulty and just as one of them had succeeded in getting clear, the submarine rushed up at full speed from the other side of the steamer striking the lifeboat as she passed, with the result that the boat was hurled against the steamer's side. The Captain was crushed to death against the hull his head being severed from his body and a sailor was so badly injured that he died soon afterwards.

The submarine torpedoed the steamer and took the crew on board. No sooner had this operation been completed than a French destroyer steamed up at full speed firing at the submarine as she came. The U-boat at once submerged. One shell from the destroyer missed her by a couple of yards.

The submarine took the steamer's crew to Zeebrugge and they say they had plenty of good food on board the submarine, but on their arrival at Zeebrugge they were taken to a military barracks where the rations served there to them were of a most meagre description."

The naval records tell a different story:

Having already dealt with one Danish steamer, the *Dansborg,* two hours earlier, the U-boat sped towards her next victim which was also flying a big Danish flag. At a distance of about a mile the gunner was ordered to fire a shell to attract the master's attention. It worked and the *Hroptatyr* slowed down. On board the submarine the master talked to the German commander and tried to reason with him, saying that he had no right to sink his ship. The young commander ignored the Dane and watched his men already swarming over the steamer planting bombs in various places.

When the rest of the crew returned in another boat with the bombing party, the submarine manoeuvred slightly and in doing so forced the bow of one boat to ride up throwing several of the men into the sea. Fortunately they could swim and were soon back in the boat.

Cast adrift the crew watched as their ship exploded and sank. Within half an hour the *Q13* appeared over the horizon and picked them up. *Q13* was disguised as the Danish steamer *Kai.*

7/53: SAN NICOLAU. *Country:* Portuguese. *Date sunk:* 16/11/16. *Tons nett:*–. *Tons gross:* 2697. *Built:* –. *Type:* SS. *Rig:* –. *Owners:* Portuguese government. *Cargo:* Timber, Lisbon for Le Havre. *Armed:* No. *Position:* 25 miles SW of Casketts (49 30 00N; 03 00 00W). *Master's name:* Amancio Jose Azeveeo. *Crew:* 37. *Crew nationality:* 36 Portuguese, 1 Brazilian.

THE end of her sailing days began at noon on November 16 for the *San Nicolau*. A submarine had surfaced alongside and fired two shells, both throwing up large columns of water. It was impressive enough for the Portuguese master to stop his ship immediately. The Germans manoeuvred to a position where they could make hand signals to the master to get his crew into the boats and come towards them.

The language was a problem but after one of the crew took the role of translator the German commander managed to obtain the details and papers he wanted. Spoken words were not necessary at the end as the commander waved his arm for them to go away.

After planting bombs on board the steamer the submarine drew back a little and fired about twelve shells into her at various places around the hull. The bombs finished the job off and she sank soon afterwards.

WORLD WAR ONE
CHANNEL WRECKS

◆

AREA EIGHT

WRECK SITES IN AREA EIGHT

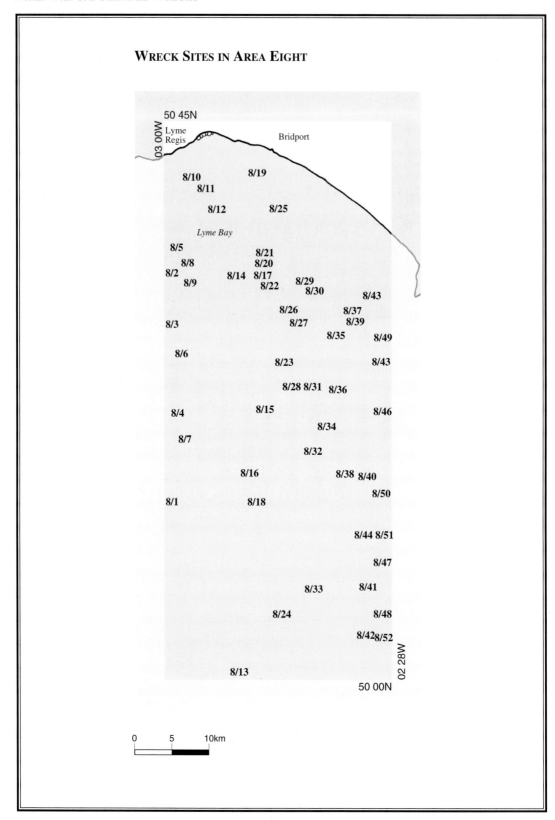

50 45N

03 00W

Lyme
Regis

Bridport

8/10
8/11

8/19

8/12

8/25

Lyme Bay

8/5

8/21
8/20

8/8

8/2

8/14 8/17

8/29

8/9

8/22

8/30

8/43

8/26

8/37

8/3

8/27

8/39

8/35

8/49

8/6

8/43

8/23

8/28 8/31 8/36

8/4

8/15

8/46

8/34

8/7

8/32

8/16

8/38 8/40

8/1

8/18

8/50

8/44 8/51

8/47

8/33

8/41

8/24

8/48

8/42 8/52

02 28W

8/13

50 00N

0   5   10km

8/1: MAY. *Country:* British.
Date sunk: 26/1/18. *Tons nett:* 24. *Tons gross:* 45.
Built: Whitstable in 1893. *Type:* SV. *Rig:* ketch.
Owners: Samuel Down, Ramsgate, Kent. *Cargo:*
Fish. *Armed:* No. *Position:* 19 miles SE of Berry
Head (50 15 00N; 03 00 00W). *Master's name:*
Samuel Down. *Crew:* 4.

SHE looked a good two miles off when the master of
the *May* first spotted the German submarine. But even
from that distance she was getting her shells fairly
close to the little sailing vessel, close enough for the
master to order his men away in the lifeboat.

As the submarine drew alongside the boat, the
commander ordered the master, the cook and the third
mate to board, their places being taken by a German
officer and two sailors. The other crew member of
the *May* had to row the men back to their ship where
they proceeded to plunder her of food, stores, clothing
and anything else they fancied. Then they planted two
bombs, one forward and one amidships.

The master described the death of his ship by
saying, "She went down like a stone."

The men were picked up by the patrol trawler *Lorna*
which landed them at Weymouth the next day.

8/2: CLYDE. *Country:* British.
Date sunk: 14/10/17. *Tons nett:* –. *Tons gross:* 146.
Built: –. *Type:* Admiralty Trawler. *Rig:* –. *Owners:*
Admiralty. *Cargo:* –. *Armed:* Yes. *Position:* Off
Sidmouth (50 33 30N; 02 59 30W). *Master's
name:* –.

THE patrol trawler 971 *Clyde.*sank after a collision
at 4.20am on October 14, 1917, with the patrol trawler
3287 *Flintshire*, off Sidmouth, Devon. *Flintshire*
survived the accident but was rendered unseaworthy.

8/3: PERRITON. *Country:* British.
Date sunk: 29/1/18. *Tons nett:* 74. *Tons gross:* 90.
Built: Minehead in 1881. *Type:* SV. *Rig:* schooner.
Owners: Edwin Whiteway Gill and others of
Rochester. *Cargo:* 140 tons flints from Dieppe
consigned to Western Point Carrying Co, Runcorn.
Armed: No. *Position:* Berry Head bearing W about
20 miles (50 29 00N; 02 59 00W). *Master's name:*
Owen George Rudge. *Crew:* 4. *Crew nationality:*
All British.

IT was an unusually painted submarine that appeared
on the surface about a mile on the port side of the
Perriton. The master described it as camouflaged and
large. As it fired a shell at another trawler which was
close by, Captain Rudge turned his vessel away.
However, a few minutes later a shell whimpered over
the bows of his schooner as a signal to him to stop.

The master obeyed the signal and told his crew to
get the small boat ready. It was while this was being
done that another shell was fired from the submarine

which smashed into the small boat as it entered the
water, completely cutting it in two and severely
injuring deck hand Richard Quale. The shells kept
coming, many of them smashing into *Perriton's* hull
opening up large holes and throwing splinters in all
directions. With no boat there was little else the crew
could do but to jump overboard.

The master managed to cling to the wreckage of
the shattered boat and also found the strength to keep
hold of his injured crewman. Twenty minutes later
the submarine came close enough to throw a line and
dragged the men towards it. The German gunner then
fired two more shells into the *Perriton* to finish her
off.

The U-boat commander not wanting to be lumbered
with four men, two of them injured – the cook had
received minor injuries as well – stopped the passing
trawler *Onyx* and handed them over. The four men
were landed at Brixham.

8/4: BAYONNE. *Country:* French.
Date sunk: 17/2/17. *Tons nett:* 2241. *Tons gross:*
2589. *Built:* 1901. *Type:* SV. *Rig:* Steel sailor.
Owners: Societe Anomyne des Violers Normando,
Rouen. *Cargo:* 1000 tons Maize, 2300 tons Barley,
New York to Ipswich. *Armed:* No. *Position:* 25
miles NE of Start Point/25 miles ENE of Start Point
(50 22 00N; 02 59 00W). *Master's name:* Albert
Thoumire. *Crew:* 27. *Crew nationality:* 23 French,
4 Americans.

ON the February 17, when *Bayonne* was off Start
Point a submarine appeared on her starboard bow and
proceeded to put two shots across her. The master
ignored them. The submarine then moved around to
the port side of *Bayonne* and fired two more shots,
which the master still ignored. Two more shots
followed which sliced through the ship's rigging and
the master ordered the ship to heave to and the men
into the boats.

The Germans placed two charges on the upper deck,
two forward, one each side abreast of the galley and
two aft at the break of the poop. When the bombs
exploded each one made no more noise than a revolver
shot. The *Bayonne* sank immediately.

The German commander told the captain that he
would give them a tow to the French coast but he
became very nervous at the approach of some ships,
their lights visible in the distance. On spotting these
the submarine made off and disappeared into the
darkness.

In his subsequent report, Captain Thoumire told
the authorities that while his ship was being sunk he
noticed a Norwegian ship called *Strella* steaming
down channel very fast and then turned to hold up
just east of Start Point. He thought these actions were
very suspicious and seemed to have some connection
with the submarine. It is not noted whether his
suspicions were correct.

One of the officers of the submarine very obligingly

gave the master a receipt for the stores they had taken and one of the German crew told the *Bayonne's* mate that their submarine was the *U-2*, but there were no markings on her.

8/5: MARGUERITE. *Country:* French. *Date sunk:* 28/6/17. *Tons nett:* 811. *Tons gross:* 1544. *Built:* 1912. *Type:* SS. *Rig:* schooner. *Owners:* Fernand Bouet of Caen. *Cargo:* In ballast, Rouen to Swansea. *Armed:* 1 x 90mm cannon. *Position:* 8 miles S of Lyme Regis/In Lyme Bay about 7 miles from shore (50 35 00N; 02 58 45W). *Master's name:* Jean Esnol. *Crew:* 21. *Crew nationality:* All French.

THE master's instructions, once he had crossed the Channel, were to hug the coast as closely as possible. However, the weather was thick and the visibility poor so the master decided that he dare not go as close as he should.

Nobody on board was aware of another danger, *UB-40* was lurking nearby, lining up the *Marguerite* for a torpedo. It struck the steamer on the port side aft in number four hold and completely destroyed the aft end.

The crew took to the boats and were soon picked up by a passing steamer the SS *Horn* which in turn transferred them to the patrol drifter *Daily Bread*, which landed them at Falmouth.

8/6: TANDIL. *Country:* British. *Date sunk:* 12/3/17. *Tons nett:* 1825. *Tons gross:* 2897. *Built:* 1900. *Type:* SS. *Rig:* –. *Owners:* Arthur Holland & Co, 2, East India Ave, London, EC3. *Cargo:* 4200 tons coal, Barry for Portland. *Armed:* No. *Position:* 20 miles W of Portland (50 27 00N; 02 58 00W). *Master's name:* Wilfred Lawson Chambers. *Crew:* 27.

ON the night of March 11, 1917, the weather was particularly bad with blinding rain and sharp flashes of lightning. Although she should not have been showing lights in normal circumstances, the master decided, in view of the weather and because of the heavy traffic around at the time, to show dimmed masthead and side lights. These lights may have caused the attack on her. Just after midnight a torpedo was fired at her port side amidships. It caused a huge explosion which killed the third engineer, two firemen and the cabin boy. The 23 remaining crew immediately abandoned the *Tandil* in two lifeboats and rowed clear. About 20 minutes later the *Tandil* sank.

The German submarine slowly approached the boats and a voice demanded to be told all the particulars of the ship. Having noted all the details, the German officer waved the boats away and the submarine turned towards new prey. A vessel had just come into sight about three miles to the south-west.

The crew were eventually picked up by the Brixham trawler *Coronet* and landed at Brixham on the same day at 9am.

U-85 was the submarine concerned.

8/7: NYASALAND. *Country:* Norwegian. *Date sunk:* 8/4/18. *Tons nett:* 203. *Tons gross:* 383. *Built:* Germany in 1898. *Type:* SS. *Rig:* schooner. *Owners:* T.E. Ebbesen, Tonsberg, Norway. *Cargo:* 393 tons coal, Cardiff to Le Havre. *Armed:* No. *Position:* 18 miles E of Start Point/S 80 deg E 20 miles from Berry Head (50 20 00N; 02 58 00W). *Master's name:* Ole Bertimus Olsen. *Crew:* 12. *Crew nationality:* 8 Norwegians, 2 Danes, 1 Swede, 1 American.

THE naval authorities were most displeased with the conduct of the master of *Nyasaland*. He picked up his route instructions from Falmouth but then chose to ignore the directions he was supposed to have taken for Le Havre.

The *Nyasaland* was undoubtedly too far out from the land. There was no wind, the sea was calm but the visibility was low, because of a haze. A small German submarine surfaced alongside the steamer and started to shell her. The master ordered the crew into the boat but he and the first mate remained on board. The shelling continued and eventually the master shouted for the boat to return to the steamer and the two men climbed in.

After questioning the crew, the German commander put his boat alongside the steamer and four sailors boarded her. They planted bombs in several places. They exploded about ten minutes later and sent her to the bottom.

The Admiralty later wrote a letter to the Norwegian authorities saying that they could offer no facilities to any vessel commanded by Ole Olsen because of his failure to comply with route instructions. War insurance would be refused to vessels commanded by him. A severe penalty and one which must have finished Olsen as a master for the rest of the war.

8/8: CHATEAU YQUEM. *Country:* French. *Date sunk:* 30/6/17. *Tons nett:* 824. *Tons gross:* 1913. *Built:* Nantes in 1914. *Type:* SS. *Rig:* schooner. *Owners:* Worms Co, Le Havre, France. *Cargo:* In ballast, Dunkirk for Barry. *Armed:* Yes. *Position:* 20 miles N 78 Deg W of Portland Bill (50 34 00N; 02 58 00W). *Master's name:* R. Cruchet. *Crew:* 28.

THE wind was strong and the sea was rough on June 30, 1917, as *Chateau Yquem* made her way to Barry Roads for orders. The master had snatched ten minutes to have dinner but his meal was soon interrupted when an explosion shook the after part of the ship. He had hardly left his seat when he realised that his ship was settling rapidly and ordered the boats to be lowered even as he raced towards the open deck. Five of his crew were wounded, four slightly and one seriously. One man, a gunner, was missing, believed killed as the main force of the explosion had been at the stern where the gun was mounted.

The ship sank in ten minutes but it was enough time for the crew to get clear. Soon afterwards they were picked up by a torpedo boat and taken into Portsmouth.

In the reports of this sinking there is a note that torpedo boat *No 81* swept the area whilst looking for the submarine. However, she was hindered by a wreck that kept snagging her cables. The wreck was noted as a Norwegian steamer sunk earlier. The only vessel that would fit in with that description would be *SS Borgund I*, (No 8/12) sunk on the same day. The position of *Borgund I*, taken by the master just before she was torpedoed, was only approximate, so it is possible that these two vessels are quite close to each other.

UB-40 was the submarine involved.

8/9: BORGA. *Country:* British.
Date sunk: 1/3/18. *Tons nett:* 638. *Tons gross:* 1046. *Built:* 1907. *Type:* SS. *Rig:* schooner. *Owners:* Managers; Mann, Macneal & Steeves, Liverpool. *Cargo:* 1350 tons coal. *Armed:* Yes. *Position:* 5-6 miles S of Lyme Regis (50 32 03N; 02 56 33W). *Master's name:* Ed T. Foley. *Crew:* 21.

BORGA sailed from Swansea on February 27, 1918, bound for Dieppe. Whilst heading up the Channel she was struck by a torpedo on the starboard side between the fore end of number two hatch and the bridge. The damage was severe and she sank within two minutes.

Five of the crew were killed but the rest managed to climb aboard the ship's raft and were eventually picked up by a patrol vessel.

U-55 was the boat involved.

8/10: BAYGITANO. *Country:* British.
Date sunk: 18/3/18. *Tons nett:* 1983. *Tons gross:* 3073. *Built:* Newcastle in 1905. *Type:* SS. *Rig:* schooner. *Owners:* The Bay SS Co, 21, Old Broad St, London. *Cargo:* In ballast, Havre to Cardiff. *Armed:* 1 x 14pdr gun. *Position:* Lyme Regis bore NE 1½ miles (50 41 45N; 02 56 00W). *Master's name:* Arthur Murrison. *Crew:* 37. *Crew nationality:* 17 British, 10 British Colonials, 10 others. *Gunners.* G. Glew, LS RNR, No 4138B Devonport; G. Duncan, AB RNR, No 9056A Portsmouth.

THE master's orders were to proceed with the convoy to Portland and then follow the coastal traffic route to Cardiff. When he got to Lyme Bay he took the ship in close to the shore as instructed, but stopped zig-zagging on account of the very hazy weather. Going close in to shore was supposed to carry some measure of safety in the belief that enemy submarines wouldn't venture into shallow water.

Lurking in Lyme Bay was the German submarine *UC-77* commanded by Oberleutnant Johannes Ries At 11.45am a torpedo smashed into the port side of the steamer and knocked out a huge hole in number four hold. Within a few minutes it was obvious to the master that his ship was going down and he gave the order for the ship to be abandoned. All but two men got clear in two lifeboats and pulled away from their ship. By this time the *Baygitano's* stern was under water but the bows were still visible. The crew in one of the boats suddenly found themselves alongside a submarine which had appeared as if from nowhere. They were questioned about the details of their ship and the U-boat then headed off to the east. It was pure luck that Oberleutnant Ries had not chosen the master's boat as he had all his confidential documents with him in an unweighted bag.

Shortly afterwards, a boat arrived from the shore. The master transferred all of the people in his boat to the shore vessel and headed back to the wreck of his ship to try and find the two missing men. The fourth engineer was in the engine room at the time and was almost certainly killed by the explosion. The first mate was seen to go back to his cabin for a pair of boots.

At the interview with the naval authorities the master was severely reprimanded for not weighting his confidential papers' bag. The report stated that Captain Murrison thought it would sink as it was.

8/11: RADAAS. *Country:* Danish.
Date sunk: 21/9/17. *Tons nett:* 1486. *Tons gross:* 2348. *Built:* 1890. *Type:* SS. *Rig:* schooner. *Owners:* Schach Steenberg Co, Copenhagen. *Cargo:* 3350 tons coal from Tyne to Bordeaux via Penzance. *Armed:* No. *Position:* Portland Bill bore SE 21 miles (50 40 00N; 02 55 00W). *Master's name:* Jorgen Wm Joogensen. *Crew:* 22. *Crew nationality:* 7 Danes, 5 Norwegians, 3 Greeks, 1 Spaniard, 1 Swede, 5 Russians.

RADAAS was making her way down Channel at eight knots and flying the Danish flag. Someone spotted the track of a torpedo on the port quarter about 100yds off and it slammed into the port side between number one hold and the forecastle, about six feet below the waterline. One man was killed. The ship started to sink rapidly and the crew just had enough time to get clear in the boats before she sank.

They were picked up by the naval vessel *Wyndham* at 7.30am and landed at Weymouth around noon the same day.

UB-40 torpedoed her.

8/12: BORGUND I. *Country:* Norwegian.
Date sunk: 30/6/17. *Tons nett:* 456. *Tons gross:* 763. *Built:* Blyth in 1883. *Type:* SS. *Rig:* schooner. *Owners:* Horgen & Telefsen, Christiania, Norway.

Cargo: 1000 tons coal from Bellamy, Cardiff to Importation Transports of Rouen. *Armed:* No. *Position:* 18 miles WNW of Portland Bill (50 38 30N; 02 53 00W). *Master's name:* A. Zachariassen. *Crew:* 15. *Crew nationality:* 12 Norwegians, 3 Swedes.

THE *Borgund I* left Port Talbot on June 28, 1917.

On the morning of the 30th the first mate was in charge of the watch on the bridge whilst the master was having breakfast. He had just taken a fix on Portland Bill which he judged to be about 18 miles distant. Suddenly, one of the crew on deck gave a shout and pointed to something. It took him a split second to see what it was, a white streak in the sea heading directly for the ship, a torpedo. He shouted to the helmsman but it was too late as it slammed into the port side. Such was the force of the explosion that it blew number one hatch cover clean off and left a gaping hole in the side of the ship.

Within seconds the master appeared on deck and ordered the boats to be lowered. Two men panicked and jumped over board and were lucky to be picked up by the first boat. However, there was no time to launch the second as the ship started to settle rapidly, forcing the master and the mate to leap clear. They were quickly picked up by the boat just minutes after *Borgund I* sank in 20 fathoms of water.

It all happened in just five minutes and as the crew stared at the debris where their ship had once been they saw that they were being watched by a periscope. Within half an hour of the periscope disappearing they were picked up by the passing steamer *Activ* and taken to Portland.

The position given for this wreck is the approximate one given by the master just prior to being torpedoed. A note in the records for the sinking of SS *Chateau Yquem*, (No 8/8) says that torpedo boat *No 81*, which was searching the area where she sank, kept snagging a Norwegian steamer sunk earlier. It is likely that this was *Borgund I* and her position given above may be inaccurate.

8/13: GUDRUN. *Country:* Norwegian. *Date sunk:* 24/5/17. *Tons nett:* 1345. *Tons gross:* 1472. *Built:* 1886. *Type:* SV. *Rig:* barque. *Owners:* W.F. Langfeldt, Christiansand, Norway. *Cargo:* 1702 tons of dyewood, Jamaica for Havre. *Armed:* No. *Position:* 30 miles SW of Portland (50 05 00N; 02 50 00W). *Master's name:* K. Skaar. *Crew:* 16. *Crew nationality:* 10 Norwegians, 4 Swedes, 2 Danes.

GUDRUN was making her way up Channel at full speed bound for Havre. The master was on deck when he saw a submarine just breaking the surface about two miles off. Within a few minutes the submarine began to fire shells at the *Gudrun*. Captain Skaar ordered the ship to be hove too and a boat to be launched. He and four men went over to the submarine

with the ship's papers and spoke with the German commander. The result was that a German officer rowed back to the *Gudrun* and ordered the remainder of the crew to take to the other boat. He then placed bombs at several places around the barque and several minutes later she blew up and sank.

The crew rowed for some time but were eventually picked up by the patrol boat *Expectation* which also had on board the crew of the recently sunk *Thyra*. All were landed at Poole.

8/14: BAMSE. *Country:* British. *Date sunk:* 17/4/18. *Tons nett:* –. *Tons gross:* 958. *Built:* Whitby in 1875. *Type:* SS. *Rig:* schooner. *Owners:* F. Le Boulanger, 7, Prospect Place, Swansea. *Cargo:* In Ballast, Rouen to Swansea. *Armed:* 1 x 18pdr gun. *Position:* 10 miles off land, 15 miles W by N from Portland Bill (50 33 00N; 02 50 00W). *Master's name:* James Anderson Wilson. *Crew:* 17. *Crew nationality:* 9 British, 3 British nationals, 3 Japanese, 2 Greeks. *Gunners:* Albert Elson, AB RN, NO CZ 5404; Wilfred Cooper, LS RN, No TZ 10086.

AS it was a dark night with continual drizzle and a strong wind, the master of the *Bamse* decided that he would stay further out to sea and would not zig-zag. This was in direct breach of his official route instructions and he paid dearly for it.

On the evening of April 17, 1918, *Bamse* left Weymouth and headed down the Channel towards her destination of Swansea. At 11.50pm a violent explosion occurred underneath the vessel. She began to settle immediately and the master realising that his ship was lost ordered the port lifeboat to be manned and cleared. As the lifeboat pulled away the master did a quick head count and realised that four men were missing. It was too late to search and as he looked back the *Bamse* disappeared below the waves.

A sea anchor was put out until daylight when a mast and sail were rigged and the lifeboat was steered towards the shore. They were eventually picked up by a patrol vessel and taken into Torquay.

When giving his account of the incident to the authorities, the master said that one of the engineers thought he heard a second explosion directly after the first. He suggested that his ship could have run into a minefield. The authorities didn't seem to agree and claimed that it was a torpedo. However, they also gave the master a severe reprimand for not following his route instructions and the Admiralty sent a letter to his company asking them to censure Captain Wilson for his disobedience.

UB-80 claimed to have torpedoed her.

8/15: L.H. CARL. *Country:* British. *Date sunk:* 20/7/17. *Tons nett:* 1198. *Tons gross:* 1900. *Built:* West Hartlepool in 1898. *Type:* SS. *Rig:* schooner. *Owners:* Lambert Bros Ltd,

85, Gracechurch St, London. *Cargo:* 2900 tons coal from L. Guerit Ltd, Cardiff to Rouen. *Armed:* 1 x 15pdr gun. *Position:* 15 miles WSW of Portland Bill. (50 23 57N; 02 46 22W) *Master's name:* Thomas Davis. *Crew:* 25. *Crew nationality:* 9 British, 16 others. *Gunners:* David Bell, Act LS RNR, No 4325B; William Hince, AB RNVR, No TZ6405.

THE loss of this vessel caused quite a lot of trouble between the master and the naval authorities. She was sailing up the Channel and passed very close to Berry Head, so close that the second mate noticed some signal flags flying at the naval lookout post ashore. He pointed them out to the master who looked through his telescope but he couldn't read them. The second mate tried and was just able to make them out and looked them up in his book to read, "Keep off the shore."

On the strength of that the master set a new course which took him away from the land by some 14 miles. *L.H. Carl* was making seven knots and following the usual zig-zag pattern so as to make life difficult for any marauding submarine. But it wasn't difficult enough for the experienced commander Oberleutnant Howaldt in *UB-40*.

Earlier the same day Howaldt had sunk the P&O steamer *Salsette* and had only just got away from the depth charges that were cast down on him by the British patrol vessels. To him, the *L.H. Carl* was an easy target. At 9.30pm a torpedo went streaking from *UB-40's* bow tube and struck the steamer square on the starboard side. The stokehold and engine room were completely wrecked along with the bridge and chart room. The force of the explosion not only tore a hole in the starboard side but also went right through the port side virtually breaking her in two. A donkeyman and a stoker who were in the engine room were both killed. The engines ground to a halt and the ship started to sink rapidly.

The boats were lowered immediately and the crew quickly pulled clear as the decks by this time were awash. The patrol vessel *Recono* appeared shortly after and picked up the crew and headed back towards the steamer to see if she could be saved. However, as they approached she broke in two and sank.

The authorities were not happy with the report of the signals. They judged that the *L.H. Carl* was too far off the land and pressed the master and officers about the signal flags they had seen. They then contacted Berry Head Station and were told that no such signal was ever given. A lot of paperwork and shaking of heads took place but there is no record of the master being cautioned or black listed.

Another report gives a slightly different position from the one given above as 50 24 30N; 2 52 30W.

8/16: HMS WELLHOLME. *Country:* British.
Date sunk: 30/1/18. *Tons nett:* –. *Tons gross:* 113. *Built:* –. *Type:* Special service. *Rig:* disguised as merchant ship. *Owners:* Admiralty. *Cargo:* –.

Armed: Yes. *Position:* 20 miles S by W of Portland Bill (50 17 00N; 02 49 00W). *Master's name:* Captain Stephen. *Crew:* –. *Crew nationality:* British.

A BRIEF report of the sinking of this special service ship, or Q-ship, was included in the general files of the period and it may be as well to include it here. The information comes from a letter written by Lieutenant Sellers to the Admiralty.

He said that at the time of the incident he was standing forward by the galley when Mr Stephen, the Captain, came to him and pointed out an object about 400yds off in the light of the sunset. He recognised it instantly as a submarine's conning tower and immediately gave the order to action stations.

The submarine moved off to their port quarter and was lost to view on the dark side of the horizon. About four minutes later a shot rang out and a shell dropped close by the ship. This was followed by a second shell which fell even closer. The third shot was a direct hit amidships right on the water line which opened up such a large hole that the ship began to settle rapidly.

They desperately tried to pin the submarine down in order to return the fire but it was firing on the move and every shot came from a different direction. Soon there was nothing more to be done as the ship was close to sinking. A lifeboat was made ready and lowered but was suddenly smashed by the main boom as the ship rolled over and sank. Fortunately, another boat stood on chocks and floated free and the crew were able to swim to it. However, in the turmoil three men were killed.

The Admiralty decided that there would be no enquiry as the loss was beyond doubt an act of war and that the captain did everything possible to save his ship.

8/17: MINERVA. *Country:* Norwegian.
Date sunk: 10/5/17. *Tons nett:* 286. *Tons gross:* 518. *Built:* Stellin in 1864. *Type:* SS. *Rig:* schooner. *Owners:* H.M. Wrangell, Haugesund, Norway. *Cargo:* In ballast, Caen for Swansea. *Armed:* No. *Position:* 15 miles W of Portland Bill/8-10 miles from the land (50 33 00N; 02 48 00W). *Master's name:* Thormod Forland. *Crew:* 12. *Crew nationality:* 5 Norwegians, 1 Swede, 1 Dane, 5 Spaniards.

THE *Minerva* left Caen on May 9, 1917. The weather was fine and she made her way round to Havre Roads for her instructions to cross the Channel to Swansea. Leaving Havre at 6.30pm she headed off across the Channel and all went well.

At 9.45 the next morning, all was not well when a German submarine appeared behind them about 1½ miles off and began to lob shells at them. The master looked ahead and could see two steamers coming straight for him and he headed towards them for safety in numbers. Steaming flat out the master was dismayed to see that he was not widening the gap between his ship and the submarine at all. If anything the U-boat was gaining on him. The *Minerva* had received several hits but then one penetrated the boiler room and the shrapnel hit a boiler bringing her to a hissing halt.

The master ordered the crew to abandon ship and get clear. As they did so the submarine went alongside *Minerva* and two Germans climbed aboard her. They placed 3 bombs along her starboard side, suspended from the deck almost to the waters edge. About 5 minutes later the bombs exploded and the *Minerva* stood up at the bows, gave a final lurch and went down by the stern.

The crew were all unhurt except for the master who had an eye injury from flying debris during the shelling. They rowed towards the shore and eventually arrived at Burton Bradstock at 3pm that day.

8/18: MEMNON. *Country:* British.

Date sunk: 12/3/17. *Tons nett:* 2042. *Tons gross:* 3203. *Built:* Belfast in 1890. *Type:* SS. *Rig:* schooner. *Owners:* Elder Dempster & Co Ltd, Liverpool. *Cargo:* 3300 tons general African produce, palm oil, ground nuts, peanuts, for Hull. *Armed:* Yes. *Position:* 20-22 miles SW of Portland Bill (50 15 00N; 02 48 00W). *Master's name:* Robert William Brisco. *Crew:* 36. *Crew nationality:* 1 Swede, 1 Norwegian, 3 Dutch, 3 American, 1 Greek, 1 Russian, 26 British. *Casualties:* A.W. Thomas, second engineer; John Irvin, third engineer; George Washington, I. Williams, Tom Peter, firemen; W. Hughes, donkeyman. All killed

THE *Memnon* had been on quite a journey as can be seen from the full description of her cargo: "130 puncheons of palm oil standing on deck on end, lashed with wires. 300 bags of ground nuts, lashed to the hatches with tarpaulins to a height of about six feet. A quantity of peanuts stowed in the hatches, shipped by various people of Lagos, Calibar, Sierra Leone, Conakray and Dacca"

She left her final port of call, Dacca, on February 22, 1917, and the Lizard was sighted at 4.40am on March 12. She turned her bow to go up Channel, the weather foggy and grey. The master was on deck having a look around to reassure himself that all was well. The First Officer, Septimus Barlow, was in charge of the watch on the bridge and had a lookout posted up in the crow's nest. The ship was pushing along nicely at eight knots.

UC66 fired a torpedo at the *Memnon*. It slammed into the starboard side of the steamer creating an enormous explosion. It struck the ship between the engine room and boilers, instantly killing six men who were in the vicinity. The master gave the order for the boats to be lowered and all hands to make for their designated boat. The master had charge of number one boat on the starboard side and the mate the port boat. Thirteen men made it into the master's

boat and seventeen into that of the mate. They pulled clear of their ship and at the same time the submarine responsible appeared and headed towards the mate's boat. When close enough a voice demanded to speak to the captain. The mate directed him to the other boat, but the German was content to talk to him and asked for the particulars of the ship.

The *Memnon* sank at 4.25pm, going down stern first. Her crew were picked up at 12.30am the next day near the Shambles by Torpedo Boat 86 and taken to Weymouth.

8/19: ST DUNSTAN. *Country:* British.

Date sunk: 23/9/17. *Tons nett:* –. *Tons gross:* –. *Built:* 1894. *Type:* SS. *Rig:* dredger. *Owners:* Admiralty. *Cargo:* none. *Armed:* No. *Position:* 1¹/₂ miles SW of Abbotsbury (50 41 00N; 02 48 00W). *Master's name:* Thomas Morgan/Sub Lieut C. Gray RNR . *Crew:* 21. *Crew nationality:* All British. *Casualties:* John Obery, first mate, drowned; E. Warren, deck hand, drowned.

THE information on this loss has been taken from a report submitted by the naval officer in command of the vessel Sub Lieutenant C. Gray.

His orders were to proceed from Portsmouth to Pembroke, Wales and from there to Haulbowline. En route he was forced to anchor in Weymouth Bay to repair a fault with the steering gear. Having sorted that problem out he continued in company with escort trawlers 273 *Fort Albert* and 615 *Horatio*.

He passed Portland Bill at a distance of half a mile and then set a course north 32 degrees west magnetic intending to follow round the coast in Lyme Bay. But when one and a half miles south by west of the Pollock Rock the ship was struck by a torpedo or mine on the port quarter.

She immediately took on a list to port and the order was given to take to the starboard lifeboat which had previously been provisioned and swung out. However, the force of the explosion had jammed the boat in the davits and by the time it was cleared it couldn't be lowered due to the rapidly increasing list of the ship. Fearing she was about to turn turtle the lieutenant ordered his men to jump and threw lifebuoys after them before following himself. A few seconds later *St Dunstan* turned over and her boilers exploded as she sank.

Having been picked up by the *Fort Albert* a muster was made of the men and it was discovered that two men were missing.

In his report Lieutenant Gray also added: "'I have the honour to recommend F. Prater, Engineer, for bravery on this occasion. On being struck, the port engine was entirely incapacitated. The telegraph connections from the bridge to engine room being so damaged that the signal to stop was not understood. Although the ship at the time had a large list to port and was in danger of capsizing, the engine room being partly full of water, this engineer went below and shut off the steam and the main valve from the starboard engine, thus saving an immediate explosion internally and adding a valuable minute to the time in which the ship floated."

Another report stated that no submarine or torpedo was seen and so the area was later swept for mines. Five were discovered and destroyed. The ship is listed by Lloyd's as mined.

8/20: AILSA CRAIG. *Country:* British. *Date sunk:* 14/4/18. *Tons nett:* 246. *Tons gross:* 601. *Built:* Troon in 1906. *Type:* SS. *Rig:* schooner. *Owners:* J. Craig & Co, 6, Royal Ave, Belfast. *Cargo:* 705 tons coal consigned to the French State Railway at Granville. *Armed:* 1 x 13pdr gun. *Position:* 12 miles NW of Portland Bill (50 33 38N; 02 47 30W). *Master's name:* Robert Millikew, 57, Wauvegaw St, Belfast. *Crew:* 15. *Crew nationality:* All British. *Gunners:* Thomas McCune, LS RNR, No D1721 Portsmouth; J. Sullivan, AB RNVR, No MZ 1784 Portsmouth; Jas Sharp, AB RNVR, No CZ 8071 Portsmouth.

THE master of the *Ailsa Craig* was on the bridge. He checked the ship's course and found it was correct at north-east by north. They were making a steady 10 knots. It was approaching the time to turn to maintain the zig-zag course which was required by the authorities. The weather wasn't particularly good and the master told the lookouts to keep a close eye on three other merchant ships which were close by.

At 7.10am Captain Millikew said he heard a distinct tap on the starboard side of the ship and this was followed by an enormous explosion. So violent was it that the decks erupted upwards and the hatch covers were blown clear into the air. The torpedo had taken the whole midship section of the ship's keel out and she was sinking very rapidly.

The crew were immediately summoned to their boat stations and within two minutes they were clear of the steamer. Three minutes later *Ailsa Craig* sank.

UB-80 claimed this sinking.

8/21: MOIDART. *Country:* British. *Date sunk:* 9/6/18. *Tons nett:* 801. *Tons gross:* 1303. *Built:* 1878. *Type:* SS. *Rig:* schooner. *Owners:* James Cormack & Co, 7, Johns Place, Leith. *Cargo:* 1550 tons coal, 80 tons steel plates, from William Mathison, Cardiff to Havre. *Armed:* Yes. *Position:* 14 miles NW of Portland Bill (50 34 00N; 02 47 18W). *Master's name:* George Skea. *Crew:* 21. *Crew nationality:* 13 British, 4 Swedes, 2 French, 1 Roumanian, 1 American. *Gunners:* W.J. Coles, AB RNR, No 51491; John Johns, LS RNVR.

AT 2am on June 9, 1918, William Drever, the first mate of *Moidart* had the watch and was on the bridge. The ship was steaming up the Channel following the coastal route and would then turn to cross to Havre. The weather was calm, a smooth sea and the visibility good even though it was dark. Looking around, the mate was very alarmed when he suddenly saw a large submarine had appeared on his starboard quarter about 400yds off. He immediately ordered the helm to put hard over to try and bring the submarine directly astern and rushed to the chartroom to rouse the master.

In less than a minute the ship was struck by a torpedo on the starboard side aft and began to settle rapidly. One minute later the steamer sank by the stern. It happened so quickly that no boats could be got away and the crew found themselves floundering in the water desperately looking for something to cling to. The German submarine glided into the middle of the floating men and, ignoring their cries for help, a voice demanded to know the ship's name.

The crew eventually found one of the boats floating but upturned and several clung to it for six hours, during which time some of them dropped off through exposure. Only six men survived the sinking and were picked up by the passing steamer *Clifton Grove* of Glasgow.

The master protested to the naval authorities about the length of time they were in the water with no assistance. The Admiralty replied that the *Moidart* had no wireless and had not let off flares so they had no way of knowing of their plight.

The submarine responsible for sinking the *Moidart* was *UC-77* commanded by Oberleutnant Johannes Ries.

The *Moidart's* gun has been raised by amateur divers for the National Maritime Museum.

8/22: VENI. *Country:* Norwegian. *Date sunk:* 10/5/17. *Tons nett:* 364. *Tons gross:* 654. *Built:* Oslo in 1901. *Type:* SS. *Rig:* schooner. *Owners:* C.H. Englhart, Oslo. *Cargo:* 777 tons coal from Newport to St Malo. *Armed:* No. *Position:* 15 miles W of Portland Bill/4-5 miles from the shore (50 32 00N; 02 47 00W). *Master's name:* Abraham Fjogctad. *Crew:* 14. *Crew nationality:* 9 Norwegians, 2 Swedes, 2 Danes, 1 Spaniard.

HAVING loaded the coal at Newport, *Veni* headed around the coast and into Falmouth for orders. She left Falmouth on May 9, 1917, at 10.30pm, with the weather moderate and sea conditions good.

The following day she was close to Portland and the master was preparing to cross the Channel. His change of course was forgotten when a U-boat appeared on the starboard side and opened fire. At that distance the *Veni* stood no chance and the master ordered the ship to be stopped and the boats lowered. On seeing this the submarine ceased firing to let the men get clear. As they did so the German commander hailed them to come towards him and ordered them on to the submarine. Using one of *Veni's* boats, several German sailors then boarded the steamer and after helping themselves to various items, planted the bombs that would send her to the bottom.

On their return the Germans pushed the master and his crew back into the boat. The master immediately rowed to the aid of his other boat which he had seen capsize and the men in her were clinging to the sides. As he made his way towards them the *Veni* exploded, heeled to port and sank.

All the crew were later picked up by a torpedo boat and landed at Weymouth.

8/23: GORIZIA. *Country:* Uruguayan. *Date sunk:* 30/4/17. *Tons nett:* 1246. *Tons gross:* 1957. *Built:* Dumbarton in 1907. *Type:* SS. *Rig:* schooner. *Owners:* Oriental Navigation Co, New York and A. Dodero, Paris. *Cargo:* 2200 tons general from New York for Le Havre, plus 102 bales of wet cotton stowed on number one hatch. *Armed:* –. *Position:* 12 miles SW by W of Portland Bill (50 26 00N; 02 45 00W). *Master's name:* George Dalmadge Rex. *Crew:* 22. *Crew nationality:* 7 Americans, 5 British, 1 Italian, 5 Chileans, 2 Spaniards, 1 Norwegian, 1 Dutch.

AFTER her Atlantic crossing *Gorizia* arrived in Falmouth on the afternoon of April 29, 1917, to check if there were any further instructions. On the same day she headed further up Channel for Portland. It was to be her last call before heading across the Channel to Havre.

At 3.45pm she was making steady progress at five knots when one of the crew noticed a thin object on the port bow at about 500yds distant. The master was alerted and he hurried on deck to confirm his worst fears that the object was the periscope of a submarine. He watched it carefully through his binoculars as it circled his ship and then slowed down and the submarine surfaced. No sooner had she surfaced than men came out on deck and within moments had the deck gun loaded. They then began to fire at the *Gorizia* and after about 12 shots the master decided he had had enough and ordered the ship to be stopped and the boats lowered.

The German gunners were finding their range and one shell penetrated the boiler room sending up clouds of steam. By then the crew had got clear of the ship and the submarine drew closer. As it approached, the German commander ordered the master to come aboard his submarine where he was asked the usual questions. When asked about his nationality the master informed him he was American to which the German replied, "I am sorry but I must sink your vessel. War is war."

The German's attention was then diverted by a cry from one of his crew. Another vessel was coming which didn't look at all friendly. It was in fact the British patrol boat *Lorna* who had heard the gunfire and was determined to give the German a taste of his own. Captain Rex was immediately ordered off by the German commander and the submarine was

quickly manoeuvered alongside the *Gorizia*. At speed the Germans placed several bombs on board her and fled. Meanwhile, 4000yds away, the commander of *Lorna* could see what was going on but powerless to do anything. In his frustration he opened fire on the submarine but was just out of range. The submarine then dived and shortly afterwards, the bombs exploded causing *Gorizia* to settle rapidly by the stern. At 6pm she sank leaving the crew to wait for *Lorna*. *Lorna* put the crew safely ashore at Weymouth.

There was some confusion afterwards as to the position of the *Gorizia*. The master's position was 50 36 00N; 02 57 00W, but the commander of *Lorna* disagreed with that and the Admiralty decided that *Lorna's* postion (given above), was correct.

8/24: FINN. *Country:* Norwegian. *Date sunk:* 19/11/16. *Tons nett:* 2473. *Tons gross:* 3806. *Built:* Sunderland in 1906. *Type:* SS. *Rig:* schooner. *Owners:* Ivar Christenson, Oslo. *Cargo:* 1000 tons coal and 3000 tons coke from Dunstan on Tyne to Genoa. *Armed:* No. *Position:* 30 miles SW by S of Portland Bill (50 06 00N; 02 45 00W). *Master's name:* Alf Foyn. *Crew:* 31. *Crew nationality:* 16 Norwegians, 2 Finns, 4 Greeks, 4 Danes, 1 Italian, 1 Swede, 1 Spanish, 2 Americans.

AT anchor in The Downs, the master of the *Finn* decided that he would wait a little longer, after being warned by the authorities that there was a lot of enemy submarine activity in the Channel. He eventually sailed later the same day and the ship made good progress down the Channel. At 2.30pm the next day the mate, Hjalmar Berg, watched in horror as a submarine headed directly towards him.

The master came on to the bridge and was greeted by the sound of a shell zipping overhead. He looked at the submarine and read the signal flags, "Bring papers to me immediately." He rang the telegraph to stop and blew the ship's whistle to inform the German commander that he understood the message.

Having rowed across to the submarine the master returned a little later accompanied by German officers. A gloomy Captain Foyn approached his mate and told him that their ship was to be sunk and that he should divide the crew into two groups, one group to take to a boat under his charge and he would take command of the other.

The boats remained alongside the steamer as the Germans planted bombs and looted the ship of navigational instruments. Then the Germans were rowed back to the submarine and both boats were tied astern. After watching the steamer sink the submarine headed off with both boats being tossed about like corks in her wake. Eventually the painter on the mate's boat broke and they were left to drift. However, it wasn't for long, as the passing steamer *Paul* of Brugge picked them up and later landed them at Portsmouth.

The master's boat was soon set adrift by the

Germans and the crew were spotted by the Swedish steamer *Corfitz Beck Friir*, picked up and landed at Weymouth.

8/25: GIBEL HAMAM. *Country:* British. *Date sunk:* 14/9/18. *Tons nett:* –. *Tons gross:* 647. *Built:* 1895. *Type:* SS. *Rig:* –. *Owners:* Watts & Watts. *Cargo:* Coal, Swansea to France. *Armed:* 1 gun aft. *Position:* Off Abbotsbury, Dorset (50 38 00N; 02 45 00W). *Master's name:* –. *Crew:* 22.

THERE is not much information in the records concerning the loss of this vessel mainly due to the fact that her sinking was so rapid that only one man survived.

A seaman, a Greek called Amanuel Markaras, was at the wheel of the *Gibel Hamam* at the time she was sunk. He said that the ship had left Swansea on September 12, 1918, bound for France. They had kept to the coastal route and the master intended to anchor for a while but was ordered by the patrol vessel *Maritana* to proceed to Portland. The master complied and sailed on. When going across Lyme Bay at 9.30pm on August 14, there was an enormous explosion and the seaman found himself floating in the water among a huge pile of wreckage. He believed the ship had struck a mine although he couldn't be sure.

At 7.30am the next morning a civilian coast walker, William Thoren, spotted the seaman drifting ashore on a piece of wreckage. This was about four miles west of Abbotsbury.

The naval authorities contacted the commander of the patrol vessel *Maritana* to ask what he had said to the master of the *Gibel Hamam*. Apparently he had found the steamer anchored in a position that was far too exposed and advised him to make for Torbay. Nothing was mentioned about Portland.

The position given is only a rough estimation. *UB-103* claimed the sinking

8/26: POLKERRIS. *Country:* French. *Date sunk:* 4/3/18. *Tons nett:* 564. *Tons gross:* 943. *Built:* 1890. *Type:* SS. *Rig:* schooner. *Owners:* Cavroy, 92, Boulevard Haussman, Paris. *Cargo:* 1140 tons coal Penarth for Rouen. *Armed:* 1 x 90mm quick fire gun. *Position:* 12 miles SW of Portland Bill (50 30 00N; 02 43 30W). *Master's name:* Theophile le Prevot. *Crew:* 22.

THERE is a certain amount of doubt as to what went on when this vessel was struck by a torpedo at 1.20am on March 4, 1918. One witness said it was hit on the starboard side and another on the port side.

Whatever the truth, *Polkerris* was hit by a torpedo as she made her way up the Channel from Falmouth. She was making around seven knots and had lookouts posted in the usual positions. She did have lights on but

they were completely masked off. Five minutes after the torpedo struck, the master observing that his ship was sinking rapidly, ordered the crew to the boats.

It was reported that the starboard lifeboat fall was damaged and the crew took to the port lifeboat and quarter boat. It's likely therefore that the torpedo did strike the starboard side. The port lifeboat with 17 men was lowered to the waterline but it capsized as the steamer started to sink. Several men were drowned but there appears to be no accurate record of the casualties. The master and four men in the quarter boat were picked up by the patrol vessel *Salvina* and taken to Weymouth. How the other survivors fared is not recorded.

8/27: SALSETTE. *Country:* British. *Date sunk:* 20/7/17. *Tons nett:* 2388. *Tons gross:* 5842. *Built:* Greenock in 1908. *Type:* SS. *Rig:* schooner. *Owners:* P & O Steamship Co, Leadenhall St, London. *Cargo:* General, London for Bombay. *Armed:* 1 x 4.7in quick fire gun. *Position:* 10 miles N 79 deg W from Portland Bill (50 29 36N; 02 43 10W). *Master's name:* Albert Borlase Armitage, Commander RNR (Retired). *Crew:* 258. *Crew nationality:* 55 Europeans, 203 others. *Gunners:* H. Bullen, OS RNR, Chatham; G. Nicolson, OS RNR, Chatham. Also carried 31 passengers including two naval officers, four naval ratings and two army officers.

THERE appears to be some confusion about the cargo *Salsette* was carrying. Some documentation has it as 20 tons of general, shipped from London and consigned to various people in Bombay and Marseilles. She also carried 23 bags of confidential mail matter for the senior naval officer of Gibraltar, the military authorities in Egypt and the Viceroy in Bombay. It was also noted that the mail was in the personal charge of the master. Other documents describe the general cargo as being much bigger, about 700 tons.

Whatever the truth, this large, elegant vessel sailed from London on July 19, 1917. As she zig-zagged her way down the Channel she passed the Shambles and was spoken to on semaphore by Torpedo Boat 85 who instructed her to pass at least four miles south of Portland Bill to keep her clear of minesweeping operations. She complied and gave the Bill a wide berth. She then set a course to steer north 47 degrees west and brought her speed up to 16.4 knots. Both the master and the first mate were on the bridge along with many lookouts and a gunner stood by the gun.

Unknown to all of them, danger was lurking very close by indeed in the form of the German submarine *UB-40*, commanded by Oberleutnant Howaldt. Howaldt had spotted the *Salsette* several miles off and positioned himself so that the big steamer would pass close by. His plan worked perfectly and Howaldt gave the order to release one of his torpedoes.

On *Salsette*, the Mate, Arthur Bertram Vaughn, went to the monkey bridge to satisfy himself that all was well when suddenly to his horror he spotted the white tell tale wake of the torpedo heading directly at the ship. He screamed to the bridge to bring the wheel hard to starboard but it was far too late. The torpedo smashed into the starboard side amidships in the stokehold and threw up an enormous column of water which destroyed everything in its path, including several lifeboats.

The master rang the engine room telegraph to stop engines. Whether it was answered is not certain as 14 men, firemen and coal trimmers, lay dead. The master quickly decided that his vessel was done for and gave the order to abandon ship. He threw his confidential papers in the weighted bag over the side and joined the rest of the survivors in the boats.

Torpedo boat *No 80* was in the area and her commander reported that he saw an explosion on a large steamer about four miles away. He signalled ML's 311 and 209 to join and close on the stricken ship. When he arrived he said he saw people in the boats leaving the ship which was sinking on an even keel but with a list to port. As *TB 80* approached the boats he suddenly caught site of broken water and a black object and at the same time the survivors in the boats were shouting, "Submarine"!. Lieutenant Clarke immediately headed directly for the submarine and quickly dropped a G-type depth charge. He was soon joined by *ML 213* who dropped another in the same spot and eventually blanketed the whole area with charges.

Meanwhile, *UB-40* sat on the bottom and waited it out. At one stage several of the depth charges came close and shook her. But Howaldt's luck held and he escaped to sink even more British shipping. On the same day he sank the steamer *L.H. Carl*.

Salsette went down some 15 minutes after being hit, and because she was so large a dan buoy was placed close to her to warn shipping. Some accurate positions were given for the Buoy at 50 29 30N; 2 45 45W, whilst transit fixes of the wreck were given as; highest part of Portland Bill N 87 degrees E, Halton Hall and Golden Cape N 5 Deg E, Portland Bill Light House S 80 deg E. All magnetic. However, the position given above is fairly accurate.

Only one of the 23 bags of confidential mail was saved, the rest went down with the ship and what they contained may never be known. However, amateur divers located the wreck around 1974 and reported that she was in very good condition lying on her port side. The depth to the bottom is 43 metres and 30 to her deck.

8/28: ROMSDALEN. *Country:* British. *Date sunk:* 17/2/17. *Tons nett:* 1632. *Tons gross:* 2746. *Built:* West Hartlepool in 1895. *Type:* SS. *Rig:* schooner. *Owners:* Harland & Co, West Hartlepool, Durham. *Cargo:* 3506 tons patent fuel and 8 railway wagons from Franklin Thomas & Co.

to Calais. *Armed:* Yes. *Position:* 35 miles E of Start Point/8-10 miles SW of Portland Bill (50 24 00N; 02 42 00W). *Master's name:* William Hopkins. *Crew:* 25.

THE *Romsdalen* was on charter to J.B. Allen & Co. of West Hartlepool and sailed from Swansea at 2pm on February 15, 1917. On February 17, at 9.40pm the ship was off Portland Bill and the Second Mate, John Rochester, was asleep in his bunk. He awoke with a start as the ship shuddered from an explosion and grabbing his clothes he made his way to the bridge. He met the gunner who told him that the ship was in a bad way and that the master wanted him to launch his lifeboat. He made for his boat on the port side and got it away successfully with ten hands. The master meanwhile, along with the first mate and twelve hands, got away in the starboard boat.

None of them were quite sure what had happened.The master didn't know if they had struck a mine or been hit with a torpedo but he pointed out that the damage occurred just below midships. The first mate said he thought they had been hit just abaft the foremast on the starboard side. Whatever the truth the *Romsdalen* sank within 20 minutes.

The survivors in the second mate's boat rowed towards Brixham but were picked up at 2.30am on the 18th by the *Levinet* of London and transferred to the patrol boat *Verbena II* at 8pm the same day. They were later landed at Brixham. The master's boat landed at 11.15am on the same day at Burton Bradstock. They were assisted ashore by a local boatman called Joseph Thorner, who used his small boat to ferry them to the beach.

U-84 claimed to have torpedoed her.

8/29: POMERANIAN. *Country:* British. *Date sunk:* 15/4/18. *Tons nett:* 2694. *Tons gross:* 4241. *Built:* 1882. *Type:* SS. *Rig:* schooner. *Owners:* Canadian Pacific Ocean Services Ltd, London. *Cargo:* 177 tons whiting, 129 tons fullers earth, 340 tons general. *Armed:* 1 x 13pdr gun. *Position:* 9 miles WNW of Portland Bill (50 33 30N; 02 41 23W). *Master's name:* Alexander Maxwell. *Crew:* 56. *Gunners:* Mr Gibbs, Mr Jeffs, Mr Goodwin.

OUT of a total complement of 56, only one man survived the sinking of the *Pomeranian*.

That survivor, William Bell, second engineer, reported to the interviewing officer that the ship's final destination was St Johns, New Brunswick. They were making their way down Channel to call in at Falmouth for orders. When off Portland Bill at 5.30am on April 15, 1918, the ship was struck by a torpedo causing a huge explosion. He was down in the engine room at the time standing by the ship's telegraph for orders when he suddenly felt the ship listing very heavily. He rushed on deck to find the ship sinking rapidly. He grabbed a lifebelt. No sooner had he put it

Only one out of the 56 crew survived the sinking of the *Pomeranian*.

on than the ship sank from beneath his feet. At that time he said the purser was with him but on looking around a few moments later he had disappeared.

He then saw a submarine just breaking the surface of the water. Unknown to Mr Bell then, it was *UC-77* commanded by Oberleutnant Johannes Ries. She glided past and then dived again. The second engineer was lucky and found a large plank floating close by and managed to hold on to it for support.

The *Pomeranian*, although sunk was resting on the bottom, with part of her fore rigging above water. William Bell managed to swim to it and climb up high enough to get himself clear. While in the rigging he said he spotted what looked like one of the ship's lifeboats but he couldn't be certain if there was anyone in it.

He was taken from the mast by the patrol ship, *Lorna* and landed at Weymouth.

The Admiralty attributed the high casualty rate to the very cold water and they criticised the master and the company for not having free floating rafts on board.

8/30: OLE LEA. *Country:* Norwegian.
Date sunk: 4/7/17. *Tons nett:* 313. *Tons gross:* 543.
Built: –. *Type:* SS. *Rig:* schooner. *Owners:* O. Kvilhang & Co, Haugesund, Norway. *Cargo:* 600 tons coal from Stevens & Co, and another of Glasgow to Electric Co, Nantes. *Armed:* No.
Position: 9 miles WNW of Portland Bill

(50 32 00N; 02 41 00W). *Master's name:* Ferdinand Henriksen. *Crew:* 15. *Crew nationality:*
8 Norwegian, 2 Spanish, 2 Portuguese, 1 Argentine, 1 Chilian, 1 Dane.

HAVING completed her lading, *Ole Lea* left Glasgow on June 30, 1917, made her way south and eventually up the English Channel. On the day of her loss the weather became hazy but she still made seven knots on an east-south-east course. She was stalked by a German submarine which suddenly surfaced on the starboard side and opened fire with her deck gun. The master ordered the engines to be stopped and after assessing the situation, ordered the crew to abandon ship.

As they pulled clear the submarine moved closer to the steamer and began pouring shells into her. It is stated in the records that she sank at 3.40am although the master said that he didn't actually see it sink himself.

The crew were picked up at 5am by a patrol boat which had heard the gunfire and came to investigate. They were later landed at Weymouth.

Ole Lea was changing her name to *Ull* at the time of her sinking.

8/31: ALGARVE. *Country:* British.
Date sunk: 20/10/17. *Tons nett:* –. *Tons gross:* 1274. *Built:* Renfrew, Glasgow, 1899. *Type:* SS. *Rig:* –. *Owners:* Letuchexau & David, Swansea.

Cargo: In ballast, Rouen for Swansea. *Armed:* Yes.
Position: 15 miles WSW from Portland Bill
(50 24 00N; 02 41 00W). *Master's name:* Mr Lewis.
Crew: 21.

THE loss of the *Algarve* resulted in the master and
17 officers and men losing their lives. Consequently it
was one of the three survivors, Boatswain Jorgos
Espinoza, who was interviewed about the loss.

He reported that the ship left Rouen on October
18, 1917, on the flood tide and was bound for
Swansea. The ship was at full speed and he was on
watch on deck when suddenly the ship was struck by
a torpedo on the port side in number three hold. She
started to settle very quickly and although the crew
managed to get into a lifeboat the ship heeled over
on top of them. Most of the men dived out of the boat
to get clear but three were not quick enough and taken
down with the ship as it sank.

The Boatswain said he was in the water for about
five minutes and then managed to find a piece of
hatchway. On looking around he saw that four sailors
were close by holding on to a gangway that had
floated free but of the rest of the crew, nothing was to
be seen.

When they were eventually found by the armed
yacht *Lorna* only three survivors remained, two
having dropped off at some time during the night.
The three were taken safely to Weymouth.

UB-38 was the submarine involved.

8/32: GERMAN SUBMARINE (possible).
Country: German. *Date sunk:* 28/11/16. *Tons
nett:* –. *Tons gross:* –. *Built:* –. *Type:* –. *Owners:* –.
Armed: Yes. *Position:* 14 miles SW by S from
Portland Bill (50 19 00N; 02 41 00W). *Master's
name:* –.

THE captain of the *Sarepta*, George Robert Wylie
RNR, reported that on the night of 27th November
27, 1916, his vessel was on patrol to the south-west of
the Shambles Light Vessel. He was in company with
Sailor King.

At about 6am the next day one of his lookouts
spotted a black object in the water and both patrol
ships altered course to investigate. The object seemed
to be very low in the water and at times it disappeared
from view. At one stage they lost it from sight only to
have it reappear astern of the *Sailor King*. Captain
Wylie by this time had identified it as an enemy
submarine and ordered his gun crew to stand by their
guns and await his order.

Both patrol vessels manoeuvred around to try and
get as close to the submarine as possible. It was barely
daylight and visibility was very poor. As the engines
slowed right down Captain Wylie heard a voice from
the submarine shout, "Ship Ahoy!" There was a pause
and the voice shouted the same again.

This time Captain Wylie replied, "Yes sir."
"Heave your ship to," came the reply.

Captain Wylie tried to get a better view but found it
difficult to see. He couldn't make out anyone on the
deck of the submarine so he decided to play along
and shouted, "All right sir," at the same time looking
to his gunners and adding, "Let fly lads."

The first shot smashed into the submarine just
below the conning tower and smoke rose up in huge
clouds. The second shot ripped into the hull close to
the water line just in front of the conning tower. Just
then four men appeared and ran to the deck gun to
return the fire. They managed to get a few off at the
Sarepta but they passed wide and high.

By this time *Sailor King* had got herself in a
position to open fire and she too joined the affray.
Captain Charles Keable RNR of the *Sailor King* stated
that he had to wait before he could fire for fear of
hitting *Sarepta* but as soon as he was clear his gunners
opened up hitting the submarine with several shells.

Both Captains reported that there was a loud
explosion followed by huge quantities of smoke and
the submarine disappeared. *Sailor King* steamed into
the smoke and found huge amounts of oil floating on
the water. The Captain and crew of both patrol vessels
were certain they had sunk the submarine.

The Admiralty wanted absolute proof that an
enemy submarine had been sunk before they would
award any prize money of up to £1000. In this case
they only awarded £200 to be divided among both
crews. German records show no submarine sunk at
this time.

8/33: GERMAN SUBMARINE UB-72.
Country: German. *Date sunk:* 12/5/18. *Tons
nett:* 520. *Tons gross:* 650. *Built:* Hamburg, 1917.
Type: UB-class, MkIII. *Owners:* German Navy.
Armed: 10 torpedoes, 10.5cm deck gun. *Position:*
25 miles SSW of Portland Bill (50 08 00N;
02 41 00W). *Master's name:* Oberleutnant Franz
Träger. *Crew:* 34. *Crew nationality:* German.

THIS successful sinking was carried out by another
submarine, the British *D-4*, commanded by Lieutenant
Claud Barrington Barry RN. He submitted his report
to his commanding officer and this information is
taken from that report.

He began his patrol on May 9, 1918. On the 16th he
noted in his log that at 5.30am an enemy submarine
was sighted about two and a half miles off. The sea
was calm and he was able to make a positive
identification that it was a UB type vessel. Five
minutes later the enemy turned and headed directly
towards the *D-4*. Not wanting to ruin his advantage
Lieutenant Barry ordered the periscope down and
moved off at a right angle. At 5.43am the periscope
was put up and the enemy was spotted again, a bit
closer making about six knots. Down went the scope
again and *D-4* was manoeuvred into a better position
for an attack.

At 5.50am the log recorded the enemy position at
about 1200 yards distant and notes, "fired upper fore

tube, allowing deflection of six knots for the enemy." Ten seconds later another Mk 8 torpedo streaked from the lower fore tube.

The gunners were ordered to stand by and make ready to man the gun instantly on surfacing, in case of a miss by the torpedoes. However, they didn't miss, or at least one didn't as a huge explosion boomed out in the distance. As *D-4* broke surface the gunners scrambled to the gun and the commander looked through his binoculars. There was a large oil patch ahead and more importantly, objects bobbing around inside it. It was soon apparent that the attack had been successful when three men were found swimming around in a dazed and exhausted state. They were picked up and taken aboard *D-4*.

After being kitted out with some dry clothes and a few tots of rum the three men were questioned by Lieutenant Barry. He noted that they were in an excited state and made a cautionary note in his report that their information should not be relied upon too heavily. They could speak no English and the questions were put to them using signs and charts. The three men were named as August Wiers, on lookout on the bridge at the time she was hit. Wilhelm Labbs, an electrician, on the switchboard at the time. And Gabriel Munyan, a stoker who was running a compressor.

The first thing they established was that their ship was *UB-72* and that their commander's name was Lieutenant Träger. He was at breakfast with the engineer officer at the time of the attack and was killed along with the other 31 men aboard her. The torpedo struck the *UB-72* clean in the engine room and she was immediately blown apart. The three survivors had no idea how they survived. They just found themselves floating on the water, sheer good luck on their part.

By using charts Lieutenant Barry was able to establish that *UB-72* had left Wilhelmshaven on March 27, 1918, and travelled to Heligoland, through the Fair Island Passage and the Shetland Isles and into the Irish sea. They made one attack on a steamer and fired two torpedoes but both of them missed. However, they soon ran into trouble themselves when a destroyer caught sight of them. The three men claimed that 72 depth charges were dropped in an attempt to kill *UB-72* but their commander blew out oil to try to deceive his attackers and dived to 92 metres. They survived to continue their patrol which took them to the Scillies then up to the Boulogne and Cherbourg areas.

It was also learned by Lieutenant Barry that *UB-72* could make 16 knots on the surface and 12 below. She carried 10 torpedoes which could be fired through four bow tubes and one at the stern. The deck gun fitted was a 105mm calibre.

UB-72 was due to return to her base between 12-16th June.

Lieutenant Barry was awarded the DSO and others of his crew were decorated.

8/34: FORGET ME NOT. *Country:* British. *Date sunk:* 12/3/17. *Tons nett:* 25. *Tons gross:* 40. *Built:* Galmpton in 1911. *Type:* FV. *Rig:* ketch. *Owners:* Mrs Ann Painter, 78, Howard St, Lowestoft. *Cargo:* None. *Armed:* No. *Position:* 12 miles SW by S from Portland Bill (50 21 00N; 02 39 00W). *Master's name:* George Pitman Burgoyne. *Crew:* 4.

THE crew of *Forget Me Not* had started to haul in fish and were having a generally good day before all the trouble started. The master and the third hand were busy icing the fish that they had already caught when a shell came whistling over the rigging. The master jumped up to see what was going on and was met with the sight of a submarine bearing down on him at an alarming rate. He immediately shouted to his men to get under way and try to make a run for it.

The submarine was fast catching them up from the south and more shells were throwing up spouts of water all around the little ship. Realising that he had no chance of escape the master and his crew jumped into their rowing boat and got clear.

The submarine manoeuvred alongside *Forget Me Not* and the master said he saw several German sailors climb aboard. By the time they left he was a long way off and couldn't see what they did to her but assumed they must have planted bombs.

The four men were soon picked up by the trawler *Day Spring* of Brixham but later transferred to the *May* of Ramsgate. She dropped them off at Brixham later on the same day.

8/35: JESSIE. *Country:* British. *Date sunk:* 27/4/17. *Tons nett:* 90. *Tons gross:* 108. *Built:* Kingston-on-Spey 1878. *Type:* SV. *Rig:* schooner. *Owners:* P. Donovan, Lamb House, Wexford, Ireland. *Cargo:* 174 tons coal from Cardiff to Carantin. *Armed:* No. *Position:* Portland Bill bore 7 miles E half N (50 28 30N; 02 38 00W). *Master's name:* William Dunne. *Crew:* 5.

THERE was nothing the master could do when the German submarine appeared from the south-west at 2pm on April 27, 1917. The *Jessie* was laid over on the port tack and making barely two knots whilst the enemy vessel was capable of 15. Three shots echoed across the water from the approaching submarine, two fell short and the third went whistling over the *Jessie's* rigging. It was enough for the master who decided that it was wise to stop.

Within a few minutes the German submarine lay alongside the *Jessie* and the commander demanded to speak to the master. He wanted to know all the details of the ship, where bound, where from, cargo and name. After noting down the details he told the crew to get into their boat and clear off. With several rifles pointed in their direction the crew had no choice whatsoever and did as they were told.

Once the vessel was abandoned the Germans put

a boarding party onto the *Jessie* and looted her of all they needed, which as far as the master could see from a distance was food and paraffin oil. They then planted two bombs, one amidships and the other forward. They exploded and sent the *Jessie* plunging down.

When asked about the submarine by the authorities the master said that she was about 100ft long and painted grey although she bore no marks to suggest what her number was. The master was censured for not destroying his confidential papers, having left them in his cabin. However, none of the crew were injured and they were eventually spotted by the patrol boat *Sarepta* and taken into Weymouth.

8/36: BROOMHILL. *Country:* British. *Date sunk:* 10/5/17. *Tons nett:* 843. *Tons gross:* 1392. *Built:* 1910. *Type:* SS. *Rig:* schooner. *Owners:* Brownhill Collieries Ltd, Newcastle. *Cargo:* 1700 tons coal from Penarth to Sheerness. *Armed:* No. *Position:* 9 miles WSW from Portland Bill (50 24 00N; 02 38 00W). *Master's name:* George Right. *Crew:* 18. *Casualties:* R. Jones, fireman; J. Jones, fireman, killed.

THERE is not a great deal of information on the circumstances of this loss. Apparently, she was proceeding on her way when a submarine appeared and started shelling her from a distance. About 12 shots were fired, six hitting her squarely killing two members of the crew and injuring another. The master attempted to outrun the submarine and headed directly for the shore but the *Broomhill's* speed was no match for the submarine which overtook her. The crew were ordered off the ship by the Germans and took to the boats. The German crew then placed bombs fore and aft on the battered vessel and she blew up at 5.45am sinking almost immediately.

The approach of a patrol boat caused the submarine to dive very quickly leaving the crew to be picked up and taken into Weymouth.

UC-61 was the submarine involved.

8/37: MARTHA. *Country:* Belgian. *Date sunk:* 7/3/18. *Tons nett:* –. *Tons gross:* 676. *Built:* –. *Type:* SS. *Rig:* –. *Owners:* Trading & Shipping Co, Belgium. *Cargo:* 800 tons coal for Calais. *Armed:* 1 x 75mm Portuguese gun. *Position:* 5 miles W by S of Portland Bill (50 30 00N; 02 36 00W). *Master's name:* Hector Blond. *Crew:* 15. *Crew nationality:* 14 Belgian, 1 British.

HAVING received her route instructions at Falmouth *Martha* proceeded up the Channel on her way to Calais. She was zig-zagging as ordered but not to any set pattern and was making a steady nine knots. A good lookout was being kept by three men on the bridge and one aft on the gun platform.

Suddenly she was stopped violently as a torpedo found its mark on the starboard side just before the

bridge and virtually destroyed the forward part of the ship. There was nothing that could be done to save the vessel as it was sinking very quickly. Within four minutes all but two of the crew were clear. A gunner called Steinwinkel and David Vanhove, a seaman, were killed by the explosion. One minute later the ship sank.

The crew pulled for the shore but were soon picked up by the steamer *Pembroke Coast* and landed safely at Plymouth.

8/38: BIDARTAISE. *Country:* French. *Date sunk:* 20/6/17. *Tons nett:* 98. *Tons gross:* 123. *Built:* 1901. *Type:* SV. *Rig:* schooner. *Owners:* G.B. Appeceix, St Servan, France. *Cargo:* In ballast, Cherbourg for Swansea. *Armed:* No. *Position:* 15 miles SSW of Portland Bill (50 17 00N; 02 36 00W). *Master's name:* Louis Picard. *Crew:* 5.

THE schooner *Bidartaise* left the port of Cherbourg at noon on June 20, 1917, and was bound for Swansea for cargo. She was under full sail and the master was on watch. Suddenly a shell whistled past his ship followed rapidly by four more. None of them were hits but the master noticed that they were getting closer each time. He decided that his position was hopeless and ordered the ship to stop and the boat to be lowered. While these preparations were going on, the submarine continued to fire. The crew pulled clear of the schooner just in time as the submarine's gunners found their mark. Soon they scored several direct hits and the *Bidartaise* went down rapidly.

The submarine then circled the crew in their boat, as if to complete a lap of honour but then spotted another sailing ship in the distance, the *Benita*, and made off after her.

Some time later the master and crew of the sunken schooner were spotted by HMS *Vanadis* and landed at Weymouth around 8am the next day.

8/39: GRANE. *Country:* Norwegian. *Date sunk:* 9/3/18. *Tons nett:* 682. *Tons gross:* 1122. *Built:* Bergen in 1899. *Type:* SS. *Rig:* schooner. *Owners:* Albert Schjelderup, Bergen, Norway. *Cargo:* 1430 tons coal from Tucker & Co, Swansea to Rouen. *Armed:* No. *Position:* 5 miles WSW of Portland Bill (50 29 25N; 02 35 10W). *Master's name:* Herman Johan Amundsen. *Crew:* 15.

SINKING as quickly as she did after being torpedoed it was amazing that so many of the crew survived. The master stated that at 9.15pm on March 9, 1918, a torpedo struck the starboard side of his ship just under the foremast. Such was the impact and damage that she sank within one minute.

The port lifeboat was launched with most of the crew in it but on touching the water, one of the davits got caught as the ship lurched over, capsizing the boat at the same time. Although upturned the boat still floated keel upwards and most of the crew managed to cling to it for support. Two men however, the cook and a seaman, were drowned. The master spotted the raft a few yards away and swam to it. He secured a line and brought it alongside the boat to provide more floatation.

At 10.15pm a torpedo boat arrived on the scene and they were landed at Weymouth.

8/40: FORTUNA. *Country:* British.
Date sunk: 3/8/16. *Tons Nett:-. Tons gross:* 110.
Built: Emsworth 1892. *Type:* SV. *Rig:* brigantine.
Owners: Albert E. Benney, Falmouth. *Cargo:* 220 tons of steel turnings, from Leconte & Fils, Havre to Swansea. *Armed:* No. *Position:* 15 miles SSW from Portland Bill (50 17 00N; 02 35 00W).
Master's name: Sydney Bate, 12, Frobisher Terrace, Falmouth. *Crew:* 5.

THE *Fortuna* was only 15 miles from safety having crossed the Channel during the day. It was 7.30pm and the master could see a barge about five miles off his starboard bow, heading towards him in an erratic way as if being chased. On looking around he spotted a submarine which was closing fast on the barge and then opened fire on it with her deck gun. Soon after, the little barge stopped and the master of *Fortuna* could see that the crew were abandoning their ship. A few minutes later the barge disappeared.

Fearing it was his turn next the master of *Fortuna* ordered all the hands on deck and to get the lifeboat ready and provisioned. His suspicions were correct as the submarine turned towards them. Within a few minutes the *Fortuna* was signalled to stop by a shell whistling over her stern. A voice ordered the crew to leave and come towards the submarine.

Alongside the enemy submarine the *Fortuna's* crew were told to get aboard and show their ship's papers while a German boarding party used their boat to plant bombs, one in the after cabin and another in number one hold. Cast adrift the crew watched as the bombs exploded and their ship went down instantly.

Some time later they joined up with the boat and crew from the barge and were found by the SS *Ioanna*. The *Fortuna's* crew accepted a lift but the barge crew decided to row for the shore as they were by then so close.

8/41: CLAN CAMERON. *Country:* British.
Date sunk: 22/12/17. *Tons nett:* 2285. *Tons gross:* 3595. *Built:* Sunderland in 1900. *Type:* SS.
Rig: schooner. *Owners:* Clan Line Steamers Ltd, 109, Hope St, Glasgow. *Cargo:* 2800 tons of tea and jute from Chittagong to London and Dundee.
Armed: 1 x 4.7in gun. *Position:* 22 miles S of Portland (50 08 00N; 02 34 00W). *Master's name:* Quentin Charles Pagan. *Crew:* 68. *Crew nationality:* 53 Lascars, 15 British. *Gunners:* Thomas Ellis, Prov LS RFR, No 187191; William George Hall, OS RNR, No ON9255A; Mark Hutchings, OS RNR, No ON2078.

THE events which led to the *Clan Cameron's* demise started at 5.40am on December 22, 1917. She was part of a convoy heading up the Channel when one of her escorts, the destroyer *Acasta*, passed close by and carrying out a sharp turn hit *Clan Cameron's* port bow. The destroyer ordered the master of *Clan Cameron* to stand by him and they were both eventually joined by the patrol vessel *Lookout*. The senior naval officer ordered the steamer to proceed towards St Catherine's at full speed.

The damage to the *Clan Cameron* was quite considerable and her fore peak was flooded but she was in no imminent danger of sinking. She headed, as ordered, for St Catherine's and was making a zig-zag course at 10 knots. Suddenly the senior gunner made signals to the bridge that he had spotted a periscope on the starboard side. At the same time the second gunner opened fire at the wake of a torpedo which was now skimming towards them. The gunner fired several shots in the hope he might have been able to hit the torpedo and detonate it but it was a hopeless gesture. They all took cover as it slammed into the side of the ship. The explosion tore a huge hole in number three hold as well as smashing the lifeboats and blowing away the side of the bridge.

As the stokehold and engine room began to fill rapidly the engines were shut down. The ship began to list heavily to starboard and the master gave the order to abandon ship using the port lifeboats. At 12.30pm an armed tug came alongside and the crew transferred to it and moved clear of their sinking ship. As they did so another explosion boomed out and a further hole appeared in the steamer's side. The submarine had remained in the vicinity and was determined that the ship would be sunk. And sink she did very soon after.

UB-58 was the submarine involved.

8/42: JOHAN. *Country:* Danish.
Date sunk: 26/12/16. *Tons nett:* 793. *Tons gross:* 828. *Built:* 1883. *Type:* SV. *Rig:* barque. *Owners:* R.K. Bagor, Marstal. *Charterers:* Messrs Thiboumery, Havre. *Cargo:* Logwood. *Armed:* No. *Position:* 22 miles NNW of Casketts (50 04 00N; 02 34 00W). *Master's name:* C.H. Boye. *Crew:* 12.
Crew nationality: 7 Danish, 1 Norwegian, 3 Russian, 1 British (Jamaican).

JOHAN sailed from Montego Bay, Jamaica, West Indies, on October 14, 1916, bound for Havre. The trip went without incident until around noon on December 26, 1916. As she made her way up the Channel the weather was bad with rain and mist but the sea conditions were calm due to a very light wind.

A submarine suddenly appeared close by her and the master noticed she had a French flag flying on her small mast on the conning tower. It was just a ruse; within a few minutes the German gunner fired a shell at the *Johan* as a signal to stop.

Two more shells followed which Captain Boye rightly assumed to be an order to abandon ship. They pulled clear in the two lifeboats within minutes and rowed over to the waiting submarine. The German commander ordered the master out of the boat and his seat was taken by several German sailors. They demanded that they be rowed over to the *Johan* to plant bombs. One was placed in the ship's lazarette aft and another in the fore peak.

The two bombs were enough to do the job and *Johan* sank at 2.45pm. Left to their own devices, the crew rowed the two boats towards shore but were picked up by a passing steamer and landed at Deal.

8/43: GERMAN SUBMARINE UB-74.

Country: German. *Date sunk:* 26/5/18. *Tons nett:* 520. *Tons gross:* 650. *Built:* Hamburg 1917. *Type:* UB-class, MkIII. *Owners:* German navy. *Armed:* 10 torpedoes, 10.5cm deck gun. *Position:* 4 miles WNW of Portland Bill (50 31 48N; 02 33 11W). *Master's name:* Oberleutnant Ernst Steindorff. *Crew:* 34. *Crew nationality:* German.

AFTER a German submarine had been spotted in the vicinity of Portland Bill, HM Yacht *Lorna*, commanded by Lieutenant Charles Loftus Tottenham, RNR, was ordered to warn traffic of the danger.

On May 26, 1918, at 8.07pm, Lieutenant Tottenham wrote in his report that he closed on the SS *Jabiru* about eight miles north-east by north of Portland Bill and ordered her master to go directly into Weymouth, keeping a sharp lookout on the way. *Lorna* kept her westerly course and at 8.40pm her commander gave the same instructions to the SS *War Cross*.

Ten minutes later a message was picked up by *Lorna's* wireless, "SOS SS two miles south west Portland Bill *Jabiru* torpedoed." Lieutenant Tottenham immediately altered course to assist and sped off in *Jabiru's* direction. At 9.14pm the wireless was buzzing again as another message was picked up from *Jabiru* saying that the torpedo had misfired and she was proceeding into port.

The wireless operator on *War Cross* had also heard the messages and was keeping his master informed. He had turned her away from the *Jabiru* hoping to steer clear of the menacing submarine lurking somewhere close by. Lieutenant Tottenham advised the master of *War Cross* to get as close to the land as possible and head for Weymouth rather than stay out in the open sea.

More and more vessels were appearing and *Lorna* pushed ahead to the south to intercept another steamer. However after three miles it was seen that the drifter *Evening Primrose* had closed with the steamer and her master was being warned. *Lorna* turned away to

the west to intercept yet another steamer. It was 9.55pm when the shout went up, a periscope, heading west about 150 feet off the port bow. *Lorna's* helm was hurled over to starboard and she responded almost instantly taking her directly over the periscope. A light grating sound was heard as *Lorna's* keel brushed over the top of the submarine's conning tower. A second later the first D type depth charge set to 50ft went over. As it splashed into the water the helm was put hard over to starboard again and another depth charge released. Two loud explosions followed and the sea erupted. The lookouts on *Lorna* watched intently for signs of a hit. Four objects were spotted bobbing about in the huge masses of bubbles that were bursting to the surface. The submarine had been hit for sure and Lieutenant Tottenham was not about to waste any time in following up his advantage. *Lorna* went directly into the middle of the disturbance and dropped yet another depth charge. As it went over the side it became evident that the four objects were men, German submariners, crying out for help. It was too late.The depth charge exploded, the force of it throwing three of the men high into the air killing them instantly. The fourth man was picked up but he was in a pitiful state, covered in oil with obvious internal injuries. He suffered an agonising three hours on board *Lorna* before dying. Also fished out of the water was a hat with 'Unterseeboots Ableilung' written on it.

However, before the rescued German died the poor fellow was able to tell Lieutenant Tottenham that his name was Lieutenant Wilhelm Ventland from Cologne, that he was from the German submarine *UB-74* commanded by Oberleutnant Ernst Steindorff, one week out of Zeebrugge. He also added that since they had been out they had torpedoed three enemy ships.

Lt. Charles Tottenham was awarded the DSO and many of the crew of the *Lorna* were also decorated

8/44: IVO.

Country: British. *Date sunk:* 3/8/16. *Tons nett:* 55. *Tons gross:* 80. *Built:* Bostal in 1902. *Type:* SV. *Rig:* barge. *Owners:* G.A. Little, Stroud, Kent. *Cargo:* In ballast, Portland for Alderney. *Armed:* No. *Position:* Portland Bill bore NNE 19 miles (50 12 00N; 02 31 00W). *Master's name:* George Day, 6, Raphael Rd, Milton, Gravesend, Kent. *Crew:* 3.

THE master first spotted the German submarine when she was five miles off. He ploughed on regardless in the hope that her commander wouldn't be interested in such a small ship, or maybe find another victim. He had left Portland, less than 20 miles away, at noon on August 3, 1916, and was due in Alderney the next day.

His worst fears were confirmed when a shell cracked across the bows of the *Ivo*. It was a signal to stop which he promptly obeyed. A voice from the submarine ordered the crew to grab some clothes and food and row to the submarine in their boat. Once on board they were questioned and told that their ship would have to be sunk. As they talked several German sailors were already planting bombs aboard the *Ivo*.

The German commander didn't cast them adrift immediately but towed them for some time. Eventually he came across another victim, a brigantine from Truro. She got the same treatment and sank within three minutes, stern first. The *Ivo's* crew were then left with the crew from the brig and the submarine made off.

Both crews were eventually picked up by passing vessels and taken to Portland. They were asked if any of them had noticed the number of the submarine but they said there were no obvious marks. One particularly observant man noticed the number 40 stamped on the hatchway ledge but it was uncertain if this was the U-boat's number.

8/45: ETHEL. *Country:* British.
Date sunk: 16/9/18. *Tons nett:* 1491. *Tons gross:* 2336. *Built:* 1898. *Type:* SS. *Rig:* schooner. *Owners:* Burdick & Cook, 34, St Mary Ave, London. *Cargo:* In ballast, Rouen to Barry Roads. *Armed:* 1 x 12pd 12cwt gun. *Position:* 4½ miles SSW of Portland Bill (50 26 18N; 02 30 26W). *Master's name:* Frederick James Lucker. *Crew:* 26. *Crew nationality:* 21 British, 1 Greek, 1 Aluvian, 2 Portuguese, 1 Peruvian. *Gunners:* L.D. Aitcheson, RNR, No 792L; C.C. Maltby, RNVR, No BZ 5731.

THE torpedo that struck the steamer *Ethel* at 2.20am on September 16, 1918, caused a lot of damage. It struck below the waterline flooding number two hold, the stokehold, the engine room, as well as smashing the bridge and charthouse, and tore up the deck on the port side.

At the time of the attack the ship was eight miles south east of Berry Head. The master had the misfortune to be blown completely overboard by the explosion but managed to keep afloat until one of the boats could pick him up.

Immediately after the explosion the First Mate, Mr A. Rice, took command and ordered the boats to be lowered as quickly as possible with all hands. The steamer was getting close to sinking.

A thick fog set in and the crew in the boats lost sight of their ship. It was still dark when the mate heard the sound of a vessel close by and asked one of the men to burn a piece of paper. It worked and they were spotted by ML 133 which first picked up the mate's boat and later found the other boat a few miles to the south.

Once ashore the master and the first mate were questioned. The naval authorities were given an explanation by the master about his position so far off the coast and they were satisfied. However, they did have cause to caution the mate for not destroying the ship's confidential papers. While being interviewed, the master was informed that HMS *Sunfish* had found his steamer still afloat and was at present under tow. The master immediately asked if he could be taken to his ship and in the words of the interviewing officer, "showed great spirit after his morning experience."

The master got a lift in a drifter from Torbay and rejoined his ship. He found her in a sorry state, being towed by the patrol trawlers, 3303 *Wyndham*, 3302 *Miura* and 3511 *John Lyons*. They were making slow progress and were eventually joined by the tug *Pilot* which speeded things up somewhat. However, the *Ethel* finally gave in and sank off Portland Bill.

UB-104 was the submarine involved.

8/46: AIRPLANE. *Country:* British.
Date sunk: 27/12/17. *Position:* 8 miles S by W of Portland Bill (50 23 00N; 02 30 00W).

THERE is just a brief mention about this in Weekly Reports which says that HM Trawler 3335 *Toronto* picked up the pilot of an airplane which had come down in the sea. The airplane was from Salisbury. They tried to get a line on it but it sank too quickly.

8/47: MARIA. *Country:* British.
Date sunk: 13/4/17. *Tons nett:* 138. *Tons gross:* 175. *Built:* Hayle in 1865. *Type:* SV. *Rig:* schooner. *Owners:* W V Kellow, Par, Cornwall. *Cargo:* 280 tons of coal from Kingham Co, Glasgow, to Cherbourg. *Armed:* No. *Position:* 25 miles SW from Portland Bill (50 10 00N; 02 30 00W). *Master's name:* William lewis. *Crew:* 4.

AFTER leaving Glasgow on January 5, 1917, *Maria* ran into some heavy storms and sustained a fair amount of damage. She limped into St Ives and was repaired there until late March. She eventually got under way again on April 12, for Cherbourg.

At 4.45pm on March 13 all hands were on deck when the watchman shouted that he could see a submarine some way off, about five miles. The master grabbed his binoculars to check. Sure enough it was a U-boat. He told the men to get their gear together and a boat ready just in case but otherwise to carry on. He reasoned that if the submarine commander was going to attack there was nothing he could do about it. And attack he did for within ten minutes shells were dropping in the water just short of the *Maria*. The master told his men to get clear and pull away.

The submarine continued shelling as she approached but stopped when alongside the crew. The commander wanted to know all the details for his log but then shouted for them to go away. One of the German lookouts had spotted a British patrol boat which was bearing down on them. The commander immediately ordered his gunner to continue shelling but it was having little effect on the *Maria*. Very hurriedly the submarine was manoeuvred closer to the sailing ship and a sailor threw a couple of bombs inside her. With that the submarine dived and was gone. *Maria* sank about five minutes later under the force of the explosions.

None of the crew were injured and they were delivered safely to Poole the next day.

8/48: ERMENILDA. *Country:* British. *Date sunk:* 4/8/16. *Tons nett:* –. *Tons gross:* 94. *Built:* –. *Type:* SV. *Rig:* –. *Owners:* Hamblin & Sons, Taunton Road, Bridgewater. *Cargo:* stone, Guernsey for Poole. *Armed:* No. *Position:* 24 miles SSW of Portland Bill (50 06 00N; 02 30 00W). *Master's name:* H. Hamblin. *Crew:* 4.

ERMENILDA had sailed from Guernsey on the August 2, 1916, and was making her way across the Channel to Poole when disaster struck. The German submarine, which surfaced close by her, had men aboard in a trice and several bombs planted. The German commander spoke very good English and politely told the crew that they had five minutes to get clear. Five minutes later the crew stopped their lifeboat a few hundred yards away and watched. The bombs exploded and *Ermenilda* sank like a stone.

Fortunately, the weather was good and the men were able to row steadily towards the coast. Eventually they were spotted by a lookout on the Russian ship *Tammerfors* which promptly altered course and picked them up. It was a nice gesture but it did not prevent her sharing the same fate as *Ermenilda* six months later.

8/49: FROGNER. *Country:* Norwegian. *Date sunk:* 29/4/18. *Tons nett:* 875. *Tons gross:* 1476. *Built:* Oslo in 1907. *Type:* SS. *Rig:* schooner. *Owners:* Fearnley & Eger, Oslo, Norway. *Cargo:* In ballast, St Malo for Newport. *Armed:* No. *Position:* 3 miles SW of Portland (50 28 20N; 02 29 30W). *Master's name:* Johan Adolf Soholt. *Crew:* 19. *Crew nationality:* 10 Norwegians, 3 Danes, 1 Greek, 2 Russian/Finns, 3 Swedes.

THE *Frogner* started her journey with a convoy when it left Cherbourg but then parted from it when she was close enough to the British coast.

At 6.10pm on April 29, 1918, the master came out of the bridge and looked out to sea over the port side. To his horror he was greeted with the sight of a torpedo speeding directly towards him. He shouted to the helmsman to put hard to port but there was no time for the ship to respond. An enormous explosion was the result as the torpedo smashed into the after hold tearing out a huge hole.

Within 30 seconds the ship's deck was flush with the sea and it was an amazing feat to get all the crew clear in the boats before she sank. There were no casualties and all were landed at Weymouth.

8/50: BENITA. *Country:* British. *Date sunk:* 20/6/17. *Tons nett:* 91. *Tons gross:* 120. *Built:* Warrington. *Type:* SV. *Rig:* schooner. *Owners:* Robert Killen of Dublin. *Cargo:* 210 tons stone from Cherbourg to John Carter of Poole. *Armed:* No. *Position:* 15 miles S of Portland Bill (50 16 00N; 02 28 00W). *Master's name:* Charles Price. *Crew:* 5.

BENITA met her end very suddenly and very rapidly as she made her way across the Channel to Poole. She was under full sail and running nicely before the wind when up popped a submarine only 500yds away. She made no attempt to communicate, but just opened fire with her deck gun. The first shot passed through the mainsail and the second hit the hull. The master realised there was nothing he could do and ordered his crew to abandon ship. They pulled clear and left their ship to her fate.

The firing stopped and the submarine eased alongside the schooner and when close enough, one of the German crew threw a bomb on board. A few minutes later the bomb exploded and blew the *Benita* almost completely to pieces. What remained sank immediately.

The crew were picked up by a patrol boat and landed at Weymouth at 9.30 the next morning.

8/51: TECWYN. *Country:* British. *Date sunk:* 21/2/17. *Tons nett:* –. *Tons gross:* 132. *Built:* –. *Type:* MV/SV. *Rig:* schooner. *Owners:* Plisson Navigation Co Ltd. *Cargo:* Flints & boulders, St. Valery for Runcorn. *Armed:* No. *Position:* 20 miles S of Portland Bill (50 12 00N; 02 28 00W). *Master's name:* Evan Owen Williams, 8, Ivy Terrace, Borthygert, Portmadoe. *Crew:* 5. *Crew nationality:* 4 British, 1 Norwegian.

THE motor on board the *Tecwyn* had been causing trouble for some time and as she crossed the Channel it was reduced to running on only one cylinder. The master had put sail up to assist but could only manage about four knots.

It was a hazy kind of day and in the distance the master could just make out the shape of a submarine. He hoped he was wrong as a few minutes later she disappeared. However, she then surfaced only a few yards from the stern of the ship. A voice boomed out ordering the crew to take to the boats.

As soon as the crew got clear a German gunner fired a shell from about 60yds away but missed the schooner. Closing the distance to about 20yds the gunner had another go and fired about 16 shells into her. Eventually she rolled over and sank.

The submarine drew close alongside the lifeboat and the master was ordered to board the submarine where he was questioned as to general details of his ship. The German commander said he was sorry for what he had done but added that even small ships had to be sunk.

The crew were picked up by the steamer *Countess* and later landed at Guernsey.

8/52: THYRA. *Country:* Danish. *Date sunk:* 24/5/17. *Tons nett:* 251. *Tons gross:* 285. *Built:* 1900. *Type:* SV. *Rig:* 3 masted schooner. *Owners:* Hans Petersen, Marstal, Denmark. *Cargo:* 300 tons of dyewood, Haiti for Le Havre. *Armed:* No. *Position:* 45 miles SSE of Start Point (50 04 00N; 02 28 00W). *Master's name:* Peter Jensen Dan. *Crew:* 8. *Crew nationality:* 7 Danes, 1 Norwegian.

THYRA had entered the English Channel and was proceeding under full sail. The master had left an able seaman at the wheel while he and the mate were talking down below. The sound of gunfire brought them both rushing on deck where they were met by the sight of a submarine about two miles off. The submarine rapidly fired about ten shells at them, of which all missed. The master, realising he could not out run his assailant ordered his crew to take to the lifeboat and get clear. From their boat they watched as the submarine poured shell after shell into their little wooden schooner and eventually she sank.

Some six hours later they were spotted by the patrol boats *Paragon* and *Expectation* and taken into Poole.

British ships standing by the victim of a U-boat attack in the Channel.

WORLD WAR ONE
CHANNEL WRECKS

◆

AREA NINE

WRECK SITES IN AREA NINE

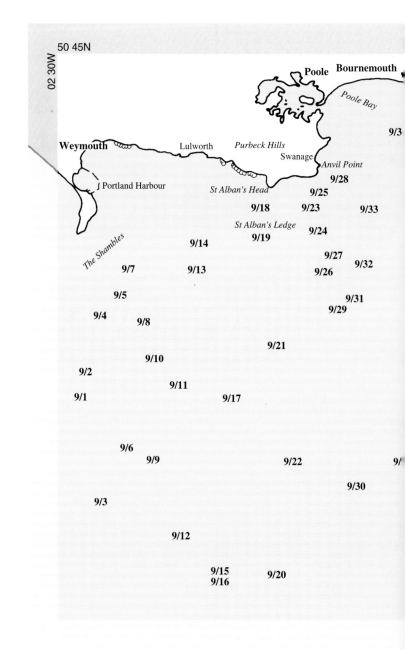

9/52
9/46
40 9/45
9/43

9/51

9/50
9/44
9/47
9/49

9/48

9/42

9/41

01 30W

50 00N

9/1: STANDARD. *Country:* Danish.
Date sunk: 20/1/17. *Tons nett:* 193. *Tons gross:* 262.
Built: 1900. *Type:* SV. *Rig:* schooner. *Owners:* C.L.
Petersen, Svendborg, Denmark. *Cargo:* 235 tons
china clay, Fowey for Leith. *Armed:* No.
Position: 13 miles S of Portland Bill (50 18 00N;
02 27 00W). *Master's name:* H.T. Rasmussen.

AT 3pm on January 20, 1917, the *Standard* was under
small sail with the First Mate, J. Wad, at the wheel. He
was scanning the horizon carefully as the schooner
zipped along. Something caught his eye and he lifted
his binoculars to try and see what it was. About two
miles off there was a vessel flying a French flag but
almost as soon as the mate made it out the flag
disappeared and was replaced with a German flag. At
the same time he realised that the vessel was a
submarine. A few seconds later a puff of smoke
appeared from the enemy's deck gun followed by a
loud bang. However, no shell was seen to fall near
the *Standard* and the mate concluded it must have
been a blank charge.
   By this time the master was by the wheel and
another bang echoed across the water. Two men
noticed that signal flags were being hoisted. Having
difficulty reading them the master ordered the ship
to heave to and he was then able to see that flags were
ordering him to row to the submarine with his ship's
papers.
   The small boat was lowered and the master,
accompanied by two seamen, went over to the waiting
submarine. The German commander examined his
papers and retaining them, ordered two of his crew
to go into the *Standard's* boat and place bombs on
the schooner. They took the master and two seamen
with them and ordered them to get the rest of the crew
into the boat and pull clear.
   The German boarding party opened the hatch covers
and placed a bomb at each end of the ship on the outer
port side. They then set about helping themselves to
provisions and when finished called the master's boat
to give them a lift back to the submarine.
   At 4pm, with her crew looking on from a distance,
the bombs exploded and the *Standard* sank almost
immediately, going down bows first.
   The crew rowed towards Portland Bill and were
eventually picked up by a tug just off the Bill at about
10.30am the next day.

9/2: GERMAN SUBMARINE (possible).
Country: German. *Date believed sunk:* 30/10/15.
Tons nett: –. *Tons gross:* –. *Built:* –. *Type:* –.
Owners: German navy. *Armed:* Yes.
Position: 11 miles S of Portland Bill (50 20 00N;
02 27 00W). *Master's name:* –. *Crew:* –. *Crew
nationality:* German.

THERE is no information available to identify the
submarine involved. The sinking appeared to be
positive and the Admiralty paid out the £1000

maximum award to the crew of the vessels involved.

At 2.25pm on the October 30, 1915, the admiralty patrol vessel *Annie Melling* was on general patrol steaming south-west at half speed with her modified sweep wires out. She was in company with armed Trawler 1541 *Trooper* who was positioned two miles on the starboard bow with the vessels *Shelomi* and *Tanager* on the port bow four miles off. All the vessels had their sweeps out looking for mines and submarines.

Captain Willis was in the wheelhouse with a seaman next to him at the wheel. He was busily scanning the horizon with his binoculars when there was a shout from a deck hand called Maclean, stationed aft to watch the beam of the sweep, "Sir, the sweep has gone!"

Captain Willis ran from the wheelhouse and jumped up onto the funnel casing and immediately ordered the leading seaman to fire the sweep charge. He ran back to the wheelhouse and put the engines full ahead and the helm hard to port with the intention of ramming whatever came up. A column of water rose into the air as the sweep charge was detonated and a long brown body broke the surface that looked like the rounded bilge of a ship. The captain estimated the submarine to be over one hundred and thirty feet in length and he could see a dark patch in the centre of it which looked every bit like a big hole but was he thought probably a dump vent.

As *Annie Melling* raced at full speed towards the rolling mass of metal the whole thing appeared to break in half and sink. As it did so a small explosion threw up another column of water and this was followed by billowing masses of bubbles and a huge slick of oil. The relatively calm sea turned almost motionless as the oil spread over the area, smoothing the water as it rippled outwards.

Annie Melling's crew watched for any tell tale objects. The air bubbles continued to rise for over an hour and then slowly stopped but the oil was still rising at dusk. A lead sounding was taken close to the submarine which showed 34 fathoms and the spot was marked with a buoy.

While this was going on the other patrol vessels had been heading towards them at full speed. The senior officer Lieutenant Barton, commanding the *Trooper*, had been watching the incident very closely through his binoculars and he later confirmed to the Admiralty that it was undoubtedly an enemy submarine.

There is a note in the records that when the Admiralty were deciding whether to award the money or not, as the object was in 34 fathoms it was out of the reach of divers; otherwise it would have been checked to make sure it was a submarine.

No submarine is reported as lost on that date in German records.

9/3: FRIGGA. *Country:* Norwegian.
Date sunk: 25/8/17. *Tons nett:* 646. *Tons gross:* 1042. *Built:* 1900. *Type:* SS. *Rig:* schooner.

Owners: Jacob Kjode of Bergen. Charterers: Furness Withy, London. *Cargo:* 1435 tons coal. *Armed:* No. *Position:* 20 miles S by E ½ E of Portland (50 10 00N; 02 25 00W). *Master's name:* Christian Brandt. *Crew:* 16. *Crew nationality:* 11 Norwegians, 2 Danes, 2 Spaniards, 1 Greek.

FRIGGA sailed from Port Talbot on August 22, 1917, and was bound for St Servan. She called in at Weymouth Roads on the 25th to join a coal convoy and left the same day at 7pm in company with 12 other vessels. *Frigga* was stationed in the convoy at position eight in a single line ahead formation.

Being part of a convoy escorted by armed patrol boats should have been safe but it wasn't to be so for the *Frigga*. A U-boat commander had been watching the convoy through the periscope and must have selected *Frigga* as the best target. A torpedo smashed into her starboard side in number three hold and she began to settle quickly.

The crew mustered rapidly. Ten went for the port lifeboat and six for the starboard. The ship sank just over two minutes later and nothing further was seen of the port boat. It was later concluded that it must have been dragged down with the ship and all in her drowned. The master and crew in the starboard boat were rescued by the escort trawler *Lapwing II*, who immediately took up the search for the submarine and any more survivors, but found nothing. The survivors were landed at Weymouth.

9/4: VALDES. *Country:* British.
Date sunk: 17/2/17. *Tons nett:* 1373. *Tons gross:* 2233. *Built:* 1914. *Type:* SS. *Rig:* schooner. *Owners:* (Managers) Yeoward Bros, 24, James St, Liverpool. *Cargo:* Full cargo of flour and hay. *Armed:* No. *Position:* 7 miles S of Portland Bill (50 24 40N; 02 24 30W). *Master's name:* L.S. Scott. *Crew:* 29. *Crew nationality:* 26 British, 3 Russians.

VALDES was officially classed at the time as an Admiralty transport. She sailed from Manchester on the February 15, 1917, and was bound for Cherbourg. The weather was fine, the sea smooth but it was a very dark night.

She was making good progress until a torpedo tore into her starboard side. The blast was so powerful that it blew the starboard lifeboat completely to pieces. The ship was in a shambles but somehow the port lifeboat was successfully launched with 20 of the crew aboard. The ship sank within six minutes and the master and seven of the crew were thrown into the sea. The master survived but nine men died in the sinking for which *U-84* claimed responsibility.

The survivors crammed as best they could into the boat and decided to row towards two steamers they could see not far away. As they got close one of the steamers blew up. She subsequently turned out to be the *Hunsworth*. The crew of the *Valdes* had had enough and turned away from any more trouble.

They were picked up eventually by the armed patrol trawler No 1983 *Sea Monarch* and, while on board her, two of the men died from exposure and shock. The bodies of the two men were taken to Portland whilst the rest of the crew were landed at Weymouth.

The *Hunsworth*, which had also been torpedoed, was found floating the next day and towed into Weymouth Bay.

9/5: W.H.L. *Country:* British. *Date sunk:* 28/1/18. *Tons nett:* 78. *Tons gross:* 92. *Built:* Falmouth in 1885. *Type:* SV. *Rig:* ketch. *Owners:* Bird & Co, St Sampson, Guernsey, Channel Isles. *Cargo:* In ballast, Cherbourg for Shoreham. *Armed:* No. *Position:* 8 miles SSE of Portland Light (50 26 00N; 02 22 00W). *Master's name:* Henry William George Wetherall. *Crew:* 4. *Crew nationality:* All British.

HEADING for Shoreham the *W.H.L.* was under full sail and running nicely before the wind. At half past midnight a German submarine suddenly appeared just off their port quarter. The crew of the *W.H.L.* expected at any moment to be shelled but instead a number of the German crew appeared on the submarine's deck with rifles and revolvers and began to fire at the ketch. The master felt he had no choice but to submit so he and his men got clear of their ship and rowed towards their assailants.

Arriving alongside the submarine they were ordered to board. Several Germans used their boat to go across to the *W.H.L.* to plant bombs as well as helping themselves to provisions and clothing. Once back in their boat the crew pulled away and watched as their ship blew up and sank stern first.

9/6: THE MACBAIN. *Country:* British. *Date sunk:* 3/3/17. *Tons nett:* 248. *Tons gross:* 291. *Built:* Arbroath in 1881. *Type:* SV. *Rig:* barquentine. *Owners:* Edward Stephens, Fore St, Fowey. *Cargo:* 150 tons ballast, Cherbourg for Fowey. *Armed:* No. *Position:* 20 miles SSE of Portland (50 14 00N; 02 21 00W). *Master's name:* George Beynon. *Crew:* 7. *Crew nationality:* 3 British, 2 Norwegians, 1 Swede, 1 Dane.

THE master of *The Macbain* looked worried as he watched the flashes of gunfire about three miles to the south-east of him. Whatever was happening meant trouble and he preferred not to be in it. He ordered every sail that could be found to be set and hoped he could get well away. However, about 15 minutes later a shell flew over the top of the ship's rigging and about a quarter of a mile off lay a German submarine. It had just dealt with another sailing vessel, *Adelaide* and her commander wanted more.

A voice from the enemy ordered the master to bring a boat which he did with two other men. The master was taken on board the submarine whilst two German sailors rowed back to the *The Macbain* with bombs which were planted fore and aft. A few minutes later the boat once again pulled clear with the rest of the crew aboard. A few more minutes and the sailing vessel had gone.

It was all over so quickly and all the crew of *The Macbain* could do was to wait for rescue in their small rowing boat. The SS *Hannah* had already picked up the crew of the *Adelaide* and did the same for *The Macbain*, landing them at Barry Roads the next day.

9/7: GERMAN SUBMARINE (possible). *Country:* German. *Date believed sunk:* 19/2/17. *Tons nett:* –. *Tons gross:* –. *Built:* –. *Type:* –. *Owners:* German navy. *Armed:* Yes. *Position:* 2 miles SSE of Shambles Light Vessel (50 28 00N; 02 21 00W). *Master's name:* –. *Crew:* –. *Crew nationality:* German.

HMTB *No 86* was on patrol near the Shambles with Lieutenant Leon S. Acheson in command. He had been warned of submarine activity in the area and had the hydrophones out listening for movement below. At 3am on February 19, 1917, the man on the phones shouted that he could hear an engine and, with no other vessels around, there was every chance that it was submarine. He was ordered to keep listening and keep shouting out. It was getting nearer and nearer to the point where it must have been extremely close indeed. At 3.30am a watchman shouted that he could see a conning tower about 500yds to port, heading in the direction of the Shambles Light Vessel.

Lieutenant Acheson immediately ordered full power, there was no need to tell the helmsman what to do! *TB 86* got within 100yds when the submarine dived. Estimating the direction and speed, the lieutenant ordered a C-Type depth charge to be dropped which emitted a huge thud followed by an enormous mushroom of water. The hydrophone was put over quickly to ascertain if the engines were still running but all was silent. Several of the crew informed the commander that they distinctly heard two explosions and also felt the pressure of both. There was no doubt in their minds that the submarine had suffered an internal explosion.

They stayed in the area for some time, but apart from oil nothing came to the surface. Nothing was heard on the hydrophones.

Even though the Admiralty agreed that the submarine was undoubtedly sunk there is no mention in the records of any prize money being paid out. However, Lieutenant Acheson was awarded the Distinguished Service Cross for his actions.

German records show no submarine sunk on that date.

9/8: ORNE. *Country:* French. *Date sunk:* 21/12/17. *Tons nett:* 444. *Tons gross:* 1280. *Built:* Nantes in 1903. *Type:* SS. *Rig:* –. *Owners:* Paul Duval, Trouville. *Cargo:* 1078 tons coal from Lysberg Ltd, Penarth to Paul Duval, Trouville. *Armed:* 2 x 90mm guns. *Position:* 6 miles SE of Shambles (50 24 30N; 02 19 00W). *Master's name:* Eugene Danee. *Crew:* 22. *Crew nationality:* All French.

THE master had been injured by the explosion which sank the *Orne*, so the first mate made the loss statement. His comments were brief.

The vessel was headed up Channel to make a crossing and was off the Shambles at 1.15am on December 21, 1917. Sea conditions were good with only light winds. Without any warning a torpedo slammed into the starboard side of the ship and blew an enormous hole in number two hold. Within seven minutes the steamer had gone down.

The force of the explosion wrecked the lifeboats and the crew had to take to the raft which was still in one piece. Whilst on the raft the mate said that he caught a glimpse of a submarine's conning tower about 100ft away. The crew were eventually picked up by the patrol vessel *Evening Primrose* and landed at Weymouth.

The naval authorities noted in the paperwork that they were dismayed to hear that the French authorities had not given the master instructions to zig-zag. French captains were in trouble throughout the war over that issue.

9/9: ADELAIDE. *Country:* British. *Date sunk:* 4/3/17. *Tons nett:* 135. *Tons gross:* 291. *Built:* Padstow in 1869. *Type:* SV. *Rig:* brigantine. *Owners:* A.E. Binney, Frobisher Terrace, Falmouth. *Cargo:* 100 tons rubbish ballast. *Armed:* No. *Position:* 20 miles SSE of Portland/42 miles NW by N from Cherbourg (50 13 00N; 02 18 00W). *Master's name:* Sidney Bate. *Crew:* 6. *Crew nationality:* All British.

THE master of the *Adelaide* couldn't make out what the strange noise was drifting across the water. It sounded every bit like a motor engine. He looked around ahead of his ship but still couldn't see anything. On looking astern he was met with the sight of a peculiar object following directly in his wake, gradually getting bigger as it rose up out of the water to reveal itself as a German submarine.

There was nothing the master could do, his six knots was no match for the submarine's speed which he estimated to be somewhere near 20. A shot rang out and a shell whistled through the rigging. Another shot smashed away the top sail yard bringing it crashing down to the deck. The master ordered his men to take to the boat and get clear. Even as the men launched their boat the submarine's gunner was still pumping shells into the *Adelaide's* wooden hull throwing huge splinters in all directions.

Once the men were clear, the master had expected the Germans to finish his ship with bombs but they didn't. Instead they headed off at full speed in pursuit of another sailing vessel which had the misfortune to wander into the area. This turned out to be the *The Macbain*. At one point the master had thought of sneaking back onto the *Adelaide* as she was still afloat, albeit in a sorry state and very low in the water, but he thought better of it. Instead he chose to drift away. Help came in the form of the government transport SS *Hannah* which later landed them at Barry Roads.

Other reports suggest that the *Adelaide* didn't sink and was towed into Brixham.

9/10: MARIE LOUISE. *Country:* French. *Date sunk:* 17/3/17. *Tons nett:* 229. *Tons gross:* 291. *Built:* 1901. *Type:* SV. *Rig:* schooner. *Owners:* Guest Eclair Boenner. *Cargo:* 500 tons of old iron, Havre for Briton Ferry. *Armed:* No. *Position:* 12 miles SE of Portland Bill (50 21 00N; 02 18 00W). *Master's name:* Le Gouyader. *Crew:* 10.

THERE is very little information concerning the sinking of this vessel. All that is recorded is that she was sunk by three bombs placed on her by an enemy submarine. The crew all got clear and were picked up the SS *Basse Indre* of Nantes and landed at Deal at 3pm on March 18, 1917.

9/11: SPIRAL. *Country:* British. *Date sunk:* 4/8/16. *Tons nett:* –. *Tons gross:* 1342. *Built:* Oslo in 1906. *Type:* SS. *Rig:* schooner. *Owners:* The Minnie SS Co Ltd, Royal Chambers, W. Hartlepool. *Cargo:* 1858 tons coal, Tyne to Bordeaux. *Armed:* No. *Position:* 40 miles WSW of St Catherines (50 19 00N; 02 15 00W). *Master's name:* Nathan Bradley. *Crew:* 20.

SHE left the Tyne on the July 27, 1916, bound for Bordeaux and while going down the east coast was attacked by a zeppelin, but was not hit.

Proceeding on her way across the Channel she settled back into routine. It was Friday August 4, 7.30am, and the master had just gone below. The chief officer was left in charge, assisted by the bosun who was on deck lookout. It was the bosun who reported that he could see what looked like a submarine 500yds off on the port quarter. His suspicions were instantly confirmed when a shell whistled overhead and splashed 20ft on the other side of the ship.

The master awoke with a start and following wartime instructions immediately burnt his secret papers. He reached the deck just in time to hear an enemy voice boom out, "Get into your boats!"

The *Spiral* was unarmed and the submarine's gunner trained his deck gun on them at point blank range.

The master took charge of one boat and the chief officer the other. The submarine *UB-18* meanwhile, approached the chief officer's boat and the German commander asked for the ship's papers. He was referred to the master who pluckily denied having them but then finding himself looking down the barrel of a revolver was told, "Don't be reckless!" He handed over the ships register, bills of lading, manifest and some personal papers.

Meanwhile, the German crew were stripping the bits they wanted from the *Spiral*; clocks, barometers and provisions. When they had had their fill they planted bombs deep in the ship and three explosions were heard, but she refused to sink. The submarine dived but about an hour later re-appeared and put an officer on board to plant another bomb which did the trick, sending *Spiral* to the bottom stern first.

As the crew settled in to begin rowing they were hailed by another lifeboat, it was the crew of the sailing vessel *Demaris* who had been sunk by the same submarine about half an hour earlier. Help came to all of them in the form of SS *Kanawha* of Liverpool which took them safely to London.

9/12: LITTLE MYSTERY. *Country:* British.
Date sunk: 30/4/17. *Tons nett:* 95. *Tons gross:* 114. *Built:* Kingsbridge in 1887. *Type:* SV. *Rig:* schooner. *Owners:* E. Stephens, Par, Cornwall. *Cargo:* 168 tons coal from Cardiff to Cherbourg. *Armed:* No. *Position:* 25 miles SSE from Portland Bill (50 07 00N; 02 15 00W). *Master's name:* John Henry Greet. *Crew:* 5.

AT 7am on April 30, 1917, the master was on deck. His ship was on the port tack skipping along nicely towards the French coast. In the distance he noticed another vessel and he got his binoculars to have a closer look. There was something peculiar about it which made him feel very uneasy. By the time he got his glasses up it seemed to have disappeared but on closer inspection he could see a periscope.

He shouted for all hands to come on deck and ordered the boat to be made ready while he destroyed his confidential sailing instructions. Soon the submarine was on the surface and alongside the port side of the *Little Mystery*. The commander appeared at the top of the conning tower with a pistol and started to fire, one bullet hitting Russian Seaman, Carl Eglit in the arm.

After the boat was launched the German commander waved the crew to come towards him. On board, the master was ordered to produce his ships papers and told that his vessel would be boarded and bombed. The master asked if he could go back to his ship to collect his personal compass and some photographs, and the commander agreed. The U-boat commander and five sailors set about the task of planting the bombs.

Cast adrift the crew of *Little Mystery* watched the bombs explode and five minutes later she sank. In about an hour the patrol vessel *Royalto* arrived on the scene and picked the men up.

9/13: IOLANTHE. *Country:* British.
Date sunk: 4/1/18. *Tons nett:* 1743. *Tons gross:* 3081. *Built:* 1904. *Type:* SS. *Rig:* schooner. *Owners:* Petersen & Co, 6, Lloyds Ave, London. *Cargo:* Hay, railway wagons and railway material. On government service, Clyde to St Helen's. *Armed:* 1 x 12pdr 12cwt gun. *Position:* 10 miles SE by E from Portland Bill (50 28 00N; 02 12 30W). *Master's name:* James Scott. *Crew:* 31. *Crew nationality:* 30 British, 1 Norwegian. *Gunners:* J. Rooke, LS RNR, No ON8657A; F.W. Thornton, AB RNVR, No TZ9875.

STEERING east by south the *Iolanthe* went past the Shambles at 10.35pm. She was making nine knots and was zig-zagging, changing every 15 minutes. A good lookout was being kept with two officers on the bridge, a man on the forecastle and a gunner by the gun. Suddenly an enormous explosion boomed out from the port side which tore a huge hole in number three hold. At that particular moment it was assumed that the ship had struck a mine.

Although badly damaged the steamer was holding up remarkably well and it was hoped that she could be coaxed gently into harbour. The crew tried to get some direction on her but she soon began to settle. Just after midnight it was obvious that the ship was about to go down and the crew took to the boats. As they pulled clear they saw a submarine and a large one at that. In fact it was *UC-75* commanded by Oberleutnant Johann Lohs.

Two patrol trawlers were soon on the scene and attempted to tow the *Iolanthe* but no sooner had they got lines aboard her than she sank. There were no casualties and all the crew were landed at Weymouth.

9/14: HMD GOLDEN SUNSET. *Country:* British.
Date sunk: 4/1/18. *Tons nett:* –. *Tons gross:* 85. *Built:* –. *Type:* patrol drifter. *Rig:* –. *Owners:* Admiralty. *Cargo:* On Admiralty service. *Armed:* Yes. *Position:* Near Shambles LV (50 30 30N; 02 12 00W). *Master's name:* –.

ONLY the barest details appear to have survived of this incident. A brief report mentions that she was sunk at 11.45pm on January 4, 1918, after a collision. The name of the other vessel involved is not given.

9/15: ILLINOIS. *Country:* American.
Date sunk: 18/3/17. *Tons nett:* 3275. *Tons gross:* 5225. *Built:* 1913. *Type:* SS. *Rig:* schooner/tanker. *Owners:* Texas SS Co, 17, Balton Place, New York. *Cargo:* In ballast, London for Port Arthur, Texas, USA. *Armed:* No. *Position:* 20 miles N of Alderney (50 03 00N; 02 10 00W). *Master's name:* H.H. Iversen. *Crew:* 34.

At 7.45am on March 18, 1917, one of the lookouts on the tanker *Illinois* spotted a submarine about three miles off. The master was called and they watched the submarine dive. The master hoped that this was the last he would see of her. But she rose to the surface again, this time much closer. The master saw movement on the submarine's deck and a few minutes later a bang was heard followed by the screaming of a shell as it passed over the ship. The second shell was much better aimed and knocked the wireless equipment out. The third penetrated the engine room forcing the engineers to shut down the engines.

The master decided that there was nothing he could do except to abandon his ship which was swiftly done. The submarine's gun kept firing at the steamer until the last boat had pulled away. The master was ordered by the German commander to bring his boats alongside and five men were ordered aboard. Their places were taken over by German sailors, each clutching a bomb.

Having rowed to the *Illinois* and back again the five crew re-joined their shipmates and rowed away. They stopped for a while and watched as the first of the bombs exploded. Within ten minutes their steamer had gone. Shortly afterwards they were spotted by the Alderney pilots' boat and towed in to Alderney.

9/16: DEMARIS. *Country:* British.
Date sunk: 4/8/16. *Tons nett:* –. *Tons gross:* 98.
Built: Goole in 1859. *Type:* SV. *Rig:* schooner.
Owners: George Brown, Lime St, Hull.
Cargo: 155 tons stone from A & F Manuel of Guernsey, to London. *Armed:* No. *Position:* 20 miles N of Alderney (50 03 00N; 02 10 00W).
Master's name: Richard Cawthorne. *Crew:* 4.

THE weather was a little hazy when *Demaris* left Guernsey at 8pm on August 2, 1916. The wind was light but the little sailing vessel ran on the port tack heading in an east-north-east direction.

Suddenly, a submarine appeared virtually alongside them and fired several rifle shots. The master ordered the sails to be taken in and the submarine came closer, making fast to the *Demaris*. At 6.15am a German officer boarded her and ordered the master to put his crew in the boat and get clear as she was to be sunk with bombs. The master had no choice and pulled clear to watch as his ship blew up and sank immediately.

The master of *Demaris* noticed that the crew of the submarine were by then hurrying and in a few moments had shut down the conning tower hatch and dived. On looking around he could see a steamer heading towards them. It was the SS *Spiral* and she was to be the submarine's next victim.

The *Spiral* shared the same fate as *Demaris* and both crews later joined together. They were spotted by a lookout on the SS *Kanawha* of Liverpool and taken to London.

9/17: MERMAID. *Country:* British.
Date sunk: 29/4/17. *Tons nett:* 57. *Tons gross:* 76.
Built: Rye in 1856. *Type:* SV. *Rig:* schooner.

Owners: Charles King, 20, Charing Cross, St Helier, Jersey. *Cargo:* In ballast, St Malo for Plymouth. *Position:* 18 miles SSW of Anvil Point (50 18 00N; 02 08 00W). *Master's name:* Henry James Richmond, 25, Dumaresq St, St Helier. *Crew:* 4.

ALTHOUGH she was over 50 years old the *Mermaid* was still a useful sailing vessel and frequently made trips across the Channel with all sorts of cargo. On April 29, 1917, she was making her way to Plymouth for a cargo. She had left St Malo at noon and the weather was set for a good crossing.

The master was busily checking his course and a seaman called Hairon was at the wheel. The master looked up for a moment to collect his thoughts and spotted a black object in the distance. He looked again and realised it was a submarine. At the same moment a shell screamed overhead and threw up a spout alongside the *Mermaid*. With the shell burst still ringing in his ears he ordered the men into the boat as another shell slammed through the mainsail.

The crew pulled clear, stood by and watched as the submarine drew alongside their abandoned ship. A few minutes later the *Mermaid* exploded and began to settle instantly. Within two minutes she had gone.

The submarine made no attempt to talk to the crew and headed off to the south-east. The crew began to row steadily northwards towards the shore. The Nowegian steamer *Bjerra* picked them up and landed them at St Helens Roads.

9/18: ARFON. *Country:* British.
Date sunk: 30/4/17. *Tons nett:* –. *Tons gross:* 227.
Built: –. *Type:* Admiralty Trawler. *Rig:* –.
Owners: Admiralty. *Cargo:* –. *Armed:* Yes.
Position: 1¹/₂ miles SSW from St Albans Head (50 33 00N; 02 04 00W). *Master's name:* J. Abrams. *Crew:* 13. *Crew nationality:* British.

THE Court of Enquiry into the loss of HMT 134 *Arfon* was held at Portland Naval Dockyard a few days after her sinking. The first witness to be called was E. McKeown RNR, commander of HMT 135 *Vera Grace* who was in company with *Arfon* at the time of her loss. He stated that both vessels were involved in sweeping operations from St Albans Head to the Shambles. Another patrol vessel *Alaska* was also in the area at the time and it was her commander who ran up the signal that he had sighted a mine. Gunfire was heard followed by a loud explosion as the mine was destroyed by rifle shots. Both *Vera Grace* and *Arfon* moved to the spot and began to sweep the area together in formation. It was 9.45am when they passed over the spot where the mine had exploded as it was well marked by the presence of many dead fish. In an instant the *Arfon* was enveloped in a ball of smoke and within a few seconds she was head down in the water so far that her propeller rose up into the air and was still turning rapidly.

Walter Gleeson a deck hand on *Arfon* said that he was abreast of the wheelhouse at the time and that the explosion occurred under the starboard, forward gallows and was so powerful that it knocked him clean off his feet. By the time he picked himself up the *Arfon* was almost under and he dived over the starboard quarter rail only to be sucked down with the sinking ship. However, he managed to gain the surface, dazed but otherwise all right and stayed afloat until picked up by the *Alaska*. Walter Gleeson added at the enquiry that he saw the cook, James Doy, come out of the galley and jump overboard but didn't know what happened to him. He also saw another man whom he couldn't identify, jump over the stern only to be caught by the propeller.

Signalman, George White, also survived and gave evidence at the enquiry. He was sitting on the wheelhouse steps at the time of the explosion and ran aft to get a lifebelt. But before he could put it on the ship sank from beneath him. The other survivor was leading seaman McIntyre but he sustained bad head and leg injuries and was still in hospital at the time of the enquiry.

Two of the survivors were picked out of the water by a boat sent from *Vera Grace* but these were later transferred to the Trinity House vessel *Warden*. She happened to be in the area and was much better equipped to deal with injuries.

The Court of Enquiry concluded that *Arfon* had been sunk by striking a mine and that no person could be held responsible for her sinking. Her commander and nine members of her crew perished in the sinking.

9/19: START. *Country:* Norwegian.
Date sunk: 22/12/17. *Tons nett:* 341. *Tons gross:* 728. *Built:* 1896. *Type:* SS. *Rig:* –. *Owners:* J. Larrsen, Skiene. *Cargo:* Coal from Swansea to Rouen. *Armed:* No. *Position:* 3½ miles S by E of St Albans Head (50 31 00N; 02 04 00W). *Master's name:* M. Mikkelsen. *Crew:* 14.

THERE is little information on this sinking. Out of 14 crew only two people survived, the master and the Swedish second mate, O. Brendtssen.

The master said that it happened at around 1.15am, when a huge explosion occurred aft which virtually blew the stern right off the *Start*. She sank in less than two minutes giving very few of the crew time to get away. He was below at the time and had no sooner made the deck than he found himself in the water. He spotted something floating close by which turned out to be the raft he had purposely left loose on deck for just such an emergency. On looking around the floating debris he could find only one other person, the second mate.

The master added that at the time, his vessel was making seven knots, he had no lights showing on the seaward side of the ship but did have dimmed lights showing on the port side. He saw no trace of a submarine or a torpedo and concluded that he struck a

mine. The Admiralty made no notes on the sinking which they usually did if they disagreed. Lloyd's, however, later recorded her as torpedoed.

9/20: VIGOURIEUX. *Country:* French.
Datesunk: 14/6/17. *Tons nett:* –. *Tons gross:* 230. *Built:* –. *Type:* SV. *Rig:* –. *Owners:* Ferrailles Metias, Paris. *Cargo:* In ballast, Cherbourg to Briton Ferry. *Armed:* No. *Position:* 20 miles N of Casketts Light (50 03 00N; 02 03 00W). *Master's name:* Carus. *Crew:* 5. *Crew nationality:* All French.

THE crew of *Vigourieux* didn't expect the treatment they got at 11am on June 14, 1917. They were making good progress across the Channel taking advantage of the fine weather and good sailing conditions. Then a submarine appeared about 600yds off and menacingly turned her bow towards the sailing ship.

The first shell missed but only just. The next six or so all found targets, bringing down rigging and tearing up planks as though shredding paper. The master told his men to get the boat to the sheltered side and get clear before they were all killed. As they left, the shelling stopped and a few minutes later the submarine was alongside the little rowing boat. Two German sailors jumped in clutching bombs and the submarine towed them back to the *Vigourieux*. The bombs were quickly hung on the outside of the ship.

Stopping 200yds off, the German commander questioned the master about his ship and also asked if there were any more vessels in the area. The master knew that there were several others but told the commander he was alone. At that moment two loud explosions boomed out and a few minutes later the *Vigourieux* had gone to the bottom.

The crew rowed for some time but with good navigation and assistance from the strong currents in the area they made Alderney safely. The Lloyds agent looked after them until arrangements were made to get them to Cherbourg.

9/21: CONCH. *Country:* British.
Date sunk: 8/12/16 *Tons Nett:*-. *Tons gross:* 5620. *Built:* Wallsend, Tyne in 1906. *Type:* SS. *Rig:* schooner/tanker. *Owners:* Anglo Saxon Petroleum Co, St Helens Court, London. *Cargo:* 7000 tons benzine, shipped at Rangoon and consigned to Thameshaven. *Armed:* Yes. *Position:* 12 miles S by W ½ W from Anvil Point (50 22 20N; 02 02 30W). *Master's name:* –. *Crew:* 60.

THE *Conch* was bound for the River Thames and London. She had sailed from Rangoon and on her way called at Gibraltar for orders on the December 7, 1916. The Chief Engineer, Herbert Raffray, from Jersey, said that the next day he went below at 5pm, leaving the watch to the fourth engineer, but was backwards and forwards from time to time. He was in his cabin at about 10.15pm when he suddenly heard an explosion and felt a heavy bump. He rushed below but found all was well down there and the engine room telegraph was still on full ahead. The rest of the engineers appeared and the second and third reported that the whole of the forward house was ablaze and that it was very difficult to get on deck. The bridge was blown to pieces and anyone in it or near to it would have stood little chance of surviving.

The fourth engineer had already burnt himself quite badly in going to rouse the others and attempts to make the deck only ended in being forced back by the flames. They had to get on deck somehow if they were going to get to the boats.

At midnight the second engineer managed to get on deck, blew the whistle and shouted to the others to come and join him. The chief engineer could then see the extent of the problem, a large gash in the ship's port side forward, spewing lighted oil. The ship was still under way making 10 knots and leaving a stream of burning oil in her wake.

The forward lifeboats were gone but they managed to dig out a little workboat which they foolishly tried to launch. With the ship still having forward movement on her the boat capsized immediately. They persevered with it and more by luck than judgement managed to get a few men in it who were towed behind the steamer.

The chief engineer tried several times to shut the engines down but couldn't get to the controls in the engine room because of the intense heat.

Eventually the boat being towed behind the ship came adrift leaving the second and third engineers on the burning steamer. The crew's boat was in a bad way and had to be baled out continually but eventually the steamer *Rattray Head* came to the rescue.

During the early hours of the next morning, five Chinese were also picked up by *Rattray Head* which stood by the tanker, which was still burning fiercely. A naval patrol boat informed *Rattray Head* that they had picked up the two engineers left on board. Soon afterwards, several patrol boats arrived on the scene, the trawlers *Maristo* and *Wimpole*, and HMDB destroyer *Nymphe*.

The *Conch* eventually sank. The gaping hole in her side was almost certainly caused by a torpedo. The initial explosion had killed the master, all the deck officers, the radio operator, two gunners and eighteen of the crew, 28 men in all.

UB-23 claimed the sinking.

9/22: NORMA. *Country:* Danish. *Date sunk:* 14/1/17. *Tons nett:* 1177. *Tons gross:* –. *Built:* 1884. *Type:* SS. *Rig:* schooner. *Owners:* C.P. Jensen, Copenhagen, Denmark. *Cargo:* 2000 tons of general and fruit/onions/wine from Valencia to London. *Armed:* No. *Position:* 34 miles SW of St Catherines (50 13 00N; 02 00 00W). *Master's name:* Jen Jepsen of Esbjerg, Denmark. *Crew:* 19.

NORMA experienced bad weather from Ushant and eventually put into Falmouth on the January 11, 1917. She left Falmouth on the 13th at 4pm and continued up the Channel.

At about 10am the next day the master was below when the mate, who was on watch, called him to come to the bridge and pointed out a submarine on the starboard bow about two miles off. They carried on at full speed making around seven knots and watched with alarm as the submarine overhauled them. Suddenly, a gun shot rang out and the master could see that the submarine had hoisted signals flags but he was unable to read them. Another shot was heard and the *Norma* was stopped giving two blasts on her whistle. The master then made out the signal which read, 'Come on board with your papers.' He ordered the answering pennant to be raised and went across with his papers to the waiting submarine, a mere ship's length off.

As the master arrived he was ordered out of the boat and a German crew rowed it back to the *Norma* complete with a set of bombs.

Whilst on the submarine the master noticed another steamer, a Norwegian, stood to on the starboard bow and he asked the German commander what he was going to do to her. "Sink her," came the reply.

The commander then gave the crew on board the *Norma* ten minutes to get in the boats and pull clear. The master's boat arrived back and he was told to get clear and join his crew. As they rowed away they stopped to watch the bombs explode and in addition watched the submarine fire four shells into her. Half an hour later the *Norma* sank stern first.

The submarine then turned towards the Norwegian steamer to continue her destructive work and as she passed the *Norma's* crew a voice was heard, "Goodbye. I hope you will be safe."

Several hours later one of the boats was picked up by the armed yacht *Maid of Honour*, which then made a search for the submarine without success. The other boat and crew was picked up by a passing ship and transferred to the *Maid of Honour*. All the survivors were taken to St Helens Roads and from there to Portsmouth.

9/23: AVANTI. *Country:* British. *Date sunk:* 2/2/18. *Tons nett:* –. *Tons gross:* 2128. *Built:* 1912. *Type:* SS. *Rig:* schooner. *Owners:* Det Forenede Dampskibsselckab, Copenhagen. *Managers:* Lambert Bros, Glasgow. *Cargo:* 3500 tons iron ore, Bilbao for W. Hartlepool. *Armed:* 1 x 12pdr 12cwt gun. *Position:* 4 miles SE by E from St Albans Head (50 33 35N; 01 57 15W). *Master's name:* A.R. Jones. *Crew:* 24. *Gunners:* George Charles Knight, OS RNR, No BZ9582; Bert Garrett, OS RNR.

THE information on this sinking was given by one of the only two survivors, George Knight. He stated that they were proceeding to Falmouth from Bilbao and all was normal. He was on watch on the gun platform when there was a huge explosion at around 6am. The ship broke completely in half and sank immediately.

Within a second or two he was in the water but luck was with him as he spotted a raft floating right next to him. He remembered seeing other members of the crew swimming around the area but only one other made it to the raft, a Spanish seaman called Francisco Lopez.

At about 8am he said a periscope from a submarine appeared and headed directly at the raft but when about 200 yds off it altered course and moved away. They were found at noon by the patrol drifter 1835 *La Parisienne* and landed at Poole.

UB-59 was the submarine involved.

9/24: GERMAN SUBMARINE (possible).

Country: German. *Date believed sunk:* 12/5/17. *Tons nett:* –. *Tons gross:* –. *Built:* –. *Type:* –. *Owners:* German navy. *Armed:* Yes. *Position:* 4 miles S of Anvil Point (50 31 36N; 01 57 00W). *Master's name:* –. *Crew:* –. *Crew nationality:* German.

CAPTAIN Peter Nicholson reported that he left Portland Harbour on May 11, 1917, in HM Trawler No 1978 *Maristo*, to relieve another patrol vessel on standard patrolling duties. He spent most of the day generally cruising his defined area, stopping every now and then to listen with the hydrophones. At 12.45pm the next day, *Maristo* was off Anvil Point when one of the lookouts shouted that he could see a submarine partially submerged in the distance. Captain Nicholson immediately gave the order to increase speed and head towards it with the intention of ramming.

As they got closer the crew could see that it was indeed a submarine and so far nobody on board it had spotted their rapid approach. When only a few hundred yards off, the submarine dived and everyone on *Maristo* thought that was the end of the matter. However, five minutes later a periscope was spotted close by on the starboard side. Once again the trawler was turned towards it and this time got very close indeed before it submerged again. Captain Nicholson reported that he saw the wake of the periscope when only 25yds off and altered his course slightly ahead of it's track. As he passed the position that he judged to be just ahead of it he ordered a D-type depth charge with a fuse set to eighty feet to be dropped. The instant it was released he ordered the helm hard to port to bring *Maristo* back over the same spot and followed up with a secondary G-type charge. Two huge explosions followed and Captain Nicholson slowed his ship down to watch and wait.

Five minutes later a lookout reported a periscope about 50yds off on the starboard side. The helmsman responded instantly and sent *Maristo* racing towards it. There appeared to be something strange about it as it seemed to make very little effort to get out of the way. One man said that he heard a bang from under the ship as though it had clipped the periscope but that was secondary as another depth charge, set much shallower to 40ft, exploded directly over the spot where the submarine had dived. A huge explosion followed which sent up an enormous spout of water into the air. Within a minute or so large amounts of oil were spreading across the water's surface and a strong smell of petrol was in the air. *Maristo's* men waited and listened on the hydrophone but all was silent down below.

Within an hour *Maristo* was joined by torpedo boats No's *34* and *37* who also took up the vigil but their commanders reached the same conclusion as Captain Nicholson, that the submarine was dead on the bottom.

Although the Admiralty accepted the fact that the submarine was most probably killed they felt that it could not be proved for certain so awarded the crew £200 instead of the maximum £1000. Captain Nicholson was awarded the DSC and others in his crew were also decorated.

There is no report of a submarine sunk on this date in German records.

9/25: KYARRA. *Country:* British.

Date sunk: 26/5/18. *Tons nett:* 4383. *Tons gross:* 6953. *Built:* 1913. *Type:* SS. *Rig:* schooner. *Owners:* Australasian United Steam Navigation Co, London. *Cargo:* 2600 tons Australian mails and confidential papers for the Governor of Australia. *Armed:* 1 x 4.7in Japanese gun. *Position:* 1½ miles S of Anvil Point/Anvil Point bore NNW 1¼ miles (50 34 50N; 01 56 30W). *Master's name:* Albert John Gladstone Donovan. *Crew:* 112. *Crew nationality:* 108 British, 2 Americans, 1 Swede, 1 Norwegian, plus 34 military ratings. *Gunners:* Walter A. Olding, L/Cpl. RMLI, No PO 8734; H.E. Tanner, Pte. No PO 12448; H.A. Redding, Pte. No PO 10329; Chas E. Sage, LS Australian Navy; R.H. O'Connor, AB Australian Navy. *Casualties:* 6.

THE *Kyarra* was bound for Australia but was to call into Devonport on her way down Channel. She carried a number of military ratings and with the large number of crew there were 147 on board.

She left Tilbury Docks on May 24, 1918, and made her way down the Channel passing the Isle of Wight the next day. The weather was good with a light westerly wind and a calm sea. Captain Donovan had his ship zig-zagging as ordered and was maintaining a comfortable 12 knots. The pilot was in charge on the bridge when suddenly there was a shout from one of the lookouts to say he had spotted a torpedo on the port side. The helm was immediately put hard over to port but the ship had no time to answer and it slammed into her amidships.

The master called for reports from below. Five people had been killed in the engine room by the explosion and to make matters worse he was told that the engine room was flooding rapidly. On looking around he could see with his own eyes that his ship was done for so he gave the order for everyone to go immediately to their boat stations and as soon as the way was off, get clear.

The *Kyarra* sank at 9.08am, 19 minutes after being struck by the torpedo.

The boats pulled to Swanage where they were taken care of and one injured man was sent to Swanage Cottage Hospital but died the next day.

The U-boat commander responsible for sinking the *Kyarra* was Oberleutnant Johann Lohs in *UB-57*.

Today the wreck of the *Kyarra*, being relatively close to shore, is visited by large number of amateur divers. She is well broken up but still resembles a large steamer in places. Many champagne bottles have been found lying around the wreckage, some still full. The wreck is owned by Kingston Branch of the British Sub-Aqua Club.

9/26: GERMAN SUBMARINE (probable).

Country: German. *Date believed sunk:* 25/3/18. *Tons nett:* –. *Tons gross:* –. *Built:* –. *Type:* –. *Owners:* German navy. *Armed:* Yes. *Position:* 7 miles S by E of Anvil Point (50 28 00N; 01 56 00W). *Master's name:* –. *Crew:* –. *Crew nationality:* German.

THE pilot of Seaplane No *1794* was John Francis McNamara, an American with the rank of Ensign, attached to the ship *Daedalus* at the sea plane station at Portland. On March 25, 1918, he took off on a regular patrol with Sub Lieutenant Sawyer on board as observer. His report states that at 1.50pm he spotted the periscope of a submarine and immediately opened the throttle to full speed for an attack. On his first pass he dropped a 100lb bomb which fell about 15 feet ahead of the periscope but directly in line with it. He climbed and circled to see the effect. About three minutes later huge quantities of air burst to the surface. Realising he had probably done some serious damage to the submarine he lined his aircraft up for another attack.

His second bomb, this time a 230 pounder, landed right in the middle of all the disturbance. The following explosion was enormous, throwing up a huge column of water and leaving oil scattered over a wide area around it. He circled for over an hour to see if anything more conclusive would come to the surface, at the same time warning merchant ships to keep clear. At 3.30pm his fuel situation forced him to leave so after signalling the submarine's position to a nearby destroyer he headed back to Portland.

The Admiralty were extremely pleased with McNamara's performance and concluded that the submarine was most probably sunk. He was recommended for the Distinguished Service Cross and was presented with it soon afterwards

German records do not show any submarine sunk on this date.

9/27: APARIMA. *Country:* British.

Date sunk: 19/11/17. *Tons nett:* 3684. *Tons gross:* 5704. *Built:* Dumbarton in 1902. *Type:* SS. *Rig:* –. *Owners:* Union SS Co Ltd, Dunedin, New Zealand. *Cargo:* In ballast, London for Barry and New York. *Armed:* 1 x 4.7in gun. *Position:* 6 miles S by W ³/₄ W from Anvil Point (50 29 45N; 01 55 00W). *Master's name:* Gerald Stanley Doorly. *Crew:* 112.

SINCE the outbreak of the war the *Aparima* had been used as a troop ship conveying New Zealand troops to Egypt and England. She was also used by the company as a training ship for cadets and her last trip was no exception; on board were 30 boys aged between 15 and 20. She had left New Zealand on September 5, 1917, fully loaded with food for London. She reached there safely in November and after discharging was taken over by the British government and dispatched in ballast for New York. She left London on November 17, with instructions to call in to Barry Docks.

Aparima sailed down the Channel on a zig-zag course as per Admiralty instructions. The master had all his usual lookouts in position but on such a dark night there was little to see. The commander of *UB-40* lurking off the Isle of Wight could see the *Aparima* well enough, and he released a torpedo. Those on board the steamer said later they heard a loud thud followed by a terrific explosion which virtually blew the stern of the vessel away. The master was blown completely off his feet but, luckily, wasn't injured. Fire broke out. Smoke added to the confusion below decks where many of the crew had been in their bunks and asleep. In five minutes she was gone.

One of lifeboats was capsized as it touched water. Despite the cold the three boats that made it rowed around the wreckage for some time looking for signs of life. One man was found on a raft and taken aboard. A total of 56 people survived but the same number had perished. One boat was picked up by a patrol vessel and another was found by the Norwegian steamer *Gelhung*.

Of the 30 cadets on board and quartered in the poop, 18 were killed. Included in the Admiralty records of this loss is a letter from a man grieving over the loss of his son and accusing the steamship company of criminal negligence.

9/28: HMD PLANTIN. *Country:* British.

Date sunk: 26/4/17. *Tons nett:* –. *Tons gross:* 84. *Built:* –. *Type:* patrol drifter. *Rig:* –. *Owners:* Admiralty. *Cargo:* –. *Armed:* Yes. *Position:* 3 miles SSE of Handfast Point, Poole Bay (50 35 48N; 01 54 00W). *Master's name:* –. *Crew:* 10.

ON April 25, 1917, HM drifter No 1440 *Plantin* had been engaged in sweeping operations to the south-south-east of Standfast Point, (called Handfast today), Poole Bay. She had just shot her sweeps

The *Aparima* was sunk off the Isle of Wight by a torpedo fired from *UB-40*.

when the skipper received a message from J.P.A. Richardson RNVR, commander of HMD 2734, *WPG1*, in charge of sweeping operations, that he was sweeping in the wrong position. The skipper of *Plantin* was about to haul in his sweeps when they suddenly raced away as though something had got caught in them.

Lieutenant Richardson on *WPG1* immediately moved over the spot while *Plantin* cut her lines and dropped a dan buoy. A depth charge was sent down which exploded and set off two further explosions in rapid succession.

Believing that they could have a crippled submarine below them the patrol vessels sent down several more depth charges but nothing significant came to the surface. *Plantin* and two other drifters were ordered to keep watch all night with their hydrophones over the side and to keep away all other traffic. At daylight the next morning another charge was exploded electrically but still nothing came to the surface to signify the presence of a submarine.

At 6am, having decided that his nets must have snagged a rock and that the strong current must have given the impression that something was caught in the sweep, the skipper of *Plantin* moved in to recover his dan buoy. As he eased up to the buoy a huge explosion boomed out from the after end of the ship sinking her almost instantly. As the other patrol vessels moved in to assist, only one man, the second hand, who was at the wheel at the time was found. The skipper and eight other ratings were killed in the explosion.

It was discovered later that a German minefield had been laid at this position. That accounted for the explosions after the depth charge was sent down. It was assumed that *Plantin* must have struck one of the other mines.

9/29: HARTBURN. *Country:* British. *Date sunk:* 15/10/17. *Tons nett:* 1494. *Tons gross:* 2367. *Built:* 1900. *Type:* SS. *Rig:* schooner. *Owners:* Capel & Co, 2, Exchange Buildings, Newcastle. *Cargo:* 880 tons of hay, 70 tons of railway trucks. *Armed:* 1 x 12pd 12cwt gun. *Position:* 20 miles E of Portland (50 25 00N; 01 54 00W). *Master's name:* Albert Newman Shelton. *Crew:* 26. *Crew nationality:* 22 British, 1 Spaniard, 1 Italian, 1 Norwegian, 1 Russian. *Gunners:* Harry Rose, LS GL RNR, No 7382A Portsmouth; H.W. Newish, AB RNVB, No B23769.

HARTBURN was on voyage from Manchester to St Helens and was in the position given at 1.30am. The sea was calm and the night clear when an explosion occurred on the starboard side amidships. A hole was blown in the side of her about eight feet below the waterline and such was the force of the explosion that a number of hay bales were forced upwards, blowing the hatch completely off number two hold.

The ship began to sink at once and the boats were lowered, remaining alongside whilst the situation was examined. Once the upper deck was awash it became obvious that she was going down and the crew pulled clear. The steamer sank a few minutes later.

The master realised that three men were missing and rowed around the area for some time but was unable to find them. One of the boats was leaking, so the master spread out the crew to compensate, and set about rowing towards the shore. They were eventually spotted and picked up by the Italian steamer *Antonio* of Genoa and taken into Weymouth Roads.

The *Hartburn* was logged as "mined".

9/30: VIKHOLMEN. *Country:* Norwegian. *Date sunk:* 10/9/17. *Tons nett:* –. *Tons gross:* 494. *Built:* –. *Type:* SS. *Rig:* –. *Owners:* –. *Cargo:* Coal, Cardiff for St Malo. *Armed:* –. *Position:* 32 miles SW of St Catherines (50 11 00N; 01 52 30W). *Master's name:* –. *Crew:* –.

This vessel was in a convoy with three others, *Gaguiel*, *Nazare* and *Marquise de Luburac*. They were being escorted by the Admiralty trawlers *John Lyons* and *Verbena*.

The information is supplied by a report from the commander of the *John Lyons*, Lieutenant Reuben Hodge.

The convoy left Weymouth Bay at 9.30pm on September 9, 1917, and had arrived off St Albans Head at 12.15am on the 10th, the course then being set for Cherbourg. The convoy was in good formation and no lights were visible apart from dimmed stern lights.

At 2.35am the watch keeper of the *John Lyons*, T. Belton, informed the captain that he had heard a dull thud and had seen red rockets astern. They immediately turned and headed for the area and met up with the other patrol vessel *Verbena* which informed them that the *Vikholmen* had been torpedoed or mined and he had on board six survivors, the master, chief mate and four deck hands. The steamer had sunk in 20 seconds giving the rest of the crew no time to get clear.

The area was searched but no trace was found of a submarine or any mines, but Lieutenant Hodge submitted in his report that he believed the steamer had struck a mine. However, the Admiralty disagreed and suggested that as the *Vikholmen* was third in line and of the shallowest draft in the convoy, the vessels ahead of her would have struck any mines first. Secondly, it was a bright moonlit night, excellent conditions for submarine activities, and in their opinion she was most likely torpedoed. And they recorded her as "torpedoed".

9/31: FLUENT. *Country:* British. *Date sunk:* 20/7/17. *Tons nett:* 2326. *Tons gross:* 3660. *Built:* 1911. *Type:* SS. *Rig:* schooner. *Owners:* J. Westoll, Sunderland. *Cargo:* 6100 tons steel and oats, New York to London. *Armed:* 1 x 12pd 12cwt gun. *Position:* 16 miles S from Anvil Point (50 26 00N; 01 52 00W). *Master's name:* Lewis Hutchinson. *Crew:* 29. *Crew nationality:* All British. *Gunners:* A. Chivers, LS RNR, No 4014 Devonport; J. Maron, LS RNR, No 486 Devonport.

FOR the last leg of her journey *Fluent* sailed out of Plymouth and headed up Channel with her escorts. The weather was particularly good, fair with light winds and a slight sea. The journey went without incident until 8.10pm.

It was described as a loud, violent explosion and the master immediately ordered the engines to be shut down to see how the ship reacted. As the eight knots fell off it soon became very apparent that she was going to sink quickly. She was beginning to settle down noticeably by the stern within minutes.

At the muster by the lifeboats it was discovered that two men had been injured by the explosion, T. Adams the ship's cook and George Bull the chief steward. All the crew including the injured men got away safely in the ship's boats and were picked up almost immediately by one of their escort vessels *Lord Stanhope*.

The *Fluent*, hung on for 40 minutes before sinking. The master was of the firm opinion that his ship had struck a mine as the explosion occurred directly under the keel of the steamer. It was also considered highly likely that any torpedo would have been spotted in the calm conditions. However, UC-65 later claimed to have sunk her with a torpedo.

9/32: HAZELWOOD. *Country:* British. *Date sunk:* 18/10/17. *Tons nett:* 2002. *Tons gross:* 3120. *Built:* 1904. *Type:* SS. *Rig:* –. *Owners:* Gascony Steamship Co Ltd, 29, Gt Helens, London. *Cargo:* Coal. *Armed:* Yes. *Position:* 8 miles E ½ E of Anvil Point (50 29 00N; 01 51 00W). *Master's name:* J.F. Anderson. *Crew:* 32.

OWING to the fact that all the 32 crew lost their lives on this vessel there is very little information in Admiralty records concerning her sinking.

She left Newcastle on October 14, 1917, and nothing more was heard from her until 10.30pm on the 18th when she reported by wireless that she had sighted an enemy submarine in position 50 31 00N; 01 47 00W. At half past midnight the steamer *Etonian* was close to this position and the master claimed he heard shouts from the water. It was a dark night and he was unable to see anything and thought it wise not to stop for fear of being attacked. About 10 minutes later he spotted a suspicious looking vessel off his starboard bow, very close with no lights and he immediately turned his helm to bring it astern as he fled zig-zagging.

Portsmouth Naval Base reported receiving the message from *Hazelwood* and immediately dispatched two patrol vessels to the area. They also reported receiving the message from *Etonian* which read 'vessel sunk at 50 29 00N; 01 51 00W.' A patrol vessel was subsequently sent to this position but nothing was found immediately in either areas. However, the next day the Drifter 237 *Tessie* picked up a bag containing *Hazelwood's* ship's papers at position 50 28 10N; 01 47 00W and later still the body of the steward was found close to the same spot.

The position given in the specification is where the *Etonian* heard the men's cries and a wreck has been found near this position by amateur divers.

9/33: BARON GARIOCH. *Country:* British.
Date sunk: 28/10/17. *Tons nett:* –. *Tons gross:*
1831. *Built:* West Hartlepool in 1895. *Type:* SS.
Rig: schooner. *Owners:* H. Hogarth & Sons,
Glasgow. *Cargo:* Water ballast, Calais for
Liverpool. *Armed:* 1 x 13pdr anti aircraft gun.
Position: 5 miles SE from Anvil Point (50 33 00N;
01 50 30W). *Master's name:* Laurence Leask.
Crew: 23. *Crew nationality:* 22 British,
1 American. *Gunners:* Herbert Horsley, AB RNVR,
(killed); Norman J. Law, LS AB RNVR, No
LZ5836. (killed).

BARON GARIOCH should have been zig-zagging but she wasn't. The master would later have to explain to the Admiralty why he had decided not to.

She left Calais on October 16, 1917, crossed the Channel and was making her way down the coast. Her route was to take her round the Lizard and up the west side to Liverpool. At 8.20am on the 28th the master was below having breakfast leaving the second mate in charge of the bridge. He had barely started to eat when a mighty explosion boomed out from the port side of the ship. The master immediately ran on deck and found his ship in a bad way. The main mast had gone, the aft part of the ship by number three hold was missing and she was settling by the stern very rapidly. The gun was deserted as the gunners had been blown overboard by the explosion.

The crew managed to get clear of the ship in the starboard lifeboat but one man, a fireman, appeared on the deck of the sinking steamer. His shipmates urged him to jump into the sea and they would pick him up, but he froze in panic and disappeared as the ship sank. After 20 minutes a patrol drifter arrived and took the survivors to Poole.

When asked why he wasn't zig-zagging by the naval authorities the master said that he had just passed a naval destroyer and several patrol trawlers and assumed with their presence around it would be quite safe to take a straight course. He was cautioned by the Admiralty against making such dangerous assumptions in the future.

UC-63 claimed this sinking

9/34: CLAN MACVEY. *Country:* British.
Date sunk: 8/8/18. *Tons nett:* 3710. *Tons gross:*
5817. *Built:* 1918. *Type:* SS. *Rig:* –. *Owners:*
Cayzer, Irvine & Co Ltd (Clan Line Steamers Ltd).
Cargo: 10,000 tons coal, Newcastle to Port Said.
Armed: 1 x 4in, 1 x 15pdr guns. *Position:* 7 miles E
by S of Poole Harbour entrance (50 39 30N;
01 46 30W). *Master's name:* Richard Cardoc Jones.
Crew: 55.

THIS loss of this fine new ship on her maiden voyage was almost over-shadowed by the row between the naval officer who went to her assistance and the master of the Clan Macvey. A court of enquiry followed.

Clan Macvey loaded with coal at Newcastle. She was to take the inshore coastal route down the Channel and call in at Falmouth before proceeding further. She crossed Poole Bay and at 7.50am on August 8, 1918, was half a mile off Anvil Point. The officer of the watch on the bridge suddenly spotted the periscope of a submarine a few hundred yards off the port beam. He immediately ordered the helm hard to port but a few seconds later a torpedo crashed into the vessel's midships and blew a hole about 80ft long. The master ordered the ship to be abandoned and within a few minutes all but seven of the crew, who were killed in the stokehold by the explosion, pulled clear.

Two miles to the south of her was the patrol trawler *Arthur Cavanagh* commanded by a Lieutenant Irvine, who immediately went to the steamer's assistance. When he got there he found that the ship was totally abandoned. He approached the master's boat and the master told him that the *Clan Macvey* would float for days. Lieutenant Irvine then suggested to him that he and some of his crew should go back on board to assist with tow lines and they would attempt to get her into the shallows. This the master refused to do.

Tow lines were made fast by the crew of the *Arthur Cavanagh* and on being joined by another patrol vessel, *Vera Grace*, they tried to pull the steamer round. The tide swept them past Swanage where Lieutenant Irvine had originally hoped to pull her in, but they managed to get her just inside Poole Bay. The biggest problem was that *Clan Macvey's* helm had been left hard to port and at every attempt to tow her with any power she would sheer off. Once more the master was asked if he would go back to his ship and suggested that if he did no more than put the helm amidships he would be doing well. But again he refused, merely adding that perhaps it should be towed by the stern.

At 10.30am two tugs arrived and took control of the stricken steamer. The *Arthur Cavanagh* was now free of the steamer but still had the master and crew on board. Once again Lieutenant Irvine asked the master if he would like to go back to his ship. He again declined but then added that he would like to be dropped off at Portsmouth. Lieutenant Irvine informed him that he would take him to Weymouth if he got permission from the Admiral and proceeded towards Anvil Point. With this the master became hysterical and in tears demanded to be put ashore at Swanage. He added that the submarine was lurking off the point and that he and his crew's safety were now in the lieutenant's hands.

Lieutenant Irvine by this time had had enough and said to the master, "Shut up that damn row or you will have your crew as bad as yourself." The lieutenant decided that perhaps it would be a good idea to get rid of him and promptly headed for

Swanage. When they reached Swanage the master then refused to get into the boat and demanded to be taken to Portsmouth. Lieutenant Irvine approached the master and told him, that if he didn't get into the boat he would personally put him in it. Eventually the master went but as he left, his parting shot was to shout at the naval men that they were "a rotten load of bastards."

Meanwhile, the two tugs *Vulcan* and *Pilot* were struggling with the crippled steamer and could only make very slow headway. She became more and more unmanageable until, at 12.10pm the next morning, her back suddenly broke and she sank amidships up to the bridge deck. The two ends of her were well clear of the water but she was in only seven fathoms of water. The wreck was a serious hazard to shipping and later she was blown up.

Cayzer, Irvine & Co, complained to the Admiralty about Lieutenant Irvine's treatment of their ship and master. However, the enquiry found, in general, that his actions were well justified.

UB-57 was the submarine involved.

9/35: ALBERDINA. *Country:* Dutch.
Date sunk: 26/2/17. *Tons nett:* –. *Tons gross:* 134.
Built: –. *Type:* SV. *Rig:* –. *Owners:* –. *Cargo:* In ballast, Havre for Teignmouth. *Armed:* No.
Position: 30 miles SW of Isle of Wight (50 13 00N; 01 46 00W). *Master's name:* –.

THERE is not a great deal of information on this sinking but the circumstances follow a familiar pattern.

She was making her way across the Channel when she was held up by a German submarine, which, after firing several shells at the *Alberdina*, shouted for the crew to leave her immediately. Once clear, a German sailor went on board and placed a bomb which exploded a few minutes after he left.

9/36: LUXOR. *Country:* British.
Date sunk: 19/3/18. *Tons nett:* 2195. *Tons gross:* 3571. *Built:* 1918. *Type:* SS. *Rig:* –. *Owners:* I. Moss & Co, Liverpool. *Cargo:* In ballast, Cherbourg for Barry. *Armed:* 1 x 4in quick fire gun.
Position: 18 miles SSE from Anvil Point (50 20 00N; 01 44 30W). *Master's name:* Robert Greenlees Muir. *Crew:* 40. *Crew nationality:* 36 British, 4 others. *Gunners:* Joseph Smith, AB RNVR, No BZ5302; George J. Godfrey, LS RFR, No 224551 Chatham; William R. Granger, AB RNVR, No BZ5734 Devonport.

GETTING the *Luxor* away from Cherbourg on March 18, 1918, turned into a complete fiasco. The master stated that the sailing time for the convoy was 8.15pm. The pilot boarded the *Luxor* at 7.45pm and ordered the vessel to weigh her anchor and follow the passing escort trawler. Other steamships should have been ready but they were not. When the escort trawler commander approached the Norwegian steamer *Jyler* and told the crew to get under way, he was told that the master and first mate were still ashore.

At around 9pm the convoy did get under way but included in the convoy was a tug which was towing a French schooner. The *Luxor* had suddenly become the lead ship and the master later complained that he was forced on numerous occasions to slow down and wait for the tug which was making little more than six knots.

At 2.10am on March 19, the first mate was on watch and somehow managed to hear what he thought was a torpedo running through the water. He looked around and sure enough spotted the white wake of a torpedo about 500yds off heading straight towards the *Luxor*. He immediately ordered the helm hard to port but the ship didn't respond quickly enough and the torpedo slammed into the starboard side.

It was all over in three minutes, but all the crew managed to get away in the boats. The escorting trawlers *Sea Monarch* and *Aerial II* were on the scene very rapidly and soon had the men out of the boats and safely on board. Both escorts then made a series of searches for the submarine and at one stage, *Aerial II's* commander reported that he had spotted the submarine and dropped two depth charges on it. He claimed that the second charge had seriously damaged the submarine but a later enquiry took the view that the submarine was probably only slightly damaged. The crew of the *Luxor* were later landed at Weymouth.

The master was not a happy man. His ship was new and he felt very bitter about the organisation at Cherbourg. He complained to the naval authorities that the tug should never have been part of such a convoy and that if he could have maintained a reasonable speed he felt that he might not have been sunk. The Admiralty agreed with him and consequently quite an international rumpus followed.

UB-57 was the submarine responsible for the sinking.

9/37: VENEZUELA. *Country:* French.
Date sunk: 14/3/18. *Tons nett:* 401. *Tons gross:* 733. *Built:* Glasgow in 1906. *Type:* SS. *Rig:* schooner. *Owners:* Societe Navigation Havraise, Havre, France. *Cargo:* 592 tons coal. *Armed:* 1 x 90mm French gun. No 840. *Position:* 9 miles E of Durlston Head (50 35 48N; 01 43 12W). *Master's name:* M. Callac. *Crew:* 28.

THE story of the *Venezuela* is an unusual one, not in the manner by which she was lost but how she disappeared without hardly any record.

She was built by Bow, McLachlan & Co at Paisley, Glasgow, and launched in 1906, although Lloyds list her as 1907. She was sold as new to Hermanos Dodero of Montevideo, Argentina. In 1918 she was sold into French ownership and was employed on the coal run from Wales to France.

Her last voyage began on March 12, 1918, at Swansea where she was loaded with coal. She called in at Falmouth for sailing instructions and then continued on her way up the Channel. This was the last time that *Venezuela* was seen and she was posted as missing.

Some clues as to her whereabouts were found when two bodies were washed ashore at Bembridge and Sandown, Isle of Wight, both wearing lifebelts marked *Venezuela* and her papers were discovered in a drawer floating in Bournemouth Bay. Nothing more was known until 1984 when amateur divers from the Swindon branch of the British Sub-Aqua Club located the wreck and discovered her name in bronze letters across the stern.

Further research revealed that the *Venezuela*, whilst crossing Bournemouth Bay in the early hours of March 14, had been attacked by the German submarine *UB-59* commanded by the U-boat ace, Erwin Wassner. Wassner's log recorded that he released two torpedoes at the steamer and although he couldn't positively identify her, there can be little doubt that it was *Venezuela*.

Since the positive identification of the wreck, the 90mm gun has been raised by Swindon BSAC and has been treated, preserved and placed on display in their clubhouse. They are also salvors in possession of the wreck.

9/38: EASTERN BELLE. *Country:* British.
Date sunk: 1/4/17. *Tons nett:* 79. *Tons gross:* 160. *Built:* Ipswich in 1883. *Type:* SV. *Rig:* ketch. *Owners:* H.W. Richards, Portsmouth. *Cargo:* 155 tons pitch from Harvey Stamshaw to Cherbourg. *Armed:* No. *Position:* 30 miles SW of St Catherines (50 09 00N; 01 42 00W). *Master's name:* Thomas William Jarrett, 7, Augerstem Rd, Portsmouth. *Crew:* 3.

IT was typical British spring weather with rain one minute, sunshine the next and then snow squalls. Throughout the night of the March 31, 1917, the *Eastern Belle* had been virtually becalmed. Sometimes the wind would get up enough to make a little headway but then die off as quickly as it came. The next morning at around 10am the mate shouted down to the master, "Come up skipper, there's a submarine."

The master hurried on deck to see that there was indeed a submarine about two miles off heading directly for them. Within a few minutes the submarine opened fire with her deck gun and shells were dropping into the water all around the sailing ship. The master reckoned it was only a matter of a few more shots before the gunner found the mark, and told his men to quit the ship. They pulled clear and waited to see what would happen.

As the submarine got within a half a mile of the ketch a snow squall set in and the crew lost sight of what was going on. Two loud explosions boomed out followed by several small ones but when the squall cleared nothing was to be seen of either the *Eastern Belle* or the submarine.

The crew pulled for the shore and were later picked up by the patrol ship *Robin II* and taken to Portsmouth.

9/39: ELIZABETH HAMPTON. *Country:* British.
Date sunk: 14/5/17. *Tons nett:* 77. *Tons gross:* 170. *Built:* Shoreham in 1867. *Type:* SV. *Rig:* schooner. *Owners:* W.H. Robertson, 2, Pierhead Chambers, Cardiff. *Cargo:* 151 tons coal from P.Rochard Cardiff to Carentan. *Armed:* No. *Position:* 25 miles SW of Dunnose Point I.O.W (50 20 00N; 01 41 00W). *Master's name:* Stephen William Bate. *Crew:* 4.

ELIZABETH HAMPTON had been having a tough time of it in the last few weeks leading up to her demise. She had been weathered in at Falmouth for nearly a month and wasn't able to leave there until April 28, 1917. She made her way up the Channel towards the Isle of Wight and stayed at St Helens until the weather became moderate enough to cross.

At noon on May 14, she was skipping along quite nicely with all the hands on deck busying themselves with normal routine work. One of the hands who had been posted as a lookout suddenly shouted to the master that he could see something that looked like a broom handle on the starboard bow about 50yds off. The "broom handle" turned into a periscope as the submarine surfaced.

The master told his men to get their belongings together and make a boat ready to leave the ship the instant it became necessary. Meanwhile, the submarine had made a full circle around the ship and approached very closely to the stern. The master decided that this was the moment and ordered his men to pull clear. A sailor from the submarine threw a line to the crew, ordering them to tie off to it and pull themselves alongside. The master was taken aboard for questioning while several German sailors rowed over to the *Elizabeth* to plant bombs and help themselves to various instruments, as well as a basket of provisions.

It was not a very nice parting remark from the German commander as he watched the master rejoin his men in the boat. His exact words according to the master were, "Now get out of it." A few minutes later the crew watched as the bombs on board their boat exploded causing pieces of timber to fly in all directions. Ten minutes later *Elizabeth Hampton* settled down by the stern and disappeared.

The crew rowed for about half an hour to the north-west and then were taken aboard by a British destroyer.

9/40: ALGERIAN. *Country:* British.
Date sunk: 12/1/16. *Tons nett:* –. *Tons gross:* 3837. *Built:* Liverpool in 1896. *Type:* SS. *Rig:* schooner. *Owners:* Ellerman Lines Ltd, 12, Moorgate St, London. *Cargo:* In ballast, Cowes for Avonmouth. *Armed:* No. *Position:* Position: S 48 W (True) Approx 2.5m from Needles (50 38 00N; 01 38 30W). *Master's name:* John Ring. *Crew:* 53.

AT 8.20am on January 12, 1916, the *Algerian* steamed out of Cowes Roads, Isle of Wight and proceeded on her way to Avonmouth. Passing the Shingles Buoy the master gave the order for full away and she was soon up to her top speed of 10 knots. The master decided to go to his chartroom and left the third mate in charge with a sharp warning to keep his eyes open. No sooner had his warning been given when there was a terrific explosion which caused the ship to shudder violently.

The hatch covers from number two hold were blown right off and she appeared to be settling down rapidly. All hands were called and within four minutes everyone had been accounted for at their stations. The master then wisely ordered all the boats away but told them to keep close to the ship while he stayed aboard to survey the situation.

On looking down into number two hold he could see the water was coming in fast and it appeared to him that the ship was holed on both sides. The vessel began to list heavily to port. He quickly looked over the side. The port plates looked all right but the starboard were all buckled and twisted from the main deck to the waterline. The bulkhead between number one and two holds was smashed and he concluded that she wouldn't float long. The master hailed a boat and left the *Algerian*.

A little later the steamer appeared to be stabilising and it began to look as though she might be saved. Admiralty drifters had now joined them, and with some volunteers the master went back aboard *Algerian* to secure towing lines. Slowly she was towed towards the Needles Channel and soon they were joined by the Lighthouse Commissioners vessel *Warden*. All was going well, they were making good headway with the flood tide, and now hoped to get her inside the boom defences at Southampton Water and beached.

When approaching the boom gateway the Admiralty ship *Robina* came alongside the stricken vessel and secured to the *Warden* on the port side. This added drag caused the *Algerian* to sheer off and miss the gateway. The master was not impressed and was even less so when the commander of *Robina* ordered him to drop anchor. He knew that if he did it would put too much strain on his already weakened ship. As the anchor bit bottom his fears were confirmed and water started to pour into number two hold. The crew once again took to the boats and looked on as the *Algerian* sank in 10 fathoms of water.

She is listed as mined by a field laid by *UC-5*.

9/41: BADGER. *Country:* British.

Date sunk: 3/8/16. *Tons nett:* 36. *Tons gross:* 89. *Built:* Glasgow in 1894. *Type:* SS. *Rig:* smack. *Owners:* Thomas Harvey, Hamshaw Chemical Works, Portsmouth. *Cargo:* 90 tons coal tar shipped by the Gas Co, Jersey. *Armed:* No. *Position:* 25 miles NE of Cape la Hague (50 06 00N; 01 38 00W). *Master's name:* Arthur George Mathews. *Crew:* 5.

HAVING been stopped by a German submarine and had bombs planted on board her, the crew of the *Badger* were told that they had six minutes to get clear.

Six minutes later they watched from a distance as the decks heaved upwards and pieces of their ship splashed into the water in all directions. However, she didn't sink. The master and crew looked around to see if the submarine had gone and saw that it was lurking about half a mile away. She came back towards the shattered ship and fired several shells into her which finished the job off.

The crew rowed for a while but were eventually spotted by a lookout on the Danish steamer *Halfdan* which picked them up and later handed them over to a patrol boat that was headed for Poole.

UB-18 is believed to be the submarine involved.

9/42: SPHENE. *Country:* British.

Date sunk: 3/8/16. *Tons nett:* 308. *Tons gross:* 740. *Built:* Glasgow in 1902. *Type:* SS. *Rig:* schooner. *Owners:* William Robertson, 45, West Nile St, Glasgow. *Cargo:* In ballast, Honfleur to Newport. *Armed:* No. *Position:* 23 miles SW of St Catherines Point (50 16 00N; 01 38 00W). *Master's name:* Richard Sterling. *Crew:* 13.

AS soon as the *Sphene* left Honfleur a thick fog came down and the master decided to anchor in Havre Roads and wait for it to clear. It lifted an hour later and *Sphene* continued on across the Channel.

At 11.30am on August 3, 1916, the master was in the chartroom when suddenly he heard a loud bang. He ran to the bridge and asked the second mate what it was, but he didn't know. They looked around and spotted movement about two miles away. Looking through binoculars the master could see that it was a submarine in the throes of attacking a sailing vessel. The master realised that the *Sphene* was probably next.

He ordered the helm hard to port immediately to see if he could put some more distance between them but at that moment a shell threw up a column of water a few yards off. It was too accurate for comfort and the master ordered the ship to heave to.

Obeying the commander's order the master and crew boarded the enemy submarine while a German sailor used their boat to plant bombs. It was all over in a few minutes and the crew were left to fend for themselves. They were picked up eventually by two French torpedo boats and taken to Cherbourg.

UB-18 was also concerned in this sinking.

9/43: HMD NEW DAWN. *Country:* British.

Date sunk: 23/3/18. *Tons nett:* –. *Tons gross:* 93. *Built:* –. *Type:* hired drifter. *Rig:* –. *Owners:* Admiralty. *Cargo:* –. *Armed:* Yes. *Position:* 3 miles SW by S half S from Needles (50 37 00N; 01 37 30W). *Master's name:* –. *Crew:* 13. *Crew nationality:* British.

THERE is little information about the sinking of the armed drifter *New Dawn*. The main details come from a report given by the commander of the drifter *Jeannies*, who was with *New Dawn* at the time. Lieutenant Rougvie said that they were sweeping a supposed minefield when suddenly *New Dawn* reported that mines were visible on the surface. *Jeannies* immediately slipped her cable and warned *Unity*, giving her orders to follow on.

Five mines could be seen on the surface and the order was given to open fire on them but it was a flood tide and they only sunk one of the mines before they started to disappear below the surface. It was decided to sweep them and a dan buoy was dropped at the eastern end to mark the start of the sweep.

At 1.30pm *New Dawn* and *Jeannies* started their trawl and managed to get four mines in the sweep but suddenly *New Dawn* struck another mine which exploded. This explosion set off the four mines in the sweep which resulted in utter chaos. *New Dawn* sank within two minutes and boats were sent in to look for survivors. Luckily 10 men were found but sadly the skipper, an engineer and a fireman were lost.

9/44: MYRTLE GROVE. *Country:* British.
Date sunk: 23/11/17. *Tons nett:* 691. *Tons gross:* 2642. *Built:* South Shields in 1894. *Type:* SS. *Rig:* –. *Owners:* Alexander & Main, Glasgow. *Cargo:* 1187 tons Hay, 6 railway wagons. *Armed:* –. *Position:* 13 miles WSW from St Catherines (50 31 00N; 01 37 00W). *Master's name:* –. *Crew:* 28.

THERE is virtually no information among the normal sources on this sinking, probably because she was not the victim of direct hostile action. In Weekly Reports it notes that *Myrtle Grove* was sunk after a collision with the Norwegian steamer *Mineral*. She was badly damaged and began to sink slowly. The Norwegian steamer *Astrea* rendered assistance and tried to tow her into Freshwater Bay but the tow line parted.

A report by a naval officer stated that had she been towed by the stern instead of by the head then he felt she would have been saved. Instead she continued to take on more and more water and eventually sank in the position given.

It was also noted by the authorities that the master of the *Myrtle Grove* abandoned his ship too early as when the patrol vessel *Tessie* went alongside there were Norwegians on board from the *Astrea*.

9/45: ALBION II. *Country:* British.
Date sunk: 13/1/16. *Tons nett:* –. *Tons gross:* 240. *Built:* –. *Type:* hired armed trawler. *Rig:* –. *Owners:* Admiralty. *Cargo:* –. *Armed:* Yes. *Position:* Needles Light bearing NE 1½ miles (50 38 30N; 01 37 00W). *Master's name:* Clark Mead. *Crew:* –. *Crew nationality:* British.

FOUR patrol vessels were assigned to sweep an area of sea to the south-west of the Needles Lighthouse on January 13, 1916. On the day previous the steamer *Algerian* had struck a mine so it was fairly certain that an enemy minefield had recently been laid. *Apley* and *Macaw* were leading the sweep, in what was known at the time as 'echelon' formation. At one stage *Apley's* sweep snagged something on the bottom and her commander was of the opinion that it was either a rock or a mine buried in the mud. However, the sweep suddenly cleared and she continued. Following astern was *Albion II* with her sweeper partner *Zena Dare*. *Albion's* gear needed some adjustment to prevent her sweeps fouling her propeller and whilst this was being sorted out one of the hands thought he saw a mine hiding behind the kite. The sweep wire was immediately veered to clear the mine but the result was that it came free and swung in towards the kite, exploding about five feet from the port side of *Albion*.

A loud explosion boomed out followed by a shock wave that knocked all the crew off their feet, but luckily nobody was injured. Down below the engineer also heard the bang and thought that his boiler had exploded. He rushed forward to check it out but found it still intact. Returning aft he was met with gallons of water rushing up from the port side deck plating and realised that the explosion was external. He checked the area thoroughly and soon spotted a large hole in the ship's bottom as well as the fact that a sea cock had been torn from the side of the ship.

Skipper Clark Mead, ordered all hands on deck and for a boat to be got ready just in case they had to leave in a hurry. The engineer reported to him that she was taking in water rapidly. Already she was well down by the stern, her bows slowly creeping up into the air and the whole vessel was being tossed about by the rough sea. The skipper decided that the best course of action was to get his men to safety and they all headed for the nearby *Zena Dare*. The senior officer on *Macaw* asked for the skipper to join him and they discussed the possibility of getting a line on the *Albion* and taking her in tow. They tried several times but the weather was just too rough. At 12.30pm, nearly an hour after the explosion, *Albion II* disappeared downwards.

After reading the reports on the incident the Admiralty decided on a Court of Enquiry which was held at the Navigation School in the Dockyard at Portsmouth on January 15, 1916. The enquiry didn't go well for the skipper after it was judged that *Apley* had almost certainly dislodged a mine from the seabed which rose up into his path. They concluded that the skipper had made a mistake in not going forward when the mine was spotted which would have brought her sweep directly astern. It could then have been pulled in and any resulting explosion would probably not have injured the ship. It was also decided that more effort should have been made to plug the hole with the use of sails over the side and that a plan should have been made to try and beach her more quickly.

It was also pointed out that it was the feeling of the enquiry that the skipper left his ship prematurely.

There was no record of the skipper receiving any punishment apart from the censure of the enquiry, but that was punishment enough.

The position of the *Albion II* when she sank was rather confused in the documents of the time. The position given in the specification is likely to be the most accurate. Another position given by *Robina*, which arrived on the scene to help, was Needles Light bearing north 17 degrees west and St Catherines bearing south 55 degrees east.

9/46: SERRANA. *Country:* British.
Date sunk: 22/1/18. *Tons nett:* 2342. *Tons gross:* 3677. *Built:* South Shields in 1905. *Type:* SS. *Rig:* schooner. *Owners:* Antilles Shipping Co Ltd, 16, Fenchurch Ave, London. *Cargo:* 1500 tons general from London & Immingham to West Indies. *Armed:* 2 x 7.5in Howitzers, 1 x 4in gun. *Position:* Sand Bar called The Bridge, Needles I.O.W. (50 39 45N; 01 36 30W). *Master's name:* Albert George Maskell. *Crew:* 46. *Crew nationality:* 45 British, 1 Swede, 12 Passengers, 1 Pilot. *Gunners:* William George Petts, L/Cpl. RMLI, No CH17406; Thomas Jennings, Pte. RMLI, No 17876; George Johnson, LS, RNR, No A6488; Malcolm Gillies, AB, RNR, No D2214; George Baker, AB, RNR, No A4227.

WITHIN two weeks the *Serrana* might have been basking in the Caribbean sunshine. The people in Barbados were looking forward to her arrival as she carried 300 tons of general cargo, 87 bags of letters and 25 bags of parcel post. However, it was not to be.

As the *Serrana* passed the Isle of Wight the master and the pilot noticed that it was getting very busy with a number of vessels around. The night was dark and it was considered too dangerous to zig-zag. This was very obliging to Oberleutnant Stöter in *UB-35*. His torpedo struck at 4.35am in the port side amidships. Within a few minutes the ship began to buckle in the centre and the water started to wash across the decks.

The master gave the order to abandon ship, and finding that he was cut off from the boats, took to a raft along with the pilot and a deck hand. Meanwhile, 40 other members of the crew and passengers got away in the boats although two passengers were drowned in the attempt to get clear.

Three men had been killed in the stokehold by the explosion and several others badly injured, mainly by the escaping steam from the ruptured pipes and boilers. Eventually, all the survivors were picked up by two patrol drifters and taken to Poole.

The *Serrana* however did not sink and was found by a patrol ship drifting close to the Needles. The master was informed and he offered to go back to the ship to try and rescue the mail bags and his confidential papers. He stated later in a letter that although he tried to reach the documents he found that the holds were

flooded and he had no way of getting to them.

The patrol boats tried for hours to take the *Serrana* in tow and they did make some progress. Several times hawsers were put on board and each time they were broken by the heavy swell and by the ship's stern rearing high in the air. In the end she went aground on the sand bar called 'The Bridge', where she eventually broke up.

9/47: JEANETTE. *Country:* French.
Date sunk: 6/4/16. *Tons nett:* –. *Tons gross:* 118. *Built:* –. *Type:* SV. *Rig:* lugger. *Owners:* Georges Vidor, Rue de la Siere, Boulogne. *Cargo:* None. *Armed:* No. *Position:* 12 miles WSW of St Catherines Point (50 30 20N; 01 35 30W). *Master's name:* Pierre Monard. *Crew:* 20.

THE fishing vessel *Jeanette* was bound for the rich fishing grounds off the southern coast of Ireland. The weather was fair when she made her crossing of the Channel and at 8.30pm on April 6, 1916, she was off St Catherines Point, just ready to bear away to the west.

As if from nowhere a submarine suddenly appeared close by the starboard side of *Jeanette* and doubled around the stern to come alongside to port. Two German sailors jumped from the submarine onto the fishing vessel and at gunpoint ordered all the crew to take to their boat immediately. Soon afterwards, two explosions boomed out and ten minutes later *Jeanette* had gone to the bottom.

The crew landed themselves in the boats on the south coast of the Isle of Wight.

9/48: KONG GUTTORM. *Country:* Norwegian.
Date sunk: 11/7/18. *Tons nett:* 920. *Tons gross:* 1350. *Built:* 1901. *Type:* SS. *Rig:* schooner. *Owners:* –. *Cargo:* In ballast, Caen for Swansea. *Armed:* –. *Position:* Portland Bill bore NW 30 miles (50 20 00N; 01 35 00W). *Master's name:* Jacobsen. *Crew:* 15.

WHAT caused the loss of this vessel was to prove something of a mystery. The patrol vessels near her at the time and the evidence given by the survivors all pointed towards there being an internal explosion.

The *Kong Guttorm* was crossing the Channel from Caen with the Havre to Weymouth convoy. From Weymouth she was due to continue down the Channel to Swansea. The patrol trawler *Christopher Dixon* led the convoy. Her commander, Lieutenant W.P. Meldrum, stated that at 1pm on July 11, 1918, he noticed that the *Kong Guttorm* and another steamer called *Channel Trader* had dropped behind. At 4pm he signalled to the patrol vessel *Merlin* to turn around and order those two ships to increase speed. Lieutenant Meldrum reduced the speed of the convoy and allowed the two steamers to catch up. At 5.55pm he was below having his tea when there was a huge explosion in the direction of one of the steamers and after rushing on deck he was just in time to see the *Kong Guttorm* sink.

Four survivors were picked up and they were questioned as to what happened. One seaman said he was on the forecastle when the explosion occurred and he immediately came out through the door only to step straight into the sea. The ship had sunk within 30 seconds. Another of the survivors stated that he thought that the ship had broken in half.

After all the evidence was analysed the naval authorities believed that because of the bad weather and the fact that no submarine activity had been reported in the area, it was unlikely that the steamer had been sunk by a torpedo. It was more likely that she had struck a mine or, because she had been carrying gas coal earlier, an internal explosion had taken place in the bunkers.

9/49: AZEMMOUR. *Country:* French.
Date sunk: 20/3/18. *Tons nett:* 750. *Tons gross:* 928. *Built:* –. *Type:* SS. *Rig:* –. *Owners:* Generalle Trans Atlantique. *Cargo:* 716 tons general. *Armed:* 1 x 90mm gun. *Position:* 12 miles W of St Catherines (50 29 00N; 01 35 00W). *Master's name:* Jean Guillaume. *Crew:* 28. *Crew nationality:* All French. *Gunners:* P. Rabbalams, J. Thibaud, J. Jehanno, E. Pontoizeau.

THE master reported that as he made his way down the Channel to Brest he felt the ship shudder as though she had been hit by something, although there was no explosion. The voyage continued and several minutes after the incident a periscope was spotted followed by the whole submarine as it surfaced. The master immediately altered course to head away from the submarine and hoped he could outrun it. It was a gallant attempt but in vain as one minute later a torpedo hit the *Azemmour's* port quarter.

The crew of the *Azemmour* didn't know it at the time but the submarine they had just had the misfortune to meet was *UB-59* commanded by Kapitanleutnant Fritz Wassner. Wassner was an 'ace' commander, responsible for sinking many thousands of tons of shipping. He was also on the British Government's list of war criminals.

The damage to *Azemmour* was severe and the crew immediately took to the boats. At 4.49am, four minutes after the explosion, the steamer went to the bottom.

Help was on hand fairly quickly in the form of the Admiralty yacht *Maid of Honour* which plucked 23 of the crew to safety. Five of the crew went down with the ship.

9/50: FLORENCE LOUISA. *Country:* British.
Date sunk: 17/5/17. *Tons nett:* 95. *Tons gross:* 150. *Built:* Bridgewater in 1876. *Type:* SV. *Rig:* schooner. *Owners:* Arthur Chard & Co, Falmouth, Cornwall. *Cargo:* 190 tons of scrap steel from Paris to the steel works at Briton Ferry. *Armed:* No. *Position:* 7-8 miles S of the Needles (50 32 00N; 01 35 00W). *Master's name:* James Prettyman. *Crew:* 4.

AT 5am on May 17, 1917, the crew of the *Florence Louisa* could just make out a shape of a submarine about one and a half miles off their port bow.

Suddenly a shell whistled across their bows. The helm was put hard down to stop the ship, and the crew made the lifeboat ready for lowering. Another shell cracked past the vessel's topgallant sail and they delayed no longer and got clear of the ship.

He looked for the submarine again but to his amazement it had disappeared. Looking around a broad grin broke across his face as racing towards him was the British Destroyer *Nymphe*. *Nymphe* took the crew on board and cast their little boat adrift in the rush to search for the submarine. For two hours they searched with no success and eventually the four crewmen were put back on board the *Florence Louisa*.

Astonished at his good luck the master got his vessel under way again and even found his lifeboat. He then headed away on a northerly course.

At 12.30pm the wind dropped and left the ship wallowing around off the Isle of Wight. Behind her a submarine appeared on the surface and within a few minutes a voice from it was shouting at the *Florence Louisa* to get the crew in the boats and leave. The crew left their ship for the second time and drifted clear of her. The submarine approached the boat and taking it in tow pulled it alongside the sailing ship. Two German sailors jumped in and quickly set about hanging a bomb in the middle of the hull about six feet below the waterline. They returned to the submarine and pushed the little boat clear, suggesting to the castaways that they would be well advised to get away as quickly as possible.

They took the advice and watched as the bomb exploded, sinking their ship. They were picked up at 3pm by a patrol boat and landed at Ventnor at 5.30pm.

9/51: BORGNY. *Country:* Norwegian.
Date sunk: 26/2/18. *Tons nett:* 1149. *Tons gross:* –. *Built:* –. *Type:* SS. *Rig:* –. *Owners:* Fred Olsen & Co, Oslo. *Cargo:* 1500 tons coal. *Armed:* No. *Position:* 3½ miles S of The Needles (50 36 00N; 01 35 00W). *Master's name:* Ole Anton Hansen. *Crew:* 17. *Crew nationality:* 11 Norwegians, 2 Swedes, 2 Danes, 1 Russian/Finn, 1 Dutch.

THE result of this sinking was an Admiralty blacklisting for the master, for sailing up the Channel with a stern light showing and for failing to comply with his instructions. The master defended his actions and sent a letter to his employers who in turn passed it on to the Admiralty.

He said that he was on passage from Newport to Rouen and had called at Falmouth for his instructions. As ordered, he kept as close to the shore as possible whilst proceeding up Channel. It was a dark night and at one stage he spotted another steamer very close behind in his wake. Fearing a collision and as the rules stated that in such circumstances a dimmed light should be shown, he put a dimmed stern light on.

Between Portland and the Shambles he was hailed by a guard boat and ordered to pass two miles off the Shambles, one mile off Anvil Point and close in around Poole Bay. He obeyed these instructions to the letter but then while heading out to pass round the Isle of Wight he was hit by a torpedo.

There is very little information on the actual sinking of the vessel apart from the fact that she sank in ten minutes.

As for the Admiralty, they relented upon reading the letter and, after checking out his story, withdrew his name from the blacklist.

9/52: MECHANICIAN. *Country:* British. *Date sunk:* 20/1/18. *Tons nett:* –. *Tons gross:* 9044. *Built:* 1900. *Type:* SS. *Rig:* –. *Owners:* Scharente SS Co Ltd, Liverpool. *Cargo:* In ballast, London to New York. *Armed:* Yes. *Position:* At SW end of Shingle Bank near Needles, Isle of Wight (50 40 00N; 01 35 00W). *Master's name:* James Nicholson. *Crew:* 102. *Gunners:* George Henry Wardroper, PO RN, James Ross, OS RNR.

MECHANICIAN was a big ship and was classed as an armed merchant cruiser. She had no cargo on board at the time of her loss but a witness at the subsequent enquiry stated that she had rubble ballast in addition to water ballast. She was bound for Plymouth and from there to America. Her problems began when she was off the Isle of Wight and was torpedoed by a German submarine. The crew said at the enquiry that the submarine had shown herself later close by.

A great deal of effort was made to try and save the *Mechanician*. At the enquiry a letter was submitted by the commander of the naval drifter *Rosebud*. He described how he and two other vessels tried to get the crippled ship under tow and through the Needles Channel to calm water. The weather was rough with a choppy sea, which combined with a large swell near the Needles. Most of the men were taken off, leaving a few to handle the hawsers.

Several times the hawsers broke and one or other of the towing vessels had to run the risk of getting close to the big rolling ship to get fresh lines attached. What they desperately needed was a proper tug but there were none available.

Good progress was made at one stage, but the ship grounded about two and a half cables west by south of the south-west Shingles Buoy. The steamer then swung beam on to the sea and soon after broke her back.

The next problem encountered was how to get the remainder of the crew off. Somehow, they succeeded but a signalman fell to his death when he slipped over the side of a hatchway. Getting the men off was handled by the drifter *Jeannies* and was described in the senior officer's report as one of the most skillful feats of seamanship he had ever witnessed.

The *Mechanician* broke completely that same night and both halves of the vessel came to rest on the inside edge of the Shingle Sands about six cables north-east of the SW Shingles Buoy.

UB-35, commanded by Oberleutnant Kurt Stöter, sank her with two torpedoes.

WORLD WAR ONE
CHANNEL WRECKS

◆

AREA TEN

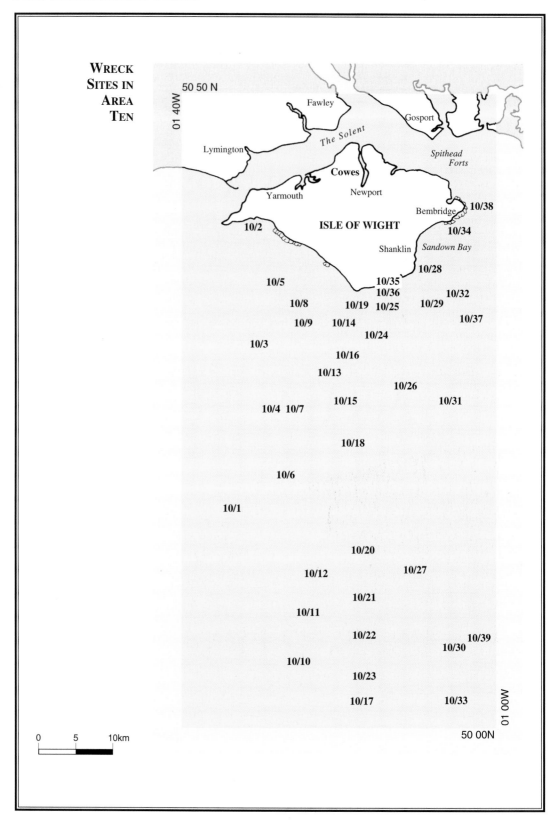

WRECK SITES IN AREA TEN

50 50 N

01 40W

Fawley

Gosport

The Solent

Spithead Forts

Lymington

Cowes

Yarmouth

Newport

Bembridge

10/38

ISLE OF WIGHT

10/2

10/34

Shanklin

Sandown Bay

10/28

10/5

10/35

10/36

10/32

10/8

10/19

10/25

10/29

10/9

10/14

10/37

10/24

10/3

10/16

10/13

10/26

10/4 10/7

10/15

10/31

10/18

10/6

10/1

10/20

10/12

10/27

10/21

10/11

10/22

10/39

10/30

10/10

10/23

10/17

10/33

01 00W

0   5   10km

50 00N

10/1: ROB ROY. *Country:* British.
Date sunk: 26/1/18. *Tons nett:* –. *Tons gross:* 93.
Built: Dalhousie in 1867. *Type:* SV. *Rig:* schooner.
Owners: Mules & Co, Pier Head Chambers,
Cardiff. *Cargo:* 35 tons flint stones as ballast,
Fécamp for Teignmouth. *Armed:* No. *Position:*
20 miles SSW of St Catherines (50 17 00N;
01 34 00W). *Master's name:* Martin Grenfell.
Crew: 5.

AFTER the sinking of this vessel, the naval authorities
noted that the master of the *Rob Roy* did not have a
very clear recollection of what happened which was
attributed to his poor health and his age, being over
70. Consequently, the information about this sinking
was gleaned from the crew.

They were some 20 miles to the south-west of St
Catherines Point at about 4pm, and the first they knew
of any danger was when a shell whistled close by. On
looking around, one of the crew saw the submarine
about a mile off heading straight towards them and
firing continually as it approached.

The master immediately ordered the crew into the
ship's boat and they pulled clear with shells still
crashing into their ship. Once close enough the
submarine stopped the bombardment and shouted for
the boat to come alongside. The commander of the
submarine ordered Able Seaman S. May to board,
and questioned him about the ship's particulars. The
result, however, was inevitable and the Germans
planted enough bombs on the *Rob Roy* to send her to
the bottom.

The crew were eventually picked up by the French
steamer *Lutece*.

10/2: WAR KNIGHT. *Country:* British.
Date sunk: 25/3/18. *Tons nett:* –. *Tons gross:* 7951.
Built: San Francisco, USA, in 1917. *Type:* SS.
Rig: –. *Owners:* Cunard SS Co/British Government.
Charterers: Furness Withy & Co, Billiter St,
London. *Cargo:* Food, ammunition and general
from Philadelphia, via New York. *Armed:* Yes.
Position: Freshwater Bay, Isle of Wight, 500yds
from shore (50 39 55N; 01 31 00W). *Master's
name:* Mr Holroyd. *Crew:* 32.

THE collision between the SS *War Knight* and the
American tanker, *O.B. Jennings*, led to a Court of
Enquiry which was convened aboard HMS *Eclipse*
on April 3, 1918.

At midnight on March 23/24, 1918, 16 ships in
company in eight columns escorted by HMS *Syringa*
and six destroyers, were proceeding on a course N
73 degrees E and carrying out number three zig-
zag. *Syringa* was about 1 mile ahead of the centre
column.

At 0030 March 24, the commanding officer of
Syringa, Maurice B.R. Blackwood RN, heard two
explosions and saw a flash, and thought that a vessel
had been torpedoed about 9-12 miles off. So he

thought he had better alter the course of the convoy to
NNE at about 1.15am. However, some of the vessels
in the convoy did not receive the signal and continued
on the original course of N 73 degrees E.

After altering course to NNE the commanding
officer of *Syringa* made the signal that the course of
the convoy would be altered to S 82 degrees E at
2.15am. Again, some of the ships in the convoy did
not receive this signal, consequently they were broken
into two groups.

The groups were separated by a few miles only,
the southern group being to the south-east of northern
group. The northern group included *Kia Ora* and *War
Knight*. The southern included *O.B. Jennings*, *Mirlo*
and *Aungban*.

In order to keep well clear of the *Kia Ora* and *War
Knight*, *O.B.Jennings* altered course further to the
west. Shortly after this the commanding officer of
O.B. Jennings observed *War Knight* turning to
starboard and, to avoid a collision, put the helm hard
to starboard. However, the *War Knight* struck her
practically at right angles, abreast the bridge on the
starboard side.

The surrounding water immediately burst into
flames, caused by burning naphtha oil pouring out of
a ruptured tank from the hold abaft the bridge on the
Jennings.

After the collision, the *O.B. Jennings* continued in
a circle to port with the little way she maintained.
War Knight remained stopped and burning all over.
The master of the *Jennings* realising the danger,
righted his helm and gave his ship a touch ahead with
the engines, and got clear of the dangerous area.

The destroyers *Garland*, *Pasley*, and *Oberon* carried
out the work of rescue, and saved 39 men of the *O.B.
Jennings* and 11 of the *War Knight*.

On board *War Knight*, many of the crew had died as
the naphtha oil flooded over the decks in sheets of
flames. One young man, an apprentice called Clayton,
carried out his specific fire duty to the letter. As the
flames engulfed the ship he ran immediately to the
ship's magazine and flooded it with water. His prompt
action undoubtedly saved the ship from a massive
explosion which would have certainly killed everyone.
Sadly, Apprentice Clayton died from his injuries, but
modestly remarked from his bed in Portsmouth Royal
Hospital, "I was only doing my duty."

The master of *O.B. Jennings*, George W. Nordston,
was mystified by the action of *War Knight*. He said at
the enquiry that *War Knight* appeared to swing
violently through 90 degrees bringing her bows at
right angles to his ship. Had she kept her previous
course there would have been plenty of room for his
earlier manoeuvre. He put forward the theory that
War Knight's steering must have jammed. However,
this was dismissed as unlikely.

The Court of Enquiry found that the orders issued
by *Syringa*, although justified, were too hurried and
sufficient time was not given to allow the whole
convoy to receive the signals. It was impossible to
say why *War Knight* turned her bows so radically.

The *War Knight* ablaze off Freshwater Bay.

The master and officers on the bridge at the time, were all killed, and 32 men were lost in all.

Later, as the *War Knight* was being towed in by destroyers, she struck a mine laid by *UC-17,* and finally had to be sunk by gunfire off Freshwater Bay, Isle of Wight.

10/3: ELEANOR. *Country:* British.
Date sunk: 12/2/18. *Tons nett:* 1239. *Tons gross:* 1980. *Built:* 1888. *Type:* SS. *Rig:* schooner. *Owners:* Ridley Sons & Co, North Shields. *Cargo:* Government stores. Listed as a mine carrier. *Armed:* 1 x 12pdr gun. *Position:* 9 miles SW by W of St Catherines (50 30 00N; 01 30 00W). *Master's name:* Arthur T. Braine. *Crew:* 36.

THE second officer of *Eleanor,* Barton Hunter, was one of the only two survivors from the crew of 36. As the only officer, he gave the information on the sinking.

He said that they were making their way down the Channel towards Falmouth and from there they were bound for Malta. At 2.04am he was in his bunk and was awakened by a loud explosion. The ship was in a terrible mess, with all the boats blown to pieces and the ship already settling badly. He ran up to the bridge with the intention of firing off a distress rocket but

as he got there another explosion rocked the ship. The next instant he found himself in the sea.

It was a very dark night and he could see nothing but he could hear men shouting for a boat to be sent to them. There was no boat and nothing he could do. He felt something bump into him and to his relief found it was a raft that had been left loose on deck.

After 15 minutes on the raft he could just make out the shape of a vessel slowly approaching him and stop. Still unable to make out what it was he heard a voice shout down to him demanding to know all the details of his ship. The second mate said he answered all the questions correctly as he feared for his life with the bows of the submarine perilously close to him.

At around 6.30am he was spotted and picked up by the steamer *Carronmore* and later taken into Poole by a patrol drifter.

UB-57 was the submarine responsible.

10/4: ESPAGNE. *Country:* Belgian.
Date sunk: 25/12/17. *Tons nett:* 230. *Tons gross:* 1463. *Built:* Antwerp in 1911. *Type:* SS. *Rig:* schooner. *Owners:* –. *Cargo:* In ballast, Havre for Newport. *Armed:* Yes. *Position:* 11 miles SW by S of St Catherines Point (50 25 00N; 01 28 00W). *Master's name:* –. *Crew:* 24.

THE sinking of this vessel happened so rapidly that out of 24 crew members only three people survived. The lamp trimmer, Emile Francois Hintjens, gave brief details of what he could remember.

He said that he was on the bridge at the wheel and it was about 5.30am. They had passed St Catherines Point and were making about nine knots. Suddenly there was an explosion and he found himself covered with wreckage. He struggled for a few moments to free himself and then made for the starboard lifeboat which he found to his horror had disappeared. The next instant he was in the water as the ship sank from beneath him.

He swam around for a while and then noticed a hatch cover floating nearby. From there he spotted three other crew members, a gunner, the mess room steward and a trimmer floating on top of an upturned boat. The four survivors were later picked up by a patrol drifter. On the way into Poole the trimmer died.

UC-71 sank the ship.

10/5: WESTVILLE. *Country:* British.
Date sunk: 31/12/17. *Tons nett:* 2048. *Tons gross:* 3207. *Built:* 1913. *Type:* SS. *Rig:* schooner. *Owners:* Balls & Stansfield, 75, Tyne St, North Shields. *Cargo:* 5200 tons coal. *Armed:* 1 x 12pdr gun. *Position:* 7 miles WNW from St Catherines Light (50 35 00N; 01 28 00W). *Master's name:* George Bell, 84, Wingrove Rd, Newcastle. *Crew:* 30. *Crew nationality:* 19 British, 11 Others. *Gunners:* H. Smart, LS RNR, No 7168A; H. Bush, LS RNVR, No 2162Z.

WESTVILLE left Blythe on December 27, 1917, bound for Blaye near Bordeaux. She steamed down the Channel on December 31, making nine knots and steering north-west by west. The master had the watch on the bridge and the first officer was on the forecastle head. It was a dark night and the ship should not have been showing any lights in accordance with admiralty instructions. However, a lookout had spotted a ship close on the starboard side and the master felt it was dangerous to proceed without some warning and ordered the bow lights to be turned on. This was to cost him dearly.

Suddenly the ship shuddered under a violent explosion from the port side which left a large hole and smashed one of the lifeboats to pieces. She started to list rapidly and the crew scrambled quickly to the remaining boats and got clear. *Westville* capsized and sank within four minutes but luckily all the crew survived.

UB-35 was the submarine responsible.

10/6: INGER. *Country:* Danish.
Date sunk: 11/12/16. *Tons nett:* –. *Tons gross:* 786. *Built:* –. *Type:* SS. *Rig:* –. *Owners:* J. Lauritzen, Copenhagen. *Cargo:* Fruit. *Armed:* No. *Position:* 15 miles SSW from St Catherines Light (50 20 00N; 01 27 00W). *Master's name:* Mads Skou. *Crew:* 15. *Crew nationality:* All Danish.

THE *Inger* left Gandia in Spain on December 1, 1916 and was bound for London. All went well until about 15 miles from St Catherines, Isle of Wight. On Monday December 11, at 1.30pm, she was steering an easterly course, making a steady seven and a half knots and was flying the Danish flag on the ensign staff so as to give no doubt as to her nationality.

One of the watch keepers noticed what he thought to be a submarine on the starboard beam about two miles off heading towards the *Inger*. The master could see that the submarine had hoisted a signal flag but couldn't read what it said, though he had a good idea. He kept full ahead as fast as the ship would go but the submarine fired a shot across the *Inger's* bows. The master was then able to read the signal which read, 'Bring your ship's papers to me.'

He realised he had no choice so ordered the ship to be stopped and a boat to be lowered. He crossed the 100yds gap which separated him from the submarine only to be greeted by an irate German commander who demanded of him, "Why didn't you stop when I signalled?" Captain Skou didn't answer.

The German then examined his papers and said, "You are bound for London?" Skou replied that he was.

"Well I must sink your ship." replied the commander.

Skou protested, "You are not allowed to do that. Fruit is not contraband."

"I call that a luxury cargo," retorted the German.

Captain Skou was becoming desperate and added, "No! It's not luxury."

The German commander began to loose his patience and eyeing Skou coldly said, "It is foodstuff and that is contraband. In any case you are bound for London and I must sink you."

Skou carried on his protest but the German waved him aside and added, "I am very sorry but it is wartime."

Orders were given and some of the German crew went over to the *Inger* and placed three bombs aboard her, one in the engine room, one in the forehold and the other on the port side outboard.

Meanwhile *Inger's* crew were ordered into a boat and Captain Skou was returned to his. He asked the German commander if they could be given a tow nearer the shore but the German shook his head and said: "I cannot do that but St Catherines light is north-north-east 23 miles."

The outboard bomb exploded first and the *Inger* heeled over to port. Then another bomb exploded and the *Inger* started to sink very slowly by the stern. The submarine moved around to her bow and fired seven shots into her fore part. About half an hour later she sank.

The submarine headed off in the direction of another steamer that was about four miles away and left the crew of the *Inger* to row for the shore. They pulled for about three hours in the direction of the coast but were eventually spotted by the Danish steamer *Anna Mirsk*, who hoisted the survivors and their boats on board and headed for Dartmouth. On arrival off the Mewstone they were lowered back down and rowed the last leg into Dartmouth.

The only consolation for Captain Skou was that the German commander had allowed him to keep his own personal chronometer and sextant. A rare act of compassion.

10/7: SOUTH WESTERN *Country:* British. *Date sunk:* 16/3/18. *Tons nett:* 278. *Tons gross:* 687. *Built:* Poplar in 1874. *Type:* SS. *Rig:* schooner. *Owners:* London & SW Railway Co, Dock House, Southampton. *Cargo:* 12½ tons general, 4 passengers, 1 bag of mail, Southampton for St. Malo. *Armed:* 1 x 13pdr mounted on Maxwell frame. *Position:* 11 miles SW of St Catherines (50 25 00N; 01 27 00W). *Master's name:* John Alfred Clark. *Crew:* 30. *Crew nationality:* All British. *Gunners:* James; Hartley.

WINDING along at 10 knots on her zig-zag course the *South Western* made good progress towards St Malo. At 11.30pm the master who was on the bridge spotted a submarine on the surface quite close to him. He immediately ordered the gunners to open fire as soon as they could but the submarine dived before they could get a shot in. A few minutes later the submarine appeared again on the starboard side of the steamer about five cables off and once again the master ordered the gunners to open fire. But they were too late as a torpedo slammed into the side of the ship and destroyed the bridge.

The master was thrown to the deck by the huge surge of water and debris caused by the explosion. He lay there for a few minutes completely dazed and unable to help himself. The rest of the crew were busy launching what lifeboats were still intact. Two were got away aft but capsized almost immediately. The rafts were then thrown over and a few of the men clung to them. By this time the master had come round enough to realise that he must get away from the sinking ship and slipped over the side. He managed to get himself to a raft and was joined there later by the First Mate, Mr Gardner.

There was some criticism later from the Admiralty concerning the two gunners whom they felt did not act with enough haste. They also took a dim view of the fact that the gunners were the first to jump overboard. However, they paid dearly for it as they were both listed as missing. In all only six people survived from the *South Western*.

Although the Admiralty's criticism of the gunners behaviour was probably a just one, it is unlikely the outcome would have been any different. The submarine responsible was *UB-59*, commanded by Kapitanleutnant Erwin Wassner. He was a very experienced U-boat commander and had already

earned his title of 'ace' by sinking over 100,000 tons of shipping.

10/8: INDUTIOMARE. *Country:* Belgian. *Date sunk:* 6/7/17. *Tons nett:* –. *Tons gross:* 2900. *Built:* –. *Type:* SS. *Rig:* –. *Owners:* Bryn & Gyllsen, chartered by Belgian government. *Cargo:* –. *Armed:* 1 x French 90mm field gun. *Position:* 5 miles W of St Catherines (50 34 00N; 01 26 00W). *Master's name:* Alphonse Leenaers. *Crew:* 25. *Crew nationality:* 18 Belgian, 5 Norwegian, 1 Swede, 1 Chilean. *Gunners:* Alfred Duchaine; Gaspar Yelleslagh; Joseph Conteur; Gustave Bol.

SHE left Newport, Wales on July 4, 1917, and called into Falmouth for her sailing instructions, leaving there on the 5th, bound for Havre.

At the time of running into trouble she was steering east by south making eight knots. The master and the second mate were on the bridge and simultaneously spotted the track of a torpedo on the starboard bow about 200yds off. The helm was immediately put hard to starboard but it was far too late and the torpedo smashed into the ship. Following the enormous explosion the ship began to settle rapidly and the crew quickly took to the lifeboats. Within two minutes of getting clear the *Indutiomare* had gone to the bottom. Three men were killed.

The survivors were later picked up by the French steamer *Thisbe* and transferred to HMS *Seahorse*. They were landed at Portsmouth at 3.45pm.

10/9: REDESMERE. *Country:* British. *Date sunk:* 28/10/17. *Tons nett:* 1323. *Tons gross:* 2123. *Built:* 1911. *Type:* SS. *Rig:* schooner. *Owners:* The Brombort SS Co Ltd, Liverpool. *Cargo:* On Admiralty service, 3600 tons coal, Barry to Southampton. *Armed:* 1 x 12pdr gun. *Position:* 6 miles WSW of St Catherines Light (50 32 00N; 01 25 00W). *Master's name:* David Jackson. *Crew:* 25. *Crew nationality:* 24 British, 1 American. *Gunners:* McMillam, LS RNVR; Proctor, AB RNVR.

REDESMERE sailed from Barry Dock on October 24, 1917, and called into Falmouth for orders on the 27th, leaving at noon the same day for Southampton. At 4am on the 28th she was steering east by north making nine knots when there was a huge explosion at the after part of the ship behind the engine room bulkhead in number three hold.

Such was the force of the explosion that the vessel sank in one minute leaving no time for the crew below to escape and consequently 19 men died.

The survivors were literally blown into the water and clung to broken hatch covers and an upturned boat. They were found about five hours later by the naval vessel *P18*.

UB-40 torpedoed her.

10/10: GERMAN SUBMARINE (claimed).
Country: German. *Date believed sunk:* 17/5/17.
Tons nett: –. *Tons gross:* –. *Built:* –. *Type:* –.
Owners: German navy. *Armed:* Yes. *Position:*
30 miles S by W of St Catherines Point (50 05 00N;
01 25 00W). *Master's name:* –. *Crew:* –. *Crew
nationality:* German.

THE information on this incident is taken mainly from
the report of the commanding officer of the special
service ship HMS *Glen*, Lieutenant R.J. Turnbull. He
stated that he left Portland naval base on the morning
of May 17, 1917, to commence his patrol. At 6.30pm
on the same day he heard the report of a gun from
somewhere close by. He immediately gave the orders
for all hands to general quarters and waited to see
what would happen next. Five minutes later another
bang was heard but this time a lookout had spotted
the flash and the commander was able to see the
source, an enemy submarine about two and a half
miles off.

Lieutenant Turnball ordered his ship to stop and
the 'abandon ship' party to get the boat away. It was a
well practiced routine to fool the submarine
commander into thinking that the *Glen*, which looked
like a merchantman from the outside, was being
abandoned and just ripe for sinking. Lieutenant
Turnbull watched as the submarine came closer. She
was of the UB type but he couldn't make out any
distinguishing marks. He could see men on the
conning tower armed with rifles taking the odd shot
but then they disappeared. The submarine slowly got
lower in the water and soon only her periscope was
showing. But she came closer, rounding the stern of
the *Glen*. At 200yds she altered course and to
Lieutenant Turnbull's delight started to surface. He
waited until she was completely on the surface and
shouted the orders to his gunners to open fire.

The first off the mark was the three pounder which
missed but the twelve pounder didn't, the shell
opening up a large hole in the submarine's body just
below the conning tower. A man appeared on the top
of the conning tower just as the next salvo went off.
The shell's impact sent him crashing down the hatch.
Glen's gunners managed to loose off another three
shells before the submarine was put into a crash dive
but as the stern rose high into the air they hit it with
another two shells. The submarine dived but with a
distinct list to port and huge volumes of air and oil
gushed across the surface of the water.

Glen manoeuvred in among the oil and watched.
For half an hour air bubbles and oil rose to the surface
making it pretty certain that the submarine was done
for. Suddenly a shout from the watch pointed to the
top of a conning tower and periscope about 400yds
off on the starboard bow. For a moment the lieutenant
wondered if it was the same submarine but realised
that it couldn't be with so much oil and air still rising
to the surface. He shouted to his gunners, "Fire as
you bear!" Several shots threw up spouts of water
close to it but it dived very quickly. It surfaced

partially again about 600yds off on the port side and
was met with the same welcome. It dived once more
but was not seen again.

The Admiralty looked into the claim by asking for
reports from several of HMS *Glen*'s crew. They all
agreed with their commander and had no doubt in
their mind that the submarine was fatally damaged.
Their Lordships decided that whilst they agreed that it
probably was sunk, and pending further evidence to
prove it, they awarded £300 pounds to the crew as
prize money. Four men were also decorated for their
services in the action.

German records show that this was *UB-18* but,
though damaged, she managed to return to Zeebrugge.

10/11: OIEKAST. *Country:* Norwegian.
Date sunk: 10/12/17. *Tons nett:* –. *Tons gross:* 600.
Built: –. *Type:* SS. *Rig:* –. *Owners:* E.M.
Ebrohronsen, Porsgrund, Norway. *Cargo:* water
ballast, Rouen for Cardiff.. *Armed:* No. *Position:*
About 25 miles N from Cape Barfleur (50 09 00N;
01 24 00W). *Master's name:* Peter Veldussen.
Crew: 14. *Crew nationality:* 2 Danes, 2 Swedes,
4 Spanish, 6 Norwegians.

THE details of this sinking were taken by the State
Police at Guernsey where the 10 survivors landed.

The ship had left Rouen on December 8, 1917. At
noon on the 10th they were steering west-north-west
making six knots when a German submarine came up
behind them very rapidly. Before the master knew
what was happening the submarine fired a shell which
hit the stern house and smashed the lamp room.
Another shot struck the funnel and yet another
knocked the steering gear out.

The master ordered his crew to take to the boats.
He took charge of one boat with nine men and the
second mate took charge of the other boat with three
men. As they pulled clear the submarine continued
the bombardment, causing the steamer to list to port
before slowly sinking.

The boats kept close together for about an hour as
they rowed towards the island of Guernsey but then
lost sight of each other.The master's boat landed at
Rocquaine. Nothing further was heard of the second
mate's boat and it was assumed that it had sunk in
the heavy seas.

10/12: BORGSTEN. *Country:* Norwegian.
Date sunk: 19/12/17. *Tons nett:* 998. *Tons gross:*
1718. *Built:* Oslo in 1913. *Type:* SS. *Rig:* four-
masted. *Owners:* Pette Olsen, Oslo, Norway.
Cargo: None. *Armed:* No. *Position:* Cape Barfleur
bearing S ½ W 30 miles (50 12 00N; 01 23 00W).
Master's name: Sverre Crosby. *Crew:* 22.

THE day before *Borgsten* was lost there was a huge
explosion on the port side. It threw those men in their
bunks to the deck and caused the ship to reel and

shudder. However, by some stroke of luck the ship was unharmed. The master thought at the time that it had been an attempt to torpedo his ship but he couldn't be certain.

The next day at 11.15pm the ship was not so lucky when without warning a torpedo slammed into the same side and practically blew the aft end completely off. Within two minutes the stern was underwater.

Most of the crew made for the lifeboats but the chief mate and a fireman were seen to leap over the side and were drowned. Two boats were lowered and the rest of the crew got clear. Five minutes later a large submarine approached them and demanded that the master should give all his ship's details. The master noted later that the submarine was huge and must have measured 300ft or more.

One boat had no oars so it was taken in tow by the other. By setting a sail and rowing they slowly made headway towards the coast. When about nine miles off St Catherines they were spotted by a patrol vessel and landed safely.

10/13: BRAAT II. *Country:* Norwegian. *Date sunk:* 7/3/18. *Tons nett:* –. *Tons gross:* 1834. *Built:* 1914. *Type:* SS. *Rig:* –. *Owners:* Hermann Jacobsen, Sarpsbourg. *Cargo:* 2780 tons coal, Newport for Rouen. *Armed:* No. *Position:* 7 miles SW by S of St Catherines (50 28 50N; 01 21 02W). *Master's name:* Caspar Greger Solberg. *Crew:* 21. *Crew nationality:* 14 Norwegians, 7 mixed nationality.

THE *Braat II* was passing the Isle of Wight at 5.30am on March 7, 1918. She was making nine knots but was not zig-zagging as she had been ordered to do at Falmouth. The master was about to order a course change which would set him across the Channel to Rouen. At that moment a torpedo slammed into the starboard side of the ship, well below the waterline at the aft end.

The damage was severe and the master immediately ordered the crew to abandon the steamer. Two men were injured in the attack, a seaman and a fireman, but their injuries were only slight.

When asked why he was not zig-zagging the master replied that the night was very dark, the visibility very poor and he was close to land. He felt that it was unsafe to do so until he was further out to sea. There appears to have been no action taken against him.

There were no casualties and all the crew were picked up by the patrol vessel *Willonyx*.

UB-30 was the submarine involved.

10/14: MOLINA. *Country:* Norwegian. *Date sunk:* 22/1/18. *Tons nett:* –. *Tons gross:* 1122. *Built:* 1905. *Type:* SS. *Rig:* –. *Owners:* J. Ringen, Haugesund. Chartered to Furness Withy. *Cargo:* In ballast, Le Havre to Swansea. *Armed:* No. *Position:* 3 miles NE by N of St Catherines (50 32 00N;

01 20 00W). *Master's name:* Roald Larsen. *Crew:* 17. *Crew nationality:* 11 Norwegians, 2 Swedes, 2 Danes, 1 Mexican, 1 American.

MOLINA was part of a convoy that had just crossed the Channel from Havre. They had sighted St Catherines and were coming in close so that they could all peel off and head for their various ports. *Molina* bore away down the Channel for Swansea and was just about to set up a zig-zag routine when there was a tremendous explosion on the port stern quarter. Such was the force of the explosion that most of the stern was blown off.

It was 1.30am, and very dark, the master ordered the ship to be abandoned immediately. The crew pulled clear and 20 minutes later *Molina* went down. They were eventually picked up by a passing steamer and taken to St Helens.

UB-35 torpedoed the *Molina*.

10/15: TWEED. *Country:* British. *Date sunk:* 13/3/18. *Tons nett:* 498. *Tons gross:* 1025. *Built:* 1892. *Type:* SS. *Rig:* schooner. *Owners:* George Sloane, 53, Bothwell St, London. *Cargo:* 600 tons government stores. 1000 drums cresol oil and general, Newhaven to Cherbourg. *Armed:* No. *Position:* 8 miles SW of St Catherines Point (50 25 54N; 01 19 36W). *Master's name:* Archibald McMillan. *Crew:* 20. *Crew nationality:* All British.

TWEED was described in contemporary documents as a passenger and cargo steamer and was on Admiralty service.

It may be of significance that the interviewing officer thought it important to ask how and where the cargo was stowed. He noted that the 1000 drums were stowed in the well deck forward and stacked on their ends, close together. Other cargo is described as cased goods stowed in the alleyways aft. What was in the cases wasn't stated but it was almost certainly stores of some description for the war effort. Perhaps the officer knew that salvage attempts would be made in view of the nature of the cargo.

Tweed was part of a convoy heading to Cherbourg on the night of March 12, 1918, making just over seven knots and had only her stern light switched on. Not much of a give away but enough for Kapitanleutnant Erwin Wassner in *UB-59* who had spent most of the night on the surface re-charging batteries. At 0.45am he spotted the convoy and picked out the *Tweed* as his most likely target with a lot of her cargo on deck clearly visible. One torpedo was enough, striking the port side just behind the engine room. She began to sink very quickly, in fact within three minutes only her bows were visible.

The survivors escaped in number four lifeboat and 13 were later picked up by the patrol trawler *Willonyx* which landed them at Portsmouth. Four of the crew were killed by the explosion and three more died trapped below decks when the ship sank.

10/16: LONDONIER. *Country:* Belgian.
Date sunk: 13/3/18. *Tons nett:* –. *Tons gross:* 1846.
Built: 1911. *Type:* SS. *Rig:* –. *Owners:* Royal
Lloyds Belgique. *Cargo:* In ballast. *Armed:* 1 x
12pdr gun. *Position:* 4½ miles S by W from
St Catherines (50 29 58N; 01 19 16W). *Master's
name:* S. Degryse. *Crew:* 37.

LONDONIER sailed from Calais and was bound for
the Bristol Channel. She was torpedoed when off St
Catherines Point. There were some questions
afterwards as to why she wasn't zig-zagging but no
record of the master's reply to the charge. In fact,
there was hardly any information at all recorded on
the Submarine Attack form. Twelve men were
reported missing. *UC-71* was the submarine involved.

10/17: ALINE MONTREUIL. *Country:* French.
Date sunk: 21/9/17. *Tons nett:* 955. *Tons
gross:* 1624. *Built:* Sunderland in 1900. *Type:* SS.
Rig: schooner. *Owners:* Montreuil & Co. *Cargo:* In
ballast, Rouen for Swansea. *Armed:* 2 x 90mm
guns. *Position:* 20 miles N of Cape Barfleur
(50 02 00N; 01 18 00W). *Master's name:* Auguste
Mette. *Crew:* 31. *Crew nationality:* All French.

ALINE MONTREUIL was part of a convoy crossing
the Channel in heavy seas in the early hours of the
morning. The master was on the bridge when the ship
was struck by a torpedo on the port side between
number two hold and the boiler room. The explosion
was so severe that it almost blew the ship in half and
she sank in 90 seconds. The master only had time to
get out of the bridge and step into the water as the
ship sank away beneath him.

A raft was carried loose on deck for just such an
emergency but only seven of the crew managed to
climb on it. Out of 31 people only two sailors, two
firemen, a steward, the boy and the master survived.

They were in a bad way in the heavy seas and it
was all they could do to hang on to the raft. Some of
the crew said that they saw the submarine responsible
for their plight pass over the wreck site and then
headed north partially submerged. At day break they
hoisted a handkerchief in the air on a plank of wood
and hoped someone would spot them. Help came at
noon when the destroyer HMS *Llewellyn* picked them
up and took them into Portsmouth the same evening.

10/18: MENDI. *Country:* British.
Date sunk: 21/2/17. *Tons nett:* –. *Tons gross:* 4230.
Built: 1905 in Glasgow. *Type:* SS. *Rig:* schooner.
Owners: British and African Steam Navigation
Company. *Cargo:* Requisitioned as army transport:
806 officers and men of the South African Native
Labour battalion, Cape Town to Le Havre.
Armed: Yes. *Position:* 12 miles S of St Catherines
(50 22 30N; 01 18 00W). *Master's name:* Henry
Yardley. *Crew:* 88. *Crew nationality:* British.

THE only information in Admiralty local records is a
report by the commanding officer of the naval patrol
vessel HMT *Grenadier*.

It stated: "At 0208 received a message to resume
patrol. At 0700 received a signal to assist a sinking
steamer 12 miles south of St Catherines. Dense fog.
Proceeded with all possible despatch, course various.
At 0815 spoke with topsail schooner the *Sydney of
Kinsale* from Cork to Portsmouth, who reported
hearing cries at 0600 to the southward. Steered to the
south. At 0830 sighted wreckage, bunker hatches,
spars etc. 0835 sighted bodies of negroes dressed in
military uniform, floating with the aid of lifebelts. A
considerable number hanging onto tank rafts. The
majority had their heads underwater, their lifebelts
were made fast too low around their bodies about the
middle. Searched thoroughly but on investigation
there was not a live person amongst them.

"I estimate there were from 300 to 400 bodies.
Amongst them were five white men, two of them
apparently stewards, had their heads above water and
well back and arms outstretched as if they had been
swimming on their backs. Hauled them aboard and
found they were dead, no papers of identification on
them. In searching found the body of the ship's fourth
officer, with papers on him indicating that he was
William Windsor Small. The address on the letter from
his mother, The Haven, 4, Clarendon, Egremont,
Cheshire, England. His head was under the water, chin
on chest, one sea boot off, hands tightly clenched.
Found one upturned boat. Righted it and took it in tow.

"Then sighted a large raft with three negroes lying
on it. One was perfectly naked, with the exception of
a singlet. They were dead. Picked up two lifebuoys
with the name *Mendi* of Liverpool painted on. There
was no name on the boat. Also found a binocular box
as used on the bridge. The binoculars were inside with
the name *Mendi* engraved on them.

"Whilst searching we heard the whistle of a
steamer, indicating she was stopped. We attempted
to close on her but failed to discover her direction,
she continually shifting position. At 0030 commenced
to return to St Helens steering north-east".

In fact, *Mendi* was in collision with the 11,493-ton
liner *Darro* in thick fog. six hundred and fifty six men
were lost, including 31 of the crew of the *Mendi*.
Others were saved by escort destroyer boats.

10/19: ORIFLAMME. *Country:* British.
Date sunk: 25/11/17. *Tons nett:* 2424. *Tons gross:*
3764. *Built:* 1899. *Type:* SS. *Rig:* tanker. *Owners:*
Lane & Macandrew. *Cargo:* 5000 tons benzine in
bulk, from New York to Havre. *Armed:* 1 x 4.7in
quick fire gun. *Position:* 9 miles S of Nab
(50 33 23N; 01 17 43W). *Master's name:* –. *Crew:*
40, plus some passengers and 1 signalman.

AFTER striking a mine at 5.45am on November 25,
1917, *Oriflamme*, although badly damaged was still
afloat. However, it was the distress rocket that was

fired which caused the problems. The explosion from the mine had caused one of benzine tanks to burst and the flames from the rocket ignited it. As flames started to spread around the deck the master had no alternative but to abandon ship.

The head count at the boat muster revealed that one man was missing. However, it was considered too dangerous to mount a search for him. What nobody on board realised was that the man was below but unconscious from the blast of the mine.

A patrol trawler soon arrived on the scene and after successfully getting a line on *Oriflamme*, managed to tow her into Sandown Bay. By then the fire had died out and men were able to get back on board her. The missing man was soon found, although still unconscious, and taken to Portsmouth Hospital.

The records are unclear about exactly what happened next but suggest that *Oriflamme* broke away from the tow and eventually capsized. She remained afloat but was considered a hazard to navigation and was sunk by gunfire from a patrol boat.

10/20: PHANTOM. *Country:* British.
Date sunk: 8/6/17. *Tons nett:* –. *Tons gross:* 251.
Built: Salcombe in 1867. *Type:* SV. *Rig:*
barquentine. *Owners:* The Plisson Steam
Navigation Co, Cambrian Buildings, Cardiff.
Cargo: 418 tons coal from E.T. Aguis Ltd, Cardiff
to Henry de la Houssaye, Fecamp. *Armed:* No.
Position: 20 miles S of St Catherines Point
(50 14 00N; 01 17 00W). *Master's name:* David
Roberts. *Crew:* 7. *Crew nationality:* 2 British,
2 Norwegian, 1 Danish, 1 Belgian, 1 Italian.

THE sailing vessel *Phantom* left Cardiff on May 15, 1917, and was bound for France via Falmouth and St Helens. She arrived at St Helens on May 31, and left on June 7, heading on a southerly magnetic course as directed. She picked up the convoy at about 8pm on the same day. At about the same time the wind dropped considerably and she struggled to make headway.

At midnight the course was altered to south-south-east and at 7.30pm the master spoke to a passing torpedo boat. The next day at about 8.15pm the sound of a shot was heard off the starboard quarter and a shell passed over the vessel. The master thought he saw a submarine about one and a half miles off. Taking no chances he ordered the ship's boat to be got ready. As the boat was being lowered the submarine opened fire again and made a direct hit on the *Phantom*. All the crew scrambled into the boat, but as they did so it filled with water, just remaining afloat. They managed to work clear of their sinking vessel while the submarine continued her bombardment. *Phantom* began to settle and sank by the head at 8.40pm. The submarine edged closer as if to check their handiwork and then made off.

The crew were left with their boat completely swamped and continually capsizing. Three men were

lost by exhaustion and drowning. The survivors were picked up at 2.30am the next day by a torpedo boat and taken to shore.

10/21: BARBARA. *Country:* British.
Date sunk: 20/10/16. *Tons nett:* 2444. *Tons gross:*
3740. *Built:* 1897. *Type:* SS. *Rig:* schooner. *Owners:*
Kent Steamship Co Ltd, Billiter St, London.
Cargo: 6000 tons refined sugar, Philadelphia for W.
Hartlepool. *Armed:* No. *Position:* 25 miles S of St
Catherines (50 10 00N; 01 17 00W). *Master's name:*
William Mayne. *Crew:* 32.

HAVING made the journey safely across the Atlantic from Philadelphia it was bad luck that she should run into trouble in the English Channel. The men on the bridge spotted an enemy submarine at about 5pm and a few minutes later the first shell passed close over the bows. The master took the shot as a warning and ordered the engines to be stopped.

The signals flying from the submarine ordered the ship to be abandoned and the master reluctantly gave the order. The crew pulled clear and watched as the submarine poured about 15 shells into the steamer. By 5.20pm she had sunk.

The crew headed for the shore and were picked up a little later by the *Victor de Chavarri* of Spain.

10/22: RIQUETTE. *Country:* French.
Date sunk: 13/11/16. *Tons nett:* 124. *Tons gross:*
250. *Built:*1905. *Type:* SV. *Rig:* schooner.
Owners: Y. Eghes, Paimpol. *Cargo:* In ballast from
Treport to Fowey. *Armed:* No. *Position:* 27 miles S
of Isle of Wight (50 07 00N; 01 17 00W). *Master's
name:* Y. Elks.*Crew:* 7.

RIQUETTE was just about making three knots at 5.10pm on November 13, 1916. The wind was light from the west and the night was dark but clear. Although the crew didn't see her straight away, a submarine had surfaced about 150yds off the *Riquette's* port side. The first the crew knew of her was when a shell went screaming over the rigging.

The submarine got closer to *Riquette* and a German officer shouted to the master to stop his ship and go to him in the ship's boat. With the submarine's deck gun trained on him the master had little choice.

Two German sailors rowed the boat back to *Riquette* armed with two bombs. They planted them quickly and headed off back to the submarine. Within a few minutes the bombs exploded, sending the schooner down almost instantly.

On board the submarine, Captain Elks was questioned by the German commander. He wanted to know all the details of his ship. He also wanted to know if he had any Englishmen on board. Why that should interest him so much he didn't say. After the questioning was over the men were allowed back in their boat and towed behind the submarine for a while.

The German commander even asked Captain Elks if he wanted to go to France or England. They were cast off and picked up later by the Danish steamer *Aurora*. She landed them safely at Deal around 5pm the next day.

Just to confuse matters, another position was reported for this sinking as 50 15 00N; 00 45 00W.

10/23: OLIVINE. *Country:* British.
Date sunk: 4/4/15. *Tons nett:* –. *Tons gross:* 634.
Built: Glasgow in 1902. *Type:* SS. *Rig:* schooner.
Owners: William Robertson, 44, West Nile St, Glasgow. *Cargo:* 751 tons granite, from St Sampsons, Guernsey, to Calais. *Armed:* No.
Position: 30 miles S of St Catherines Point (50 04 00N; 01 17 00W). *Master's name:* Archibald Samuel, 15, Elizabeth St, Glasgow. *Crew:* 12.

"ABANDON ship immediately," was the order in the signal flags which were flying from the conning tower of *U-33* as she approached the *Olivine*. The master and the first mate were on the bridge and heard a voice in good English order them to leave within 10 minutes as the ship was going to be sunk. The master could see the submarine's deck gun trained on them and her crew on deck armed with rifles. He decided he had no choice but to obey and ordered the boats to be lowered.

As the crew pulled clear the voice came again, "Five minutes are up. Look alive and get clear!"

At 5.55pm the submarine fired a torpedo at the abandoned ship but it missed. However, the second one didn't, hitting *Olivine's* starboard side and she sank 90 seconds later stem first.

The crew were picked up and landed at Portsmouth where the master made his statement. The Senior Naval Officer noted on it that he thought the master acted very tamely and made no real effort to save his vessel. The Admiralty then carried out their usual practise in such cases by blacklisting him from commanding any vessel covered under the government war risk insurance scheme. However, Captain Samuel was given the chance to explain his actions. He felt he had no chance of out-running the submarine especially as he was burning bad quality bunker coal. Also, the bridge on *Olivine* was open providing no cover from rifle fire and no other vessel was in sight to assist.

The Admiralty relented and let him off with a warning but first explained the procedure that steamers should adopt when faced with such situations. On sighting a hostile submarine the bows should be turned and the vessel made to head at full speed directly at it, thereby forcing the submarine to dive. The Admiralty claimed that in every case this method had been adopted it had worked and allowed the intended victim to escape.

10/24: ASBORG. *Country:* Norwegian.
Date sunk: 3/1/18. *Tons nett:* 1749. *Tons gross:* 2750. *Built:* Sunderland in 1896. *Type:* SS. *Rig:* schooner. *Owners:* Tho B. Heistein & Sons, Oslo, Norway. *Cargo:* 450 tons steel plates and 3350 tons coal from Furness Withy, Newcastle, to Italian Government, Leghorn. *Armed:* No. *Position:* 3 miles S of St Catherines Point (50 31 10N; 01 15 20W). *Master's name:* Johannes Johannesen. *Crew:* 25. *Crew nationality:* All Norwegian.

AT 3 oclock on the morning of January 3, 1918, the master of the *Asborg* was fast asleep in his bunk. He had left the bridge an hour previously and had passed command of the ship to the first mate. The ship was on her correct course and was set to pass St Catherines Point on the Isle of Wight about three miles off on the starboard bow.

Unknown to those on the *Asborg*, *UC-75*, commanded by Oberleutnant Johann Lohs, was lurking close by. A few minutes later a torpedo smashed into the port side causing the bunker store and the engine room to be laid wide open.

The master woke with a start and rushed on deck. The first mate and some of the crew were already preparing the starboard lifeboat and others were hauling out the gig. The steamer was settling slowly which allowed them plenty of time to get clear. The *Asborg* sank about 35 minutes later. The crew rowed for the shore and landed at St Catherines Point at about 7.30 the same morning. There were no casualties.

10/25: ISLEWORTH. *Country:* British.
Date sunk: 30/4/18. *Tons nett:* 1846. *Tons gross:* 2871. *Built:* 1896. *Type:* SS. *Rig:* –. *Owners:* Watts, Watts & Co, 7, Whittington Ave, London, EC3. *Cargo:* 4200 tons iron ore, Bilbao to Middlesbrough. *Armed:* 1 x 12pdr 12cwt gun. *Position:* 2-3 miles E of St Catherines/3 miles SW of Ventnor Pier (50 33 25N; 01 14 12W). *Master's name:* Robert Kimmond Douglas. *Crew:* 33. *Gunners:* Herbert Hopkins; Harold Swan.

THERE is not a great deal of information on the circumstances of the sinking of the *Isleworth*. She left Spain on April 24, 1918, and was heading up the Channel for Middlesbrough. The instructions she received at Falmouth were to keep close to the land and follow a zig-zag course.

When close to the Isle of Wight she was hit by an enemy torpedo at 1.30pm on April 30. The ship sank almost immediately and out of a total of 33 crew only four survived, the master, third mate and the two gunners.

UC-17 was the submarine concerned.

10/26: DONEGAL. *Country:* British.
Date sunk: 17/4/17. *Tons nett:* –. *Tons gross:* 1885. *Built:* 1904. *Type:* SS. *Rig:* –. *Owners:* Admiralty Transport. Midland Railway Co, Heysham Harbour, Lancs. *Cargo:* 690 wounded soldiers. *Armed:* 1 x

HM Transport *Donegal*, torpedoed while returning to England with wounded soldiers.

13pdr gun. *Position:* 15 miles S by W from Nab LV/19m S from Dean LV (50 27 00N; 01 11 40W). *Master's name:* John Jackson. *Crew:* 69. *Casualties:* 11 crew. No final total of wounded troops also lost.

THIS account is taken from a letter written to the Midland Railway Co by the Master, John Jackson:

"At 2.30pm on April 17, 1917, HM Transport *Donegal*, No G1862, under my command left Havre for Southampton with one medical officer, 639 wounded soldiers and four stretcher bearers. 33 of the wounded were stretcher cases and the remainder able to walk. I sailed under confidential sailing directions from the naval divisional transport officer at Havre and was accompanied by two destroyers as escorts.

"At about 3.30pm I was signalled by my escort and given fresh directions which were promptly obeyed. All went well until 7.43pm when the chief officer drew my attention to the track of a torpedo about 400yds away on our port side, just astern of one of my escorts. I immediately gave the order to the helmsman 'hard to starboard,' in an endeavour to avoid the torpedo. However, it was too late and my ship was struck near the port propeller with the result that the stern was practically blown away and carried with it the 13 pounder gun which had only been mounted the day before. One of the gunners who was standing by it is missing and must have been killed.

"At the time the vessel was struck I was on the bridge as also were the chief and third officers. I immediately gave orders for the boats to be lowered as it was very apparent that the ship was sinking. The weather was fine, a moderate sea and a light north west wind with clear visibility. The chief officer failing to find the carpenter, who I have reason to believe was killed by the explosion, personally saw that all watertight doors were closed. The boats were quickly lowered and got away with the exception of two of the port lifeboats which were smashed by the escort *Jackal* who, on seeing our predicament, hastened alongside to take off the troops and crew. The two port lifeboats could not be loaded and removed so the only alternative was for the *Jackal* to smash the boats as she came alongside. Nobody was injured in this operation.

"The starboard lifeboats had been lowered and got safely away. All buoyant seats were cast adrift ready for floating off and immediately the *Jackal* came alongside the troops were transferred to her, whilst the other escort *Liffey* circled round to protect us from any second attack. The *Jackal* having taken on all she could, which I estimate was over 500, cleared away to take up guard and allow *Liffey* to come alongside for the remainder, which I estimated to be about 30. But before she could close, my vessel, which had been gradually sinking by the stern, gave a list to starboard and began to fill very rapidly, throwing those left on board into the water. She sank at 8.33pm.

I am glad to say however, that most of those left to the last were picked up by the boats of the escorts, our own boats and also by a third destroyer which appeared on the scene whilst I was in the water. I was picked up by the dinghy of the *Jackal* and taken on board. We were all eventually taken to Southampton.

"The casualties to the troops injured in the explosion or missing are, I understand, to be about 26, but do not know definitely. The casualties to the ship's company as far as I can ascertain at present are one sailor, three firemen and a trimmer injured and removed to hospital. 11 are missing some of whom I'm afraid were killed by the explosion whilst in their bunks in the after forecastle. The buoyant seats were of great assistance to those thrown into the water and as two unknown steamers were standing by it is just possible that some of the missing men may yet turn up.

"Although the conduct and behaviour of the whole of the ship's company was excellent, I must specially mention the good service rendered by the Chief Officer, Mr Howlden; the Purser, Mr Ashcroft; the Wireless Operator, Mr Cowley; and the Signaller, W. Marshall; who stood by me on board to the last".

UC-21 was the submarine involved.

10/27: GLYNYMEL. *Country:* British. *Date sunk:* 12/3/17. *Tons nett:* 713. *Tons gross:* 1394. *Built:* 1890. *Type:* SS. *Rig:* schooner. *Owners:* Harris Bros, Swansea, Glamorgan. *Cargo:* In ballast, Havre for Swansea. *Armed:* No. *Position:* Cape Barfleur bearing SW by S 30 miles (50 12 30N; 01 11 00W). *Master's name:* Evan Thomas. *Crew:* 15. *Crew nationality:* 7 British, 8 Greeks.

AN hour after high water on March 11, 1917, *Glynymel* left Rouen and headed down the river. The weather was fine with a moderate breeze and she arrived at Havre Roads at 1.30pm leaving there at 6.30 the same evening for Swansea. At 3.30 the next morning the master was alerted by the sound of gunfire and went on deck to investigate. He immediately spotted an enemy submarine about a mile off heading directly towards him, firing shells as it approached.

The first shot struck the bridge injuring the mate and the second shot went right through the chart house. Another shot penetrated the accommodation and hit the second engineer, Robert Stote, who was killed instantly.

The master ordered her to be stopped and blew his whistle to indicate to the enemy that it was not necessary to continue firing. It worked and the bombardment ceased.

The ship's dingy had been damaged by a shell which left only one boat serviceable. All the crew crammed themselves in and pulled clear of the ship. The night was dark and the master said he couldn't see exactly what happened to the *Glynymel*. The submarine had gone very close to her and fired another 13 shells. They were followed by a dull thud which he assumed to be a torpedo, adding it was at that point *Glynymel* must have sank.

The crew were eventually picked up by the steamer *Farraline* of Leith at 9.30am and transferred to the patrol boat *Wyndham* at 1pm, three miles off the Shambles Light Ship. From there they were taken safely to Weymouth.

The submarine involved was *UC-66*.

10/28: LUIS. *Country:* British. *Date sunk:* 12/4/18. *Tons nett:* 2696. *Tons gross:* 4284. *Built:* 1916. *Type:* SS. *Rig:* schooner. *Owners:* H.C. Nielsen, West Hartlepool. *Cargo:* 6628 tons oil, food, foodstuffs, timber. *Armed:* 1 x 18pdr gun. *Position:* St Catherines bore NNW 4 miles when struck (50 36 28N; 01 09 54W). *Master's name:* Frederick Hemrich, 4, Westoe Parade, South Shields. *Crew:* 37.

LUIS was number 13 in a convoy heading up the Channel. They had just passed St Catherines Point at 10.30 in the evening of April 12, 1918. At that point the convoy wasn't zig-zagging and it was noted that *Luis* was showing a stern light but dimmed right down.

Two torpedoes were fired in rapid succession at *Luis*. The engine room and bunkers on the port side were smashed open.

In the engine room the Fourth Engineer, Mr Jeffries, lay badly injured. Several steam pipes had been ruptured and were spraying scalding steam everywhere. The Second Engineer, Robert Coulson, had also been scalded on his hands and legs but was still mobile. Through sheer determination he managed to carry his colleague up the ladder to safety. It was a gallant act but unfortunately both men later died from their injuries.

The *Luis* didn't sink immediately but remained afloat for two hours. Most of the crew were taken off but a few volunteers stayed behind to assist the master with tow lines. The steamer was eventually towed into Sandown Bay but sank about one mile south of Shanklin Pier.

Four people in total lost their lives in this sinking. For his brave conduct Robert Coulson posthumously received the Albert Medal which was presented to his wife by King George V. This medal was seen recently by viewers of the BBC's Antiques Roadshow where it was proudly shown and explained by his daughter.

UC-71 was the submarine involved.

10/29: POLO. *Country:* British. *Date sunk:* 12/2/18. *Tons nett:* 1127. *Tons gross:* 1906. *Built:* Hull in 1913. *Type:* SS. *Rig:* schooner. *Owners:* Ellerman Wilson Line Ltd, Hull. *Cargo:* 3200 tons general and coals from Hull to Malta and Alexandria. *Armed:* 1 x 4in gun. *Position:* 6 miles E by S of St Catherines (50 33 30N; 01 08 30W). *Master's name:* Tom Hornsby. *Crew:* 33. *Crew nationality:* 24 British, 9 others.

STEAMING down the Channel *Polo* was making a speed of around seven knots. The master and the mate were on the bridge, the lookouts were all in position and the lifeboats were swung out ready for any emergency. It was fortunate that the ship was so well prepared, for at 10.45pm a torpedo smashed into her port side, opening up a huge hole in number two hold.

The ship listed heavily to port and began to fill

rapidly. So severe was the list that only the port boat could be lowered, which was done immediately and 21 people got clear. The master seeing the boat clear went aft to the jolly boat but found it missing. Looking around he could see it was afloat with several men in it. The next instant he was tossed over the rail as the ship gave a violent lurch. Fortunately for him the men in the jolly boat spotted his predicament and plucked him clear. Some of the other men stayed with the starboard boat and as the steamer sank they floated free.

A count of heads revealed that three men were missing and although the area was searched for some time, no trace of them could be found.

After abandoning the jolly boat in favour of the lifeboats the crew set about pulling for the shore. They were picked up later by the patrol Drifters *Egbert* and *Olive Leaf*, and landed at Portsmouth.

10/30: WYNDHURST. *Country:* British. *Date sunk:* 6/12/17. *Tons nett:* 252. *Tons gross:* 570. *Built:* Aberdeen in 1917. *Type:* SS. *Rig:* schooner. *Owners:* Cleeves & Co, Cardiff. *Cargo:* 690 tons coal from Cleeves & Co to Cleeves Jacqueline Co, Rouen. *Armed:* 1 x 12pdr quick fire gun. *Position:* 30 miles due S of St Catherines Point (50 06 00N; 01 06 30W). *Master's name:* Thomas Parr. *Crew:* 14.

WYNDHURST was the first ship in the line of a convoy, accompanied by armed naval escorts, which left St Helens on December 6, 1917. The convoy was steering just west of south on a zig-zag course making seven knots.

The Chief Mate, George Mundle, was on the bridge with a seaman acting as lookout. It was 9pm and the night was dark but the weather fair. Suddenly there was a big explosion on the ship's starboard quarter which literally broke her in two pieces and she sank stern first within 10 seconds. The chief mate said that he was dragged down with the ship but was eventually released from her suction and surfaced. He spotted a raft close by and shouted for any men that might be nearby to swim towards him. Only two men did so, a Spanish fireman and a British seaman. Within 20 minutes one of the escorts, the tug *Great Emperor*, picked them up and landed the three men at Havre.

A naval patrol officer gave a slightly different position for this vessel as 50 07 00N; 01 08 00W.

UC-71 was the submarine concerned.

10/31: FALLODON. *Country:* British. *Date sunk:* 28/12/17. *Tons nett:* 1914. *Tons gross:* 3012. *Built:* 1903. *Type:* SS. *Rig:* schooner. *Owners:* London & Northern SS Co Ltd, Bishopsgate, London. *Cargo:* None. *Armed:* 1 x 12pdr gun. *Position:* St Catherines bearing NW by N 10-12 miles (50 26 00N; 01 06 00W). *Master's name:* Alfred Lodge. *Crew:* 31. *Crew nationality:* 25 British, 6 others.

FALLODON sailed from Havre and was destined for Glasgow. Whilst on her way down the Channel she was struck by a torpedo on the port side which blew a huge hole inwards to the engine room and also a large hole outwards on the other side.

The ship started to settle rapidly but then slowed down and sank completely some 45 minutes later. Thirty of the crew made it clear of the sinking ship but one man, the second engineer, was killed. The survivors were picked up by a French destroyer and later transferred to a British torpedo boat.

This was another victim of *UC-71*.

10/32: HIGHLAND BRIGADE. *Country:* British. *Date sunk:* 7/4/18. *Tons nett:* 3697. *Tons gross:* 5669. *Built:* Govan in 1901. *Type:* SS. *Rig:* schooner. *Owners:* Nelson Line (Liverpool) Ltd, Leadenhall St, London. *Cargo:* 1100 tons general from London to Buenos Aries and Montevideo, 11 bullocks on deck. *Armed:* 1 x 6in gun. *Position:* 5 miles S by E of St Catherines Light when hit (50 34 50N; 01 05 10W). *Master's name:* George Watson. *Crew:* 57. *Gunners:* David Mann, RNR, No B4342; Thomas O'Shea, RNR, No B8775; James Hawkins, PO No B2466.

HIGHLAND BRIGADE was on one of her regular runs to Argentina. Her instructions were to make her way down the Channel to Plymouth and from there to join the convoy for the crossing to South America.

In the early hours of April 7, 1918, *UC-71* fired a torpedo which struck her on the port side in number one hold and tore open a huge hole. The master immediately slowed the ship and asked for a damage report. The engineers reported that number two bilge was making water but not at an alarming rate. The engines were brought up to slow ahead but it was soon evident that her steering gear was badly damaged.

Two hours later the *Highland Brigade* was still afloat although settling further down in the water. A patrol vessel had just arrived in response to the SOS messages sent out on the radio and it was decided to take the steamer in tow. Most of the crew had by this time left her in the boats but the master remained behind with a few volunteers to help with the towing cables. Other vessels soon arrived including two tugs but it was not looking good. The steamer's fore deck was awash and her propeller was out of the water.

At 10am it was obvious that she was sinking and the master with his volunteers cut the tow lines and left her. At 10.30am she sank in 15 fathoms of water.

In the documentation concerning this sinking there is some controversy about the brightness of St Catherines Light. Presumably, it was the master of the *Highland Brigade* who noticed that on a clear night the light radiated out across the water. Passing ships were silhouetted, giving an enemy submarine commander an easy target. It was recommended that the brightness of the light be reduced.

10/33: KINGSDYKE. *Country:* British.
Date sunk: 17/1/18. *Tons nett:* 1066. *Tons gross:*
1710. *Built:* 1888. *Type:* SS. *Rig:* schooner.
Owners: Lowlands SS Co Ltd, Newcastle. *Cargo:*
In ballast, Rouen for Cardiff. *Armed:* Yes. *Position:*
22 miles NNE from Cape Barfleur (50 02 00N;
01 05 00W). *Master's name:* J. Hutton. *Crew:* 21.

EVEN steamers in a convoy were still far from safe
from German submarines. The *Kingsdyke* left Havre in
convoy for Cardiff. The weather was particularly good
being fine, clear and with a light wind blowing from
the south-east.

At 10.20pm *Kingsdyke* received the full force of a
torpedo from *UB-80* in her midships. So violent was
the explosion that it caused the funnel and part of the
bridge to come crashing down on the forecastle head
killing all those who were on the bridge including the
master.

The rest of the crew managed to launch a boat but
when the ship sank in just six minutes, the boat
capsized. Six of the men clung to the upturned boat
for 12 hours until they were rescued by a French torpedo
boat. Many more men had been holding on to it but
had succumbed to the cold and dropped away.
Altogether 16 men from the *Kingsdyke* lost their lives
that night.

10/34: HMS P12. *Country:* British.
Date sunk: 4/11/18. *Tons nett:* –. *Tons gross:* 613.
Built: 1915 by J.S. Whites & Co, Cowes, IOW.
Type: Patrol boat. *Rig:* P-class. *Owners:* Admiralty.
Cargo: –. *Armed:* 1 x 4in gun, 2 torpedo tubes.
Position: ¾ mile SE of Culver Cliff IOW
(50 39 25N; 01 05 00W). *Master's name:* –.
Crew: –. *Crew nationality:* British.

THE records note, in a somewhat disapproving tone,
that the vessel responsible for the sinking of HMS
P12, made no attempt to render assistance and just
continued on her course unescorted.

The vessel in question was the Belgian Transport
SS *Emanuel Nobel*, which was being escorted by *P12*
towards Havre. The records do not state exactly what
happened, but at 9.40pm on November 4, 1918,
somehow *P12* was rammed so violently by the
steamer that it literally cut her in half. The weather
couldn't have helped much and was probably the main
reason for the collision. It was blowing a full gale,
the sea was very rough with rain squalls passing
through from time to time.

Her crew had to abandon her immediately.
Fortunately another patrol vessel, *P16*, came straight
to her aid and got all the men off.

The stern section sank almost instantly after she
was abandoned but the fore part drifted for some while
before sinking in the shallows near Culver Cliff, Isle
of Wight.

10/35: BRIGITTA. *Country:* British.
Date sunk: 4/12/17. *Tons nett:* –. *Tons gross:* 2084.
Built: 1894. *Type:* SS. *Rig:* –. *Owners:* Colonial
Coal Shipping Co. *Cargo:* 2740 tons coal, Barry
for Dieppe. *Armed:* 1 x 18pdr gun. *Position:* 6 miles
SW from Nab (50 35 30N; 01 04 00W). *Master's
name:* –. *Crew:* 29.

BRIGITTA was sunk as the result of hitting a mine.
Naval Weekly Reports contained a brief mention that
she suffered an explosion at 10am on December 4,
1917. Twenty-seven survivors were brought into
Portsmouth but two were missing.

Another small piece of information came from a
naval summary which stated that *Brigitta* had struck a
mine at 9.50am. The explosion was so violent that
the fore part of the ship was completely blown away
and she sank in just four minutes. Two men were lost.

10/36: LEON. *Country:* French. *Date sunk:* 7/1/18.
Tons nett: –. *Tons gross:* 2451. *Built:* Sunderland
in 1895. *Type:* SS. *Rig:* –. *Owners:* Societe des
Houilles Agglomerees, La Rochelle. *Cargo:* 2250
tons coal, 600 tons coke, consigned to Tunis.
Armed: 2 x 90mm canons, model 77. *Position:*
9 miles E of St Catherines (50 35 30N; 01 04 00W).
Master's name: Louis R. Orchambeau. *Crew:* 34.
Crew nationality: 31 French, 1 Haitian,
2 Sengalese. *Gunners:* J. Cavarce; R. Delahaye;
J. Carrieres; A. Le Delic; J. Barence; J. Olliver;
J. Rame. *Casualties:* David Gustav, naval rating,
No 1381, St Nazaire; Lacheur Nantes, naval rating,
No 2093; Abdul El Kater; Amadou Boujoum.

IT was said at the time that the master of *Leon* was
courting disaster by the way he was behaving. He had
no flag flying, wasn't zig-zagging and he had
navigation lights on.

Commanding the German submarine *UC-75* was
Oberleutnant Johann Lohs, who had earned the title of
ace by sinking over 100,000 tons of shipping in his
career. Lohs noted in his log that the *Leon* was
behaving very strangely and for such an experienced
man it was simplicity itself to sink her.

The torpedo struck the *Leon* on the starboard side in
number two hold and blew a large hole in her.
Although taking on water steadily, the ship stayed
afloat for over an hour. The master ordered the crew to
stand by the lifeboats and await his further orders.
Four men decided that they couldn't wait and lowered
a lifeboat while the ship was still moving. The boat
capsized and the men were all lost .

Later the master gave the order to abandon her and
the rest of the crew pulled clear. Shortly after she
sank, a patrol vessel took them to St Helens.

10/37: CAMBERWELL. *Country:* British.
Date sunk: 18/5/17. *Tons nett:* 2589. *Tons
gross:* 4077. *Built:* Sunderland in 1903. *Type:* SS.

Rig: schooner. *Owners:* Well Line Ltd, 21, Moseley St, Newcastle. *Cargo:* 5000 tons general from Middlesbrough and London to Colombo, Madras and Calcutta. *Armed:* 1 x 4.7in gun. *Position:* 6 miles SE of Dunmore Head, Isle of Wight (50 32 30N; 01 03 00W). *Master's name:* Frederick Lincoln Adamson, 39, Neale St, Roker. *Crew:* 65. *Gunners:* W.T. Blacksley, L/Cpl. RMLI No 9740 Chatham; J.H. Such, Pte. RMLI No 14257 Chatham

THE deposition to the interviewing naval officer was given mainly by the Chief Officer of *Camberwell*, Edwin Lane Bush, of 34, Marlborough Street, Seaham Harbour. He was on watch at the time.

He said that they spotted the Owers at 5.15am on the May 18, 1917, and altered course to west by south to pass the Owers about one mile off. At 6am a patrol boat came close and asked for the name of the vessel followed by another 45 minutes later which signalled M.J. meaning 'alter course to port'. When the patrol boat got abeam of the *Camberwell* she asked, "Where bound?" The mate got the third mate to reply in semaphore and received the reply back,"Keep out a bit, there are mines about."

The mate immediately altered course to south-west by west and made sure that all the lookouts were alert. The sky was overcast, a moderate wind was blowing, whipping up a fairly choppy sea. At 7.10am a shout went up; a lookout had spotted a mine. The mate sent for the master who scurried up on deck, "Where's the mine?" he asked. But before a reply could be made, a huge explosion rocked the ship, blowing number one hatch cover clean off, and giving the steamer a heavy list to starboard.

All the crew apart from seven men went to their stations. The seven missing men were below at the time and were either killed by the mine or had drowned. The mate went to the starboard boat which was lowered but the Asiatics in it refused to unhook the falls. The mate reasoned with them that if they didn't do it the consequences would be disastrous for them. He headed off to the forward bridge boat and climbed in. However, there was no need to lower it, the *Camberwell* plunged down sucking the boat with it. The mate and others with him surfaced and were picked up by the master's boat. The starboard boat had managed to get unhooked and they were all floating free. All that remained visible of the *Camberwell* was part of her propeller sticking out of the water.

A destroyer was soon on the scene along with the patrol yacht *Fire Queen* and between them they took all the survivors aboard and carried them into Portsmouth.

10/38: HMS VELOX. *Country:* British. *Date sunk:* 25/10/15. *Tons nett:* –. *Tons gross:* 420. *Built:* 1902. *Type:* Destroyer. *Rig:* C-class with steam turbines. *Owners:* Admiralty. *Cargo:* –. *Armed:* 1 x 12pdr, 5 x 6pdr, 2 torpedo tubes.

Position: Off Nab Light (50 41 30N; 01 02 06W). *Master's name:* Lieutenant F. Pattinson, RNR. *Crew:* 54. *Crew nationality:* British.

THE only information in local records on this sinking comes from a letter written by the commander.

He said they went on day patrol at 7am on Monday October 25, 1915, in the area off Culver and Dunnose. An easterly gale was blowing with a very heavy sea. Shortly before noon the chief engineer reported to him that the condensers had lost suction three times and that to put the problem right the ship should find smoother water.

The captain ordered the *Velox* to be taken towards the Nab End Buoy where they could find relative shelter. At 3.45pm Lieutenant Pattinson was on the bridge with the gunner Mr Wilmore when suddenly there was an explosion aft which was followed almost immediately by another. He looked aft and saw that his cabin, the pantry, the after gun, torpedo tube and the ward room had completely disappeared.

The first lieutenant and chief engineer lay badly injured in the wreckage of the ward room and it was only with great difficulty that they were freed. Two gunners who had been at the after gun and two ward room servants were later unaccounted for, presumed to have been blown over the side.

The commander immediately ordered the boats to be swayed out, distress rockets and blank charges to be fired from the 12 pounder gun in the hope of attracting attention.

It worked as very soon a naval drifter appeared. Lieutenant Pattinson ordered her commander to make for St Helens immediately to bring a doctor. A second drifter arrived within minutes and the wounded were transferred to her. The *Velox* was by then in imminent danger of sinking and 10 men along with the commander remained on board to see if anything could be done to save her. The auxiliary vessel *Conflict* was next on the scene and a line was got on board the stricken ship. The tow was taken up very slowly and some headway made but she was too badly damaged. Shortly after, her stern dropped down, her bows rose up and she heeled over to starboard. The men left on board got off as quickly as they could and as the last man got clear the *Velox* finally settled down and was gone.

Lieutenant Pattinson said later that no submarine was seen or known to be in the vicinity and he was of the opinion that a mine was responsible for the first explosion. This in turn had exploded a depth charge that was placed at the aft end of the ship.

10/39: CLIBURN. *Country:* British. *Date sunk:* 20/10/16. *Tons nett:* 174. *Tons gross:* 440. *Built:* Workington in 1916. *Type:* SS. *Rig:* schooner. *Owners:* Stainburn SS Co Ltd, Station St, Workington. *Cargo:* 493 tons coal shipped from Swansea and consigned to Honfleur. *Armed:* No. *Position:* 30 miles SSE of St Catherines Point (50

07 00N; 01 02 00W). *Master's name:* John Charles Murray. *Crew:* 10.

THE *Cliburn* was steaming along nicely at eight and a half knots until at 4.10pm a shell crashed into the water just ahead of her forcing the master to slow down. After a few minutes a submarine appeared and fired several more shells. However, none hit the steamer.

The master brought the ship to a standstill and gave the order to abandon. The Germans followed the usual pattern at this stage in the war and used the steamer's boat to board the *Cliburn* to plant bombs, one in the engine room and one on the starboard side. Having got their boat back the crew left the submarine and rowed in the direction of the French coast passing their sinking steamer after the bombs exploded.

They were eventually picked up by the Norwegian steamer *Hardrol* and landed at Cardiff later the same day.

Another victim of a torpedo fired from a U-boat

WORLD WAR ONE
CHANNEL WRECKS

◆

AREA
ELEVEN

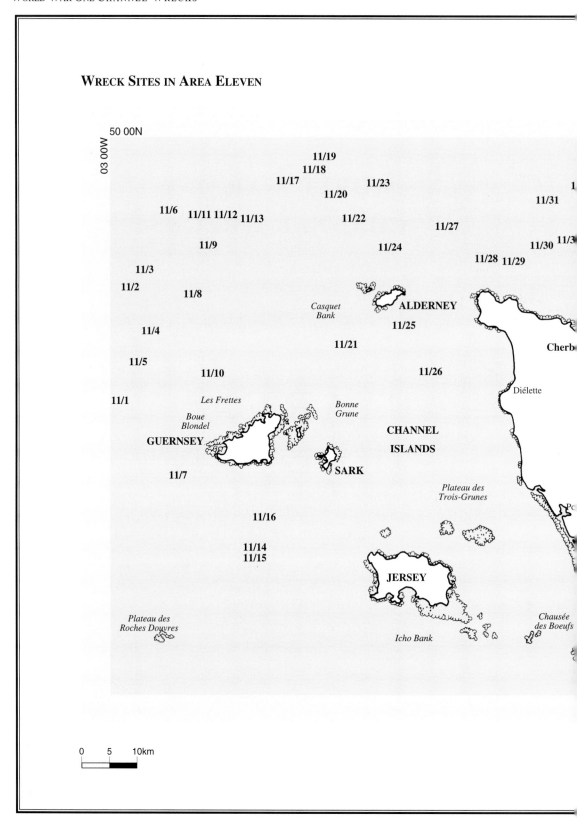

WRECK SITES IN AREA ELEVEN

50 00N
03 00W

11/19
11/18
11/17
11/20
11/23
11/31
11/6
11/11 11/12 11/13
11/22
11/27
11/9
11/24
11/30 11/3
11/3
11/28 11/29
11/2
11/8
Casquet
Bank
ALDERNEY
11/4
11/25
Cherb
11/21
11/5
11/26
11/10
Diélette
11/1
Les Frettes
Bonne
Grune
Boue
Blondel
CHANNEL
GUERNSEY
ISLANDS
11/7
SARK
Plateau des
Trois-Grunes
11/16
Pc
11/14
11/15
JERSEY
Plateau des
Roches Douvres
Chausée
des Boeufs
Icho Bank

0 5 10km

216

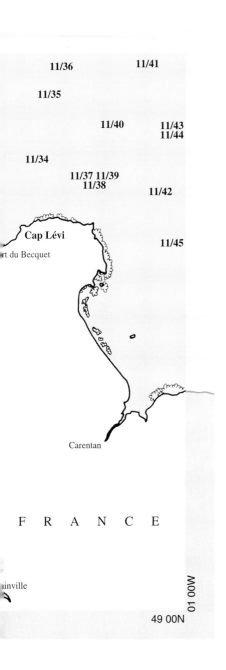

11/36   11/41

11/35

11/40   11/43
11/44

11/34

11/37 11/39
11/38   11/42

Cap Lévi   11/45

rt du Becquet

Carentan

F R A N C E

inville

01 00W

49 00N

11/1: CITY OF WINCHESTER.
Country: British. *Date sunk:* 28/3/18. *Tons nett:* 82.
Tons gross: 275. *Built:* Hull in 1877. *Type:* SV.
Rig: ketch. *Owners:* Channel/Cardiff Shipping Co
Ltd, Cardiff. *Cargo:* In ballast, St. Malo for Cardiff.
Armed: No. *Position:* 10 miles NW by W of Hanois
Light, Guernsey (49 32 00N; 02 57 00W). *Master's
name:* William Henry Organ. *Crew:* 3. *Crew
nationality:* 1 British, 2 Danes.

WITH a strong south westerly wind blowing, the *City
of Winchester* found it difficult to keep up with the
convoy crossing the Channel. About 10 miles off
Guernsey the master realised that he was on his own.

His worse fears were realised when a submarine
appeared to the south-west. He told his two crew to get
the boat ready. Fifteen minutes later the submarine
was much closer. A shot rang out and a shell ripped
through the headsails. A second shot tore through the
mainsail and a third knocked the coamings away. At
this the master and crew took to the boat. The
submarine fired two more shots, one of which missed.

Then the submarine, having got much closer, fired
three more shots into the ketch. A few minutes later
she sank stern first. The submarine drew alongside
the boat and the master was asked for the details of his
ship. He said that the German commander was only a
young man of about 23 and was taking notes while
another officer did the talking.

After about two hours of sailing their little boat in
quite heavy seas they eventually attracted the attention
of a French torpedo boat and were later landed at
White Rock, Guernsey.

11/2: RHONA. *Country:* British.
Date sunk: 27/11/16. *Tons nett:* 281. *Tons
gross:* 640. *Built:* Dublin in 1909. *Type:* SS. *Rig:*
schooner. *Owners:* Michael Murphy, 3, Beresford
Place, Dublin. *Cargo:* 713 tons coal from Cardiff to
St Servan. *Armed:* No. *Position:* 19 miles NW by N
from Guernsey (49 44 00N; 02 54 00W). *Master's
name:* Henry Banks. *Crew:* 12.

THE *Rhona* left Cardiff on the November 23, 1916,
and for a while had to take shelter behind the Isle of
Lundy owing to a gale that raged for several days.
She managed to press on but her luck ran out close
to the Channel Islands when she was attacked by a
German submarine.

After being told to leave their ship by the Germans
the crew took to two lifeboats, the mate in charge of
one and the master the other. The Germans performed
their usual trick of using one of the crew's boats to
plant bombs on the steamer forcing the crew to row
them back and forth.

After four explosions on board the *Rhona* she
lurched over and sank leaving the crew to fend for
themselves. During the night the two boats got
separated but they were both picked up the next day.
The men in the master's boat were picked up off St

Peters Port by the motor fishing vessel *Stork* and the mate with his crew by the SS *Pembroke*. There were no casualties.

UB-18 was the submarine involved.

11/3: INDUSTRY. *Country:* British. *Date sunk:* 5/9/17. *Tons nett:* 77. *Tons gross:* 91. *Built:* Cardiff in 1865. *Type:* SV. *Rig:* schooner. *Owners:* Smith Petersen & Co, Cardiff. *Cargo:* In ballast, Granville for Swansea. *Armed:* No. *Position:* 20 miles NNW from Hanois, Guernsey (49 46 00N; 02 53 00W). *Master's name:* Donald Murray. *Crew:* 4.

THE master watched with horror as the German submarine pounded the schooner *Glynn* to pieces only a few miles away from him. He could only get two knots out of his ship as the wind was so light.

The *Glynn,* in the distance, was still afloat when the submarine bore away from her and headed for the *Industry*. The crew took to the boat and pulled clear but then the submarine disappeared. The crew stayed close to the *Industry* and thought that maybe their luck was in after all. Perhaps the submarine had spotted something it didn't like and had dived to escape. They inched closer to their ship and were contemplating boarding her again. Suddenly the submarine surfaced about a quarter of a mile away and started to shell the schooner. Within a few minutes the *Industry* was sunk and the submarine turned her attention back to the *Glynn* which was still afloat. Half an hour later, she too went down.

The crew rowed all night and landed at White Rock, Guernsey at 11am the next day.

11/4: HELGE. *Country:* Swedish. *Date sunk:* 3/12/17. *Tons nett:* –. *Tons gross:* 360. *Built:* –. *Type:* SS. *Rig:* –. *Owners:* Cordelia Shipping Co, Gottenberg/Hudson Bay Co. *Cargo:* In ballast, Granville for Barry Roads. *Armed:* No. *Position:* 6 miles NW of Guernsey (49 39 00N; 02 53 00W). *Master's name:* Bengt Hugo Norin. *Crew:* 11. *Crew nationality:* 9 Swedes, 2 Danes.

HELGE called into Cherbourg for instructions before heading out across the Channel.

A submarine suddenly appeared about 2000yds away from the ship and began to fire shells at her. After seven or eight rounds had found their mark the master ordered the ship to be stopped and the crew to take to the boats. As soon as the crew were clear the submarine finished her off with another 25 rounds.

After she had sunk, the submarine came alongside the boat and asked the master all the usual questions as to her name, size and cargo. The crew were found the next morning about two miles off Start Point by the APV *Mewslade*. The only one casualty among the crew was a Swede, Carl Westerberg, who was slightly injured by wood splinters thrown up by a shell.

11/5: BRITANNIC. *Country:* British. *Date sunk:* 13/12/17. *Tons nett:* 74. *Tons gross:* 98. *Built:* Southtown in 1891. *Type:* SV. *Rig:* ketch. *Owners:* W.L. Jenkins, Baltic Buildings, Swansea. *Cargo:* 25 tons of ballast, Granville to Fowey. *Armed:* No. *Position:* 12 miles NW from Hanois, Guernsey (49 36 00N; 02 53 00W). *Master's name:* William Baker. *Crew:* 3.

THE German bombing party that went over to the *Britannic* in her own lifeboat, spent over an hour plundering her. They loaded the boat with every useful piece of equipment they could find, clocks, compasses and provisions. Just before leaving her they planted three bombs.

The master and crew of the *Britannic* could only watch from the submarine, where they were held at gunpoint. The master had realised there was nothing he could do when he first spotted the enemy vessel at 2am. The U-boat had surfaced about 150yds off and fired three shells at his ship. There was only a light breeze and the little sailing vessel was barely making headway as it was. Even if there had been wind it would have made little difference against such a fast assailant.

The boat drew back alongside the submarine, the bombing party passed up their spoils to their shipmates and ordered the three prisoners to get in and go away. The master asked if they were at least going to let them have some food and water but a German officer said "No" and waved them aside. The men rowed off. After a few minutes the sound of three explosions caused them to stop and look towards their ship. Planking flew in all directions and within two minutes she had gone.

The three men took 36 hours to reach St Peters Port, Guernsey.

11/6: GERMAN SUBMARINE (UB-19). *Country:* German. *Date sunk:* 30/11/16. *Tons nett:* 260. *Tons gross:* 290. *Built:* 1915. *Type:* UB-class II. *Owners:* German navy. *Armed:* 4 torpedoes, 5cm deck gun. *Position:* 26 miles north by west of Hanois, Guernsey (49 52 00N; 02 48 00W). *Master's Name:* Oberleutnant Erich Noodt. *Crew:* 23. *Crew nationality:* German.

FLYING aircraft was a dangerous business during the first world war as Sub-Lieutenant J.R. Ross could testify. He was involved in an incident which resulted in the destruction of an enemy submarine, but was nearly killed doing so.

He reported that he took off in his seaplane No 8379 from Portland Harbour at noon on the November 30, 1916, and headed out towards the Channel Islands on patrol. Accompanying him was mechanic, J. Redman as observer. The records are not specific as to whether he had been tipped off about a German U-boat in the area but he stated that he followed a distinct oil trace which eventually led him to the submarine.

Earlier in his flight he had spotted what he described as a 'tank steamer' and as the submarine was heading in its direction he dropped a 65lb bomb on the U-boat and headed off to warn the steamer. Pilot Ross made several attempts to signal the ship but his signals went unanswered. He decided to land next to the steamer and after doing so, discovered that the vessel was in fact HMS *Q7* pretending to be the steamer *Penshurst*. Having informed her commander of the submarine's position, the seaplane started to take off again.

However, at about 150ft Sub-Lieutenant Ross reported that the plane stalled and began to side slip into a dive. It had nearly recovered when a wing tip touched the water and slewed the whole thing around tearing off the floats. The commander of *Q7* sent a boat to assist the aircraft. They managed to get a sling on it and started the process of getting it on board.

Oberleutnant Erich Noodt in *UB-19* had been watching events through his periscope and decided the time was right to make his attack. He surfaced a few hundred yards away and began to fire shells at the *Q7*. The commander of *Q7* not wanting to blow his cover ordered the wrecked plane to be cast off and made out as if he was running away. The plan worked and very shortly the submarine caught up with *Q7*, which went into its "abandon ship" routine. Noodt moved in. At 250yds *Penshurst* opened up with her concealed guns, firing 83 shells at *UB-19,* which foundered.

Noodt and 15 others were rescued by *Penshurst* whose captain, Commander F.H. Grenfell was awarded the D.S.O. As for the pilot and observer of seaplane No 8379, they were shaken but otherwise unhurt and returned to Portland.

11/7: FIGARO. *Country:* French.
Date sunk: 26/1/18. *Tons nett*: –. *Tons gross:* 566. *Built*: –. *Type:* SS. *Rig:* –. *Owners:* Societe Importation, 9, La Place Lafayette, Rouen. *Cargo:* Coal, Brest to Rouen. *Armed:* No. *Position:* 3¹/₂ miles SW of Les Hanois Light, Guernsey (49 24 00N; 02 46 00W). *Master's name:* Yves Martin. *Crew:* 17.

THE information on this sinking is mainly taken from a statement sent to the Admiralty by the State Police of Guernsey. The master made his statement to them after landing at Rocquaine.

The master said that his ship left Brest at 3.30pm on January 25, 1918, with a cargo of coal for Rouen. At 8.45 the next morning a huge explosion occurred on the port side in number one hold. Within a minute or so the ship was listing heavily to port so the master had no choice but to order his crew to take to the boats. They had an accident with the starboard boat which resulted in two men being thrown into the sea but they were saved. They got away from the ship just in time as 10 minutes after the explosion, *Figaro* sank. Lloyd's recorded her as having been torpedoed.

11/8: GRACE. *Country:* British.
Date sunk: 29/11/16. *Tons nett:* 99. *Tons gross:* 135. *Built:* Deitziel, Holland 1866. *Type:* SV. *Rig:* schooner. *Owners:* Mrs E.L. Murdock, 3, Ladysmiths Rd, Gloucester. *Cargo:* 200 tons clay in bulk and casks from Lovering, Par to Rouen. *Armed:* No. *Position:* 40 miles SE by E of Start Point (49 43 00N; 02 44 00W). *Master's name:* Andrew Murdock. *Crew:* 3.

GRACE was making about four and a half knots at 8.30 in the morning of November 29, 1916. She was heading across the Channel for Rouen and the weather promised a good crossing. The master was looking around with his binoculars and had spotted an object about a mile off on the port beam. He tried to distinguish it but couldn't make it out for some time. Whatever it was it appeared to be heading towards him. By the time he realised that it was an enemy submarine it was too late as at the same instant a shell threw up a spout of water close alongside the ship.

The master shortened sail and waited as the submarine drew nearer. When in hailing distance a voice from the submarine in clear English ordered them to abandon their ship and approach the submarine. They did as they were told and later four Germans used their boat to plant bombs on the *Grace*. At 9.30am she blew up and sank.

The crew were put back in their lifeboat and cast adrift. They rowed for some time but were eventually spotted by a patrol vessel and taken into Falmouth.

11/9: CLEMATIS. *Country:* British.
Date sunk: 28/11/16. *Tons nett:* 22. *Tons gross*: –. *Built:* Lowestoft in 1891. *Type:* FV. *Rig:* dandy. *Owners:* John Thomas Wilson, 4, Overgang, Brixham. *Cargo:* Fish. *Armed:* No. *Position:* 40 miles SSE of Berry Head (49 48 00N; 02 42 00W). *Master's name:* John Thomas Wilson. *Crew:* 3.

THE master of *Clematis* watched the events going on about two miles off to the south-south-east through his binoculars. He couldn't quite make out the exact detail but it looked as though a submarine was attacking a schooner. He decided he wasn't going to hang around and ordered all plain sail up and put the ship over on the port tack.

Still the master watched and to his dismay saw that the submarine was heading towards him rapidly. Within a few minutes a shell threw up a spout of water close by the ship. The master ordered the sails in before joining his crew in the ship's boat.

As the submarine approached a voice called for the crew to come aboard. The Germans followed the usual pattern and used the little boat to row over to the *Clematis* to plant bombs. When they returned a few minutes later they were seen to be clutching all sorts of items plundered from the sailing ship.

The *Clematis* sank almost immediately the bombs

exploded. Her crew were ordered back in their boat and shoved clear while the U-boat headed off towards another victim.

11/10: LA MANCHE. *Country:* French.
Date sunk: 1/5/17. *Tons nett:* –. *Tons gross:* 335.
Built: –. *Type:* SV. *Rig:* 3 masted schooner.
Owners: –. *Cargo:* In ballast, Granville to Cardiff.
Armed: No. *Position:* 8 miles N of Hanois Light
(49 34 00N; 02 42 00W). *Master's name:*
T. Besnard.

THE only information available on this sinking was taken from a half completed deposition form, probably filled in from information supplied by the Guernsey Police. Apparently *La Manche* sailed from Granville on April 27, 1917, at 8pm and got herself into trouble on May 1, when she was attacked by a German submarine. Many shells were fired into her but the crew managed to get away unharmed. The vessel was finished off by bombs. The crew were set adrift and rowed themselves to Guernsey.

11/11: MIENTJE. *Country:* British.
Date sunk: 20/5/17. *Tons nett:* 93. *Tons gross:* 120.
Built: 1913. *Type:* SV. *Rig:* ketch. *Owners:*
Admiralty. *Cargo:* Shingle ballast from St Malo to Fowey. *Armed:* No. *Position:* 25 miles N of Hanois, Guernsey (49 51 00N; 02 41 00W). *Master's name:* Daniel Forshaw. *Crew:* 4.

THE details of the sinking of this vessel are explained by the information given for the sailing ship *Dana* which was in company with *Mientje*. The master of *Mientje* also made a statement to the Guernsey State Police. He added that after quitting his ship the German commander said to him, "Why do you go to sea? We shall sink all the ships and stop all the trade."

The owners of the *Mientje*, the Admiralty, later gave the master a hard time over the fact that his accounts went down with the ship, calling it a clumsy and careless thing to happen. Captain Forshaw tried to explain to them that when you have shells whistling past your ears the last thing that enters your head is whether you have got your accounts in order. He had a point but the Admiralty still took a dim view of it.

11/12: DANA. *Country:* British.
Date sunk: 20/5/17. *Tons nett:* 153. *Tons gross:* 182. *Built:* 1874. *Type:* SV. *Rig:* brigantine. *Owners:* Cornish Traders Ltd, Falmouth. *Cargo:* Shingle ballast from St Malo to Fowey. *Armed:* No. *Position:* 25 miles N of Hanois, Guernsey (49 51 00N; 02 40 00W). *Master's name:* Thomas John Hicks. *Crew:* 6.

THE information on this sinking was taken mainly from a letter written by the Guernsey State Police who interviewed the master of the *Dana* and also the master of the sailing vessel *Mientje*.

Both vessels left St Malo at 6am on May 20, 1917, and were given a tow by a steamer to a position about 10 miles south of Hanois Light, Guernsey. They were cast off and headed across the Channel. The journey went well until a German submarine appeared on the scene and began to shell the *Dana* heavily. The master ordered his men to get the boat ready while he burnt his confidential papers and threw some food into a trunk. Unfortunately, he never got chance to get the trunk into the boat as the shelling was getting more and more severe. Their boat eventually ended up alongside the submarine and three German sailors jumped in with bombs and demanded to be rowed over to the *Dana*. The master asked if he could go aboard and get the food trunk but one of the sailors said no, adding that he would get it for him.

With the bombs in place the master was ordered on board the submarine where the German commander said to him, "Now you will see your ship sink." Seconds later the bombs exploded and the master did indeed see his ship sink. Turning to the *Mientje* the commander asked, "Do you know that ship?"

The master replied, "Yes."

"Is she armed?"

"No."

The commander continued, "I know England well, it's a pity we are fighting each other, we should be together. You stand there and if that ship is armed you will die. We always take precautions and shell the ships before we go near as it's happened that when we have given them orders to leave the ship a part of the crew have gone in the boat and left a part on board, and as soon as we get close, unsuspecting any danger they open fire on us. I never thought the English people could be guilty of such a dirty trick."

The submarine towed the boat towards the *Mientje* shelling her as she edged closer and closer. After about 10 shots her crew were seen to pull clear and once more the German bombing party went to work.

Setting both crews free the submarine commander waved to them and shouted, "Have a safe and pleasant passage to the land and don't tell any lies to the Daily Mail about us." The crew landed on Sark at 9.45 the next morning.

11/13: BRIZEUX. *Country:* French.
Date sunk: 21/10/16. *Tons nett:* 1963. *Tons gross:* 2302. *Built:* 1901. *Type:* SV. *Rig:* barque. *Owners:* Societe Anonyme des Voiliers, Dunkerquois. *Cargo:* In ballast from Havre to Buenos Aires. *Armed:* No. *Position:* 12 miles NNW of Caskets (49 51 00N; 02 35 00W). *Master's name:* Louis Thomas Bourgneuf. *Crew:* 24. *Crew nationality:* All French.

At 10.50am on October 21, 1916. Captain Bourgneuf sighted the submarine off the port bow and judged it to be about half a mile off. He could see that the

Germans had raised signal flags. He knew what they meant instantly and as he heard a shell whistle close by he barked out the order to furl up the sails.

The crew pulled clear of the *Brizeux* and obeyed the command to go alongside the submarine. One of their boats was used by four German sailors who went back to sailing ship and planted several bombs on board her. While all this was going on the German commander had spotted another steamer in the distance and ordered his gunner to fire a shell at her which was promptly done. However, he was most surprised when a shell came whistling back and threw up a spout of water perilously close to the submarine. The commander hadn't noticed a big British transport that appeared in the distance and she was well armed.

The German sailors hurried back to their ship and with shells screaming all around them, dived to safety. The crew of the *Brizeux* had pulled well clear in their boats cursing their bad luck on timing. If the transport had turned up 10 minutes earlier their ship might have been saved. But it was not to be as a few moments later a huge explosion boomed out and the *Brizeux* went down.

The steamer *Tempo* had a lucky escape. It was she whom the submarine had fired on before the timely intervention of the passing transport. Grateful for his deliverance the master of the *Tempo* picked up the crew of the *Brizeux* and then went on to pick up the crew of the *Rabbi* whose ship had been sunk close by.

11/14: GERMAN SUBMARINE (UC-18).

Country: German. *Date sunk*: 19/2/17. *Tons nett*: 417. *Tons gross*: 493. *Built*: 1916. *Type*: UC-class II. *Owners*: German navy. *Armed*: 18 mines, 7 torpedoes, 8.8cm deck gun. *Position*: 12 miles W of Grosnez Point, Jersey (49 15 00N; 02 34 00W). *Master's Name*: Oberleutnant Wilhelm Kiel. *Crew*: 26. *Crew Nationality*: German.

LIEUTENANT F.A. Frank, RNR, of HMS *Q18*, reported that he left Portland on the afternoon of Thursday February 15, 1917, to patrol up as far as Dungeness and then back down the Channel to Land's End. From there he set a course across to Ushant and back up the Channel staying on the French side. He intended to pass between Jersey and Guernsey, through the Alderney race and back across the Channel towards Portland.

At 6.35am on the 19th gunfire was heard and Lieutenant Frank immediately went on the bridge to see what was happening. He asked the officer of the watch if he knew the direction of the gunfire, but he didn't. At 6.54am two more shots rang out and the shells sliced into the water ahead of *Q18*. It was now obvious to Lieutenant Frank that a submarine had fallen for *Q18*'s disguise as a small steamer called *Lady Olive* and was attacking him. It was time to put the trap into operation and the ship was brought to a standstill. He looked through his binoculars and could

just see the outline of the submarine about three miles off. The orders were given for the 'abandon ship' parties to get ready. At 7am two boats pulled away to the south to dupe the submarine commander into thinking that the ship was indeed being abandoned.

He fell for it and slowly zig-zagged his way towards the *Q18* firing occasionally as he came. Most of the shells went wide but one or two found their mark and made the ship shudder under the impacts. Still the men left on board kept silent and ready by their guns. Lieutenant Frank whispered to the gun captains to keep a sharp lookout through the scuppers as he was unsure which side the submarine would approach and gave them permission to fire as the opportunity allowed. At 7.10am the enemy was within 100yds and turned broadside on to *Q18*'s port gun crew who leapt into action. The first shell blew a huge hole out of the base of the conning tower, the second made a direct hit on the deck gun killing the gunner instantly. *Q18*'s gunners kept up their deadly bombardment and scored several hits below the submarine's water line. Another shot on the conning tower virtually demolished it and a man who had just appeared at the top was blown to pieces.

The submarine took on a list to starboard and began to belch out huge amounts of vapour. As she listed, the holes in her sides sank below the water and made her settle by the head. Within two minutes the stern was high in the air and she slipped below, blowing out huge volumes of air as she went. Lieutenant Frank rang full ahead on the engine room telegraph with the intention of getting over the top of the submarine and dropping a depth charge, just to make sure she was finished. However, the engine room didn't respond. Two of the submarine's shells had penetrated it, steam was escaping from ruptured pipes and the water rising very rapidly. It was a bitter blow to the crew. They had sunk the enemy very efficiently but at the cost of losing their own ship.

For nearly two days the 46 crew of *Q18* rowed and drifted trying to make headway to the south and land. It was exhausting and demoralising work and the commander used every method he knew to keep their spirits up. At one stage he sighted a submarine but he kept it to himself. During the second night the two boats became separated but the next day the commander's boat was spotted by the French destroyer *Dunois* which was tracking an enemy submarine. It eventually came alongside the *Q18*'s crew and told them to get aboard quickly but at that very moment a shout went up and she sped off firing her gun at a distant submarine. When she came back 16 of the men managed to get aboard her but the same thing happened again. As the destroyer pulled away her propeller took a big lump out of the cuttter leaving seven men floundering in the water.

They were all eventually landed at Cherbourg where Lieutenant Frank was relieved to find that the crew in the second cutter had been picked up by a trawler.

Lt Frank was awarded the DSM and members of his crew were also decorated and given prize money.

11/15: HMS Q18 *Country:* British.
Date sunk: 19/2/17. *Tons nett:* –. *Tons gross:* –.
Built: –. *Type:* SS. *Rig:* schooner/Q-ship. *Owners:*
Admiralty. *Cargo:* None. *Armed:* Yes. *Position:* 12
miles W of Grosnez Point, Jersey (49 15 00N;
02 34 00W). *Master's Name:* Lieutenant F.A.
Frank. *Crew:* 46. *Crew Nationality:* British.

SEE the sinking of *UC-18*, site 11/14. *Q18* was
disguised as the small merchant steamer *Lady Olive*.

11/16: DROMORE. *Country:* British.
Date sunk: 18/5/17. *Tons nett:* 106. *Tons
gross:* 268. *Built:* Paisley in 1903. *Type:* SS. *Rig:*
schooner. *Owners:* Parkley SS Co, Dunster House,
Mark Lane, London. *Cargo:* In ballast from St Malo
to Swansea. *Armed:* No. *Position:* 6 miles S of St
Martins, Guernsey (49 19 00N; 02 32 00W).
Master's name: Allan Kerr. *Crew:* 9.

DROMORE'S engines were at full ahead pushing her
along at just over eight knots. The master had gone
to his cabin leaving the mate in charge on the bridge
and was about to settle down to some paperwork when
he heard the mate yell, "Shot on port bow." He dashed
up to the bridge to see what was going on just as
another shell whimpered past the front of the bridge.
He immediately grabbed his binoculars and scanned
the sea off the port side but couldn't see anything.
Then he spotted it, a conning tower, heading directly
towards him.

Captain Kerr decided that there was nothing he
could do. He had heard of the high speeds the German
U-boats could achieve and with her only two miles
off, realised he stood no chance of getting away. He
ordered the engines to be shut down and told the crew
to take to the boat. As they pulled away from the ship
the submarine rose higher in the water and two more
shells sliced one after the other in the water close by.
This was followed by two more aimed at the steamer.
Dromore shuddered under the impact as they struck
home and let out a loud explosion as one of them
penetrated a boiler. Within two minutes she was down
by the stern and in another two she went to the bottom.

The crew were eager to get away and started to row
enthusiastically towards Guernsey. The submarine
commander left them alone and didn't stop them for
the usual questioning. They eventually reached
Guernsey at 2.45 the next morning.

11/17: FULVIO. *Country:* Norwegian. *Date sunk:*
21/10/16. *Tons nett:* –. *Tons gross:* 305. *Built:*
1909. *Type:* SS. *Rig:* schooner. *Owners:* Ragurdo,
Blockstad, Oslo. *Cargo:* 256 tons coal from Barry
Docks to Honfleur. *Armed:* No. *Position:* 12 miles
NNW from Caskets (49 55 00N; 02 29 00W).
Master's name: Johan Severin Olsen. *Crew:* 13.
Crew nationality: 6 Norwegians, 2 Greeks,
1 Uraguayan, 4 Spanish.

Fulvio was making a steady eight and a half knots
whilst crossing the Channel from Barry Docks to
Honfleur. At 8.15am the mate had the watch and was
busy writing his notes when a dull bang rang out
followed by a whoosh of air as a shell dropped into the
water a few feet behind the stern. The master was
below at the time and immediately rushed on deck to
see what all the noise was about.

The mate and the master scanned the horizon and
could only see a small vessel about three miles off.
The master had just lifted his binoculars up when there
was another bang and a shell went whimpering
overhead. Through the glasses the master could then
see clearly a German submarine heading straight
towards him. He noticed that the submarine had a small
sail up and was flying a French flag, a ruse to make
it appear like a small sailing vessel from a distance.
As it approached the *Fulvio* the French flag was
replaced by the German ensign and signal flags were
sent up to read, "Abandon your ship immediately."

The master felt he had no choice but to obey and
accordingly gave the order. Two boats pulled clear
of the ship and rowed towards the submarine. As they
approached it a voice shouted for them to come
alongside and several German sailors appeared with
rifles. Whilst the crew were being questioned and
relieved of their papers one of their boats was taken by
two German sailors back to the *Fulvio* where they
planted bombs and helped themselves to anything
they fancied.

As the crew pulled clear of the submarine the
bombs on their steamer exploded and a few minutes
later the *Fulvio* turned over on her starboard side and
sank by the stern. At the same time the submarine
turned and sped off to the west in pursuit of another
steamer.

The crew were picked up later that day by the patrol
vessel *Vanadis* and landed at Weymouth at about 8pm
the same evening.

11/18: PASCAL. *Country:* British. *Date sunk:*
17/12/16. *Tons nett:* 3541. *Tons gross:* 5587. *Built:*
1913. *Type:* SS. *Rig:* schooner. *Owners:* Lamport &
Holt, Royal Liver Buildings, Liverpool. *Cargo:*
3500 tons hay and oats from Halifax, Nova Scotia
to Cherbourg. *Armed:* No. *Position:* 12 miles N of
Casketts Light House (49 57 00N; 02 23 00W).
Master's name: Hugh Layton. *Crew:* 43.

Sunday December 17, 1916, was a day the crew of
the *Pascal* were not likely to forget. It was 4.30pm
when a shell passed very close over the bridge. A
German submarine was closing on the steamer fast
and continued its bombardment relentlessly. Several
shells smashed into the superstructure and one crashed
into the steering gear causing it to lock the helm hard
over. The *Pascal* turned and settled into a continual
circle.

The master realising the danger his crew were in
ordered all hands on deck. The engines were left

The *Pascal* was sunk in 1916 by gunfire and a single torpedo from *UB-70*.

running but as more and more shells continued to slam into the ship the third engineer volunteered to go below and shut them down.

As the ship slowed the master ordered the boats to be manned and lowered. He had hoped that the Germans would see that he intended to abandon his ship and stop firing but the shells kept coming. One shell threw up large chunks of shrapnel which killed Second Officer Howard D. Poulton and Bosun Joseph Bennett. Others were hit but not seriously injured.

Eventually one boat was cleared away with 26 men and the eldest apprentice in charge. After the master had thrown his confidential papers in the weighted bag overboard he followed with the rest of the crew in the other boat. As they left their shattered ship behind, a voice from the submarine ordered the master to come alongside. Having got what information he needed the German commander waved the lifeboat to get clear and positioned his craft for the final strike, a torpedo square into the midships of the *Pascal*.

Both lifeboats rowed towards the Channel Islands and were eventually spotted and towed to safety.

The submarine concerned was *U-70*.

11/19: PERRA. *Country:* Norwegian.
Date sunk: 27/11/16. -. *Tons nett:* –. *Tons gross:* 1688. *Built: Type:* SS. *Rig:* schooner. *Owners:* –.
Cargo: Iron ore from Bilbao to Calais. *Armed:* No.
Position: 15 miles N of Casketts (49 58 00N; 02 22 00W). *Master's name:* H.Torjassen. *Crew:* 19.

THERE is very little information on this sinking other than a letter from the master of the steamer SS *Fishpool* to the Admiralty saying that he picked up the survivors from the SS *Perra*. It was at 1pm on the November 27, 1916, whilst he was in position, Les Hanois Light, Guernsey, bearing south 12½ miles when he found the crew in their ship's lifeboats. The master of the *Perra* reported that his ship had been sunk at 7.30am that day by a German submarine.

The submarine had towed the crew in the boats for about six miles but abandoned them when another steamer had been spotted. After slipping the boats it submerged and made off for another attack.

11/20: PAN. *Country:* Norwegian.
Date sunk: 26/10/16. *Tons nett:* –. *Tons gross:* 795.
Built: –. *Type:* SS. *Rig:*–. *Owners:* Lorentz, Stabell, Bergen, Norway. *Cargo:* Coal, Barry for Caen.
Armed: No. *Position:* 20 miles WNW of Cape la Hague (49 54 00N; 02 20 00W;). *Master's name:* Richard Najhammer. *Crew:* 14. *Crew nationality:* 8 Norwegians, 1 Russian, 2 Danes, 1 Swede, 1 Spaniard, 1 British/Angolese.

The submarine appeared as if from nowhere about a quarter of a mile off and headed straight towards the *Pan* firing shells as she came. The master watched as the signals were hoisted up the small mast 'Abandon your ship immediately.'

With shells screaming all around them the crew

rapidly lowered their boats and pulled clear. As they did so the submarine moved in for the kill and poured shells into the steamer's side until she could take no more and sank.

Easing gently alongside the master's boat the German commander asked for the ship's details, her cargo, destination and all other relevant information. Satisfied with the answers he received he told the *Pan's* crew that they were free to go and motioned them away with his hand. Captain Najhammer asked the commander if he could tow them a little closer to the land. The German shook his head and said, "I have not got the time. I have many more ships to sink today."

So the crew rowed off in the general direction of the nearest land and were eventually picked up by the Norwegian steamer *Zeus* and landed at Falmouth.

11/21: RABBI. *Country:* Norwegian. *Date sunk:* 21/10/16. *Tons nett:* 511. *Tons gross:* 875. *Built:* 1904. *Type:* SS. *Rig:* schooner. *Owners:* K.M. Pedersen, Kragro, Norway. *Cargo:* 1200 tons coal from H. Goldberg, Swansea to Rouen. *Armed:* No. *Position:* 6 miles SE by S from Casketts Light (49 38 00N; 02 18 00W). *Master's name:* Anton Amundsen. *Crew:* 14. *Crew nationality:* 6 Norwegians, 2 Swedes, 2 Russians, 4 Spaniards.

RABBI was steering east-south-east magnetic and making eight knots when the master spotted what he thought was a small French fishing vessel about two miles off on his port bow. He became very suspicious when he spotted another steamer, the fellow Norwegian *Fulvio*, also in the distance but obviously sinking. He immediately altered course to render assistance but then to his horror he saw that the innocent little fishing vessel had turned into a menacing German submarine.

The first shell fell short, the next a bit closer to the *Rabbi* and the master realised he was in a hopeless situation. The Germans hoisted the signal AB, 'Abandon Ship.' Later Captain Amundsen climbed aboard the submarine from his lifeboat and spoke with the German commander. He gave him the papers he asked for and the commander very politely gave him a receipt for them. Whilst all this was going on several German sailors were busily planting bombs on the *Rabbi*, one in the engine room and another on the outside.

The crew of the *Rabbi* could only watch from the boats as their steamer blew up and sank. The submarine sped off after yet another victim, the French barque *Brizeux* and having sunk her it then attempted to sink the steamer *Tempo* which had the misfortune to be in the area at the time. The Germans began their usual routine by lobbing a shell at the steamer but in his hurry the commander hadn't noticed another steamer appear. It was a big British transport and more important, it was armed. A shell threw up a spout of water within several yards of the submarine and this was followed by another. It was some good shooting and too close for comfort for the Germans who promptly dived to get out of the way.

It was the *Tempo's* lucky day and she quickly picked up the crew of the *Rabbi* and the *Brizeux* and sped out of the area as fast as she could, making Swansea safely later that day.

11/22: JEANNE. *Country:* Danish. *Date sunk:* 5/9/16. *Tons nett:* 720. *Tons gross:* 1190. *Built:* 1904. *Type:* SS. *Rig:* –. *Owners:* Martin Carl, Copenhagen. *Cargo:* 925 tons esparto grass from Algiers to Leith. *Armed:* No. *Position:* 16 miles NE of Casketts (49 51 00N; 02 17 00W). *Master's name:* G. Olsen. *Crew:* 18. *Crew nationality:* 11 Danes, 2 French, 1 Norwegian, 4 Swedes.

THERE is very little about the circumstances of this sinking other than the fact that at around 12.15pm on September 5, 1916, she was intercepted by an enemy submarine.

Jeanne's crew were given 10 minutes to leave the ship and during that time they gathered up what belongings they could whilst the Germans planted bombs at various locations. The crew left in one of the ship's boats just a few minutes before the bombs exploded and *Jeanne* sank.

The crew were later picked up by a British patrol boat and landed at Weymouth.

11/23: BRITANNIA. *Country:* British. *Date sunk:* 5/9/16. *Tons nett:* 39. *Tons gross:* 48. *Built:* Kingsbridge in 1896. *Type:* SV. *Rig:* ketch. *Owners:* J.H. Davis, Plymouth. *Cargo:* 76 tons manure from Depass, London to Norman & Son, St Hillier, Jersey. *Armed:* No. *Position:* 12 miles N of Alderney (49 55 00N; 02 12 00W). *Master's name:* Alfred Tope.

HAVING left London at 1pm on August 27, 1916, the *Britannia* worked her way down the coast and into the Channel, putting into Newhaven on the September 3 for provisions. At 8am on the 6th she was in mid Channel heading for Jersey. The mate was at the wheel and the master was having breakfast when a gunshot rang out. The master came on deck to see what was happening and made out the shape of a submarine about two miles off. He told the mate to hold his course and a few moments later another shell crashed into the water astern of them. The mate held his course but it was hopeless trying to outrun the very swift moving submarine.

The Germans got within hailing distance and shouted to the master to leave his ship. He complied and rowed towards the submarine where their boat was forced to row back to the *Britannia* with a party of German sailors, all armed with bombs. It didn't take long for the bombs to be expertly positioned and five minutes later they exploded causing the wooden ship to list heavily to port before sinking bows first.

At 2pm the same day the crew were picked up by the French patrol ship *Cerbere* and taken to Cherbourg. They eventually got passage home on the SS *Philadelphian* which landed them at Weymouth on the September 10.

11/24: TWIG. *Country:* British.
Date sunk: 24/10/16. *Tons nett:* 95. *Tons gross:* 120. *Built:*Fareham in 1875. *Type:* SV. *Rig:* schooner. *Owners:* Thos Tyrrell, 82, Lower Main St, Arklow, Wicklow. *Cargo:* 200 tons stone shipped by Brookes Ltd, Guernsey, and consigned to Southampton. *Armed:* No. *Position:* 15 miles N of Alderney (49 48 00N; 02 11 00W). *Master's name:* John James Tyrrell. *Crew:* 5.

AT about 10pm the wind fell off to a complete calm and the *Twig* drifted gently to the south-west but then as the tide began to flood she drifted to the north east. At 8am the next morning a light breeze sprang up from the south-west and the ship was able to proceed on her way across the Channel.

About an hour later the master of the *Twig* spotted what looked like a submarine ahead of him and altered the helm slightly to take him off a converging course. A few minutes later his suspicions were confirmed when a shell splashed into the water just to the starboard side. The master looked towards the submarine and to his dismay noticed that there were in fact two of them, one behind the other. Another shell hit the water, this time a lot closer.

There was nothing the master could do, he was at the mercy of the enemy. A few minutes later one of the submarines called for a boat to be launched and to come aboard. The Germans made one of the crew stay on the submarine and the others were ordered to row a bombing party back to the *Twig*. Having completed the task the crew were cast adrift. From a safe distance they watched as their ship lurched under the explosions and sank.

At 4.30pm they were picked up by a French patrol ship and landed the next day at Boulogne.

11/25: DESPATCH. *Country:* British.
Date sunk: 30/11/17. *Tons nett:* 99. *Tons gross:* 230. *Built:* Glasgow in 1870. *Type:* SS. *Rig:* schooner. *Owners:* The Yula Steamers Trading Co Ltd, Liverpool. *Cargo:* 180 tons general from Liverpool to St Malo. *Armed:* No. *Position:* 9 miles WSW of Cape la Hague (49 40 00N; 02 10 00W). *Master's name:* Thomas Jones. *Crew:* 8.

THIS was in fact a double tragedy but there is virtually no information included in the records of the French vessel involved.

It all started when *Despatch* developed problems with the crowns on her boilers and had to put in to Cherbourg to try and get them sorted out. But the work couldn't be done at Cherbourg for some reason, so it was decided to tow her to St Malo. The task fell to Cherbourg tug No 8 and after a 250ft hawser was attached, the tow began.

All went well until 11am when a German submarine commander decided to throw both ship's crews into utter confusion. A well aimed torpedo struck the tug and the force of the explosion caused her to turn broadside on to the path of the *Despatch* which still had about eight knots of way on her. The master of *Despatch* turned his helm and shouted for the hawser to be freed but it was too late, her stern striking the tug amidships on the starboard side. The tug immediately listed heavily to port and as *Despatch* rolled right over her she sank within seconds.

A boat was lowered straight away to try and rescue any survivors from the tug but only two men were found alive. However, one of them, the skipper, was in a bad way and in need of resuscitation. The master of *Despatch* did all he could to save the skipper but was interrupted by the chief engineer who gave him the bad news that *Despatch* was taking on water rapidly.

A French torpedo boat drew alongside the steamer. *Despatch* was taken in tow yet again to see if she could be saved but by 3pm the water in her was up to the cylinders and rising. Within the hour the crew had to be taken off as she settled down by the stern but stubbornly refused to sink. A few well placed shells from the French patrol vessel's guns soon put an end to her.

11/26: BORO. *Country:* Norwegian.
Date sunk: 27/11/16. *Tons nett*: –. *Tons gross:* 819. *Built:* –. *Type:* SS. *Rig*: –. *Owners:* Jacob Rabi, Tonsberg. *Charterers:* Souppart et Mouttard, Paris. *Cargo:* Coal, Port Talbot for St Malo. *Armed:* No. *Position:* 18 miles ENE of Guernsey (49 35 00N; 02 05 00W). *Master's name:* L. Endresen. *Crew:* 13. *Crew nationality:* 8 Norwegians, 2 Greeks, 1 Dane, 1 Brazilian, 1 Portuguese.

EVEN though the master of the *Boro* was not zig-zagging, it probably would have made little difference. It was 12.45pm on November 27, 1916. *Boro* was making a steady eight knots, when a German submarine appeared close by her. Flags were flying from the small mast on the conning tower, 'AB', "Abandon Ship."

The master, realising that he had no choice in the matter, did as he was told. The crew pulled clear in the ship's boat and rowed over to the submarine. The German commander questioned the master on the details of his ship and journey. He even told the master he could speak to him in Norwegian or English. As the questioning continued, German sailors were busy planting bombs on the *Boro*. They blew up a few minutes later and sent the steamer to the bottom.

The submarine took the men in the boat in tow for about 20 minutes before casting them off. However, the weather was fine and it didn't take them long to reach shore.

11/27: AGNES CAIRNS. *Country:* British. *Date sunk:* 26/4/17. *Tons nett:* –. *Tons gross:* 146. *Built:* 1873. *Type:* SV. *Rig:* schooner. *Owners:* Joseph Penaliggon, Newquay, Cornwall. *Cargo:* 230 tons coal from Portsmouth to Guernsey. *Armed:* No. *Position:* 8 miles NE of Alderney (49 50 00N; 02 02 00W). *Master's name:* Joseph Penaliggon. *Crew:* 5.

ALL that is in the records about this vessel is that she was attacked by a German submarine at around 5.30pm on April 26, 1917, and subsequently blown up by bombs. The crew were taken in tow in their boat by the submarine towards another sailing vessel which turned out to be a French ketch but her name is unknown. After being cast adrift the crew managed to row themselves to Alderney.

11/28: USSA. *Country:* British. *Date sunk:* 3/5/17. *Tons nett:* 1077. *Tons gross:* 2066. *Built:* 1913. *Type:* SS. *Rig:* schooner. *Owners:* John Holt & Co, Liverpool. *Cargo:* 1050 tons hay and 12 railway wagons on deck, 6 fore and 6 aft, from Manchester to Cherbourg. *Armed:* 1 x 6pdr Hotchkiss gun. *Position:* 2 ¹/₂ miles NW of Western Fort, Cherbourg (49 47 30N; 01 53 00W). *Master's name:* Robert Montgomery. *Crew:* 30. *Crew nationality:* All British. *Gunners:* John J. Bourke, ON 5158 RFR; Robert Strathers, ON 1779 RNVR.

CAPTAIN Montgomery of the steamer *Ussa* was not at all happy at being told to stay out at sea. He arrived off Cherbourg at 2.30am and a patrol boat sent out from the examination vessel approached and said that he would have to wait until daylight before coming into port. Apparently it was suspected that a minefield had been laid in the western approaches to the harbour and it was deemed far too dangerous to attempt an entrance in the dark.

Captain Montgomery felt very exposed and open to attack as he kept his steamer moving around. The weather was fine and clear, the sea smooth, the perfect conditions for an enemy submarine to attack. At 4.30am a loud explosion rocked his ship from stem to stern. A huge hole had been opened up on the starboard side aft behind the engine room and *Ussa* started to settle very rapidly. The crew only just made it clear in the boats before the steamer sank in 11 fathoms of water.

The master was livid when he and his crew were picked up by a patrol vessel, convinced that his ship had been a sitting duck for a German submarine. But

the naval authorities maintained that it was much more likely he had struck a mine. This theory was strengthened by the fact that three mines were subsequently found in the area where *Ussa* sank. Other records give her as mined in a minefield laid by *UC-26*.

Because of the danger the wreck presented to shipping entering Cherbourg, it was accurately fixed as bearing north 17 degrees west, true, 1385 metres from the Fort de l'Quest on the breakwater at Cherbourg. Instructions were given for her to be dispersed with explosives.

11/29: ELLEN HARRISON. *Country:* British. *Date sunk:* 29/4/17. *Tons nett:* 72. *Tons gross:* 103. *Built:* Alverton in 1878. *Type:* SV. *Rig:* schooner. *Owners:* Patrick Donovan, Lamb House, Wexford. *Cargo:* 168 tons coal shipped by Cwmanan Colliery, Cardiff, consigned to Isigny. *Armed:* No. *Position:* 7 miles NW of Cherbourg (49 47 00N; 01 50 00W). *Master's name:* Dennis Murphy. *Crew:* 4.

HAVING picked up his sailing instructions Captain Murphy left Falmouth at 11am on April 27, 1917. He set a course to take him up the Channel and was due to call in at St Helens but on the way he decided that the weather was good enough to proceed straight across to the French coast. Unfortunately he never made his destination for at 4.30am on the 29th one of his lookouts spotted the shape of a German submarine, surfacing about three quarters of a mile off to starboard.

The master immediately called all hands to get the boat ready. He threw his sailing instructions in the weighted bag that was in permanent readiness and tossed the whole thing over the side. The submarine fired the first shell when about 500yds off but it missed. However, the rest that followed didn't and one shell burst in the rigging causing the whole lot to catch fire. By this time the crew were well clear and watched as the submarine manoeuvred alongside the schooner, several sailors jumping aboard her. Five minutes later the men left and two explosions boomed across the water. *Ellen Harrison* lurched under the force of the blasts and within a minute was gone.

The submarine didn't hang about which puzzled the master a little. He felt sure the commander would have wanted to see his papers. But the reason became clear 15 minutes later when a French torpedo boat arrived on the scene and plucked them to safety.

11/30: NORMANDY. *Country:* British. *Date sunk:* 25/1/18. *Tons nett:* 251. *Tons gross:* 617. *Built:* 1910. *Type:* SS. *Rig:* schooner. *Owners:* London & South Western Railway Co, Waterloo, London. *Cargo:* 90 tons of general, approx 3000 bags of Army mail, Southampton to Cherbourg.

Armed: 1 x 12pdr 12cwt gun. *Position:* 8 miles NNW of West Fort, Cherbourg (49 48 42N; 01 45 20W). *Master's name:* Ernest Woods. *Crew:* 20. *Crew nationality:* All British, plus 20 passengers.

NORMANDY slipped quietly out of Southampton at 8.30pm on January 24, 1918. It was a fine clear night and all lights were put out as she made the open sea. Crossing the Channel went well and the vessel averaged some 11 knots.

Down below in the engine room the watch was in the charge of the Chief Engineer, Mr Budden, who was relieved by the Second Engineer, Mr Barnes at 12.35am. Mr Barnes reported that all through his watch the engines were running sweetly at full speed until 3.50am when he heard and felt a violent explosion immediately behind the aft engine room bulkhead on the port side. He noticed instantly that the engine started to race away and he knew that the propeller shaft must have been severed. By the time he had shut off steam a few seconds later, he reported that the water was already lapping around his feet and as he made the engine room ladder he was virtually swimming.

About 90 seconds later Mr Barnes made the accommodation block but had great difficulty in getting out due to wreckage blocking all the exits. He managed to get out on deck just in the nick of time as the ship sank from beneath his feet.

In the water he managed to find a hatch cover for himself and spotted the master nearby clinging to an air tank from a lifeboat. The master was in a bad way and had a broken leg. When interviewed later, all the master could remember was giving the order to lower all boats and get clear but the ship sank in two minutes which gave no time for them to be launched.

In total only six of the crew and seven of the passengers survived the sinking. *Normandy* was torpedoed by *U-90*.

11/31: LOUIE BELL. *Country:* British.
Date sunk: 26/1/18. *Tons nett:* 94. *Tons gross:* 118. *Built:* Carrick Fergus in 1882. *Type:* SV. *Rig:* schooner. *Owners:* Fisher & Sons, Barrow-in-Furness. *Cargo:* 190 tons flints for Bridgewater Navigation Co, Runcorn. *Armed:* No. *Position:* 12 miles N of Cherbourg (49 53 00N; 01 44 00W). *Master's name:* Richard Iddon. *Crew:* 5. *Crew nationality:* 4 British, 1 Norwegian.

THE *Louie Bell* was not very long out of Cherbourg when the German submarine began the attack on her. Shells were whistling over and all around her, convincing the master that he had better get himself and his men away before the gunner finally scored a hit.

It was a hazy day and the master couldn't see the submarine clearly but he headed off in the ship's boat in the general direction from which the shells were coming. The submarine was 500yds away before he could see it clearly, her gunner still firing shells at the *Louie Bell*. The commander appeared at the top of the conning tower and ordered the men to board. He came down to greet them and began to question the master regarding his ships details. While this was going on a raiding party used the crew's boat to do a little plundering and bombing.

When they returned to the submarine the master watched in dismay as they unloaded all his instruments, brass fittings, even some of his own clothes. This was followed by two explosions from the bombs the Germans had left behind which sank the *Louie Bell* almost instantly.

The men were told to get back in their boat and head for the land as best they could. They rowed well into the night in the general direction of the French coast but it was hard going against the tide and wind. Fortunately for them they were spotted by a keen eyed watchman on the British destroyer *F52* which picked them up and dropped them safely at Plymouth.

11/32: GERMAN SUBMARINE (UB-78).
Country: German. *Date sunk:* 9/5/18. *Tons nett:* 520. *Tons gross:* 650. *Built:* 1917. *Type:* UB-class III. *Owners:* German navy. *Armed:* 10 torpedoes, 10.5cm deck gun. *Position:* 12 miles NE by E of Cap la Hague (49 49 00N; 01 41 30W). *Master's name:* Oberleutnant A. Strosberg. *Crew:* 34. *Crew Nationality:* German.

A LOOKOUT on the escort vessel *P33* shouted to his commander that he could see a dark shape ahead, a submarine, on the surface and a big one at that. She was approximately 400yds off and the commander knew that the only chance he had of getting her was if his charge, SS *Queen Alexandra*, a cross-Channel transport, could ram at full speed. He immediately signalled the steamer but there was no need, Captain Angus Keith had already spotted the U-boat and was busy barking orders to his helmsman.

As the steamer's bows responded to the helm the commander of *P33* ordered his engines to slow to allow the *Queen Alexandra* to cut in front of him and get down to business. The submarine's commander had obviously seen *P33* and was now frantically crash diving his boat. *P33*'s bow lights were put on and trained on the submarine. It was a sitting duck for the *Queen Alexandra* only yards away.

It was 12.48am precisely when the bows of the steamer sliced into the submarine just behind the conning tower. Over 785 tons at 20 knots was certain to inflict a lot of damage. The submarine was virtually cut in two.

Captain Keith knew that he had done for the enemy vessel and slowed down to examine his own ship. He was lucky, the bows were a bit buckled, his rudder and a propeller bent, but his ship was still watertight and he let *P33* get on with completing the job by depth charging.

After several well placed charges to ensure that the submarine was indeed finished, the commander of *P33* dropped a dan buoy to mark the spot and continued after *Queen Alexandra*. She maintained half speed to reduce the pressure on her damaged hull and arrived safely at Cherbourg with her cargo of soldiers from Southampton.

The commander and crew of *P33* couldn't wait to get back to the spot where the submarine was hit and at daylight found the dan buoy. A search down current soon revealed a heavy oil slick and pieces of debris, clear signs that the submarine had been mortally wounded. Several French naval patrol boats arrived on the scene to assist in the search and located an obstruction on the bottom in 32 fathoms. This was investigated later by divers and found to be the German submarine *UB-78*.

The owners of *Queen Alexandra*, John Williamson & Co of 99, Great Clyde Street, Glasgow, were delighted that their ship had played a crucial role in sinking an enemy submarine. They sent a letter to the Admiralty on June 1, to officially claim the prize money. The Admiralty agreed to pay the maximum allowed of £1000 which was divided among the crew of the steamer. The master, Angus Keith, was also awarded the DSC for his actions.

11/33: CITY OF GHENT. *Country:* British.
Date sunk: 5/9/16. *Tons nett:* –. *Tons gross:* 199. *Built:* Grimsby in 1871. *Type:* SS. *Rig:* schooner. *Owners:* Theodor Shipping Co, The Side, Newcastle. *Cargo:* 200 tons coke from Jenkins of Newcastle to Rouen. *Armed:* No. *Position:* Barfleur Light bearing SE 18 miles (49 54 00N; 01 37 00W). *Master's name:* Harry Payne. *Crew:* 9. *Crew nationality:* 7 British, 2 Swedes

THE Theodor Shipping Company had only purchased the *City of Ghent* about two months earlier from a company in Nova Scotia. Her last trip began after loading at Newcastle and crossing the Channel to arrive at Havre Roads on August 27, 1916. The master was instructed by the French naval authorities to proceed at once to Cherbourg. She arrived the following morning and remained there until September 4. Having unloaded her cargo she proceeded back to Havre at midnight.

At 7am on the September 5, the mate was in charge of the watch on the bridge and the master was in the chartroom. The peace of the morning was suddenly shattered by the sound of gunfire. The master rushed on deck and found that he was being shelled by a submarine which had taken up a position about 300yds off on his port quarter. Realising that his situation was hopeless the master stopped the ship and listened as the submarine commander ordered him to leave. He obeyed and with his crew rowed to the waiting enemy vessel. Three of his crew were ordered out of the boat onto the submarine. German officers armed with bombs took their place and demanded to be

rowed to the *City of Ghent*. There they placed the bombs, one in the engine room and the other in the fore peak.

Having delivered the Germans back to their ship the master and crew pulled clear to watch as their steamer blew up and sank. They were eventually picked up by the French torpedo boat *Francisqui* and taken to Cherbourg.

11/34: GOWRIE. *Country:* British.
Date sunk: 10/10/17. *Tons nett:* 441. *Tons gross:* 1031. *Built:* 1909. *Type:* SS. *Rig:* schooner. *Owners:* Dundee Perth & London Shipping Co, Dundee. *Cargo:* 552 bags of mails, 35 tons aircraft stores, 41 tons cranes (on deck), 5 tons oil, 406 tons supplies, 223 tons ordnance. *Armed:* No. *Position:* 12-14 miles NE of Cherbourg (49 49 00N; 01 25 00W). *Master's name:* George Boyd. *Crew:* 23. *Crew nationality:* All British.

THE Admiralty were not pleased with the actions taken by the master of the *Gowrie* his ship was lost to an enemy torpedo. She had left St Helens on October 9, 1917, and was escorted by a patrol trawler across the Channel towards Cherbourg. The weather was bad, being a dark night with a strong breeze and a heavy swell.

At 3.40am on October 10, the master was aware that he could no longer see his escort and slowed the engines down in the hope that they would meet up shortly. One of his crew then shouted that he could see a vessel off the port bow and the master looked to see if it was the missing escort. He couldn't be sure but assumed it was and put his bow lights on to help the escort locate him. It was a fatal mistake as a few moments later the master realised that it wasn't the escort trawler but an enemy submarine. Almost at the same time a torpedo slammed into the port side of the ship tearing a big hole in her below the waterline.

The master later claimed that he didn't hear the explosion or see any blast damage but a lookout named Michael Doyle, stated that a large column of water was thrown up level with the bridge and the gangway doors and rails were all broken and twisted.

The *Gowrie's* engines were stopped and the boats lowered as the ship settled more and more into the water. The crew pulled clear of the ship and stood by until 5.30am when she sank. The submarine's conning tower was spotted close by at one stage. The boats pulled for the coast and eventually made it safely into Cherbourg.

The Admiralty concluded that the master had been extremely slack with his organisation in the event of an attack and had no control over his crew. Consequently, they banned him from taking command of any Admiralty ship or any ship on Admiralty service. They also recommended that he be blacklisted on the War Risk Insurance, which effectively meant that no employer could ever employ him as a master.

George Boyd obviously accepted the criticism as he asked the Admiralty if he could continue working as a first mate and they agreed.

The submarine concerned was *U-53*.

11/35: GOOD HOPE. *Country:* British.
Date sunk: 27/4/17. *Tons nett:* 77. *Tons gross:* 86. *Built:* Boxham in 1905. *Type:* SV. *Rig:* Ketch. *Owners:* W.T. Symonds & Co, 72, Bute St, Cardiff. *Cargo:* None. *Armed:* No. *Position:* 15 miles NNW of Barfluer (49 56 00N; 01 24 00W). *Master's name:* Joseph Rands, 49, Somers Rd, Southsea. *Crew:* 4. *Crew nationality:* All British.

AT 11.15am on April 27, 1917, the master was on watch by the seaman at the wheel keeping a sharp lookout for enemy submarines. He had been warned earlier that they were about and didn't relish the idea of bumping into one. However, he didn't spot the submarine which surfaced off their starboard beam. The first he knew of it was when a shell came whistling over the rigging and splashed into the water on the other side. This was followed by a second which also missed, but only just. When he did spot the U-boat the master was surprised to see that the submarine was about two miles off. He realised that he had no chance of escape and ordered his men to get the boat ready whilst he set about burning his confidential sailing instructions.

The men left their ship in the nick of time for when they were only 20yds away a shell slammed into the stern of *Good Hope* smashing away her rudder and leaving a huge hole in the stern. She started to settle immediately and by the time the submarine arrived she had sunk.

The German commander appeared to be in a bad mood and shouted at the master to come alongside and show his papers or else. The master was in no position to refuse. After getting the information he wanted the commander's last words were: "It's a pity all you Britishers aren't killed."

The crew rowed towards the French coast and were later spotted by a torpedo boat which took them to Cherbourg.

11/36: RAGNA. *Country:* Norwegian.
Date sunk: 23/12/17. *Tons nett:* 1747. *Tons gross:* –. *Built:* –. *Type:* SS. *Rig:* –. *Owners:* N. Ragenes, Haugesund, Norway. *Cargo:* 2333 tons coal, Barry for Rouen. *Armed:* No. *Position:* 18 miles N by W of Cape Barfleur (49 59 00N; 01 22 00W). *Master's name:* Nils Jargin Nilson. *Crew:* 19. *Crew nationality:* 7 Norwegians, 6 Spaniards, 2 Russian/Finns, 2 Dutch, 2 Danes.

RAGNA was the fifth vessel in a convoy consisting of eight ships. Nobody is precisely sure what happened as it was very dark and all over with so quickly. At 2.45am she suffered a huge explosion on her port side in number four hold which blew a large hole in her. She took in water rapidly but one of the escorting trawlers HMT *Sweeper* was alongside very quickly to take the crew off.

The master wasn't sure whether he had struck a mine or had been torpedoed. However, Commander Humphries of *Sweeper* said that as he was taking the men off *Ragna*, some of his men said they saw the wake of a torpedo pass astern of them. He immediately started a search for any sign of the submarine but had no luck.

The convoy continued ahead regardless, leaving *Sweeper* with the *Ragna's* crew to catch up. They were all landed safely at St Helens later the same day.

Admiralty records list *Ragna* as "torpedoed".

11/37: DUCHESS OF CORNWALL.
Country: British. *Date sunk:* 11/4/17. *Tons nett:* 1070. *Tons gross:* 1706. *Built:* 1889. *Type:* SS. *Rig:* schooner. *Owners:* Duchess of Cornwall SS Co Ltd, Truro. *Cargo:* Government stores. *Armed:* Yes. *Position:* 5 miles N of Cape Barfleur (49 47 00N; 01 16 00W). *Master's name:* W. Irvine. *Crew:* 22.

WHAT happened in the early hours of April 11, 1917, was told by the only survivor, Gunner Sidney Beck, RNR, No 2621B. He said that they left London on April 9, bound for Boulogne. On reaching there they received new instructions to head for Havre but on arrival were told that the port of Havre was closed and they would have to go to Cherbourg.

It was a bright moonlit night and Sidney Beck was at his station by the gun. Just after midnight on April 11, he said he saw something moving through the water but assumed it was a porpoise. He turned out to be wildly wrong as a torpedo slammed into the starboard side amidships causing an enormous explosion. The steamer sank immediately leaving all those below with no chance of escape. Sidney Beck was lucky to have been on deck and found himself floating in the water. He swam around and looked for something to cling to and again was lucky in finding a large plank.

In Sidney Beck's brief letter to the Admiralty he didn't say how long he was floating around but it couldn't have been long for the time of year or he would never have survived the cold. He did mention however, that he was picked up by a patrol vessel and taken to Cherbourg.

The *Duchess* was torpedoed by *UC-26*.

11/38: CONOID. *Country:* British. *Date sunk:* 29/3/17. *Tons nett:* 140. *Tons gross:* 165. *Built:* Peterhead in 1865. *Type:* SV. *Rig:* schooner. *Owners:* T. Couch & Sons, St Austell, Cornwall. *Cargo:* 290 tons china clay, shipped by Parkyn & Peters, St Austell, and consigned to Rouen. *Armed:* No. *Position:* 3½ miles N of Cape Barfleur (49 46 00N; 01 15 00W). *Master's name:* Frank

Larscombe. *Crew:* 5. *Crew nationality:* All British.

THE scant details on the deposition made by the master of *Conoid* state that she sailed from Fowey on March 28, 1917, and crossed the Channel. Her problems began at 8am the next morning when an enemy submarine appeared almost alongside and started a crippling bombardment with her deck gun. The Germans gave the crew no chance to get themselves together and one shell even smashed their lifeboat to pieces. In desperation they dug out a small 12ft dingy and in a very choppy sea managed to get clear of their sinking vessel.

They left just in time for the *Conoid* sank within minutes of their leaving. They set a course for the French coast which was fairly close. However, it was hard going in a small boat in such rough seas. The crew landed at St Vaast-la-Hougue later the same day.

11/39: WALTER ULRIC. *Country:* British. *Date sunk:* 29/3/17. *Tons nett:* 91. *Tons gross:* 112. *Built:* 1875. *Type:* SV. *Rig:* schooner. *Owners:* A.W. Chard, Commercial Chambers, Falmouth. *Cargo:* 190 tons coal, Cardiff for Caen. *Armed:* No. *Position:* 4 miles N of Cape Barfleur (49 47 00N; 01 15 00W). *Master's name:* C. Wall. *Crew:* 6.

WALTER ULRIC was in company with the sailing vessel *Conoid*. After *Conoid* was sunk by a German submarine the surviving crew reported that they saw the submarine chase off after the *Walter Ulric* and gunfire was heard coming from her general direction. However, as darkness was falling at the time they were unable to see whether she was sunk or managed to give the submarine the slip.

The Admiralty records stated that there was no knowledge of her whereabouts and concluded that it was most likely she was sunk by the submarine. She was posted as "missing".

11/40: ROMNY. *Country:* British. *Date sunk:* 26/2/18. *Tons nett:* 525. *Tons gross:* 1024. *Built:* 1913. *Type:* SS. *Rig:* schooner. *Owners:* Det Forenede Dampskibsselckab, Copenhagen. *Charterers:* Lambert Bros, 85, Gracechurch St, London. *Cargo:* In ballast,Rouen to Swansea. *Armed:* 1 x 13pdr Vickers. *Position:* 10 miles NNE from Cape Barfleur (49 52 00N; 01 12 00W). *Master's name:* Charles Herbert Rowland. *Crew:* 25. *Crew nationality:* 15 British, 10 others.

ROMNY was part of a convoy which had set off to cross the Channel from Rouen. The convoy was formed in two columns and everything proceeded as normal for the first part of the journey. After the convoy made the next course change they continued in formation until 5.30am when gunfire was heard and the whole convoy was ordered to start zig-zagging,

a tedious routine but the best available at the time.

At 6.15am *Romny* had been singled out by Oberleutnant Ernst Steindorff, commander of the German submarine *UB-74*. He was at periscope depth judging the timing of his shot. The torpedo smashed into the *Romny's* stern. Such was the force of the explosion that about 15ft of the stern section was completely blown away, killing the two gunners instantly.

There are few other details except that the surviving 16 crew members managed to get a boat launched and were picked up by a French patrol vessel.

11/41: AMBIORIX. *Country:* Belgian. *Date sunk:* 6/12/17. *Tons nett:* –. *Tons gross:* 1444. *Built:* –. *Type:* SS. *Rig:* –. *Owners:* –. *Cargo:* –. *Armed:* –. *Position:* 20 miles NNE of Barfleur (50 00 00N; 01 07 00W). *Master's Name:* –. *Crew:* 24.

THIS information came from a brief mention in Weekly Reports which noted that the commanding officer of HMT 1162, *Sapper*, reported a collision between the SS *Primo* and the SS *Ambiorix* at 9.30pm in the above position. *Ambiorix* was the fourth ship of a line in convoy. She sank 15 minutes after the collision.

All the crew were picked up and also two of the crew from the *Primo* who had jumped overboard at the time of impact. They were all landed at Havre.

Ambiorix had been captured by the Germans in August, 1915, but was released in December 1916.

11/42: GREAVESASH. *Country:* British. *Date sunk:* 26/2/18. *Tons nett:* 687. *Tons gross:* 1263. *Built:* 1918. *Type:* SS. *Rig:* schooner. *Owners:* E.R. Newbigin, Mansion House Chambers, Newcastle. *Cargo:* In ballast,Havre to Barry Roads. *Armed:* 1 x 12pdr 12cwt gun. *Position:* 7-10 miles ENE of Barfleur (49 45 00N; 01 04 00W). *Master's name:* Albert Sydney Taylor. *Crew:* 20. *Crew nationality:* 18 British, 2 Spaniards. *Gunners:* Cuthbert Alfred Dowdeswell, Act LS RNVR, No WZ3059 Portsmouth; Daniel Collins, AB RNVR, No 1790 Portsmouth.

THIS vessel sank very rapidly after a torpedo crashed into the side of number one hold. The master said that he was in the charthouse at the time of the explosion and although he came out immediately, the ship was by then almost under. He didn't know it at the time but the German submarine *UB-74* was the culprit. Her commander, Oberleutnant Ernst Steindorff, had left Zeebrugge only the night before with his crew, refreshed after a two week break.

The speed of the sinking was confirmed by the second steward, Victor Williams, who said that he was asleep in his berth aft and on hearing the explosion rushed on deck. Finding that the deck was awash he dived into the sea and commenced swimming to what he thought was one of the ship's boats. On getting closer to the object he claimed that a torpedo came zipping past him and it appeared to come from whatever he was swimming towards. The *Greavesash* had long since sunk and there was no reason for another torpedo. He decided not to approach the object and swam away.

He eventually found 11 of his fellow crew members and all of them were eventually picked up and landed at Cherbourg. However, eight others went down with the ship.

11/43: BOAZ. *Country:* British. *Date sunk:* 31/3/17. *Tons nett:* 93. *Tons gross:* 110. *Built:* Littlehampton in 1908. *Type:* SV. *Rig:* ketch. *Owners:* The Wynnfield Shipping Co, Grimsby. *Cargo:* In ballast, Ouistreham to Poole. *Armed:* No. *Position:* 15 miles NE of Cape Barfleur (49 52 00N; 01 00 00W). *Master's name:* William Alfred Moorcraft. *Crew:* 4.

Boaz had left France on the morning of March 31, 1917, bound for Poole in Dorset. She was not a particularly fast vessel, her normal speed being only about 3 knots. She was in company with another sailing ship the *Gippeswic* and together they hugged the French coastline as close as safety would permit. At 3.30 in the afternoon *Boaz* was spotted by an enemy submarine.

In fact, the master was first to see her when she surfaced about three miles off on his starboard bow. He shouted to the helmsman to steer away and hoped he might escape, but it was too late. As the submarine caught up with *Boaz* the German gunner opened fire. Several shells threw up spouts of water all around her with one striking home and the master realised he had no choice but to stop. Obeying the signals, the crew pulled away in their boat and headed out towards the waiting submarine. The master was ordered on board for questioning while his boat and crew were used by German sailors to plant bombs on *Boaz*. Before leaving her the sailors helped themselves to various items of food and equipment. At 4pm it was all over for the *Boaz* as the bombs exploded and she sank immediately.

The crew were cast adrift to fend for themselves as the submarine raced off to attack the *Gippeswic* which shared the same fate. For 22 hours the crew rowed towards the French coast making little or no headway against the wind and tide. They were eventually spotted by a French destroyer and picked up.

11/44: GIPPESWIC. *Country:* British. *Date sunk:* 31/3/17. *Tons nett:* 92. *Tons gross:* 115. *Built:* Littlehampton in 1912. *Type:* SV. *Rig:* Ketch. *Owners:* The Wynnfield Shipping Co, Grimsby. *Cargo:* in ballast, Caen to Poole. *Armed:* No.

Position: 15 miles NE of Cape Barfleur (49 52 00N; 01 00 00W). *Master's name:* John Larking. *Crew:* 4.

THE story of the *Gippeswic* is nearly a carbon copy of that of the *Boaz*. They were in company and both heading for Poole in Dorset. The master had just witnessed the fate of his companion and was in no hurry to share the same. The crew put up as much sail as they could get on her in the hope of trying to escape but it was useless. The *Gippeswic* could barely make 3 knots in a good wind while the German submarine could do over 15.

As the submarine closed on the little ship the master ordered his men to take to the boat . The same format was followed with several German sailors going over to the *Gippeswic* and planting bombs, after helping themselves to whatever provisions they fancied. However, they were not so efficient this time. The bombs failed to sink her and she had to be finished off by the gunner.

The crew made for Barfleur and were for a time in company with the crew from the *Boaz*. They became separated during the night but after nearly 24 hours they were spotted by the French torpedo boat *Harpon* and taken to Cherbourg.

11/45: MORNING STAR. *Country:* British. *Date sunk:* 12/11/17. *Tons nett:* 86. *Tons gross:* 129. *Built:* Greenock in 1869. *Type:* MV. *Rig:* motor schooner. *Owners:* Oakley, Sollas & Co, 52, Gracechurch, London. *Cargo:* 150 tons china clay from Fowey to Rouen. *Armed:* No. *Position:* 11 miles E by S of Barfleur Point (49 40 00N; 01 00 00W). *Master's name:* John Peard. *Crew:* 5.

WHILST the master was detained on board the enemy submarine for questioning a German sailor held a rifle on the men who were alongside in the lifeboat. They were the crew of the *Morning Star*, forced by fierce shelling from the submarine to abandon her. The sailor was very sympathetic and talked to the men in good English. " I lived a long time in England, I know it well. I curse this war, I wish it was over. It is not our fault that we have to sink your ship, we just have to do our duty. I know the people back in England will not believe that but it's true." He looked away. He looked tired and hungry. The men said afterwards that all the German crew looked pale and edgy.

A German officer walked to the boat, the sailor accompanying him clutching two bombs. They climbed in with the men from *Morning Star* and ordered them to row back to their ship. They were told to wait as the officer disappeared aboard. He was gone for some time but later appeared with armfuls of the ship's equipment, flags, charts, food and many other bits and bobs. He looked around with the bombs in his hands before deciding the best place to put them. The *Morning Star's* men watched him fumbling around the ship, his hands visibly shaking, his head constantly lifting, looking first at his submarine and then around the horizon. Here was a troubled man, they all thought. After choosing the two spots he judged would do the most damage he hung the bombs and jumping back down into the boat, ordered the men to row him back to his ship.

Back on the submarine the master was still being questioned by her commander. He did not look well. The master said that he was very fidgety, breaking off sentence to shout orders and hurry people along. He was dirty, unshaven, his eyes had large bags under them. The master wondered what they had gone through to put them all in such a state.

The bombs exploded about five minute later and at 8pm *Morning Star* was no more. The crew were picked up about an hour later by a French patrol boat and taken to Cherbourg.

WORLD WAR ONE
CHANNEL WRECKS

◆

AREA
TWELVE

WRECK SITES IN AREA TWELVE

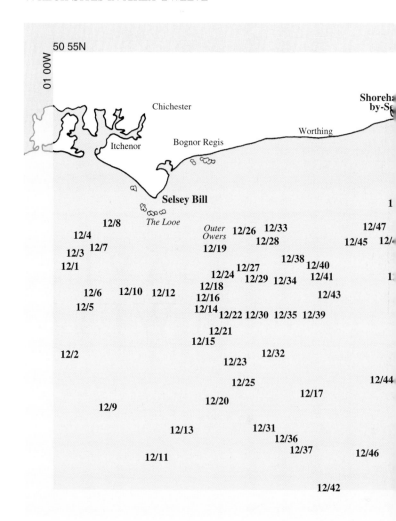

Brighton

12/63
12/66
12/64
12/65

2/56 12/57
12/58
12/59

5   12/62

12/61

12/60
12/67
50 20N

00 00

12/1: ELFORD. *Country:* British. *Date sunk:* 18/5/17. *Tons nett:* 929. *Tons gross:* 1739. *Built:* 1915. *Type:* SS. *Rig:* schooner/tanker. *Owners:* Sharp SS Co, Milburn House, Newcastle. *Cargo:* Government stores, Chatham for Cherbourg. *Armed:* No. *Position:* 2 miles S from Nab Light Vessel (50 38 06N; 00 58 30W). *Master's name:* Lieut David Gillan, RNR. *Crew:* 21.

ELFORD met her end at 2am on May 18, 1917. She was steaming down the Channel under escort at full speed. The weather was good, fine and clear and the sea was calm. Without any warning a violent explosion occurred aft, so powerful that it blew the hatch covers completely off and threw out much of the cargo.

She began to settle by the stern straight away and the master ordered all hands to their boat stations whilst he assessed the situation. After a check he concluded that she would eventually sink and ordered the boats away to a waiting escort vessel.

From the escort they watched the fate of the *Elford* which, although settling down had stabilised somewhat and the master had the idea of going back to the ship to fetch some of his papers. He had already thrown his confidential papers overboard in the weighted bag but he felt it would be useful to get some of the others. The master and mate rowed over to the stricken steamer but she was at an extremely awkward angle. They tried to get aboard but it was impossible to do with any degree of safety.

About 45 minutes after the explosion the *Elford* finally gave up and sank. It wasn't certain what had caused the explosion. Some said it was a torpedo, others a mine, but the authorities came down on the side of a mine as several had been found in the vicinity about that time.

12/2: WAPELLO. *Country:* British. *Date sunk:* 15/6/17. *Tons nett:* 3368. *Tons gross:* 5576. *Built:* 1912. *Type:* SS. *Rig:* schooner. *Owners:* The Tank Storage & Carriage Co Ltd, London. *Cargo:* Benzine. *Armed:* 1 x 12pdr 12cwt gun. *Position:* 15 miles S 58 Deg E from St Catherines (50 31 00N; 00 58 30W). *Master's name:* D. MacDonald. *Crew:* 46. *Crew nationality:* 45 British, 1 Russian. *Gunners:* A. Smith, Pte RMLI No 5804; M. Morris, Pte RMLI, No 8635.

THE tanker *Wapello* left the port of Philadelphia, USA on May 30, 1917, and was bound for Thameshaven. Her orders were to call into Falmouth which she did and left there on June 14. She proceeded up the Channel under escort and was making about nine knots. Nothing suspicious was seen by any of the lookouts, but suddenly a cry from the bridge and a hand pointed to what looked like the wake of a torpedo. The helm was immediately put hard to starboard but it was too late and it slammed into the starboard side of the ship, tearing an enormous hole in the bunker hold.

The force of the explosion killed two of the crew and the ship began to settle down in the water rapidly. The tanker was brought to a halt and the remainder of the crew came on deck making for the boats. Within a few minutes of the crew getting clear of her the *Wapello* sank.

Meanwhile, escort trawlers *Caliph* and *Lord Stanhope* had appeared on the scene and picked up the survivors. They were later landed at Portsmouth.

Oberleutnant Reinhold Salzwedel in *UC-71* had torpedoed her.

12/3: ERIN II. *Country:* British.
Date sunk: 19/10/15. *Tons nett:* –. *Tons gross:* 181.
Built: –. *Type:* Hired armed trawler. *Rig:* –.
Owners: Admiralty. *Cargo:* –. *Armed:* Yes.
Position: 3-4 cables SSW of Nab Light Vessel
(50 39 30N; 00 57 20W). *Master's name:* Lieut
E.G. Rule. *Crew:* –. *Crew nationality:* British.

LIEUTENANT Rule should have been off duty. Lieutenant Wilkinson in *Jackdaw* met *Erin II* and informed the commander that he should have gone into harbour at daylight, so with all possible speed he made to do just that. At 12.30pm the vessel was smashed to a halt by a violent explosion at her aft end and she began to sink immediately. No sooner had Lieutenant Rule ordered all the crew on deck, than the ship sank from beneath them.

Seven men were killed by what must have undoubtedly been a mine contact. Prior to the explosion Lieutenant Rule had fortunately ordered the patrol vessel *Elisi* to come within hail so she was close at hand to render assistance.

This spot was to prove a troublesome one as later events showed. On October 22, 1915, the salvage tug *Grappler* was over the wreck of the *Erin II* salvaging her guns and stores. Two divers were sent down to assess the situation and shortly after, Diver Bishop surfaced to say that *Erin's* sweeping net was obstructing his work. A line was attached to it and put around a capstan on *Grappler*. As soon as the line began to take in there was an enormous explosion under *Grappler's* bows. When the turmoil subsided, two bodies were seen in the water, Mr Stubble, a rigging inspector, and Mr Carr, a chargeman. Mr Tarrant, mate of the *Grappler* was blown off the sponson and was never seen again. The second engineer, Mr Herring, was blown overboard and swam back but later died from his injuries. Edward Hart, a rigger, was found dead, suspended by his wrist in the wreckage over the starboard bow.

Grappler was saved and towed into port.

12/4: STAR OF BUCHAN. *Country:* British.
Date sunk: 20/10/15. *Tons nett:* –. *Tons gross:*
81.*Built:* –.*Type:* Hired armed drifter. *Rig:* –.

Owners: Admiralty. *Cargo:* –. *Armed:* Yes.
Position: Nab LS bearing W by N 500yds
(50 40 00N; 00 56 40W). *Master's name:* James
May..

AT 6.30am on October 20, 1915, the crew of *Star of Buchan* were hauling in her indicator net. Most of it was on board coming up over the bows, both ends were in but something was fouling a total clearance. The captain in the wheelhouse heard the mate say that he could see something in the net. His words were followed instantly by a huge explosion.

Captain May was partly stunned and when he recovered sufficiently, saw that the whole of the fore part of his ship was blown away leaving the deck just level with the water. She sank far too quickly for the boat to be cleared and the seven men working forward were all killed. The dingy from Nab Light Ship picked up one survivor and the vessel *Desperates* picked up the remainder.

12/5: LUCKNOW. *Country:* British.
Date sunk: 18/5/17. *Tons nett:* –. *Tons gross:* 171.
Built: –. *Type:* Armed trawler. *Rig:* –. *Owners:*
Admiralty. *Cargo:* –. *Armed:* Yes. *Position:* 9 miles
E by S of Dunnose, Isle of Wight (50 35 00N;
00 56 30W). *Master's name:* –. *Crew:* –. *Crew
nationality:* British.

IN some ways it was just bad luck on the part of the *Lucknow* when she was blown up by a mine. However, a senior officer said later that the patrol trawlers involved in the incident shouldn't have been in the minefield at low water.

Lieutenant Commander J. Burn, RNR, was in command of HM yacht *Vagrant* and was in company with *Lucknow* on mine clearing operations on the Owers Inner Patrol. Some distance away the trawler *Tally Ho* signalled to *Vagrant* that mines had been spotted. *Vagrant* and *Lucknow* immediately headed off in the direction indicated by *Tally Ho* to see what they could do.

After a few minutes *Lucknow* signalled that she had spotted two floating mines and was going to open fire to sink them. She was joined by *Vagrant* and a torpedo boat who all joined in the shooting, their crews obviously eager for some target practise. One mine was successfully detonated and *Lucknow* set about the other one on her own as she had the clearest view of it. Unknown to the commander of *Lucknow* he was drifting into danger. A moment later she bumped into another mine. A huge explosion followed and according to Lieutenant Burn huge clouds of steam and smoke billowed into the air. When it cleared sufficiently to see, *Lucknow* had disappeared.

Boats were lowered from *Vagrant* and *Tally Ho* very quickly and rowed into the wreckage to find survivors. Fortunately, seven men were found but they were all seriously injured. The men were rushed to port and taken aboard the Haslar Hospital launch.

The whole incident was discussed at a Court of Enquiry and the procedure for dealing with moored mines was restated. Under no circumstances should sweepers attempt to clear mines at low water. They should be marked with a buoy and watched carefully from a safe distance as low water approaches. Once the position of the mines are known relative to the buoy they can be cleared from about two hours after low water onwards.

12/6: HMT APLEY. *Country:* British. *Date sunk:* 6/12/17. *Tons nett:* –. *Tons gross:* 250. *Built:* –. *Type:* Patrol Trawler. *Rig:* –. *Owners:* Admiralty. *Cargo:* –. *Armed:* Yes. *Position:* 4 miles SE of Culver (50 36 00N; 00 55 30W). *Master's name:* Lieutenant Frederick W. Moody, RNR. *Crew:* 17. *Crew nationality:* British

THE only report that sheds any light on the fate of the minesweeping trawler, number 143 *Apley* was in a letter from the Flag Captain to the Commander-in-Chief. The Admiralty concluded that nothing further would be gained by holding a Court of Enquiry and that is why there is little documentation.

Apley was leading four divisions of minesweepers in the vicinity of Owers at 11.30am on Thursday December 6, 1917. She had just finished her sweep and was proceeding to another area as per orders. *Apley* dropped a dan buoy to mark the position for the start of the new sweep when suddenly the shout went up from a lookout, "Mine on the starboard bow!"

The skipper asked: "Where?" But there was no time for an answer as a tremendous explosion blew the foremost half of the ship to pieces. *Apley* sank at once taking two officers and nine ratings with her. Boats were launched by other sweepers close at hand and *Manx King* and *Oxwich Castle* succeeded in finding six men alive. Her commander, Fred Moody was lost. He was described later as a capable and trustworthy minesweeping officer who had done much good work and would be difficult to replace.

12/7: HMD PELAGIA. *Country:* British. *Date sunk:* 28/11/16. *Tons nett:* –. *Tons gross:* 84. *Built:* –. *Type:* hired drifter. *Rig:* –. *Owners:* Admiralty. *Cargo:* –. *Armed:* Yes. *Position:* 1¹/₂ miles E by S of Nab Light Vessel (50 40 00N; 00 55 00W). *Master's name:* –. *Crew:* –. *Crew nationality:* British.

THE only information available on this sinking in these records comes from Weekly Reports which says *Pelagia* was sunk by a mine just south of a line of moored nets near Nab.

12/8: CORBET WOODALL. *Country:* British. *Date sunk:* 30/5/17. *Tons nett:* 544. *Tons gross:* 917. *Built:* Sunderland in 1908. *Type:* SS. *Rig:*

schooner. *Owners:* Stephenson R. Clarke, 4, St Dunstans Alley, Newcastle. *Cargo:* 1250 tons coal, South Shields for Poole. *Armed:* 1 x 3pdr Hotchkiss. *Position:* 2¹/₂ miles NE by E of Nab (50 41 30N; 00 53 30W). *Master's name:* Joseph Henry Brown. *Crew:* 16. *Gunners:* Joseph L. Bone, LS RNVR No 2800 Chatham; Stanley Clark, LS RNVR No 2583 Chatham.

WHEN *Corbet Woodall* struck a mine at 10.30am on May 30, 1917, nobody on board saw anything. The weather was certainly good enough to have spotted any lurking submarine or the tell tale white streak of a torpedo. In the conditions it could only have been a mine and a subsequent search by sweepers did reveal several of them.

She was steering west by south at the time making just over nine knots and so hit the mine with considerable impact. The explosion was enormous, on the port side just forward of the bridge. The master and mate were on the bridge at the time and were dazed by the blast. The bows went down almost instantly and the master realised that he had to get his crew clear quickly. Luckily he was well organised and the boats were always carried swung out ready for just such an emergency. By the time the crew were in the boats *Corbet Woodall's* bows were already resting on the bottom in 40ft of water.

About 10 minutes after the explosion all the crew were well clear of the steamer, when her stern suddenly plunged downwards to join the bows on the shallow bottom. Apart from a few minor injuries all escaped relatively unscathed.

12/9: GERMAN SUBMARINE (UB-81). *Country:* German. *Date sunk:* 2/12/17. *Tons nett:* 650. *Tons gross:* 520. *Built:* 1917. *Type:* UB-class III. *Owners:* German navy. *Armed:* 10 torpedoes, 10.5cm deck gun. *Position:* 17 miles ESE from St Catherines Light (50 27 00N; 00 53 30W). *Master's name:* Oberleutnant Reinhold Salzwedel. *Crew:* 34. *Crew nationality:* German.

UB-81 was a brand new submarine, but with a veteran U-boat ace in command. She left Zeebrugge on November 28, 1917. She got through the Dover Straits without any problems and on sighting several British torpedo boats off Beachy Head, dived to steer clear of them. Salzwedel's orders were to sink merchant shipping, not to get involved in fights with patrol boats.

On December 2, *UB-81* was cruising submerged at 20 metres depth about two miles south-east from Owers, when she struck a small mine aft. The damage was such that she could use her engine but couldn't fully dump her ballast. The situation worsened when her aft bulkhead started leaking, flooding the engine room. The only thing the crew could do was to remove the torpedoes from the forward tubes and pump air into the bow tanks. Soon several feet of the submarine showed above water and by sliding through a torpedo tube, several men were able to climb out to sit on her bows.

At 10.07pm HMS *P12* was returning to Portsmouth on completion of escort duty to Dieppe. Lieutenant L.W. Newberry-Boschetti, in command, said that he received a radio message from Culver to investigate a rocket seven miles south-south-east of Culver. He altered course accordingly and headed off to have a look. At 10.15pm he also saw a rocket go up and increased speed towards it. As he approached, a lookout shouted that morse was coming over on a flashlamp which read, 'SOS. We want your help, who are you?'

On closing with the area, the lieutenant said he saw what appeared to be the bows of a small vessel sticking up out of the water with several men clinging to it, shouting for help. He passed about 20yds off the vessel and turned with the intention of going alongside to rescue the men. However, the patrol boat GB *109* was close astern blocking his turn and forced him to widen the circle bringing him on to the weather side. At 10.45pm *P12* crashed into *UB-81* with tragic results. An engineer, Mr Davison, said he was standing abreast of the engine room hatch and was so close he could have touched the submarine. He reported hearing the submarine's plates give and five seconds later she plunged to the bottom.

One German sailor managed to jump aboard *P12* before *UB-81* went down. Several others were left floating around in the water shouting, "We are your prisoners." A skiff was launched and the remainder picked up by able seaman A.L. Levin, who in the words of his commander, "handled it with such skill in such bad conditions." This action later earned him a commendation.

By this time many other patrol vessels were in the area and one dropped a dan buoy to mark *UB-81's* resting place. The prisoners were all put on board *P12* and placed under the charge of Mallett, a gunner, as they made for St Helens. Two officers were among the prisoners and could speak English very well. They explained how they came to be in the situation and added that they were grateful to have been taken by the British and not the French.

Several statements were taken from the prisoners and other information came to light. Apparently she carried 10 torpedoes but had used none of them. *UB-81's* engineer said that she could make 30 knots on the surface although only nine knots underwater and could maintain it for about 50 hours.

Although the Admiralty were pleased generally with the events, they considered that *P12* should have depth charged *UB-81* after she sank to make sure she was finished. They mentioned that they did find the wreck later in 17 fathoms and that divers were going to be put down to get inside her. They refused Lieutenant Newberry-Boschetti's application for prize money on the grounds that the submarine was already sunk. *P12* had merely speeded up the process and drowned the remainder of the crew in the process.

12/10: LOWMOUNT. *Country:* British. *Date sunk:* 7/5/17. *Tons nett:* 1295. *Tons gross:* 2070. *Built:* Sunderland in 1888. *Type:* SS. *Rig:* schooner. *Owners:* A.Capel & Co, Exchange Buildings, Newcastle. *Cargo:* 2650 tons iron ore from Bilbao to Stockton-on-Tees. *Armed:* No. *Position:* 5 miles SW of Owers/4 miles SE of Nab (50 36 00N; 00 50 00W). *Master's name:* John Williams. *Crew:* 22. *Crew nationality:* 13 British, 5 Russians, 3 Spaniards, 1 Dane.

THE journey from Bilbao was fairly uneventful for the *Lowmount* until the convoy ran into a gale on May 5, 1917. So bad were the conditions that the lookouts couldn't keep track of the rest of the convoy and they lost them. The master decided to ride the worst of the storm out and eventually made St Helens at 5pm on the 7th. At 8.30 the same evening a patrol boat from the examination vessel gave *Lowmount* permission to leave and she got underway half an hour later.

The Chief Officer, John Alfred Copeman, had the watch from 8pm until midnight and said that all was well as they proceeded east up the Channel. The weather was slightly overcast but the visibility was good with only a slight swell on the sea.

At 9.40pm she passed Nab Light Vessel steering south-east half east and making a steady eight and a half knots. At 10.25pm when about four miles off Owers there was a tremendous explosion in number two hold which blew the hatches clean off and sent clouds of ore heaving into the air. The blast was so powerful that it caused the bridge to collapse and the men inside it only just got clear.

The chief officer ran to the port lifeboat and started to cut the lashings, the steamer sinking so fast that the bottom of the lifeboat was nearly touching the water. In minutes the stern was well awash and the port lifeboat just got clear.

The steward had tackled the starboard boat and he also managed to get it clear with a few men. Both boats rowed around for nearly half an hour picking up men, but five didn't make it. They were down below at the time and were either killed by the explosion or drowned by the sudden inrush of water.

Having picked up the men, the mate lit a red flare which managed to attract the attention of torpedo boat number *109*, which soon came to investigate. The crew were first taken to St Helens and from there to Portsmouth.

The master and mate of the *Lowmount* were under the impression that they had been hit by a torpedo, although nobody on board had seen any trace of a submarine. The naval authorities however, were of the opinion that she had struck a mine.

UC-70 later claimed the *Lowmount* as a victim of one of her minefields.

12/11: GERMAN SUBMARINE (possible).

Country: German. *Date sunk:* 4/9/17. *Tons nett:* –. *Tons gross:* –. *Built:* –. *Type:* –. *Owners:* German navy. *Armed:* Yes. *Position:* 23 miles SE by E of St Catherines Point (50 23 00N; 00 47 00W). *Master's name:* –. *Crew:* –. *Crew nationality:* German.

THERE is documentation in Weekly Reports that is worthy of note concerning the possible sinking of an enemy submarine.

The commander of HMML *82*, Lieutenant A.E. Durrant, reported that on September 4, 1917, he had depth charged a hostile submarine and that a French seaplane had flown over him and dropped a message which read, 'Submarine attack. Good results'.

The next day the Lieutenant made a further report on the incident. He said that after spotting the submarine's conning tower he immediately put his ship up to full speed. He got extremely close to the U-boat before she dived and he managed to drop the first depth charge directly over her. The explosion sent up an enormous column of water and several of his men said they saw large flat pieces of metal mixed in with the water. He dropped a second charge but this time the explosion caused nowhere near the amount of disturbance on the surface and he suggested that it was the rupturing of the submarine which created the large column of water on the previous charge.

There is nothing further which might substantiate the report and so far no other comments or awards of prize money from the Admiralty has been found in the records. Nor do German records have any casualties for that date or area.

12/12: AXWELL. *Country:* British.

Date sunk: 13/11/17. *Tons nett:* 784. *Tons gross:* 1442. *Built:* West Hartlepool in 1909. *Type:* SS. *Rig:* schooner. *Owners:* Broomhill Colliers Ltd, Collingwood Buildings, Newcastle. *Cargo:* 1850 tons coal from A.T. Watson, Newcastle, to R. Lyon, Rouen. *Armed:* 1 x 3pdr Vickers. *Position:* 3 miles WSW of Owers (50 36 00N; 00 46 00W). *Master's name:* William Norman Thompson.

AXWELL left Amble on November 9, 1917, and called into Southend for instructions. She left there and began her journey down the Channel before cutting across to Rouen.

At 4.45am on the 13th the second mate was on the bridge and spotted an object just off his starboard bow. The object was moving and crossing him from starboard to port. He became suspicious and decided to do what was recommended by the Admiralty and head straight towards it. By now he could just see in the darkness that it was a submarine partially submerged and a series of cat and mouse manoeuvres took place with the result that the *Axwell* struck the submarine a glancing blow along her starboard side. The submarine was forced to swing alongside the steamer and on looking over the side the second mate was able to look directly down onto the conning tower.

The submarine then made off and was soon out of sight. Meanwhile, the master, who had felt the collision, came on the bridge to find out what was going on. He ordered the ship to continue towards St Helens and after a while spotted a patrol vessel. The master turned towards the trawler with the intention of informing the commander about the submarine. He drew closer and was just about to put the megaphone to his lips when a loud explosion boomed out on the *Axwell's* port side amidships.

The ship sank rapidly and the crew made for the only two lifeboats which were intact, the explosion having destroyed the others. Fifteen minutes later the deck was awash and the crew pulled clear of the sinking ship. It was still dark and soon they lost sight of *Axwell*. The patrol vessel picked them up and began to search for two missing men but could find no trace of them. At daylight it was discovered that *Axwell* was still afloat and the master and four of his crew boarded her but found that she was completely full of water. A tow line was tried but as soon as headway was put on the steamer she lurched over and sank.

It seems that the enemy submarine commander, Oberleutnant Hans Valentiner in *UB-56*, didn't like being bumped by steamers!.

12/13: TEELIN HEAD. *Country:* British.

Date sunk: 21/1/18. *Tons nett:* 1083. *Tons gross:* 1718. *Built:* 1883. *Type:* SS. *Rig:* schooner. *Owners:* Ulster SS Co, Ulster Chambers, Belfast. *Cargo:* 1700 tons potatoes. 1520 tons consigned to Admiralty. *Armed:* 1 x 12pdr gun. *Position:* 12 miles S by W of Owers Light Vessel (50 25 00N; 00 44 00W). *Master's name:* Robert Suffern. *Crew:* 28. *Crew nationality:* 27 British, 1 Swiss (naturalised). *Gunners:* M.G. Price, RNVR, No BZ5035; J. O'Donnell, RNVR, No TZ10030.

TEELIN HEAD sailed from Belfast on January 17, 1917. She was sailing up the Channel with a convoy and had a patrol trawler escort on each beam. A German submarine was sighted about three cables off on the port side and a torpedo hit the ship in number two hold. The vessel sank very rapidly with the result that 13 people were killed including the master.

Because the master perished with his ship there is little information recorded on the Submarine Attack Form, but the sinking was later claimed by *UC-31*.

12/14: BASIL. *Country:* British.

Date sunk: 11/11/17. *Tons nett:* –. *Tons gross:* 3220. *Built:* Belfast in 1895. *Type:* SS. *Rig:* –. *Owners:* Admiralty requisitioned. *Cargo:* Munitions from Southampton to Boulogne. *Armed:* 1 x 4.7in gun *Position:* 2 miles S of Owers (50 35 00N; 00 41 00W). *Master's name:* –. *Crew:* –. *Crew nationality:* –.

Basil, formerly *Mourne*, until she changed ownership, was employed by the Admiralty ferrying men, munitions and provisions to the war front in France.

With such cargoes she would have made a prime target for enemy submarine commanders. However, it was the British weather which was to send her to the bottom. She literally ran into a fog bank at full speed and collided with the French steamer *Margaux* heading in the opposite direction.

The force of the impact was tremendous and *Margaux* just about remained afloat long enough to limp into port. *Basil* however, came the worst off and foundered with the loss of 13 men.

12/15: HMD G.S.P. *Country:* British. *Date sunk:* 2/2/17. *Tons nett:* –.*Tons gross:* 100. *Built:* –. *Type:* Patrol drifter. *Rig:* –.*Owners:* –. *Cargo:* –. *Armed:* Yes. *Position:* 6 miles S of Owers Light Vessel (50 32 00N; 00 41 00W). *Master's name:* –.*Crew:* –. *Crew nationality:* British.

THERE is only a brief mention of this incident in Weekly Reports which states that the patrol drifter 2989 *G.S.P*, had been sunk in a collision with HMS *Radiant* and five ratings were drowned.

12/16: ALGIERS. *Country:* British. *Date sunk:* 26/2/17. *Tons nett:* 1520. *Tons gross:* 2361. *Built:* 1882. *Type:* SS. *Rig:* schooner. *Owners:* Oliver & Co, Franco British SS Co, London. *Cargo:* In ballast. *Armed:* 1 x 15pdr on naval platform. *Position:* 2 miles S of Owers Light Vessel. (50 35 30N; 00 40 30W). *Master's name:* H.J. Naidley. *Crew:* 27. *Crew nationality:* 3 Norwegians, 1 Russian/Finn, 23 British. *Gunners:* H.E. Journeux, LGCLS RNR, No 6672; Arthur Worsley, AB RNVR, No 55937.

ALGIERS was listed as being on Admiralty service and loaned to the French government for coal carrying. She left Calais on February 25, 1917, bound for Barry Roads for orders. The second officer was on watch with the lookout. The master, having set the course, went below and had no sooner done so when there was a tremendous explosion. He immediately rushed back on deck to find that the fore part of the ship had been completely blown away and he feared that she would not stay afloat long enough for even one boat to be launched. However, the starboard boat was lowered and 19 of the crew managed to scramble into it. The other eight men in the watch below were either killed by the explosion or drowned by the sudden inrush of water. Within 10 minutes of the explosion the *Algiers* was on the bottom.

The naval patrol boat *Tally Ho* was in the vicinity and was guided to the lifeboat by the light that the survivors were burning. They were picked up at 3.20am and brought safely into Portsmouth. On questioning, all were of the opinion that they had been

hit by a torpedo although nobody saw anything of a submarine.

The sinking of the *Algiers* was claimed by *UC-65*.

12/17: POLPEDN. *Country:* British. *Date sunk:* 14/11/16. *Tons nett:* 944. *Tons gross:* 1510. *Built:* 1902. *Type:* SS. *Rig:* schooner. *Owners:* Farrar Groves & Co, 147, Leadenhall St, London. *Cargo:* In ballast from Dunkirk to Ayr. *Armed:* No. *Position:* 13 miles SE of Owers (50 28 00N; 00 27 00W). *Master's name:* George Henry Clarke. *Crew:* 20. *Crew nationality:* 19 British, 1 Dane.

POLPEDN is listed among the records as an Admiralty prize, previously known as *Thor*.

The weather was good during the early hours of November 14, 1916. There was no wind which made the sea dead calm. The moon was shining brightly but there was a haze to the general visibility. In such conditions the steamer should have been zig-zagging but she wasn't. When asked about this later, the master said that he didn't think it was necessary at night, and in any case he had never been given any books or instructions on how to do it.

At 3.30am, the Mate, J. Irving, and a lookout were on the bridge. Suddenly the lookout shouted out and both men looked at a submarine that had appeared on the port side. The mate was about to order the helmsman to turn away but was too late, a torpedo smashed into the port side amidships, blowing out a huge hole.

The master arrived on deck within seconds and ordered the crew to the boats. However, the boat on the port side was useless, smashed to pieces by the explosion. All the crew squeezed into the starboard boat and pulled away. They made it just in time as a minute or so later the *Polpedn* sank. From the time of being struck to sinking, took just five minutes.

The crew rowed to the northward, assisted by the calm weather. However, they didn't have to wait long for help as the patrol vessel *Villenise* spotted them and took them aboard. She later handed them over to HMT 1747 *Willonyx* which landed them at Portsmouth.

UB-38 was the submarine involved.

12/18: LIGHTFOOT. *Country:* British. *Date sunk:* 16/3/18. *Tons nett:* 1104. *Tons gross:* 1875. *Built:* 1916. *Type:* SS. *Rig:* schooner. *Owners:* Wandsworth, Wimbledon & Epsom Gas Co, London. *Cargo:* In ballast. *Armed:* 1 x 12pdr 12cwt gun. *Position:* 1 miles SE of Owers Light Vessel (50 36 30N; 00 40 00W). *Master's name:* William Henry Metcalf. *Crew:* 22. *Crew nationality:* 18 British, 1 French, 1 Norwegian, 1 Dutch, 1 Russian. *Gunners:* A. Grant, L/Cpl. RMLI, No B1979 Chatham; H. Dunn, Pte. RMLI, No B2012 Chatham.

LIGHTFOOT was heading down the Channel at her full speed of 10 knots making for Barry Roads for orders. She was not zig-zagging and the Admiralty later issued a stern warning to the master on this point but stopped short of putting him on the blacklist. At the time of her loss she was steering north by west and the sea was moderate.

The torpedo struck the *Lightfoot* on the port side in number three hold and opened up a huge hole in her. She began to sink very rapidly indeed. It was quite a considerable feat of organisation to get the crew away so quickly but escape they all did in under two minutes. Thirty seconds later the steamer sank.

One lifeboat with seven hands was picked up by the trawler *Hibernia II* and the other with 15 hands was found by the French steamer *Otto*.

UB-30 was the submarine involved.

12/19: GASCONY. *Country:* British. *Date sunk:* 6/1/18. *Tons nett:* 1942. *Tons gross:* 3133. *Built:* 1908. *Type:* SS. *Rig:* schooner. *Owners:* David MacIver Co, Liverpool. *Cargo:* Government stores, guns and carriages, hay and charcoal, consigned to Calais. *Armed:* Yes. *Position:* 2 miles NNE of Owers Light Vessel (50 39 30N; 00 39 30W). *Master's name:* William Melville. *Crew:* 39. *Crew nationality:* 37 British, 1 Norwegian, 1 Chinese. *Gunners:* Claude Brookholding Dawes, L/Cpl. RMLI.

THE loss of the steamer *Gascony* resulted in a Court of Enquiry. This was held remarkably quickly, the day after in fact. Presiding were Commander Arthur C. Heathcote, RN, President, and Lieutenant Commander William Henry Whittle, RNR.First witness was the Master, Captain William Melville.

He stated that he left Southampton water at 4pm on January 6, 1918, and discharged the pilot at the Warner Buoy. He picked up the escort boats *TB21* and *P12* east of the same buoy at about 6.50pm. Soon after, Signalman James Jones reported to the master that he had received a message from escort boat *TB21* setting out the route that the master should follow. He read the instructions which required him to pass seven miles south of Owers, seven miles south of Brighton Light Vessel and five miles south of Royal Sovereign. This was to ensure that he avoided a two mile radius mine area. The master compared the instructions with the written ones he had already received and commented to the signalman that they were altogether different.

The master said he left the bridge at 11pm to attend to some paperwork in his cabin and returned at 11.15. Three minutes later a large explosion boomed out from the port side of the steamer just behind the bridge and a huge wall of water was thrown up and over the deck. The master immediately put the telegraph to stop which was answered by the fourth engineer, James Dempsey. Dempsey said in his testimony that

he heard a dull thud followed by a loud explosion which left steam pouring out of the port boiler. He ran to the telegraph to answer the master and after shutting down the throttle went up on deck to see what was happening.

The master ordered the crew to their boat stations and to stand by whilst he made an inspection of his ship. He saw that the stokehold and engine room were filling with water. Chief Engineer Arthur Jackman, who had served on *Gascony* for nine years, joined the master at the engine room stairway and later reported in his testimony that the engine room was completely dark and full of steam. He added that there was no way anyone could have gone down there with any degree of safety.

The master sounded the forward hold and found three feet of water but the after holds were dry. Thinking over the situation the master decided to launch the forward boat with the the crew and ordered them to stand by at a safe distance. He made one more examination of his ship. Feeling satisfied that all his crew were away and that the steamer was probably going to sink shortly, he too, left the ship and rowed over to the waiting escort boat *P12*.

P12 remained close to the sinking *Gascony* all night, scanning her from time to time with powerful searchlights. She was settling by the head but at around 6am she seemed to be stable. This was cue enough for the master who immediately asked for volunteers to go back with him and see what could be done to save her. The mate and four men stepped forward straight away and were soon back aboard. At 8am a tug arrived followed 20 minutes later by a second. The six men soon had the ropes connected and *Gascony* was put under tow.

As she wasn't towing particularly well through the water, mainly because her steam steering gear had locked the rudder over, the master managed to disconnect it and get the rudder somewhere near to the ahead position. A trawler came up astern and made fast to assist the steering and also provide a quick escape route for the men aboard *Gascony* should the need arise. At 1.30pm the need did arise as the water rose rapidly in number one hold causing the steamer to drop down rapidly by the head. Fifteen minutes later she broke in two and sank like a stone.

Of all the crew members that were called to give evidence at the enquiry, only the master put forward the idea that *Gascony* had been torpedoed because he had heard a hiss just before the explosion. The others assumed that they just had struck a mine and the enquiry also concluded that *Gascony* had most likely struck a mine. They also added that if the master had put out his Otter mine defence equipment it may have been prevented. The master was also criticised for not having adequate provision in closing water tight doors below and he should have been zig-zagging.

However, information later came to light that *Gascony* had indeed been torpedoed by U-boat ace Oberleutnant Johann Lohs in *UC-75*.

12/20: MOLESEY. *Country:* British.
Date sunk: 1/12/17. *Tons nett:* –. *Tons gross:* 3218.
Built: –. *Type:* SS. *Rig:* –. *Owners:* Watts, Watts &
Co, London. *Cargo:* 4867 tons phosphates.
Armed: 1 x 4.7in Japanese quick fire gun. *Position:*
12 miles SW by W from Brighton LV (50 27 30N;
00 39 30W). *Master's name:* Richard Coverdale
Oliver. *Crew:* 32 plus 2 signalmen and 1 distressed
British seaman from Gibraltar. *Gunners:* Thomas
Butcher, No ON7888; James Woky, No ON8984;
Farnham Maggs, No ON10520.

IT was just after midnight when the torpedo slammed
into the midships of the steamer *Molesey*. However,
the resulting explosion, although severe, did not do
enough damage to sink her.

There was plenty of time for the crew to assemble at
the boats and wait for the order from the master to
abandon ship. After the master had destroyed his
confidential papers he joined his crew at the three
boats and they all successfully got clear.

About 45 minutes later a German submarine
appeared on the surface close to the three boats. The
German commander demanded to speak to the master
and after questioning him ordered him to row several
German sailors across to the *Molesey*. The steamer
was still afloat and the German commander was eager
to finish the job off.

A few well placed bombs did the trick and she sank
a few minutes after they exploded. The crew in the
boats rowed towards the shore. The master and 19
men made it safely to the Brighton Light Vessel. The
other two boats were picked up by a passing vessel
and landed at Newhaven.

Molesey was the only victim of *UB-81*.

12/21: EVADNE. *Country:* British.
Date sunk: 27/2/17. *Tons nett:* –. *Tons gross:* 189.
Built: –. *Type:* Armed trawler No 148. *Rig:* –.
Owners: Admiralty. *Cargo:* –. *Armed:* Yes.
Position: 5 miles SSE of Owers (50 33 00N;
00 39 00W). *Master's name:* John Barron. *Crew:* –.
Crew nationality: British.

ARMED trawler No 148 *Evadne*, was attached to unit
113, an auxiliary patrol based in the port of
Portsmouth. She was mainly involved in
minesweeping duties and her sweeping partner at the
time of her loss was the trawler *Sweeper*, commanded
by Lieutenant G. Foote RNR.

Both vessels were on what was known as the Owers
patrol which entailed sweeping the traffic route south
of the Owers Light Vessel. At 9.45am on February
27, 1917, they were informed by HMT *Ben Torc* from
the Newhaven patrol that two mines had been sighted
to the south. *Evadne* and *Sweeper* immediately headed
for the area. On the way *Evadne's* cables were
detached from *Sweeper* to allow her to investigate an
object that had been spotted.

The object turned out to be nothing more than a

cork fender and *Evadne* was put up to full power to
catch up with *Sweeper*. At 10.30am there was an
enormous explosion from under *Evadne's* stern, so
powerful that she sank almost immediately.

Only two men survived to give any sort of
explanation of what happened. William Devine said he
was stationed right forward under the gun platform
as lookout. He said he saw nothing before the
explosion but knew that it occurred aft as the ship
instantly went down by the stern. Ernest Ives was at
the wheel at the time of the explosion. He also
confirmed that it occurred aft and as he went out of the
charthouse door he stepped into the water just as the
ship sank. Both men were dragged down by the
suction of the ship but managed to get free and
surfaced.

Ben Torc arrived on the scene quickly and picked
the men up. She also picked up the body of another
man, William Sutherland, but nothing was seen of
the rest of the crew. The only explanation of *Evadne's*
loss was that she had struck a mine.

12/22: HIGHLAND CORRIE. *Country:* British.
Date sunk: 16/5/17. *Tons nett:* 7583. *Tons
gross:* 8700. *Built:* Glasgow in 1910. *Type:* SS. *Rig:*
schooner. *Owners:* Nelson Steam Navigation Co,
98, Leadenhall St, London. *Cargo:* 3500 tons
frozen meat from Buenos Aires and Montevideo to
London. 2 Embassy mail bags. *Armed:* 1 x 4.7in
gun. *Position:* 4 miles S of Owers Lightship
(50 34 30N; 00 38 30W). *Master's name:* Percy
Maynard Jacobs. *Crew:* 80. *Gunners:* Edward
Fitzgerald, Seaman RNR, No 5021B; John Murray,
Seaman RNR, No 4090A.

THE Embassy official at Montevideo forgot to tell
the master of the *Highland Corrie* that he should call
in at Falmouth on reaching the UK coast. The result of
this proved disastrous not only for the ship but the
official. He was later dismissed because of it.

She left Montevideo on April 18, 1917, at 5pm and
began the long voyage to the UK. The trip went well
and when off Land's End the master sent a radio
message to the Admiral at Devonport giving him his
time of arrival but he got no reply. He sent a second
message and still got no answer but picked up a report
that vessels at Land's End and the Lizard were under
attack. He decided to keep well clear of the area and
proceeded up the middle of the Channel out of harms
way, or so he thought.

At about 11.30am on May 16, the third mate was on
watch, lookouts positioned fore and aft and one in
the crow's nest. The first mate and the master had
just left the bridge and the master was about to start
his usual rounds of the ship. He headed off aft towards
the gun and then heard and felt a thud on the port side
of the ship between number two and three holds. He
dashed back to the bridge but by this time the ship
had taken on a distinct list to port which was
worsening by the second. Looking below he spotted

that the port side of the bridge and the rails were blown away and the forward port lifeboat, number four, had been smashed to pieces.

He immediately ordered the engines to be stopped and the helm put to starboard to pull the ship up quickly. He ordered the passengers to get to their boat stations which was swiftly done, followed by the crew. Nine boats in total were lowered to the water. One, unfortunately, tipped over resulting in one passenger, a doctor, never being seen again.

The people in the boats watched the *Highland Corrie* heel further over to port, so much so that her bilge keel was almost showing. Help soon arrived in the form of three patrol boats and three destroyers. The master's boat and three others were picked up by HMS *Badger* and the rest by the patrol boats. Two destroyers took the sinking ship in tow in an attempt to save her but it was useless and she turned completely over and sank.

The incident claimed the lives of six people, four passengers and two crew. The rest of the survivors were taken into Portsmouth. The mail bags which were addressed to the Secretary of State, went down with the ship.

UB-38 was the submarine which torpedoed her.

12/23: VIGDA. *Country:* Norwegian.
Date sunk: 25/2/17. *Tons nett:* 1156. *Tons gross:* 1880. *Built:* 1901. *Type:* SS. *Rig:* schooner. *Owners:* Jac Enger, Tonsberg, Norway. *Cargo:* 2630 tons coal. Chartered by French merchants. *Armed:* No. *Position:* 6 miles S of Owers (50 30 50N; 00 37 50W). *Master's name:* O. Johannsen. *Crew:* 22. *Crew nationality:* 14 Norwegians, 2 Chinese, 2 Chileans, 2 Mexicans, 1 Russian, 1 Swede.

VIGDA was proceeding down the channel having departed from Hull on February 22, 1917, and was bound for Nantes. At some stage in the journey a submarine appeared on the surface close to her and began to fire on the vessel with a machine gun. This was followed by two shells which both struck home in *Vigda's* hull. The commanding officer of the submarine called for the master to bring his ship's papers to him, which he did, as he had no other choice.

Once on board he was asked by the German commander for details of his ship such as nationality, cargo, and destination. Two of the German crew were sent over to the steamer with three bombs. One was placed in the engine room and the other two in the after hatch. The bombing party having returned to the submarine, the commander's parting words to the *Vigda's* crew were, "I give you five minutes to clear out," which they did pretty quickly. Within a few minutes of leaving her the bombs exploded and *Vigda* sank rapidly.

The patrol vessel *Lancer* picked up the crew at 1.15am on the 26th, eight miles South of the Owers.

12/24: WAR HELMET. *Country:* British.
Date sunk: 19/4/18. *Tons nett:* 5042. *Tons gross:* 8184. *Built:* Japan in 1917. *Type:* SS. *Rig:* schooner. *Owners:* Royal Mail Steam Packet Co, Southampton. *Cargo:* In ballast, London to Barry. *Armed:* 1 x 4.7in, 1 x 90mm guns. *Position:* Owers LS bearing W by S ¹/₂ S 3 miles when hit (50 37 25N; 00 37 30W). *Master's name:* Anthony Purvis. *Crew:* 86. *Crew nationality:* 20 British, 66 Chinese. *Gunners:* F. Coster, RMLI, No 7822 Plymouth; C. Ellnor, L/Cpl. RMLI, No 6181 Plymouth; H. Northfield, AB RNVR, No LZ 7604; J. Prenty, AB RNVR, No MZ 1682; F. Caddick, AB RNVR, No WZ 2240.

THE majority of the information concerning this sinking is in a letter written by the Master, Anthony Purvis.

Following Admiralty instructions received while in the Downs the master anchored his ship off Newhaven at 9pm on April 18, 1918. At 3.15am the next morning the pilot arrived and they headed off under his orders down the Channel. The ship stopped at 5am to set up and put out the Otter Mine Defence equipment which was completed at 5.40am. It was most likely that during this stop Oberleutnant Johann Lohs of the German submarine *UC-75*, decided that *War Helmet* would be his next victim. Five minutes after the steamer returned to speed a torpedo slammed into her port side aft.

The master was on the bridge at the time and he immediately ordered the crew to get to their boat stations and stand by. It was daylight and the master was able to look down into the engine room skylight. He saw that the engine room floor was covered in water and he heard the port engine race away as its propeller shaft broke. The master next learned that the steering gear was out of action and they were now helpless, drifting with the wind, a brisk force five north-westerly.

The wireless operator was ordered to send out a distress message but he found that the dynamo had been damaged and the radio equipment was useless. The master looked at the boat stations and was pleased to see all his crew, including the large number of Chinese, all calmly standing by for orders with no panic. As the gun platform became awash he ordered the boats to be lowered away.

The master said that the last he saw of the *War Helmet* she was entirely submerged from the aft end to the fore deck, her bows sticking clean out of the water with the officers cabins just awash. She lay in 12 or 13 fathoms of water.

All the crew were picked up by patrol vessels and taken to Portsmouth.

12/25: HUNGERFORD. *Country:* British.
Date sunk: 16/4/18. *Tons nett:* 3643. *Tons gross:* 5811. *Built:* 1913. *Type:* SS. *Rig:* schooner. *Owners:* G. Hleyn & Sons, Headline,

Belfast. *Cargo:* In ballast, Havre for New York. *Armed:* 1 x 12pdr 12cwt gun. *Position:* 9 miles SSE of Owers LV (50 29 00N; 00 36 00W). *Master's name:* Jas K. Moore. *Crew:* 54. *Crew nationality:* 49 British, 5 others. *Gunners:* H. Harris, RNR, No T1556; J. Martin, LS RNR No OL 1687.

AT just under 8 knots *Hungerford* was heading down the Channel, New York bound. It was dark and rough.

At 4.35am on the morning of April 16, 1918, a torpedo smashed into the ship on the port side. The force of the explosion penetrated the engine room killing two engineers and a fireman instantly.

Captain Moore ordered the ship to be abandoned which was soon done, the men in the boats standing close by to see what would become of their ship. After a while it seemed that the steamer would remain afloat and the master ordered his boat to go back to her. In the distance the patrol trawler *Alyna* was approaching and as the master climbed back onto his stricken ship the trawler pulled alongside. Lieutenant Thompson told the master to make ready to receive a wire hawser and he would try a tow but at the same time warning him that the submarine would probably fire another torpedo.

The Lieutenant was right and at 6.50am another torpedo slammed into the steamer, this time on her starboard side. The men on the patrol ship saw the wake of it about 20yds ahead and immediately searched for the submarine. However, the conditions were too bad to locate it.

Weather conditions were also making life intolerable in the lifeboats and several men died of exposure. The patrol vessel went around to each boat in turn and took the steamer's crew aboard. In all 46 men were saved.

At 7.15am *Hungerford* sank and the patrol boat headed for St Helens.

The *Hungerford* was another victim of *UC-75*.

12/26: SHIRALA. *Country:* British. *Date sunk:* 2/7/18. *Tons nett:* 3400. *Tons gross:* 5306. *Built:* Glasgow in 1901. *Type:* SS. *Rig:* schooner. *Owners:* British India Steam Navigation Co, Leadenhall St, London. *Cargo:* 5000 tons general inc 180 tons explosives, ammunition, wine, elephant tusks, 1700 tons mails. *Armed:* 1 x 4.7in quick fire gun. *Position:* Owers LV bore S 60 deg W 4 miles (50 40 55N; 00 35 10W). *Master's name:* E.G. Murray Dickinson. *Crew:* 100 plus 203 European and native passengers. *Gunners:* Angus McKay, RN, No A4894.

THE *Shirala* had a lot of people on board, the bulk of whom were Indians bound for Bombay. The records are not very precise on exactly how many people there were in total but a general estimate from all the figures given would indicate just over 300.

The ship is listed as belonging to the P&O Line and she was requisitioned by the Government for war duties. The company listed in the specification, The British India Steam Navigation Co, were the charterers for this particular voyage.

She left London on June 29, 1918, and called in at various ports along the south east and south coast for route instructions. She had on board a Trinity House Pilot, Mr Fredrick Allan, and he was on the bridge at 5.10pm on July 2. The ship was close to the Owers Light Vessel making a speed of 10 knots. Suddenly, there was an enormous explosion from under the stokehold on the port side and this was followed about 15 seconds later by another. There were conflicting views as to whether the explosions were caused by mines or torpedoes, but there was no doubt that the *Shirala* was badly damaged.

The master found that she was basically breaking in half. He immediately ordered everyone to their boat stations and to get clear. All but five people got away. The five who were lost, the Second Engineer, Malcolm Wright and four firemen, were killed in the engine room by the force of the explosion. The survivors were picked up by several patrol boats and landed at various ports but the majority were taken to Southampton.

The *Shirala* sank in 11 fathoms of water and at one stage it was expected that she would be salvaged. There is a letter in the records from the General Post Office dated a month later asking the Admiralty for details of their salvage intentions. The Admiralty replied that the vessel lay in 11 fathoms of water and was badly damaged and they felt that it wasn't worth salvaging.

However, modern times have made parts of the *Shirala's* cargo more interesting to salvors and in 1978 elephants' tusks and hundreds of brass shell cases were raised. The man responsible for the sinking of the *Shirala* was the German ace, Oberleutnant Johann Lohs in the submarine *UB-57*.

12/27: HUNTSHOLM. *Country:* British. *Date sunk:* 11/6/17. *Tons nett:* 1203. *Tons gross:* 2073. *Built:* 1914. *Type:* SS. *Rig:* schooner. *Owners:* –. *Cargo:* In ballast, Dieppe for Southampton. *Armed:* 1 x 13pdr gun. *Position:* 4 miles E by S from Owers Light Vessel (50 37 45N; 00 35 00W). *Master's name:* John Davies, Bodina, Bow St, Cardigan. *Crew:* 24. *Crew nationality:* All British. *Gunners:* John Murray RNR; Emyrs Davies RNVR.

HUNTSHOLM sailed from Dieppe at 10am on June 10, 1917, and headed for Southampton Light. She was making 11 knots and was not zig-zagging as she was too near the coast. At 1.45pm on the 11th she was suddenly struck by a torpedo on her port side amidships. One of the gunners claimed that he caught a glimpse of a periscope and saw the track of the torpedo seconds before the explosion. The torpedo struck the ship about 10ft below the waterline and blew a hole through both sides of her. The vessel started to sink by the stern and 15 minutes later she turned over on her port side and sank in 15 fathoms of water.

The crew were picked up by the patrol trawler *Balfour* and taken to safety.

This ship was a war prize, formerly the German ship *Telde*, and was torpedoed by *UB-40*.

12/28: GLENLEE. *Country:* British. *Date sunk:* 9/8/18. *Tons nett:* 3120. *Tons gross:* 4915. *Built:* 1917. *Type:* SS. *Rig:* –. *Owners:* Furness Withy & Co. *Cargo:* 2100 tons steel billets, Dunkirk for Portland. *Armed:* 1 x 4.7in 2 x 7.5in howitzers. *Position:* 5 miles E of Owers LV/Owers LV bearing WSW 1¹/₂ miles (50 40 30N; 00 34 00W). *Master's name:* George Lumsden. *Crew:* 68. *Crew nationality:* 18 British, rest Lascars, Chinese and Japanese. *Gunners:* Joseph.S. Sharwood, LS RNVR, No 4642B; John Charles Cook, AB RNVR, No BZ 483; Isaac Pedley, AB RNVR, No 10295; Albert Jubb, LS; John Watts, RNR.

THE Trinity House pilot on board the *Glenlee* confirmed that the ship had kept on her proper course from Dunkirk and was heading for Portland. They were steering south 79 degrees west and were making 11 knots. Just after midday on August 9, 1918, a huge explosion took place between numbers three and four holds. One of the gunners, Joseph Sharwood, said he was on watch at the time and he believed that the explosion took place on the starboard side. The force of the explosion was tremendous and it threw debris everywhere. One piece of debris hit him and rendered him unconscious for a few seconds. He shook himself and seeing that the ship was already about to sink, made for his lifeboat. By this time the ship's stern had already touched bottom and her bows were high in the air.

Another gunner, John Cook, said that he arrived on deck after the explosion just in time to hear the master shout the order to abandon ship. They got clear in the boats and about 15 minutes later the ship sank completely. He added that one of the gunners, John Watts, was drowned.

At this stage it wasn't certain what had caused the explosion. A few miles away the commander of a patrol vessel could see the *Glenlee* and realised she was in trouble. He immediately increased speed and headed towards her. When about a mile from her one of his lookouts spotted a submarine's periscope. The patrol vessel gave chase and dropped several depth charges but there is no record to say if he was successful. Later, 67 of the crew were picked up and landed at Littlehampton.

UB-57 was the submarine involved.

12/29: GARTLAND. *Country:* British. *Date sunk:* 3/1/18. *Tons nett:* 1683. *Tons gross:* 2613. *Built:* 1913. *Type:* SS. *Rig:* schooner. *Owners:* The Gartland SS Co Ltd, 30, Renfield St, Glasgow. *Cargo:* 3440 tons coal, Newcastle for Gibraltar. *Armed:* 1 x 3in high angle gun. *Position:* About 5 miles ESE of Owers Light Ship (50 37 00N; 00 34 00W). *Master's name:* Lawrence Fredrick Hansen. *Crew:* 27. *Gunners:* Norman MacIver, OS RNR, No 9282; Angus Murray, OS RNR, No 4399; Roderick MacIver, LS RNR, No 5411.

BOUND for Gibraltar, *Gartland* was making her way steadily down Channel. The master was on the bridge with the second officer and a lookout was on watch forward. A gunner was also stationed on the gun platform aft but in spite of all the precautions nobody spotted the submarine just below the surface off the port side. The first anyone knew of her presence was when a torpedo slammed into her amidships, bursting into the engine room and exploding. Two men, the third engineer and a fireman, were so close to the blast that they were killed instantly.

The master had to act quickly as the decks were almost awash within a minute or so. However, the crew did manage to get themselves in a boat and pull clear just as the steamer sank. They rowed for some time in the general direction of shore and were later spotted by a lookout on the steamer *Nunima* of West Hartlepool which dropped them at St Helens.

After the Admiralty had read the master's deposition of the incident they wanted to know from him why he had so few lookouts. He replied that he only had three men on board who had passed the Board of Trade's exam and he felt that with himself and an officer on the bridge, a man forward and a gunner aft, it was quite sufficient. Nothing further was mentioned on this point so presumably their Lordships were satisfied.

UB-30 was the submarine concerned.

12/30: ATLAS. *Country:* British. *Date sunk:* 13/11/17. *Tons nett:* 613. *Tons gross:* 989. *Built:* 1904. *Type:* SS. *Rig:* –. *Owners:* Admiralty. Agents William Coupland & Co, Newcastle. *Cargo:* 1300 tons coal, Warkworth for Rouen. *Armed:* 1 x 12pdr gun. *Position:* 5 miles SE of Owers Light Vessel (50 34 30N; 00 34 00W). *Master's name:* Alfred Ernest Wilson. *Crew:* 20. *Crew nationality:* 19 British, 1 Other. *Gunners:* W. Livermore, LS RNVR, No LZ 5038; H. Greasley, AB RNVR, No TZ 8721.

HEADING for Rouen, *Atlas* made her way down the Channel steering west half north at a speed of seven knots. After passing Brighton Light Vessel the master set a course that he reckoned would take the ship one mile to the south of the Owers Light Vessel. He then left the bridge in charge of the chief mate with orders to call him once they had made Owers.

The mate had just spotted the Owers Light Vessel and was about to send one of the hands to wake the master when a terrific explosion took place. Nobody had seen the torpedo but the mate stated later that he had been torpedoed two months earlier on another vessel and it was exactly the same explosion. This theory was strengthened by the patrol vessel *Cedar* which was close by. Her commander said that he and all his crew had heard the hiss of a torpedo pass under the stern of his ship.

The result was that the deck just behind the bridge of the *Atlas* was ripped up and a gaping hole left in her side. She sank seven minutes later. Fortunately all the hands were saved, and apart from cuts and bruises, all were uninjured.

The *Atlas* was claimed by *UB-56*.

12/31: HUNTSMOOR. *Country:* British. *Date sunk:* 20/2/18. *Tons nett:* 2682. *Tons gross:* 4957. *Built:* 1901. *Type:* SS. *Rig:* schooner. *Owners:* Jenkins Bros, Cardiff. *Cargo:* Coal and water ballast, Harve for Southampton. *Armed:* 1 x 6in gun. *Position:* 50 miles N 10 deg W of Havre Light (50 25 00N; 00 33 00W). *Master's name:* Robert Bates. *Crew:* 59. *Crew nationality:* 56 British, 2 Russian, 1 Italian. *Gunners:* E. Stringer; H. Miles; G. Robinson.

DETAILS of where the torpedo struck the *Huntsmoor* as she made her way from Havre to Southampton were very precise: in the fore end of number four hold, 11 feet below the waterline. However, they are less precise on the time. One witness said it was 10.30pm, another 11.20pm.

The master gave the order to abandon his rapidly sinking ship and three boats pulled clear. The master's boat containing 21 men in total was never seen again.

The crew who made statements were the Second Mate, Wilfred Rushforth, and the Second Engineer, Thomas Stubbs. They said that as they rowed away from the scene a German submarine came alongside them and demanded to know various details of the *Huntsmoor*. Not content with what he was being told, the German commander took two seamen, J. Dyer and George Searle, on board the submarine and, at gunpoint, questioned them separately. One of them was asked to spell the steamer's name eight times. Eventually they were let go and the two boats rowed towards the shore.

One boat containing 24 men was picked up and taken to the Royal Sovereign Light Vessel and the other boat with 14 men was picked up by the destroyer *Crusader*.

UB-40 was the submarine involved.

12/32: CANDIA. *Country:* British. *Date sunk:* 27/7/17. *Tons nett:* 4195. *Tons gross:* 6482. *Built:* Greenock in 1896. *Type:* SS. *Rig:* schooner. *Owners:* P&O Navigation Co, 122, Leadenhall St, London. *Cargo:* 8000 tons general from Sydney and Melbourne, Australia to London.

Armed: 1 x 4.7in gun. *Position:* 8 miles S 40 deg E from Owers LS. Sank about ¼ mile E of this (50 31 00N; 00 32 30W). *Master's name:* Charles Grant Smith. *Crew:* 98. *Crew nationality:* 20 British, 69 Lascars, 9 Goanese. *Gunners:* M. Kightly, L/Cpl. RMLI; E.C. Palmer, Pte. RMLI.

THE *Candia* sailed from Melbourne, Australia on May 26, 1917, bound for London. On Friday July 27, at 5am the ship was eight miles off the Owers Light Ship steering north 77 degrees east and making 12 knots. The master was on the bridge with the second mate and a helmsman. Suddenly, an explosion boomed out on the starboard side sending up an enormous blast which killed one of the lookouts instantly and smashed one of the lifeboats to pieces.

The ship began to settle down by the stern immediately and all hands made for the boats. They all got clear and stood by to watch their ship slip below the waves.

Meanwhile, HMT *Willonyx* was busy attending to another casualty, the SS *Bellajio* which had been torpedoed and abandoned a few miles away. Having picked up the survivors from the *Bellajio*, *Willonyx* proceeded in the direction of the *Candia* after hearing the explosion and spotting a red flare. She picked up 23 of the crew and another patrol vessel, HMD 3108 *Green Pastures*, picked up most of the rest.

Bellajio was later refloated.

UC-65 claimed to have sunk the *Candia*.

12/33: AIRPLANE. *Country:* British. *Date sunk:* 18/7/18. *Tons nett:* –. *Tons gross:* –. *Built:* –. *Type:* –. *Rig:* –. *Owners:* –. *Cargo:* –. *Armed:* –. *Position:* 10 miles E by S of Selsey Bill (50 41 00N; 00 32 00W).

THIS information comes from the commander of a patrol vessel who said that while on patrol at 2.50pm on July 18, 1918, he witnessed an aeroplane suddenly dive into the sea. He immediately proceeded to the spot but could find nothing of the plane or the pilot.

12/34: VESUVIO. *Country:* British. *Date sunk:* 6/4/16. *Tons nett:* –. *Tons gross:* 1391. *Built:* –. *Type:* SS. *Rig:* schooner. *Owners:* General Steam Navigation Co Ltd, 15, Trinity Sq, London. *Cargo:* 1100 tons of general, Sicily to London . *Armed:* No. *Position:* 6 miles E of Owers LS (50 37 00N; 00 31 00W). *Master's name:* Mr Elgar. *Crew:* 21.

VESUVIO had been to several Mediterranean ports picking up cargo as she went, finally leaving the port of Messina, Sicily, on March 22, 1916. The weather was fine and clear with a light breeze and all looked good for a quick voyage home.

The master followed the usual route orders and on calling in at Gibraltar found no more instructions so continued on his voyage. On passing the Casquets rocks near Guernsey he set a course for Beachy Head. On April 6, at 11.20am, Beachy Head was sighted. The first mate had just been relieved on the bridge by the master and second mate.

The master called the chief engineer, Mitchell Hughes, who was on deck and asked him if more speed was available. The chief had no time to reply as a terrific explosion occurred on the port side. In his statement later the chief engineer said that the boiler must have burst as a huge mass of boiling water carried away the bridge and left him choked by the smoke and sulphur fumes.

The master, second mate and the man at the wheel were all killed by the explosion. The first mate had somewhat better luck after being trapped in his bunk and managed to break down his door with a chair, making the deck dressed only in his shirt. The survivors made their way to the only lifeboat intact on the starboard side. Led by the mate were the second and third engineers and nine of the crew.

Vesuvio sank within a few minutes of the boat pulling clear and the survivors circled the area looking for other survivors. They found a steward clinging to a large citrate cask with one leg shattered and face wounds. A little later they found a trimmer floating on a hatch cover.

About 15 minutes later they were picked up by the Admiralty submarine catcher *B25*, commanded by Lieutenant Johnson and all landed safely at Newhaven.

The third engineer later claimed that he saw the wake of a torpedo just before the explosion. The chief mate made a statement but unfortunately died before he could sign it.

The Admiralty listed *Vesuvio* as "mined".

12/35: ALERT. *Country:* British. *Date sunk:* 28/11/16. *Tons nett:* –. *Tons gross:* 289. *Built:* 1897. *Type:* SS. *Rig:* steam/sailer. *Owners:* J.B. Knapton, 38, Gt Tower St, East London. *Cargo:* In ballast, Havre for Littlehampton. *Armed:* No. *Position:* 6 miles ESE of Owers (50 34 30N; 00 30 30W). *Master's name:* George Croxford. *Crew:* 10.

ALERT sailed from Havre and was bound to Littlehampton. The reports state that an enemy submarine fired shots at her and the commander demanded that they heave to. The submarine came alongside and placed a bomb in the engine room and one in the hold. The bombs exploded and the ship sank bows first.

Another report states that at 9am on November 28, 1916, the transport *Shining Cave* reported that seven miles east-south-east of Owers Light Vessel, three Littlehampton transports had been attacked by a submarine. The patrol vessel *Ben Torc* accompanied by another proceeded at full speed towards the position and at 10am, about five miles east-south-east of the Owers, they picked up two boats containing 10

survivors from the SS *Alert* sunk by bombs and gunfire from a submarine.

This submarine (*UB-39*) also sank the steamer *Alison* at about 7.45 the same morning.

12/36: GERMAN SUBMARINE (possible). *Country:* German. *Date believed sunk:* 23/10/17. *Tons nett:* –. *Tons gross:* –. *Built:* –. *Type:* –. *Owners:* German navy. *Armed:* Yes. *Position:* 13 miles S by E of Owers (50 24 30N; 00 30 30W). *Master's name:* –. *Crew:* –. *Crew nationality:* German.

LIEUTENANT Commander C.E. Hughes White was certain that he had sunk an enemy submarine whilst in command of HMS *Melampus* during the afternoon of October 23, 1917, and he was awarded the DSO for it. But there is considerable doubt about his "kill".

He reported to his senior officer that he was proceeding up the Channel with an HS lighter in tow when a lookout spotted a hostile submarine about five miles to the south of them, running fast on the surface. He immediately ordered the lighter to be slipped when about 11 miles south-south-east of Owers Light Vessel and headed after the enemy.

He made good progress towards her and got within about two miles when she dived. He had all eyes kept on the spot and made a judgement of where she was headed. Once in the area he slowed his ship down and lowered explosive sweeps, commencing a broad zig-zag pattern at 1.35pm. The starboard paravane picked up its depth straight away and ran well between 30 and 40ft. However, the port one dived only about 10ft before breaking the surface and remained there. On the fourth leg of the zig-zag, when the ship was about three miles west of the position where the submarine dived, the starboard paravane was fired at 35ft by dynamo. A huge explosion occurred throwing up an enormous mushroom of water and leaving the sea surface covered by a dark patch of oil or possibly battery fluid. The helm was put hard over and the only D-type depth charge on board was dropped to the west of the patch, exploding at 80ft. The lieutenant noted that the depth of the water according to the chart was 27 fathoms (160ft). He turned the ship again and threw two G-Type depth charges.

As *Melampus* turned sharply and came back over the spot two huge blisters, or bubbles, as he describes, came to the surface. It was far more than normal and was witnessed by several men on the bridge including Engineer Lieutenant-Commander Barker. The ship was turned again, the speed eased and brought up again to veer the port paravane which dived nicely to about 90ft or more. Once over the spot it was exploded by dynamo but nothing of significance came to the surface. The starboard paravane wire was then heaved in and the tow anchorage was found to be heavily scored by contact with a steel body. They cruised the area for some time but having no more depth charges and being responsible for the drifting

The *Moldavia,* seen here with her portholes blacked out for wartime service.

HS lighter, the commander thought it prudent to go and find it.

At first the Admiralty were not convinced that the submarine was destroyed and labelled it as probably seriously damaged. Lieutenant Hughes White and Signalman Hanwell both identified the submarine type from silhouettes as *U151-157.* The Admiralty received intelligence later that a German submarine of that type had recently been established to have been lost and it was very probable that it was operating in the area where *Melampus* made the attack. They therefore revised their classification from probable to "known".

Strangely, there is no record of any cash award being made at the time but several of the crew of *Melampus* received decorations for their part in the action.

German records show that *UC-16* was lost during that period, but evidence of bodies washed ashore in Holland indicate a sinking position 200 miles away from the Owers site and HMS *Melampus.*

12/37: MOLDAVIA. *Country:* British.
Date sunk: 23/5/18. *Tons nett:* –. *Tons gross:* 9500.
Built: 1903. *Type:* SS. *Rig:* Armed merchant cruiser. *Owners:* P&O, commandeered by Admiralty. *Cargo:* 900 American troops. *Armed:* 8 x 6in guns. *Position:* (50 24 35N; 00 28 48W).
Master's name: Captain A.H. Smyth. *Crew:* 370.
Crew nationality: British.

Naval Weekly Reports note briefly that she was torpedoed at 4.55am on May 23, 1918, 435 people were saved but 56 troops were listed as missing. One soldier died later during an amputation operation.

Other sources mention that *Moldavia* was a large liner, the sister ship of *Mongolia,* generally employed on the Australia run. She was commandeered by the government in 1915 for the war effort. On the day she was sunk she had on board a large number of troops. She was in convoy with a number of escorts around her. However, this didn't stop Oberleutnant Johann Lohs, in *UB-57,* from firing a torpedo into her.

Today the remains of the *Moldavia* lie in 50 metres of water, 24 miles off Littlehampton.

12/38: HMT SAPPER. *Country:* British.
Date sunk: 29/12/17. *Tons nett:* –. *Tons gross:* 276.
Built: –. *Type:* Patrol trawler. *Rig:* –. *Owners:* Admiralty. *Cargo:* –. *Armed:* Yes. *Position:* 8 miles E by S of Owers LV (50 38 30N; 00 28 30W).
Master's name: –. *Crew:* –. *Crew nationality:* British.

THERE is very little known about what happened to the Patrol trawler No 1162 *Sapper.* She was sent to patrol the area around the Owers Light Vessel on December 28, 1917, and reported to Culver at 9pm that she was patrolling between three to eight miles south to south-west of Owers. Her message sent on the radio was to be her last. She was repeatedly called back the next day with no response.

At 3.35am on December 29, Culver received a message from a steamer that a patrol boat had been attacked. The steamer went into St Helens and identified herself as the *Tewfikieh* from London to Malta. The master said that at 1am he was spoken to by a patrol boat but didn't know her name. The patrol boat took up station ahead as an escort until 3am when it blew up, presumably, said the master, by a torpedo.

The Admiralty were fairly certain that the patrol vessel concerned must have been *Sapper* as she was in the area and had not been seen since. They made no statement about the cause of her sinking. A search was made of the area for survivors but nothing was found.

12/39: ALISON. *Country:* British.
Date sunk: 28/11/16. *Tons nett:* – . *Tons gross:* 286. *Built:* 1848. *Type:* SS. *Rig:* schooner. *Owners:* Northwich Carrying Co Ltd, Northwich. *Cargo:* Government stores from Havre to Littlehampton. *Armed:* No. *Position:* 8 miles ESE of Owers Light Vessel (50 34 30N; 00 28 00W). *Master's name:* John Rogerson. *Crew:* 7. *Crew nationality:* British.

AT 7.30am on November 28, 1916, the master of *Alison* rushed to his cabin and grabbed his weighted bag. He stuffed his auxiliary notices into it and threw it over the side into the sea. A German submarine was bearing down on him from the north, firing shells as it approached. The Admiralty were very strict about destroying secret papers, or anything that might assist the enemy.

With the paperwork out of the way Captain Rogerson set about saving his crew. There was nothing he could do against such powerful odds. Reluctantly he ordered his men to take to the boat.

A German officer, presumably the commander, shouted to Captain Rogerson to come to the submarine. He wanted to ask him questions and also use his boat to plant bombs on the *Alison*. It was quickly done, less than a minute according to the captain, and the German sailors hurried away from the burning fuses. After the bombs exploded the steamer sank very quickly. The men were left to row to the shore as the submarine dashed off in pursuit of another ship close by, the *Alert*. She too, shared the same fate. However, another steamer, *Skinningrove*, got away when she fled at full speed.

The seven men from the *Alison* were picked up by the steamer *Southern Coast* which took them to safety the same day.

The submarine involved was *UB-39*.

12/40: JAFFA. *Country:* British.
Date sunk: 22/2/18. *Tons nett:* 760. *Tons gross:* 1383. *Built:* 1897. *Type:* SS. *Rig:* schooner. *Owners:* Ellerman Wilson Line. *Cargo:* In ballast,

Boulogne to Southampton. *Armed:* 1 x 12pdr 12cwt gun. *Position:* 9 miles E by N of Owers (50 38 30N; 00 27 00W). *Master's name:* William Newton. *Crew:* 27. *Gunners:* J. Joyce, RNR, gunlayer; D. Main, second hand.

JAFFA was obeying her route instructions and was on a zig-zag course making her full speed of eight knots. She had no lights showing at all and should have been very difficult to spot. However, at just after midnight on February 2, 1918, a torpedo crashed into the port side just under the bridge.

The engines were stopped immediately while the damage was assessed but it was obvious that she could sink at any moment. Some of the crew managed to get a boat away from the starboard side but others were not so fortunate.

As the steamer sank, people were left in the water trying to find something to cling to. The submarine surfaced close by and a voice demanded to know the ship's name. Having got that information, the submarine dived.

Seventeen of the crew eventually sailed into Littlehampton but 10 were lost.

The submarine involved was *UB-30*.

12/41: CAIRNDHU. *Country:* British.
Date sunk: 15/4/17. *Tons nett:* 2561. *Tons gross:* 4019. *Built:* Sunderland in 1911. *Type:* SS. *Rig:* schooner. *Owners:* Cairn Line SS Ltd, Akenside House, Newcastle. *Cargo:* 6250 tons coal from S.Shields to London Coal Co, Gibraltar. *Armed:* 1 x 13lb Vickers Maxim. *Position:* 25 miles WSW of Beachy Head (50 37 30N; 00 26 30W). *Master's name:* Robert Anthony Purvis. *Crew:* 38. *Crew nationality:* All British. *Gunners:* McDonald; McClean.

CAIRNDHU sailed from South Shields on the April 12, 1917, made her way down the east coast and then anchored in the Downs at 11.40am on the 15th. Having received her sailing instructions she left at 2.50pm on the same day and cleared the defensive gate at 4.48pm. The acting Third Mate, an apprentice, Thomas Daniel Healy, went on watch with the first mate at 8pm and began the usual routine of checking charts and plotting courses. The night was dark but the visibility was good despite a choppy sea. A lookout was on the forecastle head and all the lights were out. At 9pm the lights had to be switched on as a lot of traffic was in the area and it was this act which brought about her sinking.

Thomas Healy went out on deck to have a look around when, to his horror, he saw the white wake of a torpedo streaking towards the port side of the ship. Before he could move or utter a word of warning the torpedo smashed into *Cairndhu* amidships. The master was lying in his berth at the time of the explosion and upon being thrown out of his bed ran smartly up on deck to find that his ship had almost sunk. One of the hatches had been completely blown off and the ship was listing heavily to port. He ordered all hands to muster at the boats and got himself and six men to the starboard boat. Meanwhile, young Thomas Healy was busying himself with the port boat and he stated later that the mate went to lend a hand with the starboard boat and he never saw him again. Thomas Healy got his boat away with 32 men and remained close by the sinking steamer to look out for other survivors. At this point a German submarine appeared and approached the boats and demanded to know all the details of the ship. It then moved away towards the steamer and returned some five minutes later. As it did so it ran into Healy's boat nearly cutting it in half and threw many of the men into the water. A bitter Thomas Healy said later that the submarine commander had done it on purpose as he heard some of the Germans shout "Die you sons of bitches!" Seven of his men were missing; those who couldn't swim.

The third mate's boat was now totally awash with the sea constantly breaking over it. They had lost the oars and became little more than a log in the water. From time to time a wave would wash off one or two of the men who had no resistance left in them due to the cold. Eventually they spotted the lights of a steamer and managed by pure luck to attract her attention. It was the steamer *Kullerberg* of Hilsingborg and she quickly picked up the remainder of the men in that boat who by then numbered 20. They were taken to the anchorage off the Isle of Wight and eventually into Portsmouth.

Those who went with the master's boat fared a little better and were picked up at 6.30am by the SS *Fredheim* of Tonsberg and landed at Newhaven by a torpedo boat at 10am. Altogether 11 men were lost.

UB-40 was the submarine involved.

12/42: CITY OF MEXICO. *Country:* Norwegian. *Date sunk:* 22/11/16. *Tons nett: –. Tons gross:* 1511. *Built: – Type:* SS. *Rig: –. Owners: –. Cargo:* Coal, Blyth for La Rochelle. *Armed: –. Position:* 35 miles SW of Beachy Head (50 20 00N; 00 25 10W). *Master's name: –. Crew:* 21.

A BRIEF note in Weekly Reports mentions that the master of the hospital ship *Carisbrooke Castle*, now into Southampton Water, has on board the master and 20 of the crew of the SS *City of Mexico*, from Blyth to La Rochelle, sunk by submarine in the above position at 8.30am. The submarine was painted grey with a red spot on the bows.

12/43: EDEN. *Country:* Norwegian. *Date sunk:* 30/4/17. *Tons nett: –. Tons gross:* 1304. *Built: –. Type:* SS. *Rig: –. Owners: –. Cargo:* Coal, Tyne for Rouen. *Armed: –. Position:* 10 miles E by S of Owers (50 36 00N; 00 25 00W). *Master's name: –*

THE loss of the Norwegian steamer *Eden* is another which has little documentation attached to it.

The only reference to her is found in Weekly Reports which notes that at 9.50pm on April 17, 1917, *Eden* was sunk by a German submarine. The patrol vessel *Sheldon* went out to investigate after an explosion was heard and at 11am, picked up two lifeboats containing the crew of the SS *Eden*

She is recorded as torpedoed.

12/44: HOULGATE (ex-JOHN LAMBERT). *Country:* French. *Date sunk:* 22/11/16. *Tons nett:* 929. *Tons gross:* 1550. *Built: –. Type:* SS. *Rig:* schooner. *Owners:* Great Lakes & St Lawrence Transport Co. *Cargo:* Coal, Montreal for Le Havre. *Armed:* Yes. *Position:* 24 miles WSW of Beachy Head in 24 fathoms/23 miles SE of Owers LV (50 29 00N; 00 18 00W). *Master's name:* Harrison. *Crew:* 22.

WHAT information there is on the *John Lambert* is rather confusing. Some sources record her as French, others Canadian. She was Canadian and was then bought by a French company, but it is not clear which flag she was under at the time of her loss.

The French newspaper, Le Petit Havre, reported that she was attacked by a German submarine. The first shot fired at her was at 4.15pm. This shell struck her forward and holed her. Other shells followed which smashed the bridge and another penetrated the engine room. The master ordered the crew to take to the boats which was promptly done.

Even though it must have been obvious that the crew were abandoning the steamer, the submarine's gunner kept firing. Several more shells penetrated deep into her hull, one bursting the boiler. Soon after, she settled rapidly and sank.

The crew were picked up by the SS *Nordcap* at about 1am. At daybreak they were transferred to the patrol boat *St Andre* and taken to Havre.

However, the above information in the files as taken from the newspaper cannot be entirely correct. The British naval authorities reported that a patrol vessel found *John Lambert* the next morning, deserted but very much afloat. They describe her as painted a dull dark slate colour, 241ft long, 41ft beam and 15ft 6in depth. She was in a bad way though and didn't stay afloat for long.

12/45: RAMSGARTH. *Country:* British. *Date sunk:* 27/11/16. *Tons nett:* 797. *Tons gross:* 1552. *Built:* Middlesbrough in 1910. *Type:* SS. *Rig:* schooner. *Owners:* South Metropolitan Gas Co, 709, Old Kent Rd, London. *Cargo:* In water ballast, Cardiff and Brixham for Tyne. *Armed:* No. *Position:* 8 miles S of Worthing Pier/10-11 miles E of Owers LV (50 40 00N; 00 21 00W). *Master's name:* Tom Appleton. *Crew:* 19. *Crew nationality:* 10 British, 2 Japanese, 4 Italians, 3 Greeks.

At 8am on the November 27, 1916, Second Officer Percy Hillson Walke spotted a small steamer in the distance that appeared to be in trouble. He called the master to see what he could make of it and together they examined the scene through their binoculars. The ship seemed to be blowing off clouds of steam and there was a lot of activity around the lifeboats.

Suddenly they saw a lifeboat pull clear and decided that they would go in closer and help the men out. The master was about to give the order to alter course when he spotted something else. Protruding from just behind the far side of the steamer was part of a submarine. He immediately ordered the engines to be put full ahead and told the second mate to get away quickly.

The submarine commander of *UB-39* was sharp, he had already spotted the *Ramsgarth* and his gunners were taking aim at her. Several shells were fired and one eventually hit the steamer on the starboard side. Captain Appleton knew that he was in trouble. The enemy gunners had found the range and worse still the submarine was catching them up rapidly. He realised he had no chance of escape and ordered the ship to heave to, telling his crew to make for the boats and get clear.

The German commander ordered the steamer's crew aboard his submarine whilst a boarding party used their boat to plant bombs on the *Ramsgarth*. It was efficiently done and a few minutes later the steamer sank.

Having got their boat back the crew set about rowing for the shore, making Worthing Pier safely later that day.

12/46: VICTORIA. *Country:* British.

Date sunk: 16/4/17. *Tons nett:* 133. *Tons gross:* 168. *Built:* Falmouth in 1897. *Type:* SV. *Rig:* schooner. *Owners:* William Garthwaite, 94, Gracechurch St, London. *Cargo:* 290 tons coal tar pitch, shipped at Greenwich and consigned to Cherbourg. *Armed:* No. *Position:* 30 miles SW of Beachy Head (50 23 00N; 00 20 00W). *Master's name:* Maurice Evan Morris. *Crew:* 5.

THE weather was so bad that *Victoria* had three attempts to cross the Channel, each time being blown back by the ferocity of the gale. She had left Greenwich on March 27, 1917, and nearly three weeks later she still hadn't managed to get to her destination at Cherbourg. At 4.30am on April 16, the master decided to run up to Owers to find shelter and wait the storm out yet again. He was on deck with a lookout as the first light began to give a little visibility. Scanning the darkened seas he suddenly caught sight of what looked like a fishing vessel and was just about to dismiss it as such when an orange flash appeared from it. This was followed a second or two later by a shell whistling close by.

The shells kept coming. One found its mark in the side of the ship which made her reel under the impact. Another completely smashed away the fore sail bringing down tackle and rigging all over the decks. The master brought the ship to a stop. The boats were got out and the crew rowed to the stern of the ship to try and get some protection from the shells and the weather.

A few minutes later the submarine drew close to the crew's boat and the *Victoria*. The German commander shouted that he wanted to see the master and the first mate and that they should come aboard immediately.

Whilst they were being questioned several German sailors went across in their boat to the *Victoria*. Once aboard they gathered up many of the ship's instruments and whatever food they could find in the galley. Satisfied with their haul they planted bombs in the hatches and quickly left. Ten minutes later there were two loud explosions and the *Victoria* disappeared.

The master and crew were set adrift in the rough seas to fend for themselves. It was tough going, very wet and cold. It was a great relief to the men when at 10.30am, a sharp-eyed lookout on the destroyer *D 24* spotted them. They were landed safely at Portsmouth later the same day.

12/47: IKEDA. *Country:* British.

Date sunk: 21/3/18. *Tons nett:* 4760. *Tons gross:* 6311. *Built:* Stockton in 1917. *Type:* SS. *Rig:* schooner. *Owners:* J.H. Welsford, 17, Water St, Liverpool. *Cargo:* In water ballast, London for Galveston, Texas. *Armed:* 1 x 4in gun. *Position:* 7 miles W from Brighton LV (50 41 00N; 00 19 00W). *Master's name:* William Edward Price. *Crew:* 48. *Crew nationality:* –. *Gunners:* Baker; Waring; Allen.

IKEDA left the Port of London at 6am on March 20, 1918. Her destination was Galveston, Texas and she was ordered to take the usual down Channel course. The master stated later that his instructions were to keep five miles off Beachy Head and then keep close to the coast, passing to the north of the Brighton Light Vessel. From there he was to pass to the south of Owers. The Admiralty concluded that after he rounded Brighton Light Vessel the master appears to have made to the southward a little too soon.

At 3.30am on March 21, the night was dark but clear and the sea was smooth with little or no wind. A loud explosion suddenly shattered the calm night and within a few minutes the *Ikeda* was sinking.

The master ordered distress rockets to be fired and instructed the radio operators to send out an SOS. The boats were swung out in readiness and the crew mustered at their stations. Looking over the side the master could see that the circulation pumps were still going and would be a hindrance to launching the boats. He asked for a volunteer to go down into the engine room and turn them off. The chief engineer came forward without hesitation and had the job done within a few minutes.

Judging it was time to leave, the master called for the two young radio operators, Henderson and Smith, to leave their posts and join the rest of them. They were commended later, along with the chief engineer for outstanding behaviour.

Within half an hour the crew were well clear and watched as their ship sank to the bottom. A few minutes later two patrol trawlers arrived, picked the men up and landed them safely at Newhaven.

The submarine involved was *UB-40*.

12/48: C.S. 72. *Country:* British. *Date sunk:* 19/4/17. *Tons nett:* 138. *Tons gross:* 164. *Built:* Waterhuizen in 1912. *Type:* SV. *Rig:* schooner. *Owners:* On Admiralty service. *Cargo:* 245 tons carbon retorts from Dublin to Dieppe. *Armed:* No. *Position:* 15 miles S by E ½ E of Newhaven (50 40 00N; 00 17 00W). *Master's name:* Charles Leech. *Crew:* 6.

C.S. 72 was formerly the German sailing ship *Senator Dantziger*, given the official number of 136841. She is listed as being chartered in London by a French firm although it seems that her owners or managers were John Carter of Poole.

She proceeded from Dublin on April 13, 1917, bound for Dieppe. On Thursday April 19, she was 15 miles off Newhaven, under all sail making about three knots. The master was below, the mate on deck with a seaman at the wheel. Although the conditions were hazy the mate saw something in the distance that troubled him. He went to the master and told him that he thought he could see a submarine and that he had better come and look for himself. The master went on deck immediately and was greeted by a shell whistling towards him which struck the main gaff topsail. The submarine was on the starboard bow, on the surface about one and a half miles off.

The master ordered all hands on deck and into the boats, while the submarine still continued shelling. All the crew managed to get in the boats, and dropped astern of the schooner. A moment later a shell smashed into the ship on the starboard side. The men in the boat started to pull towards the submarine which fired about five shells, apparently directly at them but none hit.

The submarine then turned it's attention on the *C.S. 72* and closed in on her. After another 10 shells she sank at approximately 3pm. The submarine commander must have spotted something because he left the scene rapidly, heading off towards the north east.

The crew in the boat were picked up by the French patrol steamer *Pelican* and landed at Boulogne.

12/49: PENTYRCH. *Country:* British. *Date sunk:* 18/4/18. *Tons nett:* 2117. *Tons gross:* 3311. *Built:* 1901. *Type:* SS. *Rig:* schooner.

Owners: J.H. Lambert and J. Barnett & Co, Baltic House, Cardiff. *Cargo:* 4650 tons coal, Tyne for Genoa. *Armed:* 1 x 4in gun, marked 9 star BL. *Position:* 5 miles WNW of Brighton LV (50 43 00N; 00 16 00W). *Master's name:* Clarence Leonard Eagle. *Crew:* 32. *Gunners:* Benjamin William Tyman, RNVR, No MZ 1919 Chatham; Harry Owens, RNVR, No M 4-21; Chatham; Thomas Brown Johnson, RNVR, No TZ6583 Chatham..

ZIG-ZAGGING down the Channel as close to land as possible, *Pentyrch* was heading to the warmer climes of Genoa.

However, the commander of *UB-40* had other ideas, and sent a torpedo streaking towards her. It struck her square on the starboard beam causing a huge explosion which tore a great lump out of her side. The master ordered all hands to the boats and asked the wireless operator to send out an SOS message. The operator tried but the dynamo was damaged by the explosion and rendered the equipment useless.

The ship didn't sink immediately but gradually filled which gave the crew time to get clear. She sank about three quarters of an hour later. All were saved with the exception of a donkeyman who was killed by the explosion.

12/50: GRIS NEZ. *Country:* French. *Date sunk:* 9/3/15. *Tons nett:* 80. *Tons gross:* –. *Built:* 1900. *Type:* SV. *Rig:* steam schooner. *Owners:* Louis Boutel, Boulogne, France. *Cargo:* –. *Armed:* No. *Position:* 20 miles WSW (True) from Beachy Head (50 37 00N; 00 16 00W). *Master's name:* E. Barbe. *Crew:* 16.

THERE is very little information on this vessel. She sailed from Boulogne on March 9, 1915, and was bound for Dartmouth. While crossing the channel she was stopped by a German submarine and the crew were ordered to go on board a vessel called *R.174* which was close by. The submarine then commenced to shell the *Gris Nez* which sank at 5pm.

12/51: MOHLENPRIS. *Country:* Norwegian. *Date sunk:* 15/4/17. *Tons nett:* 388. *Tons gross:* 637. *Built:* Lubeck in 1884. *Type:* SS. *Rig:* schooner. *Owners:* Joint Stocks Co Ltd, Bergen, Norway. *Cargo:* 691 tons coal from T.P. Rose Richards Ltd, Swansea to Mory & Co, Boulogne. *Armed:* No. *Position:* 20 miles WSW of Beachy Head (50 38 00N; 00 15 00W). *Master's name:* Cains Marius Barelius. *Crew:* 13.

LEAVING Llanelly on the April 12, 1917, at 9pm sharp, the *Mohlenpris* put into Falmouth for orders on the 14th and left there at 5pm. She was bound for Treport in France and all went well for her until Sunday 15th at 6.30pm. The weather was fine and clear and they were skimming along just over seven knots. The master was in the saloon, the second mate was on watch on the bridge with a seaman at the wheel.

The master suddenly heard a gun shot and he rushed up to the bridge. He hadn't bargained for anything so spectacular. Before his eyes was not one but two submarines, one on his starboard side and the other on the port side, both about two miles off. To make matters worse both of them were firing shells towards him.

The master ordered all hands on deck and the boats to be lowered. With all the crew aboard, the boats were pulled clear of the steamer. One of the submarines approached the master's boat and ordered him to board. He was then put back into the boat with three Germans sailors and ordered to row across to the *Mohlenpris*. Once on board her the Germans looted what ever they fancied and then placed bombs at strategic locations around the vessel. Having returned to the submarine the crew pulled clear just as their ship was blown up and sank in 20 fathoms of water.

On their way to the shore the two boats were found by the Admiralty trawler *Sheldon* and all of the crew landed safely at Newhaven at 6pm on the 16th April.

12/52: CUBA. *Country:* British.
Date sunk: 15/5/17. *Tons nett:* –. *Tons gross:* 271. *Built:* –. *Type:* SV. *Rig:* barquentine. *Owners:* J.W. Finch. *Cargo:* 385 tons clay, from Teignmouth to Treport. *Armed:* No. *Position:* 18 miles ESE from Owers (50 31 30N; 00 14 30W). *Master's name:* –. *Crew:* 7.

THE attack made on the *Cuba* by a German submarine was particularly savage. From a mile off, the German gunner kept up a steady bombardment on the barquentine, many shots slicing through her rigging and some crashing into her hull. Deadly splinters of wood were hurled around the ship in all directions, injuring two of the crew.

At 7pm the master decided that he could take no more of the pounding and left in the small boat with his crew. The submarine went alongside the boat and ordered the master to board. As the German commander questioned the master, several sailors got into the boat with *Cuba's* crew and ordered them to row back to their ship. Once on board they plundered her of everything they could lay their hands on. They also planted bombs at various places which exploded soon after they left.

Having finished with the master, the German commander told him to join his crew and make for the shore. The master looked across at his ship, just in time to see her go down by the head at 7.30pm. As they rowed away from the area, another submarine surfaced close to the first. They closed together and after the commanders had some sort of conversation, made off together on the surface.

The crew from the *Cuba* must have been swept

along by the wind and tide, for they eventually landed at Fecamp in France.

12/53: PAGENTURM. *Country:* British.
Date sunk: 16/5/17. *Tons nett:* 3160. *Tons gross:* 5000. *Built:* 1909. *Type:* SS. *Rig:* –. *Owners:* On Admiralty service. *Cargo:* India Office and military stores for Mesopotamia. *Armed:* 3 x 4.7in gun. *Position:* 16 miles W from Beachy Head (50 40 00N; 00 12 00W).*Master's name:* W.H. Ross. *Crew:* 82. *Crew nationality:* 13 British, 1 Chinese, 68 Lascars.

AFTER loading at Chatham the *Pagenturm* was met by her first escort a drifter called *Try Again*, at the Elbow Buoy on Tuesday May 15, 1917. The escort convoyed the vessel to the South Goodwins and was there relieved by another patrol drifter. Progress was slow as the *Pagenturm* had to steam between half speed and slow in order to keep station with her escorts. A third drifter escorted her from the South Goodwins to the west of Folkstone Gate and a fourth saw her to Dungeness. She had to wait there for about 15 minutes and eventually made her way down Channel with the vessel *White Ear* escorting.

On the bridge of *Pagenturm* the first mate and the Pilot, Mr Ellison, were on watch and they set the vessel on a course that would take them down to Falmouth. From there they were to proceed to Barry Dock to refuel for the journey to Mesopotamia. All was going well until they were off Beachy Head, when at 5pm their progress was dramatically halted by a torpedo which slammed into the starboard side abreast of number two hold. There is very little detail available after this point except for the fact that the ship sank at 6.20pm in 18 fathoms of water. It was reported that four Lascars were missing.

UB-40 was the submarine involved. *Pagenturm* was a former German ship, taken in India at the outbreak of war.

12/54: FANELLY. *Country:* French.
Date sunk: 6/11/16. *Tons nett:* –. *Tons gross:* 309. *Built:* –. *Type:* SV. *Rig:* –. *Owners:* –. *Cargo:* In ballast, Treport for Cardiff. *Armed:* –. *Position:* 18 miles WSW of Beachy Head (50 38 00N; 00 12 00W). *Master's name:* –.

THE only reference that appears on this sinking is in the form of a letter from the British Consulate in Rouen to the Marine Department of the Board of Trade which says:

"I have the honour to inform you that the master of the British SS *WH Dwyer* of Sunderland, at Rouen from Blythe, has reported to me having picked up at sea at 8.15pm on November 6, 1916, the crew of 10 men of the French barquentine *Fanelly* of Granville. This vessel was reported to have been sunk at 10am the same day by a German submarine. The men who were in two boats had drifted about 35 miles before being picked up. They have been landed at Rouen and taken charge of by the French naval authorities at this port."

12/55: GLENARM HEAD. *Country:* British. *Date sunk:* 5/1/18. *Tons nett:* 2527. *Tons gross:* 3908. *Built:* 1897. *Type:* SS. *Rig:* schooner. *Owners:* G. Heyn & Sons, Belfast. *Cargo:* 4687 tons of ammunition, Southampton to Boulogne. *Armed:* 1 x 12pdr 12cwt gun. *Position:* 20 miles E of Owers/8½ miles, 184 degrees from Brighton LV (50 34 00N; 00 10 00W). *Master's name:* Robert Macauley. *Crew:* 41.

THERE is very little information on this sinking in the records, probably because the master perished along with his ship.

Glenarm Head sailed from Southampton on January 4, 1918, and was making about eight knots when an explosion occurred at the aft end of the ship. The vessel sank in about five minutes and two lives were lost, the master and a Mr Brookman, the deck boy.

Although there was no certain proof at the time, the Admiralty put *Glenarm Head's* loss down to being struck by a torpedo. *UB-30* claimed to have torpedoed her

12/56: TYCHO. *Country:* British. *Date sunk:* 20/5/17. *Tons nett:* 2029. *Tons gross:* 3216. *Built:* Hull in 1904. *Type:* SS. *Rig:* –. *Owners:* T. Wilson Sons & Co/Ellerman Wilson Line, Hull. *Cargo:* 5700 tons general from Bombay and Karachi to Wilson Sons & Co, Hull. *Armed:* 1 x 3pdr quick fire gun. *Position:* 16 miles W ½ S of Beachy Head (50 39 00N; 00 08 00W). *Master's name:* G.B. Williams. *Crew:* 33. *Crew nationality:* 32 British, 1 Greek. *Gunners:* H.C. Williams; W. Campbell, No 5121.

TYCHO had been steaming trouble free ever since leaving Bombay on March 25, 1917. She eventually reached Falmouth on May 19, and called in for route instructions. She left the next day at 6.05pm and made her way through dismal weather of rain, drizzle and haze.

As she made her way up Channel the first mate was on the upper bridge, the master on the lower bridge with a seaman at the wheel and another on lookout on the forecastle head. An enormous explosion took place on the starboard side of the ship abreast of number one hold. The blast was so powerful that it blew the hatch cover off which in turn smashed the side of the forecastle.

The crew immediately mustered at the boats, something they had practised many times, and the master ordered the engines to be stopped. *Tycho* was sinking rapidly and the crew lowered the boats and pulled clear of her. Some of the crew had spotted two steamers not far off and so all the boats rowed towards

them in the hope of being spotted. As they did so the *Tycho* gave a lurch and sank.

The two steamers in the distance were the *Porthkerry* and *Esperanto*. The men on *Porthkerry* had seen their plight and turned towards them to render assistance. It was a gesture of compassion that cost them dear.

The lifeboats drew alongside the *Porthkerry* and the men made ready to get aboard her. The first mate, in charge of one boat, looked back momentarily to where his ship had once been. He saw no ship but to his horror spotted the track of a torpedo heading straight at him. He had barely time to open his mouth to shout a warning when the torpedo slammed into the side of the *Porthkerry*, blowing his master's lifeboat to pieces and killing all but one in her, and punching a huge whole in the side of the *Porthkerry*. The first mate's boat was overturned by the blast, scattering the occupants in all directions.

The *Porthkerry* joined the *Tycho* on the bottom within seven minutes and all that remained on the surface was a mess of debris and bodies. The chief engineer had managed to get one boat away from *Porthkerry* and was now weaving his way in and out of the vast amount of wreckage rounding up survivors. *Porthkerry's* Third Mate, Mr Pearson, had managed to get a boat away but it capsized. He found himself in the water with several men clinging to the boat, but some were trapped under it. He dived several times and got out the cook and a seaman, an action which later earned him a commendation for his courage.

The other steamer *Esperanto* had seen all this happening. The Admiralty recommendations were clear: in such situations steamers should get out of the area as quickly as possible or risk the same fate. The master and crew were aware of the risk but could not leave their fellow seamen in trouble. They turned the ship to the wreckage and managed to pick up all those still alive. Later they handed them over to the tug *Mercedes III* which took them into Newhaven at 2am the following morning.

The *Tycho* and *Porthkerry* were torpedoed by *UB-40*.

12/57: WEGA. *Country:* British. *Date sunk:* 14/6/17. *Tons nett:* 522. *Tons gross:* 839. *Built:* 1885. *Type:* SS. *Rig:* schooner. *Owners:* –. *Cargo:* 940 tons coal. *Armed:* No. *Position:* 20 miles W by S of Royal Sovereign Light Vessel (50 39 00N; 00 08 00W). *Master's name:* George Hadden. *Crew:* 17.

THE *Wega* left Hartlepool on Sunday June 10, 1917, at 10am and was bound for Cowes, Isle of Wight. She passed Dungeness on the 14th at about noon and followed the course given to her at the Downs. The weather was foggy and the master had been on the bridge all day. As the fog cleared he decided that it was safe for him to go to his berth in the chart room and rest for a while. He was soon asleep.

At 9.45pm, Captain Hadden awoke with a choking sensation. He cleared his throat and suddenly became aware that his ship was down by the head. He saw the furniture in his cabin had been thrown around. He managed to struggle out of the chart room injuring his hand and right eye in the process. On making the deck he found that his ship was sinking rapidly and, worse still, the lifeboats had been completely destroyed by the force of the explosion.

On the last occasion that his ship had been laid up for repairs, Captain Hadden had had the foresight to have a raft made up which could be left untied on the deck for just such an emergency. The entire surviving crew would have to trust their lives to the raft.

Some of the crew were missing. The second engineer was seen by one of the men at the fore part of the raft as the ship was sinking, but then the raft crashed violently against a hatch and he vanished. As the *Wega* sank the raft was overturned by the suction of it going down and the surviving 12 men were thrown into the sea. Once again Captain Hadden had thought of just such a situation and had the raft constructed with large holes in it. Little did he realise at the time that his forsight would save his own life. As the raft turned over he found himself underneath it, but with a little help from one of his crew he scrambled through a hole to the surface. Two men, the chief engineer and the mess room steward, were struggling in the water, clinging to a small piece of wreckage. Neither could swim and were drifting further away from the raft. With no means of propelling the raft towards them the bosun, Robert Anderson, got back into the water and swam to the assistance of the two men, bringing them back to the raft one at a time.

Within half an hour help came in the form of the patrol drifter *Three Boys* which took the survivors on board and landed them at Newhaven.

On examination, the master stated that he didn't hear anything of the explosion at the time but added that everybody on board heard two distinct explosions and possibly a third which came from the engine room. Nobody saw anything of a submarine and so the conclusion was that the vessel had run into a minefield.

For his gallant conduct in rescuing his two shipmates, the Bosun, Robert Anderson, was commended for bravery, awarded a bronze medal and received a reward of £3.

Wega was torpedoed by *UC-71*.

12/58: PORTHKERRY. *Country:* British.
Date sunk: 20/5/17. *Tons nett:* 1117. *Tons gross:* 1920. *Built:* 1911. *Type:* SS. *Rig:* –. *Owners:* The Porthcawl SS Co, 49/50, The Exchange, Cardiff. *Cargo:* 2600 tons coal for the Admiralty. *Armed:* No. *Position:* 16 miles W ½ S of Beachy Head (50 38 30N; 00 07 30W). *Master's name:* Mr Ebbitt. *Crew:* 19. (see *Tycho*, 12/56).

12/59: JUPITER. *Country:* British.
Date sunk: 21/5/17. *Tons nett:* 1354. *Tons gross:* 2124. *Built:* 1901. *Type:* SS. *Rig:* schooner. *Owners:* W.R. Bradley, 9, Pier St, Hull. *Cargo:* In ballast, Dieppe to Manchester. *Armed:* 1 x Vickers 3pdr gun. *Position:* 15 miles W of Beachy Head (50 38 00N; 00 07 00W). *Master's name:* Penville. *Crew:* 25.

LEAVING Dieppe on May 20, 1917, *Jupiter* proceeded on a zig-zag course at eight knots. There was a gunner on watch aft and all the usual lookouts were in position. At 4.40am without any warning a torpedo smashed into the side of the ship and she began to fill rapidly. Within a few minutes only the ship's bows remained above water. Such was the speed of her sinking that the crew had no time to get to the boats and most of them were thrown into the sea.

As they floundered in the water a submarine appeared close by and demanded to know the name of the ship along with other details. A part of the *Jupiter's* bow was still showing and the submarine's deck gun soon came alive and pumped five shells into it, sinking it almost immediately.

As if from nowhere, another steamer appeared on the scene. It was the SS *Karoo* and on spotting her the submarine turned on her and opened fire. However, it was not to be so easy this time as *Karoo* returned the fire with some ferocity. The German commander must have felt he was pushing his luck and dived. The skipper of the *Karoo* sent a radio message that he was engaging an enemy submarine and he identified it as *U-20*. (*UB-40* later claimed to have torpedoed *Jupiter*.)

Very soon the naval vessel HMS *P50* arrived at the scene and lowered a boat to pick up the survivors. One man, a 70 year old American was found to be unconscious and had to be hauled in with a lifeline. Attempts were made to revive him but he died shortly afterwards. There were 19 lost in all.

12/60: REIME. *Country:* Norwegian.
Date sunk: 7/11/16. *Tons nett:* 1137. *Tons gross:* 1913. *Built:* 1912. *Type:* SS. *Rig:* schooner. *Owners:* Fearnley & Eger, Oslo. *Cargo:* 2050 tons coal from Tyne to Rouen. *Armed:* No. *Position:* 52 miles SW of Dungeness (50 21 00N; 00 03 00W). *Master's name:* P.C. Bull. *Crew:* 21.

JUST one form gives the basic details of this sinking. The weather was not good with a rough sea whipped up by the gale force south-westerly wind. Occasional squalls were coming through turning the visibility at times to nil. At 6pm *Reime* was stopped by a German submarine and her crew were ordered to abandon her. They had very little choice with a four inch gun trained on them and did as they were told when ordered to board the submarine. The master and the mate were held on the submarine while the crew suffered the indignity of having to row German sailors back to their steamer to plant bombs. The bombs were very effective, sinking the steamer almost immediately they exploded.

The crew rowed for some time but were eventually picked up by the passing steamer *Cratloc* of Limmerick and dropped off at Deal at 1pm the following day.

12/61: NORTHLANDS. *Country:* British. *Date sunk:* 5/4/15. *Tons nett:* –. *Tons gross:* 2776. *Built:* Hartlepool in 1900. *Type:* SS. *Rig:* schooner. *Owners:* R.G. Jones, 57, Merchants Exchange, Cardiff. *Cargo:* 4200 tons iron ore, Le Goulette for Middlesbrough. *Armed:* No. *Position:* 20 miles SW from Beachy Head (50 31 00N; 00 02 00W). *Master's name:* Albert Sidney Taylor. *Crew:* 24.

CAPTAIN Taylor had spotted an odd looking object about half a mile off on his port beam and couldn't make any sense of it. It looked like a buoy and a flagstaff about 2ft high with a small red flag on top. Maybe it was just that but he felt it was odd all the same. He went to have a look on his chart and asked the second mate to keep an eye on it. When he returned to the bridge three minutes later his suspicions were confirmed as the object had materialised into a submarine. Instead of altering his course as intended for Dungeness, the master immediately set off on a zig-zag course calling all hands on deck and warning them of the danger.

The submarine soon caught up with the *Northlands* and hoisted the signal flag, 'Stop or I'll fire!' The master felt he had no choice and ordered the engines to be shut down. Flying a new signal, the submarine at 200yds off ordered, 'Abandon at once, I am going to sink you.' The crew obeyed and left in the boats while the submarine began edging closer, her crew waving at the men in the boats to hurry up and get clear. Ten minutes later, at 11.40am, the *Northlands* was torpedoed and sunk.

The crew were picked up by the steamer SS *Topaz* of the Cockerell Line, Belgium and taken into Deal. In his statement to the authorities, Captain Taylor said that his ship was not showing any nationality flag and bore the false name *Thlan*, but the submarine commander took no steps to ascertain his nationality.

U-33 was the submarine concerned.

12/62: NOTRE DAME DES VICTOIRES. *Country:* French. *Date sunk:* 3/9/16. *Tons nett:* –. *Tons gross:* 161. *Built:* –. *Type:* SV. *Rig:* smack. *Owners:* L. Boncler of Boulogne. *Cargo:* –. *Armed:* No. *Position:* 15 miles SW of Beachy Head (50 34 00N; 00 02 00W). *Master's name:* Pierre Barbe. *Crew:* 19. *Crew nationality:* 17 Danish, 1 Swede, 1 Finn.

SHE was on passage from Weymouth to Boulogne and was approached by a German submarine. The crew were ordered to leave the vessel and a bomb placed on the outside of the hull. It exploded several minutes later but the ship refused to sink. Frustrated at being held up the German gunners fired about 10 shells into her before she finally gave in and sank.

The crew of the *Notre Dame* were later picked up by a Norwegian steamer, transferred to a British torpedo boat and subsequently landed at Portsmouth.

12/63: UNITY. *Country:* British. *Date sunk:* 2/5/18. *Tons nett:* –. *Tons gross:* 1091. *Built:* 1902. *Type:* SS. *Rig* –.: *Owners:* Lancashire & Yorkshire Railway Co. *Cargo:* Guns and ammunition, Newhaven to Calais. *Armed:* –. *Position:* 5 miles SW of Newhaven (50 43 00N; 00 02 00W). *Master's name:* –.

THERE is literally only a snippet in Weekly Reports which states that *Unity* was sunk at 7.14pm on May 3, 1917, in the above position.. Twelve of her crew died.

UB-57 sank the *Unity*

12/64: CLAN MACMILLAN. *Country:* British. *Date sunk:* 23/3/17. *Tons nett:* 2805. *Tons gross:* 4525. *Built:* Dumbarton in 1901. *Type:* SS. *Rig:* schooner. *Owners:* The Clan Line Steamers Ltd, 109, Hope St, Glasgow. *Cargo:* 50 tons coir matting from Chittagong via London to Glasgow. *Armed:* 1 x 4.7in gun. *Position:* 10 miles W of Beachy Head (50 42 50N; 00 01 00W). *Master's name:* George Young. *Crew:* 91. *Crew nationality:* 15 British, 76 Lascars. *Gunners:* Harry Ladbury, RMLI L/Cpl, No 14884 Chatham; Joseph Bennett, RMLI Pte. No 2640.

IT was a very dark and cold night with snow squalls coming through periodically. The *Clan Macmillan* was at full speed heading down the Channel. Because there was a lot of shipping around, coupled with the poor visibility during the snow showers, the master had some of the lights switched on. He went below at midnight leaving the watch in the capable hands of the mate and the third officer. About 55 minutes later the master was woken up by the sound of a loud bang. He jumped out of his bunk immediately and, dressing himself as he ran, headed to the bridge.

It was soon apparent what had happened, a torpedo striking her on the starboard side amidships had buckled her decks and opened up a large hole in her side. The master could see that she was taking in water fast and ordered all hands to get to their boat stations. Everyone was accounted for and apart from four Lascars being slightly injured they were all unhurt. About 15 minutes later the boats pulled clear of their steamer only to come face to face with the vessel that had caused them all the trouble.

The German U-boat manoeuvred into a position at right angles to the *Clan Macmillan*. The crew watched as a white streak came hurtling out of the forward torpedo tube and connected with the side of the steamer, striking her in virtually the same position as the first. She creaked and groaned after the explosion and a huge crack appeared in her; she was breaking in two.

The submarine drew alongside the boats, and an officer, presumably the commander, demanded to speak to the master. Captain Young had seen it coming and hid himself down in among the legs of his crew. They shook their heads at the commander and made out that they didn't know where the captain was, telling him only their ship's name and her tonnage. The commander seemed content with that information and headed off into the night.

By 2.45am there were three patrol trawlers around *Clan Macmillan* and at 5am when several torpedo boats turned up she still hadn't sunk. She was in a sorry state though, the crack in her midships getting worse by the minute. An hour later she gave up, broke in two and sank to the bottom.

The patrol trawler *White Ear* took her crew on board and stayed in the area whilst the steamer was still afloat. Soon after she sank they headed for the shore landing at Newhaven at 8.20am.

12/65: VASCO. *Country:* British.
Date sunk: 16/11/16. *Tons nett:* –. *Tons gross:* 1914. *Built:* 1895 by Furness Withy. *Type:* SS. *Rig:* –. *Owners:* T. Wilson & Sons. *Cargo:* 2100 tons general, Hull for Naples. *Armed:* 1 x 12pdr 12cwt gun. *Position:* 10 miles W by S of Beachy Head (50 42 00N; 00 01 00W). *Master's name:* –. *Crew:* 26.

AT 10.10pm on November 16, 1916, *Vasco* struck a mine with her bows which literally blew off the fore part of the ship. As if this were not trouble enough, about five seconds later she struck another mine further aft. The *Vasco* was in a terrible mess, and worse still, many of her crew lay dead in the wreckage.

The master was below at the time and rushed on deck. It was obvious his ship was going down, and rapidly at that. He ordered the boats away and went to the bridge. While the crew were trying to get clear he continued to blow the ship's whistle to attract attention.

Vasco sank so suddenly that many of the men who were left alive were unable to get clear in time. The chief officer managed to get the starboard boat away with five men. He also managed to find two more floating in the water.

About 45 minutes later they were picked up by the SS *Kronstadt* of Leith. When her captain had heard what had happened he steamed back to the area to search for more survivors. It paid off for one very lucky naval gunner, who was found clinging to a piece of debris.

Altogether 17 people, including the master, lost their lives in the *Vasco*.

12/66: CLODMOOR. *Country:* British.
Date sunk: 3/5/17. *Tons nett:* 2408. *Tons gross:* 3753. *Built:* Sunderland in 1902. *Type:* SS. *Rig:* –. *Owners:* Admiralty transport Moor Line Ltd, Newcastle. *Cargo:* 5777 tons wheat stowed in bulk and bags. *Armed:* 1 x Japanese 12pdr gun. *Position:* 5 miles SW of Newhaven (50 43 00N; 00 00 30W). *Master's name:* Charles Hunter. *Crew:* 30. *Crew nationality:* 1 Dutch, 1 Norwegian, 4 Greeks, 1 Portuguese, 1 American, 22 British.

CLODMOOR left the port of Bahia Blanca on March 14, 1917, and headed for cooler northern parts. She called in at Falmouth for orders and left there on May 2, at 7.50pm. Her orders were to proceed up Channel on a zig-zag course and eventually make her way north to Newcastle.

The master followed his instructions to the letter. At 4.30pm on May 3, the visibility was good about six miles and there was other traffic around. Another steamer was about three miles ahead and even an armed British trawler lay a few miles off to the south-west. The *Clodmoor* was making good speed at about eight knots and there was every reason to feel safe.

What happened next took the crew totally by surprise as a torpedo slammed into the side of her just before the bridge by number two hold, about five feet below the waterline. It blew an enormous hole in her, ripped open the upper deck and lifted the hatches completely off. The bridge and chart room were totally wrecked but by some amazing piece of luck only three men were slightly injured.

Very soon two patrol boats *Smew* and *Balfour* appeared on the scene and finding the *Clodmoor* in a bad state but still afloat, put lines on her and began to tow her towards the shore. At 6.05pm torpedo boat No 5 arrived and watched over them as the master ordered his crew to take to the boats. *Clodmoor* heeled over on her starboard side and sank by the head at 9pm in 14½ fathoms of water. *TB 5* closed on the scene to pick up the crew and later took them into Newhaven.

The examining naval officer wasn't completely convinced that it was a torpedo which had sunk the *Clodmoor* until one of the crew produced a piece of shrapnel that he found on deck before quitting the ship. An examination of the fragment made it almost certain that it was a piece of a torpedo. The examining officer also put in his report that unfortunately, some of the rescued men were the worse for drink when they were brought ashore.

UB-48 was the submarine involved.

12/67: HARPALION. *Country:* British.
Date sunk: 26/2/15. *Tons nett:* 3669. *Tons gross:* 5867. *Built:* West Hartlepool. *Type:* SS. *Rig:* schooner. *Owners:* J. and C. Harrison, London. *Cargo:* In ballast, London for Newport News. *Armed:* No. *Position:* 6½ miles W of Royal

Sovereign Light Ship when hit (50 20 00N; 00 00 30W). *Master's name:* Abraham Widdess. *Crew:* 42.

THE master of the *Harpalion* was in his cabin at 5.20pm on February 24, 1915, chatting to the Pilot, Mr Wyatt. Their conversation came to an abrupt halt as a loud thud was heard from the port side amidships followed by a huge explosion. They both ran on deck and found that they were totally enveloped by a huge cloud of steam. It was obvious to the master that the engine room had been severely damaged. Unknown to him at that moment, three of his firemen had been killed.

With the steamer listing heavily to port the master ordered the crew to take to the boats. Shortly afterwards, the torpedo boat HMS *Syser* came alongside and the commander shouted to the master that he would pick them all up. The master shouted back that he had recently spotted a submarine's periscope and the *Syser* cruised around for a while whilst the *Harpalion's* crew made ready to leave. Finding nothing of the submarine the torpedo boat took the crew off.

Harpalion didn't sink immediately. The commander of *Syser* ordered another patrol vessel *Amazon* to watch over the steamer as he was of the opinion that she could be saved. It was nearly two days later before any effort was made to get her in tow when four men from the vessel *Ariel* went aboard her to fix lines and, presumably, claim salvage. By this time the *Harpalion* was about 25 miles off Beachy Head and the weather was very rough. A tug later approached but was unable to do anything and the steamer was abandoned for the second time just after midnight on the 26th when she sank.

Though *U-8* had torpedoed her on February 24, 1915, the *Harpalion* was reported by Lloyd's as finally sinking "40 miles off Cape d'Antifer" on February 26.

WORLD WAR ONE
CHANNEL WRECKS

—◆—

AREA
THIRTEEN

WRECK SITES IN AREA THIRTEEN

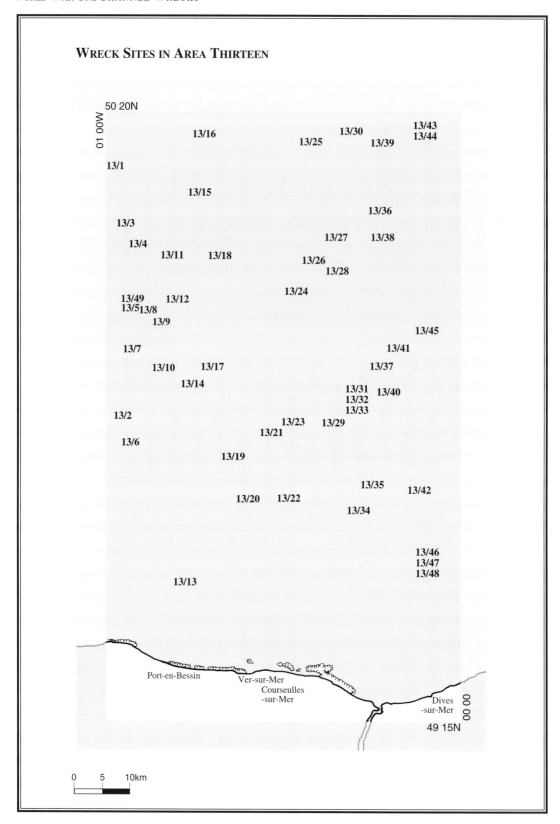

50 20N

01 00W

13/16   13/30   13/43
        13/25   13/39   13/44

13/1

13/15

13/36

13/3

13/4   13/27   13/38
13/11   13/18   13/26
        13/28

13/24

13/49   13/12
13/5 13/8
13/9

13/45

13/7

13/41

13/10   13/17   13/37
13/14

13/31 13/40
13/32
13/33

13/2

13/23 13/29
13/21

13/6

13/19

13/35   13/42

13/20 13/22

13/34

13/46
13/47
13/48

13/13

Port-en-Bessin   Ver-sur-Mer
        Courseulles
        -sur-Mer

Dives
-sur-Mer

00 00

49 15N

0   5   10km

13/1: HILDA LEA. *Country:* British.
Date sunk: 23/12/17. *Tons nett:* 793. *Tons gross:* 1330. *Built:* 1916. *Type:* SS. *Rig:* schooner. *Owners:* British Government. Managers, James Cormack & Co, Leith. *Cargo:* 1720 tons coal for Rouen. *Armed:* 1 x 90mm gun. *Position:* 23 miles SE by S of St Catherines (50 14 00N; 01 00 00W). *Master's name:* Andrew Brown. *Crew:* 22. *Crew nationality:* 21 British, 1 Swede. *Gunners:* H. Short, LS RNR, No 1412X; C. Hanson, AB RNVR, No 10930TZ; J. Hanson, AB RNVR, No 10934TZ.

IT was 9.15pm. The bright moonlit night meant that Oberleutnant R. Gebeschus could have the pick of the convoy as he watched through the periscope of *UB-35*. He chose the thirteenth ship, the *Hilda Lea*.

The first anyone knew of it on *Hilda Lea* was when one of the lookouts spotted a white wake only a few yards off the port side. But it was far too late to do anything as it slammed into her amidships, well below the waterline, penetrating the engine room. So fierce was the explosion that one donkeyman was killed instantly and a seaman wounded. To make matters worse the wrecked engine room then burst into flames.

The master knew he had to act quickly and gave the order to abandon ship. The crew managed to get away in the starboard lifeboat and a working boat, the port boats having been smashed by the explosion. They were in the nick of time for when they were only a few yards away, the steamer sank by the stern and disappeared.

The escort trawler *Sweeper* picked the crew up. As they were outward bound they had to make some transfers, once to the French destroyer *Florial*, next to *TB 110* which eventually landed them at St Helens.

13/2: CONSTANCE MARY. *Country:* British.
Date sunk: 15/12/16. *Tons nett:* –. *Tons gross:* 142. *Built:* Glasgow in 1875. *Type:* SV. *Rig:* three-masted schooner. *Owners:* Albert Westgate, Woolster St, Plymouth. *Cargo:* 260 tons of iron ore from Caen to Swansea. *Armed:* No. *Position:* 20 miles NE of Cape Barfleur (49 47 00N; 00 58 00W). *Master's name:* William Stiles, 58, Cromwell Rd, Plymouth. *Crew:* 5.

CONSTANCE MARY was well on her way to Swansea. She had loaded her cargo at Caen and left there at 11am the previous morning. Nobody on board her was aware of the large grey object which lurked behind them until a shot rang out. The shell plunged into the sea ahead. Flags ran up the conning tower mast of the U-boat ordering the master to stop, but he chose to ignore it. A few moments later another bang was followed by a second shell that threw up a spout of water alongside the *Constance*. After the third shell the master knew his situation was hopeless and ordered all the sails to be taken in.

The German commander was very blunt as the crew and the ship's dog arrived alongside the submarine in their lifeboat. The master was ordered to board for questioning whilst a bombing party went over to the *Constance*. Her sinking was neatly done by placing two bombs, one by the fore mast and the other at the mizzen. The bombing party then helped themselves to whatever took their fancy, barometer, clocks, provisions and a set of flags. Ten minutes later the *Constance Mary* was gone.

The crew rowed for three hours in a southerly direction when they were spotted by the Norwegian steamer *Storfond* of Stavanger. They were eventually landed at Barry Dock on the morning of December 18.

13/3: BISHOPSTON. *Country:* British.
Date sunk: 4/9/17. *Tons nett:* 1536. *Tons gross:* 2513. *Built:* 1916. *Type:* SS. *Rig* schooner.: *Owners:* Swansea Steamers Ltd, Gloucester House, Swansea. *Cargo:* In ballast, Le Havre for Portsmouth. *Armed:* 1 x 6pdr gun. *Position:* 30 miles S by E from St Catherines (50 08 00N; 00 57 00W). *Master's name:* Clifford F. David. *Crew:* 29. *Crew nationality:* All British. *Gunners:* C.H. Bond, AB RNVR, No WZ3550; T. Cropper, RNVR GL3, No MZ1430.

HAVING delivered her cargo, which included Royal Naval Air Service stores, to France the *Bishopston* was on her way back to Portsmouth. It was a fine, bright night and the ship was making good progress at nine knots. At 3.45am the second mate had the watch but the master was also on deck. As Mr David started to go below, something caught his eye in the distance and he realised that it was a partially submerged U-boat. Worse still, there was the tell tale white track of a torpedo heading his way. He had no time to alert the bridge and the torpedo hit the starboard side of the ship aft.

She settled down to the waterline almost immediately and many of the men had to throw themselves into the water. Some of the boats got away and most of the crew made it apart from two, presumed to have gone down with the ship. From the time of the torpedo striking to the time of sinking was two minutes.

The crew were later found by a naval patrol vessel and taken into Portsmouth

Submarine concerned was *UC-16*.

13/4: PLM 4 *Country:* French.
Date sunk: 27/12/17. *Tons nett:* 1508. *Tons gross:* 2640. *Built:* –. *Type:* SS. *Rig:* –. *Owners:* PLM Railway Co, Havre. *Cargo:* 3800 tons coal, Tyme for Le Havre. *Armed:* 1 x 90mm gun, 1 x 95mm gun. *Position:* 31 miles SE by S of St Catherines Point (50 07 00N; 00 56 00W). *Master's name:* L. Huchon. *Crew:* 32. *Crew nationality:* All

French. *Gunners:* L. Gaudez, A. Curudeau, J. Le Guinner, P. Le Baron, A. Helaile, J. Durand, F. Roussel.

CROSSING the Channel in convoy with two other steamers, the *PLM 4* was under the escort of four patrol vessels.

The first anyone knew of an attack was when the master of *PLM 4* heard and felt an explosion on the port side of his ship. He said he also heard two smaller explosions some distance away about a minute before the attack. These were depth charges dropped by the patrol vessel *Gozo* which had spotted a submarine dive about 500yds away. The steamer began to list heavily to port and was settling down by the head. The sea was rough and it proved extremely difficult for the crew to launch the boats, but they finally got clear. By then two patrol vessels were at hand and picked the crew up. However, one man, who had been washed out of a boat, had to be rescued by a boat from the patrol trawler *Everton*. He was plucked from alongside the sinking steamer just a few minutes before she sank.

13/5: SUFFOLK COAST. *Country:* British. *Date sunk:* 7/11/16. *Tons nett:* 378. *Tons gross:* 780. *Built:* Middlesbrough in 1913. *Type:* SS. *Rig:* schooner. *Owners:* Powell Bacon & Hough, Tower Buildings, Liverpool. *Cargo:* 882 tons of general from Leopold Walford & Co, Glasgow, to Henri D. Lahousaye, Fécamp. *Armed:* No. *Position:* 14 miles ESE of Cape Barfleur (49 37 00N; 00 56 00W). *Master's name:* Humphrey Ellis Williams. *Crew:* 16. *Crew nationality:* 14 British, 1 Italian, 1 Belgian.

THE *Suffolk Coast* had all but made it across the Channel when suddenly the master spotted a submarine which appeared about two miles ahead and travelled at full speed straight across his bows. The master said that it appeared to take no notice of him so he altered course very quickly for Cherbourg and hoped he could get in before the commander either spotted him or changed his mind. At the same time he ordered a signal to be flown from the mast, 'Enemy submarine in the vicinity,' in the hope that a patrol vessel would spot it and investigate.

When about six miles north-north-west of Cherbourg a French patrol vessel appeared and steamed around the *Suffolk Coast*, seemingly making a search. However, a few minutes later she left.

Thinking he was safe Captain Williams altered course again and passed three miles off Barfleur at 2.35pm. At 4pm he was back on his original course when he spotted a stationary steamer in the distance with what appeared to be a submarine alongside it. He looked through his binoculars and saw that a submarine was attacking a Norwegian steamer which was about to sink. The master immediately ordered a change of course and hoped that the submarine

hadn't spotted him. His hopes were dashed when a shell whistled over the bridge and landed in the sea ahead. This was followed by several more and the master realised he had no choice but to stop.

As the submarine drew nearer the master could read the signal which ordered him to send over his ship's papers. Captain Williams asked the mate if he would take the papers over in the boat whilst he set about destroying his secret papers. The mate returned a little later with a German officer and two sailors who promptly set about helping themselves to charts, clocks and anything else they fancied. Having loaded it all in the boat they placed three bombs, each about the size of a one pound tin of salmon, at various places around the ship. With the fuses lit the Germans informed the crew that they had better get clear which was no sooner said than done. Five minutes later the bombs exploded and the steamer sank.

It was a long row for the men in the boat and it was fifteen hours before they were picked up by a French torpedo boat and landed at St Vaast.

Submarine involved was UC-17, which had no fewer than six commanders and survived the war.

13/6: LAURA C. ANDERSON. *Country:* American. *Date sunk:* 29/8/17. *Tons nett:* 766. *Tons gross:* 960. *Built:* Bath, Maine, USA, 1891. *Type:* SV. *Rig:* 4 masted schooner. *Owners:* A.D. Cummins & Co, Philadelphia, USA. *Cargo:* 1406 tons general from New Orleans to Havre. *Armed:* No. *Position:* Cape Barfluer bearing W about 15 miles (49 45 00N; 00 55 00W). *Master's name:* Charles R. Davis Jnr, Philadelphia. *Crew:* 8. *Crew nationality:* 4 Americans, 1 Portuguese, 1 Mexican, 2 British.

HAVING completed her voyage across the Atlantic from New Orleans, *Laura C. Anderson* was making her way up the Channel towards Havre. She had been delayed by a gale which blew for several days. However, the end of the journey was near, and the master took little notice of what he thought was a French fishing boat about two miles off on his starboard beam.

Suddenly the fishing boat swung about and there followed a bang which sent a shell whistling past the schooner. The master soon realised that it was certainly no fishing vessel but a submarine and hoped that the German commander had made a mistake, not realising that the ship was American. So he ignored it and carried on. Two more shots followed, one cut the main peak halyards and the other struck the bulwarks. With this the master brought the ship to a halt and waited. The submarine wasn't getting any closer but continued to fire at the ship about every two minutes. The master felt that the German commander was being very cautious and smelt a trap, thinking that he was dealing with a Q-ship. Still the shells kept coming, each one causing more damage, so the master ordered a boat to be lowered and the crew pulled clear.

Having seen the boat leave, the submarine commander brought his vessel closer, still firing as it approached and even aimed one or two shots at the lifeboat. Eventually she drew alongside the boat and ordered the master and crew to climb aboard. Several Germans boarded the boat and were towed across by the submarine to the *Anderson* where they proceeded to loot anything they could find, before planting bombs on her. Back at the submarine the crew were returned to their boat and as the exchange was taking place the schooner blew up, turned on her port side and sank. Not content with looting the ship the Germans even took the small amount of stores the men had in their lifeboat.

About two hours later the crew were picked up by HMS *P35* which took them into Portsmouth harbour.

13/7: TELA. *Country:* British.
Date sunk: 2/5/17. *Tons nett:* 4067. *Tons gross:* 7226. *Built:* 1916. *Type:* SS. *Rig:* transport. *Owners:* Admiralty. *Cargo:* In ballast from Havre to Barry Roads. *Armed:* 1 x 4.7in gun. *Position:* 40 miles NW of Havre (49 55 00N; 00 54 00W). *Master's name:* J.C. Jackson. *Crew:* 79. *Crew nationality:* 52 British, 1 Spaniard, 3 Chileans, 1 American, 22 Dutch. *Gunners:* J. Siddle; J. Robertson.

IT is noted in an obvious hurriedly filled in Submarine Attack form that at 12.40am, *Tela* was struck by a torpedo on the port side aft causing a huge explosion. She sank very quickly but all the crew managed to get safely away in the lifeboats. They were picked up by a torpedo boat and taken to Havre.

Submarine concerned was *UB-18*.

13/8: VINAES. *Country:* Norwegian.
Date sunk: 8/6/17. *Tons nett:* 626. *Tons gross:* 1107. *Built:* –. *Type:* SS. *Rig:* –. *Owners:* Sjen Lotten of Haugesund. *Cargo:* Coal, Swansea for Rouen. *Armed:* No. *Position:* 15 miles ENE of Cape Barfleur (49 59 00N; 00 52 00W). *Master's name:* F.M. Yoiyensun. *Crew:* 12.

VINAES' orders were to proceed to St Helens Roads and join a coal convoy to cross the Channel. The convoy consisted of 15 vessels and the *Vinaes* was placed in position number 12. They all set out across the Channel in a zig-zag fashion.

At 10pm a torpedo slammed into the port side forward of *Vinaes* and she sank almost immediately.

The armed escort trawler *Alaska* was nearby and the commander, R.J. Moore, states that at 10pm he heard a heavy explosion. On looking aft he saw that the *Vinaes* was about five cables from him and could just see in the dark that she was in trouble. A boat was launched immediately which managed to find one survivor. Other survivors were picked up by adjacent ships including the Norwegian SS *Norma*.

13/9: GERMAN SUBMARINE (possible).
Country: German. *Date believed sunk:* 18/8/17.
Tons nett: –. *Tons gross:* –. *Built:* –. *Type:* –.
Owners: German navy. *Cargo:* –. *Armed:* Yes.
Position: 20 miles SE by S from Antifer
(49 58 00N; 00 50 00W). *Master's name:* –.
Crew: –. *Crew nationality:* German.

THERE is only a brief mention in Weekly Reports which says that patrol trawler *Monarch III* reported that an enemy submarine was sighted. Her commander considered that this was the same submarine which was bombed by the sea plane 9860 on the same day.

Several patrol vessels proceeded to the area and spotted a very large oily patch on the water surface with bubbles rising up through the midst of it. They dropped a depth charge and waited in the area to see if anything came to the surface but had to leave through stress of weather.

German records list no loss for this date.

13/10: WILLIAM GEORGE. *Country:* British.
Date sunk: 30/9/16. *Tons nett:* 127. *Tons gross:* 250. *Built:* Rhyl Flint 1876. *Type:* SV. *Rig:* schooner. *Owners:* Albert Westcott, 43, Woolster St, Plymouth. *Cargo:* 247 tons coal from Swansea to St Valery, France. *Armed:* No. *Position:* 10 miles NNE of Cape la Hague (49 53 00N; 00 50 00W). *Master's name:* John Smith. *Crew:* 5.

THE submarine which suddenly appeared about one mile off the *William George's* port quarter was very accurate with her shelling. So much so that the master ordered the sails to be reduced, but on reading signals from the submarine ordered his crew to abandon ship. They rowed slowly over to the submarine where the commander demanded the ship's papers and questioned the master about his voyage and destination.

After telling the crew of the *William George* to get clear the German commander edged his submarine to within 100yds of the little sailing vessel and began a bombardment. The smooth sea conditions made it an easy target and most of the shells found their mark. The German gunners seemed to be enjoying the opportunity of some target practice and were in no hurry to finish. However, in the distance the appearance of a French torpedo boat sent the Germans scurrying back to the conning tower and two minutes later the submarine dived.

The crew of the *William George* rowed back towards their ship which was settling down in the water. As they approached she lurched over and sank.

The torpedo boat turned out to be the *Durantil* which picked them up and landed them at Cherbourg.

13/11: MARGARET SUTTON. *Country:* British.
Date sunk: 2/8/16. *Tons nett:* –. *Tons gross:* 197.
Built: Cork in 1868. *Type:* SV. *Rig:* brigantine.
Owners: John H. Davis, 26, Woolster St,

Plymouth. *Cargo:* 85 tons shingle ballast, Treport to Couch, Fowey. *Armed:* No. *Position:* St Catherines Point bore NW by N 35 miles (50 05 00N; 00 47 00W). *Master's name:* William Baker. *Crew:* 5.

THE sailing vessel *Margaret Sutton*, although nearly 50 years old was still a useful ship.

She left the port of Treport on the August 1, 1916, at 11am and was bound for Fowey, Cornwall. The crossing went well and she was under full sail, on a north-north-west heading. At 9.30pm the next night an enemy submarine appeared astern of her and then came close up on the *Sutton's* starboard quarter and ordered her to stop.

The commander of the submarine shouted across for the *Sutton's* lifeboat to come and fetch two of his men. With guns pointing at him the master of the brig had no choice but to comply and his boat returned with two German sailors, both armed with bombs.

After helping themselves to the barometer, clock and compass, the unwelcome boarders demanded to be taken back to their submarine and suggested that as the bombs were timed to explode in five minutes the crew should get into the boat as well.

The bombs exploded as predicted. Five minutes later, *Margaret Sutton* was gone.

The men drifted for several hours until the Admiralty trawler *White Ear* picked them up and landed them safely at Newhaven.

The rest of the patrol made an exhaustive search to the east but found nothing except wreckage from the *Margaret Sutton* at 50 10 00N; 00 12 00W. The survivors were picked up in 50 23 00N; 00 17 00W.

13/12: DRESDEN. *Country:* British. *Date sunk:* 23/9/16. *Tons nett:* 489. *Tons gross:* 950. *Built:* Glasgow in 1865. *Type:* SS. *Rig:* schooner. *Owners:* Leith Hull & Hamburg Steam Packet Co Ltd. *Cargo:* 798 tons coke, shipped by H.R Watson of Newcastle and consigned to Rouen. *Armed:* No. *Position:* 41 miles S by E from Nab End Rock Buoy (50 00 00N; 00 47 00W). *Master's name:* John Wright, 54, Sloan St, Leith. *Crew:* 18. *Crew nationality:* 13 British, 2 Russian, 1 Spaniard, 2 Greek.

AT 5pm on September 23, 1916, the master and mate of SS *Dresden* were on the bridge. One of the crew suddenly shouted up to the bridge and pointed to an object off the port bow which looked every bit like the conning tower of a submarine. A few minutes later the whole U-boat appeared on the surface on the port side of the *Dresden* and began shelling. One shot threw up a spout of water just ahead of the steamer and another whistled between the fore mast and the funnel.

The accuracy of the shooting made the master decide that it was pointless to continue and ordered the engines to be shut down. The crew assembled at their boat stations and as the steamer came to a halt they left the ship and pulled clear. Meanwhile, the submarine had been moving closer and a voice ordering both boats alongside her. The Germans then took one of the boats to plant bombs on the *Dresden* and help themselves to the chronometer, bell and money.

Back in their boats the crew looked on as their ship exploded and sank. They rowed and sailed for many hours but were not rescued until the the next day when they were picked up by the steamer *Jaffa* of Hull and landed at St Helens.

Submarine involved was *UB-37* commanded by Oberleutnant Hans Valentiner.

13/13: TARPEIA. *Country:* British. *Date sunk:* 11/5/17. *Tons nett:* 218. *Tons gross:* 538. *Built:* 1905. *Type:* SS. *Rig:* schooner. *Owners:* Cair & Eidman Ltd of Cardiff. *Cargo:* 651 tons stone, Alderney to Treport. *Armed:* No. *Position:* 21 miles SE by E of Cape Barfleur (49 30 00N; 00 46 00W). *Master's name:* Daniel Armour. *Crew:* 13. *Crew nationality:* 10 British, 3 Greeks.

THE only information on this sinking comes from a few details written on a Submarine Attack form.

It was a bright moonlit night with very little wind and a calm sea when *Tarpeia* was approached by two German submarines, one of which opened fire on her with her deck gun. Four shells were fired in total but it's not clear if any of them hit. The master was compelled to give up and after abandoning his ship the Germans planted bombs aboard her. The bombs exploded at approximately 4.30am and she sank instantly.

The crew rowed towards the shore and were eventually spotted by a lookout on a French torpedo boat which landed them at Havre later the same day. All the crew were accounted for and there were no injuries.

German records suggest that only one submarine was involved – *UB-18*.

13/14: TAMMERFORS. *Country:* Russian. *Date sunk:* 26/2/17. *Tons nett:* –. *Tons gross:* 994. *Built:* –. *Type:* SS. *Rig:* –. *Owners:* Russian navy. *Cargo:* 1051 tons coal, 5 railway wagons. *Armed:* –. *Position:* 27 miles NE of Barfleur (49 52 00N; 00 45 20W). *Master's name:* –. *Crew:* 17. *Crew nationality:* 10 Russians, 1 British, 1 French, 2 Danish, 2 Norwegians, 1 Swede.

TAMMERFORS was part of a convoy that left St Helens on February 26, 1917, to cross the Channel. She should have been fairly safe as the fleet was protected by armed escorts but this proved no deterrent to a determined German U-boat commander.

At 10.40 that evening she was struck by a torpedo on the port bow. In one minute the main deck was under water and she began to list over to starboard. The crew lowered the starboard boats and 12 men managed to get clear, two injuring themselves in the process. Five men however, were killed instantly by the explosion of the torpedo.

As the boat got clear the master reported that he saw a faint torch light and the shadow of what he believed to be the submarine. They rowed for a while and were picked up by the French steamer *Parame* of Havre.

13/15: CONNAUGHT. *Country:* British. *Date sunk:* 3/3/17. *Tons nett:* –. *Tons gross:* 2646. *Built:* 1897. *Type:* SS. *Rig:* –. *Owners:* City of Dublin Steam Packet Co. *Cargo:* In ballast, Havre to Southampton. *Armed:* No. *Position:* 25 miles S of Owers LV (50 11 30N; 00 44 00W). *Master's name:* John Thomson. *Crew:* 77.

SUCH were the circumstances of the sinking of the *Connaught* that the Admiralty ordered a Court of Enquiry. The enquiry was convened two days after her sinking on Monday, March 5, 1917, at 10am, in the board room of the Union Castle Line offices in Southampton.

Captain John Thomson was called to give his account of events, which was all text book stuff, apart from one fact; he wasn't zig-zagging.

Connaught cleared the Whistle Buoy at Havre and dropped the pilot off. The steamer came up to her top speed of 18 knots and headed across the Channel towards Southampton. At around 12.30pm, Chief Officer Henry Alexander Wood relieved Second Officer Harry John Addison from bridge watch duties. Having finished his lunch, Harry Addison went back on the bridge around 1.30pm where he was joined by the master. The master looked around and commented to his second officer how quiet it was and added that it was remarkable that the Channel was so deserted, not another vessel in sight. He spoke too soon for a few minutes later there was a huge explosion aft.

The port engine slowed down of its own accord and stopped, while the starboard engine raced away; a sure sign that the propeller had been blown off. Captain Thomson shouted to the chief officer, who was just outside the bridge, to have the boats manned and to stand by the ship.

Captain Thomson went to his room, gathered up his confidential papers, stuffed them into the weighted bag and tossed them over the side. He then made for the Marconi room where the wireless operator was busy trying to get off an SOS. He gave the ship's position to him but it was hopeless. The aerial cables lay on the deck, blasted down by the force of the explosion.

Having a closer look at the aft section of his ship, Captain Thomson realised that three men had been working below cleaning out the aft hatches. They were missing, undoubtedly killed by the explosion. He pulled himself away from the mess and looked

over the starboard rail. All the crew except himself, the chief officer and the wireless operator, were in the boats alongside. He shouted down to them to pull away a few yards to safety. He went forward to join his two colleagues and they lowered themselves down in the jolly boat.

From a position just ahead of the steamer off the port bow, Captain Thomson surveyed the ship. He discussed the situation with the mate and they both agreed that she appeared to be stable and not sinking any further. With an air of determination the master said, "We will get back to the ship and see if we can get the wireless up." They moved around the bow of the *Connaught* to get back aboard but suddenly stopped. A periscope appeared only 200yds off. The German submarine commander had other ideas for the ship and was making it plain to the master that to go back on board would be foolish.

To push the point home, another torpedo crashed into *Connaught* on her port side amidships. A massive hole opened up causing the water to pour in. Within a few minutes she turned over and sank. The master gathered together in the boats and headed away from the area. The master glanced back to where his steamer had gone down and saw the submarine still on the surface. However, it wasn't alone, another submarine was a few hundred yards off it. He kept an eye on them and saw that one of them was heading towards him. His crew also spotted it and shouted for him to get in the largest boat and hide among the legs and coats. When the German commander asked for the master, he was told that he had been killed and went down with the ship. The German eyed them disbelievingly, but was in a hurry and settled for the name and tonnage of the ship.

It was 8pm before the crew in the boats spotted anything that might be close enough to rescue them. They waved at the passing steamer and a lookout managed to spot them. SS *Grantully Castle* picked them up and took them to Southampton.

The Court of Enquiry concluded that *Connaught* had been sunk as the result of an attack by an enemy submarine. They picked on the fact that the master had not been zig-zagging. However, he appears to have received nothing more than a caution.

The submarine concerned, according to German reports, was *U-48*.

13/16: ATHOLE. *Country:* British. *Date sunk:* 26/4/17. *Tons nett:* 109. *Tons gross:* 149. *Built:* Littlehampton in 1892. *Type:* SV. *Rig:* ketch. *Owners:* Forbes, Abbott & Lennard Ltd, Shoreham. *Cargo:* In ballast, Havre to Shoreham. *Armed:* No. *Position:* 20 miles S of Owers LV (50 18 00N; 00 41 00W). *Master's name:* John Martin McCoy. *Crew:* 5.

THE master of *Athole* followed his sailing instructions to the letter when he left the French coast and crossed the Channel very quickly. The wind throughout the night had been very strong, so strong that her top sail sheet had been carried away and couldn't be replaced until the next day after the wind had eased down. Having sorted the rigging out the master set a course to take her up Channel to Shoreham.

All was going well until 8.15am on the April 26, 1917, when a shell came whistling past the ship and landed in the water about 20yds off. This was followed by another which landed much closer. The master looked around and spotted a German submarine catching up with him rapidly.

The shelling became more accurate as the submarine got closer, causing bits of rigging to go flying in all directions. One shell set a sail on fire. The master and his crew had long since decided that enough was enough and pulled away from their stricken ship. As they did so the submarine opened fire with a machine gun but fortunately for the crew it was aimed very wide and obviously intended as encouragement for them to hurry up. After talking to the master and examining his papers the German commander left *Athole* to his gunner who dispatched her with a few well placed shells. She turned turtle at 8.45am and sank a few minutes after.

The crew rowed to the north as best they could in the choppy sea and were spotted by the crew of the patrol ship *Wheatear* when about five miles south of the Owers. They were picked up and taken to Littlehampton, landing there at about 3pm on the same day.

13/17: TOPAZ. *Country:* British.
Date sunk: 12/3/17. *Tons nett:* 270. *Tons gross:* 696. *Built:* 1896. *Type:* SS. *Rig:* schooner. *Owners:* William Robertson, 45, West Nile St, Glasgow. *Cargo:* In ballast, Houfleur for Port Talbot. *Armed:* No. *Position:* 27 miles ENE from Cape Barfleur (49 53 00N; 00 40 00W). *Master's name:* Neil McLean. *Crew:* 13. *Crew nationality:* 10 British, 2 Greek, 1 Spaniard.

BY the time the *Topaz* got permission to leave Havre Roads it was 8.50pm on March 11, 1917. She headed out across the Channel in excellent weather conditions, very calm, although quite dark as a thin layer of cloud obscured the moon. Making a steady nine knots she should have been in Port Talbot right on schedule. Just after midnight the master left the bridge and turned in. At 1.08am he was thrown out of his bunk by an enormous explosion.

Both hatches had been completely blown off and water was gushing into the ship. Within two minutes the *Topaz* was already half underwater. The order was given for all hands to abandon the ship immediately. Two minutes later the steamer had gone to the bottom.

The two boats were left floating in the calm sea. Although nobody saw anything of a submarine most of them were of the opinion that they had been struck by a torpedo. The master carried out a roll call to see if all his crew were present but found that three men

were missing, the Second Engineer, a steward and a fireman. They rowed around among the wreckage for some time but were unable to find any trace of them.

A sail was set up in one of the boats and the other fastened behind it. The master set a course that he reckoned would put them somewhere handy for Havre and hoped for the best. They eventually reached land at 6.30pm the same day but not quite where expected, ending up about 10 miles east of Le Havre.

Topaz was another victim of *UB-18*, according to German records.

13/18: CONRAD. *Country:* British.
Date sunk: 12/12/16. *Tons nett:* –. *Tons gross:* 141. *Built:* –. *Type:* SV. *Rig:* schooner. *Owners:* Fisher Alimonda & Co, 112, Fenchurch St, London. *Cargo:* Flint/stone, Dieppe for Runcorn. *Armed:* No. *Position:* 45 miles SSE of St Catherines (50 05 00N; 00 40 00W). *Master's name:* John Williams. *Crew:* 5. *Crew nationality:* 4 British, 1 Norwegian.

IT was 10.30am and the *Conrad* was well into her journey from Dieppe having left there the day before. Suddenly a shell threw up a huge column of water next to the ship. This was promptly followed by three more which landed equally as close. The master realised that the gunner on the German submarine, which now lay close to him, was merely using the *Conrad* for target practice and could pick his moment to score a direct hit. He ordered his crew into the lifeboat immediately, leaving them no time to collect clothing or food.

As they cast off a voice from the submarine ordered them to come alongside. The master was taken on board for questioning and told that while he stayed on the submarine his crew and boat would be used to row a bombing party to the *Conrad* to sink her. It was done with speed and precision. Ten minutes later the master found himself back in his own boat with his crew and cast adrift to fend for themselves.

For eight hours they drifted, cold, wet and thoroughly miserable, wondering if they would ever see the land again. At 7.30pm they had a stroke of luck when a patrol boat spotted them despite the darkness. They were landed the next day at St Helens on the Isle of Wight.

13/19: JUNO. *Country:* British.
Date sunk: 2/5/17. *Tons nett:* 825. *Tons gross:* 1384. *Built:* 1882. *Type:* SS. *Rig:* schooner. *Owners:* Bristol Steam Navigation Co, Prince St, Bristol. *Cargo:* In ballast, Rouen to Cardiff. *Armed:* No. *Position:* 17 miles E of Cape Barfleur (49 43 00N; 00 37 00W). *Master's name:* Charles James Southcliffe. *Crew:* 20.

THE master was on the lower bridge when his problems started. His ship was making good speed.

With the fine weather and a calm sea, it should have been a pleasant journey to Cardiff. He had no idea at the time that the commander of a German submarine was at that very moment lining up his ship for a torpedo. It slammed into the starboard side of the *Juno* causing a terrific explosion which penetrated the engine room, opening up a huge hole.

Within a minute the steamer was well down by the stern and the master ordered her to be abandoned. Two minutes later she sank, the boats getting clear in the nick of time. However, when the master called the roll it was found that the Steward was missing.

The crew rowed for over three hours towards the shore and were eventually picked up by the patrol vessel *Merlin*.

UB-18 again claimed responsibility.

13/20: GERMAN SUBMARINE (possible).

Country: German. *Date believed sunk:* 5/2/17. *Tons nett:* −. *Tons gross:* −. *Built:* −. *Type:* −. *Owners:* German navy. *Armed:* Yes. *Position:* 26 miles E of Cape Barfleur (49 39 00N; 00 34 00W). *Master's name:* −. *Crew:* −. *Crew nationality:* German.

LIEUTENANT Hugh Raymond, RNR, was on escort duty in command of HMS *P12*. His was the lead ship ahead of two columns of merchant steamers heading for Le Havre. *P12* was on a continual zig-zag pattern sweeping the path ahead of the convoy with her crew on full alert.

Ordinary Seaman Kettle, on the starboard bow watch blinked and looked again, he had spotted something. The object came and went in the hazy darkness about one and a half miles off, but he had seen the shape before and immediately shouted to the officer of the watch, Mr Webber, that he thought there was a submarine on the surface heading north.

Mr Webber's actions were instantaneous and shouted orders, "Port the helm, telegraph to full ahead." *P12* responded rapidly and the engineers below had her up to full speed in a trice. The captain came out of the charthouse and on hearing the facts put the whole ship to battle stations at the same time ordering the depth charges to be cleared away ready for use.

Ten minutes later another lookout shouted that he could see something in the moonbeam. It was a submarine on the surface heading north. *P12* was fortunately down beam of the submarine so was able to push ahead unseen towards it, but when about 300yds off her engines must have given her away and the submarine went into a crash dive. The wake of the submarine was clearly visible when a depth charge was thrown over the side set to explode at 80ft.

Then a huge thud set the sea rumbling beneath the ship followed by a huge column of water which threw out clouds of black smoke, sparks and oil over a wide area.

Lieutenant Raymond reported later that it was no ordinary explosion and for several minutes afterwards huge billowing masses of bubbles continued to rise to the surface. He marked the position with a buoy and made off back to his convoy to lead them safely to Le Havre. Later that same day HMS *Hind* was sent to have a look at the spot and her captain reported that at 9am large quantities of oil were still rising from the spot. He ordered a C-type depth charge to be dropped which brought up more oil and air bubbles.

There is no record of the crew being awarded any prize money by the Admiralty. Lieut. Raymond was awarded the DSC and other members of his crew were decorated. German records show no loss on this date.

13/21: SOMME. *Country:* British.

Date sunk: 30/3/17. *Tons nett:* 1090. *Tons gross:* 2600. *Built:* Sunderland in 1916. *Type:* SS. *Rig:* schooner. *Owners:* Normandy Shipping Co/Stephenson Clarke, London. *Cargo:* 2450 tons coal from Powell Duffryn of Newport to Rouen. *Armed:* 1 x 6pdr Hotchkiss. *Position:* Cape Barfleur bearing W by S 20 miles (49 46 00N; 00 30 00W). *Master's name:* Edward Sparshott, 12, Ashbrook Terr, Boldon, Durham. *Crew:* 21. *Crew nationality:* 10 British, 5 Spanish, 5 Greek, 1 Argentine.

AFTER sailing from Newport on March 27, 1917, *Somme* called into Spithead and left there under escort at 5.30pm on the 29th. The master went down to his cabin leaving the second mate on the bridge with a lookout and the gunner at the gun aft. The ship was steering south-south-east making about nine knots when she was struck by something on the starboard side just below the bridge. A big explosion followed which badly damaged the bridge followed by another which blew the covers off number four hold.

From this point onwards much confusion ensued. The boats were ordered to be lowered but no instructions were given to wait until the ship had stopped moving. Consequently some of the boats containing inexperienced crew capsized on touching the water. To add to the problem, the gunner, on spotting one of the upturned boats assumed it was an enemy submarine and opened fire. Eventually some order was restored and the master, who was last to leave, joined the other 15 survivors. The master reported that the lights of the *Somme* were last seen at 2.45am and that when he left the ship the water was already up to the hatch coamings, so it could only have been a matter of minutes before she sank. All the survivors were picked up by the armed trawler *Sapper* and taken to Portsmouth.

There was a considerable amount of controversy after this sinking about the conduct of the master and his position in the convoy. He was supposed to stay close to the convoy for the journey across the Channel and was asked by the Admiralty why he was so far to the eastward ahead of them. Also why was he showing lights? The master giving an account of his actions said that he was steaming at nine knots instead of his usual 11. The weather was thick and he couldn't see the other ships. As he understood it, the orders were that the convoy had to be in Havre Roads by daybreak and moving at anything less than nine knots would have delayed his arrival. He assumed the rest of the convoy must have been going slower than usual. The Admiralty ruled that the master had just forged ahead without due regard to instructions and consequently lost his ship. He was therefore put on the Admiralty blacklist which meant his company were unable to give him another command.

Captain Sparshott appealed to the Admiralty some five months later saying that he was still unemployed. They relented and advised his company to re-employ him. However, before they could do that he managed to get a job with the Inland Water Transport.

UB-40 claimed to have sunk the *Somme*.

13/22: JOSEPH. *Country:* British.
Date sunk: 4/5/17. *Tons nett:* 175. *Tons gross:* 205.
Built: 1875. *Type:* SV. *Rig:* brigantine. *Owners:*
F Nicholls, Whitstable, Kent. *Cargo:* 323 tons coal
from Howden Dock, N.Shields to Caen. *Armed:* No.
Position: 25 miles E of Cape Barfleur (49 39 00N;
00 28 00W). *Master's name:* George Isby, from
Swalecliffe.

AFTER leaving South Shields *Joseph* called into Southend for orders and was told to proceed to St Helens. She arrived there on the April 29, 1917, and had to wait until May 3, for new instructions. She could have sailed at any time that day but there was virtually no wind until 8pm when she slipped out to head across the Channel.

The master said he felt quite safe until midnight as there were naval patrol vessels buzzing about in every direction, but in the early hours of the next morning the *Joseph* was on her own. At 6.45 the master was on watch with two lookouts when one of them shouted that he could see a submarine about two miles off on the starboard side. At a distance of half a mile the German gunner opened fire with the deck gun. The first two shots went wide but the third dropped close to the stern of the sailing ship making the master realise that they had no chance of escape.

With all sails furled the *Joseph* wallowed as her crew pulled clear and headed off to meet the approaching submarine. The enemy used the *Joseph's* boat to do the job but their plundering was interrupted by two approaching trawlers. In a few minutes the submarine dived, one minute after that the bombs exploded and *Joseph* disappeared.

The trawlers turned out to be the British patrol vessels HMT's *Sweeper* and *Vale of Leven*.

13/23: FRANCOIS ET GEORGETTE.
Country: French. *Date sunk:* 9/6/17. *Tons nett:* –.
Tons gross: 7. *Built:* –. *Type:* FV. *Rig:* –.
Owners: –. *Cargo:* –. *Armed:* No. *Position:* 25

miles NW of La Heve (49 47 00N; 00 26 00W).
Master's name: Buquet. *Crew:* 2.

WHEN the *Georgette* had been sunk by gunfire from a German submarine the commander took her crew of two on board. The master, Monsieur Buquet, and his mate M. Lacorne complained to the German asking him why he should want to deprive a poor fishermen of a meagre livelihood. The commander replied that he had no way of telling if his ship was armed and added he suspected that it was.

The men having no boat of any use were kept on board the submarine for some time. On one occasion the German commander asked Buquet to come to the periscope and have a look at a fishing vessel. As he looked through the lens the commander asked, "Does that look an innocent character to you?"

"Yes, it does," replied Buquet.

"Very well, I will come to the surface but I will shoot you if your report is wrong."

Luckily for Buquet the fishing vessel was indeed just that and after sinking her the two Frenchmen were put into the survivors' boat. Unfortunately, there appears to be no record of this other sinking in Admiralty records, but Lloyd's lists a *Eugene Mathilde*, a 15-ton French fishing boat, sunk on the same day in the same area.

Buquet and Lacorne were kept on board the submarine for 24 hours and later told the authorities that they thought it was a UB type but did not discover her number. She had two periscopes, a four inch gun and the jaws and teeth of a shark painted on her bows.

13/24: EMLYNVERNE. *Country:* British.
Date sunk: 25/11/16. *Tons nett:* 268. *Tons gross:*
546. *Built:* Montrose in 1894. *Type:* SS. *Rig:*
schooner. *Owners:* Emlyn Jones & Co Ltd, 5, Dock
Chambers, Cardiff. *Cargo:* In ballast, Tréport for
Swansea. *Armed:* No. *Position:* 30 miles NW of
Cape Antifer (50 01 00N; 00 25 00W). *Master's
name:* Emmanuel Courby Laverick. *Crew:* 11.
Crew nationality: 5 British, 1 Japanese, 1
Portuguese, 3 Greeks, 1 Dutch.

AT 5.10am on the November 25, 1916, the *Emlynverne* was battling her way through appaling weather across the Channel. The wind was strong with frequent rain squalls which at times reduced the visibility to almost nil. It was, understandably, not welcome news to the master when the chief engineer reported that he had a defect in the high pressure cylinder and that the engines would have to be slowed down, or maybe stopped if necessary. The master didn't want to risk stopping which would leave him very vulnerable to enemy attack. Instead he put the telegraph to half ahead and decided he would make direct for St Helens Roads where he could assess the damage in safety before continuing to Swansea.

Five hours later the master heard what he hoped he wouldn't hear, gunfire. He looked around but could see nothing through the thick mist. A few minutes later the mist cleared enough for him to see a vessel astern of him which looked like a small sailing ship. The mist closed in again before he could get his glasses on it. At the same time the chief engineer reported that the problem in the engine room was getting worse and that he would have to shut the engines down for a while to put it right, there was no choice.

As the steamer slowed to a halt the inevitable happened and the mist suddenly cleared. To his dismay the master saw that the sailing ship was in fact an enemy submarine and what's more she was bearing down on him at an alarming rate. He could do nothing but wait and watch, lifting his binoculars to read the flags that were being run up the submarine's small mast, 'Abandon your ship immediately.'

The master ordered the crew to make for the boats. A loud bang boomed out across the water and a shell slammed into the port side of the ship. This was followed by another. The crew hurried into the boat on the opposite side of the ship and pulled clear very rapidly. All the while the submarine kept up her bombardment, shell after shell crashing into the ship's hull causing it to lurch at every impact. At 10.40am the *Emlynverne* could take no more and sank stern first.

The master and his crew in the boats kept rowing and hoped they would be left alone if they could get far enough away. It worked and the submarine bore away to chase another two masted steamer that was about four miles to the north-west. The *Emlynverne's* crew rigged up a sail and settled down to some serious pulling. They were not seen by any passing traffic and ended up rowing the whole distance to shore reaching Eastbourne at 10am the following day.

UB-18 was the submarine involved.

13/25: SILVIA. *Country:* British.
Date sunk: 1/4/17. *Tons nett:* 142. *Tons gross:* 164.
Built: Appledore in 1872. *Type:* SV. *Rig:* schooner.
Owners: W. Tyzzer, St Austell, Cornwall. *Cargo:*
280 tons china clay from Parkin & Peters, Par to
Rouen. *Armed:* No. *Position:* 15 miles SSE of
Owers (50 17 00N; 00 23 00W). *Master's name:*
David George Brinkworth, Par, Cornwall. *Crew:* 5.
Crew nationality: 4 British, 1 Portuguese.

THE wooden schooner *Silvia* was a fine vessel and although 45 years old had been extensively refitted only two years previously. On February 15, 1917, she made her way up to Fowey with the intention of mustering a crew. She remained there until March 23, and then having loaded a cargo and signed on a crew, she sailed up the Channel.

The weather was fine and the vessel ran well in a breeze. On reaching the examination boat at St Helens Roads they picked up their sailing instructions. At 5pm on March 31, she continued on her voyage. But all that night she was becalmed and it wasn't until

7.30 the next morning that enough wind arrived to allow her to make any headway. At 11am she was close hauled on the starboard tack making a good four knots. The master was on deck and the mate was at the wheel with a lookout beside him.

Suddenly a shell whistled through the air and knocked the end off *Silvia's* jib. On looking around, the crew were surprised to see a submarine about 100yds off their starboard side. A second bang rang out and a shell sliced off the topsails and then a third followed which smashed the bowsprit.

The master ordered the men to take to the boats. While they were doing this another two shells were fired at them but nobody was injured. As they pulled away from the schooner another four shells were fired before the submarine came alongside the lifeboat and ordered the crew aboard. The German crew then borrowed the boat to go and plant bombs on the *Silvia*, one forward and one aft. Having done this they then began to help themselves to paraffin, rope, tobacco, cigarettes and the ship's compass.

After being questioned by the German commander, the crew of the *Silvia* were ordered back into their boat and rudely told to "Clear off." As they did so the bombs exploded on board their ship and she sank at 12.15pm.

The crew rigged a sail and headed towards the land. They were eventually picked up by HMT *Hornet* and taken to the examination boat at St Helens. From there they were later taken to Portsmouth.

13/26: PEARL. *Country:* British.
Date sunk: 23/9/16. *Tons nett:* –. *Tons gross:* 613.
Built: Londonderry in 1904. *Type:* SS. *Rig:*
schooner. *Owners:* Wetherall Steamship Co Ltd,
Goole, Yorks. *Cargo:* 778 tons coal, shipped from
Llanelly and consigned to Mory & Co, Tréport,
France. *Armed:* No. *Position:* 40 miles NNW of
Havre Roads/41 miles S ¼ E from the Nab
(50 05 00N; 00 23 00W). *Master's name:* Joe Addy,
61, Bacheler St, Hull. *Crew:* 13.

THE master couldn't believe it. On his port bow he could see three vessels and one of them had fired a shell at him. Two of them were undoubtedly submarines and the third looked like a British patrol boat. It wasn't until the third vessel fired a shot that he could see it was another submarine in disguise. And what a shot. The shell dropped exactly in the ship's path, far too accurate for comfort so he ordered the ship's engines to be shut off. With one of the submarines catching him up very quickly, he ordered the boats to be lowered and with himself in charge of one and the mate the other, they drifted astern.

It was 20 minutes before the submarine arrived and a voice ordered the master to go on board. The German commander ordered one of the lifeboats to follow the submarine back to the *Pearl*. After demanding any money and the ship's papers the Germans began to steal any bits of the ship that they fancied and hung two bombs on the port bulwarks. The crew of the submarine lined their deck to watch the bang whilst Captain Addy and his crew rowed away. At 7.30pm the bombs exploded and as darkness fell the submarine was still alongside the *Pearl* as she settled down, presumably sinking soon after.

However, help was at hand. The steamer *Aline Montreuil* came close enough to be hailed by the crew of the *Pearl* and took them in tow. In the early hours of the following morning they were handed over to the patrol vessel *Willonyx* which took them into Portsmouth.

UB-37 claimed to have sunk the *Pearl*.

13/27: JERSEYMAN. *Country:* British. *Date sunk:* 24/11/16. *Tons nett:* 146. *Tons gross:* 388. *Built:* Paisley in 1883. *Type:* SS. *Rig:* schooner. *Owners:* The Channel Shipping Co, 5, Dock Chambers, Cardiff. *Cargo:* 361 tons anthracite cobbles from Swansea to Tréport. *Armed:* No. *Position:* 45 miles NW of Dieppe when damaged (50 07 00N; 00 20 00W). *Master's name:* Evan Evans. *Crew:* 12

THE force of the impact made the whole ship shudder as *Jerseyman* made her way across the Channel at around seven knots. The bosun at the wheel felt it, so did the master and the first mate who were in the chartroom. The master went onto the bridge to have a look around. No submarines were about or any sign astern of explosion debris. He wondered if the ship had struck a mine but it did not sound or feel like an explosion. He looked all around the sides of the ship but could see no obvious damage.

At 3.30pm the chief engineer came onto the bridge with a grim face to report to the master that the engine room was filling rapidly with water. It was already two feet deep over the plates and rising. They had tried to put the pumps to work on it but they appeared to be blocked with coal and no amount of effort would clear them. He went away to have another go at sorting the water problem out. At one stage the whole of the ship's crew formed a human chain with buckets to try and get on top of it, but it was useless. Several hours passed and the water continued to rise, putting the boiler fires out, leaving the ship to drift.

By 8pm it seemed obvious to the master that the ship was going to sink. He ordered the crew to take to the boats but to stay alongside the steamer to see what would happen. However, at 10pm she did sink leaving the crew to row south with the wind and sea.

The crew were split up in two boats with the master in charge of one with five men and the Mate, T.G. Jenkins, with five men in the other. The mate made a landing at Herdelot Beach at 9am the following morning and the master reached Le Bouldal at 2pm on November 26.

On considering the evidence, the Admiralty decided that the *Jerseyman* hit a submerged wreck and because the pumps were blocked she sank as a result. They consequently ruled for insurance purposes that she was not a war loss.

However, Lloyds recorded her as torpedoed and a war loss.

13/28: RED ROSE. *Country:* British. *Date sunk:* 22/5/18. *Tons nett:* –. *Tons gross:* 401. *Built:* –. *Type:* SS. *Rig:* –. *Owners:* Admiralty. *Cargo:* Government stores, Littlehampton for Le Havre. *Armed:* –. *Position:* 46 miles SSW of Newhaven (50 04 00N; 00 20 00W). *Master's name:* –.

IT was something of a mystery at the time just what happened to the transport *Red Rose*. However, recent research has shown that she was in fact torpedoed by the German submarine *UB-40*.

All that was known at the time was that HMT *White Ear*, commanded by G.W. Thannat, skipper RNR, was to escort her from Littlehampton to Havre Roads and both ships sailed at 9pm on May 21, 1918. A course was set of southerly magnetic and they maintained a speed of seven knots, *Red Rose* keeping a position on *White Ear's* port beam, two to five cables distant.

The weather was calm and sometimes very hazy. It was in one of the haze patches that the commander of *UB-40* decided to take his chance and slam a torpedo into the side of *Red Rose*. It was 3am and all that was heard on *White Ear* was a heavy explosion somewhere in the mist. She headed off in the direction of the explosion but found no wreckage and no trace at all of *Red Rose*.

For two and a half hours *White Ear* combed the area looking for the transport but after deciding that nothing more could be done, the commander turned his ship back to Littlehampton.

13/29: LISMORE. *Country:* British. *Date sunk:* 12/4/17. *Tons nett:* 630. *Tons gross:* 1305. *Built:* 1905. *Type:* SS. *Rig:* schooner. *Owners:* City of Cork SS Co, Ireland. *Cargo:* In ballast, Rouen for Portishead. *Armed:* 1 x 6pdr gun. *Position:* 19 miles NW by N of Whistle Buoy, Havre (49 47 00N; 00 20 00W). *Master's name:* Henry Blanchard. *Crew:* 24. *Crew nationality:* All British. *Gunners:* Philip Danells, Chatham; Edward Kelly, Chatham.

LISMORE was making her way across the Channel at a good speed of 12½ knots and steering a course of north-north-west. It was 8pm, all the lookouts were in position and nothing unusual was seen by any of them. Without any warning whatsoever the steamer's progress was violently halted by a torpedo smashing into her side. A huge explosion followed and within four minutes she had gone to the bottom taking five of the crew with her.

The rest of the crew managed to get to a boat and

launch it before she sank. They drifted around the wreckage completely stunned by the speed at which it happened. A few minutes later the cause of all the trouble, *UB-38*, rose up out of the water next to the boat. The conning tower opened and the commander beckoned them to come closer. Several German sailors threw the boat a line and tied it off to the stern. The commander asked the master about his ship, cargo and all the things he needed to know for his log. The master asked him if he would tow them to shore but the commander shook his head and told them they were only 10 miles off.

The crew pulled for several hours before being spotted by a patrol drifter which picked them up and landed them safely the same day.

The Admiralty also had one or two questions to put to the master, particularly about leaving Rouen earlier than his orders had stated. They also wanted to know why he was not zig-zagging. Many letters were sent back and forth with the result that they accepted his reasons for leaving Rouen early but gave him a caution about zig-zagging in future.

13/30: WARILDA. *Country:* British.
Date sunk: 3/8/18. *Tons nett:* 4477. *Tons gross:* 7713. *Built:* 1912. *Type:* SS. *Rig:* schooner. *Owners:* Adelaide SS Co. *Agents:* Yuill's Ltd, 120, Fenchurch St, London. In Government service as "ambulance transport". *Cargo:* 614 wounded soldiers, 117 crew, 70 RAMC staff. *Armed:* 1 x 4in quick fire gun. *Position:* 33 miles NW by N of Antifer (50 18 00N; 00 18 00W). *Master's name:* James Sim (Southern Australian ticket). *Crew:* 120. *Crew nationality:* –. *Gunners:*. James Carter, LS RFR; William Barton, LS RFR; John Read, LS RFR.

WARILDA was an Australian steamer, registered at Port Adelaide but requisitioned by the British government for use as a hospital ship. She was loaded with injured soldiers. The holds on the *Warilda* had been hastily converted into wards and the lowest ward was I-Ward containing 102 patients. I-Ward was purposely allocated to walking wounded with the idea that if the ship had to be evacuated they could get on deck more quickly. It was a good idea but few were to survive in I-Ward.

She left Havre on August 2, 1918, and was being escorted by two destroyers to Southampton, HMS *P39*, commanded by Lieutenant J.W. Durnford RN, and HMS *P45*, commanded by Lieutenant Rudolph Thompson RN. They made good progress, at 15 knots, steering north 10 degrees east.

Even though it was a cloudy and a dark night, the second mate on watch on the bridge spotted the shape of a submarine about 100yds off the port bow at 1.35am. He shouted to the helmsman to turn directly towards the submarine with the intention of ramming it. A few seconds later the master arrived on the bridge and endorsed the second officer's actions but the submarine was too fast and too manoeuvrable. The helm was put hard over again, this time to bring the enemy directly astern. The master watched intently to see what the German commander intended to do, when suddenly a white streak appeared from it followed seconds later by a deafening explosion deep on the port side between the engine room and, tragically, number four hold....I-Ward.

The force of the explosion caused a great deal of damage. One engine had been knocked out of action, and the engine room began to fill rapidly. But the scene in I-Ward was one of utter carnage. The explosion had occurred directly under the ward and had killed most of the patients outright. Survivors of the blast were drowned by the sudden inrush of water as the ward completely filled, setting *Warilda* heavily down by the stern. At least 101 patients died in I-Ward.

The master realised that if the engine room bulkhead held he would stand a chance of getting the rest of the people off. He ordered all the patients to be assembled on the promenade deck and the boats to be lowered down on them. Several boats were soon ready to go but the master shouted that no boat was to leave until the way had gone off the ship. One engine was still running even though the water was up to the cylinder heads, but slowly it slowed as the steam ran out and at last *Warilda* came to a halt. The first boat with wounded and nurses in it reached the water evenly but for some inexplicable reason the front fall jammed and swamped the boat resulting in the loss of two nurses. Most of the boats got clear although another on the port side fouled the Otter mine defence boom and overturned, with the loss of two officers, eight male patients and four crew.

HMS *P39* came alongside the stricken steamer and took off the rest of the patients and crew. It was no easy task. Most of the remaining patients were unable to walk so a bosun's chair was rigged, and the patients were winched across by hand. Two men in particular, Lance Corporal Booth, number 100015 and Pte Hamber, number 102681, were mentioned for their actions.

After *Warilda* had been cleared of survivors the commander of *P39* decided it might be worth trying to take the steamer in tow and lines were attached. But after 10 minutes towing the steamer could not take the pressure put upon her weakened bulkheads and she sank at 4.10am.

The Court of Enquiry was held on board HMS *Victory* at Portsmouth was told that 113 patients, one nurse, two RAMC staff and seven crew died in the sinking, but found no negligence.

UC-49 was the submarine involved, commanded by Oberleutnant H. Kükenthal (see site 5/7).

13/31: MARIA. *Country:* Belgian.
Date sunk: 29/1/18. *Tons nett:* –. *Tons gross:* 25. *Built:* –. *Type:* FV. *Rig:* –. *Owners:* –. *Cargo:* –. *Armed:* –. *Position:* 20 miles SE by E of Antifer (49 50 00N; 00 17 00W). *Master's name:* –.

THIS fishing vessel was sunk by gunfire from a German submarine along with three others, all part of the same Belgian fishing fleet. One of the names was unknown and the other two were the *De Julia* and the *Matilde Jean*.

It happened at around 3pm on January 29, 1918, when an enemy submarine went around sinking each vessel in turn. There are very few notes on this incident and no mention of any casualties among the crews.

13/32: DE JULIA. *Country:* Belgian.
Date sunk: 29/1/18. *Tons nett:* –. *Tons gross:* 25.
Built: –. *Type:* FV. *Rig:* –. *Owners:* –. *Cargo:* –.
Armed: –. *Position:* 20 miles SE by E of Antifer
(49 50 00N; 00 17 00W). *Master's name:* –.

THE Belgian fishing vessel *De Julia* was part of a fleet of four sunk by gunfire of an enemy submarine on January 29, 1918. The name of one of them was unknown but the other two were the *Maria* and the *Matilde Jean*.

13/33: MATILDE JEAN. *Country:* Belgian.
Date sunk: 29/1/18. *Tons nett:* –. *Tons gross:* 25.
Built: –. *Type:* FV. *Rig:* –. *Owners:* –. *Cargo:* –.
Armed: –. *Position:* 20 miles SE by E of Antifer
(49 50 00N; 00 17 00W). *Master's name:* –.
Crew: –. *Crew nationality:* –.

THIS vessel was part of a fishing fleet of four sunk by gunfire by an enemy submarine on January 29, 1918. The name of one of them was not recorded, but the other two were the *Maria* and the *De Julia*.

Belgian records show the "unknown" as the 25-ton fishing vessel *De Twee Marcels*.

13/34: TOKOMARU. *Country:* British.
Date sunk: 30/1/15. *Tons nett:* 3912. *Tons gross:* 6084. *Built:* Wallsend in 1893. *Type:* SS.
Rig: schooner. *Owners:* Shaw, Saville & Albion SS Co, Leadenhall St, London. *Cargo:* 700 tons frozen meat for French government. *Armed:* No. *Position:* 7 miles NW from Havre Light Ship (49 38 00N; 00 17 00W). *Master's name:* Francis Greene. *Crew:* 57.

TOKOMARU'S voyage started in Wellington, New Zealand on December 9, 1914. She called at Montevideo and Tenerife and from there she was to go to Le Havre.

All went well until she was about seven miles from Havre Light Ship. It was 9am and the master had just reduced speed ready to navigate into Havre Roads. Just then a voice shouted for the master to look off the port side. It was a periscope. Almost at the same time a huge explosion boomed out and the *Tokomaru* took on a heavy list to port.

The master ordered the crew to their stations whilst he went to his cabin to destroy his papers. He got there only to find that his cabin was nearly full of water. He joined the others and pulled clear of his ship. She went down at 10.30am.

Very soon the French minesweeper *Saint Pierre* was on the scene and picked them up. In his deposition the master noted that left on board was £62 in cash belonging to the company and £17 of his own.

U-20 claimed the sinking. Her commander, Kapitanleutnant Droescher was listed as a war criminal for this attack without warning.

13/35: FERRYHILL. *Country:* British.
Date sunk: 30/1/18. *Tons nett:* 169. *Tons gross:* 411. *Built:* 1910. *Type:* SS. *Rig:* schooner.
Owners: G.T. Gillie & Co, Baltic Chambers, Newcastle. *Cargo:* In ballast, Havre for Littlehampton. *Armed:* No. *Position:* 18 miles NW by N of Cape le Heve (49 40 00N; 00 13 00W). *Master's name:* John Adam Barron. *Crew:* 9.

AS a result of the loss of this vessel there was subsequently some argument about the fact that the master had asked for a gun to be fitted to his ship. As she sailed from Littlehampton the master saw the gun just lying on the quayside.

On her way back from Havre she encountered a German submarine which appeared on the port bow about a mile off and began to shell the *Ferryhill*. The crew were forced to abandon their ship and watch as the steamer was pounded to piece.

The steamer *Wharf* had just left Havre Roads and her master stated that he could hear firing in the distance and thought that patrol boats would be passing him shortly to investigate, but they never did. He eventually came across the crew of the *Ferryhill* and picked them up.

Apparently the submarine was in no hurry to sink the *Ferryhill* and some of the German crew had actually come on deck to take photos of the steamer sinking.

13/36: LANFRANC. *Country:* British.
Date sunk: 17/4/17. *Tons nett:* –. *Tons gross:* 6287. *Built:* 1907. *Type:* SS. *Rig:* Hospital ship. *Owners:* Booth Steamship Co Ltd. In Government service. *Cargo:* 234 British and 167 German wounded and 52 RAMC staff. *Armed:* No. *Position:* 25 miles SE of St Catherines (50 11 00N; 00 12 00W). *Master's name:* W.E. Pontet. *Crew:* 123. *Crew nationality:* British.

LANFRANC left Havre at 3.22pm on April 17, 1917, bound for Southampton. At 4.33pm the Whistle Buoy at the entrance to the barrage at Havre was rounded at a distance of one cable. The two escorts HMS *Badger* and *P37* took up their positions port and starboard about half a mile distant. At 4.52pm the course was altered to N 8 deg E mag, for a position 50 12 00 N; 00 13 00W, due allowance having been made for the flood tide. This course was steered for 38 miles. The wind was a fresh breeze from the north-north-west giving a rough sea but clear visibility.

At 7.40pm the *Lanfranc's* journey was halted abruptly by a terrible explosion which occurred on the port side abreast of the bulkhead between the engine room and number three hold. The engines were stopped and the ship, listing heavily to port, began to settle by the stern but then came to an upright position. The force of the explosion had completely shattered the two after lifeboats on the port deck along with the port quarter boat. The Marconi house on the after end of the boat deck was also wrecked and the radio gear rendered useless.

Nothing was seen of the submarine or any track of the torpedo even though a good lookout had been kept. The master was on the port side of the bridge, the officer of the watch on the starboard side and the signalman amidships. Also there was a lookout man in the crow's nest and another on the docking bridge aft.

At the time the ship was struck the escort ship *Badger* was about four points on the port bow and the escort *P37* about four points on the starboard bow, both about 1-2 miles off. Immediately after the explosion *Badger* hurried away to the south-west as if in pursuit but later returned. *P37* circled round and came close alongside *Lanfranc's* starboard side and shouted for the master to lower the boats. The master had already ordered all hands to their respective stations and to get the wounded into the boats. He also called all hands up from the engine and boiler rooms. The commanding officer of *P37* was still shouting at *Lanfranc* to lower his boats but the master quite wisely countermanded such orders until his big ship had come to a complete standstill. He had seen too many lifeboats overturned in the past by just the smallest amount of speed. When he judged it to be safe the master ordered one boat at a time to be lowered on each side to try and prevent any accidents. Eight boats got away but one boat on the starboard side went down stern first, the man on the after fall losing control on account of some wounded Germans jumping into the boat as she was passing the saloon deck. Nearly all of the occupants were thrown into the sea but were picked up by *Badger's* boats and several sailing trawlers which suddenly appeared on the scene.

The master then gave orders for the boat davits to be swung in to allow the escorts to come closer and get lines on them. The crew were to save the rest of the British wounded first and then if possible the German prisoners, who were already becoming totally unruly and had to be forced out of boats on several occasions.

Both escorts pulled away from the sinking ship at 8.15pm and circled around her picking up boats. They finally made their way from the scene at about 8.40pm when the aft deck of the *Lanfranc* was just about level with the water. She sank soon after.

The master commended the actions of the escort boats and the other boats that came to his aid.

Four British and 15 German wounded and five crew were drowned. *UB-40* was named as the attacker.

13/37: G.C. GRADWELL. *Country:* British. *Date sunk:* 2/8/16. *Tons nett:* 119. *Tons gross:* 156. *Built:* Appledore. *Type:* SV. *Rig:* schooner. *Owners:* James Edward Prettyman, Pentuan, Cornwall. *Cargo:* 255 tons grain shipped by French government for Dieppe. *Armed:* No. *Position:* 18m NW of Cape Antifer (49 53 00N; 00 11 00W). *Master's name:* –. *Crew:* 5.

WHEN dealing with small sailing vessels German U-boat commanders usually gave the crew time to get clear. The crew of the *Gradwell* got five minutes. To help them along the German sailors opened fire with rifles but nobody was hit.

The submarine came very close to the stern of the schooner and a sailor jumped aboard with four bombs which he placed at various locations around the ship. The crew were ordered to hurry themselves along, which they did very smartly. The master was asked to produce his papers. He refused at first but as a revolver was levelled at his head he wisely decided otherwise. Within a few minutes of the ship being abandoned the *Gradwell* blew up and sank.

13/38: THE MARCHIONESS. *Country:* British. *Date sunk:* 20/10/16. *Tons nett:* 218. *Tons gross:* 553. *Built:* 1900. *Type:* SS. *Rig:* schooner. *Owners:* John Hay & Sons, 58, Renfield St, Glasgow. *Cargo:* 650 tons coal, Glasgow for Fécamp. *Armed:* No. *Position:* 30 miles NW of Fecamp (50 07 00N; 00 11 00W). *Master's name:* Donald Ker. *Crew:* 11.

THE second mate turned to the master and pointed out a small object about one mile off the port bow. The master looked through his binoculars but could make nothing of it. About one minute later there was a dull thud followed by a spout of water just ahead of the ship as a shell smacked into the sea.

The master sprang into action and ordered the helmsman to steer straight for the submarine and rang the engine room to standby. He then passed the word for all the crew except the engineers on duty to come on deck and make the boats ready. This action was Admiralty text book stuff and provided the helmsman could keep his bows directly at the enemy and everyone else kept their heads down, it usually worked. But for some unknown reason the master suddenly ordered the engines to stop when about half a mile off the submarine and abandoned ship.

After a brief questioning by the German commander of *UB-18* the master pulled clear of the submarine as it began to fire shells at the steamer. Within ten minutes the *The Marchioness* had gone to the bottom.

Rowing for several hours the crew were picked up

about 25 miles south of St Catherines Point by the Norwegian steamer *Viona* and transferred to the patrol vessel *Dago*.

13/39: GRENADA. *Country:* British. *Date sunk:* 22/11/16. *Tons nett:* 2106. *Tons gross:* 2267. *Built:* Greenock in 1894. *Type:* SV. *Rig:* barque. *Owners:* Roberts, Owen & Co, 19, Old Hall St, Liverpool. *Cargo:* 1300 tons water ballast, Havre for New York. *Armed:* No. *Position:* 32 miles SW by S of Beachy Head (50 17 00N; 00 11 00W). *Master's name:* Griffith Jones. *Crew:* 22. *Crew nationality:* 9 British, 3 Norwegians, 1 Swede, 1 Dutch, 3 Finns, 2 Chileans, 2 Americans, 1 Dane.

GRENADA was to leave Havre, call in at Plymouth to take on a fresh crew and then make her way across the Atlantic to New York. At least that was the plan and at noon on the November 21, 1916, she sailed out of Havre Roads into the Channel.

At 4.20pm the next day the ship was under full sail and skimming along nicely at six knots. The master stood next to the mate who had the helm, looking around to see what traffic he had near him. The only vessel he could see was some way off and looked like a British destroyer. He lifted his binoculars to take a closer look and quickly focused the lenses. As he began to study the shape of the ship the whole of his lenses were suddenly filled with a large mass looming out of the sea only 200yds away. He lowered his glasses to be greeted by the sight of a German submarine. The master ordered the helm to go about and all the crew to come up on deck. His initial idea was to run for it but a minute later a shot rang out and a shell sliced through part of the ship's rigging. It was a hopeless situation and Captain Jones ordered the ship to be stopped and the crew to get clear in the two boats.

The master's boat went towards the submarine, but as he got within a few yards the master was surprised when the U-Boat sped past them towards the *Grenada*. With a British warship in the distance the German commander was obviously anxious to sink his victim quickly by gunfire and be off.

The British warship however, could not have been very close as try as they might to attract attention by letting off red flares, the crew in the two boats went unnoticed. Eventually they decided that they would go it alone and reached Eastbourne in the early hours of the following morning.

13/40: HUNTSLAND. *Country:* British. *Date sunk:* 6/6/18. *Tons nett:* 1757. *Tons gross:* 2871. *Built:* 1911. *Type:* SS. *Rig:* schooner. *Owners:* William Robertson, 45, West Mill St, Glasgow. *Cargo:* In Ballast, Havre for Portsmouth. *Armed:* 1 x 12pdr gun. *Position:* 16 miles NW by W from Antifer (49 50 00N; 00 10 00W). *Master's*

name: Charles George Ford. *Crew:* 39. *Crew nationality:* 37 British, 2 Others. *Gunners:* Hugh McCreath, No 8987A; James Soutar, No 2396C.

IT was a very dark night and the master of the transport *Huntsland* decided that there was no need to zig-zag. It turned out that there was every need for at 12.20am on June 6, 1918, a torpedo slammed into the starboard side of the steamer, opening up a huge hole in number four hold.

The master could see that his ship was filling and ordered a general crew muster at the boat stations. He wasn't certain that she would sink but to be safe he ordered the boats to be lowered but to stand by the steamer until daylight. He would then assess if the ship could be salvaged or not.

The ship sustained more damage than the master had realised and at 1.35am she sank stern first. The two boats set a course for Havre Roads and burned distress flares. They were spotted about four hours later by the patrol vessel *Smew* which took them to Havre.

It wasn't known then but German documents show that the German submarine responsible for this sinking was *UC-77* commanded by Oberleutnant Johannes Ries.

13/41: VANGUARD. *Country:* British. *Date sunk:* 16/11/16. *Tons nett:* 121. *Tons gross:* 240. *Built:* Sittingbourne in 1885. *Type:* SV. *Rig:* ketch. *Owners:* Alex S. Moore, 98, Leadenhall St, London. *Cargo:* In ballast, Honfleur for London. *Armed:* No. *Position:* 18 miles NW 1/2 N of Cape Antifer (49 55 00N; 00 08 00W). *Master's name:* John Galley Grigg, 142, Buckland Ave, Dover. *Crew:* 5.

AT 9.45am on the 16th the *Vanguard* was under all sail on the starboard tack with the mate at the wheel and the master beside him. After looking intently for a few seconds at an object that puzzled him the mate said, "What do you call that object to the leeward on the north west?"

The master picked up his binoculars and replied, "It looks remarkably like a submarine. Yes, it's coming our way too."

Within two minutes the submarine was much closer, close enough to fire a shell which threw up a spout of water just in front of the ketch. Understanding this to be a signal the master ordered his crew to furl the sails and prepare to abandon ship. As she slowed to a halt another shell whistled close by and the master joined his men in the lifeboat. They pulled clear, the enemy stopping just ahead of them and a voice in good English ordered them to row to the submarine.

Several of the crew were ordered to stay on the submarine's deck while their boat was rowed back to the *Vanguard*. Two German sailors boarded her and planted bombs at various places. After helping themselves to whatever they fancied the Germans were taken back to the submarine and the crew told to clear off, but not before being deprived of their oilskins and provisions.

As they rowed away from the scene the bombs exploded and the crew stopped briefly to watch their ship slide beneath the waves. They continued towards the British coast through the night and even though they were extremely exposed they kept themselves warm by steady rowing and reached St Helens Roads the next morning.

13/42: CERTO. *Country:* Norwegian.
Date sunk: 2/5/17. *Tons nett:* –. *Tons gross:* 1630. *Built:* –. *Type:* SS. *Rig:* –. *Owners:* B. Stolt Nielsen of Haugesund. *Cargo:* 2550 tons coal from Newcastle to Havre. *Armed:* No. *Position:* 10 miles N of the Whistle Buoy at Havre (49 40 00N; 00 06 00W). *Master's name:* O.N. Brasstad. *Crew:* 21.

THE only information available on this sinking is in the form of a letter from the authorities at Havre. The details are few and say that *Certo* was in a convoy from St Helens to Havre escorted by the patrol vessels *Sweeper* and *Vale of Leven*. The master had just gone below to get his dinner when there was a violent explosion on the port side of the ship. The steamer started to take on water at an alarming rate and had to be abandoned almost immediately. The crew all got clear safely and were picked up by one of the patrol ships and taken to Havre.

13/43: MARY ANNIE. *Country:* British.
Date sunk: 25/3/17. *Tons nett:* 130. *Tons gross:* 160. *Built:* Portmadoc in 1893. *Type:* SV. *Rig:* schooner. *Owners:* H.P. Thomas, Newquay, Cornwall. *Cargo:* 245 tons coal, shipped at Glasgow and consigned to Tréport, France. *Armed:* No. *Position:* 28 miles SSW of Beachy Head (50 19 00N; 00 05 00W). *Master's name:* James Henry Pappin. *Crew:* 6.

LEAVING St Helens at 9am on March 24, 1917, the *Mary Annie* made her way out across the Channel. She was doing well, on the port tack with the master on deck keeping a wary eye for marauding enemy submarines. There had been reports of intense submarine activity of late and he hoped he would be spared the experience of meeting one. He scanned the sea around his ship and saw that he was still in fairly close company with another sailing ship *Huntleys*, but something was wrong. He looked again and saw that she had stopped and worse still a submarine was laying close alongside her.

The master shouted for all the hands to come on deck and get the boat ready whilst he ran below to burn his sailing instructions. It was considered a serious offence by the naval authorities for allowing such papers to fall into enemy hands. All available

sail was put up in the hope of getting away from the submarine but it was a vain hope.

Huntleys, about half a mile away, was sinking and within a few minutes had gone. The submarine's bows turned towards *Mary Annie* and within no time at all had caught her up. A well placed shot across the bows was the warning to stop or else and the master felt he had no choice but to obey. A voice boomed out in clear English, "Bring your ship's papers."

Two German sailors ordered the crew to row them over to the schooner. They had things to do, such as help themselves to various items, the weather glass, clock, compass, flags and also as much food as they could carry. After putting the goodies in the boat they set about placing several bombs. At 6.15am the *Mary Annie* sank by the head in 40 fathoms of water.

The crews of both ships *Huntleys* and *Mary Annie* linked up and discussed the situation. Between them they agreed the best course and set about heading for the coast. The weather was favourable and they made good headway but both were eventually given a tow by the steamer *Presto* and later transferred to torpedo boat *No 3*.

13/44: HUNTLEYS. *Country:* British.
Date sunk: 25/3/17. *Tons nett:* 163. *Tons gross:* 185. *Built:* Sunderland in 1865. *Type:* SV. *Rig:* brigantine. *Owners:* J. K. Morris, 11, Drury Lane, Liverpool. *Cargo:* 310 tons pitch, shipped by Butler, Bristol and consigned to Thoumyre et Fils, Dieppe. *Armed:* No. *Position:* 28 miles SSW of Beachy Head (50 19 00N; 00 05 00W). *Master's name:* Archibald John Martin. *Crew:* 6.

HUNTLEYS spent three days at Spithead waiting for clearance and sailing instructions. She left there on March 25, 1917, and headed out across the Channel. There had been numerous reports of submarine activity in the area so it came as no surprise to the master when at 5.45am the watch keeper reported a submarine was close on the starboard quarter. The master looked for himself and could see that it was gaining on them very quickly indeed. He shouted for the boat to be got ready and set about burning his confidential papers. He was in the nick of time as a shell came whimpering over the rigging.

The crew pulled clear and had got about 40yds away when the submarine commander beckoned them towards him. The master was ordered aboard for questioning while three German sailors used his boat and crew to row back to the *Huntleys*. Several bombs were placed in positions where they would do the most damage and minutes later she went to the bottom.

After setting the crew adrift the submarine sped off to attack another vessel close by which turned out to be the schooner *Mary Annie*. She shared a similar fate and was sunk within half an hour.

Huntleys crew, meanwhile, linked with the boat from *Mary Annie* and rowed for the coast. They were spared the effort of having to row the whole distance by the SS *Presto* which took them in tow for a while before transferring them to the torpedo boat *No 3* which landed them safely at Newhaven.

13/45: RYE. *Country:* British.
Date sunk: 7/4/18. *Tons nett:* 399. *Tons gross:* 986.
Built: 1914. *Type:* SS. *Rig:* –. *Owners:* Lancs & Yorks Railway Co, Huntsbank, Manchester. *Cargo:* 600 tons military supplies, food, oil, Newhaven to Rouen. *Armed:* 1 x 90mm French gun. *Position:* 12 miles N of Cape Antifer (49 57 00N; 00 05 00W). *Master's name:* John Richard Sykes. *Crew:* 22. *Crew nationality:* 20 British, 2 others.
Gunners: J. McCall, RNVR; J.D. Owen, RNVR; J.D. Watson, LS RNVR.

THE SS *Rye* was one of two steamers crossing the Channel to Havre under the escort of HMT *Lancer II*. Unknown to both ships and their escort, they were being watched by Oberleutnant Ernst Steindorff in *UB-74*. The *Rye* presented the better target so it was she at 3.15am, who took the full force of a torpedo. It struck her directly amidships in the bunker hold and blew a large gaping hole in her side.

Nobody on board saw anything of the torpedo or *UB-74* and it was thought possible at the time that she may have hit a mine. The Admiralty later gave the verdict that she had been torpedoed although there is no evidence to suggest that in the documentation at the time. However, later documentation, and notes in *UB-74's* log revealed that it was indeed Steindorff who sank her and waited to watch her sink.

The crew took to the boats immediately and a few minutes later the steamer sank. *Lancer II* hurried to her assistance whilst the other steamer in company, *Unity*, looked on. The master of the *Unity* had heard a dull thud and wondered what was happening. However, in a letter to the authorities he said that once he saw that the *Rye* was starting to list with smoke pouring out of her funnel he increased speed and began a very erratic zig-zag course. As *Lancer II* was with the crew he didn't stop but made all speed to Havre.

All the crew from the *Rye* managed to get into the boats but unfortunately, four men were later washed out of one of them. Three drowned and one was rescued but subsequently died of exposure.

13/46: P26. *Country:* British.
Date sunk: 10/4/17. *Tons nett:* –. *Tons gross:* 613.
Built: 1915. *Type:* patrol boat. *Rig:* P-class.
Owners: Admiralty. *Cargo:* –. *Armed:* Yes, 1 x 4in gun; 2 torpedo tubes. *Position:* 1½ miles N by E of Whistle Buoy, Havre (49 32 45N; 00 05 00W). *Master's name:* –. *Crew:* –. *Crew nationality:* British.
It had been one hell of a day outside the entrance to Havre Roads on April 10, 1917. First the *Salta* had struck a mine and then one of the naval vessels trying

to render her assistance had fallen foul of the same thing. The minefield had been laid by *UC-26*.

Lieutenant B.S. Stothard RNR, commander of HMT *Diamond II*, said that he could not understand what had made the master of *Salta* turn away from the gateway until he learned later that the master had refused to enter without the assistance of a pilot. His chief officer had assured him that there was no danger but the master was adamant and turned to the north. It was his undoing as very soon after, she sank, having struck a mine.

P26 went in to help the survivors but it wasn't an easy job with the huge sea that was running and the fast current, sometimes in excess of three knots. Other vessels came to assist, *Ocean Princess*, *Dewsland* and the ill fated *Amy* who was to share the same end as *Salta* the next day.

At 1pm whilst still struggling to assist survivors from the *Salta*, *P26* also struck a mine and completely broke in two. HMD *Druid* went to her assistance and with some very skilled seamanship managed to save most of her crew.

13/47: AMY. *Country:* British.
Date sunk: 11/4/17. *Tons nett:* –. *Tons gross:* 270.
Built: –. *Type:* hired trawler. *Rig:* –. *Owners:* Admiralty. *Cargo:* –. *Armed:* Yes. *Position:* About 1½ miles N by E of Whistle Buoy, Havre (49 32 30N; 00 05 00W). *Master's name:* –. *Crew:* –. *Crew nationality:* British.

UC-26's minefield, laid just outside the boom defences to Havre Roads, certainly proved effective, sinking no less than three vessels. As well as HMT *Amy*, the patrol boat *P26* fell foul of it as did the large hospital ship *Salta*.

However, the loss of *Amy* could have been avoided according to the Senior Naval Officer, Lieutenant B.S. Stothard RNR, commander of HMT *Diamond II*. He reported that on Wednesday April 11, 1917, at 11.25am, *Amy* struck a mine and was lost with all hands but one. He made the point that the commander of *Amy* was perfectly aware of the position of the minefield as he had put a dan buoy close to it only the previous day. *Amy* was busy putting out her kite in order to start sweeping to clear the mines but in doing so her skipper had not paid attention to the strong wind and four knot current that was running. Consequently she drifted into the minefield and in spite of several vessels trying to signal her of the danger she eventually struck a mine.

One of her colleagues, HMT *Hatano* went directly in to her assistance even though *Diamond* was signalling her to stay clear. One man was picked up but the rest were not found.

13/48: SALTA. *Country:* British. *Date sunk:* 10/4/17. *Tons nett:* –. *Tons gross:* 7284. *Built:* 1911. *Type:* SS. *Rig:* hospital ship. *Owners:*

The hospital ship *Salta,* which struck a mine near the entrance to Havre.

Managers. H.E. Moss, Liverpool. *Cargo: –. Armed:* No. *Position:* 1¹/₂ miles N by E of Whistle Buoy, Havre (49 32 00N; 00 05 00W). *Master's name:* Mr Eastaway. *Crew: –. Crew nationality:* British, French, Russians, Belgians, 2 American firemen, 30 Arab firemen

The big steamer *Salta,* formally a French merchant vessel running between Marseilles and America, had been requisitioned and was sailing under a British flag as a hospital ship.

Salta's bridge watch put the engine room to standby at 11.20am and a few minutes later a trawler came up and hoisted the signal,'follow me.' She was escorted towards another British escort vessel *Diamond* which led her towards the examination vessel and handed her over.

As *Diamond* left her she signalled to *Salta* that she was free to enter Havre as soon as the examination vessel had finished with her. *Salta* acknowledged the signal. The chief officer was about to take *Salta* through the gateway to the entrance for Havre but the master stopped the process, saying that he would not proceed further without a pilot. The mate insisted that they must in view of the danger from mines but the master was adamant and turned his ship to the north.

Puzzled by what *Salta* was up to, the commander of *Diamond* signalled frantically on his whistle, 'You are standing into danger!' With that the master

immediately put the engines full astern and gave three blasts on the whistle. He held her astern for about four minutes which got her back into some semblance of order and went ahead again to swing around and line up for the gateway. Suddenly an enormous explosion boomed out from the after end of the vessel as a mine contacted her hull, opening up a huge hole in the engine room and number three hold.

It was 11.45am when the explosion occurred and within 10 minutes *Salta* was on the bottom, taking with her nine nurses, 42 RAMC staff and 79 crew. A letter in the records from the British Consulate at Havre explained that they only managed to recover 13 bodies from the wreck, no doubt due to the very fast currents that occur off Havre.

13/49: CHATBURN. *Country:* British. *Date sunk:* 1/3/17. *Tons nett:* 1224. *Tons gross:* 1942. *Built:* W.Hartlepool in 1894. *Type:* SS. *Rig:* schooner. *Owners:* F.Yeoman & Sons, Exchange Buildings, Cardiff. *Cargo:* 2600 tons coal, shipped by Wearmouth Coaling Co, Sunderland and consigned to Paris Gas Co, Rouen. *Armed:* No. *Position:* 22 miles NE from Cape Barfleur (50 00 00N; 00 55 00W). *Master's name:* Thomas Arthur Watkins. *Crew:* 22. *Crew nationality:* 19 British, 1 Norwegian, 1 Swede, 1 Belgian.

CAPTAIN Watkins' orders were to leave Sunderland and head south to make St Helens, Isle of Wight, as soon as possible to join a convoy crossing the Channel. He did just that and left with the convoy on March 1, 1917, at 4pm. The weather for the crossing was good with a light wind and a slight haze. The journey went well with all the vessels staying in formation and all maintaining a good speed. The armed patrol ships were in position and appeared to be in control, affording their convoy every protection.

It was with some amazement therefore that the officer of the watch suddenly spotted the conning tower of a submarine off the port bow and he instinctively shouted for the helm to be turned hard to port. The ship responded but before she could complete her turn a torpedo slammed into the midships of the steamer creating a huge explosion.

The master could see that his ship was settling down rapidly by the head and ordered all the crew to take to the boats. As they were getting the last few people in, one man, a donkeyman, alarmed at the angle the ship was taking, jumped overboard. The *Chatburn* had started sinking so rapidly that there was no time to shut down the engines. As her stern started to rise up her propeller was still turning and unfortunately the swimming donkeyman had his right leg broken by one of the blades. However, he was rescued by his shipmates.

Within minutes one of the escort patrol boats, *Willonyx* was on the scene and picked the men up. They reached Havre early the next morning.

The *Chatburn* was torpedoed by *UB-18*.

WORLD WAR ONE
CHANNEL WRECKS

◆

AREA
FOURTEEN

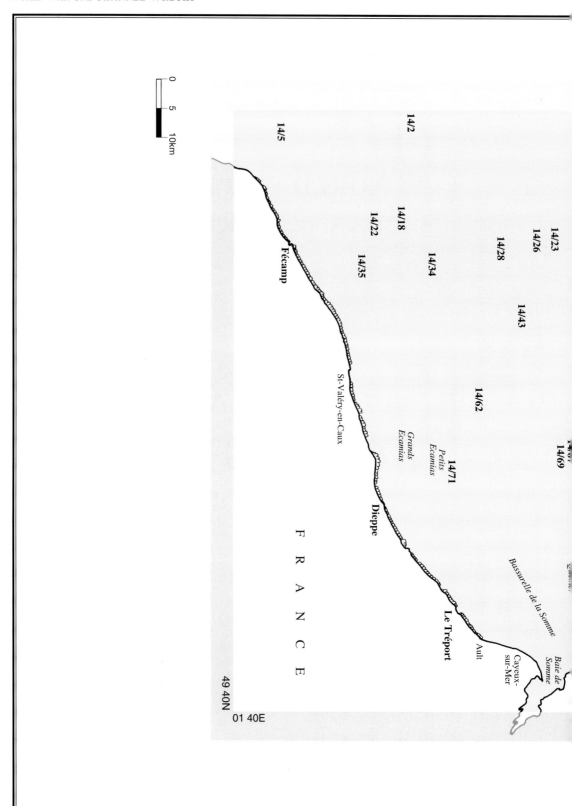

Wreck Sites in Area Fourteen

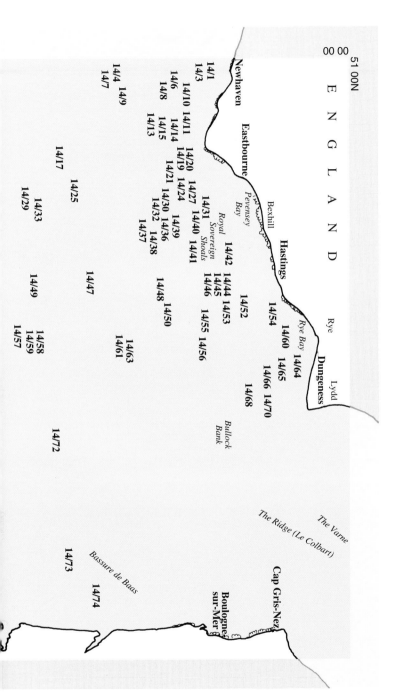

51 00N

00 00

ENGLAND

Newhaven

Eastbourne

Pevensey Bay

Bexhill

Hastings

Rye Bay

Rye

Dungeness

Lydd

14/1
14/3
14/10 14/11
14/6
14/8
14/13
14/4 14/9
14/7

14/15

14/14

14/20
14/19 14/24
14/21 14/27 14/40 14/41
14/30 14/39
14/32 14/36
14/38

14/17

14/25

14/31

Royal
Sovereign
Shoals

14/33
14/29

14/42

14/44 14/53
14/45
14/46 14/55 14/56

14/37

14/47

14/48 14/50

14/52

14/54

14/60 14/64
14/65
14/66 14/70

14/49

14/58
14/59
14/57

14/63
14/61

14/68

Bullock
Bank

14/72

The Varne

The Ridge (Le Colbart)

14/73

Bassure de Baas

14/74

Cap Gris-Nez

Boulogne-
sur-Mer

14/1: CITY OF BRISBANE. *Country:* British.
Date sunk: 13/8/18. *Tons nett:* 4510. *Tons gross:*
7094. *Built:* 1918. *Type:* SS. *Rig:* schooner.
Owners: Ellerman Hall Line, Liverpool.
Cargo: In ballast, London for Buenos Aires.
Armed: 1 x 4in and 2 x 7.5in Howitzers.
Position: 3 miles SW of Newhaven (50 44 25N;
00 00 50E). *Master's name:* Ernest Mason.
Crew: 98. *Crew nationality:* 93 British, 4
Portuguese, 1 Swede, 1 passenger (US army
doctor). *Gunners:* William Munay, Seaman RNR,
No DZ 353CH; David Cannon, LS RNR, No. AZ
692CH; George Richards, PO 1 RFR, No 17551Y;
Jas Bowland, AB RNVR, No Z 3190; Hercules
Scott, Seaman RNR, No A 7543BO.

HEADING for warmer climes the *City of Brisbane*
left London and made her way down the Channel.
She was steering north 60 degrees west and making 13
knots at 5.30pm on August 13, 1918.
    The bridge could not have been better attended with
the master, the Pilot, J.J. Ellison, and first mate. The
lookouts were in position and it was one of these that
suddenly shouted that he could see the wake of a
torpedo. There was no time to do anything as a few
seconds later it struck the ship on the port side aft by
number five hold. The whole side of the ship aft was
completely blown in and laid the engine room wide
open to the sea. The torpedo was fired by Oberleutnant
Johann Lohs in the submarine *UB-57*.
    Within a few minutes the stern of the vessel was
on the seabed and the master ordered the crew to the
lifeboats. All managed to get clear with no casualties
and they watched as about half an hour later their ship
sank in 12 fathoms of water.

14/2: S.D. *Country:* British. *Date sunk:* 2/8/16.
Tons nett: 99. *Tons gross:* 131. *Built:* 1902.
Type: SV. *Rig:* Wooden barge. *Owners:* Smeed
Dean Co Ltd, Sittingborne, Kent. *Cargo:* 223 tons
wheat, from Cherbourg to Dieppe. *Armed:* No.
Position: 18 miles NNW from Cape Antifer
(49 59 00N; 00 01 00E). *Master's name:* Alfred
Thomas Dorrell. *Crew:* 4.

THERE was hardly any wind and the *S.D.* was
struggling to make any headway at all. All possible
sail was up but she was barely making two knots.
    It was ideal weather for enemy submarines to pick
on small boats and before long one appeared and
passed the *S.D.* by about half a mile. The master
wondered if he had been spared but saw that the
submarine was going to sink another vessel. The *G.C.
Gradwell* was close by and the commander of the
submarine decided that he would sink her first.
    Then it was the turn of the barge which was
ordered to come alongside by the German
commander. He produced a revolver which was
levelled at the master of the *S.D.* and demanded to
know all the details of his ship and voyage. Once the

crew were clear two shells were fired into the stern of
the barge and she sank in a few minutes.
    The crew were later picked up by the SS *Marena* of
Liverpool and landed safely at Havre.

14/3: HMT LANCER II. *Country:* British.
 Date sunk: 18/7/18. *Tons nett:* –. *Tons gross:* 275.
Built: –. *Type:* Patrol boat. *Rig:* trawler. *Owners:* –.
Cargo: –. *Armed:* Yes. *Position:* 2/3 miles SW of
Newhaven Breakwater (50 44 10N; 00 01 10E).
Master's name: –.

THERE are only very brief details of the sinking of
Lancer II which happened at 2.20am, when HM yacht
Vagrant, sailing without lights ran into *Lancer II* and
put a big hole in her. *Vagrant* took her in tow but she
sank in 12 fathoms of water in the approximate
position given.

14/4: ARACATACA. *Country:* British.
Date sunk: 18/4/17. *Tons nett:* –. *Tons gross:* 4154.
Built: –. *Type:* SS. *Rig:* –. *Owners:* –. *Cargo:* –.
Armed: –. *Position:* 12 miles S of Newhaven
(50 35 00N; 00 04 00E). *Master's name:* –.
Crew: –.

THIS sinking is something of a mystery. Weekly
Reports state that *Aracataca* was sunk after a collision
with the French steamer *Moliere*. The brief report
goes on to say that two rafts containing 14 men were
picked up but no other information was given.
    Because the loss was not caused through enemy
action, any documentation would have been filed
separately. However, a search of the records to date
has failed to find anything further. The *Moliere* of
1545 tons, obviously survived the collision. She was
torpedoed by a U-boat on May 27, 1918, in the Bristol
Channel.

14/5: GERMAN SUBMARINE (UB-26).
Country: German. *Date sunk:* 5/4/16. *Tons nett:*
260. *Tons gross:* 290. *Built:* 1915. *Type:* UB-class,
Mark II. *Owners:* German Navy. *Armed:* 1 x 50mm
deck gun, 4 torpedoes. *Position:* Cape Antifer
bearing SE 5 miles (49 45 00N; 00 04 00E).
Master's name: Oberleutnant Wilhelm Smiths.
Crew: 23. *Crew nationality:* German.

SIX Admiralty drifters with anti-submarine nets and
depth charges were sent in the Spring of 1916 to
operate off the port of Le Havre. The Allies had
noted that the approaches to Havre were a favourite
area for the submarines of the Flanders Flotilla. On
the morning of April 5, their hunch paid off. A U-
boat was spotted trying to attack a steamer not far
off the port, and the drifters were so well placed that
as the U-boat tried to escape her periscope banged
the bottom of the drifter called *Comrades*. The other

drifters shot their nets and the drifter *Endurance* soon realised that the submarine was tangled in her nets. The French torpedo-boat *Trombe* made three runs over the net markers dropping a depth charge each time. Oberleutnant Wilhelm Smiths in *UB-26*, burned out his batteries trying to get free and when they caught fire, he surfaced. All her crew and Oberleutnant Smiths were taken off before she sank. *UB-26* was easily raised from such shallow water and after repairs went into service with the French Navy as the *Roland Morillot*.

The drifters were awarded the maximum £1000 prize money to be shared among them. There are varying stories in the records concerning this incident, but the one above is a fair description of what really happened.

14/6: FORTUNA. *Country:* Dutch.

Date sunk: 22/10/16. *Tons nett:* –. *Tons gross: 1254. Built:* –. *Type:* SS. *Rig:* –. *Owners:* –. *Cargo:* Cement, Rotterdam for Cardiff. *Armed:* –. *Position:* 7½ miles SW by W from Beachy Head (50 40 30N; 00 05 00E). *Master's name:* –. *Crew:* 25. *Crew nationality:* Dutch.

THERE is only a brief mention of this loss in Weekly Reports which stated that at 10.40am, six miles west of Beachy Head, a lifeboat and one dinghy containing 10 survivors were picked up from the SS *Fortuna* of Amsterdam, which was sunk at 1am near the above position.

Other records show that she struck a mine in a field laid by *UC-60*.

14/7: EDUARD. *Country:* British.

Date sunk: 16/4/17. *Tons nett:* 400. *Tons gross:* 476.*Built:* Of iron at Lubeck. *Type:* SV. *Rig:* schooner. *Owners:* Admiralty/Fisher Alimonda & Co, 112 Fenchurch St. *Cargo:* Shingle ballast, London for Port Talbot. *Armed:* No. *Position:* Beachy Head bearing NE 12 miles (50 34 00N; 00 05 00E). *Master's name:* William John Price. *Crew:* 10.

EDUARD was a former German sailing vessel and valued by the Admiralty Marshal at £3238. She was the largest sailing vessel under the administration of the Admiralty and carried nearly 7000 tons of cargo.

She left Regents Canal Dock at 7am and finally cleared the Downs at 1pm on Saturday April 7, 1917. On the 9th she came to anchor at Dungeness East Roads and remained there through bad weather until the 15th.

On April 16, at 4am, Beachy Head was bearing north at a distance of about 7 miles. At 7.30 the ship was tacked and the master was on deck with a sailor at the wheel. She was close hauled and making about 2 knots.

The first indication of trouble was gunfire and a shot tearing through the forward sails. A submarine was about a mile off. The master ordered the boats to be got ready and then rushed below to burn his secret papers. Meanwhile the crew got into the boats. The submarine continued to fire and another shot brought down the topmast followed by the mizzen mast and the fore yard. As the crew got clear of the ship the submarine's gunner aimed a few shots at the fleeing boat.

Having got alongside the boat the submarine's commander ordered all of the *Eduard's* crew to board. Four German crew members then took the boat over to the schooner and placed bombs on her. The job took three minutes and at the same time as the bombing party returned to the submarine the *Eduard* blew up and sank.

Having been freed the crew rowed towards the shore and were picked up by the Admiralty trawler *Balfour* which landed them at Newhaven the same evening.

14/8: T.R. THOMPSON. *Country:* British.

Date sunk: 29/3/18. *Tons nett: 2261. Tons gross: 3538. Built:* 1897. *Type:* SS. *Rig:* schooner. *Owners:* J. Westoll, 13, John Street, Sunderland. *Cargo:* 5600 tons iron ore, Benisaf to Middlesbrough. *Armed:* 1 x 4.7in gun on stern. *Position:* 10 miles W by S of Beachy Head (50 40 08N; 00 05 38E). *Master's name:* W.J. Shewan. *Crew:* 36.

THE sinking of the *T.R. Thompson* was so quick that 33 of her crew were killed. Only three men survived to tell the tale. However, because they were two seaman and an apprentice they could give very little in the way of technical details of just what happened to their ship.

The fact that the sinking occurred at 3.50am was probably a great deal to do with why so many perished. Coupled with the fact that she sank in a few moments makes it likely that most of the crew were trapped below as she went down.

The steamer's last journey began when she left Benisaf, Algeria, on March 14, 1918, heading for Middlesbrough. At the time of her sinking the weather was hazy with a brisk westerly wind that turned the sea up to be quite choppy. The survivors said that there was a tremendous explosion and the next thing they could remember was finding themselves in the water. The explosion was heard by the crew of a trawler in the area who steered their ship into the wreckage where they found the three men.

Their Lordships of the Admiralty noted that this loss had occurred in a locality which had frequently been mined in the past. However, mine sweeping operations had failed to locate any at this time. They concluded that the *T.R. Thompson* was most probably sunk by a torpedo.

They were right. The *T.R. Thompson* was a victim of *UB-57,* commanded by Johann Lohs.

14/9: BRENDA. *Country:* British.
Date sunk: 7/1/17. *Tons nett:* 225. *Tons gross:* 249.
Built: 1879. *Type:* SV. *Rig:* brigantine. *Owners:*
Albert Moore, New St, Padstow, Cornwall.
Cargo: 162 tons patent manure in bags from De
Pass & Co, London to Fowey. *Armed:* No.
Position: 10 miles SSW of Beachy Head/12 miles
due S of Newhaven (50 35 00N; 00 06 30E).
Master's name: Albert Moore. *Crew:* 7.

THE weather was fine and clear at 6.30am on January
6, 1917. The wind was fresh north-westerly as the
wooden brig *Brenda* sailed out of the port of London.
It should have been a quick trip down the Channel
but trouble started when they spotted a submarine on
the port quarter about four miles off. The master
ordered three men on deck to keep a close eye on her
as she moved on the surface at about 13 knots.
Suddenly there was a dull bang in the distance and a
shell came whistling towards them. It sliced into the
water about three yards from the port bow, throwing
up a large spout of water. Another two shots followed,
both of which missed but were too close for comfort.
The master decided that he was in a pretty hopeless
situation and didn't stand a chance of out-running the
submarine. He collected his papers and ordered his
crew into the lifeboats.

As they pulled clear the submarine passed between
them and the *Brenda* and poured twelve shells into
her. Satisfied that they had done enough damage, the
submarine moved over to the men in the boats and
demanded the ships papers. As Captain Moore handed
them over the commander of the submarine became
very agitated as he glanced between them and the
horizon. A ship was approaching and the commander
ordered the submarine's crew to beat a hasty retreat
below. A few moments later the submarine dived.

The approaching vessel turned out to be the
Admiralty trawler *Ben Tore*. She arrived just as the
Brenda sank at 12.30pm in 20 fathoms of water. *Ben
Tore* took the men aboard and their boats in tow and
headed for Newhaven Harbour, arriving there at 10pm.

14/10: MIRA. *Country:* British.
Date sunk: 11/10/17. *Tons nett:* 2397. *Tons gross:*
3700. *Built:* 1901. *Type:* SS. *Rig:* tanker *Owners:*
Stephens & Sutton & Stephens, Prudential
Buildings, Newcastle. *Cargo:* 5226 tons fuel oil.
Armed: Yes. *Position:* 4 miles SW ½ W from
Beachy Head (50 41 06N; 00 08 25E). *Master's
name:* John Davies. *Crew:* 37.

MIRA'S journey for Dover originally started from
Port Arthur, Texas, USA, but it was from Norfolk,
Virginia that she joined the convoy to cross the
Atlantic. The fleet of steamers were in the charge of
the armed merchant cruiser *Bostonian*, and the whole
convoy was flanked by American destroyers.

At 8am on October 10, 1917, the American
destroyers were relieved by several British destroyers
and the convoy continued up the Channel. It wasn't
until they were approximately 25 miles south-east of
Start Point at 5.10pm, that the trouble began. The lead
ship *Bostonian* was hit by a torpedo and a little while
later received another one to finish her off (see 7/42).
The destroyers began to blanket the area to try and
catch the offending submarine, but, the submarine
had long gone.

The convoy then continued up the Channel
unmolested. At 7am the next morning *Mira* was
lagging behind the convoy. By 7.50am she was some
seven miles behind and the senior patrol officer on
board HMS *Lucifer*, detailed HMS *P45* to watch over
her.

At 12.25pm *Mira's* wake came to an abrupt halt
with a huge explosion on her starboard side just
forward of the bridge. Lieutenant H.J. Carndoff of
P45, said he saw the explosion and realised that *Mira*
was badly damaged. Whatever had caused it wasn't
relevant to Captain Davies at the time. His ship was
badly holed and sinking rapidly. What's more the
explosion had jammed his steering gear and she
started turning in large circles out of control.

P45 raced up to *Mira's* assistance immediately and
after waiting for her to kill her engines he went
alongside. Most of the crew, apart from some
volunteers, left *Mira* and boarded HMT *Mikado*.
Lieutenant Carndoff meanwhile assessed the situation
and decided that *Mira* wasn't sinking too quickly and
there might be a chance of beaching her.

He passed up his six inch manilla hawser and
instructed the volunteer crew to make it fast to *Mira's*
bows. The tow started to work and the lieutenant
lined up a spot in his mind between Seaford and
Beachy Head where he would put her. However, the
hawser slipped off, not having been connected
properly. *P45* doubled back to pass a line again but it
was plain that *Mira* was settling down much more
rapidly. The volunteer crew were ordered off and the
patrol vessel *Balfour* picked them up. At 1 15pm,
Mira went down.

The Admiralty were not happy at the way the
escorts had conducted themselves. There had been
some problems over "signalling slackness", as they
called it, and also the wrong route had been taken
when approaching Beachy Head. It was enough for
them to order a Court of Enquiry. The Enquiry was
held at 11am on October 18, 1917, at HM Navigation
School, Portsmouth. Most of the witnesses called were
naval patrol commanders, although Captain John
Davies of *Mira* was called first.

Lieutenant Edward Chricheley Thornton, RN,
commander of HMS *Lucifer* was questioned about
his route instructions and his signalling. Dozens of
pages of signal books are bound in with the enquiry
papers. Lieutenant Richard Cowell Coppock, of HMT
Mikado, was called for the same kind of questioning.
Lieutenant Frederick Alfred Tollemache, RN,
commander of *P31*, also had to go through the same
grilling about his orders and signals, as did Lieutenant
Carndoff from *P45*.

The end result was that the enquiry found *Mira* had been sunk as a result of striking a mine. No blame was attributable to the commander of *P45*, he was merely following orders. Blame was attributed to Lieutenant Thornton, as he hadn't followed his instructions precisely to the letter. Lieutenant Tollemache of *P31* was also criticised for a signalling error but it all now looks very trivial. At the back of the enquiry papers there is a letter sent by the Admiral to all naval staff about the importance of following procedures to the letter. No disciplinary action seems to have followed.

German records say that the mine which sank *Mira* was laid by *UC-50*.

14/11: CAIRNTORR. *Country:* British.
Date sunk: 21/3/15. *Tons nett:* –. *Tons gross:* 3588.
Built: Sunderland in 1904. *Type:* SS. *Rig:* schooner.
Owners: Cairn Line Steamships Ltd. Newcastle-on-Tyne. *Cargo:* 5300 tons coal, Tyne to Genoa.
Armed: No. *Position:* Beachy Head bearing NE by N 4-5 miles (50 41 06N; 00 11 00E). *Master's name:* Robert Anthony Purvis. *Crew:* 32.

BY flying the Norwegian flag the master of *Cairntorr* had hoped it would afford him some protection against attack. Sadly, he was mistaken.

She left Dunstan, Newcastle, on Friday, March 19, 1915. On Sunday *Cairntorr* was off the Sussex coast and the master had just gone into his chartroom leaving his first mate, Otto Grund, on the bridge. An alert seaman on the forward lookout post suddenly shouted to Grund and pointed to port. Grund snatched up his binoculars and saw what he first thought to be a trail of wreckage, but then saw a torpedo about 600yds off his port beam. He ordered the helm hard to port but the torpedo smashed into the steamer's midships.

Returning at that moment to the bridge the master ordered the crew to muster at their boat stations and had the ship's whistle blown to try and attract attention. He looked across at his ship and saw she was badly holed and the inrush of water was causing her to settle. As a precaution he ordered the crew to get into the boats and to pull clear while he and his first mate remained on board to see how the ship would react.

A little later the tug *Alert* appeared on the scene and a line was attached to the stricken vessel. She was towed for a while but at 6pm she sank in 17 fathoms of water. The crew were all landed at Newhaven.

The submarine involved was *UB-34*.

14/12: PRINCESS MAY. *Country:* British.
Date sunk: 21/10/16. *Tons nett:* 86. *Tons gross:* 104. *Built:* Poole in 1894. *Type:* SV. *Rig:* ketch.
Owners: W.T. Whitmore, Main Rd, Harwich.
Cargo: 90 tons of cattle bones, Havre to London.
Armed: No. *Position:* 25 miles S of Beachy Head (50 20 00N; 00 13 00E). *Master's name:* Alfred Henry Smith. *Crew:* 4.

THE master of the sailing barge *Princess May* heard gunfire and, about a mile to the north-west, could see a German submarine on the surface attacking a motor barge. He altered course in the hope that he could get away. He looked again, the other ship, *Grit*, was in big trouble, flames leaping up high into the air with clouds of billowing smoke.

At 9.30am the first shell whistled over the bow of the *Princess May*. It was a clear warning to the master. He ordered the ship to stop and with his crew climbed into the boat to row over to the waiting enemy. The U-boat commander positioned his submarine down tide and wind of the barge, enabling one of his men to get aboard her with a bomb. Meanwhile, the master who had been kept on board handed over his ship's papers to the German commander. It was all he had, having destroyed his confidential ones earlier. His boat returned a few minutes later with his crew and the German seaman.

The bomb on board the sailing barge exploded but it seemed at first to have little effect. The master said that half an hour later they could still see *Princess May* afloat. However, about 15 minutes later she disappeared. Her crew made for the shore which was fairly hard going in the choppy sea. At about 1.30pm a patrol trawler spotted them and they were landed at Newhaven later that day.

14/13: SEVEN SEAS. *Country:* British.
Date sunk: 1/4/15. *Tons nett:* –. *Tons gross:* 1194.
Built: Dundee in 1888. *Type:* SS. *Rig:* schooner.
Owners: Leach & Co Ltd, Mark Lane, Station Buildings, London. *Cargo:* In ballast, London for Liverpool. *Armed:* No. *Position:* 6 miles S of Beachy Head (50 38 00N; 00 13 00E). *Master's name:* –. *Crew:* 17.

SEVEN SEAS sailed from London on April 1, 1915, in the early hours of the morning to begin her journey round the bottom of the country and up the west side to Liverpool. She steamed south and was making good progress until close to Beachy Head.

The second engineer said that at 4pm he had just come up from the engine room and was sitting on the companion steps. Suddenly he was shaken by a massive bang and saw a huge column of water thrown high into the air. Realising that the ship had been torpedoed he ran to the starboard lifeboat and there found five or six others. Together they managed to get into the boat but had no time to lower it when the steamer suddenly sank.

As the ship went under, the suction ripped the lifeboat clear of the falls, turning it over and tossing the men in every direction. The second engineer managed to climb onto a hatch cover that floated close by and was able to transfer himself onto the keel of the upturned lifeboat. He was later picked up by the destroyer *Flint* along with a donkeyman, four firemen and two sailors, all eventually landing at Newhaven. Although eight people were saved, nine, including the master perished. *U-37* claimed to have torpedoed her.

14/14: BORNEO. *Country:* British.
Date sunk: 18/6/17. *Tons nett:* –. *Tons gross:* 211.
Built: –. *Type:* Admiralty trawler. *Rig:* mine-sweeper. *Owners:* Admiralty. *Cargo:* –. *Armed:* Yes. *Position:* 5 miles S by W of Beachy Head (50 40 00N; 00 14 00E). *Master's name:* –.
Crew: –. *Crew nationality:* British.

THE commander of naval vessel *TB22* reported to his senior officer in the early hours of June 18, 1917, that he had discovered an enemy minefield off Beachy Head. Two sweepers were sent straight away to search the area and destroy the mines, they were *Grenadier* and her sweeping partner *Borneo*.

They got on with the job and soon the mines were being located and sunk by rifles using mine sinking ammunition. Lieutenant Christopher McCready RNVR, commander of *ML 529* said that he was sent out with Lieutenant H.G. Phillips, senior commander in HMT *Ocean Queen*, to find and assist *Grenadier* and *Borneo* and that they caught up with them at about 3.45pm. Lieutenant Phillips went aboard *ML 529* and was taken over to *Grenadier* to give her commander further minesweeping instructions. Whilst this was going on another mine had been located by *Borneo*, making 10 in total for the area. *ML 529* and *Grenadier* approached the mine and blew it up with rifle fire.

It was 5.50pm and the disturbance from the exploding mine was just beginning to die away when there was another explosion. Mathew McCrindle, a deck hand on *Borneo*, said in a statement from a hospital bed at Newhaven, that he was standing on lookout in the bows at the time. The rest of the crew were near the winch when there was a huge explosion from directly under the ship. He put his hands over his head to try and shield himself from the sharpnel but he was hit with a piece. The *Borneo* was completely blown to pieces but by some miracle he found himself floating in the water. For 10 minutes he swam around before being picked up by *ML 529*.

The mate of *Grenadier*, James Frederick Ostcliffe, said that they went in among the wreckage straight away and found one man wounded, another unhurt, but also found two dead men.

A Court of Enquiry was held at 2pm on Saturday June 23, 1917, at the Royal Navy Barracks, Newhaven. The court's findings were that *Borneo* had sunk by misadventure in striking a submerged enemy mine, but that no person present was in any way responsible for the sinking.

14/15: BRAUNTON. *Country:* British.
Date sunk: 7/4/16. *Tons nett:*-. *Tons gross:* 4575.
Built: Stockton in 1911. *Type:* SS. *Rig:* schooner.

Owners: The Tatem Steam Navigation Co, Cambrian Buildings, Cardiff. *Cargo:* 1800 tons government stores, including shells and shellcases, Halifax, Nova Scotia to British Government. *Armed:* No. *Position:* Beachy Head bearing N by E 4¹/₂ miles (50 39 30N; 00 14 00E). *Master's name:* George Burdon Sherbon. *Crew:* 29.

Having travelled all the way from Nova Scotia, *Braunton's* first stop was Boulogne. From there she was to cross the Channel and make her way round the British coast to Newport.

It was 1.30pm when she slipped out of Boulogne on the high water and the master followed his route instructions to the letter. The crossing went well until the ship was off Beachy Head.

The first mate was on the bridge with a seaman on lookout on the forecastle head. The steamer had lights on but at half power. Without any warning, there was an explosion in number four and five holds causing the ship to shudder and start to settle down. The engines were ordered full astern in a bid to slow her while the boats were launched. With all the crew accounted for the boats pulled clear of the stricken ship. As they did so the *Braunton* sank down by the stern and in a few moments was gone.

The crew were spotted soon after by a patrol boat and all taken to Newhaven.

Although there is no mention in the records of any submarine or torpedo being spotted by the crew, the sinking of the *Braunton* is listed by the Admiralty as torpedoed.

German records say she was torpedoed by *UB-29*.

14/16: GRIT. *Country:* British.
Date sunk: 21/10/16. *Tons nett:* 79. *Tons gross:* 147. *Built:* Greenhithe in 1910. *Type:* SV/MV. *Rig:* schooner. *Owners:* T. Eberhardt, Greenhithe, Kent. *Cargo:* None, from Havre to London. *Armed:* No. *Position:* 25 miles S of Beachy Head (50 19 00N; 00 14 00E). *Master's name:* Ernest Francis Milton. *Crew:* 5.

THE *Grit* was classed as a motor barge but at the time only had her engines ticking over enough to maintain the generator. All her sails were up and she was making around three knots. The master was at the wheel, the mate aft and a lookout up forward. At around 7am the lookout shouted to the master that he could see something odd off the starboard bow. The master looked and couldn't make it out either, but then it disappeared. About 15 minutes later another object appeared about 80yds off the starboard quarter. It was easily recognisable as a periscope which gradually circled the ship, passed under her stern and surfaced about 20yds off her port side.

A man appeared at the top of the conning tower with a rifle and fired several shots at the *Grit's* rigging. The master understood the message as 'stop and leave your ship.' The order was given and the men rowed across in the ship's boat to the submarine. Two German sailors jumped in and forced them at gunpoint to row to the *Grit*. They tried but owing to the wind and tide pushing the schooner away they couldn't catch up with her. The Germans abandoned the idea and got back on board the submarine. Sixteen shells later the *Grit* caught fire. She was also sinking rapidly.

Meanwhile, the submarine's commander directed his attention to another ship that had the misfortune to appear on the scene, the sailing barge *Princess May* (see 14/12).

14/17: GERMAN SUBMARINE (UC-65).
Country: German. *Date sunk:* 3/11/17. *Tons nett:* 420. *Tons gross:* 500. *Built:* 1916. *Type:* UC-class, Mark II. *Owners:* German navy. *Armed:* 1 x 88mm deck gun, 7 torpedoes, 18 mines. Position: 16 miles S of Beachy Head (50 28 00N; 00 17 00E). *Master's name:* Kapitanleutnant Klaus Lafrenz. *Crew:* 26. *Crew nationality:* German.

THE commander of the British submarine *C-15*, Lieutenant Edgar H. Dolphin, was described by his senior officer as a capable and energetic officer, who had seen a lot of action in the time he commanded *C-15*, from September 1916 to the present date. His successful attack on the German submarine *UC-65* was another feather in his cap.

Extracts from Lieutenant Dolphin's log were included in the report to the Admiralty and are summarised as follows:

He proceeded to St Helens anchorage and joined HMT *Willonyx*. At 11.30am he went out into the Channel on normal patrol duties. At 2.43pm an enemy submarine was sighted, on the surface bearing about five points on the port bow. He dived deeper to get closer to it and came up again to periscope depth. At 3.12pm he sighted the submarine again only 400yds ahead. Lieutenant Dolphin ordered a double shot to be fired and two torpedoes were released from his bow tubes. It was a cunning move on the part of Lieutenant Dolphin. Two torpedoes, expertly released, meant that whichever way the enemy turned, there was no escape. Sure enough one hit the submarine square on, while the other passed alongside as Kapitan-leutnant Klaus Lafrenz took avoiding action with *UC-65*.

Six survivors were spotted straight away but by the time *C-15* got to them only five were picked up, one of whom was Lafrenz. Lieutenant Dolphin questioned them one at a time to get what information he could while they were still shocked. They informed him that their vessel was *UC-65*, homeward bound having used up 5 torpedoes and laid 18 mines.

Lieutenant Dolphin was awarded the DSO and other members of *C-15*'s crew were also decorated.

14/18: DULWICH. *Country:* British.
Date sunk: 15/2/15. *Tons nett:* 2081. *Tons gross:* 3289. *Built:* Stockton in 1893. *Type:* SS. *Rig:* schooner. *Owners:* The Britain SS Co Ltd, 7, Withington Ave, London. *Cargo:* 4675 tons coal, Hull for Rouen. *Armed:* No. *Position:* 27 miles NNE from Cape la Heve (49 58 00N; 00 18 00E). *Master's name:* John Alan Hunter. *Crew:* 31

DULWICH was engaged in the coal run from Hull to Rouen and she left on February 15, 1915. It was a fairly uneventful crossing until, without any warning, a torpedo slammed into number three hold in the fore part of the ship. The hatches were smashed to pieces by the explosion and the steamer started to settle immediately. Two boats were swung out and 22 of the crew manned one and nine the other. They pulled clear and several minutes later the *Dulwich* sank. As the steamer went down the German submarine responsible surfaced. It soon disappeared as a French patrol boat appeared and later took the shipwrecked men to Havre.

U-16 claimed the *Dulwich*.

14/19: LALEN MENDI. *Country:* Spanish.
Date sunk: 17/11/17. *Tons nett:* 1325. *Tons gross:* 2138. *Built:* 1895. *Type:* SS. *Rig:* schooner. *Owners:* Sota y Ayner, Bilbao. *Cargo:* 3100 tons coal consigned to the Electric Co, Barcelona. *Armed:* No. *Position:* 4 miles S of Beachy Head (50 40 24N; 00 18 00E). *Master's name:* Ciriaco Echevarr. *Crew:* 22. *Crew nationality:* All Spanish.

THERE is not much information about this sinking mainly because the master could speak very little English.

The *Lalen Mendi* sailed from Middlesbrough on November 11, 1917, and made her way down the coast calling at various ports as per sailing instructions. On the day of her loss the weather was calm and the sea smooth, ideal conditions for submarines. She was struck on the starboard side by a torpedo and very severely holed. The force of the explosion damaged one of the lifeboats but it was lowered anyway. Upon touching the water it disintegrated and five of the men in it were drowned. The vessel sank in four minutes.

The survivors were eventually picked up by a torpedo boat.

14/20: RIO PARANA. *Country:* British.
Date sunk: 24/2/15. *Tons nett:* 2605. *Tons gross:* 4015. *Built:* West Hartlepool in 1902. *Type:* SS. *Rig:* schooner. *Owners:* –. *Cargo:* 6560 tons coal loaded at Dunstan on Tyne for Porto Ferrajo. *Armed:* No. *Position:* 4 miles SE of Beachy Head (50 40 40N; 00 18 00E). *Master's name:* John Williams. *Crew:* 31.

At 3.15 in the afternoon, *Rio Parana* was heading down the Channel and passing Beachy Head. The master had left the bridge for a while to answer the call of nature. He had just arrived at the heads when an enormous explosion rocked his ship.

Back on deck he could see that the steamer had been hit on the starboard side in number two hold either by a mine or a torpedo and, worse still, she was starting to list heavily. Most of the doors on the starboard side had been ripped open and the saloon was wrecked and full of water.

The boats were lowered within minutes and by the time they were ready for launching the water was level with the main deck. As the boats pulled clear the steamer sank. Fortunately all the crew were accounted for. Within half an hour they were safely aboard a torpedo boat and taken to Newhaven.

The master could not be sure at the time if his ship had been struck by a mine or a torpedo. However, the Admiralty made the point that several vessels had been sunk in the area at the same time and the crews had seen a submarine. Consequently the *Rio Parana* is listed as having been torpedoed.

U-8 claimed to have torpedoed her.

14/21: HMT BALFOUR. *Country:* British.
Date sunk: 13/5/18. *Tons nett:* –. *Tons gross:* 285.
Built: –. *Type:* Armed Trawler. *Rig:* –. *Owners:* –.
Cargo: –. *Armed:* Yes. *Position:* 5 miles WSW of Royal Sovereign LV (50 40 00N; 00 20 00E).
Master's name: Arnold Herbert Howe.
Gunners: Herbert Ogden Martyn, LS; Cyril Stanley Marshall, AB RNVR; Wallace Barham, AB; George Girling, AB.

IT all began when *Balfour* received a message to join up with the Lancs & Yorks Railway owned steamer, *Nidd*, and escort her to Dieppe. This she did and took up her station ahead of the *Nidd* a few miles from the Royal Sovereign Light Vessel. At 9.45pm everything was proceeding as normal on the *Balfour* but exciting events were taking place on the *Nidd*.

The Master of *Nidd*, John Waterhouse Kitwood, reported to the enquiry that he suddenly felt a large shock from beneath his ship under number two hold and wondered what on earth he had hit. It appeared to rumble along his ship's keel, more on the starboard side as his starboard otter mine defence boom had also been struck. He ordered the engines to be shut down and for the starboard Otter to be hove in. On examination of the otter it was found to be badly damaged and something that looked like an aerial caught up in it. A few minutes later a lookout shouted, "Submarine astern about 400yds." The submarine commander had obviously been forced to surface by the collision with *Nidd's* keel. Captain Kitwood ordered the engines to full ahead and passed word to the gunners at the stern to fire at will. Their first shot appeared to hit the submarine.

Back on *Balfour*, the signalman had noted the message from *Nidd* and passed it to his skipper who rushed to the bridge to see for himself. Sure enough there was a submarine and he put the *Balfour* hard to

starboard to have a go at the enemy. Men rushed to their quarters, guns were manned and depth charges brought to the ready. In fact so much attention was being paid to the submarine that nobody gave a thought to where the steamer *Nidd* was.

It was the Second Hand, James Howard, who first spotted the impending collision and shouted to the skipper that *Nidd* was about to strike. There was no time to take evasive action. However, a smart piece of thinking on James Howard's part at least made the impact less dangerous as he sprinted to the depth charges and replaced the keys to render them safe. It was an act which later earned him the praises of the Admiralty. A moment later the *Nidd's* bows were embedded in the port side of the *Balfour's* midships and began to push her through the water. The steamer recoiled back but her smart thinking master put the engines ahead again to plug the hole and allow the men from *Balfour* to climb aboard the *Nidd*. There was no other option open to the crew of the *Balfour* as she was sinking rapidly.

The Court of Enquiry, in summing up the evidence, reported that no blame could be attached to the master of *Nidd* in any way and that the fault lay entirely with the commander of *Balfour*. There was no documentation to say if Arnold Howe received any punishment for his error. However, the crew of *Nidd* were rewarded for their efforts in attacking the submarine and were awarded £100 to be shared between them.

14/22: HARRIET WILLIAMS. *Country:* British.
Date sunk: 28/2/17. *Tons nett:* –. *Tons gross:* 156.
Built: –. *Type:* SV. *Rig:* –. *Owners:* E. Stevens, Par, Cornwall. *Cargo:* Pitch in bulk, London for Havre.
Armed: No. *Position:* 15 miles NNE of Antifer (49 55 00N; 00 20 00E). *Master's name:* G. Bishop.
Crew: 6. *Crew nationality:* British.

HARRIET WILLIAMS sailed from Gravesend on February 23, 1917, bound for Havre. The weather was fine with calm sea conditions. She met her end when an enemy submarine appeared alongside and the crew were ordered to leave. Bombs were placed on board and a few minutes later she exploded and sank.

The crew reached the French coast later that evening.

14/23: LAURA. *Country:* British.
Date sunk: 8/9/17. *Tons nett:* 85. *Tons gross:* 180.
Built: –. *Type:* SV. *Rig:* ketch. *Owners:* Andersen & Co, Whitstable. *Cargo:* 180 tons china clay from Par to A. Peecourt, Paris via Rouen. *Armed:* No.
Position: 25 miles N of Fecamp (50 15 00N; 00 22 00E). *Master's name:* Porter Fred Aylmore.
Crew: 4.

LAURA had been in St Helens Roads, Isle of Wight for over five weeks waiting for the weather to improve. It was a relief to the crew to be able to leave on September 7, 1917, and put to sea. The journey across the Channel was pretty straight forward although quite slow due to the light winds, her average speed being only two knots. The weather was better but every now and then thick blankets of fog would roll in.

The master was on deck when something whined over the ship's rigging. It was followed 30 seconds later by another which threw up a spout of water alongside. The master realised he was being shelled but could not see where they were coming from. Another shell arrived, this time streaking through the rigging bringing down bits of tackle. The master ordered his men into the boats and they pulled clear.

A few minutes later the crew were able to see a German submarine about a mile off, closing on them rapidly. Her commander appeared on the conning tower as she drew alongside the men, ordering the master and the mate to board for questioning while the other two men were forced to row two German sailors back to the *Laura*.

The master said that the German commander asked some very strange questions about two sailing vessels he had attacked recently, one called *Ethel* and the other *Ellen Beatrice*. He wanted to know what he knew about them. Of course the master, and the mate for that matter, knew nothing of them. He then proceeded to take the men's photographs, probably as a means of striking fear into them. He said that if they were caught at sea again they would be shot. Other submarine commanders had been known to use the same threatening tactics, in the hope that others would refuse to go to sea.

By then the boarding party had returned, clutching some charts from *Laura*, after leaving behind two bombs. As the master and mate were put back in their boat the bombs exploded and *Laura* sank almost immediately.

The four men rowed the 25 miles to the French coast and made Fecamp at 1am on September 9.

14/24: BRANKSOME CHINE. *Country:* British.
Date sunk: 23/2/15. *Tons nett:* –. *Tons gross:* 2026. *Built:* 1899. *Type:* SS. *Rig:* schooner. *Owners:* Branksome Chine SS Co, James St, Cardiff. *Cargo:* 3090 tons of coal, Grimsby for Portsmouth. *Armed:* No. *Position:* Beachy Head bore W by N 6 miles (50 41 00N; 00 23 00E). *Master's name:* Francis James Ausley. *Crew:* 21.

BRANKSOME CHINE sailed from Grimsby Roads on February 21, 1915. At around 2.15pm on the 23rd she was struck by a torpedo from a German submarine. According to the officer of the patrol boat who assisted the survivors, the weather was clear with a calm sea.

The survivors reported that the torpedo struck the ship on the starboard side in number two hold between the fore mast and the bridge. They could see the coal washing out of the side of the ship and realised that she would sink quickly. She first took on a list to

starboard and then to port, filling rapidly. Before the lifeboat was lowered she had already settled down to the upper deck. The crew got clear and reported later that the ship was still afloat between 6 and 7pm. A search until midnight by a patrol boat failed to find her.

U-8 was the submarine involved (see 14/20).

14/25: CATERHAM. *Country:* British.
Date sunk: 13/11/16. *Tons nett:* 1084. *Tons gross:* 1777. *Built:* Sunderland in 1886. *Type:* SS. *Rig:* schooner. *Owners:* John Harrison, Ceylon House, Eastcheap, London. *Cargo:* In ballast, Rouen for Newcastle. *Armed:* No. *Position:* 15 miles SSE of Beachy Head (50 30 00N; 00 23 00E). *Master's name:* William Ferguson Coronie, 6, Saule Terrace, Edinburgh. *Crew:* 21.

IT was quite a foggy day as *Caterham* made her way up the Channel towards the Dover Straits with the visibility less than a mile. She was making a steady nine knots with the second mate in charge on the bridge, the master having just gone aft. Suddenly a bang echoed across the water, followed a few seconds later by the whistle of a shell which embedded itself in the forecastle head. The master dashed to the bridge and saw an enemy submarine about half a mile off on the starboard beam.

When the third shell passed extremely close to the bridge the master decided he had better stop and gave the orders accordingly. He grabbed his confidential sailing instructions, stuffed them into the weighted bag and quickly tossed them overboard. Still the submarine was firing but fortunately the shells were going wide. However, it was no time to hang around and the crew got into the boats and pulled clear. A figure appeared on the submarine's conning tower and beckoned the men over.

The master and five men were ordered aboard to be greeted by the commander. He was not a patient man, demanding to know the ship's name, tonnage and other details. Meanwhile, three German sailors used one of the *Caterham's* boats to row over to her and plant bombs.

When the bombs exploded the *Caterham* refused to sink, forcing the submarine commander to manoeuvre around her, firing shells into selected spots. At about 9.10am she plunged to the bottom.

Her crew were by this time well away, rowing for the shore. At 3.30pm they were picked up by HMS *Amazon* which took them to Dover.

UB-38 was the U-boat involved.

14/26: EZEL. *Country:* British. *Date sunk:* 8/9/17.
Tons nett: 140. *Tons gross:* 160. *Built:* Cardiff in 1873. *Type:* SV. *Rig:* schooner. *Owners:* Mrs Davies, Stanley House, Cardigan. *Cargo:* 270 tons China clay, Teignmouth to Treport. *Armed:* No. *Position:* 30 miles S of Beachy Head/20 miles N of

St Valery (50 13 00N; 00 23 00E). *Master's name:* John Jones. *Crew:* 5. *Crew nationality:* British.

FOR nearly two weeks the *Ezel* waited in St Helens Roads, Isle of Wight, for more favourable weather to make her crossing over to France. Her chance came on September 7, 1917, when at 7am she raised her anchor and headed off as ordered, hugging the coast up to Beachy Head. Setting a new course of south half east she turned off to cross the Channel heading for St Valery.

In comparison to the recent bad weather of strong winds and rain the master found himself again in bad weather, but this time through the lack of wind. With all sails set the *Ezel* was barely making a knot but it was enough for steerage and she plodded on steadily towards her goal about 20 miles off. A German submarine commander however, watched through his periscope as the little boat floated by about 200yds off.

On the *Ezel*, the master who was at the wheel, had spotted the menace. He shouted to his crew who were all on deck to make the boat ready and be prepared to leave instantly. The submarine commander took his time, but 10 minutes later the U-boat was on the surface heading around the stern of the *Ezel*, coming to a stop abreast of her port side. The first shell from the enemy went clean over the ship, a warning to the master to get clear immediately. The crew wasted no time and began to launch their boat. Another shell screamed past very close to the men smashing its way into the schooner's forward quarter. The crew got clear just in time as the German gunners began a rapid bombardment firing about eight shells in quick succession.

At 1.50pm the shot ridden *Ezel* gave in to the onslaught and sank bow first. The submarine slowly made her way alongside the lifeboat and a German officer jumped aboard their boat ordering the men to empty their pockets. Spotting the Bills of Lading from the master's pocket he snatched them away and headed off back on board his ship leaving the crew to start the long pull towards the coast.

It was 6am the following morning before they were seen about six miles off Beachy Head by the armed trawler *Tessie* which landed them at Hove later that day.

14/27: HMS ARIADNE. *Country:* British. *Date sunk:* 26/7/17. *Tons nett:* –. *Tons gross:* 11000. *Built:* 1898. *Type:* cruiser. *Rig:* converted to minelayer. *Owners:* Admiralty. *Cargo:* 400 mines. *Armed:* 4 x 6in, 1 x 4in guns. *Position:* 2 miles WSW of Royal Sovereign LV (50 42 45N; 00 23 21E). *Master's name:* Captain Harry Hesketh-Smyth. *Crew:* 304. *Crew nationality:* British.

INFORMATION regarding this sinking is taken from the report made by the commander of HMS *Peregrine* which, together with HMS *Norman*, were sent to escort HMS *Ariadne* to Portsmouth.

They headed off in formation with the two escorts forming a submarine screen, *Peregrine* on the port bow and *Norman* on the starboard. They didn't know it then, but they were being watched by Kapitan Otto Steinbrinck in *UC-65*. Suddenly a large explosion boomed out from *Ariadne* at 2.21pm. The escorts closed and were told that *Ariadne* had been struck by a torpedo. Both escorts peeled off and began to search around the stricken ship which had started to list heavily. At 3.09pm *Peregrine* was about three miles away, continuing the search for the submarine, when another explosion came from *Ariadne*, whereupon she heeled over and sank about seven minutes later.

The commander of *Peregrine* thought that a boiler must have exploded but it was believed later that it was the result of a second torpedo striking home.

Ariadne's crew were taken off and her commanding officer transferred his command to the *Peregrine*.

Thirty-eight men were killed and nine seriously wounded. Otto Steinbrinck, in his log, says he fired only once and that torpedo struck the port side amidships.

14/28: THE DUKE. *Country:* British. *Date sunk:* 20/10/16. *Tons nett:* 156. *Tons gross:* 376. *Built:* 1890. *Type:* SS. *Rig:* three-mast, mutton sails. *Owners:* J. Hay & Sons, 58, Renfield St, Glasgow. *Cargo:* In ballast, Rouen for Newhaven. *Armed:* No. *Position:* 40 miles NNE of Havre (50 08 00N; 00 24 00E). *Master's name:* Neil Smith. *Crew:* 10. *Crew nationality:* British.

THE weather was bad. The wind blowing close to force eight made the sea very rough, but the visibility was good. At 9.15am the second mate had the watch when he heard a bang in the distance. A submarine, a big one flying the German ensign, was heading straight towards him very quickly. He put the telegraph to stop and the engineers responded, as did the master who suddenly appeared on the bridge.

Captain Smith ordered the engines back up again and told the second mate that at least they should have a go at getting away. "Keep the submarine directly behind for as long as you can," he shouted, and raced off to collect his confidential papers to throw in the stokehold furnace.

On his return to the bridge he saw that the submarine was much closer. A shell landed only a few feet away alongside the ship. The next shot went clean into the rigging bringing down all sorts of gear onto the deck. It was enough for the master and he ordered the engines to be shut down again. As the submarine closed on them he told the crew to get the two boats ready and to pull clear.

A German officer appeared on top of the conning tower and motioned the men to come to the submarine. They did just that and tried to keep the boats on the shelter side of it, out of the worst of the weather. The German commander planned to

HMS *Ariadne* was used as a mine-layer. A torpedo from *UC-65* detonated her cargo, killing 38 men.

put a bombing party on board *The Duke* and two sailors got into one of the boats. However, getting back on board the steamer was another matter and they soon gave up the idea and returned to the submarine. The gunner appeared and started to fill *The Duke* full of holes, getting as many as close to the waterline as he could. It worked well, the steamer settling lower in the water with every shot until finally, at 10.30am, she lurched down by the head and was gone.

The crew in the boats had a rough time of it. They were extremely pleased when the little French fishing boat *TR 330* appeared, took them aboard and landed them at Trouville. Captain Smith wrote of them later in his letter to the Admiralty, "There are no words to praise highly enough the manner in which the fishermen treated us, sharing all the food they had and giving us dry clothes. " He asked their Lordships to consider compensating them for their generosity and they agreed.

14/29: LAURA ANN. *Country:* British. *Date sunk:* 5/6/17. *Tons nett:* 88. *Tons gross:* 116. *Built:* Southtown in 1855. *Type:* SV. *Rig:* schooner. *Owners:* Richard Gibbs Foster, Lennox House, Gloucester. *Cargo:* 195 tons boulders from Treport to Runcorn. *Armed:* No. *Position:* 20 miles SSE of Beachy Head (50 26 00N; 00 25 00E). *Master's name:* Christopher Wall. *Crew:* 4. *Crew nationality:* British.

ALTHOUGH *Laura Ann* was over 60 years old she was rebuilt in 1874. However, her last journey began when she left Treport at noon on June 4, 1917.

She had crossed the Channel and was heading for the relative security of the British coast where she would bear westward. At 7am on the morning of June 5, the Mate, Thomas Wall, who was the master's son, was at the wheel while his father was below having a breakfast. The weather was good with light winds and a reasonable sea, all the sails were up and filled nicely. Then an enemy submarine surfaced about 200yds off on his starboard quarter. As it broke surface several men appeared with rifles and began to send bullets whizzing through the sails. The master, on hearing the commotion came on deck and strode aft to the wheelhouse. He never reached it, a bullet hit him in the head, killing him instantly.

The mate, horrified at seeing his father gunned down, recovered himself enough to take command, ordering the rest of the crew into the boat. They pulled clear and headed away towards the waiting submarine. The mate had nothing to say to the German commander but just did as he was told when several sailors got in their boat armed with bombs. After ferrying them over to *Laura Ann* they watched as the enemy planted bombs. After dropping them back on the submarine the three men pulled away as fast as they could. The expected explosion never came though and on looking back, the submarine was seen alongside the sailing vessel with men aboard, the bombs having failed to detonate. Eventually at 7.30am they exploded, not only sinking *Laura Ann* but taking the body of the master down with her.

The men didn't have to wait long for help, torpedo boat *No 3* was soon on the scene. The three men and their boat were taken aboard and landed later the same morning at Newhaven.

14/30: WESTERN COAST. *Country:* British.
Date sunk: 24/2/15. *Tons nett:* 487. *Tons gross:* 1165. *Built:* Middlesbrough in 1913. *Type:* SS. *Rig:* schooner. *Owners:* Powell Bacon Hough Lines Ltd, Liverpool. *Cargo:* General, 1200 tons, London to Plymouth and Liverpool. *Armed:* No.
Position: Beachy Head bearing NW by W 8 miles (50 40 00N; 00 25 00E). *Master's name:* James Ratcliff.

HAVING taken on board a pilot, William George Kelly, at Gravesend, *Western Coast* headed off down the Channel.

At 3.40pm she was eight miles from Berry Head and was spotted by Kapitan-leutnant A. Stoch in *U-8*.

The master had gone off watch an hour earlier and was fast asleep in his bunk leaving Second Mate, Thomas William Gardener, and the pilot on the bridge. Seeing that all was going well the pilot left the bridge to get his lunch and told the second mate to keep a sharp lookout, especially for submarines. Thomas Gardener continued looking around when a few minutes later he spotted what looked like a sinking steamer to the south. After looking again through his binoculars he could see that a patrol vessel was pulling away from the stricken vessel. He was just about to call the master when he was virtually thrown off his feet by a huge explosion. Recovering himself he could see that his ship had been hit by a torpedo on port side in number two hold.

The master was awake in an instant and grabbing his clothes rushed onto the bridge. He could see that

his ship was settling down rapidly by the head and ordered the crew to make for their boat stations. He then put the engines to full astern. This took the momentum off the steamer and allowed the boats to be lowered in safety.

Within three or four minutes of leaving their ship the crew watched as she leaned over to port and sank. They began to row for the shore but were soon picked up by the SS *Osceola* of the Anglo American Oil Company. The master of the *Osceola* had been watching another steamer at the time, the same one that the second mate of *Western Coast* had been watching, and was heading to her assistance. This steamer turned out to be the *Rio Parana* but on seeing a British torpedo boat heading towards her and then witnessing the *Western Coast* hit, *Osceola's* master turned to her aid instead.

14/31: UMBA. *Country:* British.
Date sunk: 30/4/18. *Tons nett:* 1271. *Tons gross:* 2042. *Built:* 1903. *Type:* SS. *Rig:* schooner. *Owners:* British government (war prize). *Cargo:* In ballast, Dunkirk to Barry. *Armed:* 1 x Russian 6pdr gun. *Position:* 1 mile S of Royal Sovieregn LV (50 44 00N; 00 26 00E). *Master's name:* Young. *Crew:* 25. *Crew nationality:* 22 British, 1 Chilean, 1 Russian, 1 W.African.

BECAUSE 20 of the *Umba's* crew were killed, including the master, there is very little information on the circumstances of this loss.

She originally sailed from Manchester and delivered cargo to Dunkirk and left that port bound for Barry Roads. She met her end at 1.40am on April 30, 1918, when a huge explosion tore a massive hole in her side allowing her to fill with water almost instantly. Those who were not killed by the blast were asleep in their berths and went down with the ship. Five however, suddenly found themselves in the water and were picked up, very shaken but otherwise unhurt.

The *Umba* was torpedoed by *UB-57*.

14/32: LISBON. *Country:* British.
Date sunk: 30/5/17. *Tons nett:* 724. *Tons gross:* 1203. *Built:* 1910. *Type:* SS. *Rig:* –. *Owners:* Ellerman Lines Ltd, 12, Moorgate St, London. *Cargo:* Admiralty stores and 16 cylinders of gas on deck, from Newhaven to Boulogne. *Armed:* Yes. *Position:* 5 miles S of Royal Sovereign LV (50 38 30N; 00 26 00E). *Master's name:* Isaac R. Jones. *Crew:* 23 plus 2 gunners.

IT was very dark in the early hours of May 30, 1917, although the wind was light and the sea calm. It was 1 o'clock when the watch keepers on board the *Lisbon* suddenly felt their ship tremble and heard a large explosion. Nobody was sure what had happened, whether they had been hit by a torpedo or had struck a mine. One thing was certain, the ship was sinking very fast. Orders were given to make for the lifeboats and the crew ran to their respective stations. On reaching the starboard boat it was found to be completely smashed by the force of the explosion. All got into the port boat.

They got clear in the nick of time as the steamer sank ten minutes after the explosion into 25 fathoms of water. However, three men were missing, the chief gunner, chief steward and second mate. The crew rowed around the area for some time and succeeded in finding the second mate and the chief gunner, but there was no trace of the chief steward.

The boat was found later by HMTB 80, the crew taken aboard and looked after as much as possible. Some of them were hurt. The master and second mate suffering from shock. Both gunners were severely cut about their faces, and the third engineer was badly bruised. They were later transferred to the patrol trawler Lord de Ramsay and landed at Newhaven at 5.30am the same day.

The Admiralty lists her as mined.

14/33: BERNICIA. *Country:* British.
Date sunk: 13/11/16. *Tons nett:* 448. *Tons gross:* 957. *Built:* Leith in 1912. *Type:* SS. *Rig:* schooner. *Owners:* James Curries Co, 16, Bernard St, Leith. *Cargo:* In ballast, Havre to London. *Armed:* No. *Position:* 20 miles SSE from Beachy Head (50 26 00N; 00 26 00E). *Master's name:* Arthur Macdonald Cadman. *Crew:* 20.

AS the weather was hazy a particularly good lookout was being kept on the *Bernicia*. The master and the mate, W. Hunter were on the bridge, a seaman, B.J. Storm was at the wheel and another seaman, F. Gunn, was on lookout on the forecastle head. Owing to the thick weather the German submarine which had sneaked up on them was not seen until a shell screached over the rigging. She was about three quarters of a mile off the port quarter, approaching rapidly, firing shells every 30 seconds.

It was 9.05am and the master got message to the engineers below that he wanted every bit of steam they could muster, telling the helmsman to keep the submarine directly astern. Still the shells kept coming, one made a direct hit on a hatch trunkway throwing up huge splinters of wood in all directions. The master realised he had no chance of escape so he put the telegraph to stop, hoisted a flag and blew the whistle to indicate to the submarine commander that he had surrendered.

The crew left *Bernicia* in two boats and rowed as ordered to the submarine. The master and mate were told to come aboard while one of their boats was used by three armed German sailors to go over to the steamer. They stayed on board her for nearly an hour, returning with instruments, clothes, provisions and even brass fittings wrenched from various places. They also left something behind, three bombs planted in positions where they would do the most damage.

Seeing the boat returning the German commander informed the master of the direction and distance to land. At the same moment the bombs on the steamer exploded. The steamer lurched under each impact and a hole appeared in her starboard side exposing the engine room. Within a few minutes she turned over and sank.

The crew headed north and managed to keep both boats together. They made the Royal Sovereign Light Vessel at about 6.30pm and were looked after by the crew. The next day they were taken off by a patrol ship and landed at Newhaven.
The submarine concerned was *UB-38*.

14/34: PERSEVERANCE. *Country:* British.
Date sunk: 23/9/17. *Tons nett:* 98. *Tons gross:* –. *Built:* Port Mellon 1874. *Type:* SV. *Rig:* schooner. *Owners:* C.W.S. Could, Barnstaple, Devon. *Cargo:* 190 tons china clay, St Austell to Treport. *Armed:* No. *Position:* 14 miles off St Valery, France (50 02 00N; 00 26 00E). *Master's name:* James Larcombe. *Crew:* 5. *Crew nationality:* British.

THERE was nothing subtle about the tactics the German submarine commander used when he attacked the *Perseverance*. He surfaced his ship a few hundred yards off the little ship's port side and ordered his men to pound her to pieces with the deck gun. With little wind she was a sitting target and the first shell smashed into her side throwing lumps of timber in all directions. Captain Larcombe gave the order to abandon ship, which was very quickly done. It was just as well as over 30 more shells found their mark on the schooner, sending her to the bottom, a splintered wreck.

The crew watched helplessly as their ship disappeared, suddenly finding themselves alongside the submarine. The master was ordered by the German commander to board where he was relieved of the papers he had hurriedly stuffed into his pocket before leaving. They were nothing important, just Bills of Lading and the ship's register. His secret sailing instructions had been tossed over board in the weighted bag. Satisfied that he had nothing more on him, the commander waved the master back to his boat, the crew then pulling clear to head for the French coast.

Fortunately, the weather was good and at 8pm, when about a mile off St Valery, they were picked up by the Danish SS *Algo*, arriving at Deal the next day.

14/35: EXPRESS. *Country:* British.
Date sunk: 4/4/17. *Tons nett:* 98. *Tons gross:* 217. *Built:* South Shields in 1869. *Type:* SS. *Rig:* schooner. *Owners:* A.F. Henry & McGregor, Dock Place, Leith. *Cargo:* None. *Armed:* No. *Position:* 9 miles NNE from Fecamp (49 54 00N; 00 26 00E). *Master's name:* William Anderson. *Crew:* 8.

JUST after midday on April 3, 1917, the master spotted a dark object in the water just off the starboard bow. It appeared to have a wash behind it and he guessed that it was a submarine. There was no time to hesitate and he shouted to the helmsman, George Foulis, to head directly for it. It was a good piece of manoeuvring by the helmsman and the ship shuddered as the keel of the steamer made contact and creaked its way along it. The master looked back to see if anything appeared but only saw the object briefly before it disappeared.

Within a few minutes an engineer reported to the bridge that the midship section of the ship was taking in water very rapidly. He said they would put all three steam pumps on it but it looked pretty severe. The *Express* was some 20 miles north-west of Antifer so the master ordered a new course to be set back towards the French coast.

By 3am the ship was six miles from Antifer and the water had gained so much in the engine room that the fires went out. *Express* was then just drifting. The master had a look over the side of the steamer and could see the damage with quite large holes all down one side. Large sheets of canvass were thrown over and tied to the sides which did slow down the inrush of water but it was nowhere near enough.

At 8.30am it was decided out of desperation to send the mate and three hands in a boat to try to make the shore to get some help. All day they waited but no help arrived. At 7.50 in the evening the master realised that his ship was done for and with the remainder of his crew, took to the second boat. Half an hour later the *Express* sank leaving the crew to row for the shore. Help did eventually arrive when the patrol boat *Alsace* picked them up and landed them at Fecamp.

From the vague description of the object and the amount of damage done to the steamer it seems more likely that she ran over a wreck, not a submarine.

Certainly, both the Admiralty and Lloyd's do not list her as a war casualty.

14/36: GLENARTNEY. *Country:* British. *Date sunk:* 18/3/15. *Tons nett:* –. *Tons gross:* 5201. *Built:* Whitechurch in 1911. *Type:* SS. *Rig:* –. *Owners:* Caledonia Steamship Co, 14, St Vincent Place, Glasgow. *Cargo:* 7661 tons rice and rice meal from Siam Forest Co, Bangkok, to D.M. Horn & Co, London. *Armed:* No. *Position:* 4 miles S of Royal Soveriegn LV (50 39 30N; 00 26 20E). *Master's name:* John Craig. *Crew:* 40.

THE *Glenartney* was loaded at Bangkok and was bound for London via Colombo, Port Said and Algiers. She left Algiers on the March 11, 1915. The weather on the voyage was generally good and she made on average 12 knots.

On the 18th, whilst steaming up the Channel, the master on the bridge, noticed another steamer of about 2000 tons on his starboard quarter heading in the same direction about one and a half miles off. That ship then altered course to bear more southerly which

puzzled him as that would take her towards the shoals. Becoming more inquisitive he looked through his binoculars only to be met with the sight of a torpedo skimming straight towards him. He at once ordered the helm to starboard and the ship started to respond but not quickly enough. The torpedo smashed into *Glenartney's* starboard side about 10ft from the sternpost blowing a big hole in her.

Both the ship's lifeboats were manned and lowered but one capsized throwing three men into the water. Two were picked up, but the other, John McLean, couldn't be found. Standing by the *Glenartney*, the crew watched her sink stern first before they rowed off towards the Royal Sovereign Lightship. They hadn't gone far when they were spotted by the naval torpedo boat *No.3* which took them safely into Newhaven.

Captain Craig was very suspicious of the steamer he had been observing in the moments leading up to the torpedo strike. It crossed his mind that it could have been acting as a parent ship to the submarine. It had made some very odd manoeuvres and had made no attempt to assist him. The Navy made a search to locate the steamer. Eventually, she was found to be the SS *Strathfillan*. Her master said he had indeed seen the attack on the *Glenartney* but then saw the submarine heading for him and only by fleeing at full speed did he save his own ship.

U-34 claimed the *Glenartney*.

14/37: VASILLISA OLGA. *Country:* Greek. *Date sunk:* 11/2/17. *Tons nett:* 916. *Tons gross:* 1456. *Built:* 1870. *Type:* SS. *Rig:* schooner. *Owners:* Andreciades Piraeus. *Cargo:* 1666 tons coal, Port Talbot to Dunkirk. *Armed:* No. *Position:* 5 miles S of the Royal Sovereign Light Vessel (50 38 30N; 00 26 30E). *Master's name:* S. Papapeteos. *Crew:* 20.

DETAILS of this sinking are taken from a report by W. Brewster, commander of patrol vessel HMD *Evadne*, Portsmouth. There is little else in the records possibly due to language difficulties between the interviewing officer and the Greek master.

Captain Brewster wrote: "Sir, I have the honour to report that on February 11, 1917, whilst escorting SS *Sanda Isabelle* from Anvil Point to Folkstone Gate, at 7am, 3½ miles south by west from the Royal Sovereign Light Vessel, we picked up a lifeboat with the crew of 20 men from the Greek SS *Vasclissa Olga* sunk by bombs from an enemy submarine at 4am on the 11th. The vessel left Port Talbot on the 8th and was bound for Dunkirk laden with coal.

"On being relieved of the convoy at Folkstone Gate I made signal for permission to land the crew. At 12.10pm I received a reply to proceed to the Downs and report to the guardship. I reported to the guardship at 4.15pm and received permission from guard at 6.45 to land the Greek crew at Deal Pier. The crew were all landed and handed over to customs officials at 8pm."

14/38: MEDEA. *Country:* Dutch.
Date sunk: 25/3/15. *Tons nett:* 714. *Tons gross:*
1235. *Built:* 1913. *Type:* SS. *Rig:* schooner.
Owners: Koninklijke Nederlandshe Stoomboot,
Maatschabbij. *Cargo:* 1200 tons of oranges, Spain
to Whynright & Co, London. *Armed:* No.
Position: 5 miles S of Royal Sovereign LV
(50 39 00N; 00 27 00E). *Master's name:* A.F.M.
Van Balkon. *Crew:* 24.

THE Valencia district of Spain is where the *Medea's*
cargo is described as originating. Heading for London,
Medea called at the Isle of Wight and was told by a
naval trawler to go into Sandown Bay for examination.
Having been checked out and as there were no fresh
orders for her, she continued on her way.

On March 25, 1915, with conditions calm but
foggy, the German submarine *U-28* was able to close
quietly with the *Medea* off her port quarter and hoisted
the signal 'send boat.'

The first mate climbed into the lifeboat clutching
the ships papers and headed for the submarine. He
was confident there wouldn't be a problem as the
Medea was Dutch and her papers were in order. She
also flew the correct Dutch flag and had Medea of
Amsterdam in big letters on her side.

After looking at the ship's papers the German
commander, Oberleutnant Baron Von Forstner, told
the mate that his crew should take to the boats as he
intended to sink her, an unusual action at this early
stage of the war. Having no choice in the matter
Medea's men rowed clear of their ship and watched
the submarine's deck gun pound her until she sank.
The submarine took the ship's boats in tow but slipped
them ten minutes later and dived. The crew were
found soon after by *HMS Teviot*.

14/39: ALAUNIA. *Country:* British.
Date sunk: 19/10/16. *Tons nett:* 8261. *Tons
gross:* 13405. *Built:* 1913. *Type:* SS. *Rig:* schooner.
Owners: Cunard SS Co, Pierhead, Liverpool.
Cargo: 8000 tons general from New York to
London. *Armed:* 1 x 4.7in gun. *Position:* 2 miles S
by E from Royal Soveriegn LV (50 41 00N;
00 27 15E). *Master's name:* Horace Mills Benison.
Crew: 187 plus 180 passengers.

HER final journey began when she left New York in
early October and arrived at Falmouth on the 17th to
discharge mails and passengers. She left there at 1pm
on the 18th and headed up the channel for London.
At 4am the log entry put the ship at four miles off
Beachy Head with the master, first and third officers
on the bridge. The liner was speeding along at 15
knots, fast enough to give even the best U-boat a run
for her money.

At 4.30am she suffered a huge explosion directly
under her keel, thought at first by all concerned to
have been a torpedo attack. However, later information
revealed that she had run into an enemy minefield.

The explosion was enormous, so powerful that both
propeller shafts were completely disabled, bringing
the ship to an abrupt halt. Captain Benison sounded
the general alarm, ordering all persons to go to their
boat stations and standby. Meanwhile, he wanted to
know what the situation was below and shouted for the
chief engineer to give him a report. It wasn't good,
the engine room was flooding, the water was up to
the stokehold plates and increasing rapidly. Because
the propeller shafts had been severed the engines were
useless and had been shut down.

After instructing the radio operator to start sending
SOS messages the master ordered the boats away.
Two left quickly and smoothly, made easy by the light
wind and calm sea. But on spotting an approaching
patrol boat the master stopped any more from
launching and ordered those already in the water to
stay close. Torpedo boat *No 3* arrived at 5am and
began to take off passengers and crew. The steamer
was riding steady on two anchors, still settling but
nowhere near to being life threatening. More and more
patrol boats arrived. At one stage there were two patrol
boats and five naval destroyers around her.

The abandoning continued and one at a time the
boats were lowered down to the waterline to the
waiting patrol boats. Through lack of experience by
some of the crew, one boat was lowered too quickly
and threw several people into the water.
Unfortunately, this resulted in two men being
drowned, the second steward and a trimmer. The
master with his immediate officers were the last to
leave and ended up in patrol boat *TB3*. The majority of
the crew were being taken to Dover but the master
wanted to stay close to his ship to see what would
become of her.

The patrol ship *P3*, commanded by A J Landon,
arrived at 6.30am and later commented that the *Alaunia*
was upright and it was difficult to discern that anything
was wrong with her. He was surprised to find that
nobody was on board and eventually found the master
on *TB3*. He went alongside and asked if he had
abandoned the steamer to which Benison replied he
had, so Landon then asked if he could put his men
aboard to try and get her in tow. The master agreed
but added that he thought it might be dangerous.

The *Alaunia* had started to list slightly but Captain
Landon thought it was well worth trying a tow as it
would take just two miles to beach her. A tug had
been sent for but was very slow in coming. A party of
men from *P3* boarded the steamer and set about
getting her ready to tow but had great difficulty
bringing in the anchors. *Alaunia's* master said it was
ridiculous trying and too dangerous with the ship
listing at 45 degrees. Captain Landon said it was
nowhere near as bad as that and claimed that if a tow
had been tried two hours earlier she could have been
beached.

At 9am a tug arrived but by then it was too late.
The steamer had settled down very low in the water
with a list to port and at 9.20am she rolled over and
sank by the stern.

The SS *Alaunia*, passing through the Suez Canal in 1915. She sank the following year after hitting a mine.

The Admiralty were adamant that the master had prematurely left his ship and that he was responsible for not getting her in tow sooner. All the wheels for a full enquiry were set in motion but months later a lot of the witnesses were just not available because of their war service. In the end it was decided to abandon the enquiry, and to get on with fighting the war.

UC-16 laid the minefield which sank the *Alunia*.

14/40: F.D. LAMBERT. *Country:* British. *Date sunk:* 13/2/17. *Tons nett:* 1330. *Tons gross:* 2195. *Built:* 1892. *Type:* SS. *Rig:* schooner. *Owners:* James Westoll, 13, John St, Sunderland. *Cargo:* 2800 tons coal, Newcastle to Savona. *Armed:* 1 x 13pdr gun. *Position:* 1 mile E of Royal Sovereign LV (50 43 20N; 00 27 40E). *Master's name:* W.C. Lamb. *Crew:* 26. *Crew nationality:* 20 British, 2 Swedish, 1 Dutch, 1 Spanish, 1 French, 1 Chinese. *Gunners:* George Sinclair, LS RNR, No 3485 C; David J Harris, AB RNVR, No 8631.

F.D. LAMBERT was zig-zagging her way along, making a little over eight knots. The weather wasn't bad but the sea had quite a swell to it and every now and again a small squall would come through. The officer of the watch had just completed his routine checks and could see about a mile ahead that he was still in company with the SS *Wyndham*.

The torpedo struck the steamer on the port side just abreast of the foremast. A huge explosion followed, throwing up an enormous wave of water and blowing the hatch covers clean off. The damage was severe, a large hole in her side letting in water at a dangerously fast rate. She started to settle rapidly and the master gave the order to abandon.

The operation was smoothly done and 22 men got away just moments before the steamer went down. Four men were left behind but they shouted that they would drag out the small jolly boat and would be all right. It was a dark night but even so some of the men said they could see the shape of a submarine's conning tower about 50yds away.

The 22 men were eventually spotted by I.A. Smith, the commander of HMAT No 2661, *Fuji*, who picked them up. On hearing that a boat with four men was missing he made enquiries, and found they had reached the Royal Sovereign Light Ship. Most of the crew were taken to Dover.

14/41: LULLINGTON. *Country:* British. *Date sunk:* 8/2/17. *Tons nett:* 1821. *Tons gross:* 2816. *Built:* 1903 *Type:* SS. *Rig:* schooner. *Owners:* Bell Symondson Co, 32, Lime St, London. *Cargo:* 4220 tons coal, Blyth for Rouen. *Armed:* No. *Position:* 3 miles E of Royal Sovereign LV (50 43 00N; 00 32 00E). *Master's name:* W. Miller. *Crew:* 26.

THE master stood on the foredeck and wondered what it was that had just passed down the starboard side of his ship. It was dark, moving very fast against his ship's eight knots, just below the surface and made a large swirl as it passed by. He didn't have to wait long to find out as a few minutes later a torpedo slammed into his port side near number two hold throwing up such a spout of water that it drenched him where he stood.

The ship settled rapidly. Captain Miller ordered the crew away in the boats which was quickly done. In ten minutes the ship was gone.

A few miles away the commander of the patrol trawler *Highlander*, Lieut Brotchie RNR, was slipping his sweep wires. He had heard the explosion and could see that something was very wrong just on the horizon. Heading off at full speed he put out a radio message that a submarine was in sight. By the time he reached the area there was no sign of the *Lullington*, no wreckage or crew. He decided that the crew must have got clear and correctly gathered that they would have made for the Royal Sovereign Light Ship. He headed off towards it to make sure and found one of the boats, the other had already made it.

The Admiralty were not impressed with the fact that the *Lullington* was not zig-zagging as ordered and ask the master for an explanation. Presumably he had a reason but his explanation is not included in the records.

14/42: HMT AGATE. *Country:* British.
Date sunk: 14/3/18. *Tons nett:* –. *Tons gross:* 248. *Built:* –. *Type:* patrol trawler. *Rig:* minesweeper. *Owners:* Admiralty. *Cargo:* –. *Armed:* Yes. *Position:* 6 miles ENE of Royal Sovereign LV (50 46 15N; 00 34 03E). *Master's name:* –. *Crew:* 11.

THE Court of Enquiry into the sinking of HMT 1635, *Agate*, was held at The Pavilion, The Naval Pier, Dover, on Monday March 18, 1918. It was not a long enquiry and few people were called to give evidence. The judgement of the court was that *Agate* had struck a mine and everything had been done to save her. Blame for her loss could not be attributed to anyone.

Agate was on mine sweeping duties in the area around the Royal Sovereign Light Vessel. The vessel in command of the whole sweeping operation was HMS *Attentive III*, captained by Lieutenant Graham Alexander Deuchar, RNR. He was called to give evidence and to clarify the orders he had been given.

Agate's sweeping partner was HMT *Actaeon*. *Agate's* first officer, Herbert Jack Lynton, said that they connected up with *Actaeon* at 6.30am and commenced the sweep a few minutes after. They had been sweeping for about 10 minutes when there was a huge explosion from under the forefoot. The blast was so violent that it blew him completely over the side into the water. Somewhat stunned he managed to get back to the *Agate* and hauled himself aboard. He saw the skipper lying on the deck and rushed to his assistance. He had a nasty gash on his head which was bleeding quite heavily, and was very dazed. The skipper was still in hospital when the Court of Enquiry was held and therefore unable to attend.

John Henry Southwick, engineman, RNR, said that he was down in the engine room at the time of the explosion and felt a huge shock. He rushed up on deck to see what was going on and witnessed a scene of utter chaos. Several men had been blown over the side, the skipper was lying injured and the *Agate* was sinking rapidly.

Close by *Agate*, Charles Joseph Sheldon, RNR, Skipper of HMT *Delphine*, had seen what happened. He immediately sent some of his crew in a boat to help. They managed to rescue seven of the *Agate's* crew. However, four of those were injured and all of them were suffering from shock. Four men were missing.

Agate sank very soon after in 10 fathoms of water.

14/43: EBENEZER. *Country:* British.
Date sunk: 15/7/17. *Tons nett:* 149. *Tons gross:* 300. *Built:* Kingston in 1860. *Type:* SV. *Rig:* brigantine. *Owners:* John Hyland, 61, King St, Garston, Liverpool. *Cargo:* 299 tons steam coal, Garston for Dieppe. *Armed:* No. *Position:* 25 miles NW of Dieppe (50 11 00N; 00 35 00E). *Master's name:* Charles Hunter. *Crew:* 6. *Crew nationality:* British.

WHEN a shell threw up a large spout of water about 100yds ahead of the *Ebenezer*, the master quickly scanned the area around the ship. Apart from what looked like a drifter three miles off there was nothing else in sight. Again he heard a hiss and another shell sliced into the water ahead. He concluded that it could only have come from the drifter. Deciding that whatever it was he was going to get as far away from it as possible he shouted to his crew to get the ship more close hauled to wind. *Ebenezer* responded well to the change but it was not enough. Minutes later the drifter had got much closer but even more to the master's alarm she had changed into a German submarine.

The commander of the submarine wasted no time in ordering the master of the *Ebenezer* to take to his boat and come to him. The master was taken on board the enemy vessel while some of the German crew used his boat to plant several bombs on the little brig. When they returned the master was angry to see that they had looted his ship and were carrying food, clothes, ropes, instruments – in fact just about anything that wasn't nailed down.

As Captain Hunter and his crew were set adrift his ship sank as the bombs exploded. He asked the German commander if he would at least give his boat a tow a bit closer to the French coast but the commander just waved him aside, telling him to head for England instead. It was 3pm when they set off on the long haul to land and at 9pm they were still going. However, a French patrol boat spotted them and landed them at Poole in the early hours of the following morning.

14/44: BRODERICK. *Country:* British.
Date sunk: 29/4/18. *Tons nett:* 2786. *Tons gross:*
4321. *Built:* Stockton in 1890. *Type:* SS. *Rig:* –.
Owners: The Broderick SS Co, 19/21, Bury St,
London. *Cargo:* In ballast with 50 prize cattle,
London and Dunkirk to Venezuela. *Armed:* 1 x
4.7in Japanese gun. *Position:* 7 miles SSE of
Hastings (50 46 20N; 00 37 45E). *Master's
name:* George Ernest Copper. *Crew:* 67. *Crew
nationality:* 20 British, 2 Swedish, 45 Chinese.

THE main cargo of the *Broderick* was walking around
in pens on her deck and described as 50 prize cattle.

It was 1.10pm when the first torpedo struck the
Broderick on her port side in number two hold. The
damage wasn't that bad although she was taking on
water and a nasty vibration had started up in the
engine room. The master decided that he would turn
the stern of the ship to bear directly away from where
he believed the submarine to be and try to make a run
for it towards Dungeness.

It went well for half an hour. The master had sent
out a wireless message that he was under attack and
hoped that a patrol vessel would come to his rescue
very soon. The commander of the submarine,
Oberleutnant Johann Lohs, however, had other ideas
and postioned himself for another shot at the steamer.
It was another direct hit on the port side that slowed
the *Broderick* down completely, leaving her in such a
sinking state that the master had no choice but to order
her to be abandoned. As if that were not trouble
enough the large contingent of Chinese crew decided
rush the boats, complete with bags and belongings.
It took Captain Copper some time to restore order
and to convince the Chinese crew that they could not
take bags with them, there was simply no room.

The boats were ordered to stand off the steamer
and wait for help. *Broderick* settled lower and lower in
the water until finally at 4.40pm she sank by the head.
The position was virtually the same as that of another
steamer, the *Carlisle Castle*, which had been sunk
two months earlier. Help did come eventually for the
crew of the *Broderick* in the form of the Hastings
Lifeboat and several patrol trawlers.

14/45: CARLISLE CASTLE. *Country:* British.
Date sunk: 14/2/18. *Tons nett:* 2709. *Tons
gross:* 4325. *Built:* 1913. *Type:* SS. *Rig:* –. *Owners:*
The Union Castle SS Co Ltd. *Cargo:* 5300 tons
grain, oil, fuel & general. *Armed:* 1 x 4.7in Japanese
gun. *Position:* 8 miles E by N of Royal Sovereign
LV (50 46 00N; 00 38 00E). *Master's name:*
Charles John Duncan. *Crew:* 48. *Crew nationality:*
39 British, 3 Belgians, 3 Danes, 1 Russian, 2
Americans. *Gunners:* Wells; Kerrison.

THE whole journey from the USA to the Channel had
not been a good one for the *Carlisle Castle*. The
weather had been bad during the crossing and the
steamer's steering gear packed up at one stage, forcing

the convoy to leave her behind. The engineers
eventually sorted out the steering problem and she
made it on her own to Falmouth.

Her cargo was too valuable to be left to go up the
Channel unescorted so the patrol vessel *Venetia II*
accompanied her as far as Start Point where HMT
Buffalo II took over. At first all was well but after a
while the superior speed of *Carlisle Castle* meant that
she lost her escort and continued up to St Catherines
Point, once again on her own. Here she was stopped
by another patrol trawler who ordered the master to
follow him into St Helens.

After the master explained the situation he was
instructed to proceed up to Beachy Head with the
escort *Magnolia III* and at 11pm on February 13, both
ships set off. There should have been another patrol
vessel waiting at Beachy Head but there wasn't, so
the commander of *Magnolia III* obtained permission to
stay with the steamer. On several occasions the
commander of *Magnolia III* signalled to Captain
Duncan to slow down as he was finding it hard to
keep up. It was on one of those occasions, when a
mile and a half separated the the two ships, that the
waiting enemy submarine commander (Johann Lohs in
UB-57) decided to strike.

The commander of *Magnolia III* had seen the
periscope but was too far away to do anything about it.
He ordered his gunners to fire a couple of shells at
the periscope but by then it was too late, the torpedo
had smashed into the starboard side of the steamer
opening up a huge hole.

Captain Duncan turned towards the shore. The ship
was settling down fast and he rang down to the engine
room to reduce power. He got no answer, the fourth
engineer of the watch, Mr Walker, was lying dead,
killed by the explosion. Within a few minutes flames
were leaping out of the funnel and number one hatch,
leaving the master no alternative but to abandon ship.

The boats pulled clear of the stricken steamer at
8.25am, ten minutes later *Carlisle Castle* sank.
Magnolia III was at hand to pick the men up and was
soon speeding up and down looking for the enemy
submarine, but without success.

The Admiralty made a lot of enquiries about this
sinking and ended up sending a letter to the owners of
the *Carlisle Castle*. They pointed out that the only
time a master of a merchant ship could be forgiven
for leaving an escort vessel behind was if the escort
fell below seven knots in speed. The *Magnolia III*
had been making nine knots and Captain Duncan had
been signalled several times to slow down in order
to keep station. However, they added little more than
a caution for him to be more careful in future.

14/46: GERMAN SUBMARINE (possible).
Country: German. *Date believed sunk:* 7/4/18. *Tons
nett:* –. *Tons gross:* –. *Built:* –. *Type:* –. *Owners:*
German navy. *Armed:* Yes. *Position:* 12 miles S by
W of Dungeness (50 44 00N; 00 38 00E). *Master's
name:* –. *Crew:* –. *Crew nationality:* German.

ALTHOUGH there was no definite proof that this attack was completely successful the Admiralty gave it the tag of 'Probably sunk'.

The vessel concerned was the patrol vessel *P12*, commanded by Lieutenant George L.H. Deane, RNR. His report stated that he was in company with *P75* escorting two steamers, *Massasoit* and *Mockta*. It was 2.25pm on April 7, 1918, when one of the watch on the bridge shouted that he could see the top of the conning tower of a submarine about 200yds off the starboard bow. It looked as though the submarine was about to take up a position to sink the *Mockta* with a torpedo. Orders were given to put the helm to starboard and to aim for a position about 25yds ahead of the enemy vessel.

As the periscope turned the German commander spotted *P12* bearing down on him. Within seconds the periscope disappeared as the submarine crash-dived, but *P12* had already launched the first depth charge. In his report, Lieutenant Deane said that as the first charge, set to 50ft, went over he felt a slight jolt as if his ship had made contact with the conning tower of the submarine, others on board *P12* felt it too.

Lieutenant Deane continued to drop depth charges to form what he described as, a diamond shape, returning to the position where the first had been dropped. On arrival at the spot he said that huge volumes of oil were rising to the surface amid a steady stream of bubbles. By this time *P75* had also joined in the attack and after dropping depth charges ahead of the last known track of the submarine, met *P12* at the spot where the oil was still surfacing. Six hours later it was reported that oil and bubbles were still rising. It was noted in the records that attempts were to be made at some stage later to put divers down to check.

Although there are no reports confirming this sinking, two people were rewarded for their efforts in the action. Lieutenant Deane was awarded the DSC, and a gunner, Webber, was mentioned in the Gazette.

German records show no loss for this date.

14/47: ALICE. *Country:* French.
Date sunk: 21/11/16. *Tons nett:* 449. *Tons gross:* 822. *Built:*1911. *Type:* SS. *Rig:* schooner. *Owners:* Leraux Hensey, 5, Rue de Harcourt, Rouen. *Cargo:* 1160 tons coal, South Shields to Rouen. *Armed:* No. *Position:* 19 miles SE from Beachy Head (50 32 00N; 00 38 00E). *Master's name:* F. Poerean. *Crew:* 14.

THE Admiralty accused the master of not adhering to his sailing instructions. The position he gave as being sunk put him a long way from his given route and they wanted to know why.

The master said that he spotted what looked like a sailing vessel about two miles off flying French colours. At first he thought it was just that, but then realised that it was a German submarine flying French colours to fool him. It certainly worked as later the submarine was alongside *Alice*, her commander demanding that the master and his crew abandon their ship and bring the ship's papers over to him.

The master did as he was told and ordered his crew to take to the boats, but before he left he threw his confidential sailing instructions into the furnace. The master was taken on board the submarine and questioned about his ship. While this was going on several German sailors forced his crew to row them over to the *Alice* where they planted bombs. It was a smooth operation as ten minutes later the steamer went to the bottom.

The men were found by the Danish steamer *Sigrin* and taken on board. Later they were transferred to the patrol trawler No 289 *Glenboyne* and landed at Dover.

It is not clearly recorded why the master was in the position he was and although the Admiralty were not impressed with him there is no record of them putting him on the blacklist.

14/48: CONCORD. *Country:* British.
Date sunk: 22/3/15. *Tons nett:* –. *Tons gross:* 2861. *Built:* Sunderland in 1902. *Type:* SS. *Rig:* schooner. *Owners:* Thomas Smailer & Son, Victoria Place, Whitby, Yorks. *Cargo:* 4450 tons grain, Gwesto of Rosario to Bouge & Co, Leith. *Armed:* No. *Position:* 9m SE from Royal Sovereign LV (50 39 00N; 00 39 00E). *Master's name:* Edgar Calver. *Crew:* 26.

HAVING made the long run from Rosario in South America, *Concord* had only to negotiate the English Channel and run up to Scotland. According to war time rules her lifeboats were swung out in readiness as she steamed along at a steady nine knots.

On March 22, 1915, her journey came to an abrupt end when a torpedo smashed into her starboard side. Such was the violence of the explosion that it almost ripped the side of the ship out, filling the stokehold and engine room with water and totally destroying the two port lifeboats. Amazingly, all the crew managed to get on deck and 23 of them piled into the starboard lifeboat while the other three took to the gig. Later one of the men was transferred from the lifeboat to the gig as it was in imminent danger of joining the *Concord* which had by this time sunk. All the crew were found by the naval patrol boat *Wren* which took them to Dover. *U-34* was the U-boat involved.

14/49: ELDRA. *Country:* British.
Date sunk: 19/10/17. *Tons nett:* 190. *Tons gross:* 227. *Built:* Plymouth in 1873. *Type:* SV. *Rig:* Barque. *Owners:* J. Johnson Brown & Co, Newcastle. *Cargo:* 372 tons anthracite. *Armed:* No. *Position:* 35 miles NW of Treport (50 25 00N; 00 39 00E). *Master's name:* Walter Hicks Truscott. *Crew:* 6. *Crew nationality:* 5 British, 1 Belgian.

ELDRA'S luck ran out when one of the watchmen noticed the shape of a conning tower about four miles to the north-west. At first the master wasn't sure if it was a submarine but it was soon confirmed when a shell threw up a spout of water

The master realised that there was nothing he could do but to abandon his ship or face more and more shells. Even as they pulled clear of their ship the submarine's gun kept firing and each shot was closer. Eventually the enemy came alongside their boat and ordered them aboard. The master had his hands tied to a rail. The rest of the crew were herded together at gunpoint as an officer watched their boat being rowed by a German bombing party over to the *Eldra*. He turned to the men and warned them that if a man was found to be left on the *Eldra* when his men boarded the master would be shot immediately.

The raiding party did a thorough job and luckily for the master all the crew had left in the boat.After placing the bombs in places where they would do the most damage, the raiders helped themselves to food and instruments. A few minutes later the two bombs exploded sending the little ship to the bottom.

When back at the submarine the Germans for some reason tried to hoist the boat on board the submarine, maybe they intended to take the crew closer to shore, but they only succeeded in capsizing it, spilling all the equipment out. The crew were then told to leave but with no paddles could only float and go with the wind and tide. They managed to take up some inner seating planks to act as paddles and put the boat before the wind. It worked well and at 3am on October 20, they landed near Fecamp.

The position given is the position generally accepted where the incident took place. However, there are several given in the documents. One is 42 miles south-east of Owers Light and another 35 miles north-west of Dieppe.

14/50: BLACKWOOD. *Country:* British.
Date sunk: 9/3/15. *Tons nett:* –. *Tons gross:* 1230.
Built: Blyth in 1907. *Type:* SS. *Rig:* schooner.
Owners: Tyneside Hull Ltd, Millburn House, Newcastle-on-Tyne. *Cargo:* 1627 tons coal, Ashington Coal Co, Blyth, to Woruis & Co, Havre.
Armed: No. *Position:* 18 miles SW by S of Dungeness L.H. (50 40 00N; 00 42 00E). *Master's name:* John Souter. *Crew:* 17.

BLACKWOOD sailed from Blyth on March 7, 1915, at 7am on the high tide. The weather was good and the wind light. She made good progress and was abreast of Dungeness on the 9th at about 4am when a new course was set to south-west magnetic for Cape Antifer. The first mate was on the bridge and logged that she was making nine knots.

At 6.10am the peace of the voyage was shattered when the ship suddenly shuddered under an explosion on the port side amidships. A torpedo had slammed into the side of her and according to the crew they heard the plates of number two stokehold bulkhead rip open.

The master and crew were on deck immediately and subsequently reported that they could see a submarine on the port beam about two and a half miles away. The boats were ordered to be lowered and the crew got clear of their rapidly sinking ship. When about half a mile clear of her the crew reported seeing another submarine and another steamer. The first submarine had been heading in the direction of the steamer which later disappeared. This was most likely to have been the SS *Beeswing* which probably shared a similar fate (see 15/2).

Blackwood disappeared at about 6.30am. Her crew were found by the trawler *H.R.B.* of Ramsgate at 9am and landed safely ashore at Newhaven.

U-35 claimed to have torpedoed her.

14/51: MAINE. *Country:* French.
Date sunk: 21/11/17. *Tons nett:* –. *Tons gross:* 773.
Built: –. *Type:* SS. *Rig:* –. *Owners:* London, Brighton & French State Railways. *Cargo:* 522 tons ammunition, 5 tons medical stores, 76 tons blankets, Newhaven for Dieppe. *Armed:* Yes.
Position: S 16 deg E from Beachy Head 37 miles (50 17 00N; 00 42 00E). *Master's name:* Jean Maller. *Crew:* 35. *Crew nationality:* 28 French, 7 British.

THE account of the sinking is given by the commanding officer of the auxiliary patrol vessel *Smew*, who escorted *Maine* out of Newhaven at 5.15pm on November 21, 1917. He stated that they set a course south-east for 10 miles then altered course to south by east half east. At 9pm *Maine* signalled that she was stopping to put her sweeps out and they continued at reduced speed as it was not safe to enter Dieppe before 2am.

At 10.20pm the commander of *Smew* stated that he heard an explosion in the direction of the *Maine* and concluded that she had probably struck a mine. He looked in the direction of the steamer only to be met five seconds later by a terrific explosion. Such was the severity of the blast that pieces of debris fell onto the decks of *Smew* and flames leapt over 100ft into the air. *Maine* had been completely blown to pieces as the initial explosion set off the ammunition in her holds.

Smew immediately closed in on the spot and sent a boat in among the scattered wreckage. A thorough search was made but only one man was discovered alive.

14/52: ST EMILION. *Country:* French.
Date sunk: 27/7/17. *Tons nett:* 658. *Tons gross:* 1111. *Built:* 1916. *Type:* SS. *Rig:* schooner.
Owners: Messrs Worms & Co, Paris. *Cargo:* 1440 tons nitrate of ammonia in 5583 casks, Skien, Norway, for Rouen. *Armed:* No. *Position:* 12 miles W by S of Dungeness (50 47 40N; 00 42 40E).
Master's name: J. Svendsen. *Crew:* 17.

ST EMILION picked up her cargo at Skien, a large consignment of casks of nitrate of ammonia, and headed for Rouen. There is not a lot of information in the records of exactly what happened but a large explosion occurred in the hold before the bridge. The master said it was more on the starboard side but couldn't be sure. It wasn't known if she had struck a mine or had fallen victim to a German submarine.

The master stated that the explosion was so violent that it upset a paraffin lamp in the charthouse which burst into flames. He tried desperately to put it out but it was no use. Because of the fire he was unable to get to his confidential papers so instead set about saving his crew. The fire or the papers mattered little in the end as 35 minutes later *St Emilion* leaned over on her starboard side and sank bow first.

The master and crew had got clear in the ship's boat and were rescued by HMAD *Majesty*. All of them were uninjured and landed safely in the early hours of the following morning when they were handed over to Messrs Hammond & Co, who housed them at the sailors home at Dover.

Lloyd's listed her as mined.

14/53: WAR MONARCH. *Country:* British. *Date sunk:* 14/2/18. *Tons nett:* 6104. *Tons gross:* 7887. *Built:* 1917. *Type:* SS. *Rig:* schooner. *Owners:* Cunard SS Co, 51, Bishopsgate, London. *Cargo:* 9200 tons coal, 300 tons pig iron for Genoa. *Armed:* 1 x 4.7in gun. *Position:* 11 miles E by N from Royal Sovereign LV (50 46 00N; 00 43 00E). *Master's name:* Robert Baker. *Crew:* 41. *Gunners:* Act Bombadier Gilmour, RMA; Ernest Jackson, RMA; James William Trigg, RMA, No ON 8331.

THE commander of patrol boat *P49* said that he spotted a steamer at 8.20 on the evening of February 14, 1918, showing dimmed side lights and appeared to be stationary. He sent several signals by lamp to her but failed to get any response. He continued cautiously toward her and came across a lifeboat containing 17 men from the steamer *War Monarch*.

After leaving Hull on February 11, *War Monarch* steamed south calling in at Southend for orders which directed her to go on to Portsmouth. At 7.30pm on the 14th, the first mate who had the watch said that he saw a light ahead which forced him to alter course slightly. As he made the manoeuvre a huge explosion tore out a large lump of the steamer's starboard side causing water to pour into the engine room. Although nobody actually spotted anything it was strongly suspected by all concerned that a torpedo from an enemy U-boat was responsible.

It was obvious to the master that the ship was settling down rapidly and the damage being so severe there was no alternative but to abandon ship. Two boats were launched, one commanded by the master and the other in the hands of the first mate. With the weather being fine the master decided it would be wise to stay near the sinking steamer and wait for help. One of the boats did manage to stray away in the darkness but was intercepted by the trawler *Boy Leslie*.

At 8.40pm, the crew rescued by *P49*, watched as their ship finally gave in to the rising water as she rolled over and sank.

UB-57 claimed to have torpedoed her.

14/54: EFEU. *Country:* Norwegian. *Date sunk:* 22/3/17. *Tons nett:* –. *Tons gross:* –. *Built:* Portland, USA, 1909. *Type:* SV. *Rig:* 4 masted schooner. *Owners:* H.T. Realfsen, Skein, Norway. *Cargo:* In ballast, Falmouth to Porsgrund, Norway. *Armed:* No. *Position:* 10 miles WSW of Dungeness (50 51 00N; 00 44 00E). *Master's name:* George Johansen. *Crew:* 10.

THE weather was calm with a smooth sea allowing the master of the *Efeu* to hug the coast. However, it also allowed the commander of a German submarine to go in close and attack her, firing seven shells in rapid succession.

The master had given the order to abandon ship after the first shell sliced through his rigging. They pulled clear leaving the *Efeu* to the mercy of the enemy who gave her little, pounding her with another 16 shells until she could take no more. The master half expected to be questioned by the German commander but he ignored the men in the boat and sped away, perhaps feeling a little vulnerable at being so close to the shore.

The crew drifted in the boat through the night, the weather remaining kind to them throughout. At around 5.15am they were spotted by a lookout on the minesweeper No 576 *Kylemore*, which picked them up about seven miles south-west of Beachy Head and landed them at Eastbourne.

14/55: EUPHORBIA. *Country:* British. *Date sunk:* 1/12/17. *Tons nett:* 1887. *Tons gross:* 3109. *Built:* 1916. *Type:* SS. *Rig:* –. *Owners:* Robinson & Sons, North Shields. *Cargo:* 4700 tons of rice ex Burma, 150 bales of hides ex Durban, 225 cases of crayfish and 414 bags of beans ex Capetown, all for London. *Armed:* 1 x 4.7in Japanese gun. *Position:* 12 miles E of Royal Sovereign LV (50 44 00N; 00 46 00E). *Master's name:* Charles Hunter. *Crew:* 35. *Gunner:* John Macleay, AB RNR, No C1533.

THE circumstances surrounding the sinking of the *Euphorbia* are very similar to those of the *Rydal Hall*, both vessels being on the same course about a mile apart.

Euphorbia soon found herself in what the master considered to be a minefield, a large explosion occurring between number three hold and the engine room. The ship filled with water almost instantly and several men were killed in the engine room.

The crew did manage to get some boats away and headed for the oncoming steamer *Rydal Hall*, her master having by this time realised that something was very wrong. It was while the *Rydal Hall* was trying to pick up one of the boats that she too suffered a huge explosion which tore a long gash in her starboard side.

A lot of confusion and chaos was the result, *Rydal Hall* sinking almost as fast as the *Euphorbia*. Out of the 35 crew only 21 from *Euphorbia* were picked up by HMS *John Pascoe*.

After reading the accounts of this loss the Admiralty were not at all impressed. They made a strong point that both ships should have been zig-zagging and whereby they accepted the masters 'lame excuses' for why they were not, they gave both of them a stern warning to adhere to sailing instructions in the future.

UC-75 torpedoed her.

14/56: RYDAL HALL. *Country:* British. *Date sunk:* 1/12/17. *Tons nett:* 2139. *Tons gross:* 3314. *Built:* 1889. *Type:* SS. *Rig:* s schooner. *Owners:* Hall Line Ltd, Tower Buildings, Liverpool. *Cargo:* 4300 tons manganese ore, jute, linseed oil, Calcutta to Dunkirk. *Armed:* 1 x 12pdr gun. *Position:* 12 miles E of Royal Sovereign LV (50 44 00N; 00 45 00E). *Master's name:* George Naylor. *Crew:* 59. *Crew nationality:* 56 British, 2 Philippinos, 1 Swede. *Gunners:* Richard Roberts, LS, No B2389 Devonport; David Robertson, AB, RNVR, No CZ6090.

RYDAL HALL was following in the wake of another steamer called *Euphorbia* when at 3.30am a watchman shouted that *Euphorbia* had suddenly put her helm to starboard. Another watchman on deck reported to the master that he could hear people shouting, "Hold on, being mined," or words to that effect. The master ordered the engines to be put full astern to slow the ship down.

Moving slowly into the area the master could see that the crew of *Euphorbia* had abandoned their ship and were making towards the *Rydal Hall*. One boat came alongside to starboard and the men were helped aboard. Another boat was pointed out to the helmsman in the distance and the *Rydal Hall* slowly made her way towards it. She got very close to the boat when suddenly a huge explosion boomed out from amidships blowing a gash in the steamer's side about 80ft long.

By the time the master had surveyed the damage the *Rydal Hall* was already well down in the water. He went to the chartroom to gather his papers but found that it was flooded. The two lifeboats on the starboard side had been smashed by the explosion and the port boats were not big enough to take all the crew. The master left the port boats in the capable hands of the first mate, Mr Snow, and with the chief engineer, Mr Faulds, went forward to free the raft he

had made for just such an emergency. The two men arrived at the raft with some difficulty as the main deck was by then well awash and found that the quartermaster, Mr Ruperts, was already on the raft having cut its lashings. It was just as well for no sooner had the master and chief engineer jumped onto it, than the ship sank leaving the raft floating free.

The three men heard many cries from all around and using bits of wood paddled around the area as best they could. They succeeded in finding three of *Euphorbia's* crew but soon the raft was taken away by the wind and tide. The men on the raft were found later that morning by HMS *John Pascoe*, commanded by Lieutenant Lawrence, and landed at Plymouth. Altogether 23 men perished.

The Admiralty were not very happy with the conduct of the masters of both steamers. Their sailing instructions had specifically stated that they should have been zig-zagging and had they done so the outcome might have been far less tragic. In a letter written by Captain Naylor to the Admiralty, he made the point that he wasn't zig-zagging because he had been instructed by an escort boat to stop doing so.

UC-75 torpedoed her.

14/57: ACHILLE ADAM. *Country:* British. *Date sunk:* 23/3/17. *Tons nett:* 212. *Tons gross:* 460. *Built:* 1887. *Type:* SS. *Rig:* schooner. *Owners:* SE & Chatham Railway Company, London Bridge. *Cargo:* In ballast, St Valery sur Somme to Newhaven. *Armed:* No. *Position:* 30 miles NW of Cayeux (50 24 00N; 00 47 00E). *Master's name:* Robert Hitchings Kilbee. *Crew:* 14 plus 3 soldiers.

"TO the master of *Achille Adam*. Being in all respects ready for sea, you will leave by the 11.20am tide today, when clear of the Somme, anchor in a safe position until dusk then proceed to Newhaven." These were the precise instructions given to Captain Kilbee by the Naval Transport Office just before he left St Valery on March 23, 1917. However, he did not follow them to the letter and consequently, said the Admiralty, lost his ship.

She sailed in company with the steamer *Exchange*, which shared a similar fate, passing the Bell Buoy at the mouth of the river at 11.25am. Both vessels having the same orders, they should have anchored close to Cayeux and waited until dusk. Instead the masters chose to carry straight on out to sea. At 1.30pm a German submarine appeared close to the *Achille Adam*, opening fire on her with such ferocity that two of the crew were killed and several others injured. The master was ordered to abandon his ship and go to the submarine.

After being questioned, the master asked the German commander for some bandages to treat his injured men but the commander replied that he had none. The men were told to clear off and the submarine moved in to sink the steamer with a few more shells before turning her attention to the *Exchange* nearby.

In the boat were three officers, three firemen, two seamen and three RMLI soldiers. Some of them were injured worse than others, but none were prepared for the long wait before being found. It wasn't until 4.45pm the next day that HMS *Alarm* spotted them, more than 26 hours later. Three had died of exposure during the night and one died just before being picked up.

The master was asked by the Admiralty to explain his actions, why he had not anchored as ordered and waited until dusk. Captain Kilbee replied from his hospital bed that he had always anchored and waited for dusk in the past but on that particular day the weather was too bad. The sea was heavy with a strong flood tide against wind situation. His orders were to anchor in a safe place until dusk but he could not find a safe place and as he had no other instructions, except that in such cases masters should use their own discretion, he decided to proceed.

The Admiralty did not take it any further. However, reading the notes passed around internally, they appeared to have expected nothing more of civilians, who would always try and find loopholes in their instructions.

14/58: MARGARET. *Country:* British.
Date sunk: 17/12/16. *Tons nett:* 20. *Tons gross:* 54. *Built:* Kirkintillock in 1905. *Type:* SV. *Rig:* schooner. *Owners:* W.E. Colebrook, Strand, Rye, Sussex. *Cargo:* None. *Armed:* No. *Position:* 8 miles SW by W of Dungeness (50 50 30N; 00 47 30E). *Master's name:* Mr Ford. *Crew:* 7.

MARGARET was in the fishing grounds off Dungeness at about 8.30am on December 17, 1916. The trawl was out and she began her track towards Hastings. It was a good run, scooping up plenty of fish. When off Hastings the master turned his ship and headed back towards Dungeness for another run. It proved to be even more successful and half way between the two points it became necessary to empty the trawl net.

All hands got involved in getting the trawl in, all totally unaware that they were in great danger. The 17 year old deck boy, Thomas Apps, was sent forward to fetch something. This was a stroke of luck on his part, for as he got there *Margaret* was completely blown to pieces. The young lad found himself floundering in the water, amid debris which had once been his ship.

The patrol trawler 3206 *Elysian* was close by. Her commander said later that they all heard a loud explosion and were just in time to see the pieces of *Margaret* sink. Two boats were sent into the wreckage but only young Thomas Apps was found alive.

The conclusion was that a mine had got caught up in *Margaret's* nets and exploded just as the net was being winched over the side.

14/59: EXCHANGE. *Country:* British.
Date sunk: 23/3/17. *Tons nett:* 96. *Tons gross:* 279. *Built:* 1884. *Type:* SS. *Rig:* schooner. *Owners:* Manchester, Liverpool & N.Wales SS Co Ltd, Liverpool. *Cargo:* In ballast from St Valery sur Somme for Newhaven. *Armed:* No. *Position:* 30 miles NW of Cayeux (50 24 30N; 00 47 30E). *Master's name:* Charles Edwards. *Crew:* 8.

EXCHANGE left St Valery sur Somme in company with the steamer *Achille Adam*, passing the Bell Buoy in the river at 11.25am on March 23, 1917. Her orders were to anchor at the mouth of the river and wait until dusk before proceeding to Newhaven. However, along with the master of the *Achille Adam*, Captain Edwards decided that the weather was too rough to anchor safely and pressed onwards out to sea.

Whether this action caused the loss of both ships or not was a sore point with the Admiralty, but the fact remains that at around 2pm the same day, a German submarine attacked both steamers unmercifully. The *Achille Adam* was the first to go, two of her men being killed during the shelling but four more died from exposure in the lifeboat during the night. *Exchange* was next but fared much worse, not a single person survived to tell the story.

14/60: CONSTER. *Country:* British.
Date sunk: 7/11/18. *Tons nett:* –. *Tons gross:* 25. *Built:* Rye in 1878. *Type:* SV. *Rig:* ketch. *Owners:* Thomas Borcham, 7, Margarets Terrace, Rye, Sussex. *Cargo:* –. *Armed:* No. *Position:* 2 miles SW of Gas Buoy, Rye Bay (50 52 00N; 00 48 00E). *Master's name:* Thomas Borcham. *Crew:* 3.

THERE is little in the records about this sinking. The *Conster* was trawling and had the misfortune to snag a mine in her nets. A huge explosion occurred close to the surface which sank the vessel almost instantly.

14/61: UTOPIA. *Country:* British.
Date sunk: 2/3/17. *Tons nett:* –. *Tons gross:* 160. *Built:* Rye in 1860. *Type:* SV. *Rig:* brigantine. *Owners:* Jas & Murdock, Poole, Dorset. *Cargo:* 295 tons pitch from Watkins & Tickett, London to De Parce, Rouen. *Armed:* No. *Position:* 20 miles SSW of Dungeness (50 35 00N; 00 48 00E). *Master's name:* John Petersen. *Crew:* 6. *Crew nationality:* 5 British, 1 Dutch.

THE master of *Utopia* had tried to follow the instructions given to him at Southend, to stay as close to the French coast as possible. But the wind had dropped off to a virtual calm allowing his vessel to drift towards Dungeness. The master was on deck with two seaman waiting for the wind. They were not alone with their troubles. About half a mile to the south was another sailing vessel, *Gazelle*, also wallowing with slack sails. Captain Petersen spotted a black speck about two miles off, low in the water and definitely heading towards his ship. He watched as the object got closer and closer until it was clearly a submarine.

The first shell whimpered over the *Utopia's* rigging. That was enough for the master who ordered his men to take to the boat. By the time they launched it another two shells had cracked by but fortunately both went wide. The crew pulled away to the north and hoped the Germans would leave them alone. Fifteen minutes later three more shots were heard by the crew and they turned to see their ship go down a few minutes later. The submarine's crew paid no attention to the men but sped off after another victim, the *Gazelle*.

At 9pm the six men of the *Utopia* were spotted by Commander H. Humphrey of HMAT No 1602, *Returno*, who picked them up and landed them safely at Dover.

14/62: NETTA. *Country:* British.
Date sunk: 3/9/16. *Tons nett:* 177. *Tons gross:* 370.
Built: Montrose in 1909. *Type:* SS. *Rig:* schooner.
Owners: G.B. Gillie, Baltic Chambers, Newcastle.
Cargo: Water ballast, Rouen to Newcastle.
Armed: No. *Position:* 35 miles NE from Cape Antifer (50 06 30N; 00 48 00E). *Master's name:* Norris Henry Finch. *Crew:* 10.

A LARGE German submarine surfaced very close to *Netta* and fired a shell at her. It wasn't a direct hit but it ripped the canvas away from the bridge, making it very clear to the master that her commander meant business. The master put the telegraph to stop and waited to see what the next move would be. A minute or so later a stream of flags appeared on the submarine's short mast which read, 'Abandon your ship and come to me.'

The master asked the mate to go with him and together they rowed the 200yds or so to the waiting submarine. The commander ordered the master aboard and informed him that his ship was to be sunk. It was pointless to argue, the boat was already being rowed back to the steamer by two sailors clutching bombs.

Not content with planting two bombs the German sailors helped themselves to clocks, barometers, provisions and anything else they could carry. Herding the rest of the crew into the boat they set off back to the submarine with their haul and waited for the bombs to do their work. Two loud explosions boomed out, one from the forward hold and another from the engine room. *Netta* lurched under each impact and began to settle. Seven minutes later she went down by the stern.

The crew were cast adrift and left to their own devices. They took it in shifts to row towards the shore and made good headway but were eventually picked up by the Norwegian steamer *Electra* and brought into The Downs the next day.

14/63: GAZELLE. *Country:* British.
Date sunk: 2/3/17. *Tons nett:* –. *Tons gross:* 91.
Built: Ipswich in 1877. *Type:* SV. *Rig:* ketch.
Owners: W.E. Colebrook, Rye, Sussex.
Cargo: 193 tons pitch from Blagden, Waygh & Co, London to Havre. *Armed:* No. *Position:* 20 miles SSW of Dungeness (50 35 30N; 00 48 30E).
Master's name: Henry John Clothier. *Crew:* 4.
Crew nationality: All British.

CAPTAIN Henry Clothier watched in horror as the submarine attacked the sailing vessel *Utopia* about half a mile away. He saw her crew row away just as the Germans approached and fired three more shells into her hull. She lurched and bucked under each impact and began to settle at once, her head getting lower as her stern rose up. A few minutes later she was gone. The submarine turned her bows towards *Gazelle*.

Captain Clothier looked at his son next to him and said, "We've got no chance, there's nothing we can do, even if we had wind we wouldn't be able to out run it. We'd better abandon ship and be quick about it." The men pulled clear just as the shelling started. Several hit the *Gazelle* knocking off bits of rigging and generally sending lumps of timber flying in all directions. As the enemy ship drew closer a voice shouted to the men in the boat, "Come here, now!"

They pulled alongside the submarine. Her commander asked for the master, ordering him to board and proceeded to question him, where bound, where from and so on. After being pressed to produce any papers he might have the master reluctantly pulled several from his pocket, the register, manifest and bills of lading, the German officer keeping them all. Fortunately, he had no confidential papers.

While all this was going on, two German sailors had been busy in his lifeboat, making his men row them over to the *Gazelle* which was still afloat. Once alongside they attached a bomb to the starboard fore chain plates and rowed away again very quickly. The bomb exploded – sinking the *Gazelle* instantly.

The Admiralty trawler *Returno* had already found the crew of the *Utopia*. They told her commander that the submarine made off after the *Gazelle*, so it didn't take Commander Humphrey long to find her crew. They were taken on board, landing at 7am the next morning at Dover.

14/64: LA SOMME. *Country:* French.
Date sunk: 29/4/18. *Tons nett:* –. *Tons gross:* 790.
Built: –. *Type:* SS. *Rig:* schooner. *Owners:* Compagnie des Chemin de Fer Du Nord, Calais.
Cargo: In ballast, Swansea to Dieppe. *Armed:* 2 x 90mm guns. *Position:* 5 miles WSW of Dungeness (50 53 00N; 00 52 00E). *Master's name:* Louis Babelaire. *Crew:* 32.

AS she was heading for Dieppe it was strange that *La Somme* was so far to the north-east, perhaps she had orders to call in elsewhere before crossing the

Channel. However, nothing was mentioned about this in the master's statement.

Whatever caused the explosion, *La Somme* suffered a very violent one, so violent in fact that the ship was literally blown into two pieces. The fore part sank almost instantly leaving a section of the stern showing above water. Considering the force of the explosion it was remarkable that there were so few casualties. However, it seems that only one man was killed. This is not stated in the record, but is assumed by the number of men mentioned as being in the ship's boats – 31 of the crew managed to launch two of the ship's boats and got clear of the wreck.

The weather was misty with a strong wind and it may have been this that caused the boats to get separated. One boat made it with 19 men to Hastings. The other boat with 10 men was picked up by the steamer *Querida* and taken to Dover.

14/65: SALYBIA. *Country:* British.

Date sunk: 24/3/16. *Tons nett:* 2131. *Tons gross:* 3351. *Built:* South Shields in 1904. *Type:* SS. *Rig:* schooner. *Owners:* Scrutton Sons & Co, 16, Fenchurch Ave, London. *Cargo:* 4000 tons rum, sugar and general from Dominica, West Indies to London. *Armed:* No. *Position:* 4 miles SW by W from Dungeness (50 52 00N; 00 53 00E). *Master's name:* Stephen Wilkinson. *Crew:* 42, plus 7 passengers.

THE journey for *Salybia* was almost over, having tramped through the Caribbean, across the Atlantic and most of the way up the English Channel, London, her final destination, was just around the corner. She was not alone, there were several other steamers around, three on her port side and one directly astern. On the bridge with the second mate, the master looked at the clock, it was 5.50pm. He walked over to the starboard side and saw a white streak, a torpedo only yards away from the ship.

There was no time to do anything, he didn't even have time to shout to the helmsman before the torpedo struck. A huge explosion rocked the ship from the starboard side, tearing the bottom out of the after holds. Proof of this was seen immediately as her cargo began to spill out and float behind the stricken steamer. She began to settle down, and it was obvious to all on board that she wouldn't float for long.

The boats were lowered in an orderly fashion and all the passengers and crew got away safely, but only just in time as the *Salybia* sank a few minutes later. They stayed together and began to row for the shore but help was at hand in the form of the smack *Ena* of Lowestoft. She was only a small vessel but willingly took all the people on board. It was a struggle for her to make any headway but she managed to get herself into the lee of Dungeness and dropped anchor. The master eventually managed to contact a patrol vessel, HMAT 1960 *Strathdevon*, which towed them to shore.

UB-29 was the submarine involved.

14/66: KILLELLAN. *Country:* British.

Date sunk: 8/11/16. *Tons nett:* 1214. *Tons gross:* 1971. *Built:* 1914. *Type:* SS. *Rig:* schooner. *Owners:* Atlas SS Co Ltd, Montreal, Canada. *Cargo:* 2300 tons coal from Tyne to Rouen. *Armed:* No. *Position:* 15 miles W by S of Colbert Light Ship/5 miles SSW of Dungeness (50 50 00N; 00 56 00E). *Master's name:* Chas Sauter. *Crew:* 18.

THE weather was atrocious on the day that the *Killellan* ran into trouble. Although visibility was good, the wind was described as west-south-west force 10 and not surprisingly, the sea was rough.

The master said that the first he knew of any trouble was when he heard something pass over the rigging of his ship. It was difficult to make out any noises above the howl of the wind. He looked around to see if he could spot anything obvious and eventually saw the conning tower of a submarine appearing on and off in the heavy seas. The ship was making very little headway so it wasn't long before the submarine caught up and flew the signal flag to abandon ship.

The master ordered the crew to get the boats ready while he went below to destroy his confidential papers. As he did this he felt and heard a bang against the side of his ship followed by a large explosion. Guessing that the submarine had fired a torpedo he quickly put his secret papers in a weighted bag and tossed it over the side. Running to the boats he found that they had already been launched by the crew and were several yards off. However, his dilemma was solved for him as another torpedo slammed into the ship, penetrating the engine room and causing the boilers to explode. An instant later the master was floating in the water.

The crew drifted away from the master and finally couldn't see him at all in the huge waves. They were eventually spotted by the trawler *Pointer* and later transferred to the patrol trawler *Jacamar*, landing the next day at Dover. The master was also lucky, a patrol vessel was in the area and found him clinging to wreckage.

UB-40 was the submarine concerned.

14/67: DOLLY VARDEN. *Country:* British.

Date sunk: 14/11/17. *Tons nett:* 164. *Tons gross:* 201. *Built:* Bideford in 1871. *Type:* SV. *Rig:* Schooner. *Owners:* Anderson & Co, Whitstable, Kent. *Cargo:* In ballast, Dieppe to Newcastle. *Armed:* No. *Position:* 20 miles NW of Treport, France (50 16 00N; 00 57 00E). *Master's name:* John Phillips. *Crew:* 7.

THERE was not a lot written about the sinking of the *Dolly Varden*. Apparently a German submarine appeared on the surface and at long distance began to fire shells at her. It commenced a steady bombardment as it headed closer and closer to the ship, each shot getting more accurate than the previous one. The master realised he could do nothing about it and abandoned the ship after the first shell struck. The gunners on the submarine did not stop until the schooner sank, then casually turned away not showing the slightest interest in the men in the boat.

At 7.20pm the same day the crew of *Dolly Varden*, assisted by the wind and a small sail they had rigged up, found themselves about five miles from their original destination of Treport. A Belgian fishing vessel picked them up.

14/68: AUSTRALIER. *Country:* British. *Date sunk:* 29/4/18. *Tons nett:* 2364. *Tons gross:* 3637. *Built:* 1906. *Type:* SS. *Rig:* schooner. *Owners:* Lloyds Royal Belge Co, 101, Leadenhall St, London. *Cargo:* 6300 tons iron ore, Bilbao for Tees. *Armed:* 1 x 4in gun. *Position:* 5 miles SW from Dungeness (50 48 20N; 00 57 30E). *Master's name:* Richard Steel, West Kilbride. *Crew:* 35. *Crew nationality:* 33 British, 2 Greek. *Gunners:* Alexander Rois, RNR, No A772; Alexander Cargill, RNR, No A3806; W. Mackay, RNR, No A6741..

ALTHOUGH she was under the watchful eye of a naval escort, the destroyer *Arun*, it still didn't save the *Australier* from becoming another war casualty.

The journey was going well although the visibility was poor and the sky heavily overcast. HMS *Arun* was zig-zagging in front of the the steamer to protect her but suddenly the *Australier* was brought to a shuddering halt by a huge explosion. The blast was so powerful it opened up a large hole near number one hold and blew the hatch cover clean off. Five men were killed by the blast and within a minute the ship was so far down in the water it was feared that not a single boat could be launched. However, one did get clear with a few men but three minutes later the steamer went to the bottom leaving the rest of the men floundering in the water. A boat from HMS *Arun* was soon among the men plucking them to safety and they were landed later at Portsmouth.

The master of the *Australier* said that he thought his ship had struck a mine. Most of the surviving crew were convinced that they had struck a mine. Indeed one of the lookouts stated that he saw a mine directly under the bow of the ship but before he could report it to the master, the explosion had already happened. However, the Admiralty thought differently. They pointed out that a German submarine was known to have been operating in the very area in which the steamer sank and was most probably responsible for her sinking. Perhaps they knew more than they cared to say in their notes at the time.

UB-57 claimed to have torpedoed her.

14/69: KIA ORA. *Country:* British. *Date sunk:* 8/2/18. *Tons nett:* –. *Tons gross:* 99. *Built:* Greenwich in 1907. *Type:* MV. *Rig:* barge. *Owners:* Wynnfield Shipping Co, Grimsby.

Cargo: In ballast, Dieppe for Shoreham. *Armed:* No. *Position:* 20 miles N by W of Dieppe (50 15 00N; 00 58 00E). *Master's name:* George Cogger. *Crew:* 5.

THE *Kia Ora* was at one time a plain yacht and had only recently been converted by having a new 90hp Kromhout motor installed.

The master said that he was to proceed from Dieppe to Shoreham via Boulogne and left on the morning of February 8, 1918. At 8.30am when about six miles north-east of Dieppe the top mast broke off taking the sail with it over the side. Not wanting to loose this valuable piece of equipment the motor was stopped and the ship allowed to run with the wind to retrieve the mast.

By 10.20am they had the mast and sail stowed safely aboard and were about to continue their journey when a submarine suddenly appeared about half a mile off. Within a few minutes the shells were flying, making it quite clear to the master that he had to abandon ship. The crew pulled clear and headed away from the *Kia Ora* and the approaching submarine, but the German commander altered course and went alongside the crew's boat. Three men were taken aboard the submarine, replaced with German sailors and towed back to the abandoned ship.

The enemy raiders searched the ship from top to bottom looking for anything they felt could be eaten, drunk or might be of value. They even made the crew remove their watches and threw them in the swag bag. Before leaving they left a bomb in the forecastle and hurried away. The bomb exploded but didn't do enough damage to sink her so it was left to the submarine's gunner to finish the job off. *Kia Ora* sank at about 1.40pm.

There are no details about the crew reaching the shore but they did survive to tell the tale. The master was taken ill soon after and the statement on the incident had to be made by the mate, Alfred Attree. However, the file did contain a letter from the master confirming what happened.

The owners of the *Kia Ora* said in a letter to the Admiralty that they felt the loss of this vessel badly as only the year before they lost two fine sailing ships the *Boaz* and the *Gippeswic*.

14/70: GERMAN SUBMARINE (UC-50). *Country:* German. *Date sunk:* 4/2/18. *Tons nett:* 420. *Tons gross:* 500. *Built:* 1916. *Type:* UC-class minelayer. *Owners:* German navy. *Armed:* 18 mines, 7 torpedoes. *Position:* 5 miles S 15 Deg W of Dungeness (50 50 00N; 00 58 00E). *Master's name:* Kapitan-Leutnant R. Seuffer. *Crew:* 26. *Crew nationality:* German.

THE vessel concerned in sinking this submarine was HMS *Zubian* commanded by Lieutenant H.T. Hartnoll, RN, who made this report:

"At 5.30am on February 4, 1918, on the port bow

about two cables off, a large enemy submarine was sighted with two masts up and ensign flying. Lieutenant W. Campbell, RNR, who was officer of the watch and who sighted her, immediately altered course towards her and increased speed to 25 knots, at the same time calling me. When I took over, the submarine was ahead about three quarters of a cable rapidly submerging and turning away, disappearing below the surface 30-40yds ahead of *Zubian's* bow. The swirl was plainly visible.

"A depth charge, type D, set to 80ft was released on the swirl and large quantities of oil appeared on the surface, so much so that a considerable amount was thrown on the upper deck tubes aft screen and over all the men aft as far forward as the after funnel. When the helm was put over to release the next depth charge, whilst getting into position a track was observed proceeding from the first area of oil. This was followed and a second depth charge, type D, set to 40ft was dropped. Another large area of oil was observed. The submarine appeared stationary and a Dan Buoy was dropped as a mark. *Zubian* then followed up the oil track and released two G charges at separate times set to 80ft. A large amount of oil was seen from then until dawn at 6.30am. The breadth of the oil track where it first showed on the surface was at least 25ft wide and was then taken away by the tide. This track was clearly defined for a least two miles.

"At 6.35am *P12* arrived on the spot and released six D type depth charges from chutes and throwers on the spot, one cable in front of the oil and another large quantity of oil was seen. At 7.30am, *P50* and *Fawn* joined up and both released depth charges at the end of the oil track. They were stationed astern of *Zubian* and by blue pendant were brought across at right angles to and ahead of the track and two more depth charges simultaneously exploded. At this time five more ships consisting of Flotilla Leaders, more destroyers, P boats and trawlers had arrived and dropped depth charges in the vicinity of the Dan Buoy.

"*Zubian* was then sent to scout 10 miles to the southward and on returning it was found that the Dan Buoy had dragged. The area where the oil track originated was searched for and found again, another buoy being dropped on the spot where oil was coming up in small bubbles. At 12.35pm *Greyhound* was told to drop a depth charge close to the buoy which she did and another patch of oil appeared. The buoy parted its moorings and the oil track was not discovered any more. At 2.15pm another buoy was put down by *P11* on a mark dropped by *Zubian* in approximately the same position as the second one and trawlers started to sweep around it. Whilst sweeping a big bubble of oil was observed to come up two cables to the eastward of this buoy. At 3.30pm *P11* was told to drop a depth charge to the west of this patch to allow for the tide. On passing over the area where the depth charge was dropped a piece of cardboard exuding oil and what looked like a verey pistol cartridge was observed but were not picked up.

"At 1.15pm the three destroyers, *P11* and *TB15* who were detailed to assist *Zubian* were spread on lines of patrol in case the third buoy's position was wrong and the submarine might attempt to escape. *Syren* who was patrolling to westward observed some oil and released a depth charge on it. *P11* was sent to her assistance but no result was reported.

"Original dead reckoning position of the submarine is four and three quarter miles south 39 degrees west of Dungeness Light Vessel. The submarine believed to be sunk four and a half miles south 20 degrees west from Dungeness Light Vessel by cross bearings. The distance between these two spots being one and a quarter miles.

"I wish to bring to your attention the good lookout kept by Lieutenant William Campbell, RNR, who spotted the submarine. Leading Signalman, E.J. Bedford, No ONJ 8852, states that he did not see the submarine long enough to make out any salient features. Seaman, Frank Webb, No ONJ 59755, lookout on the roof of the fore bridge states that he saw the submarine clearly and says she looked the same as the one sunk by *Q18* on February 19, 1917, off Guernsey, in which ship he was serving at the time."

The Admiralty decided to allow the maximum prize money of £1000 but instead of sharing it among the crews of the vessels concerned, gave it instead to the Mayor of Dover's fund. This fund was set up for the widows and children of local crewmen lost on several trawlers which ran into minefields.

The submarine sunk in this action was later identified as *UC-50*. There were no survivors.

Lieutenant Hartnoll was awarded the DSO and others of his crew were also decorated.

14/71: TEESBOROUGH. *Country:* British. *Date sunk:* 3/9/16. *Tons nett:* 114. *Tons gross:* 308. *Built:* Goole in 1912. *Type:* SS. *Rig:* schooner. *Owners:* Albert Chester, Albert Rd, Middlesbrough. *Cargo:* In ballast, Fecamp to London. *Armed:* No. *Position:* 30 miles NE by E of Fecamp (50 03 00N; 01 00 00E). *Master's name:* Richard Pizey. *Crew:* 8.

AT 6am the master had just gone to his cabin to turn the lights out when he heard an explosion. His immediate thoughts were that the ship had struck a mine so he rushed up on deck to check the extent of the damage. On looking around he saw that it was not a mine but a shell which had struck the engine room skylight, smashing it to pieces. He shouted to a man nearby to go and muster the crew by the boat. As the man ran forward another shell came whistling in and hit the break of the forecastle sending up showers of wood, injuring the messenger in the process.

The master looked to windward and saw a submarine very low in the water, heading directly towards him at about 10 knots. The master ordered his men to get clear. An officer on the submarine motioned the crew to come towards him. Alongside, the German commander told the master to get aboard and questioned him about his ship's papers. Meanwhile, two German sailors forced the rest of the crew to row them back to the steamer to plant bombs. After helping themselves to a clock and other instruments they planted one bomb in the hold and another in the engine room.

Left to fend for themselves the crew watched as the bombs exploded. The effect was devastating, the steamer rocking from side to side through the blast, settling down by stern and sinking a few minutes later. The men rowed for about six hours in the direction of shore and rigged up a sail to assist them. However, they were in luck as a lookout on the steamer *Hitterroy* spotted them and they were all landed at Deal about 10.30pm the same day.

14/72: C.A. JAQUES. *Country:* British. *Date sunk:* 1/5/17. *Tons nett:* 1590. *Tons gross:* 2105. *Built:* 1909. *Type:* SS. *Rig:* schooner. *Owners:* The Canada SS Line Ltd, Montreal, Canada. *Cargo:* In ballast, Havre to Tyne. *Armed:* No. *Position:* 26 miles NW by N of Treport (50 27 00N; 01 04 00E). *Master's name:* B.P. Powell, Canada. *Crew:* 20.

EVEN though she was in a large convoy escorted by several armed French trawlers, the *C.A.Jaques* fell as easy prey to *UB-18*. The weather must have helped as well being clear with a light breeze and smooth sea. It was 5.50am, the convoy making generally around seven knots.

The torpedo struck the steamer on the port side aft, causing a huge explosion and tearing a large hole in her bottom. Three men were killed by the blast in the engine room. The rest of the crew tried to get the boats clear, but found that the explosion had rendered the lowering gear useless. She was sinking very rapidly, so much so that the crew had only one option open to them, to jump for their lives.

All managed to get clear of the ship as her bows started to rise into the air. Within four minutes of the explosion she had disappeared. Help was very close by as several other steamers in the convoy came forward to lend a hand, while the patrol trawlers dashed frantically back and forth to try and keep the submarine at bay.

All the survivors were transferred from the various steamers to a patrol trawler which landed them the same day at Boulogne.

14/73: ALFRED. *Country:* British. *Date sunk:* 12/6/17. *Tons nett:* 100. *Tons gross:* 130. *Built:* Elms Horn in 1904. *Type:* SV. *Rig:* schooner. *Owners:* The Admiralty, Whitehall, London. *Cargo:* 190 tons coal, Howden to Cannes. *Armed:* No. *Position:* 15 miles SSW of Boulogne/10 miles NW from Haut Banc Point

(50 29 00N; 01 24 00E). *Master's name:* Thomas Newman. *Crew:* 5. *Crew nationality:* 3 British, 2 Danish.

THE master spotted the periscope when it was about a mile and a half astern and called the mate. He too looked through the binoculars and agreed with the master, it was a submarine and she was gaining on them fast. Captain Newman asked the mate to keep an eye on it while he destroyed his confidential papers.

There was hardly any wind at all; it had been like that for over 12 hours. *Alfred* was barely making a knot, hardly the sort of speed to escape marauding submarines. The submarine surfaced about 60yds off the ship's starboard quarter, and an officer appeared on the conning tower. He pointed a revolver at the *Alfred* and fired four shots, the bullets passing through the mainsail. He shouted, "Heave to. You have seen me long enough, why didn't you stop? Get your boat out and come alongside immediately."

The master did as he was told, and rowed over to the submarine leaving the mate in charge. The German commander eyed him coldly, asking him question after question about his ship, where she had come from and where bound. Then he seemed to change tack and told Newman that he was once on the Hamburg Amerikan Line. The master wondered what was going on when the German produced a camera and took a picture of him. He then explained that this would remind him of what Captain Newman looked like and if he caught him trading again he would be shot.

Meanwhile the *Alfred's* boat was being rowed back, not by the master but by a German officer and a sailor, each armed and carrying bombs. They proceeded to loot all the provisions they could find along with anything else that took their fancy. On planting the bombs the officer told the crew, "Your ship will be down in seven minutes."

The mate and the crew wasted no time in getting into the boat. On arriving at the submarine to collect the master they were told to wait. A few moments later the German commander appeared with two men. They were French seamen who had been on board the submarine for two days. The commander ushered them towards the master saying, "Here are two of your allies. You are 15 miles from Boulogne." The master learned from the men that their ship had been sunk by the submarine near Havre and as they had no boat were forced to remain as prisoners.

The men rigged up a sail and made off for the land. They didn't have to wait long to get assistance. At around 4pm the French fishing boat No *2631* from Le Crotoy came in sight and picked them up. They were landed at Le Crotoy about 9.30 the same evening.

14/74: RHEA. *Country:* British. *Date sunk:* 22/6/18. *Tons nett:* 736. *Tons gross:* 1308. *Built:* Rotterdam in 1917. *Type:* SS. *Rig:* schooner. *Owners:* Lewis Lougher, Devon

Buildings, James St, Cardiff. *Cargo:* 1700 tons coke from Armstrong Lord, Newcastle to Rouen and Paris. *Armed:* Yes. *Position:* 10 miles S by W of Cape d'Alprech (50 32 30N; 01 29 30E). *Master's name:* John Edward Palmer. *Crew:* 23.

ARRIVING off Boulogne at 1pm on June 22, 1918, the master spoke with the examination vessel and was told to wait off the port to join a convoy that would be leaving within the hour. The master waited as ordered and at 2.15pm took up his position as the fifth vessel among a convoy of nine proceeding south.

The weather wasn't particularly good with a strong north-westerly wind whipping up the sea. At 4.15 the same afternoon the master was in charge on the bridge when he felt a slight bump followed by a huge explosion from the starboard side around number three hatch. The *Rhea* was badly holed and taking on water fast. Being quite close to the coast Captain Palmer thought of beaching his ship to prevent her becoming a total loss, as she was already settling down by the stern. However, on trying to turn her head he found that she wouldn't respond, the explosion obviously having knocked out her steering gear.

There was no choice but to abandon her which was done in the two boats. The master said that the *Rhea* first took on a list to starboard then rolled over to port before lying on her beam and sinking. Two men were slightly injured by the explosion but otherwise all the crew reached the shore safely.

It was the general consensus afterwards that the *Rhea* had almost certainly struck a mine as nobody among the convoy had spotted any trace of a submarine or torpedo. She was listed by the Admiralty and Lloyd's as "mined".

Aerial view of a burning merchant ship after being attacked by a German submarine.

WORLD WAR ONE
CHANNEL WRECKS

◆

UNCHARTED WRECKS

This section deals with vessels that were known to have been lost in the Channel but have no positive position. Some are listed as "missing and untraced vessels" by Lloyd's.

15/1: ORIOLE. *Country:* British. *Date sunk:* 30/1/15. *Tons nett:* –. *Tons gross:* 1489. *Built:* –. *Type:* SS. *Rig:* –. *Owners:* The General Steam Navigation Co Ltd, Trinity Square, London. *Cargo:* 9 casks iodine, 51 tons rubber, 350 tons meat and fish, 150 tons lead, 500 tons rice, 33 tons tea and clothing. *Armed:* No. *Position:* Unknown. *Master's name:* William G. Dale. *Crew:* 21. *Crew nationality:* British..

THIS is one of the early losses of the war and one of the many mysteries. She loaded in the River Thames at Norwoods Buoys between January 25-29, 1915, and was taken down the river by the Trinity House Pilot, Mr Fishenden, who generally did the company's work and whose son was the first mate of the ship. He left the ship at 3.30pm on January 29 just below the Ovens Buoy. She was bound for Havre with her cargo for British troops and should have arrived there the following morning.

Oriole did not arrive and much confusion ensued over what had happened to her. The company, anxious to find out what had become of their ship, wrote several letters to the Admiralty. Their Lordships knew little and could only add to the mystery by stating that one of their patrol boats had seen *Oriole* off Dover at 10.30am on January 30 and had spoken to the captain. They hadn't boarded her as they said they knew her and were quite adamant that it was Captain Dale with whom they had spoken. To confuse matters even more they said that he had told them he was bound for Bordeaux and would be there on February 2. The company were naturally very perplexed as Captain Dale could have had no doubt as to his instructions, which were clearly to proceed to Havre.

Whatever the truth, *Oriole* was never seen again. However, two clues as to her fate were reported in the form of two lifebuoys washed up near Rye marked *Oriole* on February 6 and Lloyds Weekly Index reports for March 25 that a stained envelope embossed with the company logo had been found near Guernsey with the words '*Oriole torpedoed*' written on the front of it.

15/2: BEESWING. *Country:* British. *Date sunk:* 9/3/15. *Tons nett:* –. *Tons gross:*2002. *Built:* –. *Type:* SS. *Rig:* –. *Owners:* J. Crass & Co, 3, Queen St, Quayside, Newcastle. *Cargo:* coal, Tyne for Dieppe. *Armed:* No. *Position:* Unknown. *Master's name:* –.

THE loss of this vessel is not included in the official lists. It is mentioned in Naval Weekly Reports when the company who owned her wrote to the Admiralty, asking if they had any news of her. The Admiralty first thought that the vessel *Beethoven* belonging to the same company had been torpedoed but she was subsequently found to be safe. The Admiralty contacted the Ambassador in Berlin asking if any prisoners had been taken from the vessel *Beeswing*. The reply was none, so it was concluded that she was torpedoed with the loss of all hands.

This was most likely the vessel seen by the crew of the SS *Blackwood* (See 14/50) after their steamer was sunk by a German submarine.

15/3: ASGER RYG. *Country:* Danish. *Date sunk:* 8/4/16. *Tons nett:* –. *Tons gross:* 1134. *Built:* –. *Type:* SS. *Rig:* –. *Owners:* –. *Cargo:* 1275 tons coal, Tyne for Algiers. *Armed:* –. *Position:* Off the Isle of Wight. *Master's name:* –.

THE loss of the Danish steamer *Asger Ryg* is another mystery of the period. Her last voyage began when she left the Tyne loaded with coal for Algeria. She was last seen as she passed Beachy Head on April 6, 1916, but after that was never seen again.

Evidence of her fate turned up a few days later on April 9, when Lieutenant W.C.G. Smith of HMT *Warter Priory*, found a waterlogged, white painted lifeboat about 27 miles south-east of Nab. The boat had been badly knocked around and after noting the name *Asger Ryg* he rammed and sank it.

15/4: HMT KLONDYKE. *Country:* British. *Date sunk:* 4/6/16. *Tons nett:* –. *Tons gross:* 155. *Built:* –. *Type:* Hired trawler No 647. *Rig:* –. *Owners:* Admiralty. *Cargo:* –. *Armed:* Yes. *Position:* Off Owers Light Vessel. *Master's name:* –.

AT 1am on June 4, 1916, trawler *Klondyke*, while on patrol, was run down and sunk by the SS *Hindoo*. At the time, *Klondyke* was going slow to let *Hindoo* close on her in order to warn her to pass clear of a danger off Beachy Head.

One Royal Navy rating was drowned. The skipper said that the remainder of the crew owed their lives to the Colwill Life Saving Float which supported them for 20 minutes in the water and proved most satisfactory. They were unable to get their lifeboat out as the bows of the steamer had wrecked it.

15/5: HMD FAME. *Country:* British. *Date sunk:* 22/10/16. *Tons nett:* –. *Tons gross:* 68. *Built:* –. *Type:* SV. *Rig:.* –. *Owners:* –. *Cargo:* –.

Armed: Yes. *Position:* Ran ashore on Hook Sands, Poole. *Master's name:* –.

AT about 6.45am the drifter *Fame*, on passage from North Shields to Poole, ran ashore on Hook Sands at the entrance to Poole Harbour. It was hoped that she could have been saved but the weather was so bad that all attempts to get her off were thwarted and she became a total loss. A Court of Enquiry was convened to look into the causes but the paperwork has either been destroyed or lost within other, unconnected, files.

15/6: CHARLES FECAMP. *Country:* –.
Date sunk: 10/11/16. *Tons nett:* –. *Tons gross:* –.
Built: –. *Type:* –. *Rig:* –. *Owners:* –. *Cargo:* –.
Armed: –. *Position:* Unknown. *Master's name:* –.

THE only indication that this casualty occurred is from a small report in Naval Weekly Reports noting that on November 10, 1916, at 10am, patrol vessel 2962 *Orvicto* struck wreckage, damaging her propeller off Grove Point, Portland and picked up a lifeboat marked *Charles Fecamp*.

On the same day patrol vessel number 2956 *Wimpole* reported finding a lifebuoy painted mauve grey marked *A15*, 25 miles E of Start Point.

15/7: ALFONS MARCELINE. *Country:* Belgian.
Date sunk: 15/11/16. *Tons nett:* –. *Tons gross:* 60.
Built: –. *Type:* SV. *Rig:* trawler. *Owners:* –.
Cargo: –. *Armed:* –. *Position:* Unknown. *Master's name:* –.

THIS vessel just disappeared somewhere in the Channel and was presumed to have been sunk by an enemy submarine. The only information on her is taken from a letter written by the Belgian authorities to the Admiralty asking if they have details as to her fate.

The Belgians stated that she left Havre on the November 15, 1916, bound for the British coast and that the weather had been particularly bad since. It could be that she was sunk in the gale. The Admiralty replied that they have no news of her other than a snippet of information taken from a German telegram originating in Berlin that a Belgian smack had been sunk by one of their submarines.

15/8: COATH. *Country:* British.
Date sunk: 12/12/16. *Tons nett:* 504. *Tons gross:* 975. *Built:* 1883. *Type:* SS. *Rig:* –. *Owners:* George Bazeley & Sons Ltd, Penzance. *Cargo:* None. *Armed:* No. *Position:* Unknown. *Master's name:* –. *Crew:* 16.

COATH left Newhaven on the December 8, 1916, and made her way across the Channel. The Admiralty reported that she arrived at Havre and left there at 1am on the 12th having discharged her cargo at Rouen. Nothing more was ever heard from her and it was presumed she was sunk either by an enemy submarine or mine somewhere in the Channel.

15/9: JOSHUA. *Country:* British.
Date sunk: 13/10/17. *Tons nett:* –. *Tons gross:* 60.
Built: 1867. *Type:* SV. *Rig:* ketch. *Owners:* Anglo French Coasting Co Ltd, Manchester. *Cargo:* 110 tons china clay, Fowey to Dieppe. *Armed:* No. *Position:* Unknown. Off Isle of Wight. *Master's name:* Jarratt. *Crew:* 3.

THERE is virtually no information on this sinking at all. The authorities at the time learned from a German radio broadcast that one of their submarines had sunk a sailing barge called *Joshua* off the Isle of Wight. She left Fowey on October 10, 1917, and was never heard of again. The only positive clue to back up the German radio claim was that the mate's body was washed ashore at Yarmouth.

15/10: BRITANNIA. *Country:* British.
Date sunk: 18/10/17. *Tons nett:* –. *Tons gross:* 765.
Built: –. *Type:* SS. *Rig:* –. *Owners:* –. *Cargo:* Pig iron, Middlesbrough for St. Malo. *Armed:* Yes. *Position:* Unknown. *Master's name:* –. *Crew:* 22.

THE loss of the *Britannia* is yet another one of those vessels that just disappeared. It is stated in the official records at the time that she sailed from the UK on October 18, 1917, bound for St Malo, France. She dropped her pilot off at Deal who, as it turned out, was the last person to see her.

The notes say that there was considerable enemy submarine activity on October 18-19, between Portland Bill and the Isle of Wight and it is likely she was sunk somewhere around that area.

There is a letter in the records to say that the Northern England Protecting and Indemnity Assurance Company, had been asking the Admiralty for details of her. The Admiralty gave them the only information they had at the time and added that she was most probably sunk by a torpedo.

15/11: LITTLE GEM. *Country:* British.
Date sunk: 13/12/17. *Tons nett:* 99. *Tons gross:* 114. *Built:* 1893. *Type:* SV. *Rig:* schooner.
Owners: Edward Stephens, Fowey. *Cargo:* 170 tons fishing salt from Oporto to Gaultois, Newfoundland. *Armed:* No. *Position:* Unknown. *Master's name:* W.J. Rundell. *Crew:* 5.

THE only information available in the records is a telegram from the Admiralty to say the *Little Gem* was sunk by a submarine with no survivors. There is no evidence to say where they got the information from and the only position given is, off the Channel Islands.

15/12: CHARLES. *Country:* British.
Date sunk: 18/12/17. *Tons nett:* –. *Tons gross:* 78.
Built: –. *Type:* SV. *Rig:* –. *Owners:* –. *Cargo:* Iron
ore, Granville to Swansea. *Armed:* No. *Position:*
Unknown. *Master's name:* –.

THIS is another case of a small sailing vessel going
missing without a trace. The only mention in the
official records is in the form a letter from the Sailing
Vessel Mutual Insurance Company, to the Admiralty.
They wanted to know if any information was available
on the fate of the *Charles*. The Admiralty replied that
she put in to Guernsey on December 16. 1917, for
shelter. However, since leaving there nothing has been
heard of her apart from a German communique, which
stated that one of their submarines sunk her on the
18th. The Admiralty added that they knew nothing
more of her but confirmed the German claim.

15/13: ML 52. *Country:* British.
Date sunk: 29/11/17. *Tons nett:* –. *Tons gross:* 37.
Built: –. *Type:* MV. *Rig:* –. *Owners:* Admiralty.
Cargo: –. *Armed:* –. *Position:* Unknown. Sandown
Bay. *Master's name:* –.

THERE is only a snippet in Weekly Reports which
says that *ML 52* was loaned to Blockhouse for
attendance on a submarine. During some stage of the
operations she caught fire in Sandown Bay. It was
hoped that salvage operations would be successful or
that at least the engine would be salved.

15/14: HMD PISCATORIAL II.
Country: British. *Date sunk:* 29/12/17. *Tons nett:* –.
Tons gross: 93. *Built:* –. *Type:* Patrol drifter. *Rig:* –.
Owners: –. *Cargo:* –. *Armed:* Yes.
Position: Unknown. Disappeared off Newhaven.
Master's name: –.

PISCATORIAL II, No 3300 left Newhaven on
December 28, 1917, for her patrol between Beachy
Head and Newhaven. Nothing was seen or heard of
her again. The only clue as to her fate is that at 7am
Cuckmere reported hearing an explosion which could
not be accounted for. The next morning at 11.35, the
patrol vessel *Micado* found wreckage about four miles
south of Newhaven but couldn't find anything to
identify the vessel to which it belonged.
   As she was never heard from or seen again and as
Piscatorial II was in the same area where the
wreckage was found, it was assumed by the authorities
that she had been sunk, most probably by striking a
mine.

15/15: NAOMI. *Country:* British.
Date sunk: 15/2/18. *Tons nett:* –. *Tons gross:* 27.
Built: –. *Type:* SV. *Rig:* –. *Owners:* R. Turner,
Barbican, Plymouth. *Cargo:* –. *Armed:* No.

Position: Unknown. *Master's name:* Tucker.
Crew: 3.

THE only information about this loss is that she left
Plymouth to go out to the fishing grounds and was
never seen again. No wreckage or remains of the crew
were reported in the few days after her disappearance
and it was concluded that she must have fallen prey to
a German submarine.

15/16: THETIS. *Country:* British.
Date sunk: 27/4/18. *Tons nett:* –. *Tons gross:* 25.
Built: 1872. *Type:* SV. *Rig:* ketch. *Owners:* I.W.
Kingston, 8, Church Street, Poole. *Cargo:* 60 tons
pitch. *Armed:* No. *Position:* Unknown. *Master's
name:* Weadick (Dane). *Crew:* 2.

THERE is no information on this vessel other than
the fact that she left Southampton on April 23, 1918,
bound for St Malo. She called in at Lymington Roads
on the 27th but was never seen again after that.
   The Liverpool and London War Risks Association
wrote to the Admiralty to ask if they knew what had
happened to the vessel but they didn't. They noted
however that the weather had been bad and there had
been considerable submarine activity in the area, so
they assumed she had been sunk by an enemy
submarine. The Admiralty did ask for a report from
the Needles Naval Station to know when she passed
them but there is no record of the reply.

15/17: HMT REMINDO. *Country:* British.
Date sunk: 2/2/18. *Tons nett:* –. *Tons gross:* 256.
Built: –. *Type:* Patrol Trawler. *Rig:* –. *Owners:* –.
Cargo: –. *Armed:* Yes. *Position:* Unknown.
Master's name: –.

The only information available on this sinking is that
she went missing while on patrol off Portland.

15/18: HMT MICHAEL CLEMENTS.
Country: British. *Date sunk:* 8/8/18. *Tons nett:* –.
Tons gross: 324. *Built:* –. *Type:* Patrol vessel.
Rig: trawler. *Owners:* –. *Cargo:* –. *Armed:* Yes.
Position: Off St Catherines Point. *Master's name:* –.

THIS is another one of the reported collisions that
occurred from time to time among patrol trawlers.
Apart from a mention that it happened, there is no
other information to hand.

15/19: SEAPLANE No 4414. *Country:* British.
Date sunk: 2/9/18. *Tons nett:* –. *Tons gross:* –.
Built: –. *Type:* Patrol aircraft. *Owners:* RAF.
Armed: Yes. *Position:* Unknown. In Solent 5 miles
E of Magpie when crashed. *Crew:* 2. *Crew
nationality:* British.

THIS incident was reported by the patrol vessel *DB 076* which went to the aircraft's assistance. The plane was taken in tow but when a short distance from Magpie she turned over and sank.

A party from Magpie assisted the RAF party in sweeping operations to locate it but owing to the strong tides and difficulty that would be experienced in carrying out diving operations, the officer commanding No 10 group, RAF Warsash, decided to abandon the salvage.

15/20: SEAPLANE No 1708. *Country:* British. *Date sunk:* 4/9/18. *Tons nett:* −. *Tons gross:* −. *Built:* −. *Type:* Patrol aircraft. *Owners:* RAF. *Armed:* Yes. *Position:* Crashed off St Albans Head. *Crew:* 2. *Crew nationality:* British.

THIS information was provided by the commanders of armed trawlers 1983 *Sea Monarch* and *Thomas Foley*. The plane from Calshot was seen to crash and the trawlers picked up the pilot and an observer. They took the aircraft in tow but it broke adrift during the night and sank.

15/21: BIDART. *Country:* French. *Date sunk:* 31/8/18. *Tons nett:* 900. *Tons gross:* 1737. *Built:* −. *Type:* SS. *Rig:* −. *Owners:* −. *Cargo:* Coal, Newport for Le Havre. *Armed:* −. *Position:* Inside the Skerries Bank. *Master's name:* −.

ONLY the briefest of mentions in Weekly Reports shed any light on the sinking of the *Bidart* as the result of a collision.

Apparently, the other vessel involved was the SS *Wexford Coast,* a Q-ship. The weather was fine and clear at the time which makes the incident even more unusual. *Bidart* remained afloat for two hours but eventually rolled over and sank. All the crew managed to get clear of her and were picked up by HMS *Opossum* and taken to Dartmouth.

15/22: GUERNSEY. *Country:* British. *Date sunk:* 9/4/15. *Tons nett:* −. *Tons gross:* −. *Built:* −. *Type:* SS. *Rig:* −. *Owners:* −. *Cargo:* −. *Armed:* −. *Position:* Unknown. Off Cape La Hague. *Master's name:* Berrow. *Crew:* 19.

THERE is a very brief mention of this loss in the early records of the war but it has not been picked out as a war casualty. The few letters and telegrams sent back and forth between the Admiralty and the British Consulate General at Havre, do not give any indication of the cause of her sinking.

Seven of the crew including the master perished. The 12 survivors were taken to Cherbourg and a few days later, on to Southampton.

15/23: REWARD. *Country:* British. *Date sunk:* 12/3/17. *Tons nett:* 146. *Tons gross:* 172. *Built:* 1878. *Type:* SV. *Rig:* schooner. *Owners:* William Albert Jenkins, Baltic Buildings, Swansea. *Cargo:* 285 tons coal. *Armed:* No. *Position:* Unknown. *Master's name:* John Cawsey. *Crew:* 5.

THERE is little known about this vessel other than the fact that she left Falmouth on March 12, 1917, bound for Guernsey.

15/24: TANKERTON TOWER. *Country:* British. *Date sunk:* 16/3/17. *Tons nett:* 99. *Tons gross:* −. *Built:* 1833. *Type:* SV. *Rig:* −. *Owners:* Norman Bell Leslie, 59, Dock St, Dundee. *Cargo:* 200 tons stone. *Armed:* No. *Position:* Unknown. *Master's name:* Charles Gen.

THIS is another one of those vessels that just disappeared. The last that was ever seen of her was when she left St Valery on the Somme on March 16, 1917, bound for Liverpool. It was decided that she must have been lost through enemy action somewhere in the English Channel.

15/25: ST ROGATIEN. *Country:* French. *Date sunk:* 17/11/16. *Tons nett:* −. *Tons gross:* 1581. *Built:* −. *Type:* SV. *Rig:* −. *Owners:* −. *Cargo:* In ballast, Dieppe for Nantes. *Armed:* −. *Position:* Unknown. Between Beachy Head and Dieppe. *Master's name:* −.

THERE is only a note from the Coastguard concerning this vessel to say that at 6.30pm on November 17, 1916, four French merchant seamen landed on the East Beach and were taken to the Selsey Hotel by G. Arnell, a local fisherman. They reported that their sailing vessel from Nantes was torpedoed at 9am on the same day. They said they were bound from Dieppe to Buenos Aires.

15/26: GRANT. *Country:* British. *Date sunk:* 8/1/17. *Tons nett:* 122. *Tons gross:* 273. *Built:* 1881. *Type:* SS. *Rig:* single masted. *Owners:* Jones Grainger & Co, 10, Byward St, London. *Cargo:* 330 tons flints from Le Hourdel to Runcorn. *Armed:* No. *Position:* Unknown. *Master's name:* S. Grant. *Crew:* 8.

ALTHOUGH the *Grant* was quite an old vessel she had been refitted in 1915 and was in excellent condition. This added fuel to the theory at the time that she must have been sunk by enemy action somewhere in the English Channel.

She was loaded at Hourdel with flints and the master wrote a letter from there to his employers saying that he had not been given his full cargo. He had asked for more but had been refused. *Grant* sailed from Hourdel on January 8, 1917, and was to call in at Dartmouth for bunkers before continuing her journey to Runcorn. She never reached Dartmouth and was never seen again.

When asked for information, the Admiralty stated that they knew nothing of her whereabouts but added that there was considerable enemy submarine activity in the area at the time and it was highly likely she had been sunk.

15/27: HOMOCEA. *Country:* British.
Date sunk: 10/3/17. *Tons nett:* 39. *Tons gross:* 58.
Built: 1900. *Type:* SV. *Rig:* schooner.
Owners: Joseph Jacobs, Navy Hotel, Plymouth.
Cargo: –. *Armed:* No. *Position:* Unknown. Off Treport. *Master's name:* Georges Lermet.
Crew: 18.

THERE is virtually no information at all on the circumstances of this loss. It is mentioned in the records that the trawler was probably torpedoed off Treport while fishing but there is nothing to back it up. All that is known for certain is that she was never seen again.

15/28: NORTH WALES. *Country:* British.
Date sunk: 24/10/16. *Tons nett:* 2382. *Tons gross:* 3691. *Built:* 1905. *Type:* SS. *Rig:* schooner.
Owners: North Wales Shipping Co Ltd, Newcastle.
Cargo: In ballast. *Armed:* No. *Position:* Unknown.
Master's name: G. Owen. *Crew:* 30.

THIS is one of those losses whereby nobody survived to tell the tale. *North Wales* was last seen when the pilot left her off the Isle of Wight on November 24, 1916, to proceed to Montreal.

Nothing was ever seen of her again but the first clue as to her fate came a few weeks later when wreckage and bodies washed up near Penzance, were believed to have come from the *North Wales*.

15/29: SERBISTAN. *Country:* British.
Date sunk: 17/11/16. *Tons nett:* 1851. *Tons gross:* 2934. *Built:* 1896. *Type:* SS. *Rig:* schooner.
Owners: Strick Line Ltd, Baltic House, London.
Cargo: –. *Armed:* No. *Position:* Unknown. Off Lizard. *Master's name:* J. Griffiths. *Crew:* 24.

THERE is a certain amount of confusion about the loss of this vessel. The official government publication of First World War Losses state that *Serbistan* was chased by a German submarine but she escaped and lived to sail another day. The contemporary documents of the time tell a different story.

She left Brest Roads on November 16, 1916, in company with another steamer the *Bayhowel*, both bound for Cardiff. The master of *Bayhowel* said that

they were attacked by a German submarine in the middle of the journey and as a consequence were split up. He said that he last saw the *Serbistan* on the morning of November 17, 1916. *Bayhowel* duly arrived at Cardiff but there was no sign of *Serbistan* for many days.

The first clue as to her fate came from a report by the master of the trawler *Tezenta* who passed through quantities of wreckage about 12 miles south of the Lizard. The master stopped in among the wreckage to look around and found papers and cases of cargo all pointing to the name of *Serbistan*. He picked up several of the cases and found that they contained war material, as it was described. The authorities at Falmouth made enquiries about what *Serbistan* was carrying and the cases matched the description. More proof of her demise came when a log book marked *Serbistan* and other cases of war materials were washed up at Sennen Cove, Cornwall, some days later. Notes written some time after her disappearance stated that other parts of her cargo such as aircraft parts, shell cases, even parts of airplanes themselves were also washed ashore.

All this indicates that she was sunk by an enemy submarine somewhere south of the Lizard.

15/30: WHORLTON. *Country:* British.
Date sunk: 11/1/18. *Tons nett:* 884. *Tons gross:* –.
Built: 1908. *Type:* SS. *Rig:* two-masted.
Owners: Furness Whithy & Co. *Cargo:* –.
Armed: Yes. *Position:* Unknown. Between the Downs and Southampton. *Master's name:* Alexander Gordon. *Crew:* 17.

WHORLTON left Purfleet in the Thames on January 5, 1918, bound for Dunkirk. She arrived at the Downs and was given instructions to call at Southampton in the afternoon of the January 11. She sailed from the Downs directly afterwards and nothing more was heard of her again.

Some debris was found later washed up near Beachy Head which could have come from the *Whorlton*. The Admiralty decided that she must have been sunk by a submarine somewhere in the vicinity of Beachy Head.

15/31: KURLAND. *Country:* Belgian.
Date sunk: 10/12/17. *Tons nett:* –. *Tons gross:* 1964. *Built:* –. *Type:* SS. *Rig:* –. *Owners:* –.
Cargo: Ammunition for the Belgian government from New York to Calais. *Armed:* 1 x 75mm French gun. *Position:* Unknown. Off St Catherines Point.
Master's name: G. Nyland.

THE only reason that this sinking was discovered was when she was mentioned in another sea area, South West Approaches. It was noted that she was attacked by a submarine which chased her for some time, but the master managed to shake her off. The notes went

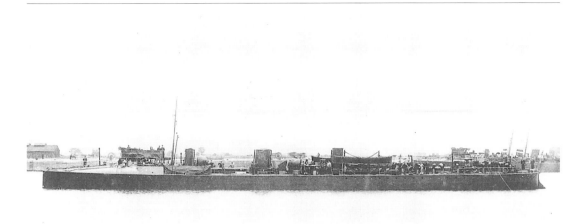

HMS *Bittern* – all hands went down with her after a collision with a steamer.

on to add that she continued up the Channel and, when off St Catherines Point, collided with another steamer and sank.

15/32: EMLYNDENE. *Country:* British. *Date sunk:* 11/12/17. *Tons nett:* 220. *Tons gross:* –. *Built:* 1903. *Type:* SS. *Rig:* The Emlyn Line Ltd, Cardiff. *Owners:* –. *Cargo:* 577 tons coal, Cardiff to Granville. *Armed:* Yes. *Position:* Unknown. *Master's name:* T. Lamb. *Crew:* 14.

EMLYNDENE sailed from Cardiff at 2.30am on December 11, 1917, never to be seen again. There is no evidence at all as to what happened to her. There was considerable submarine activity in the western part of the Channel at that time.

15/33: GOELAND II. *Country:* French. *Date sunk:* 4/1/18. *Tons nett:* –. *Tons gross:* –. *Built:* –. *Type:* Patrol vessel. *Rig:* –. *Owners:* –. *Cargo:* –. *Armed:* Yes. *Position:* Unknown. *Master's name:* –.

GOELAND II was a French patrol boat and the first indication of her loss came with the discovery of one man found drifting on a raft. The master of the American steamer, *A.A. Raven*, said later that while in convoy from Brest to the Lizard, at 7.45pm on January 5, 1918, 25 miles north from Ushant light, he saw a man on a raft hollering and whistling for help. The man was duly picked up and said that his name was Ronald Pierre Marie, 24 years of age, military number 8173 a fireman from the patrol vessel *Goeland II* of Brest. His ship was engaged in escorting a three masted schooner at 9pm the previous day, when off the Isle de Veis, they encountered a submarine which they engaged in combat. The second or third shot from the submarine exploded the boilers and his ship started to sink.

The crew managed to lower one boat but he and another man managed to get on the raft and floated free when the *Goeland* sank. Unfortunately his companion died about 10 hours previously and his body was still on the raft. The dead man's name was Maleo Louis from Bordeaux. Both the man and the body were turned over to the naval authorities at Penzance.

15/34: HMS BITTERN. *Country:* British. *Date sunk:* 4/4/18. *Tons nett:* –. *Tons gross:* 360. *Built:* 1897. *Type:* Destroyer. *Rig:* –. *Owners:* Admiralty. *Cargo:* –. *Armed:* 1 x 12pdr, 5 x 6pdr, 2 torpedo tubes. *Position:* Unknown. *Master's name:* –.

Even though warships were usually better documented than most, the loss of the *Bittern* seems to have gone almost unnoticed. A search of the records where her loss would normally have been kept turned out to be completely fruitless. The only mention of her loss was found in Weekly Reports which stated that she was lost during the early hours as the result of a collision. The position is also very vague as 'in the Channel.' The total lack of information in these records is probably due to the fact that all hands were lost with the ship after she was in collision with the steamer *Kenilworth*

Sport divers believe they have found her at 50 33 40; 02 37 24W.

WORLD WAR ONE
CHANNEL WRECKS

◆

INDEX

Note: British Navy vessels are indexed by their prefix, ie, HMD, HMS, HMT, followed by their name. U-boats are indexed under German Submarine, followed by their identification letters and number. In the case of German Submarine with no following letters and number, these are possible U-boat wreck sites and are indexed by area.

Name	Date Sunk	Wreck Number	Name	Date Sunk	Wreck Number
Abeja	9/3/17	7/15	Athole	26/4/17	13/16
Achille Adam	23/3/17	14/57	Atlantis	3/10/18	1/24
Acorn	26/9/17	6/42	Atlas	13/11/17	12/30
Adams	17/10/17	1/71	Auguste Conseil	12/3/15	2/39
Addax	29/1/18	5/29	Australbush	13/11/17	2/43
Adelaide	4/3/17	9/9	Australier	29/4/18	14/68
Adolf Andersen	17/11/17	3/37	Avance	21/3/17	5/38
Afric	12/2/17	2/21	Avanti	2/2/18	9/23
Afrique	25/9/16	3/4	Axpe Mendi	7/6/18	3/13
Agnes Cairns	26/4/17	11/27	Axwell	13/11/17	12/12
Agnete	24/4/18	6/2	Azemmour	20/3/18	9/49
Aigle	26/4/17	4/9			
Ailsa Craig	14/4/18	8/20	Badger	3/8/16	9/41
Airplane	27/12/17	8/46	Bagdale	1/5/17	3/22
Airplane	18/7/18	12/33	Ballarat	25/4/17	1/26
Airship C8	9/6/16	7/22	Bamse	17/4/18	8/14
Alaunia	19/10/16	14/39	Bamse	2/10/18	1/61
Alberdina	26/2/17	9/35	Barbara	20/10/16	10/21
Albion	30/9/15	1/64	Barbro	14/10/17	3/50
Alcyone	1/8/17	7/36	Bargany	24/12/16	3/32
Aldershot	23/9/18	6/24	Baron Garioch	28/10/17	9/33
Alert	28/11/16	12/35	Basil	11/11/17	12/14
Alfred	12/6/17	14/73	Basuta	8/2/18	3/12
Algarve	20/10/17	8/31	Baychattan	11/10/17	4/28
Algerian	12/1/16	9/40	Baygitano	18/3/18	8/10
Algiers	26/2/17	12/16	Bayonne	17/2/17	8/4
Alice	21/11/16	14/47	Beata	17/3/18	1/51
Alice	24/3/17	2/26	Beatrice	20/7/17	2/2
Alice Marie	19/12/17	6/11	Beechtree	10/2/17	6/28
Aline Montreuil	21/9/17	10/17	Beeswing	9/3/15	15/2
Alison	28/11/16	12/39	Begona No. 3	23/5/17	3/29
Allendale	27/3/18	3/23	Begonia	21/3/18	3/1
Almond Branch	27/11/17	2/11	Behrend	30/11/16	6/49
Alphonse Marceline	15/11/16	15/7	Belle Ile	27/11/16	7/16
Ambiorix	6/12/17	11/41	Bellucia	7/7/17	1/43
Amelie	13/11/17	4/16	Benita	20/6/17	8/50
Amphitrite	28/11/16	5/37	Benito	26/12/17	2/14
Amy	11/4/17	13/47	Bernicia	13/11/16	14/33
Anna	13/5/17	3/47	Bidart	31/8/18	15/21
Anna Maria	2/2/17	3/16	Bidartaise	20/6/17	8/38
Anne Yvonne	17/3/18	1/46	Bishopston	4/9/17	13/3
Aparima	19/11/17	9/27	Blackwood	9/3/15	14/50
Aracataca	18/4/17	14/4	Bleamoor	27/11/17	5/12
Arvor	21/7/18	3/21	Boaz	31/3/17	11/43
Arvor	17/3/18	1/45	Bob	29/11/17	4/32
Asaba	6/12/17	1/32	Boma	11/6/18	5/27
Asborg	3/1/18	10/24	Border Knight	4/11/17	1/44
Asger Ryg	8/4/16	15/3	Borg	10/6/18	1/54

NAME	DATE SUNK	WRECK NUMBER	NAME	DATE SUNK	WRECK NUMBER
Echunga	5/9/17	3/18	*Foylemore*	16/12/17	2/18
Eden	30/4/17	12/43	*Francis*	5/9/17	7/19
Eduard	16/4/17	14/7	*Francis*	23/4/18	1/38
Efeu	22/3/17	14/54	*Francois et Georgette*	9/6/17	13/23
Einar Jarl	12/3/17	6/43	*Fremona*	31/7/17	3/51
Eldra	18/10/17	14/49	*Frigga*	25/8/17	9/3
Eleanor	12/2/18	10/3	*Frisco*	16/5/17	4/21
Elford	18/5/17	12/1	*Frogner*	29/4/18	8/49
Eliza Anne	17/3/18	2/33	*Fulvio*	21/10/16	11/17
Elizabeth	8/9/17	6/29			
Elizabeth Hampton	14/5/17	9/39	*G.C. Gradwell*	2/8/16	13/37
Ellen Harrison	29/4/17	11/29	*G.L.C.*	12/5/17	2/27
Elsa	24/1/18	5/2	*Galicia*	12/5/17	5/6
Emilie Gallienne	13/8/17	7/1	*Gallia*	24/10/17	5/35
Emlyndene	11/12/17	15/32	*Gallier*	2/1/18	1/2
Emlynverne	25/11/16	13/24	*Garm*	25/8/17	6/22
Emma	5/9/17	7/18	*Garthclyde*	15/10/17	1/6
Endeavour	24/3/17	4/6	*Gartland*	3/1/18	12/29
Endymion	31/3/17	7/46	*Gascony*	6/1/18	12/19
Energy	21/2/17	2/47	*Gauntlet*	18/6/17	7/31
Enigma	24/3/17	2/37	*Gazelle*	2/3/17	14/63
Epsilon	31/1/17	1/67	*Gefion*	25/10/17	5/22
Erato	1/9/17	1/58	*General Leman*	29/1/18	5/32
Eric Calvert	22/4/18	1/68	*George M. Embiricos*	22/10/16	7/11
Ermenilda	4/8/16	8/48	German Submarine	2/12/16	1/15
Eros	20/3/18	1/20	German Submarine	24/10/16	1/21
Espagne	25/12/17	10/4	German Submarine	20/8/17	4/27
Ethel	16/9/18	8/45	German Submarine	8/6/18	5/39
Ethel	22/1/17	6/14	German Submarine	10/7/17	7/30
Ethiope	28/5/15	7/7	German Submarine	28/11/16	8/32
Eugenie	16/11/16	3/17	German Submarine	30/10/15	9/2
Eumaeus	26/2/18	3/49	German Submarine	19/2/17	9/7
Euphorbia	1/12/17	14/55	German Submarine	12/5/17	9/24
Eva	31/12/16	1/36	German Submarine	25/3/18	9/26
Eveline	20/12/17	6/17	German Submarine	17/5/17	10/10
Exchange	23/3/17	14/59	German Submarine	30/11/16	11/6
Express	4/4/17	14/35	German Submarine	4/9/17	12/11
Ezel	8/9/17	14/26	German Submarine	23/10/17	12/36
			German Submarine	18/8/17	13/9
F.D. Lambert	13/2/17	14/40	German Submarine	5/2/17	13/20
Facto	16/9/17	1/14	German Submarine	8/4/16	14/5
Fallodon	28/12/17	10/31	German Submarine	7/4/18	14/46
Fanelly	6/11/16	12/54	German Submarine *U-85*	12/3/17	7/41
Farn	19/11/17	6/10	German Submarine *U-93*	7/1/18	1/42
Farraline	2/11/17	3/40	German Submarine *UB-72*	12/5/18	8/33
Favourite	9/9/16	6/37	German Submarine *UB-74*	26/5/18	8/43
Ferryhill	30/1/18	13/35	German Submarine *UB-78*	9/5/18	11/32
Figaro	26/1/18	11/7	German Submarine *UB-81*	2/12/17	12/9
Finn	19/11/16	8/24	German Submarine *UB-113*	23/9/18	5/1
Florence Louisa	17/5/17	9/50	German Submarine *UC-18*	19/2/17	11/14
Florence Muspratt	5/9/17	7/21	German Submarine *UC-49*	8/8/18	5/7
Fluent	20/7/17	9/31	German Submarine *UC-50*	4/2/18	14/70
Forget Me Not	12/3/17	8/34	German Submarine *UC-51*	17/11/17	4/29
Fortuna	22/10/16	14/6	German Submarine *UC-65*	3/11/17	14/17
Fortuna	3/8/16	8/40	German Submarine *UC-66*	12/6/17	1/48

NAME	DATE SUNK	WRECK NUMBER	NAME	DATE SUNK	WRECK NUMBER
Irma	13/9/16	3/3	Little Mystery	30/4/17	9/12
Isleworth	30/4/18	10/25	Livonia	3/12/17	4/11
Ivo	3/8/16	8/44	Lizzie Ellen	28/6/17	7/25
			Lockwood	2/4/15	2/45
Jaffa	22/2/18	12/40	Lofoten	3/2/18	6/15
Jeanette	6/4/16	9/47	Londonier	13/3/18	10/16
Jeanne	5/9/16	11/22	Lord Stewart	16/9/18	5/18
Jerseyman	24/11/16	13/27	Lorle	11/6/18	1/35
Jessie	27/4/17	8/35	Louie Bell	26/1/18	11/31
Joachim Brinch Lund	16/11/16	7/5	Lowmount	7/5/17	12/10
Johan	28/12/16	8/42	Luis	12/4/18	10/28
John Lambert	22/11/16	12/44	Lullington	8/2/17	14/41
John W. Pearn	1/5/17	5/24	Luxor	19/3/18	9/36
Joseph	4/5/17	13/22	Lydie	9/2/18	1/62
Joshua	13/10/17	15/9			
Juno	2/5/17	13/19	M.L. 52	29/11/17	15/13
Jupiter	21/5/17	12/59	Mabel Baird	22/12/17	1/27
Jutland	19/11/17	3/39	Madame Midas	23/3/18	3/11
			Maine	23/3/17	4/12
K.L.M.	21/2/17	2/23	Maine	21/11/17	14/51
Kalibia	30/11/17	1/11	Mar Baltico	23/3/18	3/26
Kate & Annie	19/6/17	7/37	Margaret	17/12/16	14/58
Kendal Castle	15/9/18	5/9	Margaret Sutton	2/8/16	13/11
Kia Ora	8/2/18	14/69	Marguerite	28/6/17	8/5
Killellan	8/11/16	14/66	Maria	13/4/17	8/47
Kilmaho	16/5/17	1/16	Maria	29/1/18	13/31
Kingsdyke	17/1/18	10/33	Marie Louise	17/3/17	9/10
Kong Guttorm	11/7/18	9/48	Marjorie	9/6/17	2/7
Krosfond	22/11/17	1/65	Martha	7/3/18	8/37
Kurland	10/12/17	15/31	Martin	14/1/17	3/14
Kyarra	26/5/18	9/25	Mary Ann	19/6/17	7/39
			Mary Annie	25/3/17	13/43
L.H. Carl	20/7/17	8/15	Matilde Jean	29/1/18	13/33
La Blanca	23/11/17	6/27	May	26/1/18	8/1
La Manche	1/5/17	11/10	Mayflower	24/3/17	4/2
La Negra	3/9/17	7/8	Mechanician	20/1/18	9/52
La Roche Jacquelin	14/11/16	1/8	Medea	25/3/15	14/38
La Somme	29/4/18	14/64	Medina	28/4/17	6/9
Lady Cory Wright	26/3/18	1/39	Memnon	12/3/17	8/18
Lady of the Lake	28/11/16	7/49	Mendi	21/2/17	10/18
Lady Olive	19/2/17	11/15	Mermaid	29/4/17	9/17
Laertes	1/8/17	4/26	Merton Hall	11/2/18	3/28
Lalen Mendi	17/11/17	14/19	Mientje	20/5/17	11/11
Lanfranc	17/4/17	13/36	Minerva	10/5/17	8/17
Laura	8/9/17	14/23	Miniota	31/8/17	7/50
Laura Ann	5/6/17	14/29	Minnie Coles	23/11/17	7/51
Laura C.Anderson	29/8/17	13/6	Mira	11/10/17	14/10
Le Lamentin	26/2/17	7/24	Mizpah	3/12/16	7/2
Leanora	21/2/18	5/11	Mohlenpris	15/4/17	12/51
Leon	7/1/18	10/36	Moidart	9/6/18	8/21
Libourne	29/9/18	1/33	Moldavia	23/5/18	12/37
Lightfoot	16/3/18	12/18	Molesey	11/12/17	12/20
Lisbon	30/5/17	14/32	Molina	22/1/18	10/14
Lismore	12/4/17	13/29	Monarch	21/2/17	7/4
Little Gem	13/12/17	15/11	Monksgarth	19/8/17	3/34

NAME	DATE SUNK	WRECK NUMBER	NAME	DATE SUNK	WRECK NUMBER
S.D.	2/8/16	14/2	*Teesborough*	3/9/16	14/71
Sabia	24/11/17	1/72	*Tela*	2/5/17	13/7
Saga	8/12/16	7/12	*The Duke*	20/10/16	14/28
Salsette	20/7/17	8/27	*The Macbain*	3/3/17	9/6
Salta	10/4/17	13/48	*The Marchioness*	20/10/16	13/38
Salybia	24/3/16	14/65	*Theodor*	5/9/17	7/17
San Nicolau	16/11/16	7/53	*Theodoros Pangalos*	3/3/17	3/2
Satanita	24/3/17	2/25	*Thetis*	27/4/18	15/16
Sea Lark	28/11/16	6/40	*Thisbe*	6/9/17	1/25
Seaplane *No. 4414*	2/9/18	15/19	*Thyra*	24/5/17	8/52
Seaplane *No. 1708*	4/9/18	15/20	*Tiro*	29/12/17	1/22
Secundo	20/10/16	7/13	*Toftwood*	13/1/17	7/14
Seeker	3/12/16	7/32	*Tokomaru*	30/1/15	13/34
Serbistan	17/11/16	15/29	*Tom Roper*	21/10/17	7/38
Serrana	22/1/18	9/46	*Topaz*	12/3/17	13/17
Seven Seas	1/4/15	14/13	*Torbay Lass*	8/6/17	6/16
Sevilla	25/4/18	5/10	*Torridal*	15/11/16	3/45
Shirala	2/7/18	12/26	*Torridge*	6/9/16	7/9
Sidmouth	24/10/16	1/1	*Tregenna*	26/12/17	2/12
Silvia	1/4/17	13/25	*Tremeadow*	19/1/17	3/42
Sir Joseph	16/3/17	7/26	*Trevarrack*	16/11/16	7/28
Sjaelland	25/5/17	6/46	*Tullochmoor*	28/5/15	3/8
Skaala	26/12/17	4/14	*Tweed*	13/3/18	10/15
Skaraas	23/5/18	1/56	*Twig*	24/10/16	11/24
Snowdrop	20/2/18	2/28	*Tycho*	20/5/17	12/56
Snyg	26/2/18	3/36	*Tyne*	17/6/17	1/9
Somme	30/3/17	13/21			
Sommeina	15/9/17	1/66	*Ula*	9/1/18	2/4
Sonnie	11/8/17	3/38	*Ull*	4/7/17	8/30
South Western	16/3/18	10/7	*Umba*	30/4/18	14/31
Sparkling Foam	15/3/18	5/41	*Union*	28/12/16	7/33
Spennymoor	28/5/15	2/15	*Unity*	2/5/18	12/63
Sphene	3/8/16	9/42	*Ursa*	17/9/18	5/31
Spiral	4/8/16	9/11	*Uskmoor*	5/3/18	4/18
St Andre	19/12/17	2/19	*Ussa*	3/5/17	11/28
St Dunstan	23/9/17	8/19	*Utopia*	2/3/17	14/61
St Emilion	27/7/17	14/52	*Valdes*	17/2/17	9/4
St George	21/5/15	6/20	*Vanguard*	16/11/16	13/41
St Rogatien	17/11/16	15/25	*Varuna*	4/1/18	6/45
Standard	20/1/17	9/1	*Vasco*	16/11/16	12/65
Stanhope	17/6/17	4/22	*Vasillisa Olga*	11/2/17	14/37
Start	22/12/17	9/19	*Vav*	4/12/17	1/34
Stockforce	30/7/18	4/7	*Veda*	2/1/18	2/20
Stryn	10/6/18	5/13	*Venborg*	23/3/18	3/31
Suffolk Coast	7/11/16	13/5	*Venezuela*	14/3/18	9/37
			Veni	10/5/17	8/22
T.R. Thompson	29/3/18	14/8	*Veronica*	11/11/16	6/21
Tagus	6/9/16	3/48	*Vesuvio*	6/4/16	12/34
Tammerfors	26/2/17	13/14	*Victoria*	16/4/17	12/46
Tandil	12/3/17	8/6	*Victoria*	17/11/17	2/17
Tankerton Tower	16/3/17	15/24	*Victoria II*	6/7/17	3/20
Tarpeia	11/5/17	13/13	*Vigda*	25/2/17	12/23
Tasmania	3/10/17	4/8	*Vigourieux*	14/6/17	9/20
Tecwyn	21/2/17	8/51	*Vigrid*	31/12/17	1/18
Teelin Head	21/1/18	12/13	*Vikholmen*	10/9/17	9/30

NAME	DATE SUNK	WRECK NUMBER
Ville de Thann	27/11/17	2/5
Villebois de Mareiul	1/10/16	1/5
Vinaes	8/6/17	13/8
Visborg	27/11/16	6/30
Volnay	14/12/17	1/60
Vulcan	28/11/16	6/50
W.H. Dwyer	26/8/17	5/33
W.H.L.	28/1/18	9/5
Waikawa	19/10/17	6/7
Walter Ulric	29/3/17	11/39
Wapello	15/6/17	12/2
War Firth	4/9/18	3/27
War Helmet	19/4/18	12/24
War Knight	25/3/18	10/2
War Monarch	14/2/18	14/53
War Tune	9/12/17	1/59
Warilda	3/8/18	13/30
Warsaw	20/12/17	6/6
Wega	14/6/17	12/57
Westergate	21/4/18	6/48
Western Coast	17/11/17	2/22
Western Coast	24/2/15	14/30
Westlands	23/11/17	3/46
Westville	31/12/17	10/5
Westwood	3/10/18	1/28
Whorlton	11/1/18	15/30
Wilhelm	7/6/17	2/6
William George	30/9/16	13/10
Wreathier	3/12/17	4/10
Wyndhurst	6/12/17	10/30
Yrsa	3/12/16	7/40
Yvonne	6/9/16	2/10
Zeta	23/1/17	1/4